RESEARCH ESSAYS

ON

ANCIENT EGYPT

FREDERICK MONDERSON

SUMON PUBLISHERS

SuMon Publishers
PO Box 160347
Brooklyn, New York 11216

sumonpublishers.com@sumonpublishers.com
blackfolksbooks.com@blackfolksbooks.com
fredsegypt.com@fredsegypt.com blackegyptbooks.com@blackegyptbooks.com

Copyright Frederick Monderson/ SuMon Publishers, 2011 All Rights Reserved.

No part of this book may be reproduced, stored in a retrieval system, or transmitted by any means without the written permission of the author.

ISBN – 978-1-61023-005-6
LCCN - 2010908036

In the Tribute to Professor George Simmonds, "Unsung Hero," Dr. Fred Monderson sat at the feet of his heroes, Brother X, Michael Carter, Dr. Leonard Jeffries, El Hombre Brath, Dr. Lewis, Prof. George Simmonds, Dr. ben-Jochannan, Sister Camille Yarbrough, among others.

PREFACE

Despite tremendous archaeological, artistic and literary progress, the subject of research on ancient Egypt is still in an interpretative mess because of the great misrepresentation in presentation of this discipline.   Ancient Egypt is a commercial bonanza and in this, the marketing is principally to a European and

American audience, misinformed of their role in creation of this Nile Valley culture, developed in the formative reclamation of the archaeological history more than a century ago. Importantly, this view has extended to this day. As such, the "definitive" interpretation of ancient Egyptian history and culture is fraught with omission and distortion since the role of Africa and Africans has been ruled out of the natural order and process of this important Nile Valley cultural experience. While most European and American writers skirt the issue of the racial origins of the ancient Egyptians and in default promote a "white" origin particularly as this is fed most visitors to the ancient land; such a contention is fraught with misinformation, some of it misguided either through ignorance or in support of the now still generally accepted false view of an extra-African origin of the Egyptians. Regarding this issue, for example, Wade Nobles in *Kemet and the African World View* has stated: "This latter point is understood if one understands that the political control of knowledge is a necessary condition for white supremacy; and, that in this regard as Diop has pointed out, the common denominator characterizing the study of ancient Egypt by white Egyptologists has been their seemingly desperate pathological necessity and unrelenting attempt to refute ancient Africa's blackness. Consequently, information regarding ancient Africa has been destroyed, distorted, falsified, suppressed and intentionally made unclear."

While David O'Connor, himself a white American writer, has informed this researcher, "The Egyptians were not white;" this revelation contradicts a false yet powerfully promoted contention that the Egyptians were in fact "white" or Caucasian. Such a view believed by many and postulated, as an example, by John David Wortham in *The Genesis of British Egyptology: 1549-1906* (Norman, Oklahoma: University of Oklahoma Press, 1971: 93) is stated thus: "Augustus Bozzi Granville, a physician and a student of Coptic, undertook the earliest nineteenth-century dissection of a mummy at his London home in 1825. From his detailed dissection he correctly concluded that the ancient Egyptians were Caucasian. He also succeeded in clearing up many erroneous ideas about the embalming process. Among other things, he proved the correctness of Herodotus' assertion that the ancient Egyptians had, when preparing a cadaver for burial, extracted the pituitary through the nostrils." Naturally Herodotus only heard of mummification practices and this is believed, yet his **observation** that the ancient Egyptians had "thick lips, broad noses and were burnt of skin" is not believed. We know James H. Breasted the American Egyptologist initially described the Egyptians as "brown skinned" before he began his revisionism about the "great white race." We know many of the mummies including that of Rameses II had "brown skin."

John Romer in *Valley of the Kings* (1981) (1994: 85) exhibits a photograph of a head from the tomb of Seti I with the following caption: "Salt sold many of the antiquities that Belzoni found in the royal tombs to the British Museum. This fine head from a broken statue of a young god or king was carved in cedar wood and coated with black resin. Unlike the similar figures found in Tutankhamon's tomb these statues were not, apparently, covered in gold leaf."

Now, in an interesting article entitled "Egyptian Mummy" among Antiquarian and Philosophical Studies in *The Gentleman's Magazine* of October 1820, pp. 349-350, in describing a mummy donated by Mr. Joshua Heywood to the Hunterian Museum at Glasgow, the writer states: "The body, shrouded in from fifty to sixty folds of coarse pale brick-red colored linen, is deposited in a strong wooden coffin, fashioned so as to bear a rude resemblance to the human shape. At the upper extremity is carved a face, the features of which (as in the case with all Egyptian sculpture) are very much of the Negro cast." We know the Egyptians loved the color red because they associated it with the sun, a solar and special phenomenon. They considered themselves special! Dr. Cheikh Anta Diop said the Egyptians painted themselves red to be distinguished from other Africans. Even Dr. Ben has often said, "The Egyptians painted themselves red with the Henna plant. Even young brides were painted red with Henna." Going back to the most ancient African "Bushman Art" and even art among the "Tassili Frescoes" red was the favorite color; again like gold, it was considered to be of a divine nature!

The article continued, "Though the features were very much collapsed, the face was no where divested of skin. The skin itself was of a chestnut-brown color. The brow was well shaped, though, if any way defective, narrow; and to some it may be interesting to learn, the organ of music was prominent. The nose, though slightly compressed, retained enough of its original shape to be recognized as Roman." Even further, the gentleman wrote, "One circumstance must have struck all who had an opportunity of seeing the above interesting examination; namely, *the dissimilarity of the features to what we are taught to believe were those of the inhabitants of Egypt* [This writer's emphasis], at the remote period at which the custom of embalming existed in that country. A moment's reflection will suffice to convince us that this circumstance can in no way throw discredit on the antiquity of the genuine character of the mummy."

The writer goes on to say, "Mr. Millar, portrait painter in Glasgow, is at present finishing a likeness in oil of the face and surrounding parts. As they appeared immediately after they were exposed; and was completely successful in the accuracy of the likeness before the exposure to the air had converted the face from a brown to a sable hue, which it did in the short period of three hours."

Accepting Wortham's mummy in a "one swallow so its summer" analogy would be like comparing this *Gentleman's Magazine* article's contention that the mummy had a "Roman nose" and was "brown skin" means the Romans were brown, Black or African!

Dr. Cheikh Anta Diop, privileged to be part of the scientific team that examined and treated the mummy of Rameses II in Paris as it decayed, has revealed so much radiation was administered to the mummy in treatment it turned from brown to white! Nevertheless, Arthur G. Brodeur in *The Pageant of Civilization* (1931) has described the Egyptians as "swarthy" and equally that "Egyptian civilization is African in form and soul." (31) Yet, he continued, "The Egyptian was never negroid (sic), and was no more mixed with negro stock than the modern European." On the other hand, Margaret Murray in *The Splendor that was Egypt* (1949) (1966: 31) says of Aahmes founder of the Eighteenth Dynasty: "As the mummy of King Aahmes has been preserved, his personal appearance is known. He was a strongly built man, broad-shouldered, and with curly brown hair; he was not good-looking for he had projecting front teeth, and his portrait suggests an admixture of negro blood."

Gaston Maspero described Seti's priest Maherpra as "Negroid but not Negro!" In critical comparative contrast, J.A. Rogers has shown in *Sex and Race*, Vol. 2 (1944: 306-309) how Beethoven's biographers described him. Pardon the lengthy descriptions but this has relevance to how the Egyptians were, particularly not "Caucasian." Beethoven's color has been described by: Fischer as "black-brownish;" Grillparzer "dark;" Bettina von Arnim "brown;" Weber "dark;" Schindler "red and brown;" Fannio Giannatasio "swarthy complexion," "mulatto;" Mary Byron "swarthy;" Prince Esterhazy "blackamoor;" Frederick Hertz "dark eyes and skin" and "slightly Negroid traits;" Bruno Springer (1940) "negro ancestry;" Emil Ludwig "dark;" and Thayer as "moor." Thus, in comparison, the contention is any and all of these descriptions can be applied to the ancient Egyptians and these are far removed from "Caucasian." Brooks has argued, "No Egyptian Pharaoh could sit at a southern lunch counter to enjoy a cup of coffee before de-segregation." And so confusion reigns as regards the ancient Egyptians, or so the story goes!

Nevertheless, the first four Introductory chapters of this work, *Research Essays on Ancient Egypt*, brings the reader up to date on some aspects of current trends in African physical anthropology and recent developments at preservation and beautification of the ancient monuments of Egypt so as to be attractive in its commercial potential and safety security-wise.

Above and apart, the first and last chapters, "Who were the Ancient Egyptians" and "The Conspiracy Against Ancient Egypt" tackle the pros and cons of this issue in a synthesis that gives Africans more credit than is currently recognized in some circles. The other chapters, not only puts meat on the bones of the subject but also clothes it in the cultural and historical cultural dynamics that has endeared Egypt to all lovers of this genre over the ages.

Images of photographs, illustrations, papyrus art and even temple site ticket stubs adds a unique dimension of visual imagery enhancing this work, a contemporary classic, that will prove useful to students, scholars, laymen and even tourists who may find it equally a Guidebook.

PREFACE ADDEND

The spelling of names of kings, gods and places has a tendency to appear different according to the author mentioned or quoted. For example, the God Ra's name is sometimes spelt Re or Ra. Amon's is given as Amon, Amen, Amun, and equally as Amon-Ra, Amen-Ra or Amun-Ra. The kings Amenhotep is sometimes spelt Amenhotep, Amenophis or Thutmose is shown as Thutmose, Thutmosis, Tutmosis, Tautmes and so on. Khufu, Khafre and Menkaure are given as Cheops, Chephren and Mycerenius, etc. Thebes, Thebaid, Abydos and so on, were Waset, and Abtu of the ancients. Even the gods' names Osiris for Ausar and Isis for Auset, etc., have been Hellenized. Many of the names adopted within the last two centuries use Graeco-Roman designations as a reinforcement of the "Conspiracy Against Ancient Egypt," rather than the indigenous names the people used to describe themselves in time perspective. That is to say, it becomes problematic when describing Old, Middle or New Kingdom persons with names used during the Graeco-Roman Period, but this is what is going on now. Therefore, the reader is asked to focus on the people, gods, industries, culture and places rather than the spelling of the names. In addition, since these **Research Essays** are a result of a collection of lectures over an extended period of time, there may be duplications of the information presented and hence, the reader is asked to be lenient in criticism, in this respect. This repetition is unavoidable but perhaps reinforces the overall message of the text. Nevertheless, happy reading to all!

Dr. Frederick Monderson displays some of his books offered for sale at Brooklyn Book Fair, September 2010 at Boro Hall.

Two Ladies Title of the Pharaoh. The vulture goddess Nekhbet of the South and the cobra Goddess Wadjet of the north, were protectors of the Pharaoh.

ABOUT THE AUTHOR

Frederick Monderson is a retired college professor and school teacher who taught African History in the City University of New York and American History and Government in the New York public schools. He has written nearly 900 articles in the New York Black Press, *Daily Challenge, Afro Times* and *New American* newspapers. In this venture, Monderson lends his expertise as a historian, Egyptologist, journalist and author of several books including *Michael Jackson: The Last Dance, 50 on Point, Black Nationalism: Alive and Well, Barack Obama: Ready, Fit to Lead, Barack Obama: Master of Washington, D.C., Sonny Carson: The Final Triumph*, and on ancient Egypt *Seven Letters to Mike Tyson on Egyptian Temples, 10 Poems Praising Great Blacks for Mike Tyson, Intrigue Through Time, Temple of Karnak: The Majestic Architecture of Ancient Kemet, Where are the Kamite Kings?, Abydos and Osiris, Temple of Luxor, Medinet Habu: Mortuary Temple of Rameses III, The Quintessential Book on Ancient Egypt: "Holy Land"* (A Novel on Egypt), *Hatshepsut's Temple at Deir el Bahari, The Majesty of Egyptian Gods and Temples* (a book of Egyptian Poems), *Egypt Essays on Ancient Kemet, The Ramesseum: Mortuary Temple of Rameses II, The Colonnade: Then and Now, Reflections on Ancient Kemet, Grassroots View of Ancient Egypt and*

Glory of the Ancestors: *19 Letters to O.J. Simpson on Ancient African History*. A student of the esteemed Dr. Yosef ben-Jochannan, Dr. Monderson conducts tours to Egypt.

For Tour information, Please contact Orleane Brooks-Williams at Nostrand Travel, 730 Nostrand Avenue, Brooklyn, New York 11216. Phone Number 718-756-5300.

From the Middle Kingdom, the "White Chapel" in Karnak's Open Air Museum begs the question, 'Why is this Negro face front and center in this particular panel or "Holy Spot" with all the paraphernalia of pharaonic rule?'

RESEARCH ESSAYS ON ANCIENT EGYPT

Table of Contents

Research Essays Captions	3
Preface	18
Foreword	26
1. Introduction I	27
2. Introduction II: Eternal, Yet Changing Egypt, 2005	44
3. Introduction III Reflections On Egypt 2008	61
4. Introduction IV Egypt 2010	69
5. Who Were the Ancient Egyptians?	75
6. The Religion of Ancient Egypt	120

FREDERICK MONDERSON

7.	The Egyptian Temple	161
8.	The History of Egypt	197
9.	The Archaeology of Egypt	240
10.	The Architecture of Egypt	266
11.	The Power of One	293
12.	Metals, Men and Materials	305
13.	The Art of Ancient Egypt	320
14.	Egyptian Warfare	362
15.	Egyptian Technology	380
16.	Science in Ancient Egypt	391
17.	Gold of Egypt	425
18.	Pharaonic Taxation	459

RESEARCH ESSAYS ON ANCIENT EGYPT

19.	The King	488
20.	The Conspiracy Against Ancient Egypt	523
21.	Suggestions for Further Reading	572
22	Comparing Egyptian Chronology	578
23.	Index	581

Research Essays 1. The four gods of Abu Simbel, (right to left) Ra-Horakhty, Rameses II, Amon and Ptah as they sit in the Sanctuary.

FREDERICK MONDERSON

Research Essays Captions

Research Essays Cover. (1) Entrance Pylon of Luxor Temple with its still standing Obelisk and seated statues of Rameses II while to the left, part of the Mosque of Abu Haggag; (2) as the gods Thoth and Ra-Horakhty are accompanied in their barque, Sennufer stands backing them in another frame; (3) model Kashida Maloney of Brooklyn, New York, stands near bust statue of Hathor on grounds of the Cairo Museum of Egyptian Antiquities.

Research Essays 1. Abu Simbel Temple of Rameses II. The four gods of Abu Simbel, (right to left) Ra-Horakhty, Rameses II, Amon and Ptah as they sit in the Sanctuary.

Research Essays 1a. Abu Simbel Temple of Rameses II. Horus, Khonsu Hathor on Pillars in the twin Temple of Nefertari.

Research Essays 1b. Abu Simbel Temple of Rameses II. Kashida Maloney of Brooklyn, New York, stands before the entrance façade with four colossal seated statues and the backdrop.

Research Essays 1c. Abu Simbel Temple of Rameses II. The "Prisoners" at the base of one of the seated colossal statues.

Research Essays 1d. Abu Simbel Temple of Rameses II. Another of the "Prisoner" illustration at another base of a seated colossal statue.

Research Essays 2. Abu Simbel Temple of Rameses II. Close-up of entrance facade with seated statues, God Ra-Horakhty, titulary deity and uraeus on the cornice overhead.

Research Essays 3. Abu Simbel Temple of Rameses II. Close-up of two middle statues, one missing head to the left and the other preserved with image of Ra-Horakhty in rear, while twin Rameses in Blue or War Crown, make a Presentation of Ma'at to the God, tutelary deity of the Temple.

Research Essays 4. Abu Simbel Temple of Rameses II. Plan of the two Temples of Rameses and his Queen Nefertari.

Research Essays 5. Abu Simbel Temple of Rameses II. Entrance hypostyle hall of Rameses' Temple, with 8 colossal Osiride standing remains of the Vulture Goddess on the ceiling.

Research Essays 6. Abu Simbel Temple of Rameses II. Close-up Of one of the standing colossal statues in the entrance hall.

Research Essays 6a. Abu Simbel Temple of Rameses II. Rameses offers a bouquet and pours a libation to Khnum, god of the Cataract.

Research Essays 6b. Abu Simbel Temple of Rameses II. Looking up at two seated right side colossal statues with female figures between their legs and images of Rameses and Ra-Horakhty above the entrance.

RESEARCH ESSAYS ON ANCIENT EGYPT

Research Essays 6c.   Abu Simbel Temple of Rameses II. The Nile Gods unite the land beneath the cartouche of Rameses II.

Research Essays 7.   Abu Simbel Temple of Rameses II. Rameses smites a kneeling enemy before Ra-Horakhty while Nefertari stands at his rear.

Research Essays 8.   Abu Simbel Temple of Rameses II. Rameses wears the Double Crown and makes a Presentation of flowers while pouring a libation to Khnum, God of the Cataract.

Research Essays 8a.   Abu Simbel Temple of Rameses II. Beneath the pedestal of the seated colossal and miniature female figures, the King as a colossal figure wearing the lion skin outfit.

Research Essays 8b.   Abu Simbel Temple of Rameses II. Another view of the above image, beneath the pedestal of the seated colossal and miniature female figures, the King as a colossal figure wearing the lion skin outfit.

Research Essays 9.   Abu Simbel Temple of Rameses II. Entrance Façade of Nefertari's Temple with statues of Rameses, Nefertari and Hathor.

Research Essays 10.   Abu Simbel Temple of Rameses II. Nefertari holds a sistrum and makes a Presentation of flowers to enthroned Hathor, Goddess of her Temple.

Research Essays 11.   Abu Simbel Temple of Rameses II. Rameses in Blue or War Crown offers two bouquets to enthroned Hathor in horns and disk, while Nefertari offers flowers and holds a sistrum in her Temple.

Research Essays 11a.   Abu Simbel Temple of Rameses II. Plaque commemorating the safeguarding and reconstruction of Abu Simbel temples during Gamal Abdul-Nasser's Presidency in 1968.

Research Essays 12.   Temple of Isis on Agilka Island. Visitors and guards at the entrance landing while the Kiosk of Trajan stands in the rear.

Research Essays 13.   Temple of Isis on Agilka Island. The Western Colonnade with its 32 columns on the Dromos to the Entrance Pylon.

Research Essays 14.   Temple of Isis on Agilka Island. The Eastern Colonnade with its 17 Columns and Entrance Pylon in the rear.

Research Essays 15.   Temple of Isis on Agilka Island. The First Pylon with illustrations of the King in different attitudes making Presentations to the Gods, and below Isis straddling the entrance. Through the door opening, Isis can be seen on the First Pylon to her Temple proper. To the right, is the northern end of the Eastern Colonnade. Notice the steps in ascent inwards the Temple.

Research Essays 16.   Temple of Isis on Agilka Island. Close-up of two columns with varied capitals, and high abacus or die below the architrave. In the rear, illustrations on a wall.

FREDERICK MONDERSON

Research Essays 16a. Temple of Isis on Agilka Island. In Osiris Crown, pharaoh offers two sistrums to Isis enthroned as Hathor with her son as a child at her rear.

Research Essays 16b. Temple of Isis on Agilka Island. In the small Hathor Chapel, an ape plays a tambourine while another plays a stringed instrument. Notice the uraei on the top of the engaged screen.

Research Essays 17. Temple of Isis on Agilka Island. The King in plumes; notice his tail, as he offers two "Eye of Horus" to enthroned Horus in Double Crown beside Isis also enthroned.

Research Essays 17a. Isis Temple on Agilka Island. Pharaoh in Nemes Headdress, surmounted by Osiris crown of horns, uraei with disks, white crown with disks and with straight beard and wearing tails, offers two vessels to Hours in Double Crown.

Research Essays 18. Temple of Isis on Agilka Island. Two sister Goddesses, Hathor and Isis. Notice the exposed breasts.

Research Essays 18a. Temple of Isis on Agilka Island. Off the beaten path and from the rear of the three temples on the Dromos, panoramic view of the Pylons that guard the temple of the goddess.

Research Essays 19. Temple of Isis on Agilka Island. In rear of the Temple, Pharaoh Presents a scepter to Horus wearing the Double Crown while Isis as Hathor stands to the God's rear.

Research Essays 20. Temple of Isis on Agilka Island. Close-up view of the Kiosk of Trajan with its magnificent screened colonnade with high abacus below the overhead architrave.

Research Essays 21. Temple of Isis on Agilka Island. The King in Double Crown makes a Presentation of 3 feathers, Ma'at, to Osiris with Isis to the God's rear.

Research Essays 21a. Temple of Isis on Agilka Island. In Red Crown and wearing necklace, Pharaoh offers two vessels to Isis as Hathor.

Research Essays 22. Temple of Isis on Agilka Island. Isis out front holding a symbol of her power before Horus in Double Crown and with Hathor at their rear.

Research Essays 22a. Temple of Isis on Agilka Island. While Nephthys sits enthroned behind Isis nursing Horus, Khnum makes the child no his potter's wheel, while Thoth sits at his rear.

Research Essays 22b. Columns of the Second Eastern Colonnade in the Court of Isis's Temple proper.

Research Essays 22c. Returning from the temple of Isis, a local bird does a river dive near the rocks in background.

Research Essays 22d. On a river boat and with Trajan's Kiosk in the distant rear, native Egyptian Guide Shawgi Abd el-Rady relaxes after an interesting tour of the Temple of Isis.

RESEARCH ESSAYS ON ANCIENT EGYPT

Research Essays 23. View of the Old Cataract Hotel at Aswan from beside the Pool.

Research Essays 24. View of the New Cataract Hotel from beside the pathway near Old Cataract Hotel at Aswan.

Research Essays 24a. An assortment of Nubian jewelry for sale in the Aswan area.

Research Essays 25. Two Brothers, American and Nubian on the pathway beside the Old Cataract Hotel at Aswan.

Research Essays 26. The Outer Enclosure Wall encompassing the Temples of Karnak with the Northern Group to the left, the Central Group in the middle and the Southern Group to the right. That is the Temple of Montu to the left, Amon-Ra center, and Mut to the right.

Research Essays 27. View of Plans of the Temples of Karnak within the Outer Enclosure Wall.

Research Essays 28. Plan of the Temple of Amon-Ra at Karnak.

Research Essays 29. Temple of Amon-Ra at Karnak. Sphinxes before the Southern Colonnade within the Great Court and with the inner face of the southern half of the First Pylon to the right. The last column of the colonnade is unfinished giving evidence of how these columns were erected before being pounded smooth.

Research Essays 30. Temple of Amon-Ra at Karnak. The Processional Colonnade with its open umbel capitals beside the ruins of the hypostyle hall. To the right openings are remains of clerestory windows.

Research Essays 31. Temple of Amon-Ra at Karnak. Twin statues of Amon-Ra and Rameses II just beside the first column at the entrance to the hypostyle hall.

Research Essays 32. Temple of Amon-Ra at Karnak. Decorated columns of the hypostyle hall with their open umbel capitals and ruins of windows of the clerestory that let light into the hall.

Research Essays 33. Temple of Amon-Ra at Karnak. Evidence of repairs to columns of the hypostyle hall with their closed bud capitals, abacus and overhead architrave, all decorated.

Research Essays 34. Temple of Amon-Ra at Karnak. View of the two obelisks, Hatshepsut's left and that of her father, Thutmose I, right.

Research Essays 35. Temple of Amon-Ra at Karnak. Defaced statue of Queen Hatshepsut just before the Sanctuary.

Research Essays 36. Kashida Maloney of Brooklyn, New York, stands before a broken and repaired statue just outside Luxor Temple.

FREDERICK MONDERSON

Research Essays 37. Temple of Amon-Ra at Karnak. "Girdle Wall" of Rameses II. Nefertari, left; Rameses in Blue or War Crown offers a plant to Amon-Ra, center; Rameses offers two bouquets to a defaced deity.

Research Essays 38. Temple of Amon-Ra at Karnak. "Girdle Wall" of Rameses II. The King offers a plant and two obelisks to Amon-Ra.

Research Essays 39. Temple of Amon-Ra at Karnak. "Girdle Wall" of Rameses II. With a Goddess to his rear, Rameses offers a disfigured image to Khonsu of the Theban Triad.

Research Essays 40. Temple of Amon-Ra at Karnak. "Girdle Wall" of Rameses II. With a goddess to his rear, Rameses offers three vessels to Amon-Ra.

Research Essays 41. Hatshepsut's Temple at Deir el Bahari. From the "Bird's Eye View," from the cliff, end of First Court with First Ramp and Lower Colonnade, Second Court with Second Ramp and Middle Colonnade, Upper Terrace and Upper Colonnade and beyond, Upper Court with Sanctuary against the face of the Mountain. Mentuhotep II's Middle Kingdom Temple is further ahead.

Research Essays 42. Hatshepsut's Temple at Deir el Bahari. Black-top entrance to the Temple with First and Second Security Posts and the essential features of the structure including two Ramps seeming to join and Lower, Middle and Upper Colonnades.

Research Essays 43. Hatshepsut's Temple at Deir el Bahari. One of two trees brought by the Punt Expedition and planted in front of the Temple.

Research Essays 44. Hatshepsut's Temple at Deir el Bahari. Close-up of the two Ramps and Lower, Middle and Upper Colonnades.

Research Essays 45. Hatshepsut's Temple at Deir el Bahari. Northern half of the Lower Colonnade with its broken columns to the rear of square pillars.

Research Essays 46. Hatshepsut's Temple at Deir el Bahari. From slightly south-east, view of the Portico to the Sanctuary in the Upper Court.

Research Essays 47. Hatshepsut's Temple at Deir el Bahari. View of the Anubis Shrine (left) and the true unfinished Northern Colonnade (right) in the Second Court.

Research Essays 48. Hatshepsut's Temple at Deir el Bahari. A surviving broken head of an Osiride Figure of the Queen on the Upper Terrace.

Research Essays 49. Hatshepsut's Temple at Deir el Bahari. Close-up of three remaining Osiride Figures of the Queen that escaped destructive agents of her enemies in Thutmose III's backlash. She wears the white crown, with beard and holds the symbols of power, a whip and flail.

Research Essays 49a. Hatshepsut's Temple at Deir el Bahari. Author and photographer Dr. Fred Monderson adjusts his hat but notice the pavement in the Court and the Ramp towards the Upper Terrace seem immaculately finished.

RESEARCH ESSAYS ON ANCIENT EGYPT

Research Essays 50. Hatshepsut's Temple at Deir el Bahari. Visitor makes a phone call, perhaps to relate what a wonderful experience the Temple really is.

Research Essays 51. Temple of Luxor. From the southwest, view of the tip of the Processional Colonnade, ruins of the "Ramesseum Front," entrance Pylon, Obelisk and Minaret of Mosque of Abu Haggag, Patron Saint of Luxor.

Research Essays 52. Temple of Luxor. From the west, view of the magnificent Processional Colonnade with its 14 imposing columns with open umbel capitals, abacus and architrave overhead. The walls below, on both sides, depict the voyage from and to Karnak in celebration of the Opet Festival.

Research Essays 53. Temple of Luxor. From the southwest, view of the Papyrus bud columns of the Court of Amenhotep III.

Research Essays 54. Temple of Luxor. From the west, another view of the columns of the Court of Amenhotep III.

Research Essays 55. Temple of Luxor. From the west, a further view of columns of the Court of Amenhotep III.

Research Essays 56. Temple of Luxor. In the "Ramesseum Front," the Kiosk of Hatshepsut, usurped by Thutmose III and repaired by Rameses II.

Research Essays 56a. Plan of the Temple of Luxor with names of its builders.

Research Essays 57. Ramesseum, Mortuary Temple of Rameses II. View of the hypostyle hall with columns and clerestory (right) and vestibule with Osiride Figures and columns.

Research Essays 58. Ramesseum, Mortuary Temple of Rameses II. A better view of the columns and Osiride Figures within the porch.

Research Essays 59. Ramesseum, Mortuary Temple of Rameses II. Rameses kneels to make a Presentation to the enthroned Theban Triad of Amon-Ra, Mut and Khonsu.

Research Essays 60. Medinet Habu, Mortuary Temple of Rameses III. Entrance facade, called a Migdol, with the First Pylon in the rear.

Research Essays 61. Medinet Habu, Mortuary Temple of Rameses III. Rameses smites captives before Amon-Ra who offers him the curved sword on the left side of the Temple's Entrance Pylon.

Research Essays 62. Medinet Habu, Mortuary Temple of Rameses III. Rameses smites captives before Ra-Horakhty who offers him the curved sword on the right side of the Temple's Entrance Pylon.

Research Essays 63. Medinet Habu, Mortuary Temple of Rameses III. Defaced Osiride Figures in the First Court. Notice the small female figure near the foot of the statue.

FREDERICK MONDERSON

Research Essays 63a. Medinet Habu, Mortuary Temple of Rameses III. Rameses grasps Egypt's enemies by the hair and prepares to administer the death-blow.

Research Essays 64. Medinet Habu, Mortuary Temple of Rameses III. Pillar and column in the Second Court.

Research Essays 64a. Medinet Habu, Mortuary Temple of Rameses III. Heads of the Egyptians at the time of Rameses III. How interesting that heads or faces of statues always seems to be "purposefully defaced!"

Research Essays 65. Medinet Habu, Mortuary Temple of Rameses III. View of the Ark at rest with much decorative color remaining.

Research Essays 65a. Medinet Habu, Mortuary Temple of Rameses III. In Blue or War Crown, Rameses holds an ankh, wears a long flowing gown, with apron sporting uraei and above a hawk hovers overhead while further above, uraei signal he's in the temple.

Research Essays 66. Medinet Habu, Mortuary Temple of Rameses III. Rameses in Blue or War Crown kneels to Present Ma'at as his name to enthroned Ra-Horakhty.

Research Essays 67. Medinet Habu, Mortuary Temple of Rameses III. The author stands before the feet of two broken seated statues.

Research Essays 67a. Rameses III before enthroned Nile God with Thoth as an ibis at his rear.

Research Essays 68. Medinet Habu, Mortuary Temple of Rameses III. Rameses offers an ape to Amon-Ra and then he stands alone in the Blue or War Crown. Notice his see-thru flowing dress or galibeah.

Research Essays 69. Medinet Habu, Mortuary Temple of Rameses III. In White Crown, Rameses gestures while his cartouche stands nearby.

Research Essays 70. Medinet Habu, Mortuary Temple of Rameses III. Illustrations of vessels.

Research Essays 70a. Medinet Habu, Mortuary Temple of Rameses III. Rameses in Blue Crown and long flowing gown, holds scepters and stands above prisoners.

Research Essays 71. Medinet Habu, Mortuary Temple of Rameses III. Rameses faces and prepares to incense two divinities. Notice his long-flowing dress.

Research Essays 72. Medinet Habu, Mortuary Temple of Rameses III. While Goddess Mut stands behind Rameses who kneels before enthroned Amon-Ra, Khonsu stands behind his father, the first of the Theban Triad. Notice the Uraeus overhead indicating they're in the temple.

Research Essays 73. Mortuary Temple of Seti I at Abydos. Entrance facade of Osiris Temple at Abydos, built by Seti I of the 19th Dynasty.

RESEARCH ESSAYS ON ANCIENT EGYPT

Research Essays 74. Mortuary Temple of Seti I at Abydos. Seti in necklace, sash and long-flowing dress holds objects as he bows to Amon-Ra, who is all blue!

Research Essays 75. Mortuary Temple of Seti I at Abydos. Seti pours a Libation to Amon-Ra as Min, his ithyphallic alter ego.

Research Essays 76. Mortuary Temple of Seti I at Abydos. Seti prepares to incense and pours a libation to enthroned Ra-Horakhty in Double Crown.

Research Essays 77. Mortuary Temple of Seti I at Abydos. Ra-Horakhty embraces Seti and makes him an offer.

Research Essays 78. Mortuary Temple of Seti I at Abydos. Seti makes a Presentation to enthroned Amon-Ra in plumes. Notice the hawk above the King's head and his cartouches.

Research Essays 79. Mortuary Temple of Seti I at Abydos. The God Anubis embraces Seti who also touches the divinity. Notice the hawk above Seti's head.

Research Essays 80. Mortuary Temple of Seti I at Abydos. Isis as Hathor offers life to the nostrils of Seti.

Research Essays 81. Mortuary Temple of Seti I at Abydos. Seti offers a plant to Moon God Khonsu with side plat or lock of hair, indicative of youth.

Research Essays 82. View of the surrounding terrain in the Valley of the Kings.

Research Essays 82a. Sign indicating all you need to know regarding the "Glory of the Ancient" culture in the Valley of the Kings.

Research Essays 82b. A list of the major tombs of the Valley of the Kings.

Research Essays 83. Valley of the Kings. Tomb of Thutmose III of the 18th Dynasty.

Research Essays 84. Valley of the Kings. Tomb of Thutmose III contains decoration with the *Litany of Ra* and the complete *Imy-dwat*.

Research Essays 85. Valley of the Kings. Tomb of Tutankhamen contains decoration with the *Book of the Dead, King with Gods*, the *Opening of the Mouth Ritual* and the *Imy-dwat*.

Research Essays 86. Valley of the Kings. Tomb of Seti I contains decoration with the *Book of Gates; King with Gods;* the *Opening of the Mouth Ritual; Astronomical Scenes;* the *Book of the Heavenly Cow,* the *Litany of Ra,* and the *Imy-dwat*.

Research Essays 87. An alabaster factory with its exterior richly illustrated.

FREDERICK MONDERSON

Research Essays 88. Part of the rich variety of objects offered for sale at the Alabaster Factory.
Research Essays 89. More of the wide assortment of objects offered for sale at the Alabaster Factory.
Research Essays 89a. View of the surrounding landscape with some evidence of tombs (openings) of people of means.
Research Essays 89b. Scenes from the tomb of Vizier Rekhmara showing boat people, individuals bringing gifts and giving out instructions to workers.
Research Essays 90. Still more of the wonderful offering for sale at the Alabaster Factory.
Research Essays 91. Kom Ombo Temple to Gods Haroeis and Sobek. Majestic architecture of Kom Ombo's entrance with twin sun disk and twin uraeus on the cornice overhead. Notice the varied capitals and the twin nature of the Temple.
Research Essays 92. Kom Ombo Temple to Gods Haroeis and Sobek. Another view of the entrance, the wall, colonnade in the Court and the massive columns, capitals, architrave and twin disks overhead.
Research Essays 93. Kom Ombo Temple to Gods Haroeis and Sobek. Frontal view of the entrance with the left side dedicated to the Elder (Horus) Haroeis and the right to Sobek, the Crocodile God.
Research Essays 94. Kom Ombo Temple to Gods Haroeis and Sobek. Close-up of the intricacies of one of the varied capitals of the colonnade in the hypostyle hall.
Research Essays 95. Kom Ombo Temple to Gods Haroeis and Sobek. Twenty-three uraei Adorn this ledge above the cartouches.
Research Essays 96. Kom Ombo Temple to Gods Haroeis and Sobek. Skyward view of a wonderful contrast of two of the varied capitals below the architrave.
Research Essays 97. Kom Ombo Temple to Gods Haroeis and Sobek. The Garden at Kom Ombo Temple.
Research Essays 98. Kom Ombo Temple to Gods Haroeis and Sobek. Pharaoh holds the *aba scepter* before Horus in White Crown and Hathor in horns and disk.
Research Essays 99. Kom Ombo Temple to Gods Haroeis and Sobek. Ra-Horakhty makes a Presentation to the King.
Research Essays 99a. Kom Ombo Temple to Gods Haroeis and Sobek. Picturesque view of the Peristyle Court and twin entrance to the temple, its massive columns, all against a clear, blue sky in the rear.
Research Essays 99b. Another view of the colonnade of the Court.
Research Essays 100. Kom Ombo Temple to Gods Haroeis and Sobek. On a wall, twin deities of the Temple, Horus left and Sobek Right.

RESEARCH ESSAYS ON ANCIENT EGYPT

Research Essays 101. Kom Ombo Temple to Gods Haroeis and Sobek. Khonsu, the Moon God, of the Theban Triad stands majestically, yet defaced.

Research Essays 102. Kom Ombo Temple to Gods Haroeis and Sobek. Twin sphinxes in Double Crowns sport uraei and disks overhead.

Research Essays 103. Kom Ombo Temple to Gods Haroeis and Sobek. On a column, Goddess Hathor in the Queen Mother Crown. Notice her right breast exposed.

Research Essays 104. Kom Ombo Temple to Gods Haroeis and Sobek. The Goddess of building Seshat with her breast exposed stands next to Horus in Red and White Double Crown.

Research Essays 105. Kom Ombo Temple to Gods Haroeis and Sobek. On a column, God Sobek, Lord of Ombos.

Research Essays 106. Kom Ombo Temple to Gods Haroeis and Sobek. All the Gods, Thoth, Hathor, Bastet, Haroeis, Horus, perform a Laying of Hands ritual on the Pharaoh.

Research Essays 107. Kom Ombo Temple to Gods Haroeis and Sobek. Horus' Sanctuary in rear of the Temple.

Research Essays 108. Kom Ombo Temple to Gods Haroeis and Sobek. Sobek's Sanctuary in rear of the Temple.

Research Essays 108a. Kom Ombo Temple to Gods Haroeis and Sobek. Pharaoh and an assistant make a Presentation to Haroeis, the Elder Horus with Hathor at his rear. Notice the king's and his attendant's see-through gown.

Research Essays 108b. Kom Ombo Temple to Gods Haroeis and Sobek. Beyond the decorated wall, the uraei and disks on the architrave and the majestic columns with their different capitals.

Research Essays 108c. Kom Ombo Temple to Gods Haroeis and Sobek. On a column, the king wears the White Crown, necklace, straight beard and long flowing gown as he offers a sphinx to one of the deities of the temple.

Research Essays 108d. Kom Ombo Temple to Gods Haroeis and Sobek. Defaced figures give some understanding of how zealots destroyed much of ancient Egypt.

Research Essays 109. Kom Ombo Temple to Gods Haroeis and Sobek. From the rear, both Sanctuaries and the respective aisles of each God.

Research Essays 110. Kom Ombo Temple to Gods Haroeis and Sobek. On a rear wall, colossal sculpture and accompanying inscriptions. Notice the 10 crocodiles sacred to Sobek.

Research Essays 111. Kom Ombo Temple to Gods Haroeis and Sobek. Some scholars believe, from the makeup and decoration of the Apron, this depiction is probably that of Imhotep, builder of the Step Pyramid at Sakkara.

FREDERICK MONDERSON

Research Essays 112. Kom Ombo Temple to Gods Haroeis and Sobek. Even further, this colossal relief also depicts a person of great importance.

Research Essays 113. Edfu Temple of Horus the Falcon. Defaced King and his Queen make a Presentation to falcon image of the Temple while Horus stands before them in Double Crown.

Research Essays 114. Edfu Temple of Horus the Falcon. As the King prepares to incense the Goddess he looks to his rear at Anubi figures holding aloft an image of the God.

Research Essays 114a. Native Egyptian Antiquities Guide Shawgi Abed el Rady stands beside the back wall in the "Corridor of Victory" at Edfu Temple.

Research Essays 115. Edfu Temple of Horus the Falcon. Second part of the previous frame where the image of the God is hoisted by Anubi-like figures.

Research Essays 116. Edfu Temple of Horus the Falcon. Multiple images (above) the King gestures to images of falcons with seated divinities and (below) the King Presents to a falcon and the God aloft with lions in attendance as the Queen sports the Red Crown.

Research Essays 116a. Edfu Temple of Horus the Falcon. Pharaoh offers two vases to Amon as Min while Horus sits enthroned with Isis at his rear who seems to be saying "I've got your back, Brother."

Research Essays 116b. Edfu Temple of Horus the Falcon. Defaced figure wearing the Osiris Crown with horns, White Crown with feathers and Uraei with disks.

Research Essays 117. Edfu Temple of Horus the Falcon. Image of Thoth, God of Writing and intellect as he does his recording.

Research Essays 118. Cairo Museum of Egyptian Antiquities. A black goose. The Goose is also symbolic of Amon-Ra.

Research Essays 119. Cairo Museum of Egyptian Antiquities. One of two wooden statues of Tutankhamon dressed in gold and painted black to represent his color.

Research Essays 120. Cairo Museum of Egyptian Antiquities. The other statue of the boy-King that adorns the entrance to the gallery that houses his treasure.

Research Essays 121. Cairo Museum of Egyptian Antiquities. Bronze plaque of the boy-King striking a lion.

Research Essays 122. Cairo Museum of Egyptian Antiquities. Bronze plaque of the boy-King smiting his Nubian enemies who are painted black as he is shown previously.

Research Essays 123. Cairo Museum of Egyptian Antiquities. Part of the ushabti entourage Tutankhamon took with him to the otherworld.

RESEARCH ESSAYS ON ANCIENT EGYPT

Research Essays 124. Cairo Museum of Egyptian Antiquities. More of the ushabti entourage Tutankhamon took with him to the next world.
Research Essays 125. Cairo Museum of Egyptian Antiquities. Sphinx statue of Queen Hatshepsut.
Research Essays 126. Cairo Museum of Egyptian Antiquities. Kneeling statue of Queen Hatshepsut.
Research Essays 127. Cairo Museum of Egyptian Antiquities. Papyrus of deceased female making a salutation to the enthroned image of Osiris, God of the Dead, painted black, and while to his rear Khepre sails his boat above the great serpent.
Research Essays 128. Cairo Museum of Egyptian Antiquities. The great God Geb painted black and in reposed position on a hill encircled by the serpent.
Research Essays 129. Cairo Museum of Egyptian Antiquities. Here's another image of Osiris painted black in his shrine as he receives supplication of a deceased female. Other deities are in the background.
Research Essays 130. Ghizeh Plateau. The Sphinx of Ghizeh in its majestic splendor against the wonderful blue sky.
Research Essays 131. Ghizeh Plateau. Causeway to the Great Pyramid of Khufu of the 4th Dynasty.
Research Essays 132. Ghizeh Plateau. The Pyramid of Khafre viewed from the desert.
Research Essays 133. Ghizeh Plateau. The massive stone supports and architraves within the vicinity of the pyramids.
Research Essays 134. Columns adorn a Carpet Factory on road from Sakkara.
Research Essays 135. Memphis Museum. The alabaster Sphinx of Memphis that adorns the grounds of the museum.
Research Essays 135a. Suten Bat title of the Pharaoh with symbol of Ma'at, goddess of goodness.
Research Essays 136. Memphis Museum. Visitors mill around the fallen colossal statue of Rameses II around which the Memphis Museum is built. Notice the uraeus on his brow, the beard and the cartouche and dagger at his waist.
Research Essays 137. Memphis Museum. Anubis sits atop a granite sarcophagus on the grounds of the Museum.
Research Essays 137a. Ptah, great god of artisans and Memphis, a bald headed dwarf or pygmy.
Research Essays 138. The Step-Pyramid of Sakkara built by Imhotep for Pharaoh Zoser, 3rd Dynasty, c. 2600 B.C. This structure remains standing and intact, attesting to its architectural magnificence.

FREDERICK MONDERSON

Research Essays 138a. Memorabilia for sale on grounds of Sakkara, home of the step-Pyramid.
Research Essays 138b. Another of the vendors plying his wares in the grounds of the Memphis Museum.
Research Essays 138c. Side view of the Sphinx of Memphis.
Research Essays 138d. Remains of columns on the grounds of Memphis Museum.
Research Essays 138e. Side view of colossal statue of Rameses II and remains exhibited in and outside of cases as two ladies stroll along enjoying the view.
Research Essays 138f. Artifacts for sale outside of Theban sites.
Research Essays 139. Images of figures from a tomb at Sakkara. Interestingly, it's always the face that is attacked and one has to ask why!
Research Essays 139a. Two images of Noblemen from Sakkara holding their staff and Aba Scepter. Notice the little figure beside the staff of authority.
Research Essays 139b. Goddess Mut is the principal figure with portion of the White Crown visible to the right, from a tomb at Sakkara.
Research Essays 139c. Sign identifying Tombs of Nobles at Sakkara, open to visitors including Nefer-her-En-Ptah, Ruka-Ptah, Niankh-Khnum, Khnum-Hoteb all needing special tickets of 30 Egyptian Pounds each to visit.
Research Essays 140. On a trip to a Nubian Village at Aswan, a tumultuous turnout welcomed African American visitors and these folks followed them to the waterside.
Research Essays 140a. Two images of Anubis painted blue are looked over by two Eye of Horus in the Tomb of Senufer, taken back in 2003.
Research Essay 140b. Sennufer stands before Thoth and other gods, one wearing the red and white Double Crown in the tomb of Sennufer, picture taken back in 2003.
Research Essays 141a. and b. Two statues of very hard stone are included to give an example of broken noses.

RESEARCH ESSAYS ILLUSTRATIONS

Research Essays Illustration 1. Ancient Egyptian Universe as seen from down in the Valley of the Nile River.
Research Essays Illustration 2. The Sky Goddess Nut spanning the Heavens and encompassing the 12 hours of the day as represented by the divinities of that hour.

RESEARCH ESSAYS ON ANCIENT EGYPT

Research Essays Illustration 3. The Sky Goddess Nut spanning the Heavens between the 24 hours of the day. She gives birth to the sun in the morning and swallows it at day's end.

Research Essays Illustration 4. The Air God Shu separates the Sky Goddess Nut from the Earth Goddess Geb, while Thoth the God of Wisdom, looks on holding a feather as symbol of truth.

Research Essays Illustration 5. The Rising Sun, with Goddesses and Baboons in adoration.

Research Essays Illustration 6. The Setting Sun. A perched falcon with Sun-disk, kneeling Anubi and Horuses, the two Goddesses Isis (right) and Nephthys (left), kneel before lions with disks before the sacred tree.

Research Essays Illustration 7. Drama in the Heavens as the Celestial Cow is attended to by deities of various persuasions.

Research Essays Illustration 8. A curve representing approximately the variation in 25,920 years of the length of the year indicated by the helical rising of the Star Sirius.

Research Essays Illustration 9. Position and Movement of the Stars as viewed on a Celestial Globe and Pyramid Data.

Research Essays Illustration 10. The Sphinx buried in sand with the Great Pyramid of Khufu in the rear. Notice how high the people are which indicates how much of the desert has encroached on these monuments.

Research Essays Illustration 11. Petrie's Triangulation of the Pyramids of Ghizeh.

Research Essays Illustration 12. Topographical Plan of the Pyramids of Gizeh.

Research Essays Illustration 13. Mereruka, the Vizier of King Teti, seeming to walk through the false door in his mastaba.

Research Essays Illustration 13a. The twelve Egyptian Months of three Seasons.

Research Essays Illustration 14. Mythological animals from the Egyptian desert.

Research Essays Illustration 15. More mythological figures from the Egyptian desert.

Research Essays Illustration 16. The famous Egyptian uraeus that guards the Pharaoh.

Research Essays Illustration 17. Majestic bird of Egypt. Imagine stepping out with its flair, as the claws and beak speak volumes.

Research Essays Illustration 18. Some of the birds of Egypt.

Research Essays Illustration 19. Animals from the sculptures of ancient Egypt.

FREDERICK MONDERSON

Research Essays Illustration 20. Vases, with one and two handles.
Research Essays Illustration 21. Birds and fishes as represented in other shapes.
Research Essays Illustration 22. Different boxes with lids shaped differently.
Research Essays Illustration 23. Egyptian sailing boats in full sail.
Research Essays Illustration 24. Plants from the sculptures.
Research Essays Illustration 25. Fishing and fowling scenes
Research Essays Illustration 26. Bird traps, one with a bird caught in it, and the others are all open and empty.
Research Essays Illustration 27. Herdsmen giving an account of the cattle.
Research Essays Illustration 28. Dom and Date Palm trees.
Research Essays Illustration 29. Bellows. Thebes.
Research Essays Illustration 30. Donkey carrying a load of grain sheaves in the Pyramid Age
Research Essays Illustration 31. Tools: Blades and hooks.
Research Essays Illustration 32. Tools: Rope, chisels, cutting tools, hook, etc.
Research Essays Illustration 33. Jewelry, rings, Eye of Horus, etc.
Research Essays Illustration 34. Tools: Chisels, pot, etc.
Research Essays Illustration 35. Tools: Basket, axe blades, cutter and chisel.
Research Essays Illustration 36. Tools: Stone axes.
Research Essays Illustration 37. Tools: Float and brick making mold.
Research Essays Illustration 38. Tools: Drill head, drill bow, drill stock and fire stick and fire stock.
Research Essays Illustration 39. Goldsmiths making jewelry, smelting and weighing gold, superintending and clerks at work. Beni-Hassan.
Research Essays Illustration 40. Preparing the flax, beating it, and making it into twine and cloth. Beni-Hassan.
Research Essays Illustration 41. Tools: Mirror, vases, borers, etc.
Research Essays Illustration 42. Tools: Axe blades, cutting tools, etc.

RESEARCH ESSAYS ON ANCIENT EGYPT

Research Essays Illustration 43. Tools: Rake, hoes, sickles of wood with fling saw teeth and grain winnower.

Research Essays Illustration 44. Men dressing stone (1), sculpting a sphinx (2), and making seated and standing colossals of stone (3).

Research Essays Illustration 45. Potters making earthenware vases. Beni-Hassan.

Research Essays Illustration 46. The Nomes of Upper Egypt.

Research Essays Illustration 47. The Nomes of Middle Egypt.

Research Essays Illustration 48. The Nomes of Lower Egypt.

Research essays Illustration 49. Part I: Cutting and twisting thongs of leather; and Part II: Carpenters plying their trade.

Research Essays Illustration 50. Men throwing a spear. Beni-Hassan.

Research Essays Illustration 51. Sandal-makers and men employed in polishing a column. Beni-Hassan.

Research Essays Illustration 52. Vases of different sizes and shapes without, with one and with two handles.

Research Essays Illustration 53. Mode of transporting a colossus from the quarries, from a lithographic drawing of Mr. Bankes.

Research Essays Illustration 54. Loading and transporting precious cargo.

Research Essays Illustration 55. Marking cattle with a hot iron. Thebes.

Research Essays Illustration 56. Male dancers being accompanied by musicians and applauded by females.

Research Essays Illustration 57. Boat in full sail on the river.

Research Essays Illustration 58. Bringing home the game: A gazelle, porcupines, and a hare. Beni-Hassan.

Research Essays Illustration 59. Nubians bringing tribute.

Research Essays Illustration 60. Conjurers or thimble rig.

Research Essays Illustration 61. Cattle rescued from the inundation. Beni-Hassan.

Research Essays Illustration 62. Diverse jobs. Cutting the wheat with a sickle; lining up the asses; loading the animals; emptying the wheat in silos.

Research Essays Illustration 63. An ass fetching the falcon on its back.

Research Essays Illustration 64. The Tritura. Thebes.

FREDERICK MONDERSON

Research Essays Illustration 65. Two women working the loom.

Research Essays Illustration 66. Some plants and animals brought back from Paunit or Punt.

Research Essays Illustration 67. Herdsmen and poulterer treating sick animals and geese. Beni-Hassan.

Research Essays Illustration 68. Asiatics bringing tribute.

Research Essays Illustration 68a. More Asiatics with their tribute.

Research Essays Illustration 68b. Even more Asiatics who look nothing like the ancient Egyptians.

Research Essays Illustration 69. Painting of a temple's columned hall with Bedouin just hanging out.

Research Essays Illustration 70. Harvest scene. Thebes.

Research Essays Illustration 71. View of the rapids of the river at Aswan.

Research Essays Illustration 72. Map of Egypt and the Nile Valley to the Second Cataract.

Research Essays Illustration 73. A chariot of the New Empire in the Cairo Museum.

Research Essays Illustration 74. Harvest scene. Thebes.

Research Essays Illustration 75. The Court of Amenhotep III at the Temple of Luxor, from the northeast, during the Inundation.

Research Essays Illustration 75a. Another view of the Court of Amenhotep III from the Northeast near the Mosque of Abu Haggag.

Research Essays Illustration 76. The Luxor Temple Processional Colonnade.

Research Essays Illustration 77. Cooks and Confectioners. In the Tomb of Rameses III at Thebes.

Research Essays Illustration 78. Front of the state chariot of Thutmose IV.

Research Essays Illustration 79. Twin sentinels of Amenhotep III placed before his temple at Thebes.

Research Essays Illustration 80. Pretty well preserved head of the mummy of Seti I.

Research Essays Illustration 81. The Temple of Karnak's Processional Colonnade, during early clearance of the enclosure.

Research Essays Illustration 82. Funeral boat or Baris, with shrine.

RESEARCH ESSAYS ON ANCIENT EGYPT

Research Essays Illustration 83. Villa and garden of an Egyptian Noble of the Old Kingdom (After Perrot and Chipiez) (Breasted 1923).

Research Essays Illustration 84. View of Karnak from the south, atop the roof of the Temple of Khonsu, of the Theban Triad.

Research Essays Illustration 85. The Funeral Procession – The Mourners. The Oxen Dragging the Mummy to his last home.

Research Essays Illustration 86. Workmen drilling out stone vessels.

Research Essays Illustration 87. Funeral Rites – The Opening of the Mouth Ceremony performed by the priest in lion skin outfit.

Research Essays Illustration 88. Khuenaten worshipping the Solar Disk with his wife Nefertiti and a daughter.

Research Essays Illustration 89. Head of Amenhotep IV, Khuenaten, Ikhnaton, wearing the Blue or War Crown.

Research Essays Illustration 90. Funeral Rites at the Tomb. Winged Soul descending a ladder to the Mummy.

Research Essays Illustration 91. Great Temple of Karnak and the Nile Valley at Thebes seen from an Airplane.

Research Essays Illustration 92. The Weighing of the Soul in the Judgment.

Research Essays Illustration 93. Part of the Fleet of Queen Hatshepsut loading in the Land of Punt.

Research Essays Illustration 94. *Book of the Dead*. Spearing Khepre and Uraei on Guard.

Research Essays Illustration 95. Winged Sun-Disk, a symbol of the Sun-God.

Research Essays Illustration 96. Soul with symbols of Life and Breath revisiting the mummied body.

Research Essays Illustration 97. Relief representing Thutmose III making an offering to a God at Gebel Dosha.

Research Essays Illustration 98. *Book of the Dead*. Adjusting the sails for smooth sailing.

Research Essays Illustration 99. *Book of the Dead*. Chapter XXXIX in a Pyramid of Sakkara. From Lepsius' *Denkmaler*.

Research Essays Illustration 100. *Book of the Dead*. Chapter XXXIV, Sakkara, from Lepsius' *Denkmaler*.

Research Essays Illustration 101. Spearing the Gazelle.

FREDERICK MONDERSON

Research Essays Illustration 102.   *Book of the Dead.* Spearing the Snake, in Chapter XXXIX, *Papyrus Musee du Louvre*, 93.

Research Essays Illustration 103.   *Book of the Dead.* With jars and before the monster.

Research Essays Illustration 104.   Sailing with the Gods, from the Tomb of Rameses IV.

Research Essays Illustration 105.   *Book of the Dead.* Khepre in a Basket and Spearing the Crocodile.

Research Essays Illustration 106.   *Book of the Dead.* Vignettes from the Tomb of Rameses IX, Tomb of Seti I, and a *Leyden Papyrus*.

Research Essays Illustration 107.   *Book of the Dead.* Vignettes of the bird beak, from the *Papyrus of Ani, Nicholson Papyrus* and *Papyrus of Ani*.

Research Essays Illustration 108.   *Book of the Dead.* Chapter XXXIII. From a Papyrus, Leyden Museum, IV. Time to do the Chop-Chop of the snake and cockroach.

Research Essays Illustration 109.   *Book of the Dead.* Chapter LVII and LVIII from a Papyrus in British Museum, No. 9,949 and *Papyrus of Ani*.

Research Essays Illustration 110.   *Book of the Dead.* Water from the Cool Pool and the Tree with a Halo in Chapter LXI and Chapter LXIV from the *Papyrus du Louvre*, 11,193.

Research Essays Illustration 111.   War-Galley; the sail being pulled up during the action. Thebes.

Research Essays Illustration 112.   *Book of the Dead.* Vignettes of pouring the refreshment found at Sakkara in Lepsius' *Denkmaler* and Lanzone's *Egyptian Dictionary*.

Research Essays Illustration 113.   Spearing the Hippopotamus.

Research Essays Illustration 114.   Manner from the Tree Goddess, in Lepsius' *Todtenbuch*.

Research Essays Illustration 115.   Pleasure-boat towed round a pond. Thebes.

Research Essays Illustration 116.   A party of guests, to whom wine, ointment, and garlands are brought. Sweet-smelling cones are on their heads, as a sort of perfume ointment. From Thebes, and in the British Museum.

Research Essays Illustration 117.   A party of guests entertained with music and the dance.

Research Essays Illustration 118.   Geese brought and numbered. British Museum – from Thebes.

Research Essays Illustration 119.   Part 1. Fowling scene. Part 2. Spearing fish with the bident.

Research Essays Illustration 120.   While the deceased Ani and his wife enter Osiris' Hall of Judgment, Anubis adjusts the scale, Thoth records,

RESEARCH ESSAYS ON ANCIENT EGYPT

Am-Mit, eater of the dead, waits, and the Gods of the jury sit overhead.

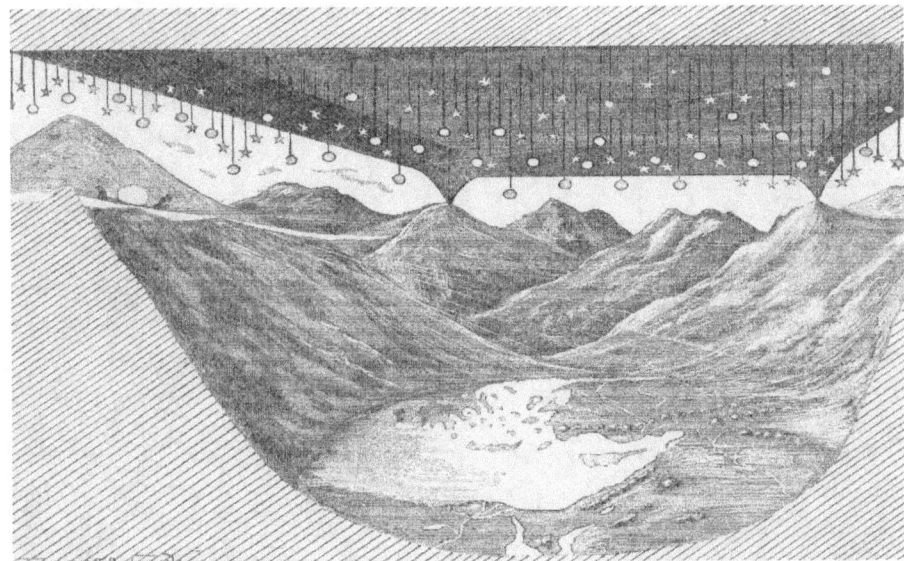

Research Essays Illustration 1. Ancient Egyptian Universe as seen from down in the Valley of the Nile River.

RESEARCH ESSAYS PLAN OF TEMPLES

Temple of Hatshepsut at Deir el Bahari 1550 B.C.
Plan of the Great Temple of Karnak
General Plan of the Temples of Karnak
Temple of Luxor
Temple of Osiris at Abydos built by Seti I and Rameses II
Plan of the Temple of Dendera
Karnak Under the Ptolemies
Temple of Hours at Edfu
Temple of Esneh, with restorations by Grand-Bey

FREDERICK MONDERSON

Research Essays 1a. Abu Simbel Temple of Rameses II. Horus, Khonsu Hathor on Pillars in the twin Temple of Nefertari.

RESEARCH ESSAYS PAPYRUS ART

Research Essays Papyrus Art 1. The Tree Goddess offers libation as Ma'at (feather) genuflects and Isis backs enthroned Osiris with Thoth and Am-Mit before the god while an Eye of Horus hangs over Thoth, looking!

Research Essays Papyrus Art 2. Geese feeding by the waterside with fishes nearby in the river.

Research Essays Papyrus Art 3. Hathor introduces Nefertari as Ma'at stretches her wings before enthroned Isis as Horus and two goddesses stands behind the goddess.

Research Essays Papyrus Art 4. The Psychostasia. As Anubis introduces the deceased, he adjusts the scales as "Am-Mit" sits waiting; Thoth records and Horus introduces the "victor" to enthroned Osiris as Isis and Nephthys back the god and the Four Sons of Horus defend.

RESEARCH ESSAYS ON ANCIENT EGYPT

Research Essays Papyrus Art 5. Two vultures and Uraei stand above two "Eye of Horus" as Anubis adjusts the scales for Judgment of a deceased female; while Thoth, the Baboon, records her situation and she presents to Osiris backed by Isis and Nephthys.

Research Essays Papyrus Art 6. Goddess with wings extended is encircled by two Horuses in Double Crowns and wings with uraei.

Research Essays Papyrus Art 7. The King stands before Hathor (left) and Presents to Horus as Ra-Horakhty in Double Crown, while the Son of Ra cartouches hangs overhead.

Research Essays Papyrus Art 8. Akhnaton (Ikhnaten) and his wife and child each make a Presentation to the hands of the sun disk, the Aten.

Research Essays Papyrus Art 9. Image of Golden mask of King Tutankhamon.

Research Essays Papyrus Art 10. Enthroned Ra-Horakhty sits beside Goddess Hathor.

Research Essays Papyrus Art 11. Tutankhamon rides in his chariot and shoots at birds.

Research Essays Papyrus Art 12. Queen presents two jars to enthroned Hathor.

Research Essays Papyrus Art 13. Tutankhamon sits enthroned and being attended by his queen.

Research Essays Papyrus Art 14. Ma'at kneels before enthroned Hathor in Queen Mother Crown comprising a vulture headdress, and atop a mortar, horns and a sun disk.

Research Essays Papyrus Art 15. Tutankhamon and his wife out hunting in the marshes (left) and he being embraced by her (right).

Research Essays Papyrus Art 16. Horus in double crown holds the hands of his Queen.

Research Essays Papyrus Art 17. Goddess Hathor holds the hand of Queen Nefertari.

Research Essays Papyrus Art 18. Attended by Thoth and Amun, Isis sits in the papyrus field nursing Horus as two goddesses stand nearby.

Research Essays Papyrus Art 19. Hunting in the mashes with the wife and child as fishes swim in the river nearby.

Research Essays Papyrus Art 20. Egyptian birds nest in a beautiful tree.

Research Essays Papyrus Art 21. The Golden Mask of King Tutankhamon.

FREDERICK MONDERSON

Research Essays Papyrus Art 22. Goddess Nuit spanning the heavens where she gives birth to the sun in the morning and swallows it up at evening time.

RESEARCH ESSAYS TEMPLE SITE TICKETS

Research Essays Temple Ticket 1. Philae Temple. Price of entrance is fifty Egyptian Pounds.
Research Essays Temple Ticket 2. Edfu Temple. Price of entrance is fifty Egyptian Pounds.
Research Essays Temple Ticket 3. Karnak Temple. Price of entrance is sixty-five Egyptian 50 Pounds.
Research Essays Temple Ticket 4. Camera Stand Permit at twenty Egyptian Pounds per site.
Research Essays Temple Ticket 5. Open-Air Museum at Karnak Temple. Price of entrance is twenty-five Egyptian Pounds.
Research Essays Temple Ticket 6. Luxor Temple. Price of entrance is fifty Egyptian Pounds.
Research Essays Temple Ticket 7. Deir el Bahari Temple. Price of entrance is thirty Egyptian Pounds.
Research Essays Temple Ticket 8. Deir el Bahari Temple Taftaf. Price of ride is two Egyptian Pounds.
Research Essays Temple Ticket 9. Ramesseum Temple. Price of entrance is thirty Egyptian Pounds.
Research Essays Temple Ticket 10. Medinet Habu Temple. Price of entrance is thirty Egyptian Pounds.
Research Essays Temple Ticket 11. Olwet Abdel Qurna. Price of entrance is twenty-five Egyptian Pounds.
Research Essays Temple Ticket 12. Abydos Temple. Price of entrance is thirty Egyptian Pounds.
Research Essays Temple Ticket 13. Dendera Temple. Price of entrance is thirty-five Egyptian Pounds.
Research Essays Temple Ticket 14. Ticket used by native Egyptians at such places as the Pyramids.
Research Essays Temple Ticket 15. Another ticket used by native Egyptians at a temple site.
Research Essays Temple Ticket 16. Imhotep Museum and Sakkara. Price of entrance is sixty Egyptian Pounds.

RESEARCH ESSAYS ON ANCIENT EGYPT

Research Essays Temple Ticket 17. Sakkara New Tombs. Price of entrance is thirty Egyptian Pounds.

Research Essays Temple Ticket 18. Mit Rahina Museum. Price of entrance is thirty-five Egyptian Pounds.

Research Essays Temple Ticket 19. Cairo Museum of Egyptian Antiquities. Price of entrance is sixty Egyptian Pounds.

FOREWORD

One particular papyrus in the Cairo Museum depicts a woman of light color before Osiris, enthroned and painted black. This particular scene raises several questions if we accept the notion of (a) Painted black for the funerary ceremony; and (b) Osiris being black because he is god of the dead, in an infernal region. (c) Is there evidence that all other internments, royal and noble, had statues "painted black for the funeral ceremony?"

1. If confined to the infernal region and so painted why is Osiris also shown as green and red? Several other issues are brought to mind in this regard.
2. The infernal region can be equated with heaven, paradise, etc., thus, are we to believe such a place of eternal bliss and heavenly joy would be considered "black" even bleak, as such a color is generally portrayed.
3. Are we to believe only kings and gods are painted black for the funerary ceremony while others are not so represented, particularly the female in the above papyrus?
4. Should we ask, Why is Maherpra 'Negroid but not Negro' is painted black and so many others are not?
5. If the 11th Dynasty lady of Mentuhotep II, Kemsit, is painted black and is considered a Negro; but Mentuhotep, also painted black, is so for the "funeral ceremony" only instead of Smith's "black flesh" is this an issue?
6. Tutankhamon is painted black "for the funeral ceremony" but the people on the plaque whom he tramples are also painted black, but they are Negroes and he is not. We know there were other statues so painted in the tombs of Seti I, Rameses I, Amenhotep I, etc.
7. Aahmes-Nefertari is painted black, but this is only "because 19th Dynasty artisans chose to so represent her." Still, many on her line are shown to have "Negro" traits. Bunsen says she's Ethiopian and a lady with the highest social titles.
8. Perhaps the critics could explain or rationalize why surviving evidence of the Gods Geb, Min, Amon, in addition to Osiris are painted black. Let us not forget, when the great God Ra created the world, his first act was to create

FREDERICK MONDERSON

Nubians, black people, even before he made Egyptians! Or, are we to believe Nubians are Caucasians. Diop calls this the "absurd conclusion."

9. Of course, surviving evidence of Caucasian Egyptians is generally speculative; though, when the Egyptians represented "white people" they refer to inhabitants of the Northland.

10. It is amazing how critics of the African, Negro, black origins of the Egyptians, try to refute all credible, surviving evidence, but proffer speculative evidence of Caucasian origins despite reports of objective western commentators, to the contrary.

1. INTRODUCTION I.

Before I took a trip to Egypt I tried to read and learn as much about the culture as I could. For years I researched the topic and within the academic domain, I took courses that enabled me to better understand the history, culture and geography. I studied archaeology, anthropology, history, art, and architecture, and began to study the rudimentary elements of the language, hieroglyphics, called *Medu Netcher* by the ancient Egyptian Africans.

In the 1980s I traveled to Egypt with Dr. ben-Jochannan. I had known him for some years, was familiar with his books, and decided why not go with experience.

Research Essays Papyrus Art 1. The Tree Goddess offers libation as Ma'at (feather) genuflects and Isis backs enthroned Osiris with Thoth and Am-Mit before the god while an Eye of Horus hangs over Thoth, looking.

RESEARCH ESSAYS ON ANCIENT EGYPT

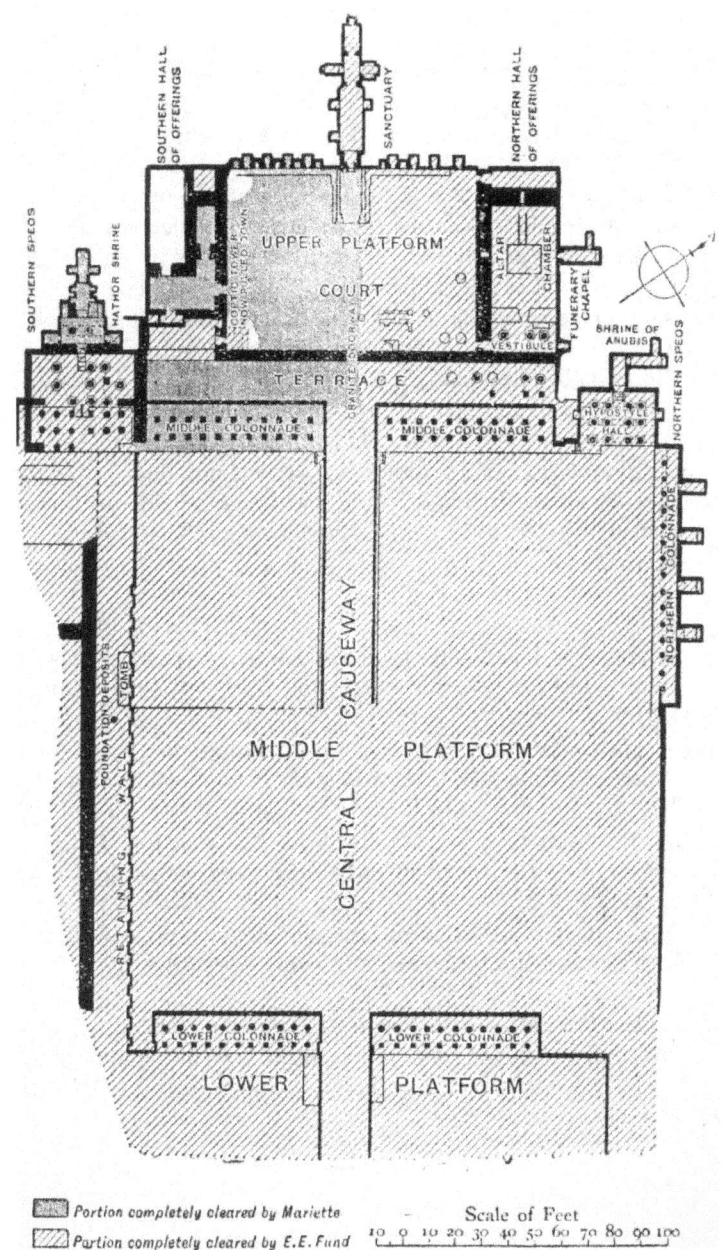

Temple of Hatshepsut at Deir el Bahari, 1550 B.C.

FREDERICK MONDERSON

It was a good tour. The Doctor made us aware of the things that were important to the observant. He always taught respect for the culture and proper attire particularly in the temples. He said: "Do not enter the Sanctuary!" In ancient times, only the Pharaoh and his High Priest could enter the Sanctuary where the God resided! He was also cognizant of the fact and reminded his students that African-Americans, who go to Egypt, are some of the most knowledgeable visitors, of that culture to that ancient land. Insisting we prepare before making the educational trip, he also made us aware of the architectural features of the temple that one has to pay attention to. With most temples, there is a Quay at the riverside where boats dock, and then perhaps a canal, he pointed out, then the path leading to the entrance generally called an Avenue of Sphinxes. This leads towards the Pylon or entranceway. Beyond this is the Courtyard. Here you may find an altar, some statues and perhaps a chapel. Perhaps there is another Pylon, but generally, there is a large hypostyle hall and sometimes a succeeding smaller hypostyle hall. Beyond this is the Sanctuary or "Holy of Holies," often surrounded by a number of smaller rooms that serve some function relating to the god and ritual of the temple worship. A flight of stairs leads to the roof where there may be a chapel to which the god is taken on certain festive days, to greet his counterpart, the Sun God.

Beyond the temple there are generally a number of outbuildings, some for members of the priesthood, and other rooms added as subsidiary places of worship of the deity. Nearby there is a Sacred Lake, fed by underground streams from the Nile River. Oftentimes there is a Nilometer nearby to predict the level of the river but also to aid in determining the level of taxes for surrounding areas. In the much later Graeco-Roman times a Mammisi was added, as a place where the deity's offspring was born. Gardens grew flowers for the daily services. Temple staff cultivated domestic crops that were adjuncts to their crafts and skills that had attained high levels of creativity. There were oftentimes schools of art, medicine and general knowledge, viz., astronomy, mathematics, hydrostatics, etc., in which young priests and members of the government's bureaucracy were trained. These are some insights to the temple and some of the secrets it holds.

In those areas where African-Americans are lacking an understanding of historical process, then research and history are wonderful tools of enlightenment. Dr. John H. Clarke viewed history as a road map that tells where you have been, where you are, and where you are going!

Malcolm X said "history is a good teacher."

RESEARCH ESSAYS ON ANCIENT EGYPT

Research Essays 1b. Abu Simbel Temple of Rameses II. Visitor Kashida Maloney of Brooklyn, New York, stands before the entrance facade with four colossal seated statues and the backdrop.

It is important that we look to our esteemed elders who have spent lifetimes researching this subject, and then listen to what they say. An accepted belief is that any scholar, who spends a lifetime, say, thirty years or so, researching an issue such as Egypt, ought to have reached some clearly defined conclusions about the cultural history of these ancient Africans. After lengthy careers, Martin Delaney,

FREDERICK MONDERSON

Edward Wilmot Blyden, W.E.B. DuBois, Marcus Garvey, Drusilla Dunjee, Carter G. Woodson, John Huggins, Dr. Yosef ben-Jochannan, Dr. John H. Clarke, Dr. Ivan Van Sertima, Dr. Jacob Carruthers, Dr. Cheikh Anta Diop, Dr. Theophile Obenga, and a whole host of others, have come to the conclusion that the history of the Nile Valley has been shaped to glorify Europe and Europeans and vilify Africa, and by its extension, her sons and daughters, at home and abroad.

In this modern world, it is a well-guarded secret if any scholars of European ancestry have made some of the same findings as African and African-American scholars. If so, they have not shouted it out, yet! That is, beyond the revelations of scholars as Denon, Higgins, Massey, Dart, and Kersey Graves, among select others.

Research Essays 1c. Abu Simbel Temple of Rameses II. The prisoners at the base of one of the seated colossal statues.

Nevertheless, Egypt is important because it is the foundation of all knowledge, viz., agriculture, science, medicine, government, architecture, art, trade, navigation, quarrying, and some may even add imperialism, and equally been the victim of distortion and omission. For instance, a good example is given by W.J. Perry in *The Growth of Civilization* quoting G. Elliot Smith in the second edition of *The Ancient Egyptians*, who noted: "The Egyptians did a great deal more than merely invent agriculture and devise the earliest statecraft and religion. Not only did they devise methods of working wood and stone and the art of architecture, they seem also to have been inventors of linen and of the craft of weaving, of the use of gold and copper, and the making of metal tools and implements. They were the first people to measure the year and to devise a calendar, and later on to substitute for the rough calculation based upon the date of the annual Nile flood the exact measurement based upon the observation of the sun's movement. They also invented shipbuilding and constructed the first sea-going ships. In a thousand and one of the details of our common civilization the originality of Egyptian civilization is revealed. The art of shaving, the use of wigs, the wearing of hats, the invention of the kilt and of the sandal and subsequently of a variety of other articles of dress, many of our musical instruments, chairs and beds, cushions, jewelry and jewel-cases, lamps — these are merely a few of the items picked at random out of our ancient heritage from the Nile Valley." Equating the African with these beginnings has not bided well for racist, Western, European and American historiography. When that writer said "our" ancient heritage, which he uses three times, he meant this legacy is not humanity's nor African, but European! And this is a distortion of history.

Research Essays Illustration 2. The Sky Goddess Nut spanning the Heavens and encompassing the 12 hours of the day as represented by the divinities of those hours.

FREDERICK MONDERSON

Because of such a distorted position, we give praise to the intellectual and research genius of Cheikh Anta Diop who has so eloquently demolished the myth of Europe and Asia in Africa. He has bequeathed a legacy of impeccable academic and historical research that in turn challenges the African and African-American scholar to defend Egypt as African!

It is clear; the history of the Nile Valley experience is so long that it boggles the imagination. Pardon me while I make known some dates that demonstrate the progress of early man in Africa. This, then, represents the precursors from which the "peopling of the Nile Valley" emerged.

A recent note in a local newspaper indicated a reinforcement of the scientific belief that man originated in Africa. We do know the earliest primate in the human evolutionary experience dates to 30 million years ago and appropriately is called *Aegyptopithecus*. That is Ape of Egypt. We know of *Proconsul* at 25 million; *Dyropithecus*, "fire using ape," at 20 million; *Kenyapithecus wickeri* at 15 million, who divided into 3 apelike creatures as: *Gigantopithecus* 9-1 million, who became extinct. *Sivapithecus* became the modern apes, chimpanzees and they evolved between 9-1 million. The third is *Ramapithecus* who further subdivided into three species in a period of around 6 million years and this process began some 12-13 million years ago.

Research Essays 1d. Abu Simbel Temple of Rameses II. Another of the prisoner illustration at another base of a seated colossal statue.

RESEARCH ESSAYS ON ANCIENT EGYPT

Research Essays 2. Abu Simbel Temple of Rameses II. Close-up of entrance facade with seated statues, God Ra-Horakhty, titulary deity and uraeus on cornice overhead.

The three species from *Ramapithecus* were *Australopithecus Robustus* with a brain capacity of 400 cc (cranial capacity) occurring somewhere between 3.5 to 1.5 million years. He was very awkward. *Australopithecus Africanus*, his counterpart, was more graceful with a cranial capacity of between 450 and 550 at about the same 3.5 to 1.5 million years ago. *Homo habilis*, "skillful man," had a cranial capacity at 700 and lived around 2 million years ago.

The latter two, *Australopithecus Africanus* and *Homo habilis,* have been called "near man," and "true man." "Near man," used tools, anything he could find in the environment, such as sticks, stones, twigs, anything. He never used his brains. He died out! "True man" on the other hand, fashioned tools. When he wanted a tool, he made it. He made tools to a "set and regular pattern." This demand challenged his brain to develop and so, in the process, he overcame his environment while his counterpart became its victim.

We know of the rich fossil grounds of East Africa such as in Kenya, Tanzania and Ethiopia, where Johansson found "Lucy" dated at 3 million.

FREDERICK MONDERSON

Mary Leakey and husband Louis Leakey, the anthropologists, found bones they dated as "firm" at 3.25 million years ago. There have been subsequent older finds of fossils.

Thus, in that long march of human history and the dance of the growth of mankind, Mother Africa, did well as a nurturer.

The difference in all of this was the cranial or brain capacity.

Homo erectus, or erect, standing man, was dated at 1.6 *million* years. If only we could envision a tunnel where *Homo habilis*, "true man," entered at 1.6 million years and emerged in South Africa around 300,000 years ago possessing a brain capacity of 1200-1350 cc.

The recent article previously mentioned, credits man with leaving Africa around 40,000 to 50,000 years ago to populate the earth. Between 40,000 and 28,000 proto-humans emerged. Modern man, "true, true man," emerged between 32,000 and 25,000 years ago.

Today's man has a cranial capacity or cc of 1350-1500.

Dr. Ivan Van Sertima, in a lecture regarding this idea of the origin of man in Africa, stated the following. He made known, that man emerged in Africa is a given. However, he continued, the racists have argued when man left Africa to populate the world as stated above, those remaining in Africa remained stagnant.

RESEARCH ESSAYS ON ANCIENT EGYPT

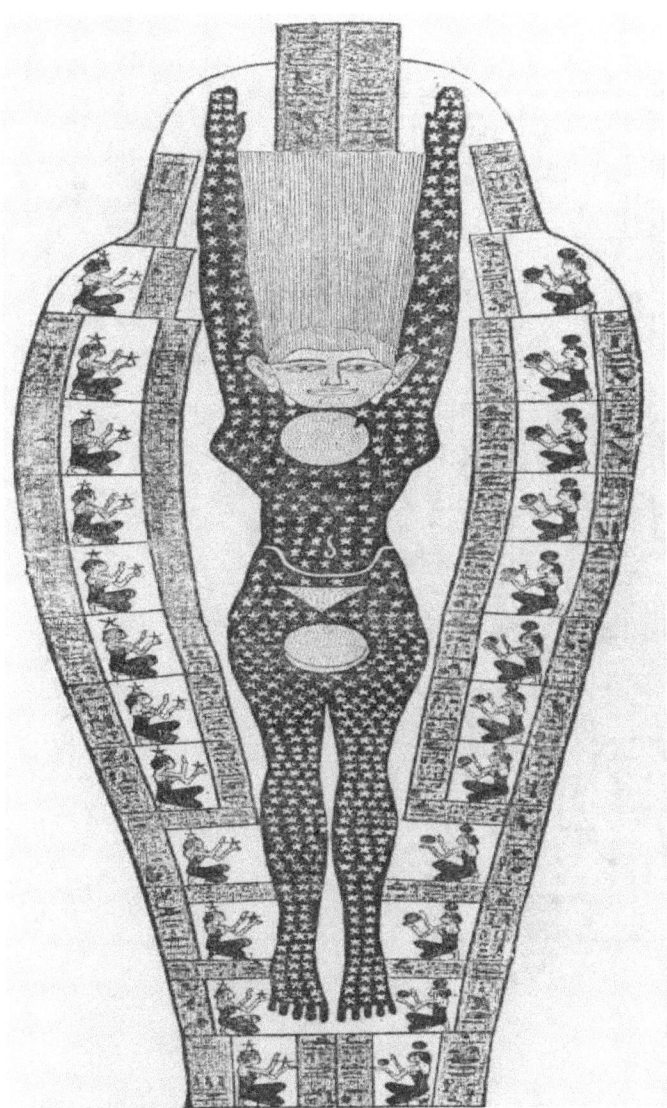

Research Essays Illustration 3. Sky Goddess Nuit spanning the Heavens between the 24 hours of the day. She gives birth to the sun in the morning and swallows it at day's end.

FREDERICK MONDERSON

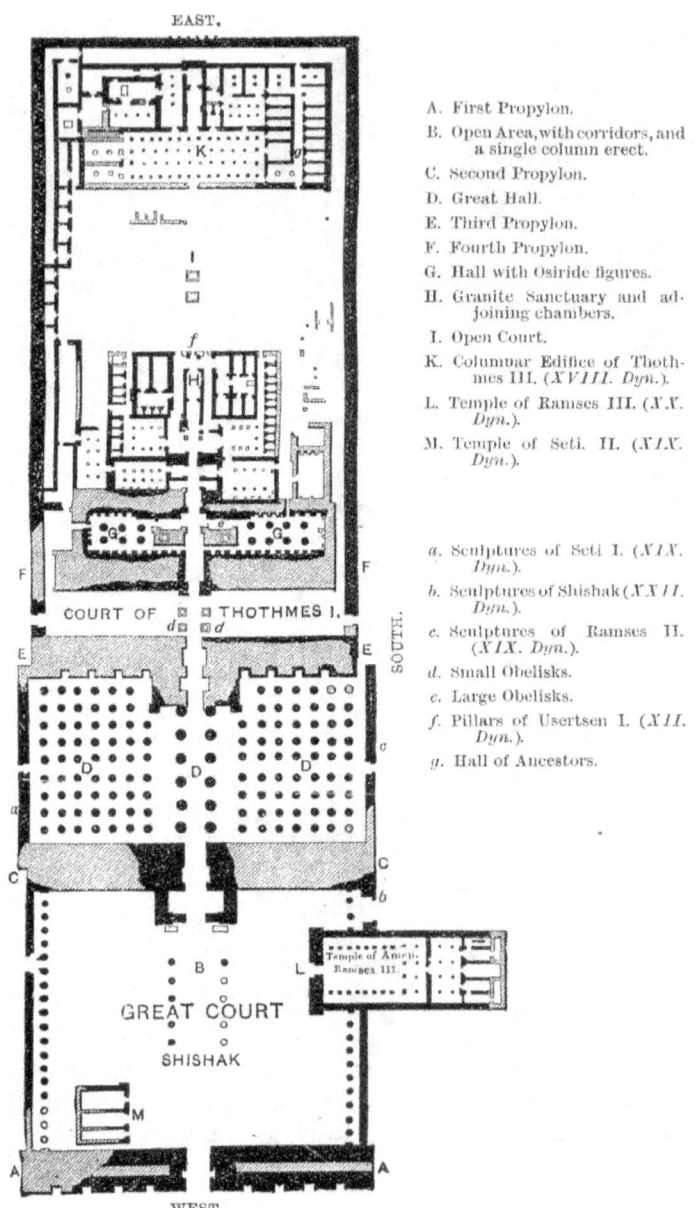

Plan of the Great Temple of Karnak

RESEARCH ESSAYS ON ANCIENT EGYPT

Man who reached Europe and Asia developed fully and then had to come back to Egypt and Africa and civilize their poor fellows. This is pure poppycock, but the racists have used this line of argument to show, among others, the civilization of Egypt and the Nile Valley was brought there by invading people of a "white morphology." This argument took the form of the "Hamitic Hypothesis," but was subsequently discredited. However, those with a racist bent still cling to the notion of a "white Egypt" despite the overwhelming evidence to the contrary.

Nevertheless, regarding early man in Africa, it is generally asked, 'Where do we get all this information?' Well, scientists worked in fields of archaeology, anthropology, paleoanthropology, psychology, anatomy, sociology, biology, zoology, linguistics, botany, primatology and taphonomy, a process of death and decay and fossilization. Much of this is found in the strata of the earth's surface. The science of stratigraphy is a geologic study of the strata of the earth dealing with its origin, composition, distribution and succession of strata.

Regarding humanity's development, this entire process was engineered and motivated by a philosophic calculus, or as we say, the three characteristics that govern the survival of man in any given environment – that is - move, adapt or die!

Man is a primate among a most diverse and complex set of similar beings.

In the suborder *Prosimil* and *anthropoidea* there is a super-family *ceboidea*. There are three super-families including *ceboidea*, *cercopithecoidea* and *hominoidea*. Others as *pliopithecoidea* and *oreopithecidae* are extinct.

The *pongidae* are the great apes. Man is a *hominoidea*.
The earliest *hominoidea* belongs to the genus *Ramapithecus*. Hominoidea is similar to *Australopithecinae*.

We know that *Australopithecus paranthropus*, "near man," of South Africa, lived around the time of *Zinjanthropus Boise* about 1.75 million years ago.

In all this Linnaean classification, we have come to characterize early man in Africa as being a nomadic hunter and gatherer.

More correctly, recent DNA research has traced the human family, not simply to Africa, but to a single female who roamed the East African plains some 200,000 years ago. She is probably the first "Eve."

FREDERICK MONDERSON

Nevertheless, we can clearly define some basic traits of early man. These were the use of tools - his primitive technology, the stone axe; bipedalism or upright posture; development of a large brain and the development of culture. The latter is characterized as rudimentary use of tools such as the hand-axe, chopping pebble tools, and use of fire. We could add the acquisition of primitive language, because of necessity. In addition, division of labor and family relationships are other factors that developed. Men became hunters and women collectors of food.

In this mix, early man began development of home bases to which members of the band returned as they forged communal hunting and communal living cultures and practices. As culture emerged, so too did different type of sites of occupancy. To complement the living sites there were butchering sites where they cut up animals of the hunt. Workshop sites or floors were where tools were made. In quarry sites he extracted flints and minerals. Ceremonial sites were where cultural functions were performed. Lastly, burial sites such as graves and later tombs were final resting places for the dead.

Research Essays 3. Abu Simbel Temple of Rameses II. Close-up of two middle statues, one missing head to the left and the other preserved with image of Ra-Horakhty in rear, while twin Rameses in Blue or War Crown, make a Presentation of Ma'at to the God, tutelary deity of the temple.

RESEARCH ESSAYS ON ANCIENT EGYPT

In this tunnel into time, man, essentially and principally African man, gradually advanced the threshold of humanity and blazed a trail of intellectual inquisitiveness and emerging scientific experimentation that ensured our future existence.

Therefore, we came to realize the difference between "true man," *Homo Habilis*, and "near man," *Zinjanthropus*, is the growth of the brain through the daring of experimentation.

The physiological trait that is most discernible is that man emerged with the opposable thumb and forefinger and flat feet, while his lesser relatives had opposable big toe and flat hands.

Research Essays Illustration 4. The Air God Shu separates the Sky Goddess Nut from the Earth Goddess Geb, while Thoth the God of Wisdom, looks on holding a feather as symbol of truth.

Therefore, in this evolution of physiological and technological change, as stated, "true man" made tools to a set and regular pattern, while "near man" used, but did not make tools. He utilized natural objects of his environment but did not transform them to a "set and regular pattern" as did "true man." This is why "near man" died out. Here then is the lesson for all people: "Use your brain rightly, before you become a victim of your environment."

FREDERICK MONDERSON

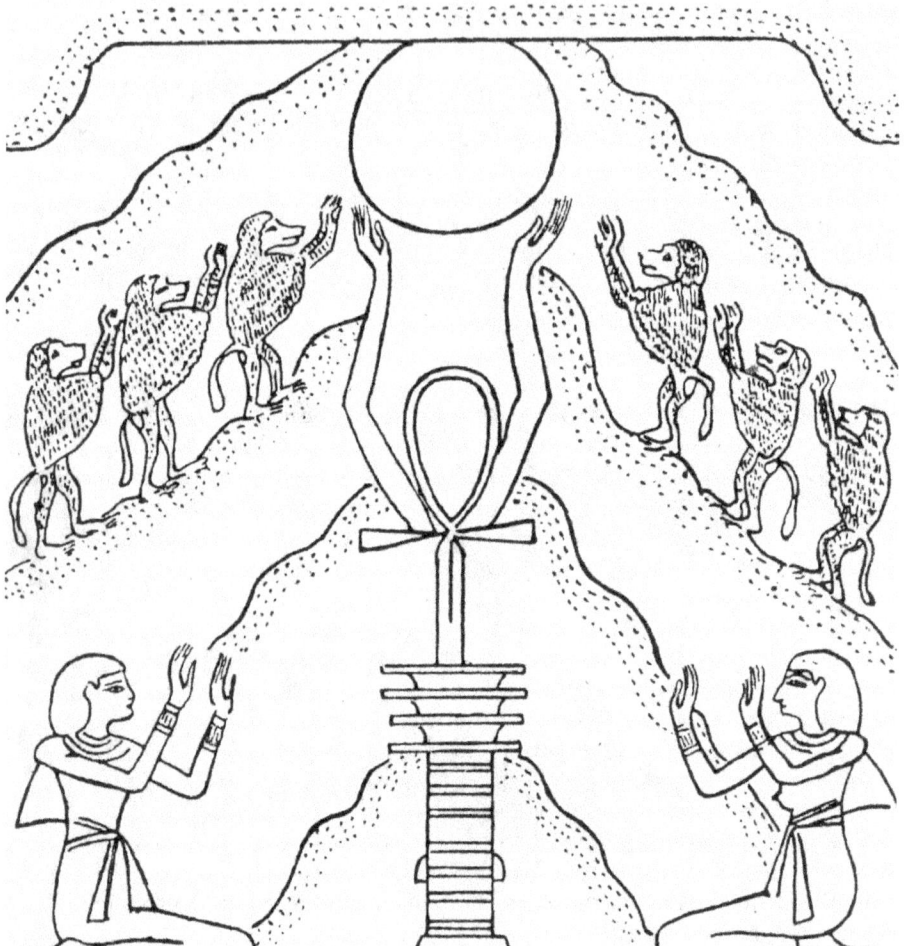

Research Essays Illustration 5. The Rising Sun, with Goddesses and Baboons in adoration.

RESEARCH ESSAYS ON ANCIENT EGYPT

Research Essays Temple Ticket 1. Philae Temple. Price of entrance is fifty Egyptian Pounds.

The repertoire of materials available for making tools included stone, wood, bone, vines, shells, skin, sinew or intestines, ivory, bark, resin, gum, leaves and any and all natural products.

For hunting early man skillfully used concealed traps, pitfalls, deadfalls and spring traps particularly in the savanna region. All this drama occurred in the Stone Age and most of it in Africa. The Stone Age is divided into 3 periods. The Early Stone Age lasted anywhere from 1.7 million to 60,000 years; the Middle Stone Age, 60,000 to 10,000 years ago. These two are generally called the Paleolithic, with the epi-palaeolithic occurring at the end, say "percussion methods." The New Stone Age, or Neolithic Period, 12,000-8,000 is associated with farming when early man made tools by the chipping method.

In the Paleolithic or Old Stone Age, man was a hunter and gatherer. His food supply consisted essentially 90 percent meat and 10 percent "agri-vegetation." By the New Stone Age, he became sedentary and his food supply changed to 10 percent meats and 90 percent "agri-produce." He started living in villages. Fishing became an important industry to supplement his diet.

He struggled with the challenges of shelter; fire for cooked food; and to provide warmth. Protection from animals and other predators was became a principal

FREDERICK MONDERSON

concern. Still, planning for the next day's hunt became a forerunner of his organizational ability and strategy. While he repaired his tools by the campfire, he began to philosophize, paint and ask questions regarding his existence.

During this period man is considered a parasite on nature. Not only did he gather his food, he used poison on arrows, spears and barbs. From 15,000 to 8,000 years ago he moved up the cultural scale to barbarian before he would begin to emerge into what later became civilization. In this he domesticated plants and animals and began the practice of agriculture that characterized him as cooperating with nature.

All this characterized the African's ability to experiment and innovate in the creation of culture and contribute to the birth of civilization and the pageantry of human destiny.

We know so much about this early period from three methods of dating. These are C-14 that date things for a few thousand years. *Potassium Argon* from 40,000 to 1.5 million and *Thermoluminesence* date into the millions. There is a fourth method of dating called *Dendochronology*, used primarily in the American southwest where giant trees grow. Scholars are able to tell the age of a tree by the rings on its inside.

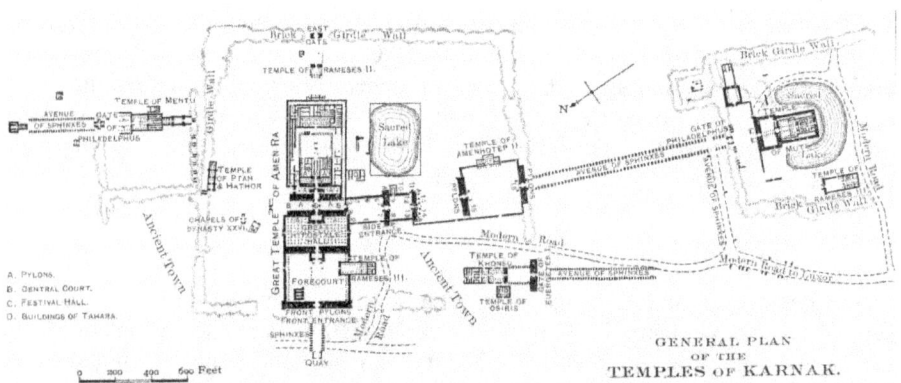

General Plan of the Temples of Karnak.

RESEARCH ESSAYS ON ANCIENT EGYPT

2. INTRODUCTION II

ETERNAL, YET CHANGING EGYPT – 2005
By

Dr. Fred Monderson

Dr. Jacob Carruthers ends his book *Mdw Ntr: Divine Speech* with a quote from the ancient Egyptian philosopher Ptahhotep: "The limits of art are never achieved; the skills of the artist are never perfected."

When I visited the Temple of Karnak recently, Brother Abdul, the Patriarch of that august complex was deeply moved and expressed the strongest sentiments of condolences to the Brothers and Sisters in the United States. He mentioned how he grieved tremendously for the losses of the "Nubian Brothers and Sisters" who were victimized by Hurricane Katrina. Interestingly, in many places in Egypt, people of all walks of life were saddened by the devastation of the hurricane. Some, particularly Nubians, were outraged by the delayed official response to that devastated region and people, purportedly due to race, class and poverty. One thing is certain, many, many Egyptians have a great fondness for Americans and Nubians are equally enthused by "Nubian Americans."

I have traveled to Egypt on many occasions and besides that first time this was the most memorable, and special of all my trips. Perhaps it was because I was traveling with my niece *Kash* and we had a wonderfully accommodating guide in the person of Hassan Elian. He was knowledgeable, kind, considerate and helpful and took us many places including a wedding in his village at Luxor. This was indeed a special trip, because on my previous trip I had a bad experience. Nevertheless, the wonderfully enlightening experience of this trip seems to have exorcised the bad taste of the last one with the insulting ignorance I was subjected to in 2003!

FREDERICK MONDERSON

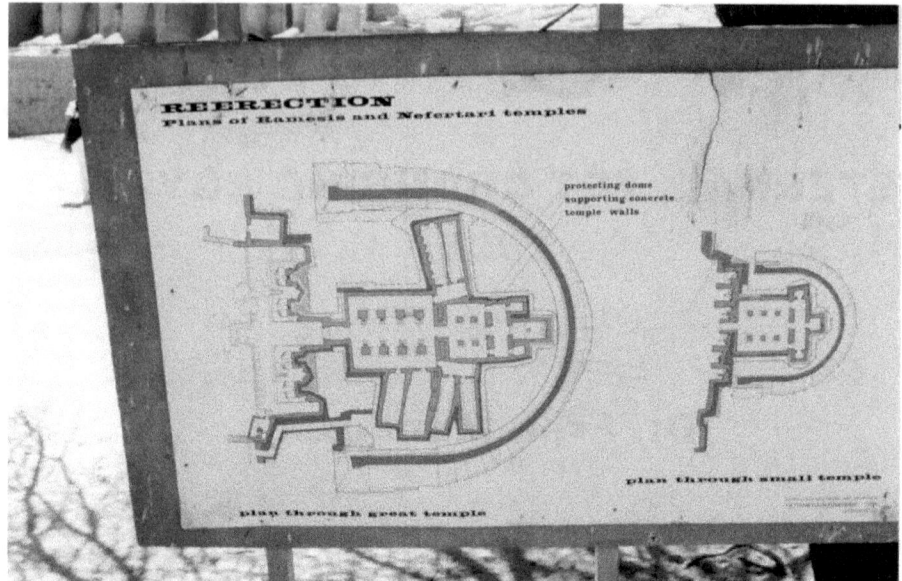

Research Essays 4. Abu Simbel Temple of Rameses II. Plan of the two Temples of Rameses and his Queen Nefertari.

This time we flew from New York into Cairo, over-nighted and then onto Aswan and Abu Simbel. Informed that photography was no longer permitted in the Cairo Museum, this was also the case at Abu Simbel. Nonetheless, photography aside, the spectacular twin temples of Rameses II and his wife Queen Nefertari (the Nubian) at Abu Simbel that took 20 years to build, were always enjoyable, enlightening and a wonderful site to behold. Ludwig Burckhardt was the first European to view the magnificent structure in 1813 and four years later the "strongman Egyptologist" Belzoni, cleared the entrance and entered the temple in 1817.

The 4-seated colossus of the pharaoh with his wife beside him, at the temple's entrance; Ra-Horakhty on the cornice beneath the uraei and 22 baboons, the prisoners on the base of the seated statues; and the other smaller statues as well as the illustrations on the outside, are not only inviting but a promise of the artistic beauty and wonderful scenery within. Besides Ra-Horakhty, Amon and Ptah as well as the deified Rameses II, are the gods worshipped in this temple as seen seated in the Sanctuary.

RESEARCH ESSAYS ON ANCIENT EGYPT

Research Essays Illustration 6. The Setting Sun. A perched falcon with Sun-disk, kneeling Anubi and Horuses, the two Goddesses, Isis (right) and Nephthys (left), kneeling before lions with disks before the sacred tree.

The vulture decoration of the ceiling and the 8 colossal Osiride standing statues in the hypostyle hall or pronaos; Rameses attacking his enemies at the Battle of Kadesh; the king worshipping and ritualizing the gods; making offerings and being embraced by the divinities; are scenes well preserved and beautifully done. The decorated columns of the king in different attitudes with the gods, various gods enthroned, along with side rooms depicting the king mainly in kneeling attitudes and making Presentations before the divinities, are all stunning sights to behold. Also of interest is the blend of color in the various parts of the temple. As the

FREDERICK MONDERSON

visitor faces the Sanctuary, the four-seated gods in Abu Simbel are (from right to left) Ra-Horakhty, the defied Rameses II, Amon and Ptah. Interestingly, this temple was built so the rays of the sun at rising would bathe the persons of Ra-Horakhty, Rameses and Amon on February 20 and October 20 of each year. Ptah was not to be touched by the sun's rays though he sat next to Amon. Some scholars say it's the 22nd day of the months. Nevertheless, with all of modern technological advancements, when the temple was moved to a higher elevation to avoid the river, this feat was never able to be duplicated. That is, the actual sun bathing the gods on the appointed days was never duplicated as in olden days.

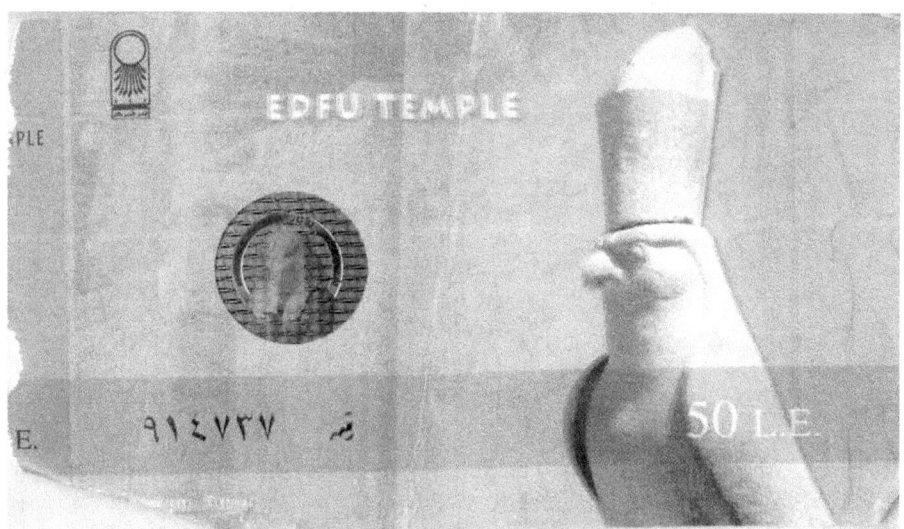

Research Essays Temple Ticket 2. Edfu Temple. Price of entrance is fifty Egyptian Pounds.

RESEARCH ESSAYS ON ANCIENT EGYPT

Research Essays Illustration 7. Drama in the Heavens as the Celestial Cow is attended to by deities of various persuasions.

The Temple of Nefertari, "possessor of charm, beauty and love," was dedicated to Hathor, Goddess of love. It is fronted by four standing statues of the king interspersed by two statues of the Queen and Hathor. The hypostyle hall or pronaos has 6 pillars with beautiful Hathor Head Capitals. The decorations are pretty well preserved with good color in which the goddess is shown in a papyrus thicket boat being presented with flowers by Rameses. Nefertari is shown embracing Rameses while gods including Thoth are on the pillars and walls.

Next is Isis Temple of Philae, a classical Graeco-Roman temple complex representing much earlier worships of Osiris and his faithful sister and wife. The architecture is superb with pylons, colonnades, temples, Nilometers, kiosk, courts, and chapels, all rich in decoration. The Temple of Kalabsha to God Mendulese, Rameses II's Temple of Beit Wali and that of Gerf Hussein in the Aswan vicinity, are also masterpieces. The Old and New Cataract Hotels and the Oberoi are all beautiful accommodation with wonderful gardens and service. The weather and climate of Aswan, the Nubian Museum, Kitchener's Garden, the High and Low

FREDERICK MONDERSON

Dams, Lotus Memorial, Unfinished Obelisk, Mausoleum of Aga Khan and Tombs of the Nobles, as well as shopping in the Aswan Sook (market) make this region a quite memorable and enjoyable city in Upper Egypt.

The five-day, four-night Nile Cruise from Aswan includes stops at Kom Ombo, Edfu and Esneh with passage through the Locks on way to Luxor, and is a pleasant, while exhilarating, experience. After leaving Aswan, we visited Kom Ombo, Edfu and Esneh before arriving at Luxor, all along the sail down the Nile was informative, enlightening and relaxing. The temples were delightful. The food on board daily was a sumptuous 3-meal buffet banquet designed to please the appetite, but also to add pounds to the waistline. Of course, the pool on board helped ease the heat; the masseur helped with the tension, the disco was entertaining and the cool Nile wind was most pleasant and enjoyable.

The first stop, Kom Ombo Temple, at the water's edge, was dedicated to two gods, the elder Horus, Haroeis, and the crocodile god, Sobek. This twin temple had twin protective winged disks with uraei on the cornice above the entrances, and two aisles, two hypostyle halls, two sanctuaries, respective decorations, two corridors as well as two priesthoods in service to the two deities. Like so many other temples, much is destroyed but what remains is sufficiently enlightening. The reliefs are beautiful, being a mixture of sunk and raised; while the ceiling boasts painted illustrations of the protective vulture goddess. There is one Nilometer. On the back wall along the outer corridor there are several colossal reliefs as well as one showing Isis in the birth chair, a table with medical instruments and a basin with water for the physician to wash his hands after any "operation." Other illustrations include a pair of ears for the priests to hear petitions of the faithful. In this temple like so many Graeco-Roman temples the art is a bit more liberal and a bit more of the Queen's and Goddess' anatomy are evident. There is a Nilometer just outside the enclosure wall of Kom Ombo.

The next stop on the Nile cruise was Edfu Temple of God Horus. This is the best preserved of all the temples of Egypt consisting of an intact Girdle or Enclosure Wall, a huge Pylon entrance, a three-sided roofed peristyle Colonnade Court with statues of the falcon god at the entrance pylon and in the Great Court before the hypostyle hall. The temple proper includes an outer hypostyle hall or vestibule, an inner hypostyle hall, and two antechambers before the Sanctuary. All this is surrounded by an outer corridor. There are adjacent rooms to the sanctuary for garments, liquid and solid offerings, incense, and books and implements concerned with the ritual of the temple.

RESEARCH ESSAYS ON ANCIENT EGYPT

Research Essays 5. Abu Simbel Temple of Rameses II. Entrance Hypostyle Hall of Rameses' Temple, housing 8 standing colossal Osiride Statues of the King with deities in the Sanctuary in the rear. Notice remains of the Vulture Goddess on the ceiling.

There is an inner passage round the temple called the "Corridor of Victory." One version of the Legend has it, after Seth killed his brother Osiris, and the "Immaculate Conception" as depicted at Abydos; Horus now grown to manhood, engaged his uncle and his band of traitors in armed combat. Battling him throughout the country, Horus finally captured and slew Seth at Edfu. There he

FREDERICK MONDERSON

built the temple and established mechanisms, a priesthood, to check the aspirations of the "followers of Seth." The "Corridor of Victory" recounts much of the battle in illustration with other features in the life of the god. There is a Nilometer to the east along the "Corridor of Victory" in the Girdle Wall. There is also evidence that an old Nilometer existed to the southeast of the temple. That is beyond the mammisi, which is now viewed at the front of the temple since the modern means of entrance has changed. In addition, Edfu shows evidence of columns below the present temple informing that the spot was sacred before Graeco-Roman times. In fact, a cartouche of Hatshepsut was found in this temple's court and removed to the Cairo Museum because of its rarity.

The significant change at Edfu is the carriage ride from the Nile Cruiser that does not bring visitors to the old entrance, through the village, one entered from the rear along the outer corridor. The present entrance is from a new and buildup area where the carriages park in an orderly fashion. Then you walk along a newly built pathway lined with shops and enter through the Mammisi.

Research Essays Illustration 8. A Curve representing approximately the variation in 25,920 Years of the Length of the Year Indicated by the Heliacal Rising of Sirius.

RESEARCH ESSAYS ON ANCIENT EGYPT

There is an inner passage round the temple called the "Corridor of Victory." One version of the Legend has it, after Seth killed his brother Osiris, and the Immaculate Conception as depicted at Abydos; Horus now grown to manhood, engaged his uncle and his band of traitors in armed combat. Battling him throughout the country, Horus finally captured and slew Seth at Edfu. There he built the temple and established mechanisms, a priesthood, to check the aspirations of the followers of Seth. The "Corridor of Victory" recounts much of the battle in illustration with other features in the life of the god. There is a Nilometer to the east along the "Corridor of Victory" in the Girdle Wall. There is also evidence that an old Nilometer existed to the southeast of the temple. That is beyond the mammisi, which is now viewed at the front of the temple since the modern means of entrance has changed. In addition, Edfu shows evidence of columns below the present temple informing that the spot was sacred before Graeco-Roman times. In fact, a cartouche of Hatshepsut was found in this temple and removed to the Cairo Museum because of its rarity.

The significant change at Edfu is the carriage ride from the Nile Cruiser that does not bring visitors to the old entrance, through the village, one entered from the rear along the outer corridor. The present entrance is from a new and buildup area where the carriages park in an orderly fashion. Then you walk along a newly built pathway lined with shops and enter through the Mammisi.

Esneh is a temple of which only the hypostyle hall has survived, some 30 feet below the city. Dedicated to the God Khnum who made man on his potter's wheel; there are several unique features of this temple. The present temple replaces an older XVIIIth Dynasty structure with possible connections to even earlier times. There are 24 massive decorated columns in this hall, each with a different type of capital. The temple is profusely illustrated both in and outside with Ptolemaic pharaohs and Roman emperors depicted. Being that far below the street level, it is beginning to suffer damage as the water-table-level has begun eroding the structure. There is talk of relocating the building so it may be better preserved.

A zodiac can be observed on the ceiling, though much of this is covered with black soot. This black soot comes from the fires modern inhabitants lit while living in the temple, during the last few hundred years before it was cleared. Another zodiac is found at Dendera temple of Hathor that we did not visit. Shortness of our trip precluded a visit to Abydos as well.

On a rear wall inside the hall, Isis sits on the birth chair; it's probably the only place, certainly the only one that has survived, depicting a baby in the embryonic sac. Nearby, Khnum is seen making man on his potter's wheel. Khnum is depicted in large size higher up on a rear wall. After the walk around Esneh temple, we retrace our steps; return to the boat and sail through the locks before our arrival at Luxor.

The Old Kingdom capital was Memphis and its funerary location was Sakkara and the Ghizeh Plateau. However, Luxor became the national capital during the Middle and New Kingdoms. The east bank is considered the land of the living and the west bank, the land of the dead. More appropriately, Simpkins (1992: 4) tells us: "The west is the land of dreams and deep shadows, the resting place of those that are there." In this respect, the east bank contains worship temples while on the west bank there are mortuary temples, or temples to the dead kings who became gods. However, this is not wholly exclusive. As such then, deceased persons were buried across the river, where Kings were interred in the Valley of the Kings; Queens in the Valley of the Queens; Nobles in the Valley of the Nobles; and Artisans in the Valley of the Artisans. The latter were confined and lived in the village of Deir el Medina because they knew the secrets of the mortuary structures. Equally too, on this west bank, nearly every New Kingdom pharaoh built a mortuary temple, his "Mansion of Millions of Years," in which he was worshipped as Osiris. Naturally, the poor people were probably buried in cemeteries in the desert and this dry soil quickly aided the process of natural mummification.

On the east bank of the river at Luxor, the worship temples of Karnak (*Ipet Isut*) and Luxor (*Southern Isut* or the God's harem) epitomizes the majesty, the power and the glory of New Empire Egypt. Nearby are temples of the Goddess Mut and Montu the war god. It took two thousand years to build Karnak as numerous pharaohs vied with each other to please the god Amon who dwelt therein. Together with his wife Mut and son Khonsu, these deities comprised the Theban Triad. Karnak had a whole social and religious system of individuals who thrived within the sphinxes, pylons, courts, chapels, kiosks, halls, doorways, processional way, colonnades, twin axis, porches, porticoes, temples, statues, obelisks, pillars, a sacred lake, as well as painted, sunk and raised relief decorations. Complementing this there were stewards, priests and priestesses, cooks, wine makers, gardeners, slaves, artisans, teachers, guards and a whole lot more. Dr. ben-Jochannan recommended that his students visit the hypostyle hall at Karnak at least six times to fully understand the magnificence of this structure.

Regarding the hypostyle hall at Karnak Temple of God Amon, *Baedeker's Guide to Egypt* (1929: 284) makes known: "The breadth of this great hall is 338 ft., its depth 170 ft., its area 6000 sq. yards, an area spacious enough to accommodate the entire cathedral of Notre Dame at Paris. One hundred and thirty-four columns arranged in sixteen rows supported the roof, of which the two central rows are higher than the others and consist of lotus-columns with open capitals, while the

RESEARCH ESSAYS ON ANCIENT EGYPT

other rows have clustered columns with closed capitals. The hall is divided into nave and aisles. The nave, itself divided into three aisles, is c. 79 ft. in height. The roof is supported by the two central rows of columns and one of the lower rows on each side, the deficiency in the height of the latter being met by placing square pillars above them. The spaces between these pillars were occupied with windows with stone lattice-work (one on the South side is still almost perfect). The side-aisles are 33 ft. lower than the nave."

Baedeker continued to confirm: "The columns are not monolithic but are built up of semi-drums, 3 ½ ft. in height and 6 ½ ft. in diameter. The material is reddish-brown sandstone. Each of the twelve columns in the two central rows is 11 ¾ ft. in diameter and upwards of 33 ft. in circumference, i.e., as thick as Trajan's Column in Rome or the Vendome Column in Paris. It requires six men with outstretched arms to span one of these columns. Their height is 69 ft., that of the capitals 11 ft. The remaining hundred and twenty-two columns are each 42 ½ ft. in height and 27 ½ ft. in circumference."

We now turn to the Temple of Luxor, built to celebrate the Festival of Opet for which Amon left his Karnak abode to spend time there with his wife Goddess Mut. Amenhotep III built the original temple but several pharaohs decorated, added or did restoration as well as injurious work to the temple. Tutankhamon decorated the colonnade, Horemheb and Seti I and Seti II did restoration work to it, Rameses II added the pylon, changed the axis, added a columned peristyle court with seated and standing statues and Alexander the Great redecorated the inner hypostyle hall and rebuilt the Sanctuary of the main temple. Akhenaton erased the name of Amon where it could be found. Seti I replaced many of these.

The Temple of Luxor therefore consists of an outer court of Rameses II called the "Ramesseum front," beyond the Pylon, an inner pylon to the original temple, the Processional Colonnade and Court of Amenhotep III, the hypostyle hall and two inner chambers fronting the Sanctuary. Beyond the Sanctuary are a large hall with 12 columns and a central chamber of 4 columns with 2 smaller flanking chambers with 2 columns each.

FREDERICK MONDERSON

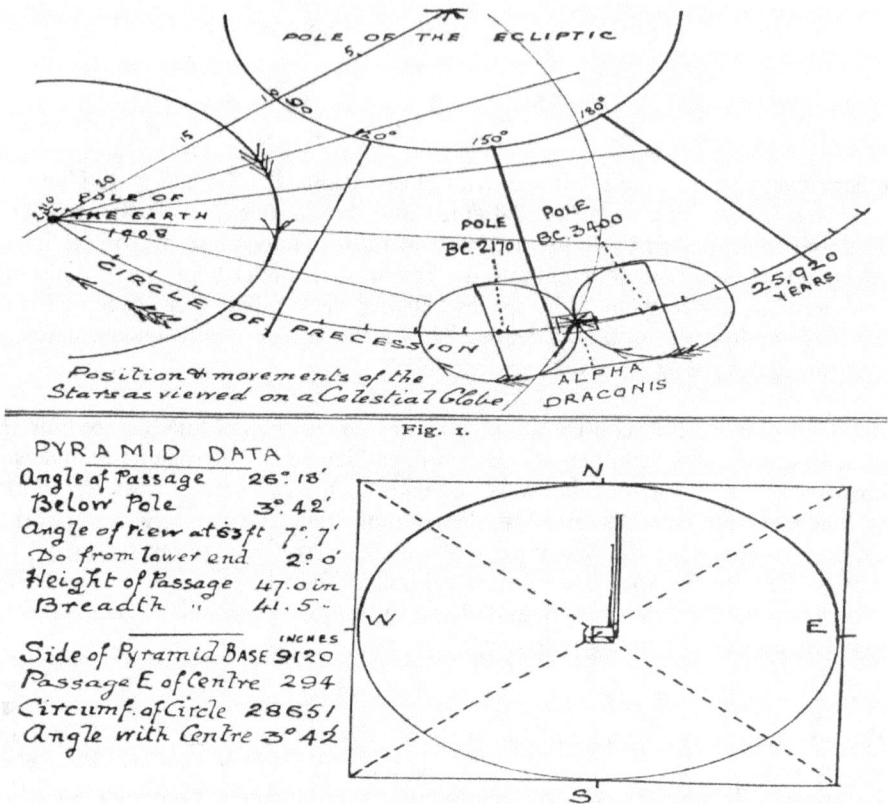

Research Essays Illustration 9. Position and Movement of the Stars as viewed on a Celestial Globe and Pyramid Data.

The Opet Festival, depicted and decorated by Tutankhamon, flanks the walls alongside the 14 columns of the Processional Colonnade. On entering, the right side represents the procession coming from Karnak along the river and the left side represents the procession returning to Karnak from Luxor, by land.

Next is the return flight to Cairo. There the hallmark of Egypt, the pyramids and sphinx are monumental and attractive. More importantly, the Cairo Museum is still an exciting place as ever for an entrance fee of 65 Egyptian pounds, and security is even more upgraded. Metal detectors greet the visitor, "pat downs" is the order and all cameras must be checked! There is no photography in the Cairo Museum of Egyptian Antiquities at this time. There are more security people in the museum, and cameras have been installed throughout. However, for an additional 75 Egyptian Pounds, a visitor can view the Egyptian mummies in a separate room. This too is new!

RESEARCH ESSAYS ON ANCIENT EGYPT

Research Essays 6. Abu Simbel Temple of Rameses II. Close-up of one of the standing colossal statues in the entrance hall.

There are over 120,000 pieces of antiquities in the Museum and 1 replica, the Rosetta Stone. The original Rosetta Stone is in the British Museum in London. This precious artifact is the basis upon which Jean Francois Champollion was able to decipher the hieroglyphic language in 1822. Found by the French at a place called Rosetta in 1798, it is a tri-lingual inscription (Hieroglyphic, Demotic and Greek) recounting the pharaoh Ptolemy Epiphanes' dealings with priests who praised him, in the three languages, for his generous relations with the temples.

FREDERICK MONDERSON

For the most part the average tour of the Cairo Museum takes two hours but there is so much to see, only the major pieces as Tutankhamon treasures, some papyrus and a few other pieces including statues and sphinxes are covered. There is a bookstore on the first floor. Thus, anyone with an interest in ancient Egypt must return to the Cairo Museum to broaden his or her understanding of the culture. The grounds are landscaped with greenery and statues and photography is permitted outside here.

Research Essays Papyrus Art 2. Geese feeding by the waterside with fishes nearby in the river.

Throughout Egypt, the Tourist Police do an outstanding job of providing protection for tourists, whether it's at the Museums, at temples and at tomb sites, on the streets and on lengthy trips they provide guarded convoys, all to ensure that no harm come to visitors. Hence, the police should be commended so people ought not to be afraid to travel to Egypt, for they will experience a remarkable collection of historically important sites and scenes that will remain imbedded in their memories forever. African-Americans must go to Egypt to see and experience the rich cultural heritage that awaits them, created by the African ancestors. Hence, we must go to Egypt as Dr. ben-Jochannan has insisted!

RESEARCH ESSAYS ON ANCIENT EGYPT

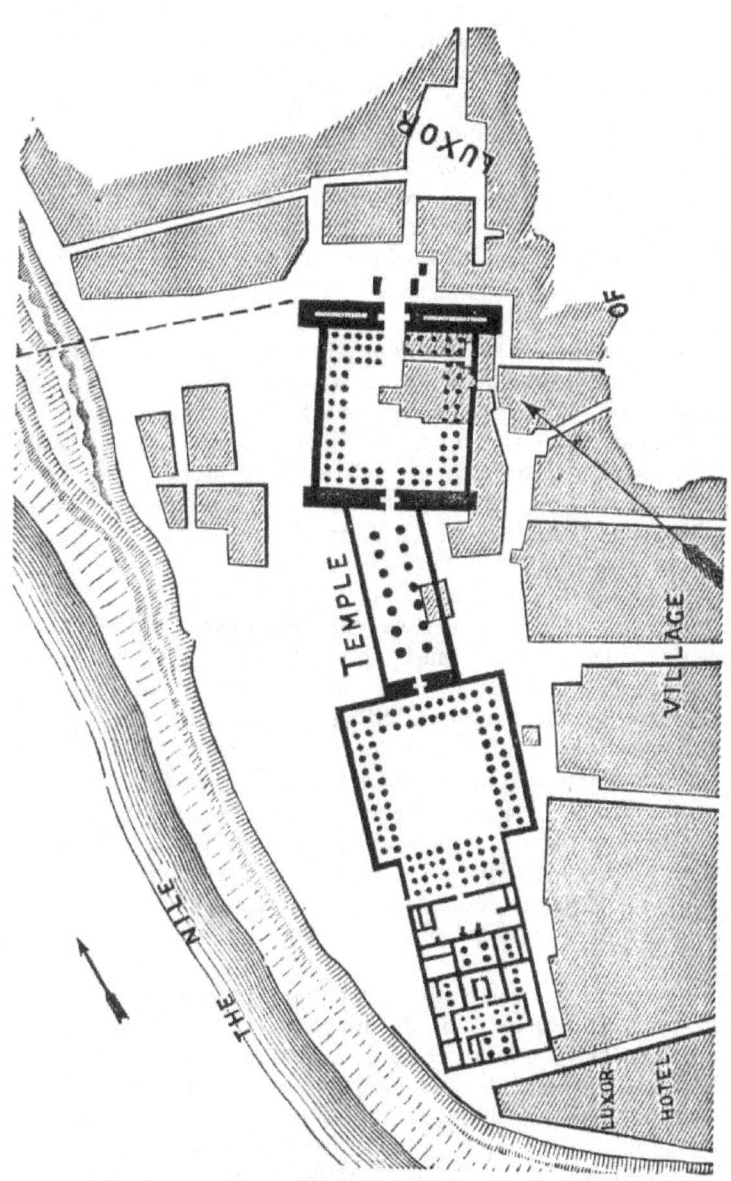

The Temple of Luxor

FREDERICK MONDERSON

What is memorable about this trip is the manner of respect and appreciation the Egyptians have for Americans, the love Nubians have for their "Nubian brothers and sisters" who come to visit, and the wonderfully enlightening transformation one experiences in the profoundly religious, spiritual, artistic, philosophic, cultural, historical and photographic adventure that's part of this pilgrimage to the "Holy Land," Egypt. The growth in outlook is noticeable when one considers the maxims of the great philosophers of Egypt, viz., Ptahhotep, Meryukare, Dua Khety, and the literary tradition of the *Pyramid Text, Coffin Text, Book of the Dead* or *Book of Coming Forth by Day*, as well as so many others seen in the tombs of the kings, the *Book of Gates, Book of the Am Duat*, and more. Then there are other wisdom works of literature as the *Book of Khun Anup, Book of Knowing the Appearance of Ra, Book of Maa-Khere* and so on.

All this is reinforced in the knowledge that from this early burst of Egyptian, African, creative expressions, religion, cosmology, cosmogony, theology, metaphysics, art, architecture, the colonnade, science, medicine, surgery, mathematics, stone construction, river transportation developed. Geometry, astronomy, farming, astrology, as well as creation of a thousand household, domestic, civic, military, political, religious and scientific and surgical implements were added in the cultural and geographical effluence called the "gift of the Nile."

Now, everyone should know why we must visit Egypt for a reinforcement of the intellectual foundation the ancient Egyptian Africans bequeathed to the world. In so doing we can and must set the young on the road to imbibe in this knowledge to embolden them, for the sometimes difficult, still challenging, journey they must experience in today's world. In this they must know that good speech is preferred to babble; truth and justice to untruth or injustice (*isfit*); good listening is a virtue; respect for elders is respect for self; to practice self-control and silence is wonderful; ma'at is the essence of wisdom and prudence as well as balance, order and truth. The practice of these ethical principles will cultivate good individuals who will become model citizens, and in turn will help improve the next generation, and in that, perhaps, wealth will become a "divine gift."

Perhaps it's best to end this with a quote from Dr. Carruthers (1995: 139) who informed: "'The Instructions of Ptahhotep' contained a collection of maxims which instructed the youth in the correct values, attitudes, and modes of behavior suited for those who would become civil servants from the office of prime minister down. Indeed, in all probability, the future pharaohs also received this education alongside some of the children from various ranks including the poorest. Although the Meryukare text states that the Pharaoh is born wise [though the Ptahhotep text says 'no one is born wise'] this is a trope signifying that the pharaohship is wise because of its inherent resources, its advisors and the records of officeholders. These students were taught what was expected of a good official.

RESEARCH ESSAYS ON ANCIENT EGYPT

A good official was wise and knowledgeable about the country and the people. He was advised to listen and learn from people in all walks of life, especially the so-called uneducated. He understood that listening was the major source of acquiring knowledge and wisdom. Above all, he understood that Ma'at (Truth and Justice) was the foundation of all existence and that it must be adhered to in all actions."

Research Essays Illustration 10. The Sphinx buried in sand with the Great Pyramid of Khufu in the rear. Notice how high the people are which indicates how much of the desert has encroached on these monuments.

Research Essays Temple Ticket 3. Karnak Temple. Price of entrance is sixty-five Egyptian Pounds.

FREDERICK MONDERSON

3. INTRODUCTION III: EGYPT 2008
By

Dr. Fred Monderson

Egypt today is a changing culture, yet, in some respects while change has come, other things remain the same. In the first instance, changes are due to the economic realities of the tourist industry and the dynamics of the "exchange rate" for foreign currency. Nevertheless, gone are the days when you could visit the monuments for cheap. Remember when it was 20 Egyptian pounds for the Valley of the Kings? Now it is 75 Egyptian Pounds. Remember when it was 20 Egyptian Pounds for the Cairo Museum? Now it's 65 Pounds! And, those people who have waited until now to visit will pay the price, for, as Dr. ben-Jochannan has said: "You must visit the great Hypostyle Hall at Karnak Temple in Luxor six times before you begin to comprehend the significance and accomplishment of those ancient Africans."

Everywhere one goes, particularly a black man traveling alone, the question is always, 'Where are you from?' When the answer is New York, USA, the response is always: "Welcome, America, ah, America is Number One.' In one of the temples I visited, to the same question and reply, one Egyptian said to me: "America! Welcome! We like Americans, we don't like Bush!" I could only reply, "Many Americans don't like Bush either." In the Cairo Museum an American woman talking to an official said: "It's getting so we don't want to say we're Americans because George Bush is such a jackass. All he wants is war."

However, it's a different story with the Nubians and Black Egyptians. It's always: "Brother! Welcome Brother." Master of Karnak Temple, Brother Abdul sends his deepest respect to the 'Nubian Brothers and sisters in America.' He's getting up there in years, for those who are familiar with this amazing brother, but he's supervising an enormous over-haul, development and beautification of Karnak. He may be retiring soon. Brother Shawgi also sends his warmest regards to Dr. ben-Jochannan. The talk is always, how Dr. Ben helped so many people. He would drop 10 Pounds here, 25 Pounds there, and 50 Pounds here and there. He was especially helpful to the Daboud Nubian Village. In every hotel he used, the baggage handlers, kitchen and house-keeping staff, everyone got an envelope.

RESEARCH ESSAYS ON ANCIENT EGYPT

Research Essays Papyrus Art 3. Hathor introduces Nefertari as Ma'at stretches her wings before enthroned Isis as Horus and two goddesses stand behind the goddess.

Naturally the security apparatus in the temples is ongoing to protect the antiquities and the tourists. Besides the north face of Rameses II's "Girdle Wall" at Karnak an enormous wiring system is being installed as electric potential in the temple is being overhauled. Near the eastern gate a systematic archaeological dig is in progress. Elsewhere to the east and south of the Great Lake and along the southern Courts as well as the temples of Khonsu and Opet, archaeological digs and restoration work continues to make new revelations. Karnak is still as busy as a beehive with visitors from Europe and now the Asian nations of China, Japan and Korea. More important, however, is the enormous beautification taking place on the frontage of Karnak. The two "speakezies" selling film and other accessories north of the ticket booth have been upgraded with a few new bazaars added. Beyond or south of the new gated walkway to the temple, a security corridor separated the new esplanade being developed and beautified to put Karnak's entrance on a more professional and world class attractive standard. In two or three years it will be a site to behold. Luxor Temple still attracts its visitors and the best time to visit is still early afternoon when the sun throws backs its reflection on the colonnades and other structures, and equally the "Girdle Wall of Rameses II" at Karnak Temple.

Across the river on the west bank where you get the customary 3 tombs in the Valley of the Kings, most visitors are familiar with the Eastern Valley housing its 65 tombs. However, a Western Valley has been opened up and the tombs of Aye, who succeeded Tutankhamon and the "magnificent" Amenhotep III, have been located. The former is now open to visitors while the latter is being prepared for opening within the next year. Naturally, there's no video in the Valley or other photography in tombs in the Valley of the Kings. Those earlier visitors who took photos years ago now appreciate those early opportunities.

FREDERICK MONDERSON

Medinet Habu, Mortuary Temple of Rameses III retains its wonderfully beautiful color depictions recounting the reign of this, the last of the imperial warrior pharaohs of the New Kingdom.

Research Essays Temple Ticket 4. Camera Stand Permit at twenty Egyptian Pounds per site.

People should not be afraid to take a trip to Egypt to view the antiquities. This cultural, historical, art and architectural as well as religious, spiritual and metaphysics and photography adventure is well worth the outlay of about $3200.00 for 15 days. Today, at $3900.00 for 15 days, it's still a bargain. The Tourist Police go to extraordinary lengths to guarantee security of visitors. A case in point! I was part of a convoy to visit Abydos and Dendera. As I rode in a private car, the police were very excited and concerned, 'We have an American with us.' Oftentimes they would say to my driver and guide, 'Do you have the American?' So I say, go to Egypt like Dr. ben-Jochannan has said, "Visit Egypt, visit Karnak Temple's Hypostyle Hall six times," make the spiritual connection with the legacy of the ancient Africans along the banks of the Nile, who gave the world so much.

Abydos Temple of Osiris built by Seti I has always been the highpoint of any trip to Egypt because it not only has the best colored illustrations in all the Nile Valley; it is the world's earliest site of pilgrimage, equally boasting levels of 10 temples dating back 5000 years. It is also the foremost site of the "Immaculate Conception." This phenomenon, involving the God Osiris and Goddess Isis is

RESEARCH ESSAYS ON ANCIENT EGYPT

remarkable, for their union produced Horus or Heru, after Osiris' unfortunate death at the hands of his evil brother Seth. Even more important, however, this unique temple has 2 courts, 2 hypostyle halls and 7 entrances for 7 shrines to 7 deities, Horus, Isis, Osiris, Amon-Ra, Ra-Horakhty, Ptah and the deified Seti I. These were the gods of the Osiris cycle, the great gods of the empire and the deified builder of the temple. Rameses II closed all but the middle of his father Seti's 7 entrances. The Abydos Tablet listing 76 kings from Menes to Seti is also located here intact or *in situ*.

The Osireion or tomb of Osiris is also located here at Abydos. It is the only Nile Valley structure or tomb completely surrounded by water with an underground passage that leads into the desert. There are 5 convoys in and out of Luxor every day. So the security police in arranging and administering as well as operationalizing the safety of visitors have got it down to a science, particularly the long trips to Abydos and Dendera. They communicate with elements stationed along the route that halt traffic so the convoy could whiz past, real VIP style; it's a sight to behold.

Well, the convoy to Edfu, Kom Ombo and Aswan again enjoyed the same VIP treatment in the drive-thru from and back to Luxor. For those familiar, the new entrance at Edfu is from the south not the north, in a newly developed and orderly plaza. Here carriages, which bring the tourists from the cruisers, park to await their passengers' return for the 12-minute trek back to the boats. I often wondered where the black people from America are. "Ever since Dr. Ben stopped coming" said Shawgi, "I have not worked with any Black groups. My brother Farouk has had the same complaint. The few Black groups who come don't give us the jobs like Dr. Ben did!"

From the time I started going to Egypt with Dr. ben-Jochannan in the 1980s, he introduced us to Shawgi and Farouk. These are the most authentic Black Egyptians, Nubians, who give a more correct view of the history of "our ancestors" so we should support them!

Edfu is a beautiful Graeco-Roman temple, very well preserved with a magnificently illustrated Pylon entrance, a Peristyle Court with two hawks before the Pronaos or Hypostyle Hall just as outside the Pylon where two other hawks were also placed. Only one of the former remains intact and visitors rush to take photographs beside it. The "Sphinx of Edfu" is no longer inside the gate but has been moved to the Plaza. Repairs continue in the "Corridor of Victory" where the struggle between Horus and Seth is vividly depicted with Isis and other deities assisting Horus, the avenger of his dead father, Osiris.

The Most unusual thing happened at Kom Ombo. After an hour at this temple, the convoy left for Aswan. Shawgi said: "My brother, there is no need to go to Aswan with the convoy, let's wait until they return in 4 hours. So I was alone in the temple to roam and get all the photos I wanted, uninterrupted. We then joined the convoy on its return and headed back to Luxor.

The Temple of Isis at Philae, now on Agilka Island, remains a beauty to behold, a joy to experience. It is also an art and architectural wonder compelling one to envision how its august nature could have withstood all the challenges of history and retain its picturesqueness, with such stately majesty. The East Colonnade, with its 16 frontal columns and 1 on the southern end and the western colonnade with its 32 columns on the dromos; the Kiosk of Nectanebo, the altar on the dromos, all before the decorated First Pylon with its two stone lion sentinels, mesmerizes the visitor. You pass this portal into the Courtyard of the Temple of Isis proper, with a second East Colonnade of 10 columns facing the Mammisi with 7 columns in front and 7 in rear as viewed from the river. Then you behold the Second or First Pylon proper to the Temple of Isis.

When the visitor considers the trauma this temple experienced down through the years from the vicissitudes of nature and the flooding Nile, invading forces, Christian and Muslim adherents and fanatics, modern plunderers and antiquities collectors and the dynamics of visitors presence and proclivities, one has to laud the builders of antiquity whose mastery of the art of construction has deified time and man and all their challenges. One should never forget the floral beauty of the capitals of columns in this temple, each with a separate and distinct work of art that continues to amaze lovers of this genre of art and architecture.

In retrospect, the greatest architectural and artistic remains are located in Upper Egypt. Throughout most of dynastic rule there was always a distinction between the east and west bank of the Nile and Upper and Lower Egypt. Some scholars refer to the east bank as the land of the living and the west bank as the land of the dead. Equally, of the two principal types of temples, worship or god temple and mortuary or king temple, some have argued the former belongs to the east while the latter belongs to the west bank.

Of course, this is not always true. For example, moving from south to north, Abu Simbel, a worship temple is on the west bank. Philae, on the other hand, is in the Nile. However, Esneh and Edfu, worship temples are on the west bank. The Valley of the Kings, Queens, Nobles and Artisans are on the west bank as they are associated with mortuary practice and place of final rest. Equally, during the New Kingdom, practically every king built his or her mortuary temple on the west bank, the Plain of Thebes. Seti I of the 19th Dynasty built his mortuary temple at Kurneh and another at Abydos, dedicated to Osiris and six other deities including him. Both temples are on the west bank.

On the other hand, Dendera, while a worship temple to Goddess Hathor is on the west bank, and the temples of Kom Ombo, Luxor and Karnak, all worship

RESEARCH ESSAYS ON ANCIENT EGYPT

temples, are on the east bank. Also, the temple of Montu, the war god and that of Mut, wife of Amon are on the east bank adjoining Karnak. There is a worship temple to Hathor near Deir el Medina on the west bank at Thebes, while some scholars have argued Seti I's Hypostyle Hall is a mortuary temple or "mansion of Millions of years" in the Karnak worship complex.

Research Essays Temple Ticket 5. The Open-Air Museum at Karnak. Price of entrance is twenty-five Egyptian Pounds.

Finally, the Cairo Museum of Egyptian Antiquities has made many changes. Naturally security is very tight at the entrance. You have to check your camera as no photographs are permitted inside. Cameras have been installed throughout the museum for security reasons. There is the same rush to view Tutankhamon's treasuries. Some pieces of his display are on loan. The cost to view the Royal Mummies is up from 75 to 100 Egyptian Pounds.

Two unusual things happened while I visited the Museum. It rained that day while I waited to enter. In all my years in Egypt I never saw rain both in Upper or Lower Egypt. Second, in the Hall of Tutankhamon, they were removing his mask from its case to put it in another case and I had the privilege to see this and some golden necklaces in their natural state.

FREDERICK MONDERSON

Research Essays 6a. Abu Simbel Temple of Rameses II. Rameses offers a bouquet and pours a libation to Khnum, god of the Cataract.

RESEARCH ESSAYS ON ANCIENT EGYPT

The chariots, vases, coffins, statues, sphinxes, etc., are still there, catching dust yet, they attract an enormous amount of visitors. Unfortunately, there are few or no noticeably Nubian or Black guides in the museum so the visitors, when it comes to issues of ethnicity, are given incorrect information that, in a way reinforces prejudices. Maspero's famous description of Maherpra, the 18th Dynasty nobleman, as being "Negroid but not Negro," should be equated with being "Caucasoid but not Caucasian;" is still in that part of the museum that is not generally visited. There is no place card that gives an accurate description of the 11th Dynasty Theban King Mentuhotep's statue, which W. Stephenson Smith in the *Art and Architecture of Ancient Egypt* described as having "black flesh." This gives many of the young Egyptian Guides the opportunity to give European tourists inaccurate information about this important Middle Kingdom monarch who united the two lands. Yet, they claim "My Professor at the Cairo University taught me Mentuhotep was painted black for the funeral ceremony."

All in all, Egypt is as warm, entertaining, enlightening and educational as any culture on earth. The tombs, temples, art and photographic opportunities give the visitor a rush that is a spiritual and philosophic as well as cultural and historic awakening and its well worth the trip. Read the books and visit Egypt to get a real grasp of the intellectual, scientific, art and architectural and medical foundations early Africans established in the Valley of the Nile. This will go a long way to enlighten people about this proud African heritage and legacy.

Research Essays 6b. Abu Simbel Temple of Rameses II. Looking up at two seated right side colossal statues with female figures between their legs and images of Rameses and Ra-Horakhty above the entrance.

FREDERICK MONDERSON

4. INTRODUCTION IV: EGYPT 2010
By

Dr. Fred Monderson

As the digs unfold and the monuments continue to tell their remarkable story, modern Egypt is undergoing tremendously rapid changes of beautifying the landscape while imposing more and more restrictions on the increasing number of visitors who come to behold the ancient treasures. Still, in a society that takes great pride in and benefits tremendously from its wonderful history, there is a hospitality the Egyptians extends that beckons the visitor return to the Nile River country for the museums, pyramids, temples, tombs, food, shopping, balloon rides, horse-drawn carriage rides and ancient and modern architecture as well as the warm reception that goes along with it.

The dollar is holding at 5.68 Egyptian pounds, tipping is still the rule and it behooves the tourist to haggle, haggle, haggle; negotiate, negotiate, negotiate; bargain, bargain and more bargain for everything from taxi or horse-drawn buggy rides to purchasing cartouches, gold, silver, books, clothing, etc., you name it.

The Egyptian authorities have long realized the value of their ancient history to modern antiquarian lovers and are doing whatever it takes to extend the welcome mat and to beautify the esplanade of the monuments to protect these treasures and enhance the ambiance which in turn encourages more visits and greater foreign exchange benefits to the nation.

On a whirlwind 10-day tour, this writer visited 10 Egyptian temples with the exception of Abu Simbel and Kom Ombo, previously visited. At mighty Karnak the entrance reconstruction is complete though the digging continues. Oldsters who are familiar with the old entrance layout to Karnak will be surprised to know the old shops are gone and the entire area, from the street to the pylon is a reconstructed plaza square with a park-like atmosphere where the gate and entrance is some 1500 meters removed. The customary metal detectors and the numerous antiquities police officers ensure safety on the grounds and also help protect the monuments. Such security precautions are designed to assure visitors who may be fearful of coming; but the show of force quickly allays such fears and people feel relaxed not simply at Karnak but at all sites on the circuit.

The venerable Brother Abdul is no longer in charge at Karnak due to health concerns. Still, he sends his greetings and well-wishes to the "Nubian brothers and

RESEARCH ESSAYS ON ANCIENT EGYPT

sisters" in America. More important, however, in exasperation he complained "I'm angry Nubian brothers and sisters do not come to Egypt as in the days of Dr. Ben." Further, he implored, "Dr. Fred, you should become the next Dr. Ben and bring our people to view our ancient heritage. Too many may be going to other places that teach them nothing about their ancestral culture. And those that do come need to use the Nubian guides." All I could say, I'll deliver your concerns.

Karnak is still as beautiful as ever from the walk through the sphinxes entrancing the Pylon and Great Court with Seti's Kiosk to the left, the northern and southern colonnades with their sphinxes, the mud ramp inside the southern half of the Pylon, two altars, a sphinx of Tutankhamon, Taharka's Kiosk, two standing statues of Rameses II and the perpendicular temple of Rameses III, all giving access to Rameses I and Horemheb's Second Pylon that entrances the Hypostyle Hall.

This magnificent building consists of 134 columns, 122 in two wings separated by 12 larger; and the largest columns in any building worldwide; columns that comprises the Processional Colonnade. While opinions vary at to its beauty, profusely illustrated with the temple rituals, it represents a "papyrus thicket at creation" when the god arose from the waters and created the world. It also reflects the caliber of architect who could plan and execute a work with such boldness and immensity that not only has defied time in its duration of existence, but it also staggers the imagination with the architecture itself and the decoration.

Pylons Three, Four, Five and Six were built by Amenhotep III and Thutmose I and III and encompass the Courts housing Thutmose I's and Hatshepsut's single standing obelisks with statues, decorated walls, and colonnades all before the Sanctuary where Dr. Ben has forbidden his students to enter. Beyond the Sanctuary, the Middle Kingdom Court esplanades the *Akh Menu*, festival temple of Thutmose III.

The "Girdle Wall" of Rameses II is still breathtaking in its fabulously illustrated depiction of the king before the gods in a multitude of attitudes. The "Coca Cola Temple" still serves the thirsty visitor beside the Sacred Lake, while the Sacred Scarab has been moved some 50 feet to the west near the Eastern Wall of the "Cachette Court." A distinct addition to the temple, pictographic and textual signs stand illustrating specific monuments on the temple plan in English, French and Arabic languages, the Open Air Museum, Courts along the north-south axis with their Pylons continue to exhibit their wonderful architecture, illustrated depiction and broken statues and stones. Work continues on the restoration of the temple of Khonsu. The Temples of Mut and Montu remain closed to visitors. Still, the ruins of the some 22 temples in the Northern, Central and Southern Groups remain a rich, rewarding and enjoyable experience to behold. Sound and Light Show, as

FREDERICK MONDERSON

regular feature at all popular temples as Karnak, Luxor, Philae and even the pyramids, is evening entertainment.

The Western entrance to the Temple of Luxor is now closed and visitors enter from the East. The area in front of the Pylon is undergoing extensive rehabilitation and the Avenue of Sphinxes there has been beautified. Even more important, work has commenced on mapping, excavating, repairing and replacing the Sphinxes of the buried Avenue of Sphinxes linking Luxor with Karnak. Naturally, all the immediate houses and businesses along this route have been cleared. Therefore, the mud-brick Sphinx Road, a major thoroughfare is not only congested but passage is terribly uncomfortable, much to the consternation of visitors and locals alike. Restoration of the walls of the Processional Colonnade at Luxor Temple depicting the procession from Karnak to Luxor and back for the Opet Festival continues to illustratively beautify this area. The "Free Open Air Museum" to the east of the temple of Luxor displays more than 50,000 pieces of broken stone recovered from the temple.

The temple of Deir el Bahari has instituted an interactive video of the Discovery Channel's expose on the recent research identifying the mummy of Queen Hatshepsut. In addition, old photographs line the walls depicting the work of clearance of the temple as well as a new plan of the temple imitating limestone of which the temple was built that guides use as a teaching tool for their groups before entering the temple. The two Ramps; First and Second Courts; Lower, Middle and Upper Colonnades; and the True Northern Colonnade; the Fishes and Birds Colonnade; the Punt and Birth Colonnades; the Anubis and Hathor Shrines; Upper Terrace and Upper Court, still exhibit their wonderful architectural features, beautiful artistic depiction and ancient color while the magnetic attraction to the Sanctuary door still evokes the wonder exuded when the temple was in use that in combination makes this temple the beautiful and magnificent work of art that it is.

Medinet Habu is still just as beautiful while the Ramesseum is undergoing extensive renovation, nearly complete that not only highlights the architectural features of the temple proper with its statues, columns, Hypostyle Halls and arched rear area, but has substantially reconstructed the magazine storage area, priests' quarters, kitchens, school and there's much more to see.

Cameras are no longer permitted in the Valley of the Kings and no more climbing the mountain under threat of arrest. Yes, that is correct! Years ago, you could take pictures in the tombs, then without flash; then there was 'no photos in the tombs,' only outside the tombs. Now, there are no more cameras in the Valley of the Kings, period! Here you must leave your camera at the security area. This ban also applies to the Cairo Museum of Egyptian Antiquities. Again, you must check your camera before entering the Museum. However, you could take pictures on the

RESEARCH ESSAYS ON ANCIENT EGYPT

grounds of the Museum. For that matter, no photos are permitted in any Museum in Egypt. How things have changed!

Naturally, the price for all sites has risen. For example, the prices now in Egyptian pounds are as follows: Karnak 65; Open Air Museum 25; Luxor 50; Ramesseum 30; Medinet Habu 30; Valley of the Kings 75; Philae 50; Dendera 35; Deir el Bahari 30; Egyptian Museum in Cairo 60; Royal Mummies in the Museum 100; Sakkara's Imhotep Museum 60; Sakkara New Tombs 30; Olwet Abdel Qurna 25; Memphis (Mit Rahina) 35; Photography at Archaeological Sites (Use of a stand) 20 pounds at each site; Riding the Taftaf at Deir el Bahari and the Valley of the Kings 2 pounds. If you rent a private taxi to any site and they wait for you, there is a 5 pound parking charge, not to the taxi but to the government, for which you get a ticket. Add this to the expected tips everywhere. If a man such as move a chair for you, he holds out his hand to shake yours, but in fact is expecting a tip.

Edfu Temple's entrance has been changed and reconstructed with the passageway strategically placed between bazaars. Here merchants display their attractive and inviting merchandise as they pester you with the chant of cheap prices where instead the goods are overpriced. Once pass this merchant gauntlet, the magnificent intact entrance pylon welcomes all to come see its treasures.

The great Peristyle Court with its 32 roofed columns, the Pronaos or Hypostyle Hall with 18 massive screened columns, the Second Hypostyle Hall with its 12 smaller columns, two vestibules before the Sanctuary and 14 rooms for vestments, liquid and solid offerings connected with the temple ritual extends this site back to the most ancient times, though the present temple was built between 237 B.C. and 17 B.C. The temple had a library at its entrance.

In the myth of the Revenge of Osiris, after Horus had defeated Seth, he and the "Followers of Horus" built the temple on the spot where the slaying took place. The temple was built and rebuilt from that time onward. There is a spot in the temple where, protruding from the ground are a set of columns which testify to the degree of which the most ancient site has built up and been built on so that the present temple literally sits on top of the columns of the earlier temple.

The "Corridor of Victory" vividly depicts the struggle and final capture of Seth disguised as a hippopotamus. Incidentally, Edfu is the only site in Egypt that boasts two Nilometers for measuring the volume of the river; one inside the temple and an old one to the south of the temple itself. The plan of the temple, the resident god and pharaoh and Goddess Seshat breaking ground are also shown.

The river voyage to Philae Temple of Goddess Isis (Now Agilka Island) is one of the most exhilarating experiences as the temple seems to literally rise out of the Nile in the approach, beginning a photographic bonanza. The rear of the Birth

FREDERICK MONDERSON

House is a photographer's treasure. Upon landing, the stairs, Kiosk of Nectanebo with its beautifully illustrated depictions and Hathor heads; the Forecourt lined by an Eastern Colonnade of 17 columns and a Western Colonnade of 32 columns, both roofed, esplanade the temples of Arsnuphis, Imhotep and Mandulese. At the end of this court steps rise to entrance the massive decorated pylon before which stand 2 stone lions. Passing through the Pylon gateway, the visitor enters the Court of the Temple of Isis.

Here the front of the columned Birth House on the west and the facing Second Eastern Colonnade display columns with capitals of varied styles. Three Hypostyle Halls stand before the Sanctuary. Very well decorated, this temple was also host to St. Stephen Church after Emperor Justinian closed the temple in 535-537 A.D. Evidence of earlier occupation of this site is dated to an altar and relief blocks of Taharka of the 25th Dynasty; while Psamtek II built the Kiosk and a temple of Amasis of the 26th Dynasty attest to the holiness of the site before Ptolemaic times. Prior to this the Island of Elephantine was the site of occupation in this region and may have sported such a temple taking it back to the beginning of dynastic times. Nevertheless, in the Temple of Isis, the last of the hieroglyphics (A.D. 394) and latest Demotic writing (A.D. 452) can be found. There is a small temple to Hathor to the east with a small courtyard in which the God Bes is shown playing a tambourine, an ape plays a stringed instrument and Pharaoh offers a necklace to the goddess.

A little further east, the magnificent Kiosk of Trajan is a beautiful and monumental testimony to Egyptian building techniques though it was erected during foreign, Roman rule. Each of its 16 columns has a distinctly different capital, here as well as the Eastern and Western Colonnades flanking the entrance. This feature is also evident at Edfu and Dendera where each column in the Peristyle Court and the Outer Hypostyle Hall has a different capital.

Seti I's 19th Dynasty temple to Osiris at Abydos has been described as possessing the most beautiful illustration in the entire Valley of the Nile. Its famed 42 steps lead to a First Pylon and First Court, now destroyed; then a Second Pylon and Second Court, also destroyed. An illustrated Pillared entrance leads through 7 doorways, all but one now closed. A First Colonnaded Hall leads to a Second Colonnaded Hall that give rise to an elevated Platform before the Chapels of the seven divinities, viz., Horus, Isis, Osiris, Ra-Horakhty, Amon, Ptah and the deified Seti I, worshipped in this temple.

While popular belief holds the temple was dedicated to Osiris, it is in fact built as a memorial monument to Seti's predecessor kings of the earliest dynasties buried in the desert at Abydos. The axis points in this direction so when the king faces the resident divinities he was also facing his ancestor kings. This temple hosts *in situ* the Abydos Tablet of which 76 ancestor kings are listed from Menes to Rameses I and Seti is the final one. There are 5 blank cartouches of "kings who have

RESEARCH ESSAYS ON ANCIENT EGYPT

transgressed against the state." These are those associated with the Amarna Heresy including Akhenaton, Smenkare, Tutankhamon and Aye. Hatshepsut's name is also included because she chose to rule as King, wore a beard, dressed as a man, built a tomb in the Valley of the Kings and built Deir el Bahari temple, larger than her ancestor, Mentuhotep II of the 11th Dynasty. In the passage leading out to the Osireion, Rameses is shown teaching young Merenptah how to lasso the bull.

The Pyramids are still fixtures on the Giza horizon, while Sakkara boasts the testament of Imhotep's Step Pyramid for Pharaoh Zoser of the 3rd Dynasty, beginning the colonnade concept and initiating the glorious history of Egyptian architecture. Three new tombs were recently discovered at Sakkara; the tomb of the two brothers Niankhnuun and Khnumhotep; Irukaptah; and the Mastaba tomb of Nefer and Kahay. There is a separate charge of 30 Egyptian pounds to view these tombs. All in all, while there are changes, it's all for the betterment and sustainability of the monuments and their history. Meanwhile, many persons invite American Nubian brothers and sisters come home to the culture of the ancestors built in Egypt, Northeast Africa.

Research Essays 6c. Abu Simbel Temple of Rameses II. The Nile Gods unite the land beneath the cartouche of Rameses II.

FREDERICK MONDERSON

5. Who were the Ancient Egyptians?
By
Dr. Fred Monderson

I.   Introduction

The "great researcher" Danny Kaye in his monumental and groundbreaking musical work *The King's New Clothes* eloquently articulated and identified that the king was not wearing anything, as he paraded before the people. He was embarrassingly naked! Equally, Baron de Montesquieu, author of the *Spirit of the Laws*, has argued that man should 'act as if your actions,' and in this case, writings, 'can become a universal law.' Now, when we examine some early writings on Egypt by what we can easily call pseudo-scientific writers, in view of historical revelations, their work certainly emerges as questionable and pejorative at best. At worst, it appears somewhat dishonest, vindictive and mean-spirited, some say racist! Prof. John H. Clarke, in his Introduction to Anthony Browder's *Nile Valley Contributions to Civilization* (1992: 9) puts it best in the statement: "Except for Egypt, African people have been programmed out of the respectable commentary of history. Europeans have claimed the non-African creation of Egypt in order to downgrade the position of African people in world history. They have laid the foundation of what they called Western civilization on a structure that the Western mind did not create. In doing so, they have used no logic!"

Research Essays Papyrus Art 4. The Psychostasia. As Anubis introduces the deceased, he adjusts the scales as "Am-Mit" sits waiting; Thoth records and Horus introduces the "victor" to enthroned Osiris as Isis and Nephthys back the god and the Four Sons of Horus defend.

RESEARCH ESSAYS ON ANCIENT EGYPT

Research Essays 7. Abu Simbel Temple of Rameses II. Rameses smites a kneeling enemy before Ra-Horakhty while Nefertari stands at his rear.

Let us not forget, modern interpretation of the culture of ancient Egypt/Kemet is oriented as Europeans ascended the Nile from north to south as opposed to the flow of the river and culture from South to north and therein lies the conundrum; some say misinterpretation, some say racist, view of ancient Egypt and its relationship with Africa or should we say, Africa's relationship with Egypt, "Ethiopia's eldest daughter."

As an example, we know the Tigris-Euphrates Rivers flowed from north to south. The comparative view would be to argue civilization ascended the river by an invading force. This is the type of argument being presented in the European conception of culture ascending the Nile River.

Conversely, because of its relation to the Nile, at its headwaters, the ancients believed the Ethiopians influenced Egypt. The Ethiopians, in fact, argued they colonized Egypt, since the peoples of the Nile were the same, being only shades of difference in color. Culturally, many modern scholars not only read the ancients but also saw the resemblance and depicted such in their works. Khamit Indus Kush in his book, *The Missing Pages of "His-Story"* (1993: 42) quotes several people affirming the connection between Egypt and Ethiopia. First, Basil Davidson in

FREDERICK MONDERSON

"The Ancient World and Africa, Whose Roots?" (*Race and Class*, XXIX, Autumn 1987, No. 2, p. 2) wrote: "The ancient Egyptians were black (in any variant you may prefer) - or, as I myself think, it more useful to say, were African, is a belief which has been in Europe since about 1830."

The American Egyptologist George Gliddon in *Ancient Egypt: The New World* (1843: 59) has pointed out: "The advocates of the African origin of the Egyptians cling to the superior antiquity of the pyramids of Meroe as a proof of the origin of civilization in Ethiopia, and its consequent descent into Egypt." Again, according to Kush, Professor Rosellini: "Accepts and continues the doctrine, of the descent of civilization from Ethiopia and the African origin of the Egyptians." Prof. Naumann equally believed: "We will first deal with the Ethiopians, as they are the nearest neighbors of the Egyptians, and further because it is historically affirmed that the latter originally migrated from Ethiopia. Indeed, the music of the Ethiopians offers strong internal evidence in support of the assertion." In *Prehistoric Nations* (New York: 1898, p. 276) John D. Baldwin wrote: "Diodorus Siculus adds to his statement that the laws, customs, religious observances, and letters of the ancient Egyptians closely resemble those of the Ethiopians, 'the colony still observing the customs of their ancestors.'"
And on and on!

Bruce Williams of the University of Chicago discovered, from the remains of Qustul, in Nubia, evidence of Pharaonic regalia, viz., white crown, sailing boat, enthroned king, scepter and flail, incense burner, palace facade, etc., dated two hundred years before such appear in Egypt. Dr. Clarke previously had said the Tasians, Badarians, the people from Merimde and Badari, all prehistoric Egyptians, were Negroes. In fact, he said, the Egyptian civilization was "rehearsed in Ethiopia before it made its debut on the stage in Egypt."

The reason for the great hunger for Egypt is best explained in a quote from W.J. Perry in his *The Growth of Civilization*, Penguin Books (1924) (1937: 48-49) where he quotes G. Elliot Smith in *The Ancient Egyptians*: "The Egyptians did a great deal more than merely invent agriculture and devise the earliest statecraft and religion. Not only did they devise the methods of working wood and stone and the art of architecture, they seem also to have been the inventors of linen and of the craft of weaving, of the use of gold and copper, and the making of metal tools and implements. They were the first people to measure the year and to devise a calendar, and later on to substitute for the rough calculation based upon the date the observation of the sun's movements. They also invented shipbuilding and constructed the first sea-going ships. In a thousand and one of the details of our common civilization the originality of Egyptian civilization is revealed. The art of shaving, the use of wigs, the wearing of hats, the invention of the kilt and of the sandal and subsequently of a variety of other articles of dress, many of our musical

RESEARCH ESSAYS ON ANCIENT EGYPT

instruments, chairs and beds, cushions, jewelry and jewel-cases, lamps – these are merely a few of the items picked at random out of our ancient heritage from the Nile valley."

Interestingly, however, when he uses the term "our" he means Europeans, not all of humanity or Africans. This, then, is what is at stake and must be corrected!

Research Essays Temple Ticket 6. Luxor Temple. Price of entrance is fifty Egyptian Pounds.

In the aftermath of the Slave Trade and Slavery, the western world could not admit at the back of their civilization, such were the creations of the people they were enslaving. In fact, this is affirmed by Count Volney in his *Ruins of Empires*, p. 16.

FREDERICK MONDERSON

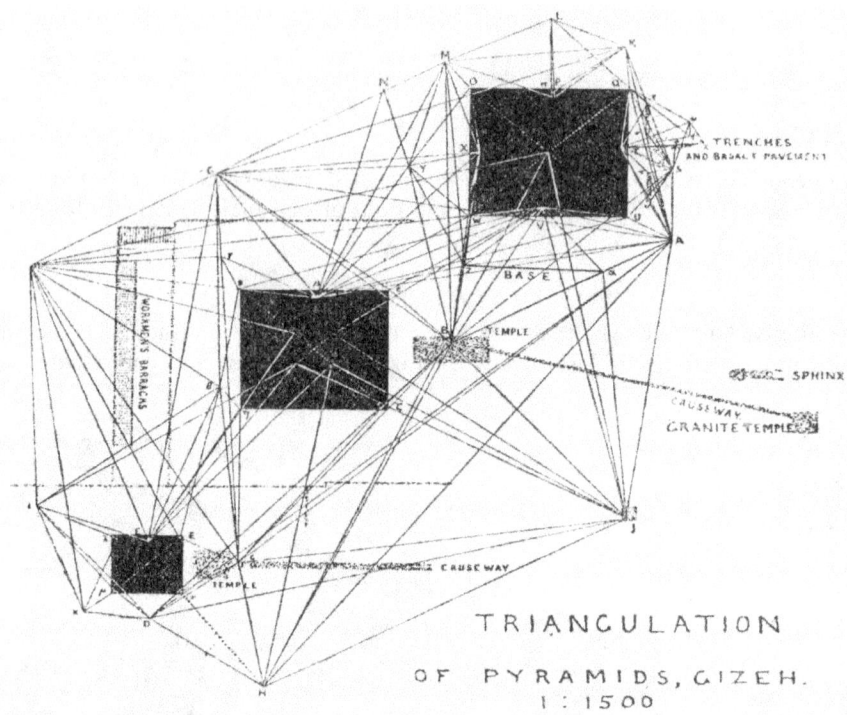

Research Essays Illustration 11. Petrie's Triangulation of the Pyramids of Ghizeh.

Nonetheless, commenting on the significance of ancient Egyptian contribution to civilization, Margaret Murray in *The Splendor that Was Egypt*, New York: Hawthorn Books, Inc., (1949) (1969: xvi) has written the following reinforcing the view previously expressed and attributed to G. Elliot Smith: "For every student of our modern civilization Egypt is the great storehouse from which to obtain information, for within the narrow limits of that country are preserved the origins of most (perhaps all) of our knowledge. In Egypt are found the first beginnings of material culture – building, agriculture, horticulture, clothing (even cooking as an art); the beginnings of the sciences – physics, astronomy, medicine, engineering; the beginning of the imponderables – law, government, and religion. In every aspect of life Egypt has influenced Europe, and though the centuries may have modified the custom or idea, the origin is clearly visible. Centuries before Ptolemy Philadelphus founded his great temple of the Muses at Alexandria, Egypt was to the Greek the embodiment of all wisdom and knowledge. In their generous enthusiasm the Greeks continually recorded that opinion; and by their writings they passed on to later generations that wisdom of the Egyptians which they had learnt orally from the learned men of the Nile Valley."

RESEARCH ESSAYS ON ANCIENT EGYPT

Further, in her explanation, Murray (1969: xvii) revealed: "Egypt was the supreme power in the Mediterranean area during the whole of the Bronze Age and a great part of the Iron Age; and as our present culture is directly due to the Mediterranean civilization of the Bronze Age, it follows that it has its roots in ancient Egypt. It is to Egypt that we owe our division of time; the twelve months and three hundred and sixty-five days of the year; the twelve hours of the day and the twelve hours of the night are due to the work of the Egyptian astronomers. The earliest clocks, the clepsydra, were the invention of Egyptian physicists. The earliest known intelligible writing is the Egyptian, so also are the earliest recorded historical events. It is due to the passion of the Egyptians for making records that so much has been preserved of their history and their literature, of their religious beliefs and their religious ritual. This passion for writing made them invent the first actual writing materials – pens, ink, paper – materials which could be packed in a small compass, were light to carry, and easy to use."

Murray (1969: xvii) continued highlighting Egyptian contributions even more, by contrasting this earliest culture with subsequent civilizations in the human drama and pointing out how Egyptian accomplishments have left them in the dark. She wrote: "The splendor of Egypt was not a mere mushroom growth lasting but a few hundred years. Where Greece and Rome can count their supremacy by the century, Egypt counts hers by the millennium, and the remains of that splendor can even now eclipse the remains of any other country in the world. According to the Greeks there were Seven Wonders of the World; these were the Pyramids of Egypt; the Hanging Gardens of Babylon; the statue of Zeus at Olympia; the Temple of Diana at Ephesus; the Tomb of Mausoleum; the Colossus of Rhodes; and the Lighthouse of Alexandria. Of all these great and splendid works, what remains to the present day? Babylon and its gardens are a heap of rubble, as ruined as a bombed city; the statue of Zeus was destroyed long ago; the Temple of Diana is utterly demolished, leaving only a few foundations; fragments of the Mausoleum are preserved in museums where they are a source of interest to experts only; the Colossus of Rhodes survives only in legend, so completely has it disappeared; the Lighthouse of Alexandria has perished almost without a trace. Of the Seven Wonders the Pyramids of Egypt alone remain almost intact, they still tower above the desert sands, dominating the scene, defying the destroying hand of Time and the still more destructive hand of Man. They line the western shore of the Nile for more than a hundred miles, and are the most stupendous and impressive as they are the most ancient of all the great buildings of the world."

Equally too, Lester Brooks in *Great Civilizations of Ancient Africa* (1971: 28) confirms: "From the cemeteries dating back before 3200 B.C., anthropologists have identified remains they label 'Eurobond' (indicating those of Cro-Magnon types), "Negroid" and some Asian types, with the 'Europoids' predominating in the north and the 'Negroids' predominating in the south. As one expert puts it, 'the races were fused on the banks of the Nile well before Pharaonic civilization came into being. These people were black by the operating definition of skin color as well as by the general physical characteristics they had then.'" Even further, Brooks (1971: 28-29) continued: "The Greeks were surprised twenty-five hundred years ago to discover that the Egyptians were the darkest-skinned peoples of the so-called Near East. Typically they were - and are today – not homogeneous. Their skin color ranges from red-black to yellow. Their hair is black and wavy, curly or wooly; their eyes are bright and black; their bodies are lean and muscular, generally tending to tallness. Egyptian noses usually are large and straight, but frequently aquiline; their jaws generally tend to thrust forward with fleshy lips, often curled back. We can say without the slightest hesitation that the ancient Egyptians would have been considered Negroes by American standards, and until the passage of the Civil Rights Act of 1964 not one of the Egyptian Pharaohs could have bought a cup of coffee in a white drug store in the southern states of the U.S.A."

Research Essays Papyrus Art 5. Two Vultures and Uraei stand above Eyes of Horus as Anubis adjusts the scales for Judgment of a deceased female; while Thoth, the Baboon, records her situation and she presents to Osiris backed by Isis and Nephthys.

RESEARCH ESSAYS ON ANCIENT EGYPT

Research Essays 8. Abu Simbel Temple of Rameses II. Rameses wears the Double Crown and makes a Presentation of flowers while pouring a libation to Khnum, God of the Cataract.

In his "Argument for A Negro Origin" in *African Origin of Civilization: Myth or Reality*, Cheikh Anta Diop (1974: 134-155) cites "Totemism," "Circumcision," "Kingship," "Cosmogony," "Social Organization," "Matriarchy," "Kingship of the Meroitic Sudan and Egypt," "Cradles of Civilization Located in the Heart of Negro Lands," and "Languages," as evidence for his position. His two-cradle theory for ice and sun environments and their influences, and patriarchy as opposed to matriarchy, viz., Europeans in the North and Africans in the South, were very convincing. Brooks (1971: 29) on the other hand sheds more light on this situation: "What African elements can be discovered in the extremely sophisticated civilization of Egypt? Among others, the complicated religious beliefs wherein tribalism, animism and taboos had extraordinary force – with special rites for the major activities such as planting, harvesting, fishing, hunting and war, in addition to the *rites du passage* – birth, marriage, death." Further he points out: "We think of African witch doctors with fantastic, colorful costumes. Look again at a formal portrait of a Pharaoh. Note that, he wears an enormous headdress. From his 'double crown' sprout the head of a vulture and the 'fire-spitting' flamed head of a female hooded cobra, supposedly capable of consuming rebels in flames. The pharaoh was the son of the falcon-god, and was considered a falcon himself, endowed with magical powers and an all-seeing eye. From his waist hangs an animal tail; on his shaven chin he wears a false beard, which is, itself, considered a god. In his hand he carries a scepter with the head of the god Seth atop it – recognizable in the curious curved snout, long, straight ears and almond-shaped eyes."

Adding even more to this fanfare, Brooks demonstrates further: "In processions, banners are carried before the king. These banners bear the symbols of the many powerful brother gods who have blessed him and whose aid is his to command." Of course he also wears arm bands, a necklace, rings, a girdle or apron with Uraeus, sandals and carries a dagger, a flail, and either a mace or bow and arrows, with which to slay his enemies, who as a god and superhuman on the battlefield could slay 'hundreds of enemies at a stroke all by himself.' 'His eyes scrutinize the depths of every being.' Nothing is impossible for him: 'Everything which he ordains comes about.'"

In this respect then, the answer to the question of "Who were the ancient Egyptians?" should not have done so, but still has baffled, confused, contradicted and often been obfuscated by modern scholars, viz., historians, journalists, archaeologists, anthropologists, and every other form of commentator particularly those who use the film and video medium as well as persons involved in printing, dissemination and distribution of information relative to Egypt. All this has left many scholars, students, and average citizens in a state of confusion. Quite frankly, these latter have been misinformed intentionally, unintentionally and because of the falsity fed the previous generations upon whose "facts" they have come to rely. Truthfully, and upon close examination, generation after generation of scholars and lay people, have been misinformed regarding the origin of the ancient Egyptians. Much of this has been intentional and when it has not been so it has been due to ignorance. Some of it is traceable to Wilhelm Hegel and other German scholars, who held, for much of the 19th Century that 'Africa was outside the realm of history,' and by extension the Egyptians were an Asiatic people in the "Middle East" being part of the "Fertile Crescent."

RESEARCH ESSAYS ON ANCIENT EGYPT

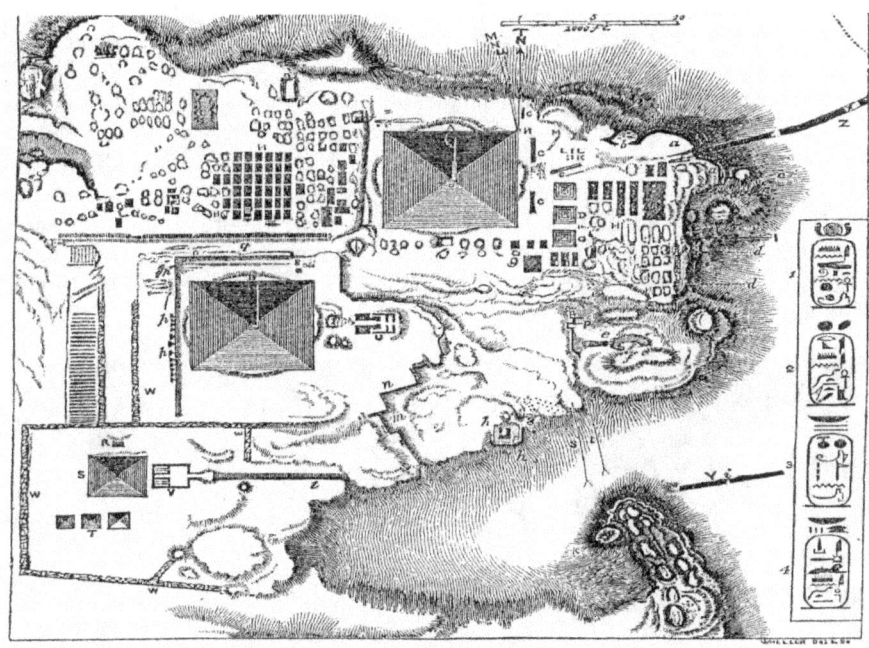

TOPOGRAPHICAL PLAN OF THE PYRAMIDS OF GIZEH.

A. Entrance to the Great Pyramid.
B. Entrance to the Second Pyramid.
C C. Long pits, by some supposed for mixing the mortar.
D. Pyramid of the daughter of Cheops (Herodotus, ii. 126).
E. Pavement of black stones (basaltic trap), the same as found on the causeways of the pyramids of Saqqâra.
F. Remains of masonry.
G. Round enclosures of crude brick, of Arab date, at N.E. angle of this pyramid.
H. Tombs of individuals, with deep pits.
I. The tomb of numbers.
K. Two inclined passages, meeting underground, apparently once belonging to a small pyramid that stood over them.
L L. The rock is here cut to a level surface.
M. A narrow and shallow trench cut in the rock.
N. A square space cut in the rock, probably to receive and support the corner stone of the casing of the pyramid.
P. Here stood a tomb which has received the title of the Temple of Osiris.
Q. Tomb of trades, to west of tombs H.
R. A pit cased with stone, of modern date.
S. The Third Pyramid.
T. Three small pyramids.
U, V. Ruined buildings, whose original use it is now difficult to determine.
W W W. Fragments of stone, arranged in the manner of a wall.
X. A few palms and sycamores, with a well.
Y. Southern stone causeway.
Z. Northern causeway, repaired by the Caliphs.
a. Tombs cut in the rock.
b. Masonry.
c. Black stones.
d, d. Tombs cut in the rock.
e. The sphinx.
f. Pits, probably unopened.
g. Pits.
h. Stone ruin on a rock.
i. Doorway, or passage, through the causeway.
k. A grotto in the rock.
l. Inclined causeway, part of Y.
m, n. Tombs in the rock.
o. Some hieroglyphics on the rock.
p. Tombs cut in the scarp of the rock.
q. Stone wall.
r. Steps cut in the rock, near the N.W. angle of the Great Pyramid.
s, t. Magnetic south, in 1832 and 1836, corresponding to M N; T N being 'true north.'
The names 1 and 2 are of king Ergamenes, mentioned by Diodorus (lib. iii. s. 6), and another Ethiopian monarch, found at Dakkeh.

Research Essays Illustration 12. Topographical Plan of the Pyramids of Gizeh.

Still more significant, it is understandable this position was enunciated during the greatest humiliation, degradation and inhumanity against Africans, that is at the height of the slave trade, slavery, the emergence of the abolition movement to outlaw the slave trade, and in aftermath of the American, French and Haitian revolutions and the discovery of the Rosetta Stone. Millennia prior to that most people believed the Egyptians were Africans and black! However, in unfolding world history and after the discovery of the Rosetta Stone in 1799, Champollion, DeSacy, and Young became involved in the process of decipherment of the hieroglyphic script, which the ancient Egyptians had named *Medu Netcher*. Of these, Champollion was the most successful deciphering hieroglyphics in 1822. This gave birth to the discipline of Egyptology and an effervescence of societies was founded fueling an antiquarian movement. His brother Champollion-Figeac has falsified the older antiquarian pioneer's intent, based on his studious observations; and others much as Herodotus' observations about the ancient Egyptians, has conveniently been ignored. Following Champollion's observations and work, the mad dash for antiquities resulted in what Brian Fagan later dubbed "The Rape of the Nile."

Research Essays 8a. Abu Simbel Temple of Rameses II. Beneath the pedestal of the seated colossal and miniature female figures, the King as a colossal figure wearing the lion skin outfit.

RESEARCH ESSAYS ON ANCIENT EGYPT

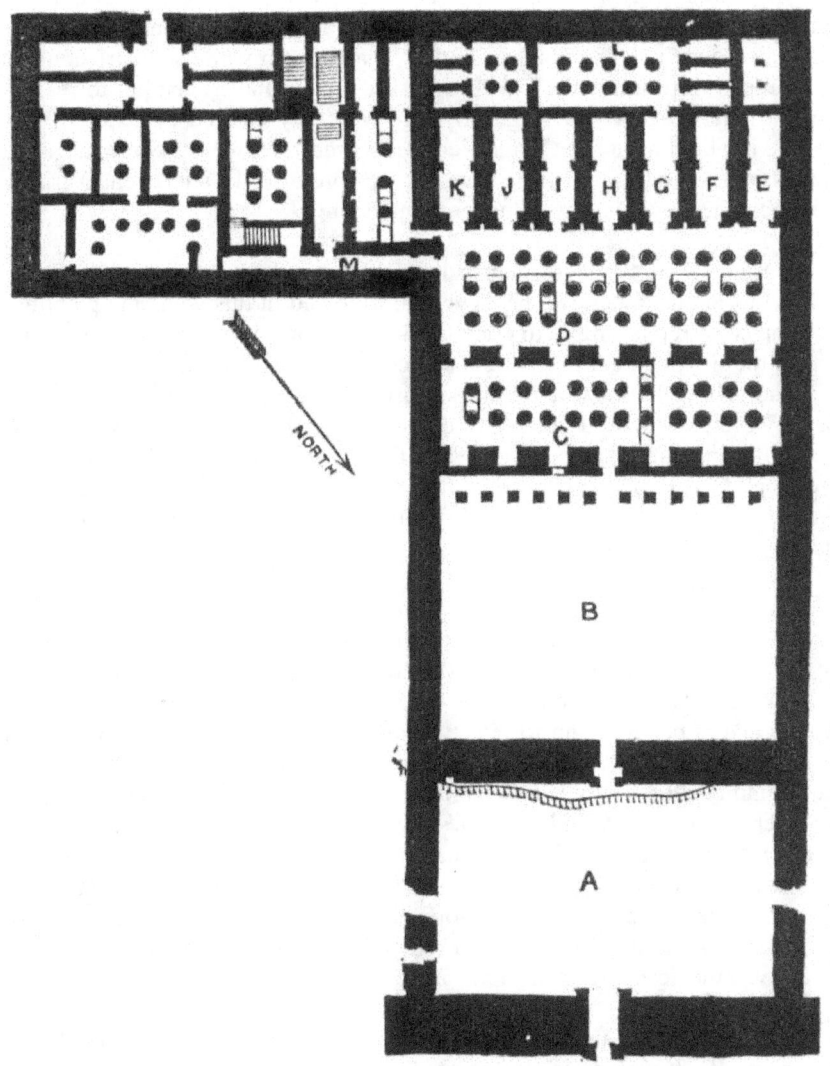

Temple of Osiris at Abydos built by Seti I and Rameses II.

Now, when it comes to the ancient Egyptians there is an unbridgeable chasm, because most white people believe the ancient Egyptians were white, and most blacks with any sense of historical understanding believe the ancient Egyptians were black! Nevertheless, a lot of ink has been spilled on the color of these early Egyptian Africans. This is particularly so of the "red color" of the Egyptians. Let

FREDERICK MONDERSON

me say at this point, I don't have all the answers! However, while we have heard of "red white men," "black white men," and "white white men," one thing is certain, the ancient Egyptians were not white! David O'Connor, a Curator at the Philadelphia Museum has confirmed such to this author! That is not to say others have not also done so! The point is, if this "mainstream white scholar" could say the "Egyptians were not white!" then the issue should have been put to rest long ago, but it is not! Let us not forget, if there were any painted evidence of white Egyptians, it would have been magnified many times. However, while the ancient Egyptians were painted red, they were also painted black; and even Osiris was painted green but Egyptians were never painted white!

From the time of the Stone Age, man has had a penchant for red as his favorite color and this led us to believe the Egyptian, followed in this vein, and painting of himself the color red is simply to demonstrate love for this color. Gay Robbins has informed, the Egyptian believed red and even gold had a solar connection and as a people who believed they were divinely chosen they used red to depict themselves. They, however, also used black to depict themselves, (Thutmose I, Ahmes-Nefertari, Tutankhamon, among survivals) though they never used white for such a depiction! Cheikh Anta Diop said the Egyptians painted themselves red to distinguish themselves from other Africans since they considered themselves special.

In September 2005, a young female guide in the Cairo Museum, in referring to the statue of Mentuhotep II found in his Middle Kingdom temple at Deir el Bahari, told this writer: "He was painted black because he was dead." Obviously she did not know, and is being taught to falsely propagate such by saying 'My Professor told me this at the American University in Cairo!' For though found in 1904, untold commentators wrote and spoke on Egypt without ever mentioning Mentuhotep II, until in 1959, he was described by E. Stephenson Smith in *The Art and Architecture of Ancient Egypt* as having "black flesh!" The guide even told this researcher she never saw Osiris, God of the Dead, painted black! So I searched him out in the Museum and found numerous examples, not just of Osiris but other kings as well. We must also remember; these wooden models are what have survived the destructive elements of time and man!

In the Cairo Museum, Number J 95,655 Osiris in White Crown is painted green. However, in JE 36,465 Osiris is painted black; JE, 95,645 Osiris is black; J, 26,228 Osiris is black; J, 35,669 Osiris is black; papyrus B 24 Osiris is black. This is a lengthy papyrus depicting a winged snake with 4 feet; as 4 goddesses ride 4 uraei with double heads. Then 7 goddesses ride a lengthy snake crossing a river while 6 goddesses pull the snake's tongue as it stands behind a line of 6 goddesses and 6 gods led by Khepre towards the deceased with his back towards Nephthys and Isis standing behind enthroned black Osiris who greets the deceased who in turn offers a plant.

RESEARCH ESSAYS ON ANCIENT EGYPT

Research Essays 8b. Abu Simbel Temple of Rameses II. Another view of the above image, beneath the pedestal of the seated colossal and miniature female figures, the King as a colossal figure wearing the lion skin outfit.

In Room 12 is housed funerary furnishing from royal tombs.

Statue No. 2374 – made of wood, Osiris is painted black.
Statue No. 2372 – made of wood, Osiris is painted black.

In this room, Case GL contains 9 large Afro wigs. These were discovered in the "Deir el Bahari Cache" in 1881.

Wooden statues Numbers 3827, 3836, 3834, 3832, 3824, are all painted black. The wooden duck Number 3838 and a wooden panther No. 3840 and wooden panther No. 3842 are all painted black. In front and outside Room 12 large wooden statues 3834a and 3834b are painted black.

In room No. 22, 9 wooden statues, painted black, are placed above Case J.

4 wooden statues are above Case I
4 wooden statues above Case O
4 wooden statues above Case P
7 wooden statues above Case R

FREDERICK MONDERSON

7 wooden statues above Case T

These are all painted black. Still, who knows what is in the basement. We must remember the place cards for much in the Museum was done by Gaston Maspero. He, incidentally, in the 19th Century, described Maherpra, as "Negroid but not Negro." He probably did not even use capitals. However, contemporary with such a description, the biographers of the musical genius Beethoven described him as "black," "swarthy," "Negroid," "Negro," etc. I ask that you to do the math!

Conversely, Dr. Yosef ben-Jochannan said the Egyptians were painted "red" because they were dead. Even further, that the Henna plant is used to paint particularly young brides red, as part of a cultural ceremony. Now, in the Tomb of Rekhmara, the Vizier, the numerous individuals are all painted red. As a reminder, Cheikh Anta Diop says the Egyptians painted themselves red to distinguish themselves from other African blacks. All this notwithstanding, there are pictorial "survivals" of Egyptians and gods painted black, viz., Amon, Min, Thutmose I, Tutankhamon, Seti I, Ahmose-Nefertari, wife and sister of Ahmose and their brother Kamose whose mother Ahotep and her father Sekenenra Tao must have been black to have produced their "coal black Ethiopian" daughter. Let's face it, in *Red Land, Black Land*, red represented barrenness of the desert; and blackness represented fertility of the cultivable land. Osiris was black so he represented resurrection and eternal life! In fact, Osiris was called "the Great Black!" Theophile Obenga has reminded all Kemet or the "black land" referred to the people not the land itself.

Rameses II's wife Nefertari was Nubian. Yet she is painted red in her tomb in the Valley of the Queens. Ahmes Nefertari was Ethiopian and painted black. In December 2005, someone called this writer to look at a program on the History Channel entitled *Black Pharaohs* about the 25th Dynasty who were Nubian and black as we know. In a fleeting glance the camera showed an image of Tanutemon, one of these black pharaohs and lo and behold, this ruler was painted red in the tomb! Let us not forget also, images in the tomb of the nobles at Aswan also show these southernmost Egyptians, where Nubia interacts significantly with Egypt and who were essentially black, also painted red. What does all this mean? It means the Egyptians were African not European or Asiatic, black not white and Egypt was and is still located in Africa not the Middle East or Asia. Now what is the evidence for all of this?

RESEARCH ESSAYS ON ANCIENT EGYPT

Research Essays 9. Abu Simbel Temple of Rameses II. Entrance facade of Nefertari's Temple with statues of Rameses, Nefertari and Hathor.

Thus, this presentation will focus on a chronological approach showing how principally eyewitnesses portrayed the ancient Africans of the Nile Valley, Egypt; first, and as interest intensified in modern times, how Egypt was viewed particularly in the 19th and 20th Centuries of our era. One thing is certain as European writers, historians and antiquarians first encountered Egypt they "colored" their reports to appease an emerging reading public in Europe. With time, African scholars did significant research unearthing the distortions, omissions, and misrepresentations and revealed what they had found. Despite profound scholarship by blacks, European writers and their American cohorts have found it difficult to accept the revealed facts or have refused to deal with the issue, sidestepping it. African research has been attacked in the most vituperative manner, minutely scrutinized and dismissed in the most unprofessional manner as if such effort was grounded in malice. Those Europeans who bucked the trend and wrote otherwise of the distortion, were ostracized and their works equally subject to the most insidious criticism.

For example, much confusion has been created as European scholars, not finding any evidence of "White Egyptians" have emphasized "Red Egyptians" as being "Red Egyptian White men." Let me give this example and pose a question before we begin. Murnane (1983: 231) in discussing the Sanctuary area of the Temple of Karnak where the god Amon-Ra dwelt, wrote: "The walls are covered with scenes illustrating the episodes of the offering rite with Amun appearing in his usual anthropomorphic guise and also in the ithyphallic form he shares with Min, the god of fertility." For many this description is obscure! Further, another writer Michael Haag's Cadogan series in *Cairo, Luxor, Aswan* (2000: 212) wrote: "On the north side of the sanctuary, where there was much rebuilding a wall erected by Hatshepsut was found concealed behind a later wall of Thutmosis III, thus preserving the original freshness of the coloring. The wall has now been removed to a nearby room, and shows Amon, his flesh painted red and with one foot in front of the other, and also Amon in the guise of the ithyphallic Min, a harvest god, often amalgamated with Amon, his flesh painted black." Let us remember, while Amon is here represented with "his flesh painted red," in the back room at Medinet Habu, he is shown enthroned and his skin is painted black there. He is also painted blue here and at Karnak beside the *Akh Menu*!

Now the serious first question is: "Why would white red men be worshipping black Gods?" Equally too, another question is, "Why did Murnane not refer to the color of Amon, as Min, being black?" Elsewhere, in the *Journal of Egyptian Archaeology* Amon has been described as "so black, he was blue!" Many writers have a tendency to skillfully dance around the question of the race of the Egyptians, particularly when evidence indicates they were black! It's all part of the conspiracy. Much further, when evidence surfaces depicting Egyptians "painted black" the logical explanation given is there were painted black because either they were dead or for the death ceremony. Yet, while no evidence exists to show Egyptians white, the assumption and propagated falsity is that they were white! Again, a very good reason the white writer affirmed to this researcher "The Egyptians were not white" is simply because today men of reasonable intellect know the falsity of a white Egypt is just that, falsity.

II. Classical Writers

a. **Homer** - Most scholarship seems to date Homer to about 800 B.C. However, this may be incorrect, even though we know he is "credited" with writing the *Iliad* and the *Odyssey*. Several things need to be looked at in relation to dating of Homer and even questioning his originality. First, we are told that Abu Simbel temple of Rameses II has the earliest examples of Greek writing and this writing is dated to the 7th Century B.C. Now, if Homer wrote the *Odyssey* and *Iliad* then it cannot be 800 B.C., as previously thought. Second, Cheikh Anta Diop says, if Homer visited Egypt it had to be in the 8th Century during the time of the Twenty-fifth Ethiopian Dynasty and much of his descriptions may be representative of later events in Egypt. Interestingly, Murray's *Handbook for Egypt* (1888) informs: "In the Ramesseum, North face of the South East Wall of the 2nd area is a scene of combat that very much resembles what Homer tells us of his Odyssey."

RESEARCH ESSAYS ON ANCIENT EGYPT

Research Essays Illustration 13. Mereruka, the Vizier of King Teti, seeming to walk through the false door in his mastaba.

b.   **Herodotus** 480-425 B.C. - Herodotus visited Egypt around 450 B.C. and wrote his *Histories* devoting Book II *Euterpe* to Egypt. Diop (1989) argued in "Origins of the Ancient Egyptians" in *Egypt Revisited* Edited by Ivan Van Sertima, and quotes the father of history in regard to the Origins of the Colchians: "It is in fact manifest that the Colchidians are Egyptians by race ... several Egyptians told me that in their opinion the Colchidians were descended from soldiers of Sesostris. I had conjectured as much myself from two pointers, firstly because they have black skins and kinky hair (to tell the truth this proves nothing for other peoples have them too) and secondly and more reliably for the reason that alone among mankind the Egyptians and Ethiopians have practiced circumcision since time immemorial." Herodotus says further that the Egyptians have "thick lips, broad noses and are burnt of skin," meaning they are black. Practically everything else Herodotus wrote about was accepted as observed fact other than that the Egyptians had "wooly hair, thick lips, broad noses and were burnt of skin." Much of what he heard or theorized could be considered conjecture, but his observations cannot be disputed! Naturally, he never said black as compared to what or whom!

c. **Aristotle** 384-322 B.C. - Aristotle in his work *Physiognomonica* made a somewhat controversial statement regarding the ancient Egyptians. He said: "The Egyptians and Ethiopians are cowards because they are black" and of the Nordics he equally said "whites are also cowards" because they are white. He was seeking to affirm that the middle ground, perhaps a "Mediterranean Race," type was the ideal. Now, while his science of cowards was wrong, for we know as proven by the many wars Africans in particular have fought; however, his description of the Egyptians and Ethiopians is essentially correct. This is one incidence in which this great philosopher and scientist was both wrong and right on the same issue.

d. **Diodorus Siculus** of Sicily 63-14 B.C. - Diodorus held to the view that Ethiopians colonized Egypt. Diop says, according to Diodorus: "The Ethiopians say that the Egyptians are one of their colonies, which was brought into Egypt by Osiris. They even allege that this country was originally under water, but that the Nile, dragging much mud as it flowed from Ethiopia, had finally filled it in and made it a part of the continent. ... They add that from them, as from authors and their ancestors, the Egyptians got most of their laws." Inadvertently Diodorus tells us the origin of Osiris as being Central African!

e. **Diogenes** says of **Zeno**, founder of the Stoic School 333-261 B.C. that he was "tall and black" and "people called him an Egyptian vine-shoot."

f. **Ammianus Marcellinus** 33-100 A.D. notes that the "men of Egypt are mostly brown or black with a skinny and desiccated look." He says further that the Colchians were "an ancient race of Egyptian origin."

RESEARCH ESSAYS ON ANCIENT EGYPT

Egyptian Name.	Meaning.	Civil Year.	In the Sacred Year the Month begins	In the Alexandrian year the Month begins
	1st month of Spring	Thoth	July 25	August 29.
	2nd ,, ,, ,,	Paophi	August 19	September 28.
	3rd ,, ,, ,,	Athyr	September 18	October 28.
	4th ,, ,, ,,	Choiak	October 18	November 27.
	1st ,, ,, Summer or Ploughing Season	Tybi	November 17	December 27.
	2nd ,, ,, ,,	Mechir	December 17	January 26.
	3rd ,, ,, ,,	Phamenoth	January 16	February 25.
	4th ,, ,, ,,	Pharmuthi	February 15	March 27.
	1st ,, ,, Inundation	Pachons	March 17	April 26.
	2nd ,, ,, ,,	Payni	April 16	May 26.
	3rd ,, ,, ,,	Epiphi	May 16	June 25.
	4th ,, ,, ,,	Mesore	June 15	July 25.

THE EGYPTIAN CALENDAR.

Research Essays Illustration 13a. The twelve Egyptian Months of three Seasons.

g. **Count Volney**, one of the Savants who followed Napoleon to Egypt at the end of the 18th Century, made the following statement regarding the ancient Egyptians from observations of the Copts. According to Diop (1989) Volney wrote: "All of them are puffy-faced, heavy-eyed and thick-lipped, in a word, real mulatto faces. I was tempted to attribute this to the climate until, on visiting the Sphinx; the look of it gave me the clue to the enigma. Beholding that head characteristically Negro in all its features, I recalled the well-known passage of Herodotus, which reads: 'For my part I consider the Colchoi are a colony of the Egyptians because, like them, they are black-skinned and kinky-haired.' In other words the ancient Egyptians were true Negroes of the same stock as all the autochthonous peoples of Africa and from that datum one sees how their race, after centuries of mixing with the blood of Romans and Greeks, must have lost the full blackness of its original color but retained the impress of its original mould. It is even possible to apply this observation very widely and posit in principle that physiognomy is a kind of record usable in many cases for disputing or elucidating the evidence of history on the origins of the peoples …."

FREDERICK MONDERSON

Research Essays 10. Abu Simbel Temple of Rameses II. Nefertari holds a Sistrum and makes a Presentation of flowers to enthroned Hathor, Goddess of her Temple.

III. To the Mid-19th Century

In a chapter entitled "Modern Falsification of History" Cheikh Anta Diop's *African Origin of Civilization: Myth or Reality* discusses Domeny de Rienzi's contention that: "It is true that back in the distant past, the dark red Hindu and Egyptian race dominated culturally the yellow and black races, and even our own white race then inhabiting western Asia. At that time our race was rather savage and sometimes tattooed, as I have seen it depicted on the tomb of Sesostris I in the valley of Biban-el-Moluk at Thebes, the city of the gods."

RESEARCH ESSAYS ON ANCIENT EGYPT

This is interesting, for if we believe the Egyptians were white and migrated to Africa leaving no evidence of the prototype of Egyptian culture in their place of origin in Western Asia, how did Thebes in Upper Egypt become the "city of their gods." Equally, any claim of a western Asian origin of the Egyptians ties them to the white race. However, let us not forget, Nubia and Central Africa was "God's land." Again, we have the absolutely absurd conclusion that whites from western Asia considered Africa as their "God's land!"

We should be aware, every people who migrated from one place to the next, retained some reference to their ancestral home. Contrary to popular western prognostication, the Egyptians never associated Mesopotamia or Southwest Africa with their origins. In fact, the record seems to indicate at least one reference to origins and this was made by Hunefer, 19th Dynasty priest of Seti I, whose papyrus, *Papyrus of Hunefer* now in the British Museum, states: "We came from the foothills of the Mountains of the Moon where the God Hapi dwells." This area is the plains of the East African mountain range. Inadvertently, he also identified the place of the origin of Osiris also called Hapi, equally a god of the Nile. As Wortham submitted one modern 1825 mummy dissection to prove the ancient Egyptians were Caucasian how then would we regard the ancients Hunefer's and Diodorus' contentions as to the origin of Osiris (Hapi) and the Egyptians?

a. **Jean Jacques Champollion** the Younger set to work and was successful in deciphering the hieroglyphic script, as we know, in 1822. Within ten years he was dead. However, his extensive work did unleash an interest in antiquarian studies. Diop quotes Champollion from a letter to his brother Champollion-Figeac, who twisted his brother's words, thus helping to bring about the falsification of Egyptian history and the continued removal of Africans from this important part of African history. He mentions four groups of people starting with the Egyptians shown with a dark red color. "There can be no uncertainty about the racial identity of the man who comes next: he belongs to the black race, designated under the general term *Nahasi*. The third represent a very different aspect; his skin color borders on yellow or tan; he has a strongly aquiline nose, thick, black pointed beard, and wears a short garment of varied colors; these are called *Namou*. Finally, the last one is what we call flesh-colored, a white skin of the most delicate shade, a nose straight or slightly arched, blue eyes, blond or reddish beard, tall [in] stature and very slender, clad in a hairy ox-skin, a veritable savage tattooed on various parts of his body; he is called *Tamhou*." He wrote elsewhere: "We find there Egyptians and Africans represented in the same way."

Even more striking, Diop argues in comparison with many West African blacks whom he names and finally states: "If the Egyptians were white, then all these fore-mentioned Negro peoples and so many others in Africa are also whites. Thus we reach the absurd conclusion that blacks are basically whites." Even further, he writes: "On these numerous bas-reliefs, we see that, under the Eighteenth Dynasty, all the specimens of the white race were placed behind the blacks; in particular, the

Research Essays 11. Abu Simbel Temple of Rameses II. Rameses in Blue or War Crown offers two bouquets to enthroned Hathor in horns and disk, while Nefertari offers flowers and holds a sistrum in her Temple.

'blond beast' of Gobineau and the Nazis, a tattooed savage, dressed in animal skin, instead of being at the start of all civilization, was still essentially untouched by it and occupied the last echelon of humanity."

b. **Karl Lepsius** - Diop tells us Karl Lepsius offered a "Canon of proportion" in his *Discoveries in Egypt, Ethiopia and the Peninsula of Sinai in the Years 1842-1848* (London: 1852) that denotes: "The proportions of the perfect Egyptian body; it has short arms and is Negroid or Negritian. From the anthropological point of view, the Egyptian comes after the Polynesians, Samoyeds, Europeans, and is immediately followed by African Negroes and Tasmanians. Besides, there is a scientific tendency to find in Africa, after excluding foreign influences, from the Mediterranean to the Cape, from the Atlantic to the Indian Ocean, nothing but Negroes or Negroids of various colors. The ancient Egyptians were Negroes, but Negroes to the last degree."

c. **Garner Wilkinson** – An English nobleman, spent several years in Egypt, particularly Thebes, during mid-19th Century. He did extensive research and produced significant works on the Egyptian culture that is still consulted by experts in the field.

IV. To 1900

a. **Auguste Mariette** – Was of an age when great interest in Egypt very early attracted many scholars from different countries, in the aftermath of Napoleon's discovery of the Rosetta Stone and Champollion's decipherment of the language. However, his vision seemed different from most of his age principally bent of antiquities acquisition. Ruffle (1977: 8-9) best puts the man and his time in perspective. "With funds from King Friedrich Wilhelm IV of Prussia, Richard Lepsius made a great survey of the monuments (published in a mammoth twelve-volume work) and collected many objects, which formed the basis of the great Berlin collection. The increasing scholarly interest highlighted the need for orderly and controlled excavation. Auguste Mariette, who was sent by the Louvre to collect antiquities in Egypt, realized this. With the support of the Khedive he founded the Egyptian Museum and Antiquities Service and became its first director, often pushing through his scientific policies in the teeth of opposition from other European Egyptologists."

FREDERICK MONDERSON

"Mariette's concern was matched by the painstaking methodology preached by William Matthew Flinders Petrie, grandson of the explorer of Australia and the first person to hold a chair in Egyptology [in England] – University College, London. This chair had been founded by Amelia Edwards whose un-intentional Nile cruise – she had gone there when a sketching holiday in France was rained off – had filled her with an enthusiasm for Egypt that led her to found not only Petrie's chair but also the Egypt Exploration Fund. Other learned societies were also formed – notably the *Deutsche Orient Gesellschaft* in 1888 and the *Mission Archaeologique Francaise* in 1880, later the *Institut Francais d'Archaeologie Orientale*."

b.   **Brugsch-Bey** – Karl Heinrich Brugsch-Bey in his *Egypt Under the Pharaohs* (London: John Murray, 1902: 2-3) has argued: "Suffice it to say, however, that, according to ethnology, the Egyptians appear to form a third branch of the Caucasian race, the family called Cushite; and this much may be regarded as certain, that in the earliest ages of humanity, far beyond all historical remembrance, the Egyptians, for reasons unknown to us, left the soil of their early home, took their way towards the setting sun, and finally crossed that bridge of nations the Isthmus of Suez, to find a new fatherland on the banks of the Nile."

Many of these individuals generally argue on speculation and offer no facts to support their contentions. Let us not forget, these people came as bakers "with empty hands and white skins." What else are we to believe? According to Manetho, the gods ruled Egypt, then the demi-gods and later the manes before the unification. By this time, after millennia of preparation and finally unification and its many benefits, political, religious, economic, artistic, architectural, and social, the foundation of dynastic culture became firmly implanted. What evidence is there that these Caucasians did anything more than just push the dough of the bread in the oven.

c.   **Adolf Erman** – German scholar extraordinaire. It's been argued Erman was probably the only modern who understood exactly what the Egyptians meant in their language. Nevertheless, Charles Finch in "Black Roots of Egypt's Glory" in *Great Black Leaders: Ancient and Modern* (1988: 140-141) has written: "As the 19th century wore on, German scholars began applying their meticulous methods of research to the study of ancient Egyptian language. Finding many similarities in words and syntax between Egyptian and the Semitic languages, the Germans unhesitatingly proclaimed Egyptian to belong to this group. As a result, their leading Egyptologists Eber, Erman and Brugsch – concluded that the impetus for Egyptian civilization itself came from a western Asiatic or Semitic source. Like others, they saw in the human figures on the Egyptian monuments – many colored a reddish-brown – evidence of a non-African 'Mediterranean race.' Anthropologically speaking, no such race ever existed, but that did not trouble

RESEARCH ESSAYS ON ANCIENT EGYPT

them overmuch and the term has remained in vogue to this day." Obviously, there was a turn around because Erman later wrote in *Life in Ancient Egypt* (New York: Macmillan, 1894: 32) confirming: "The inhabitants of Libya, Egypt and Ethiopia have probably belonged to the same race since prehistoric times. In physical structure they are still Africans." Otherwise he implied they were all white!

d.   **Gaston Maspero** – French Egyptian expert has written extensively on the history and culture. However, his take is that the ancient Egyptians were of European origin, crossed over to North Africa and entered Egypt from the west. What a pity! Lhote in "Tassili Frescoes" identified Negroes in the Sahara between 7000 and 6000 B.C. Why could these blacks not be able to enter the Nile Valley from the Sahara but whites could cross over to North Africa from Europe and then follow essentially the same route into the Valley?

e.   **William Matthew Flinders Petrie** (1853-1942) - The "Father of modern archaeology," did extensive research in Egypt and was one of the most prolific writers of his day, influencing a great many people with his, now considered, racist views. Stuart Tyson Smith in "Race" in Donald B. Redford's Edited *The Oxford Encyclopedia of Ancient Egypt* Vol. 3, (2001: 111) has written the following: "The origins of the modern conception of race derive from the work of nineteenth-century anthropologists like L.H. Morgan and E.B. Taylor, who developed 'scientific' unilinear evolutionary theoretical models for the development of human beings from 'Savagery' to 'Civilization.' Racial groups were ranked by evolutionary categories, linked to intellectual capacities, based on elaborate cranial measurements; supposedly, this provided causal links between phenotype (observable) traits, mental capacities, and socio-political dominance. This model not coincidentally reinforced the existing European-American domination of third-world peoples with the claim of scientifically 'objective' methodologies based on race and evolution." Even further, Smith continued: "The unilinear evolutionary model did influence some early Egyptologists. W. M. Flinders Petrie used it to develop his notion of the 'Dynastic Race,' to explain the rapid development of Egyptian civilization. In part this was based on prevailing models of culture change that emphasized migration as an explanation for cultural change, but, ultimately, racist notions drove the model. The implication was that Egypt had a 'white' or 'brown' ruling class dominating a native 'black' African underclass who supplied the labor to build Egypt's great monuments. The Egyptological community as a whole never enthusiastically accepted Petrie's model, although the idea persisted through a few enthusiasts. James Henry Breasted echoed the sentiments of most contemporary Egyptologists in seeing the Egyptians as indigenous, but as a brown rather than black race, related to other northeastern Africans. It is interesting to note that the Egyptians became 'White' for a classroom textbook, presumably reflecting the racism of the day. The last serious argument in support of the Dynastic Race theory appeared in Walter Emery's *Archaic Egypt* (New York, 1961)."

Research Essays Illustration 14. Mythological animals from the Egyptian desert.

Research Essays 11a. Abu Simbel Temple of Rameses II. Plaque commemorating the safeguarding and reconstruction of Abu Simbel temples during Gamal Abdul-Nasser's Presidency in 1968.

f. **Ernest Alfred Wallis Budge** - Wallis Budge was Keeper of Egyptian and Assyrian Antiquities at the British Museum and a prolific writer who wrote about *The Gods of the Egyptians, The Mummy, Egyptian Magic*, an *Egyptian Hieroglyphic Dictionary*, and a whole lot more. Regarding Budge, Finch (1988) states: "Unusual for an Egyptologist, he had conducted extensive research

RESEARCH ESSAYS ON ANCIENT EGYPT

among the peoples of the Sudan and Ethiopia – encountering cultural practices, religious ideas and languages which showed clear and identifiable linkages to ancient Egypt. It became clear to Budge that everything about ancient Egypt could be understood only by reference to Africa; there was nothing fundamentally Asiatic about Egyptian culture. In 1920, in his massive and erudite '*Egyptian Hieroglyphic Dictionary*,' Budge, reversing a 100-year trend and his own earlier opinion, classified Egyptian as an African rather than a Semitic language."

Then again, we know the Egyptian religious writing is the oldest in the world. By the First Dynasty, the *Book of the Dead* was a compilation of much earlier works, which means Egyptian writing certainly took some time to develop into that state. How come the people from Asia or wherever they came from never invented Hieroglyphics in their point of origin, nor probably had any writing until they came to the Nile Valley? The answer debunks Brugsch-Bey. Certainly Diop, Arnett and even Winkler show the development of rudimentary forms of Hieroglyphs in the Upper Nile region dating as early as 6000 B.C.

g. **Canon George Rawlinson**, in the *Story of the Nations: Egypt* (1893: 23-24) stated: "It is generally answered that they came from Asia; but this is not much more than a conjecture. The physical type of the Egyptians is different from that of any known Asiatic nation. The Egyptians had no traditions that at all connected them with Asia. Their language, indeed, in historic times was partially Semitic, and allied to the Hebrew, the Phoenician, and the Aramaic; but the relationship was remote, and may be partly accounted for by later intercourse, without involving original derivation. The fundamental character of the Egyptian in respect of physical type, language, and tone of thought, is Nigritic. The Egyptians were not Negroes, but they bore a resemblance to the Negro, which is indisputable. Their type differs from the Caucasian in exactly those respects which when exaggerated produce the Negro. They were darker, had thicker lips, lower foreheads, larger heads, more advancing jaws, a flatter foot, and a more attenuated frame. It is quite conceivable that the Negro type was produced by a gradual degeneration from that which we find in Egypt. It is even conceivable that the Egyptian type was produced by gradual advance and amelioration from that of the Negro."

FREDERICK MONDERSON

Research Essays 12. Temple of Isis on Agilka Island. Visitors and guards at the entrance landing, while the Kiosk of Trajan stands in the rear.

h.   **M. le Vicomte J. de Rouge** is mentioned in an article in *American Journal of Archaeology*, Vol. 1 (1897: 393-95) where he raises the question of "The Origin of the Egyptian Race" and attempted to "prove the theory of the Asiatic derivation." Emphasizing statues found belonging to the third, fifth and sixth dynasties, he stated: "The types of the faces do not belong to the later Egyptian style, but possess elements of the more refined Semitic organization; and this fact is used by the writer as a proof of the importation of a fully developed civilization into Egypt." Essentially, the article argues there are three theories as to the origin of the Egyptian race: (1) that the entry of the population into Egypt was made by way of Asia, passing through the Isthmus of Suez; (2) that Egypt became occupied by a colony which came in part from Asia, but passed through Ethiopia; (3) that the majority of the Egyptian population had its origin in Africa and passed into Egypt by the west and southwest." This last is a more recent theory which has been in a measure accepted by M. Maspero, and is supported by a large number of students of natural history and of ethnology, while the theory of the Asiatic origin is based on linguistic comparisons and a study of the monuments, especially the primitive monuments of Babylonia."

He says further: "The Egyptians seem not to have preserved any tradition or indication, or even memory, of their foreign origin, for they consider themselves as autochthones, and regard their country as the cradle of the human race." In addition, he argues: "The most ancient monuments discovered up to this time appear to belong to the third dynasty, such as the recently discovered bas-relief of

RESEARCH ESSAYS ON ANCIENT EGYPT

King Sozir; that of Prince Ra-hotpu and of Princess Nofrit, etc. The statues of the two last mentioned royal personages show that the art of sculpture was already in an advanced stage of development, and the types of the faces, with their aquiline noses and thin lips, recall the Semitic race rather than the Egyptian. The great sphinx of Ghizeh, which is perhaps the most ancient relic of Egyptian art, is also anterior to the fourth dynasty." He never says anything more regarding the "Negro features" of the Sphinx. Of course, Dr. ben-Jochannan, the master-teacher, told of Hunefer, a priest of King Seti I, during Ramesside times; who, in *The Papyrus of Hunefer*, noted "We came from the headwaters of the Nile, at the foothills of the mountains of the moon where the God Hapi dwells." This area is in the East African region of Mounts Ruwenzori, Kenya and Kilimanjaro near Uganda and Kenya.

Research Essays Temple Ticket 7. Deir el Bahari Temple. Price of entrance is thirty Egyptian Pounds.

i.   **Edouard Naville**, a Swiss Archaeologist, cleared the two Deir el Bahari complexes of Hatshepsut and Mentuhotep II. The *American Journal of Archaeology* XVIII (1913: 202) reported Edouard Naville presented a paper on "The African Origin of Egyptian Civilization" in *R. Arch* XXII (1913, pp. 47-65) that states essentially: "The rise of Egyptian civilization after the Neolithic period was due to conquest by an African people from the South, called Anou. The people who caused the changes when the Thinite period ends and the Memphite period begins may have been Asiatic but they brought in no important new elements, - they merely gave a new impulse to the existing civilization." This means these Asiatics comprised the third and fourth dynasties ruling at Memphis and all they brought were their "pretty white selves." However, Petrie mentioned the founder of the third dynasty was Ethiopian from his features in the Sinai. Notwithstanding, from the images, Snefru of the third and Khufu, Khafre and Menkaure, builders of the fourth dynasty Ghizeh Pyramids, were, by operating definitions, black!

Research Essays Illustration 15. More mythological figures from the Egyptian desert.

j.   **G. Elliot Smith** in *The Ancient Egyptians and Their Influence Upon the Civilization of Europe* (London and New York: Harper and Brothers, 1911: 32-39) informs: "Even such eminent scholars as de Rouge, Heinrich Brugsch, and Ebers, among many others, claimed that Egypt derived her language as well as much of her culture and knowledge of the arts from Asia; and Hommel and others went much further, and claimed that the whole Egyptian civilization was Babylonian in origin …."

"De Morgan and his collaborators claim that the Ancient Egyptian language and mode of writing, the importation into Egypt of the knowledge of metals, and of such crafts as brick-making and tomb-construction, and even the fauna and flora of the country in ancient times, all point to Babylonia as the place where the roots of Egyptian civilization should be sought."

"But, under Dr. Reisner's critical analysis of the foundations upon which these speculations were supposed to have been based, practically the whole of the elaborate edifice has tumbled to the ground. As Eduard Meyer has said, 'the suggestion that a culture, or even its chief elements, can be derived from another people is unthinkable and historically false: but influences must have been at work, and the Egyptians and Babylonians must have given and taken.'"

RESEARCH ESSAYS ON ANCIENT EGYPT

Research Essays 13. Temple of Isis on Agilka Island. The Western Colonnade with its 32-columns on the Dromos to the entrance Pylon.

"Dr. Reisner has proved the indigenous origin of Egyptian civilization in the Nile Valley, and has revealed the complete absence of any evidence to show, or even to suggest, that the language, mode of writing, the knowledge of copper, or the distinctive arts and crafts were imported."

"Schweinfurth argued that the 'invaders' of Egypt – the stereotyped phrase used by so many writers, tacitly assuming as a fact the idea of an immigration into Egypt – came from Southern Arabia (Sabaea or Hadramut), across the Straits of Bab el-Mandeb, thence through Abyssinia and the eastern Desert into Nubia, from which they spread along the banks of the Nile into Egypt …."

"Lortet and Gaillard, the most recent writers to discuss the fauna of Ancient Egypt, protest against the conclusions of Duerst that certain of the domestic animals of Ancient Egypt were brought from Asia; and they tell us that the animals known to have lived in Egypt at the time of the Ancient Empire were all African, that is, local in origin …."

FREDERICK MONDERSON

Referring to previous statements, and that preceding his book by almost a century, "Blumenbach began the serious study of the physical characters of the Ancient Egyptians. Since then a considerable number of scholars have contributed to the discussion of the significance of the anatomical evidence – in America, Nott, Gliddon, and Meigs might be mentioned as pioneers; in France, Perrier, Pruner, Broca, Quatrefages, Hamy, Fouquet, Zabarowski, Cantre, Lortet, and Verneau have made contributions of varying importance; in German-speaking countries, Carus, Czermak, Virchow, Hartmenn, Emile Schmidt, Stahr, and Oetteking may be mentioned; in England, Bernard Davis, Huxley, Owen, Petrie, Garson, Randall-MacIver, Thomson, Macalister, Karl Pearson and his school of biometricans, Myers and Keith represent some of the outstanding names of those who have written about the craniology of the Egyptians; and last, but by no means least, Italy has added the important and highly suggestive writings of Sergi, Biasutti, and Giuffrida-Ruggeri."

G. Elliot Smith, the anatomist from the University of Manchester examined the mummies and is the author of "Diffusionist theory" that Egyptian culture spread far and wide influencing many people with its contributions to human civilization development. His book, *The Ancient Egyptians and Their Influence Upon the Civilization of Europe* is a classic.

Some guides have commented on his bitterness, for, after having examined the mummies, he was ushered from the room without his notes. This may have led to some enmity towards the ancient Egyptians.

V.   To 1950

a.   **Randall MacIver** did a study in 1905 and came to the conclusion that there were two peoples living in Egypt, side by side, Africans and Europeans. His position had been, whites were in occupation in the north and blacks in the south. There was much discussion about this but it forces us to wonder how the critics in Europe, England especially, could come to agreement on this so later disputed fact. And even more, entertain a thought the ancient Egyptians were Caucasians.

b.   **Arthur Weigall** – Young and impetuous, he was an Englishman who first studied with Petrie at Abydos. He wrote a book entitled *Flights into Antiquity* in which he entitled a chapter, "Exploits of a Nigger King," dealing with the XXV Dynasty. The title of this chapter signals his contempt for Africans and thus he would not have seen Egypt as African and black. He is the writer who claimed Rameses II was Syrian. Which begs the question, 'Why would Rameses, in the Battle of Kadesh, call on an African god, Amon, saying his ancestors had worshipped the god for time immemorial, and sought his help at that crucial and

RESEARCH ESSAYS ON ANCIENT EGYPT

challenging time.' Imagine a Syrian, Asiatic, calling upon an African god while doing battle in Asia! Further, imagine this same Syrian calling upon and even worshipping an African god whose alter ego, Min, was black! We also know Amon was black. This also questions the contention that Osiris was black simply because of his role as god of the dead. Fact is, the straw men arguments easily fall apart!

Research Essays 14. Temple of Isis on Agilka Island. The Eastern Colonnade with its 17 columns and entrance Pylon in the rear.

c.   **James Henry Breasted**, pioneering American Egyptologist - Charles S. Finch III again in "The Black Roots of Egypt's Glory" quotes James Henry Breasted who wrote: "Unfitted by ages of tropical life for any effective intrusion among the White Race, the Negro and Negroid people remained without any influence on the development of civilization."

FREDERICK MONDERSON

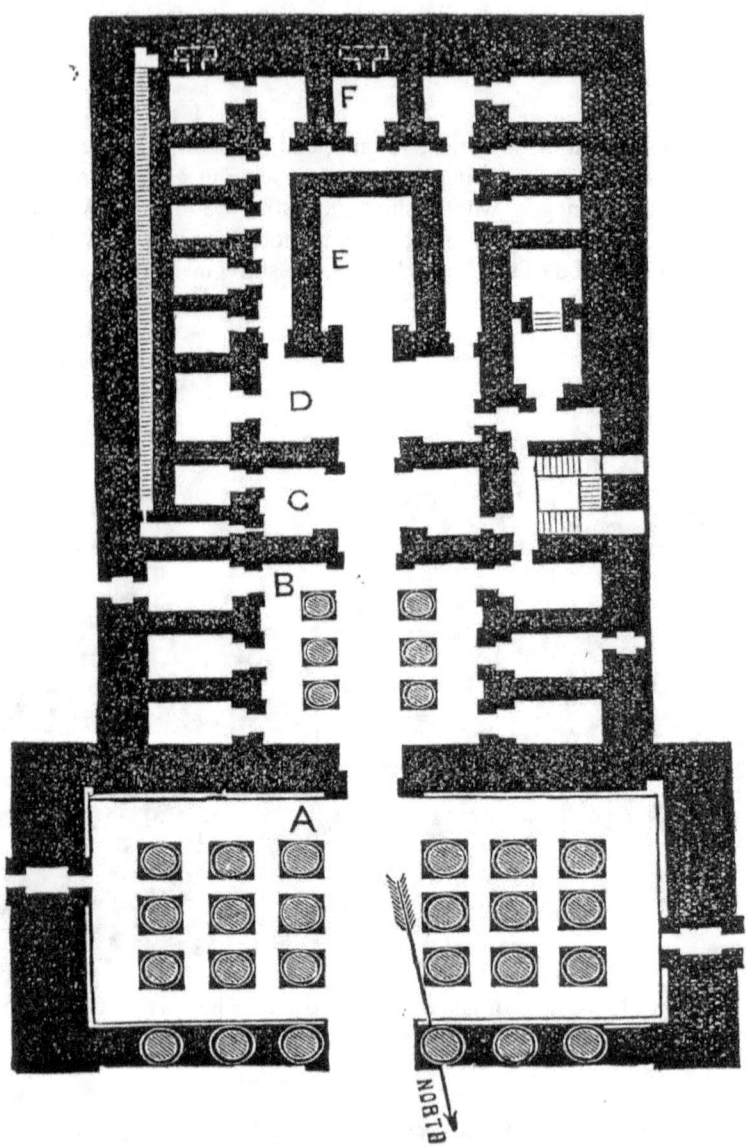

Plan of the Temple of Dendera.

It is amazing that people of Breasted's hue could write about such significant historical issues with such profound racial venom. Breasted's *History of Egypt, Ancient Records of Egypt, Ancient Times* and *The Development of Religion and Thought in Ancient Egypt* are classic "primary sources of the primary sources" of ancient Egypt. The thought of a German American writing about a people of

RESEARCH ESSAYS ON ANCIENT EGYPT

ancient Africa and could entertain the above quote raises a whole series of questions about intent and influence. We need never forget, Goethe believed, "wherever Germans went, they corrupted whatever culture they found!"

You mean to tell me, while writing his *Records of Ancient Egypt* in 1905, by the time his *Ancient Times* was published in 1916 where he described the Egyptians as "brown people," he did not know Mentuhotep II had "black flesh" even though his statue was discovered in 1904. Perhaps also, the gold of Tutankhamon blinded Breasted to the young king's black skin. In his *Ancient Times* published in 1916, Breasted described the ancient Egyptians as "brown people." However, when he re-issued it in 1935, he only dealt with "the great white race." Some have argued, because Rockefeller gave monies to fund his Oriental Studies Program, this turn-around was the 'quid pro quo." Again, nowhere does Breasted refer to Mentuhotep's "black flesh" nor does he recognize this in Tutankhamon.

Nevertheless, it is well known that the resurrection and reclamation of ancient Egypt occurred in the 19th Century and early part of the 20th Century. However, in this period of "The Rape of the Nile" there was a consistent cry about destruction of the ancient culture both by natives and European plunderers seeking treasure and collectibles. Often reports would be made that natives were destroying sites whether for purposes of fuel or in order to secure and sell antiquities to anyone who would buy them. Generally Europeans who wanted to draw attention to the problem and help to preserve the ancient record made these reports. However, very seldom did the finger get pointed or identify European plunderers and all that is said is that this or that antique was damaged.

One has to entertain a credible question, with today's hindsight, which is, 'How accurate is the work of the Breasteds?' or, 'Has there been any distortion, omission or exclusion in their work?' In the reconstruction of the role of blacks in ancient Egypt, evidence has to be gleaned from fragments and from the honest reports of men of good will, simply because much of racially relevant material has been destroyed in the trampled-over state. However, as more and more research focuses on these fragments they emerge larger than originally thought, for "truth crushed to the earth shall rise." In this, the work of racist and pseudo-scientific writers and historians are highlighted and the smoke and mirrors they constructed around the historical truth are now being blown away; and the true and marked naked prejudice of their writings and thinking that have misinformed for so long, are finally being blown away. And there they stand, "naked, without clothes" in a world of political and historical correctness.

FREDERICK MONDERSON

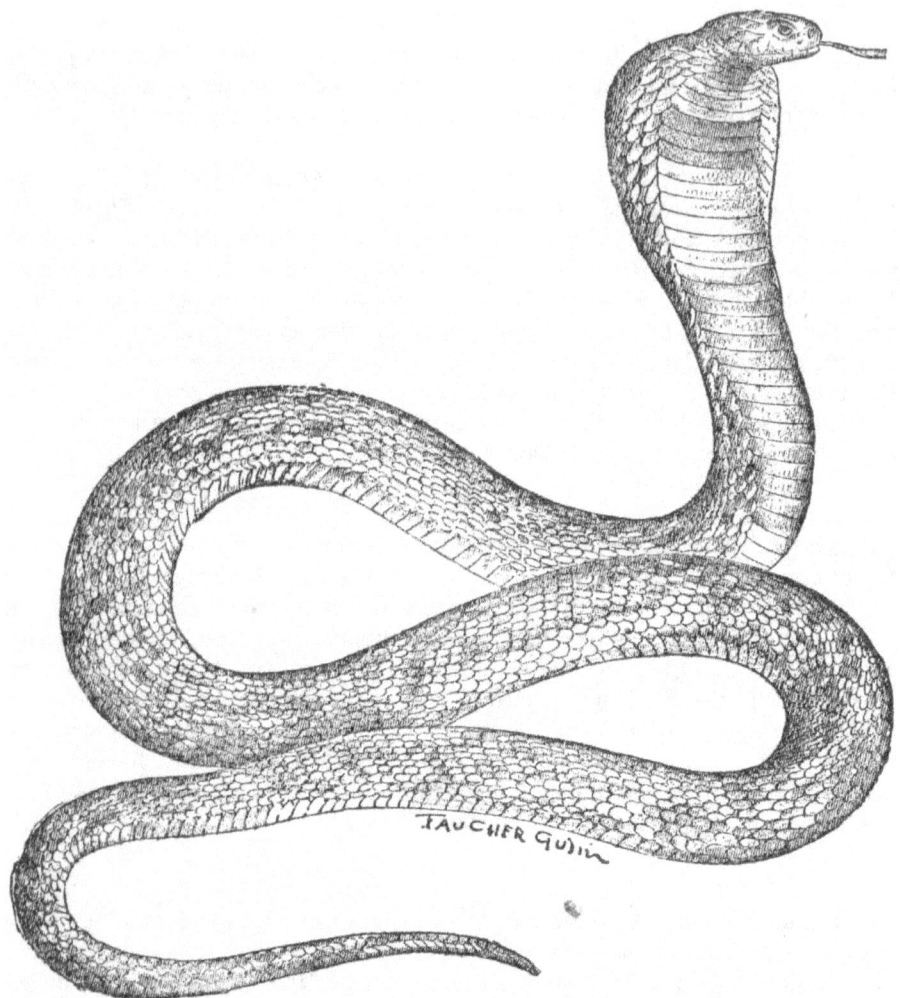

Research Essays Illustration 16. The famous Egyptian uraeus that guards the Pharaoh.

d. **T. Eric Peet,** an Oxford scholar, was part of the Egypt Exploration Fund staff. He was critical of Akhnaton in an article entitled "The Problem with Akhnaton." While doing important work in the reclamation of Egypt, he too had the same false conception that the Egyptians were white!

RESEARCH ESSAYS ON ANCIENT EGYPT

VI. The Black Challenge To 2000

a.　　**W.E.B. DuBois** began *The Negro* (Oxford University Press (1915) 1970: 140) by affirming Negro blood ran in the veins of the Egyptians, but held they were mulatto! He wrote: "With mulatto Egypt Black Africa was always in close touch, so much so that to some all evidence of Negro uplift seems Egyptian in origin." He continued this in his *The World and Africa* but could not fully defend the argument of a black Egypt. Yet, in *The World and Africa* (1946) (1971: 91-92) he quotes Palgrave who says: "As to faces, the peculiarities of the Negro countenance are well known in caricature; but a truer pattern may be seen by those who wish to study it any day among the statues of the Egyptian rooms in the British Museum: that large gentle eyes, the full but not over protruding lips, the rounded contour, and the good-natured, easy sensuous expression. This is the genuine African model; one not often to be met with in European or American thoroughfares, where the plastic African too readily acquires the careful look and even the irregularity of the features that surrounded him; but which is common enough in the villages and fields where he dwells after his own fashion among his own people; most common of all in the tranquil seclusion and congenial climate of Surinam plantation. There you may find also, a type neither Asiatic nor European, but distinctly African; with much of the independence and vigor in the male physiognomy and something that approaches, if it does not quite reach, beauty in the female. Rameses and his queen were cast in no other mould." Such a claim flies in the face of those museum displays that misrepresents in catering to please European and American visitors.

b.　　**Carter G. Woodson**, the "father of Black History" in *The Mis-Education of the Negro* (Trenton, New Jersey: Africa World Press, 1993: 154) wrote: "We should not underrate the achievements of Mesopotamia, Greece and Rome; but we should give equally to the integral African kingdoms, the Songhay empire, and Ethiopia, which through Egypt decidedly influenced the civilization of the Mediterranean world."

c.　　**J.E. Harris** (Editor) of *Pillars in Ethiopian History* (Howard University Press) (1981: 6-7) has discussed the work of William Leo Hansberry, who, at Howard University began teaching about Negro Civilizations of Ancient Africa and developed the following courses:

1.　　**NEGRO PEOPLES IN THE CULTURES AND CIVILIZATIONS OF PREHISTORIC AND PROTOHISTORIC**

FREDERICK MONDERSON

TIMES. This was a survey course based on the latest archaeological and anthropological findings concerning the Paleolithic and Neolithic cultures of Africa, the pre-dynastic civilization of Ancient Egypt, and relations to the proto-historic and early historic civilizations of the eastern Mediterranean, and western and southern Asia.

Research Essays 15. Temple of Isis on Agilka Island. The First Pylon with illustrations of the King in different attitudes making Presentations to the Gods and below Isis straddling the entrance. Through the door opening, Isis can be seen on the First Pylon to her Temple proper. To the right is the northern end of the Eastern Colonnade. Notice the steps in ascent inwards the Temple.

2. **THE ANCIENT CIVILIZATIONS OF ETHIOPIA**. This course was a survey from about 4000 B.C., covering the general areas encompassed by the present-day countries of Sudan and Ethiopia. Hansberry relied on Egyptian, Hebrew, and Greek sources as well as archaeological and anthropological data from several expeditions, including the Harvard-Boston Expeditions at Kerma, Napata, and Meroe.

3. **THE CIVILIZATIONS OF WEST AFRICA IN MEDIEVAL AND EARLY MODERN TIMES**. This course surveyed the political and

RESEARCH ESSAYS ON ANCIENT EGYPT

cultural developments of Ghana, Mali, Songhay and Yorubaland as portrayed in Arab chronicles, and the archaeological and anthropological evidence in English, French and German investigations.

d. **Prof. John H. Clarke** in John G. Jackson's *Introduction to African Civilization* (1970: 12) says "the 19th Century German scholar Arnold Herman Hereen" in discussing trade between the Carthaginians, Ethiopians and Egyptians: "gave more support to the concept of the southern African origin of Egyptian civilization."

Research Essays Illustration 17. Majestic bird of Egypt. Imagine stepping out with its flair, as the beak and claws speak volumes.

FREDERICK MONDERSON

e.   **Yosef A.A. ben-Jochannan** wrote extensively and very early began carrying people to Egypt to experience the monuments and he meticulously pointed out disparities in reporting by Western and American writers. He made a special effort to point out, in the Cairo Museum the role Gaston Maspero played in shaping the interpretation of ancient Egypt by creating the "Place Cards" of the cases. He particularly pointed to Maspero's determination that Maherpra was "Negroid but not Negro." This was tremendously important because Maherpra's papyrus specifically points out the place of "Origin of the Egyptians" and from whence the God Hapi (Osiris) came.

f.   **J.A. Rogers** in *Sex and Race* Vol. I (1967: 42), echoing sentiments similar to Diop's contention that "The true Negro is nothing more than a cigar-store concoction," says essentially Herman Junker, who had written about "The First Appearance of the Negroes in History" *Journal of Egyptian Archaeology* (1924) was mistaken in looking for Negro traits in the graves of 5000 to 3600 B.C. "The Ethiopians, or Nubians, who were described by Herodotus, Diodorus Siculus, Ammianus and others as black and woolly-haired, were Hamites, he declares." Rogers continued: "It is no wonder he did not find any of that type, however, because the kind of Negro created by the right-wing ethnologists is a rarity. It is no more characteristic of the race than the ape-like creature of the bogs that was once used to represent the Irish was true of all Irishmen. Winwood Reade said, 'The typical Negro is a rare variety even among Negroes.' Frobinus says also, 'Open an illustrated geography and compare 'The Type of the African Negro,' the bluish-black fellow of the protuberant lips, the flattened nose, the stupid expression, and the short curly hair with the tall, bronze figures from Dark Africa with which we have of late become familiar, their almost fine-cut features, slightly arched nose, long hair …. In other respects, too, the genuine African of the interior bears no resemblance to the accepted Negro type.'"

Even further, Rogers mentions: "Livingstone said that the Negro face as he saw it reminded him more of that on the monuments of ancient Assyria than that of the popular white fancy." Sir Harry Johnston, foremost authority on the African Negro said: "The Hamite, that Negroid stock which was the main stock of the ancient Egyptians, is best represented at the present day by the Somali, Galla, and the blood of Abyssinia and Nubia. Sergi compares pictorially the features of Rameses with that of Mtesa, noted Negro king of Uganda, and shows the marked resemblance. Sir M.W. Flinders Petrie, famed Egyptologist, says that the Pharaohs of the X dynasty were of the Galla type, and the Gallas are clearly what are known in our day as Negroes. He tells further of seeing one day on a train a man whose features were 'the exact living type' of a statue of ancient Libya, and discovered that the man was an American mulatto."

RESEARCH ESSAYS ON ANCIENT EGYPT

Research Essays 16. Temple of Isis on Agilka Island. Close-up of two columns with varied capitals, and high abacus or die below the architrave. In the rear, illustrations on a wall.

g.   **Ivan Van Sertima** in his "Race and Origins of the Egyptians" in *Egypt Revisited* has argued: "The African claim to Egyptian civilization rests upon a vast body of evidence. Some are cultural (ritual practices of the ancient Egyptian can be traced to the African – his totemism, circumcision, form of the divine kingship are distinct from that of the Asian); some are linguistic (Diop demonstrated convincingly at the UNESCO debate in 1974 that the Egyptians belonged beyond question to the family of African languages); some indicate a shared techno-complex (the forerunners of mummification and pyramid-building are found south of Egypt in pre-dynastic times). Most important, however, are the physical evidences. The Greeks saw the Egyptians and described the typical Egyptian circa 500 B.C. as dark-skinned with wooly hair. Studies in ancient Egyptian crania by Falkenburger tried to prove that only one-third of the Egyptians were of the classical Negroid type and that most of them were Euro-African or, to use the term invented by Sergi "the brown Mediterranean race" classification. Chatterjee and Kumar in a 1965 study ... analyzed crania from pre-dynastic Egypt and compared them with skulls of the Old Kingdom as well as the much later Middle Kingdom (12th and 13th dynasties) and found that all these skulls in respect to 'long head, broad face, low orbit and broad nasal aperture have the same characteristic features of the Negroid type.'"

VII. So Here We Are! – We must affirm, articulate, teach, preach and fight to defend Egypt as African and Negro or black. This is essentially what our intellectual ancestors, researchers, historians, lecturers, writers and activists, who, after their many years, sometimes more than thirty years of research have discovered, as being omitted and distorted regarding the history of the Ancient Egyptians.

Research Essays 16a. Temple of Isis on Agilka Island. In Osiris Crown, pharaoh offers two sistrums to Isis enthroned as Hathor with her son as a child at her rear.

VIII. Conclusions

As more and more evidence is unearthed and equally more Afrocentric scholarship unmasks untruths, distortions and omissions through vigorous analytic examination, the effort of African historiographic reconstruction will not only correct the historical record but also expose the prejudice and vindictiveness involved in earlier writers' works. Some years ago, while a student at Oxford University I met a black Englishman who, in discussion, told me, 'In any debate between a black Historian and a white Historian, the black will always win. All he has to do is to show what white men have been doing all around the world and with any sense of conscience the white man has to back-pedal.' Hence, despite efforts to 'hold back the dawn,' unmistakable truths are changing the minds of some while others 'prefer not to discuss such.' They simply skirt around the issues, and with today's knowledge and vision, are ashamed that their mentors, teacher and predecessors had been wrong and prejudiced in reporting the history of black men and women who began humanity along the civilization pageantry of art, architecture, medicine, science, agriculture, astronomy, knowledge, period! It is reassuring to show that despite Breasted's venom, black men and women have given and continue to give knowledge and enlightenment to all who seek the truth.

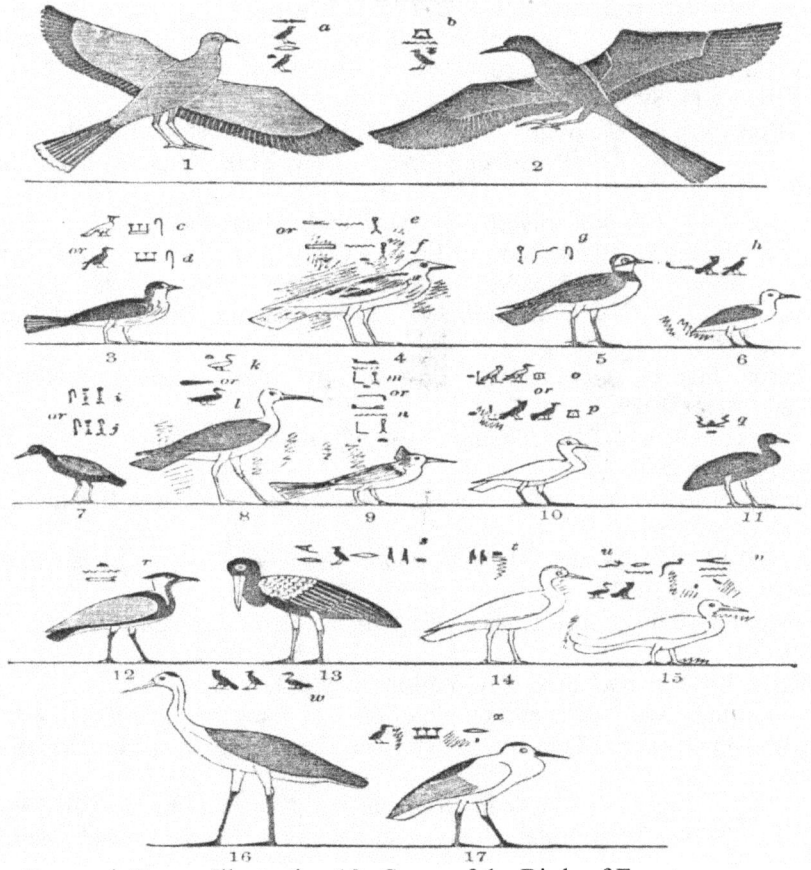

Research Essays Illustration 18. Some of the Birds of Egypt.

IX. References

Brooks, Lester. *Great Civilizations of Ancient Egypt*. New York: Four Winds Press, 1971.

Browder, Anthony. *Nile Valley Contributions to Civilization*. Washington, D.C.: The Institute of Karmic Guidance, 1992.

Clegg, Legrand H.H. "Black Rulers of the Golden Age" in *Nile Valley Civilizations* Edited by Ivan Van Sertima (1985) (1986: 39-68).

Diop, Cheikh Anta. *The African Origin of Civilization: Myth or Reality*. New York: Lawrence Hill and Company, (1967) 1974.

_____. "Origin of the Ancient Egyptians" in *Egypt Revisited*, (Edited by Ivan Van Sertima) New Brunswick, New Jersey: Transaction Publishers, (1989: 9-37).

Du Bois, W.E.B. *The Negro*. New York: Oxford University Press, (1915) 1973.

_____. *The World and Africa*. New York: International Publishers, (1946) 1971.

Erman, Adolf. *Life in Ancient Egypt*. New York: Macmillan, 1894.

Finch, Charles S. "Black Roots of Egypt's Glory." *Great Black Leaders: Ancient and Modern*. Edited by Ivan Van Sertima. Transaction Books, (1988: 139-143).

Harris, J.E. *Pillars in Ethiopian History*. Washington, DC: Howard University Press, 1981.

Jackson, John G. *Introduction to African Civilizations*. Secaucus, New Jersey: Citadel Press, 1970.

Kush, Khamit Indus. *The Missing Pages of "His-Story."* Laurelton, New York: D and J Books, 1993.

Murray, Margaret A. *The Splendor That Was Egypt*. New York: Hawthorn Books, Inc., (1949) 1969.

Perry, W.J. *The Growth of Civilization*. Hammondsworth, England: Penguin Books, (1924) 1937.

Rawlinson, George. *The Story of the Nations: Egypt*. London: T. Fisher Unwin, 1893.

Rogers, J.A. *Sex and Race*. New York: Helga M. Rogers, 1967.

Van Sertima, Ivan. "Race and Origin of the Egyptians" in *Egypt Revisited*. Edited by Ivan Van Sertima. Transaction Publishers. New Brunswick, New Jersey, (1989: 3-8).

_____. "African Origin of the Ancient Egyptian Civilization" in *Egypt: Child of Africa*. Edited by Ivan Van Sertima. New Brunswick, New Jersey, (1994) 1995.

Woodson, Carter G. *The Mis-Education of the Negro*. Trenton, New Jersey: Africa World Press, (1990) 1993.

RESEARCH ESSAYS ON ANCIENT EGYPT

Research Essays 16b. Temple of Isis on Agilka Island. In the small Hathor Chapel, an ape plays a tambourine while another plays a stringed instrument. Notice the uraei on the top of the engaged screen.

6.   The Religion of Ancient Egypt
By

Dr. Fred Monderson

I.   Introduction

The Religion of Ancient Egypt is arguably the oldest on record, dating back several millennia before Unification under Menes. This is probably before any other culture, perhaps only the Ethiopians southwards of Egypt, experienced such joys of sweet communion with deity.

Unquestionably it also influenced the manner in which other cultures enjoyed this wonderful experience. Equally too, theirs' is certainly one of the oldest written forms of religious writings. For that matter they bestow on us the oldest form of writing period. Importantly, their equally oldest religious literature, discovered as it was in the pyramids remained unchanged for millennia. This enabled scholars to understand not only Egyptian writing but also their literature as well, housed as it was in their architecture, adding also much about their skills as builders and administrators. Significantly, the writings discovered in the pyramids represented a process of religious development that probably extended for millennia back into the past.

However, and particularly for the problems of origins, Wallis Budge in *Egyptian Religion* (1900) (1991: 18) offers an interesting caveat, while affirming: "There is no evidence whatever to guide us in formulating the theory that it was brought into Egypt by immigrants from the East." Again, Budge (1991: 18-19) continued: "All that is known is that it existed there at a period so remote that it is useless to attempt to measure by years the interval of time which has elapsed since it grew up and established itself in the minds of men, and that it is exceedingly doubtful if we shall ever have any definite knowledge on this interesting point." Even more, Budge (1991) pointed out: "But though we know nothing about the period of the origin in Egypt of the belief in the existence of an almighty God who was One, the inscriptions show us that this Being was called by a name which was something like *Neter*, the picture sign for which was an axe-head, made probably of stone, let into a long wooden handle." That far back in time, some scholars have argued, the Egyptians were probably not very far removed from thinking like animals or savage peoples. Nevertheless, if we accept the view of science and the origins of man in Africa, this development may extend back thousands of years, the emergence of religious consciousness in this part of Africa.

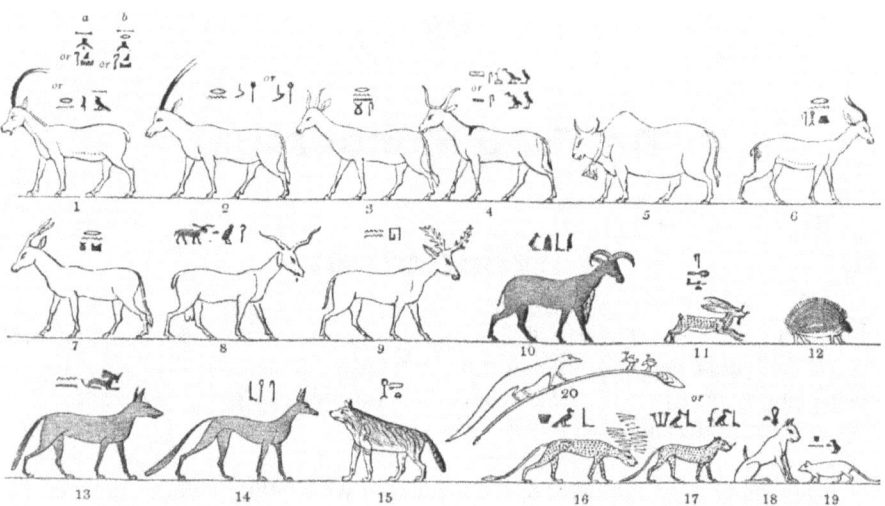

Research Essays Illustration 19. Animals from the sculptures of ancient Egypt.

RESEARCH ESSAYS ON ANCIENT EGYPT

Notwithstanding, bridging this gap and positing a view of earlier Egyptian religiosity, even further, Budge (1991: 23) affirmed: "As a matter of fact, we know nothing of their ideas of God before they developed sufficiently to build the monuments which we know they built, and before they possessed the religion, and civilization, and complex social system which their writings have revealed to us ...." In this respect, "the primitive god was an essential feature of the family, and the fortunes of the god varied with the fortunes of the family; the god of the city in which a man lived was regarded as the ruler of the city, and the people of that city no more thought of neglecting to provide him with what they considered to be due to his rank and position than they thought of neglecting to supply their own wants. In fact, the god of the city became the center of the social fabric of that city, and every inhabitant thereof inherited automatically certain duties, the neglect of which brought stated pains and penalties upon him." However, what we do know of the early Egyptian religion with certainty is contained in their earliest writing called the *Pyramid Texts*.

Research Essays 17.   Temple of Isis on Agilka Island.   The King in plumes; notice his tail, offers two "Eye of Horus" to enthroned Horus in Double Crown beside Isis also enthroned.

FREDERICK MONDERSON

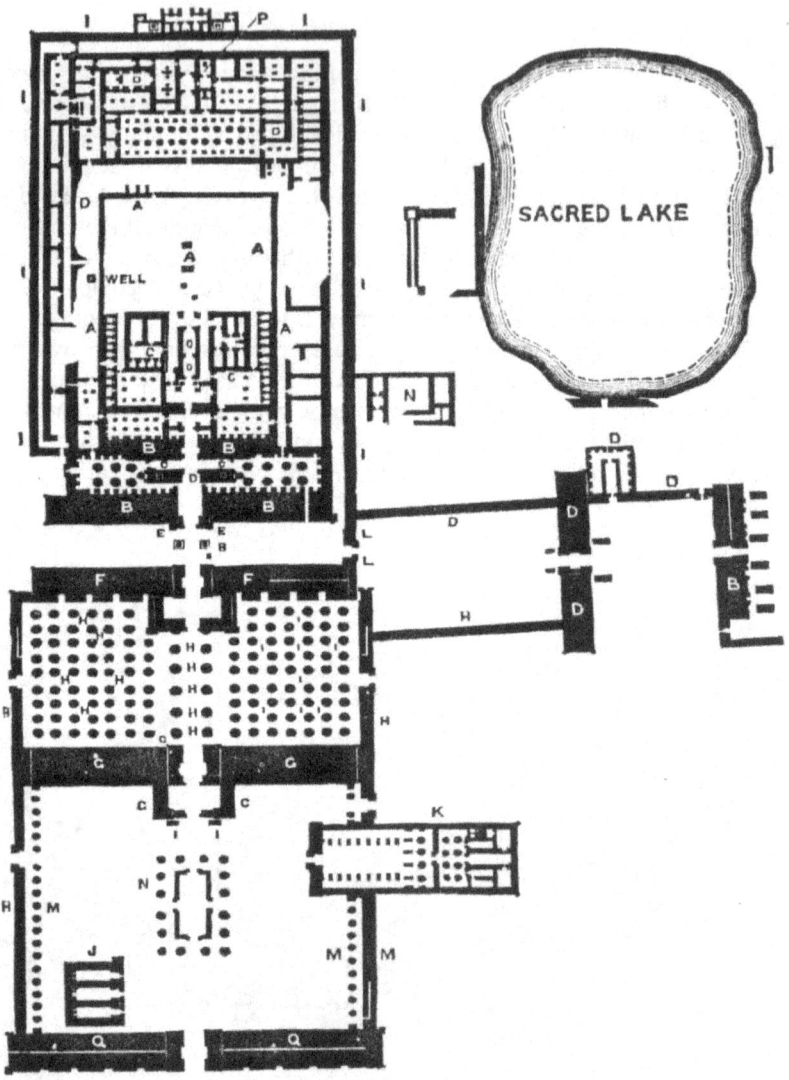

Karnak under the Ptolemies. From Mariette, *Karnak*, Pl. VII.

A. Walls standing before the time of Thothmes I.
B. Pylons built by Thothmes I.
C. Walls and obelisks of Hatshepset.
D. Walls, pylon, etc., of Thothmes III.
E. Gateway of Thothmes IV.
F. Pylon of Amenophis III.
G. Pylon of Rameses I.
H. Walls and columns of Seti I.
I. Columns, walls, and statues of Rameses II.
J. Temple of Seti II.
K. Temple of Rameses III.
L. Gateway of Rameses IX.
M. Pillars and walls of the XXIInd dynasty.
N. Pillars of Tirhakah.
O. Corridor of Philip III. of Macedon.
P. Chamber and shrine of Alexander II.
Q. Pylon built by the Ptolemies.

Temple of Karnak: Under the Ptolemies.

RESEARCH ESSAYS ON ANCIENT EGYPT

Now, as Egyptian discoveries and scholarship unfolded, modern scholars in the 19th Century coined the name *Book of the Dead* that was really the *Book of Per-em-hru* or the *Book of Coming Forth by Day*. As such, the *Book of the Dead* evolved from the *Pyramid Texts* of the Old Kingdom and the *Coffin Texts* of the Middle Kingdom. In essence, these are a collection of spells that guided the soul in the afterlife and encompassed the judgment and what happened to individuals after death. In the mechanics of this early religious literature, *Book of the Dead*, Flinders Petrie (1906: 78) informs: "We can distinguish certain groups of chapters, an Osirian section on the kingdom of Osiris and the service of it, a theological section, a set of incantations, formulae for the restoration of the heart, for the protection of the soul from spirits and serpents in the hours of night, charms to escape from periods ordained by the gods, an account of the paradise of Osiris, a different version of the kingdom and judgment of Osiris, a Heliopolitan doctrine about the *ba*, and its powers of transformation entirely apart from all that is stated elsewhere, the account of the reunion of soul and body, magic formulae for entering the Osirian kingdom, another account of the judgment of Osiris, charms for the preservation of the mummy and for making efficacious amulets, together with various portions of popular beliefs." These ideas, therefore, cover the widest conception of the human intellect as it relates to the idea that death is not the final human experience. Equally, in anticipation of this drama, social tenets of Ma'at guided the individual's action in his daily life.

In his *From Fetish to God in Ancient Egypt*, Budge (1934: 3-4) also provided the explanation of the theological significance of the Egyptian belief system. He wrote, "The foundation of the popular opinion about the religious beliefs of the ancient EGYPTIANS was laid by the great pioneer of Egyptology E. DE ROUGE' about the middle of the last century. He stated that the EGYPTIANS believed in One self-existent, supreme, eternal, almighty god, who created the world and everything in it, and endowed man with an immortal soul, which was capable of receiving punishments and rewards. DE ROUGE's words were to all intents and purposes a paraphrase of the passage in NEWTON'S *Principia* in which the great scientist expressed his belief in the Unity of God who is supreme, infinite, omnipotent, omniscient, and absolutely perfect. Who is present always and everywhere! The various works of creation are the product of his ideas, and his existence is proclaimed by them."

FREDERICK MONDERSON

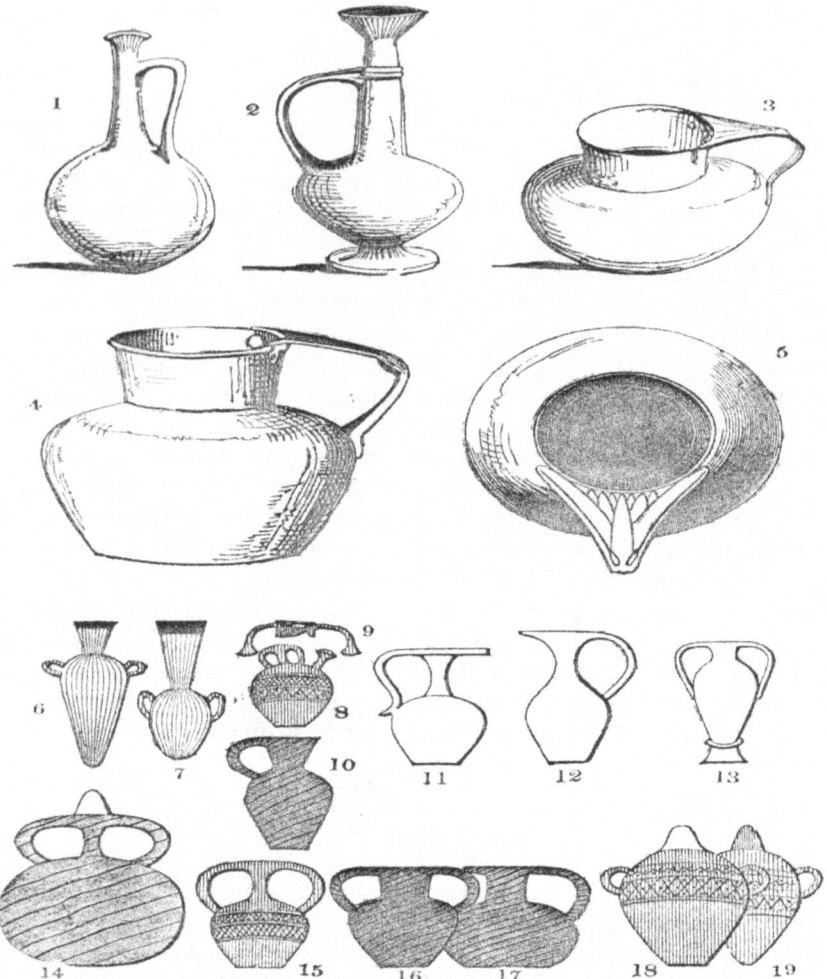

Research Illustration 20. Vases, with one and two handles.

Notwithstanding, other than the *Book of the Dead*, there were, in addition, other literature as the *Book of Gates* and *Book of Am-Duat* that describe the drama that unfolds as the Sun God traverses the domain of the underworld. The *Book of Gates* describes the gates of the hours of the night. The *Book of Am-Duat* describes the successive hours of the night through which the boat of the sun god passes and the various monsters who tried to impede his journey so as not to arise on the horizon the next day.

Generally speaking, the *Book of Am-Duat* or *Book of What is in the Underworld* represents the beliefs of the Theban locality held by the Priests of Amen-Ra; while

RESEARCH ESSAYS ON ANCIENT EGYPT

the *Book of Gates* are those held by the Priests of Osiris. These religious literatures are very old and extend to the earliest periods of Egyptian history, to a time before they were actually written. Nevertheless, we do know, by the time of the First Dynasty, a *Book of the Dead* was found in the temple of King Sempti. There was another found during the reign of King Menkaure of the Fourth Dynasty. Even at these early times, these books were revisions of much earlier works. Additionally, over time the "Chapters" or *Book of the Dead* went through many versions or Recensions. These revisions were the "Heliopolitan Recension" done by the Priests of Ra at Heliopolis in the Old Kingdom. There were also revisions made as in the "Theban Recension" of the New Kingdom, and the "Saite Recension" of the Late Period of the XXVIth Dynasty. Over the years, through the editing, revision, duplications and expansions the "Chapters" were expanded to as many as 175 with certain chapters as number 125 becoming tremendously important. Nonetheless, the texts written on the walls of the pyramids remained unchanged until discovery in the 19th century of our era.

Budge (1934: 25) adds more to our understanding of ancient Egyptian religious literature in the statement: "Among the earliest examples of religious drama may be mentioned the 'Book of Opening of the Mouth,' and the 'Book of the Liturgy of Funeral Offerings.' In the first work the ritual acts and the spells are enumerated which were believed to have the effect of enabling the deceased to breathe, think, speak, walk, etc., in spite of the fact that his body was rough bound tightly with funerary swathing. In the second work, the object of which was to maintain the life of the deceased in the Other World, the KHERI HEB or chief priestly magician presents to a statue of the deceased a long series of offerings of meat, drink, unguents, wearing apparel, etc. As he presents each he repeats a spell, the effect of which could be used by the deceased in the Other World. Every act in every 'mystery' had originally a special signification, or was symbolic of some well-known happening. Eventually the meanings of such actions were forgotten in many cases, but the repetition of the actions never ceased."

FREDERICK MONDERSON

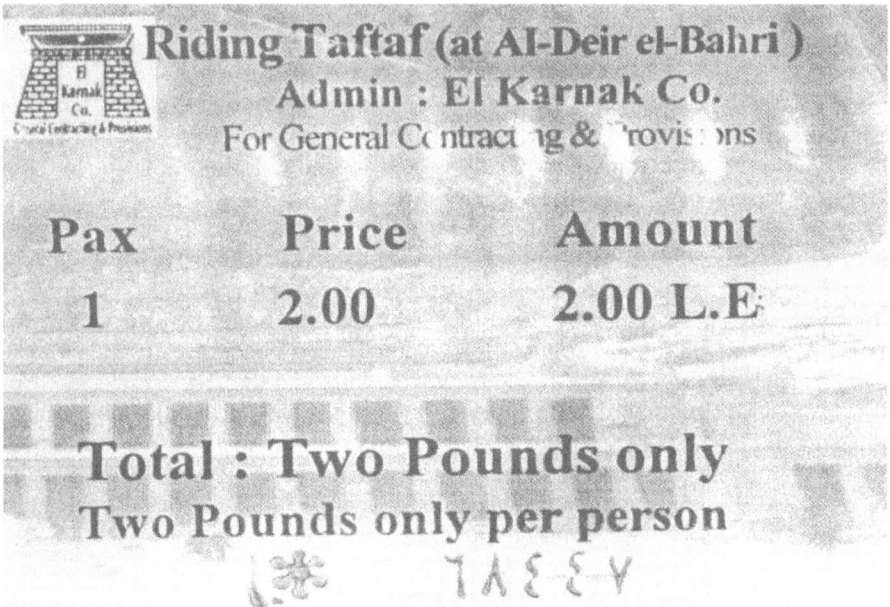

Research Essays Temple Ticket 8. Deir el Bahari Temple Taftaf. Price of ride is two Egyptian Pounds. This is the same amount charged in the Valley of the Kings.

Notwithstanding, these and so much more have shown that the religion of ancient Egypt is very unique. Even more so, than the three western religions of Judaism, Christianity and Islam which some scholars consider their foundation, have threads linking Egyptian Religion with eastern and even New World ritual and practice. Thus, the religion of ancient Egypt is very unique in that it is one of the earliest to emerge from the mist of antiquity at the crossroad of the ancient world. Principally it is a monotheistic religion emphasizing the unity of god that in later dynasties had elements of polytheism. It was solar or celestial and anthropomorphic and subterranean and boasted colorful representations of its principal gods, who in many respects, were manifestation of the same principle rather than the many gods the simple minded encounters.

RESEARCH ESSAYS ON ANCIENT EGYPT

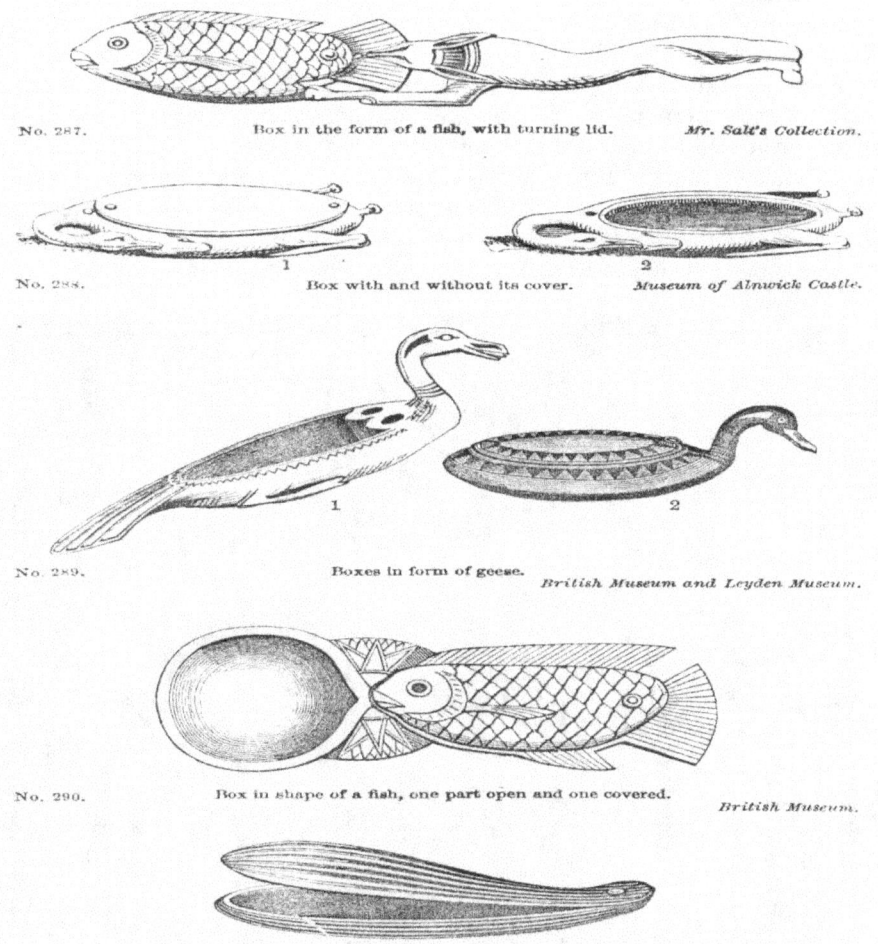

Research Essays Illustration 21. Birds and fishes as represented in other shapes.

Explaining some aspects of the ancient Egyptian religious belief and godhead, G.K. Osei (1983) tells us: "The creator is an active force. He commands; he guides; he inspires; and he ordains man's destiny." This "Oneness," is again underscored by Budge (1934: 4-5) who offers the clarification: "There is no doubt that monotheism was a tenet of the Egyptian Faith, but it was entirely different from the monotheism of Christian peoples. When the EGYPTIAN called his god 'One,' or the 'One One,' or the 'Only one,' he meant exactly what he said and what the Muslim means today when he says, 'There is no god but God.' And that god was the sun in the sky from which he received light and heat and the food whereon he lived. The EGYPTIAN in his hymns called many gods 'One,' but these gods were all forms of the Sun god, and, as I understand it, he was a monotheist pure and simple as a sun-worshipper. It avails nothing to call his monotheism 'henotheism.' A time came when Osiris was associated with Khepri, the sun at dawn, and with RA at noon-day, and with Temu as the setting sun, and the Pyramid Texts make it clear that under the VIth dynasty Osiris usurped all the attributes and powers of the 'Sun, the One lord of heaven.' There was, of course, a time when men thought that the Sun-god had no counterpart, no offspring, and no associate or equal." Thus, there was clearly a combining of gods in this early period. However, let us also seek to understand; while the sun was a manifestation of God, it was actually the magical, mystical essence behind the sun which was actually god. As such, god was a sort of "power behind the throne."

Research Essays 17a. Isis Temple on Agilka Island. Pharaoh in Nemes Headdress, surmounted by Osiris crown of horns, uraei with disks, white crown with disks and with straight beard and wearing tails, offers two vessels to Hours in Double Crown.

RESEARCH ESSAYS ON ANCIENT EGYPT

The religion of ancient Egypt is also unique because the principle of divine right was enshrined in the belief of god working in the king as guardian of the state. In this respect, Frankfort (1961: 30) has disclosed: "The Egyptian state was not a man-made alternative to other forms of political organization. It was god-given, established when the world was created; and it continued to form part of the universal order. In the person of Pharaoh a superhuman being had taken charge of the affairs of man. And this great blessing, which ensured the well-being of the nation, was not due to a fortunate accident but had been foreseen in the divine plan. The monarchy then was as old as the world, for the creator himself had assumed kingly office on the day of creation." Even further, Frankfort (1961: 30-31) in referring to the great god, continued: "Pharaoh was his descendant and his successor. The word 'state' was absent from the language because all the significant aspects of the state were concentrated in the king. He was the fountainhead of all authority, all power, and all wealth. The famous saying of Louis XIV, *l'etat c'est moi*, was levity and presumption when it was uttered, but could have been offered by Pharaoh as a statement of fact in which his subjects concurred. It would have summed up adequately their political philosophy."

Jacob Carruthers (1984: 81) equally affirms: "Here is the embodiment of what we call "Royalty" and "Kingship." In fact, Heru (Horus) is usually associated with the idea of divine kingship." Even further, Carruthers (1984: 82-83) elaborates on the role of the king as an embodiment of Horus whose throne he occupies "to establish conditions where enlightenment will prevail over ignorance."

The religion of ancient Egypt very early established the notions of heaven and hell and the philosophical tenets and principles that applied, thereto, viz., Ma'at, reverence, deference, etc., that guided the individual's ethical behavior and standards of conduct as such related to the expectations of this other worldly drama and reality. The religion of ancient Egypt is again unique in that it presented the earliest comprehensive religious writings that have survived, unchanged and unedited until discovered in the 19th Century. In this early manifestation of the creative Egyptian, African, mind, the religion established parameters and paradigms of religious experience people would forever more aspire to. In this Ma'at was a powerful social utility that was also a tremendous dynamo creating ethical standards to guide and shape the society. As a result, later civilizations benefited tremendously owing a great debt to this ancient Egyptian, African, experience.

The religion of ancient Egypt with its many and essentially African characteristics boasted several principal deities worshipped at different centers throughout the nation. An established Priesthood serviced each deity, and in order to avoid conflict, they tried to synchronize their dogma. The king, as the gods' representative on earth, built temples throughout the land and though favoring one god in one particular time, was also beneficent to the others. In the evolved practice, their architecture developed decorative features in stone as a lasting testament to their god. In their building practice, different types of temples were constructed to the god, the king and nation. The effort gave birth to the decorative arts and a number of industries that fed the ubiquitous religious demands.

Research Essays 18. Temple of Isis on Agilka Island. Two sister Goddesses, Hathor and Isis. Notice the exposed breasts.

RESEARCH ESSAYS ON ANCIENT EGYPT

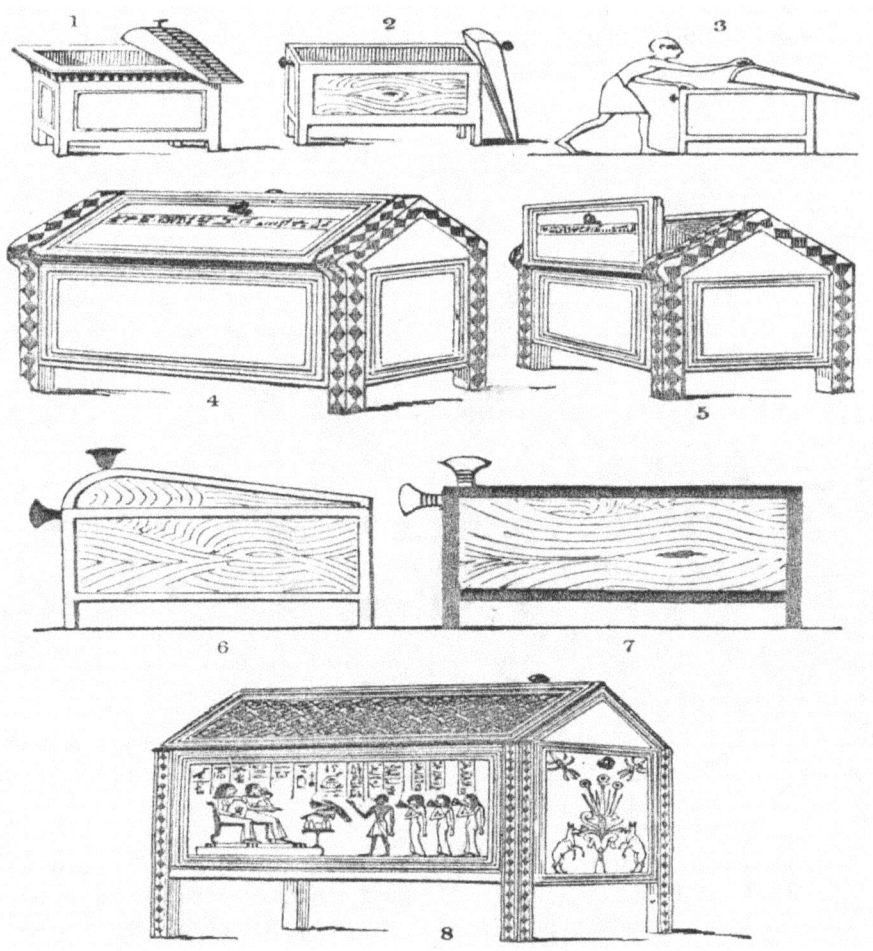

Research Essays 22. Different boxes with lids shaped differently.

The religion of ancient Egypt is unique because very early it preached the dynamics of the afterlife and so became a true engine of molding social and ethical practice. The science of the funeral, tombs, mummification, the judgment, the negative confessions, the philosophic maxim of Ma'at, and reward for the good life, were all themes and practices that later civilizations came to emulate. For worshipping and ritualizing the gods, a priesthood developed that managed the god's estate and catered to the religious aspirations of the people. In the relationship that developed with the gods, Egypt became an imperialist nation sanctioned by a divine spirit. As such, imperial pharaohs conquered and heaped untold wealth on their divinity resulting in the building of enormous structures for religious ritual worship that gave in turn birth to the development of the arts, science, medicine, etc. that equally grew out of the experiment. In the totality of this interaction, religion helped to advance science that in turn advanced civilization and thus Africa, through Egypt and the Nile Valley, can be considered the mother of experimentation and invention.

Research Essays 18a. Temple of Isis on Agilka Island. Off the beaten path and from the rear of the three temples on the Dromos, panoramic view of the Pylons that guard the temple of the goddess.

The unmistakable fact of all this is that the *Pyramid Texts, Coffin Texts* and *Book of the Dead* are the oldest religious literature and monotheism is the basis of Egyptian religion. In this Egyptian, African, religious drama, while the fortunes of other gods rose and fell, the worship of Osiris remained consistent throughout. In the practice of worship and ritualizing the gods, temples became larger, more durable and decorative, all this while the social and ethical rewards of Egyptian religion helped advance the cause of humanity. A bureaucracy aided religious worship, managed the god's estate, catered to the afterlife requirements of the individual souls and thus religion advanced the development of knowledge and civilization. All this the African bequeathed to the world, while not getting the proper credit for this legacy in the much distorted and falsified modern conception of humanity's long march along the evolutionary path of human development.

In the enormous compendium of the *Book of the Dead*, there are more than 172 "Chapters" and some versions of "Chapters" are duplicates. Still some "Chapters" seem more important than others and "Chapter" 125 is probably the most important. It is comprised of 4 parts, an Introduction, the Negative Confessions, Conclusion, and Psychostasia or Weighing of the Heart. The latter part, takes place in presence of 12 great gods of Egypt, who are Ra-Harmachis, Temu, Shu, Tefnut, Seb, Nut, Isis, Nephthys, Horus, Hathor, Hu and Sa. Thoth and Anubis are also involved in weighing the heart. However, the *Papyrus of Hunefer* mentions 14 gods and the *Turin Papyrus* lists the 42 gods to whom the Negative Confession was recited.

Why there are 42 Confessions is not certain. Some scholars such as Dr. ben-Jochannan believe they are part of a larger body of 147 Confessions. However, we do know for sure, the "eater of the dead," Am-mitt, was a woman, whose "Forepart is that of a crocodile, her hind part is that of a hippopotamus, and her middle is that of a lion." Why a woman we do not know. Yet, she stood at the judgment hoping the deceased would fail that process, not having lived by the tents of Ma'at, and then become her "lunch."

No one knows when the Judgment actually happens, whether immediately upon death or whether there is a waiting period or whether it's after the burial or mummification. One thing is certain, each soul is judged individually and the deceased hoped, when the body was being weighed against the heart in the Hall of African Judgment, his (or her) heart would not speak negatively against him and this was determined by the life he lived on earth. Now, after a successful Judgment he attained to the heavenly "Elysian Fields" with its components of "Fields of Reeds," "Field of Peace," etc. In the earthy preparation for this process, Reid (1925: 117) believed: "The Egyptian ideal was to avoid those things that are denied and to do those things that are affirmed."

Symbolism, whether of logic or magic, was very much part of the Egyptian conception of cosmological, theological, metaphysical or equality in social matters. While there appeared four principal gods, Ra, Ptah, Amon and Osiris; their realms, solar or celestial and subterranean were oftentimes not contradictory but complimentary and fused. Throughout, the belief was held that the god gave everything to Egypt and Egypt should give everything to the god. Such a view therefore pervaded every aspect of their earthly and otherworldly existence. In all of this, magic played an important part in the society, and magical provision for the dead in the future life became an accepted fact from the earliest times.

THE NEGATIVE CONFESSIONS

FREDERICK MONDERSON

1. I have not done Iniquity
2. I have not robbed with violence
3. I have not done violence to any man
4. I have not committed theft
5. I have not slain man or woman
6. I have not made light the bushel
7. I have not acted deceitfully
8. I have not purloined the things which belong to God
9. I have not uttered falsehood
10. I have not carried away food
11. I have not uttered evil words
12. I have not attacked any man
13. I have not killed the beasts that are the property of God
14. I have not acted deceitfully
15. I have not laid waste the land which has been ploughed
16. I have never pried into matters to make mischief
17. I have not set my mouth in motion against any man
18. I have not given away to wrath concerning myself …
19. I have not defiled the wife of a man
20. I have not committed any sin against purity
21. I have not struck fear into any man
22. I have not encroached upon sacred times and seasons
23. I have not been a man of anger
24. I have not made myself deaf to the words of right and truth
25. I have not stirred up strife
26. I have made no man to weep
27. I have not committed acts of impurity, nor laid with men
28. I have not eaten my heart
29. I have abused no man
30. I have not acted with violence
31. I have not judged hastily
32. I have not taken vengeance upon the god
33. I have not multiplied my speech over much
34. I have not acted with deceit, and I have not worked wickedness
35. I have not uttered curses on the king
36. I have not fouled water
37. I have not made haughty my voice
38. I have not cursed the god
39. I have not behaved with insolence
40. I have not sought for distinctions
41. I have not increased my wealth, except with such things as are justly mine own possessions
42. I have not thought scorn of the god who is in my city

RESEARCH ESSAYS ON ANCIENT EGYPT

These "Confessions" helped mold the social, moral and ethical conduct of the life of the ancient Africans, Kamites, called Egyptians of the Upper and Lower Kingdoms, also known as Tawi.

Research Essays Temple Ticket 9. Ramesseum Temple. Price of entrance is thirty Egyptian Pounds.

II. The Antiquity of Egyptian Religion

It is difficult to establish the antiquity of ancient Egyptian religion but suffice to say that by the time of the Badarian, Amratian and Gerzean pre-dynastic culture sequence, religious expressions were already evident in the graves of these early people. The objects included in the "goods of the grave," attest to belief in an afterlife and in a god figure. For example, warriors were buried with their weaponry, farmers their implements and craftsmen their tools so as to continue their "professions" in the next life. Those who could afford it had interred with them magical emblems that would later be replaced by the *Book of the Dead* to help as guide in the afterlife drama. Stepping out of the mist of prehistory, by the time of Unification at the First Dynasty, Narmer established the worship of Ptah at Memphis. On his slate palette the Goddess Hathor, whose origin is Nubian, is evident and this lets us believe their creation stories were perhaps, at least, centuries old by this time. Given that, Ra's worship at Heliopolis may have been contemporary or preceded by the religious worship of the upper kingdom. Many of the creator gods were already in existence. So having established the prehistoric origins of Ra, Ptah, Thoth, and since Narmer was a Theban, it's easy to accept Amon and his family as being in existence even though they did not come into prominence until much later. Given these gods, certainly the followers of Horus precede Narmer; thus we can assume Osiris his father, whom the ancients believed went north from Nubia or Ethiopia must have been around, though he does not become prominent at Abydos until around the second and third dynasties. Petrie found large wooden statues of Min at Koptos that are painted black dating to this earliest period. These are now housed in the Ashmolean Museum in Oxford, England. This puts Min among the earliest company of gods.

That aside, we can easily say, "Essentially, two main religious systems emerged in Egypt. First, the state cults were organized, with the temples and priesthood to ensure the survival of the gods, Egypt and the King." Then there is the term we apply today called "household gods" that fits the second category of deities. Margaret Murray in *The Temples of Egypt* says of these "household gods," that: "They were worshipped at small, domestic shrines, and had neither temple, divine cults or priesthood, but were approached by people at all levels of society for help and guidance in everyday matters."

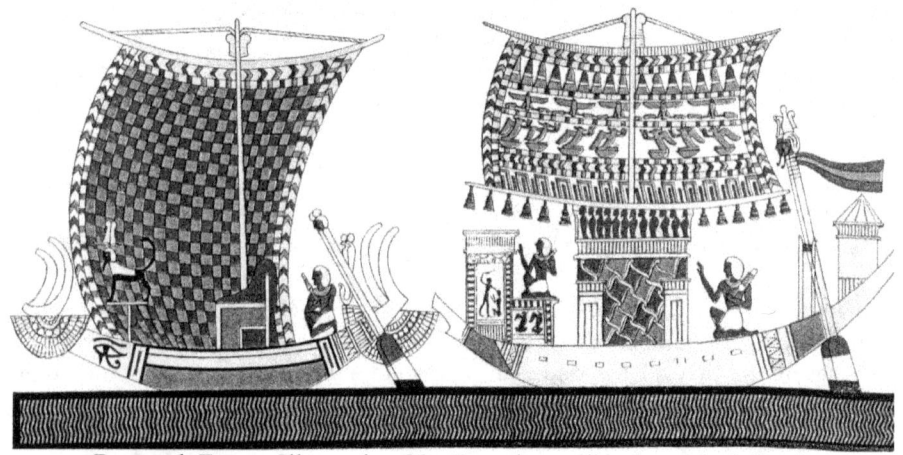

Research Essays Illustration 23. Egyptian sailing boats in full sail.

As religious expressions expanded, rituals played an important part in the mortuary or god or cult temples. Murray adds further: "In the cult temple, there were two main types of ritual. The most important ritual (known as the Daily Temple Ritual) was carried out three times per day for the resident god in every temple and dramatized the common-place events of everyday existence, providing food, clothing, washing and regular attendance for the god's cult-statue in his sanctuary. The second type of ritual, the festivals, varied in content from one temple to another, each being based on the mythology of the particular resident

RESEARCH ESSAYS ON ANCIENT EGYPT

deity. These were celebrated at regular, often yearly intervals and marked special events in the god's life, such as marriage, death and resurrection. A main feature of most festivals was the procession of the god's statue outside the temple giving the crowds their only opportunity to see the deity and participate in the worship."

There was also a royal ancestor or mortuary cult festival where the daily offerings from the divine temple worship was presented to the king's dead ancestors so that they could one day welcome him into their company.

Rawlinson's *Ancient Egypt* (1893: 38) explained the dual, common and divine, nature of Egyptian Religion in the following statement: "Beside the common popular religion, the belief of the masses, there was another which prevailed among the priests and among the educated. The primary doctrine of this esoteric religion was the real essential unity of the Divine Nature. The sacred texts, known only to the priests and to the initiated, taught that there was a single Being, 'the sole producer of all things both in heaven and earth, himself not produced of any,' 'the only true living God, self-originated,' 'who exists from the beginning,' 'who has made all things, but was not himself been made.' This Being seems never to have been represented by any material, even symbolical, form. It is thought that he had no name, or, if he had, that it must have been unlawful to pronounce or write it. He was a pure spirit, perfect in every respect – all wise, almighty, and supremely good. It is of him that the Egyptian poets use such expressions as the following: 'He is not graven in marble; he is not beheld; his abode is not known; no shrine is found with painted figures of him; there is no building that can contain him;' and, again: 'Unknown is his name in heaven; he doth not manifest his forms; vain are all representations;' and yet again: 'His commencement is from the beginning; he is the God who has existed from old time; there is no God without him; no mother bore him; no father hath begotten him; he is a god-goddess, created from himself; all gods came into existence when he began.'"

FREDERICK MONDERSON

Research Essays 19. Temple of Isis on Agilka Island. In rear of the Temple, Pharaoh Presents a scepter to Horus wearing the Double Crown while Isis as Hathor stands to the God's rear.

Even further, Rawlinson (1893: 38-39) continued: "The other gods, the gods of the popular mythology were understood in the esoteric religion to be either personified attributes of the Deity, or parts of the nature which he had created, considered as informed and inspired by him. Num or Kneph represented the creative mind, Phthah the creative hand, or act of creating; Maut represented matter, Ra the sun, Khons the moon, Seb the earth, Khem the generative power in nature, Nut the upper hemispheres of the heavens, Athor the lower world or under hemisphere; Thoth personified the Divine Wisdom, Ammon perhaps the Divine mysteriousness or incomprehensibility, Osiris the Divine Goodness. It is difficult in many cases to fix on the exact quality, act, or part of nature intended; but the principle admits of no doubt. No educated Egyptian conceived of the popular gods as really separate and distinct gods. All knew that there was but One God, and understood that, when worshipped was offered to Khem, or Kheph, or Maut, or Thoth, or Ammon, the One God was worshipped under some one of his forms or in some one of his aspects. He was every god, and thus all the gods' names were interchangeable, and in one and the same hymn we may find a god, say Ammon, addressed also as Ra and Khem and Tum and Horus and Khepra; or Hapi; or Osiris as Ra and Thoth; or, in fact, any god invoked as almost any other. If there be a limit, it is in respect of the evil deities, whose names are not given to the good ones."

RESEARCH ESSAYS ON ANCIENT EGYPT

III. The Egyptian Holy Books have exerted a tremendous influence on the religion and social behavior and practice of man in the Nile Valley.

a. **The Pyramid Texts** were found in pyramids of the 5th and 6th Dynasties of Kings Unas, Teta (Teti), Pepi I, Merenra and Pepi II at Sakkara. R. Engelback in *Introduction to Egyptian Archaeology with special reference to the Egyptian Museum, Cairo* (1961: 225) is of the view: "They are written in a far more ancient language, however, probably of the IIIrd Dynasty or even earlier, and as such are of extreme importance in the study of the ancient language. The texts are exclusively connected with the welfare of the dead king; they consist of incantations whereby his place in the sky and the other prerogatives of a dead king are assured to him, and they also incorporate the ritual which was recited in connection with the daily offerings made in the pyramid-temples. The discovery, quite recently, of an almost complete version of the Pyramid Texts on the walls of a tomb of a noble of the XIIth Dynasty at El-Lisht, shows that these texts were known some 500 years after the VIth Dynasty, and were, at any rate in this case, applied to a non-royal personage. During the IXth to XIth Dynasties, many excerpts from the Pyramid Texts are found written, usually in ink, inside the large coffins of that period. These are now known as the Coffin Texts."

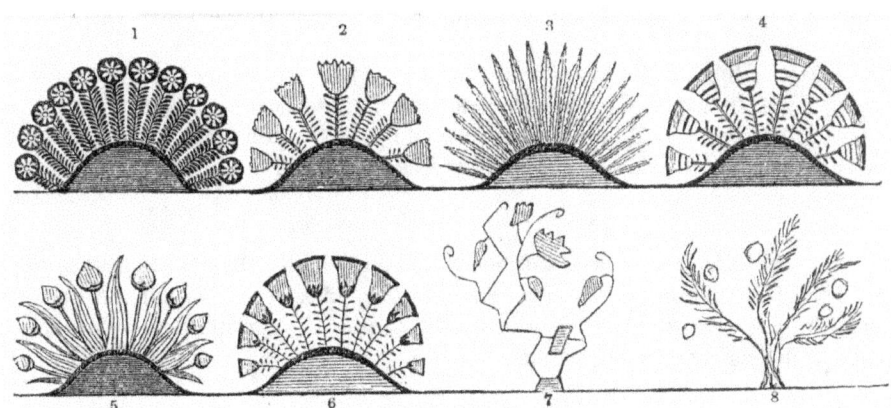

Research Essays Illustration 24. Plants from the sculptures.

He concluded: "A curious feature in the Pyramid Texts is that figures of fishes are never found; the religious or other reason for this is unknown." Even more important, there are no illustrations in the Pyramid Texts. Budge in *Egyptian Heaven and Hell* (1905: 3) offers the explanation: "That the Egyptians possessed artistic skill sufficient to illustrate the religious and general works which their theologians wrote or revised, under their earliest dynasties of kings of all Egypt, is evident from the plain and colored bas-reliefs which adorn the walls of their mastabas, or bench-shaped tombs, and we can only point out and wonder at the fact that the royal pyramids contain neither painted nor sculptured vignettes, especially as pictures are much needed to break the monotony of the hundreds of lines of large hieroglyphics, painted in a bluish-green color, which must have dazzled the eyes even of an Egyptian."

b.   **The Coffin Texts** of the Middle Kingdom were a continuation of the Pyramid Texts of the Old Kingdom that were now written on the insides and outsides of coffins as opposed to being written on the walls of pyramids. We are told: "The Coffin Texts contain an important collection of spells composed on behalf of non-royal personages and comprise incantations against hunger, thirst and manifold dangers of the Underworld, and incantations for enabling the deceased to assume whatever form he pleased, and incantations by virtue of which he could remain in the enjoyment of his former pastimes and partake of the society of his relatives and friends. Part of the interest of the Coffin Texts lies in the fact that they form a link between the Pyramid Text and the later 'Book of the Dead;' spells from both compilations occurring in them. The Coffin Texts appear to have been anciently called 'The Book of Justifying a Man in the Underworld;' when read by priests, the spells were called 'transfigurations' or 'spiritualizations.' No complete copy of the Coffin Texts has been found on papyrus, but spells from it occur on New Kingdom papyri. Mutilations of figures of animals, birds and serpents also occasionally occur on some versions of the Coffin Texts."

The Book of the Dead's magical spells, were to be recited by the dead man, to protect himself from injury, demons and the 'second death.' They were also to enable him to emerge from his tomb, to accompany the gods, to secure acquittal at the Judgment, and be able to enjoy the fruits of heaven or the Elysian Fields.

c.   **The Book of the Dead** continued the religious traditions of the Old and Middle Kingdoms, only now the religious ideas were written on papyrus called books, consisting of "Chapters" of the rituals. Naturally they incorporated much of the earlier religious beliefs.

In part, for example, C.W. Goodwin (1873: 104) discusses: "The 115th Chapter of the Turin Book of the Dead" containing "a very remarkable legend relating to the city of *An* or Heliopolis. This chapter belongs to a group of ten extending from the 107th to the 116th all of which have reference to the recognition by the deceased person of the Ba-u or Spirits of certain localities where he meets them. Several of these chapters contain very antique legends explanatory of the ceremonies observed in certain towns. Thus, Chap 112 professes to explain the origin of the worship of Horus in the town of Pa. Chap 113 had a legend explanatory of the commemoration of the finding of the bands of Horus in the word of *Chem*. The 115th Chapter .... Contains ... an account of the destruction and reproduction of the race of man in the city of Heliopolis." Continuing: "The title of the chapter is 'The Chapter of going forth to heaven, of penetrating the shrine, of knowing the spirits of Heliopolis.' The word *ammahu* translated 'shrine' appears to be specially applied to that part of an Egyptian temple where the sacred relics of the gods or heroes were deposited. King Piankhi is said to have visited the holy place called Zersa near Heliopolis and there to have offered oblations to Tum and his circle of gods in the house of the circle of gods, in which is the shrine (*ammahu*) of the gods."

Accordingly, the story continued: "'I was a great one in time past among the great ones.' 'I was a creature among the creatures.' Gods and men are all described as being created with the exception of Ra the self produced. The meaning of this passage is that the deceased claims to have appeared as a created being in some primeval period of time, and to have played a part in a previous state of existence upon the earth. He says: 'I appeared before One-eye.' One eye in this case may be an epithet for the Sun, the eye and light of creation. 'When the circumference of darkness was opened, I was one among you.' 'I know the spirits of An.'"

Research Essays 20. Temple of Isis on Agilka Island. Close-up view of the Kiosk of Trajan with its magnificent screened colonnade with high abacus below the overhead architrave.

FREDERICK MONDERSON

As the explanation goes: "The passage is one of great difficulty, although all the words of which it is composed are known. The reading Atum, of the Hays papyrus, does not help us and appears to be a mistake. 'The most glorious Atum proceeds from it, even to the limits of the things which are visible.' 'I know how the woman was made from An.' Literally, the curly haired, is the name of a curled wig worn by the priest in certain ceremonies. It is a title of Hathor, and is applied to the votaresses of Hathor. 'This took the form of a curly haired woman.' 'Then he took the form of a curly haired woman.' 'It is the curly headed of An.'"

Again, C.W. Goodwin discussed: "On the 112th Chapter of the Ritual" (Nov-Dec 1871: 144-147) and "Another Chapter of the Knowledge of the Spirits of Pa." The deceased addresses the Great Body dwelling in Zxati (16th Nome of Lower Egypt, the Mendesian) in the city of Anpu or Anu, also the bird-catcher who reigned in Pa. These personages are styled 'the elders who are without end.' 'Do you not know wherefore the town of Pa was given to Horus?'

"'Horus says to Ra, Grant that I may see the creatures of thy eyes, see as it (thy eye) sees them.' Ra says to Horus, 'Look I pray thee, at this black hog.' Said Horus to Ra, 'Behold my eye is as though Anepu had made an incision in my eye. Then we were grieved at heart.'"

Research Essays Illustration 25. Fishing and fowling scenes.

He continued: "Anpu said to the gods: 'Put him upon his bed; he will get well. It was Seth who came and took the form of a black hog. Then he fomented the wound of the eye of Horus. These words explain the cause of the accident. When Ra invited Horus to look at a black pig as one of his own creations, the evil Set came and presented himself in the form of that animal, and Horus looked upon not only a creation of Set, but Set himself. Hence the injury to his eye.' Said Horus to the gods – Who are about him – 'When Horus was in his childhood the cattle of the gods were his oxen, his goats, his pigs – They are Amesta, Hapi, Tau-ma-f, and Kabh-senu-f, whose father is Horus, whose mother is Isis.' Horus says to Ra. – 'Grant me my brother in Pa and my brother in Xen, to be within me (in my power) and to be with me, for an eternal portion.'"

IV.   The Centers of Worship

There are several other features of the religion of ancient Egypt that sets it apart from so many ancient religious beliefs. Its monotheistic nature is affirmed by Budge (1934: 44) who holds: "There is no doubt that the EGYPTIANS included monotheism among their dogmas, but it is impossible to say when their theologians evolved it. Two forms of it existed, a higher and a lower. The higher is the monotheism of Ptah of Memphis, the spirit God, the Eternal Mind, who existed before everything else, and created matter by thought, and the lower is the monotheism of Ra of Heliopolis. But the African monotheism of 3800 B.C. or earlier, though not to be compared with that of modern Christian people, is a remarkable spiritual achievement."

a.   **Ra** was worshipped at Heliopolis and was considered one of the oldest Egyptian gods. "Temu or Ra, the great god of Heliopolis, was a material being, and the source whence he came was NUNU, the great primeval abyss of water. Water existed before Ra and was regarded as the oldest thing in the world, and therefore the 'father of the gods.' The cult of Ra, i.e., worship of the Sun-god, was well established at Heliopolis long before the union of the North and the South by MENES …. The Pyramid Texts show that he had recourse to masturbation in order to produce the twins Shu and Tefnut and the peoples of the Sudan. His cult was gross and material, and the benefits which the Egyptians hoped to receive from him, were material, virility, fecundity, robust health, and abundant offspring both human and animal …. As men expected Ra to give them great material prosperity on earth, so after death, in heaven they rely upon him to provide them with divine meat and drink and apparel, and unstinted gratification of their carnal appetites. In no prayer to Ra can be found a petition by the suppliant for spiritual gifts, or any expression indicating his need of divine help, for his soul. During the great festivals when a statue of the god was carried by the priests round the town or through the country the people in crowds appeared before him, for by this act they discharged a religious obligation and, so to say, acquired merit, and they expected the god to give them in return health, strength, virility, and prosperity."

FREDERICK MONDERSON

Interesting enough, when the argument is made for an Egyptian origin outside of Africa, one has to wonder why their great god Ra made the "people of Nubia" so early in his work of creation! Are we to believe the Europeans who migrated to Egypt very early created the people of Nubia? Or, should we also believe the Nubians were Europeans? Nevertheless, the Nubians were created before the Egyptians. How interesting!

b.   **Ptah** was worshipped at Memphis after Unification when Narmer or Menes established the beginning of the first dynasty and Dynastic period. He was a god of creation as well as a patron of the arts and artisans. While considered 'Father of the gods' Ptah Nunu and 'god of the great abyss of water,' he wears the solar disk and plumes. As Ptah-Tanen 'the oldest earth-god in Egypt,' he holds the crown of Seker (horns, disk and plumes) and also holds the triple scepter. However, in his most popular form as Ptah of Memphis he is shown as a mummy god, with arms emerging, from his closely-fitted garment, at his chest and holding his scepter, wearing a beard and menat hanging from the back of his neck.

He was also a pygmy god. The pygmies originated in Central Africa, source of earliest gold and it's no wonder some of the earliest goldsmiths are pygmies. Equally, these pygmies knew how to dance the "dance of the gods" coming, as they did from "the land of the gods!"

Continuing, Budge (1934: 13-14) added: "From the text which was rescued from oblivion by SHABAKA we learn that PTAH, the Great and Mighty, had eight principal forms among which were PTAH-NUN, and PTAH-TANEN. He therefore preceded NUN and TANEN in existence and he was their creator, and he created them by an effort of his heart or mind. Thus PTAH was the oldest being the priests could imagine, and he was the Eternal Heart or Mind and was self-created. The male part of PTAH begot TEM or TEMU or RA, and his female portion was the mother of the Sun-god of Heliopolis. And, like Ra, Ptah was the father and mother of men, and he conceived and fashioned and made the gods. Tem was a form or figure of Ra …. Tem produced the gods Shu and Tefnut by masturbation and self-impregnation, whereas Ptah produced the gods by the motions of thoughts of his mind. Horus, the oldest Sun-god in Egypt, acted as the heart or mind of Ptah, and Thoth, the god of wisdom, as his tongue. What the heart of Ptah thought passed on to Thoth who translated it into words, which were uttered by the one great almighty mouth, from which everything which is hath come, and everything which is to be shall come. Though Thoth was the Word-god, his actual creative power was derived from the magical pronouncement by Ptah, who alone knew how to utter the words with the correct intonation."

c.   **Amon or Amen**, later **Amon-Ra** or **Amen-Ra** rose to prominence in the Middle and New Kingdom after the successes of his Theban

RESEARCH ESSAYS ON ANCIENT EGYPT

adherents. He dominated the country and the ancient world for more than a good millennium until Egypt became too weak to defend itself and continue its imperialist policies. He was on the same level as Ptah, even possessing some of his powers. Budge (1934: 17-18), quoting Sir Alan Gardener explained the nature and attributes of Amen, Amun or Amon in the following:

I. Amen's origin. He was self-created and as he fashioned himself none knoweth his forms. He existed first as the Eight Gods of Khenemu (Hermopolis), [The head of this Ogdoad was Thoth.] then he completed them and became one. He became in primeval times, no other being existed, there was no god before him; there was no other god with him to declare his form; all the gods came into being after him. He had no mother by whom his name was made; he had no other who begot him, saying, 'It is even myself.' He shaped his own egg; he mingled his seed with his body to make his egg to come into being within himself. He took the form of Tanen in order to give birth to the Pautti (Companies of the?) gods.

II. The hiddenness of Amen. His body is hidden in the Chiefs. He is hidden as Amen at the head of the gods. Amen is one; he hides himself from the gods and conceals himself from them.

III. His oneness. His Unity is absolute.

IV. He was a Trinity, i.e., he had three persons, or characters.

V. His name. His name is more helpful to a man than hundreds of thousands of helpers. The gods cannot pray to him because his name is unknown to them. The man who utters the secret name of Amen falls down and dies a violent death. His name is victory.

VI. Amen as lord of time. He makes the years, rules the months; ordains nights and days. The night is as the day to him. He the One Watcher neither slumbers nor sleeps.

VII. The beneficence of Amen. He breaks evil spells, expels sicknesses from the bodies of men. He, the Physician, heals the Eye, he destroys the Evil Eye (?), he releases men from hell, he abrogates the Destinies (or Fates) of men at his good pleasure, he hears all petitions and is present immediately he is invoked, he prolongs or shortens the lives of men at will, to the man he loves he adds to what Fate has decreed for him, and to the man who sets him in his heart he is more than millions. He was a

Bull for his town, a Lion for his people, a Hawk that destroyed his attackers, and at the sound of his roaring the earth quaked."

"From what has been said above it is quite clear that there was a monotheistic element in the Egyptian Religion. The Spirit-god Ptah was One, the material god Ra was One, and Amen who was claimed by his priests to be both Spirit and Matter was One." And even Ptah, Ra and Amen were considered one in unity.

d.   **Osiris** was worshiped in several places throughout the land of ancient Egypt but his head was buried at Abydos and his heart was buried at Philae. As a result these two locations became the principal centers for his worship. However, while Philae was given status it did not accord with Abydos where his principal mysteries were conducted. From the earliest times kings chose to be buried at Abydos. They built temples there as Petrie has confirmed finding 10 successive layers of temples; nobles erected stela if they could not be buried at Abydos; the dead, as indicated in illustrations, made the pilgrimage to Abydos to be near the god symbolically; and today this site boasts a surviving temple of the New Kingdom. The temple of Seti I at Abydos is a significant survival from the Ramesside Period and it boasts the finest surviving religious art of the entire land.

Research Essays 21. Temple of Isis on Agilka Island. The King in Double Crown makes a Presentation of 3 feathers, Ma'at, to Osiris with Isis to the God's rear.

RESEARCH ESSAYS ON ANCIENT EGYPT

e.   In addition to the above state centers of worship, Hermopolis boasted the cosmology of the Ogdoad, worship of the 8 gods with **Thoth** at its head. This notwithstanding, Thoth belonged to the Ra cycle of gods. Denise M. Doxey in *The Oxford Encyclopedia of Ancient Egypt* Vol. 3 (2001: 398-400), in explaining that Thoth was associated with science, medicine, cosmology, writing, nature and the afterlife as well as music, states: "As a moon god, Thoth regulated the season and lunar phases and counted the stars. Hence, he was associated with astronomy, mathematics and accounting. As the god of scribes and writing, Thoth, 'the lord of the sacred word,' personified divine speech. Seshat, the goddess of writing and literature, was said to be either his wife or daughter. By the Middle Kingdom, Thoth as a god of wisdom and justice was connected with Maat, the personification of rightness and world order. The Greeks viewed him as the source of all wisdom and the creator of languages."

"At Hermopolis, Thoth was worshipped as a cosmogenic deity, believed to have risen on a mound from the primeval chaos to create the Ogdoad consisting of Nun and Naunet, Heh, Heket, Kek, Keket, Amun and Amaunet, coordinated male and female couples representing various forces of nature. In solar religion, Thoth and Ma'at navigated the bark of Re." Even further, Doxey continued: "The principal cult center of Thoth was Hermopolis, ancient Egyptian Khenemu, near the modern town of el-Ashmunein. This was the site of a major new Kingdom temple, at which Amenhotep III claims to have dedicated a pair of thirty-ton quartzite baboons."

Research Essays 21a. Temple of Isis on Agilka Island. In Red Crown and wearing necklace, Pharaoh offers two vessels to Isis as Hathor.

FREDERICK MONDERSON

As an explanation of Thoth's creative powers, Maspero (1891: 2) has written: "The voice without speech was reputed to have the same effect as the two combined, and had been, according to certain Egyptian schools, the agent of Creation." That is: "The Supreme God who is reputed to be the God of Creation, opens his mouth, and the gods come out of it, either the gods generally, or some particular god. Once come forth, the gods each set to work on that which they were predestined to accomplish. These texts have hitherto been translated under the influence of the preconceived idea that what was here meant was a formula, and not an emission of the voice: but this is only an instinctive interpretation, and the Egyptian phrases simply state the fact of a Divine mouth opening and gods issuing from it."

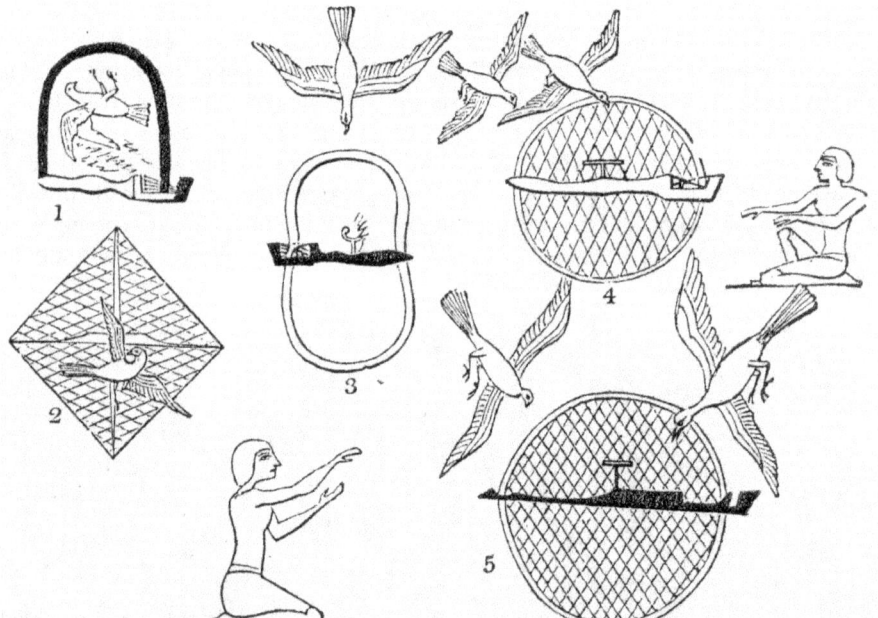

Research Essays Illustration 26. Bird traps, one with a bird caught in it, and the others are all open and empty.

He goes on to quote from a magical book in Greek that says, *inter al*, the magician addresses himself to Thoth. "'I invoke thee,' he says, 'Oh Hermes, thou who containest everything in every speech and dialect, as thou was first celebrated by the subordinate, the Sun, to whom the care of everything is entrusted.' The solar forms then salute *Thoth*, who answers them thus: 'And speaking, the god clapped his hands, and burst seven times bursts of laughter. *Kha, Kha, Kha, Kha, Kha,*

Kha, Kha, and when he had done laughing, seven gods were born,' one for each burst of laughter, as we see. When Hermes first laughed, light appeared, to light everything; and the Creation began to take place. He laughed six times in succession, and each burst of laughter gave birth to a fresh being and a fresh phenomenon; the earth, feeling the sound, in its turn gave utterance to a cry and bowed itself, and the waters were divided into three bodies (*masses*). Then were born Destiny, Justice, Opportunity, the Soul. The last, at its birth, first laughed, then wept, whereupon the god gave forth a breath, bent him towards the earth and produced the serpent Python, which is possessed of universal prescience. At the sight of the dragon the god was struck with stupor, and clacked his lips, whereupon an armed being appeared. The god, seeing this was again struck with stupor, as at sight of a more powerful one than himself, and, lowering his eyes towards the earth, exclaimed, *Iao*! The god who is master of everything was born of the reach of that sound."

V. The Temple as Sanctuary for the Gods and Place of Worship and Ritual

a.   The nature of the temple architecture was dictated by the geography, period, royal family or dynasty in power, and the wealth they possessed in order to endow their god. Since the house of the god was a thing of eternity, the building was constructed in stone and had to be quarried at some distance where good stone was located. This endeavor gave birth to a number of enterprises and disciplines. Once the stone was removed to the place of erection, the structure was further finished and beautified with elaborate artistic renderings that depicted the ritual and other facets of the pharaoh's existence, as it related to worship of his god.

b.   Pylon and Court were parts of the temple entrance that the visitor encountered as well as the pharaoh when he came to pay homage to his god. The pylon was generally decorated on the outer face and there were openings for flagstaves that flew flags of the god, nome and nation.

FREDERICK MONDERSON

Research Essays 22.   Temple of Isis on Agilka Island. Isis out front holding a symbol of her power before Horus in Double Crown and with Hathor at their rear.

c.   Halls and Colonnades were decorated features that carried the various themes and rituals of the temple and showcased the wealth of the particular god worshipped there. In some respects this architectural feature became "the glory of Egypt."

d.   The Sanctuary was the place where the divinity rested in absolute darkness that only the pharaoh or high priest dared to enter. Interestingly enough, as one ventured deep into the temple, the floor rose and the ceiling sank so that the Sanctuary became the highest point in the structure. In the Sanctuary there was an altar upon which the lustrations of the god were performed. However, incense, as part of the ritual, was never burnt on the altar, but in an incenser in some corner of this inner recess.

e.   Adjoining chambers were designed to accommodate the vestments and liquid and solid offerings of the ritual, as well as the elements of the god's toilet. Oftentimes these adjoining chambers contained a library as well as served as a bark station for the god's ark or boat. Sometimes these adjoining chambers were decorated.

RESEARCH ESSAYS ON ANCIENT EGYPT

Research Essays 22a. Temple of Isis on Agilka Island. While Nephthys sits enthroned behind Isis nursing Horus, Khnum makes the child on his potter's wheel, while Thoth sits at his rear.

VI.   The Afterlife Dynamic

a.   The tomb was an important part of the individual existence and great effort was made to prepare and furnish it correctly since he hoped to dwell there for an eternity. The nature of the tomb varied with the time period referenced in the religion and the particular individual interred there. In the Old Kingdom, the pharaoh was buried in pyramids and before that in the earliest tombs, as at Abydos. Here at Abydos, there were real tombs and cenotaphs or dummy tombs were at Sakkara, burial site of the Memphis capital. These eternal resting places were decorated with 'goods of the grave;' or as the Cairo Museum calls them, 'funerary furniture.' The 'dummy tombs' or cenotaphs at Sakkara were duplicates with the exception of the body of the deceased. However, they contained much the deceased would require in the other world. The only thing missing was the body. By the time of the Old Kingdom, officials preferred to be buried near the king's pyramid, so much so that since he was assured the immortality of heaven, being in his shadow enabled them to share in his good fortune. By the time of the Middle and New Kingdom, there developed what was called "democratization of the afterlife," in that now practically everyone could get to heaven, as did the king, providing one lived the good life as dictated by the tenets of Ma'at.

FREDERICK MONDERSON

Research Essays 22b. Columns of the Second Eastern Colonnade in the Court of Isis's Temple proper.

Tombs of the kings, queens, nobles and artisans of the New Kingdom were dug into the mountains at Thebes, and were equally and tremendously decorated with scenes of this world and the next. While some tombs depicted social themes, others emphasized the afterlife and were replete with literary themes outlining the drama of the underworld. Most Middle Kingdom tombs have not been found and when this happens, it would provide a bonanza of religious, artistic and social factual data that would further refine our understanding of Egyptian belief and practices.

RESEARCH ESSAYS ON ANCIENT EGYPT

Research Essays 22c. Returning from the temple of Isis, a local bird does a river dive near the rocks in background.

b. Mummification began very early in the Old Kingdom and reached a high state of perfection by the time of the New Kingdom. In fact, some scholars see mummification as beginning in Nubia before dynastic rule. However, great effort was made to mummify the deceased in preparation for the dynamics of the afterlife. Herodotus tells us there were three types of mummification based on the economic status of the deceased with the wealthy being more elaborate in their choice of preparation and decoration. This mummification process aided the development of science, medicine and treatment of the sick as well as dead. It also helped in creating a written record of anatomy and physiology as well as a medicinal pharmacopeia.

c. The Judgment was an important part of the Egyptian's other-worldly experience and seems he prepared for it from the earliest times of his existence or social and economic readiness. In order to get to the Judgment, once dead, the individual had to navigate a set of pylons and portals with dangerous obstacles seeking to impede his entry in the Underworld as he headed to the Hall of Judgment. By having the right knowledge and words of power he was able to gain entry and arrive at the Hall of African Judgment where his heart was weighed against a feather of truth, Ma'at. This was called the Psychostasia where sometimes as few as a dozen and as many as forty-two judges sat and observed the process. Thoth and Anubis as well as Am-mit 'searched' the deceased before finding him guilty or 'true of voice.' Upon the latter it was announced by Thoth and the assessors or jurors affirmed his findings, then the deceased was introduced to Osiris, the Egyptian god of the dead.

Research Essays 22d. On a river boat and with Trajan's Kiosk in the distant rear, native Egyptian Guide Shawgi Abd el-Rady relaxes after an interesting tour of the Temple of Isis.

d.   Before the actual weighing of the heart against the feather of Ma'at the deceased was made to make the 42 Negative Confessions affirming that he did not commit those unacceptable behaviors. The Negative Confessions were said to the 42 assessors but some scholars, such as Dr. ben-Jochannan, believed they were part of a greater body of more than 147 such confessions. Equally there was a body of 'positive confessions' the deceased made as well indicating he had done these things.

e.   The notion of standing before your god at the end of your existence was a horrifying feeling and inherently it steered individuals to live a positive and constructive lifestyle. This does not, however, lead us to believe all Egyptians lived right and truthfully.

RESEARCH ESSAYS ON ANCIENT EGYPT

Research Essays 23. View of the Old Cataract Hotel at Aswan from beside the Pool.

f.   The reward for the good life lived on earth is peace of mind in this world and eternal bliss in the next. Some people believe goodness is an outstanding moral virtue that allows the individual to live in harmony with his surroundings, people, places and even things and animals. "It makes you sleep sound at nights." However, the whole notion of goodness is an essential prerequisite of being able to survive the judgment and live among the immortals in the next life to enjoy the eternal bliss of heaven.

VII. Worship and Ritualizing the Gods

a.   The Priesthood very early developed into a professional organization with a many-faceted functionality. This gained them the power of not only being protectors of the god because of their close relationship, but also having a significant impact on the society in general because of their technical, intellectual and scientific know-how. As full-time intermediaries between the gods and king and people, their power grew immensely. Very early they acquired a tax-free status and came into control of much wealth because of the perennial endowments they became guardians over, in order to propagate the memories of deceased persons. Soon kings and nobles were not only lavishing great wealth on the gods and by extension on the priesthood, but they also became very wary and afraid of the power of this multi-faceted body that could interpret the wishes of divinity.

The article "Religion" in Ian Shaw and Paul Nicholson *The British Museum Dictionary of Ancient Egypt*, (1995) (2003: 244-245) states: "Ancient Egyptian state religion was concerned with the maintenance of the divine order; this entailed ensuring that life was conducted in accordance with Maat, and preventing the encroachment of chaos. In such a system it was necessary for religion to permeate every aspect of life, so that it was embedded in society and politics, rather than being a separate category. The Egyptian view of the universe was capable of incorporating a whole series of apparently contradictory creation myths. This holistic view also led to the treatment of prayer, magic and science as realistic and comparative alternatives, as a result it made good sense to combine what might now be described as medical treatment with a certain amount of ritual and recitation of prayers, each component of the overall treatment giving the same aim; to suppress evil and maintain the harmony of the universe."

The temples and their attendant priests therefore served as a perpetual means of stabilizing the universe. Each day they attended to the needs of the god (who was thought to be manifested in the cult image), made offerings to him, and thus kept the forces of chaos at bay. A distinction is sometimes made between, on the one hand, the important state gods (Horus or Isis) and local deities (Banebdjedet at Mendes), and, on the other hand, the "popular' or 'household' deities such as Bes and Taweret."

b.   An important function of the priesthood, beside worshipping and ritualizing the gods, was the responsibility of managing the estate of the divinity. This economic responsibility allowed the priesthood to venture into and play an essential role in the society. They collected taxes, owned their own land and farms, maintained ships on the Nile River that carried the merchandise of food, arts and crafts they manufactured for purposes of trade. There were towns given as endowments and they had to manage these so their prosperity could be multiplied. The priesthood owned untold cattle, chickens, hectares of land, ships, slaves, gardens, orchards, vessels of wine, beer, oil, and the technical sophistication to engage in all forms of trade and craft, from building, quarrying, and transportation to artistry. They built, educated others, extended the realms of science, pursued mathematics, medicine; engineering, farming, and essentially "managed the society," while serving their god. Their power became so immense the pharaohs, weak ones that is, kept a close eye on this religious power that also combined economic, scientific and moral power having political implications. This latter became so acute that the priesthood was able to seize power after the collapse of the New Kingdom.

RESEARCH ESSAYS ON ANCIENT EGYPT

Research Essays Temple Ticket 10. Medinet Habu Temple. Price of entrance is thirty Egyptian Pounds.

c.   Circumstances in relationship within the society and challenges from neighbors created an imperialist outlook and pharaohs took the sword to nations abroad while they quelled resistance at home. Warrior pharaohs pursued an imperialist policy of conquest and incorporation into their very extensive empires with demands of tribute on the nations they conquered and allied with. Much of the ensuing wealth they accumulated from their exploits abroad was lavished on the gods and priesthood, enabling them to build fabulous temples with the wealthiest decorations and enormous gifts of gold. In their relationship with the gods they were given his blessing which translated into victories with attendant wealth that in turn became temple endowments. This state of affairs continued for centuries and as the nation grew wealthier, the priesthood benefited and the god became wealthier, and so this continued. When there were no young, vigorous and strong pharaohs to defend Egypt, their numerous enemies were attracted by the wealth of the state and priests whose fortunes were untold. The temples then were, for moral and economic reasons, the first targets of invading forces that looted the holy places, desecrated the sanctuaries of the gods, and carried off much of their wealth and people.

FREDERICK MONDERSON

Research Essays 24. View of the New Cataract Hotel from beside the pathway near Old Cataract Hotel at Aswan.

d.   Religion advanced science because of its essential role in the society since the principal proponents were also the intellectual elite and this beat back the mist of ignorance. Astronomy, medicine, mathematics, government, law, education, building, quarrying, farming, arts and crafts, trade, theology, theogony, metaphysics, mummification, perhaps even warfare, sanctioned, those essential ingredients that propel society and civilization, can be traced to the practice of religion and praise of the gods. Thus, the Nile River whose effluence flowed from Central Africa manifested in a tremendous gift that enlightened Egypt and the world.

References

Budge, E.A. Wallis. *The Egyptian Heaven and Hell.* New York: Dover Publications, (1905) 1996.
_____. *Egyptian Religion.* New York: Carol Publishing Group: A Citadel Press Book, (1900) 1991.
_____. *From Fetish to God in Ancient Egypt.* London: Oxford University Press, 1934.
Doxey, Denise M. "Religion." *The Oxford Encyclopedia of Ancient Egypt* Vol. 3. London: Oxford University Press, (2001: 398-400).

RESEARCH ESSAYS ON ANCIENT EGYPT

Frankfort, Henri. *Ancient Egyptian Religion.* New York: Harper and Row, Publishers, (1946) 1961.
Goodwin, C.W. "On the 112th Chapter of the Ritual. (November-December, 1871: 144-147).
_____. "The 115th Chapter of the Turin Book of the Dead." (1873: 104).
Maspero, Gaston. "Creation by Voice and the Ennead of Heliopolis." 9th *International Congress of Orientalists,* (1-10 September, 1891: 1-10).
Murray, Margaret. *Egyptian Temples,* London: Sampson Low, Marston and Co., Ltd., 1931.
Osei, G. K. *African Contributions to Civilization.* London: African Publication Society, 1983.
Rawlinson. *The Story of the Nations: Ancient Egypt.* London: T. Fisher Unwin and New York: G.P. Putnam's Sons, 1893.
Shaw, Ian and Paul Nicholson. "Religion." *The British Museum Dictionary of Ancient Egypt.* London: The British Museum, (1995) (2003: 244-245).
Shorter, Alan W. *The Egyptian Gods: A Handbook.* London: Routledge and Kegan Paul, (1937) 1981.

Research Essays Temple Ticket 11. Olwet Abdel Qurna. Price of entrance is twenty-five Egyptian Pounds.

FREDERICK MONDERSON

Research Essays 24a. An assortment of Nubian Jewelry for sale in the Aswan area.

7. The Egyptian Temple

By

Dr. Fred Monderson

I. Introduction

The Egyptian temple was one of the most fascinating structures of the ancient Nile Valley civilization of Kemet, Tawi (the two lands), and now modern Egypt. Not simply a repository for the god worshipped therein, but it also shaped the beliefs and practices of the culture that has impacted heavily on the consciousness of man throughout history. The temple helped expand architectural designs, the extraction and transportation of stone, and the ancillary crafts that decorated and made livable and prosperous the enclosure. In addition, it furthered the development of knowledge, expanded the practice of the arts, encouraged experimentation and the furtherance of science and stimulated the growth of trade and accumulation of wealth. Naturally, the propagation of religious activities was its primary concern. The attendant great occurrences connected with the temple depended heavily on

RESEARCH ESSAYS ON ANCIENT EGYPT

the Nile River whose gifts flowed from the bosom of Africa. Thus, in all this, the Nile Valley experience was an African and by today's standards, black culture, first of its kind to become conscious of its intellectual, philosophical, esoteric, moral and spiritual, creativity.

Africans of ancient Kemet, Egypt, along the Nile, unquestionably enlightened the world through religious thought and practice, theosophy, theology, metaphysics, science and social, ethical and material accomplishments! As much, argued the great African intellect, Cheikh Anta Diop, in systematic, interdisciplinary, erudite, irrefutable and well thought-out scholarship, entitled *African Origin of Civilization: Myth or Reality*. Also, a number of dedicated African and African-American writers and scholars, including Martin Delaney, Henry Highland Garnett, W.E.B. DuBois, Carter G. Woodson, George G.M. James, John G. Jackson, Yosef ben-Jochannan, Ben Carruthers, John H. Clarke, Leonard James, Theophile Obenga, Molefi Asante and Ivan Van Sertima, after many years of research and teaching, have asserted the exact idea. This then, is the idea to advocate!

Research Essays 25. Two Brothers, American-Nubian and Egyptian-Nubian on the pathway beside the Old Cataract Hotel at Aswan.

FREDERICK MONDERSON

In this historical experiment, the great achievement and gift of this North-east African culture was its theosophical, religious, architectural, artistic, scientific and moral genius embodied in the ancient Egyptian or Kemet temple. The Egyptian temple, therefore, was a work of divinely inspired art! This creation, unlike the Jewish Synagogue, Greek or Roman Temple, Muslim Mosque, or Christian Cathedral was unique and today still evokes and exudes profound theological and cosmological spiritualism, posing thoughtful questions for scholars still seeking to define it. It was an edifice essentially erected by a king in honor of some divinity. Sometimes it was in honor of a king to be worshipped as a divinity upon his death, or of a triad of divinities, to whom he wished to pay special homage. This was all either in return for benefits received or for some future favors.

In the sculptures and paintings on the walls and columns of various temples, the king is shown as the principal figure. He is larger than all others, except the God and sometimes shown on the same plane as the divinity. On the outside, he is shown waging war with the enemies of Egypt whether philosophical, spiritual or those actually taken in battle and who are generally brought home as captives. At other times of peace, he offers gifts and sacrifices on the inside. There the prayers are said in his name and so too the ritual of the temple that praises the god. He leads the procession in which are carried the statues and emblems of the divinities and the drama. Therefore, whether cult, mortuary, sun, rock-cut, terraced, valley, or processional temple, even kiosks, chapels, or "birth houses" and "soul houses" that deserve mention, these structures were an integral part of the Nile Valley culture that helped shape the morality, and social and religious beliefs and practices these ancient Egyptian, African, people bequeathed the world in their practice of intellectual consciousness and religion and spirituality.

The temple therefore came to play an important part in fostering much of the wealth, opulence and civilization development we associate with ancient Egypt. Barbara Watterson's *The Gods of Ancient Egypt* (1984) (1996: 17) has disclosed particularly in regards economics: "Ancient Egyptian temples were big business. The temple was a landowner: the ordinary Egyptians could and did rent land from it. It was the repository for legal documents, the place where births and marriages were registered and contracts drawn up. Schools were centered on temples: scribes, artists and doctors were trained there. Most Egyptians were illiterate; temple scribes were therefore employed to draw up documents and write such letters as were necessary. Doctor-priests trained and based in temples tended the ailments of the Egyptians, and some temples even had rudimentary hospitals within their precincts where the sick could receive treatment, which often consisted of magical as well as medical methods."

RESEARCH ESSAYS ON ANCIENT EGYPT

Research Essays Illustration 27. Herdsmen giving an account of the cattle.

All this notwithstanding, the idea of the Egyptian temple is an evolved concept dating to the time of the emergence of the gods, who needed to be sheltered on earth, and thus, instructed their adherents of the specifications of their homes or earthly abode. Their priests, in turn, were equally active creators of the civilization and as early as the time of the Old Kingdom had begun to play an important role not simply in religious, mortuary, but also in civic and social matters. So much so, for this early period, Indus Khamit Kush in *The Missing Pages of "His-Story"* (1993: 25) could quote Robert Forest Wilson in *The Living Pageant of the Nile* (The Bobs Merrill Company, Indianapolis, 1924, p. 31) who wrote regarding Egypt of this age: "She had refined her system of law and government, invented taxation, developed an intricate economic system, vastly expanded the tastes and needs of her individuals, gone into foreign trade, applied state aid to agriculture, made a start with most of the common sciences, produced philosophers, erected some of the mightiest buildings the world has ever seen, discovered beauty in art, and done a thousand other things – and over the face of the rest of the earth the primeval darkness yet rested." In all this, the temple played a principal role for the priests were the great teachers and philosophers who helped mold ethical outlook and much of the general practice of the society.

As the art of temple building developed, and within the sacred enclosure, no public worship was performed, the faithful did not congregate for public prayer, and no commoner was admitted into the inner portals of the temple except the priests. Individuals high in the social echelon were welcomed into the Great Open Court, but no further! Nevertheless, writes Maspero, the "Temple was built as an image of the world, as the Egyptian imagined it to be." Importantly, Adolf Erman in *Handbook of Egyptian Religion* (1907: 6) commented on the temple in this early age of the world or consciousness of the ancient Egyptian of pre-dynastic times, and revealed: "Their temples were huts with walls of plaited wicker-work, the front of the roof was adorned with projecting wooden beams. A few short posts and two high masts in front of the building were added to provide shelter decoration. The altar consisted of a reed mat, and for the celebration of festivals, simple bowers were erected."

Research Essays 26. The Outer Enclosure Wall encompassing the Temples of Karnak with the Northern Group to the left, the Central Group in the middle and the Southern Group to the right. That is Montu left, Amon-Ra center and Mut to the right.

Comparatively and continuing this elaboration, Aldred (1980: 144) makes known: "The Egyptian temple, 'the god's house,' had its origins in the prehistoric reed or palm-leaf booth, similar to the maize-stalk shelter that the peasant even today erects in his fields to shield his beasts and himself from the cold winds of winter and the burning heat of summer. In the beginning, the god had arisen on the primeval mound above the waters of Chaos, and by magic the shrine was built around him with a fence to keep off intruders, and a rag of cloth on a pole to show that the place was sacred and taboo. As the work of creation continued and light appeared on the face of the waters, the god of the Void lifted the sky from the new marshy earth, and kept it in position on its four pole-like supports. Thus the temple as the abode of the god grew to its final form, not as an architectural concept so much as myth made tangible in stone. This finite model of the universe at its beginning is visible in the primal Egyptian temple, and determines its

RESEARCH ESSAYS ON ANCIENT EGYPT

decoration. The sanctuary, housing the image of the god, is built on the highest point of the ground, on a sort of hillock representing the primeval mound, and is a stone interpretation of the prehistoric reed hut, which is clearly discernible as a small house within a larger dwelling. Except here, in the elemental darkness, prevailing before the First Time."

Sauneron in Posener (1962: 281) offers another somewhat similar view: "The Egyptian temple was a functional building, devoted to the most essential work of earthly life, namely, the maintenance of the creation. Obscure forces of chaos existed before the world was created, and, although they were cast away to the outer edge of the world, they nevertheless continued to threaten it; the equilibrium which maintained the visible world and the various forms of life was the fact of a creation daily renewed. Every evening, in the darkness, the world again was in danger of falling into a sleep from which there would be no awakening, the return of the sun the next morning happily drove away the risk. Only the gods, by their ceaseless efforts, preserved the precarious existence of this essential vulnerable universe. These gods, universal forces in different places under different forms, lived on earth in their "houses" – the temples. The function of this building and of its personnel was to protect the gods from attacks by hostile forces, to nourish them and keep them in perfect condition, in order to facilitate their cosmic task and to keep from them any influence which could impede their action."

A posited view of this divine dynamic is offered by A.T. Mann in *Sacred Architecture* (1993: 13) who explained, the: "spiritual is the active, dynamic aspect of the psyche, which is independent of forms, and yet is an essence, which seeks expression in and through the world. Those forms into which spiritual energy flow reflect a sense of the divine and a science of such forms has developed throughout history, a science based on symbolism."

Somewhat similarly, Byron E. Shafer in *Temples of Ancient Egypt* (1998: 2) supplies an interesting description of cosmological forces at work where he points out: "Temples and rituals were loci for the creative interplay of sacred space and sacred time. Sacred space is 'a place of clarification (a focusing lens) where men and gods are held to be transparent to one another' and 'a point of communication,' the 'paradoxical point of passage from one mode of being to another.' In sacred space one is oriented to the cosmos and immersed in primordial order; there one experiences truth and renews life. Over time, such space appears unchanged and unchanging, 'stable enough to endure without growing old or losing any of its parts.'"

Even further, Shafer (1998: 2) continued: "What has been said of sacred place can, for the most part, be said of sacred time as well. It is a moment, or season, or cycle of such clarification and communication, orientation and immersion, experience and renewal. Time, however, is not so stable a dimension of order as space. Egyptians experienced time as a spiral of patterned repetitions, a coil of countless rebirths. The purest moment of sacred time was the first, the moment of creation, when the existent and its order emerged from the nonexistent and its aspect of disorder. Subsequently, time, as a component of order, proved vulnerable to chaos. So, for example, the intervals between sunrise and sunset came to change from day to day and season to season, and the beginning of each new 365-day year came to rotate slowly backward relative to the seasons and the helical rising of the star Sirius. Because of order's ongoing vulnerability to chaos, Egyptians needed to conceive of creation not as a single past event but as a series of 'first times,' of sacred regenerative moments recurring regularly within the sacred space of temples through the media of rituals and architecture."

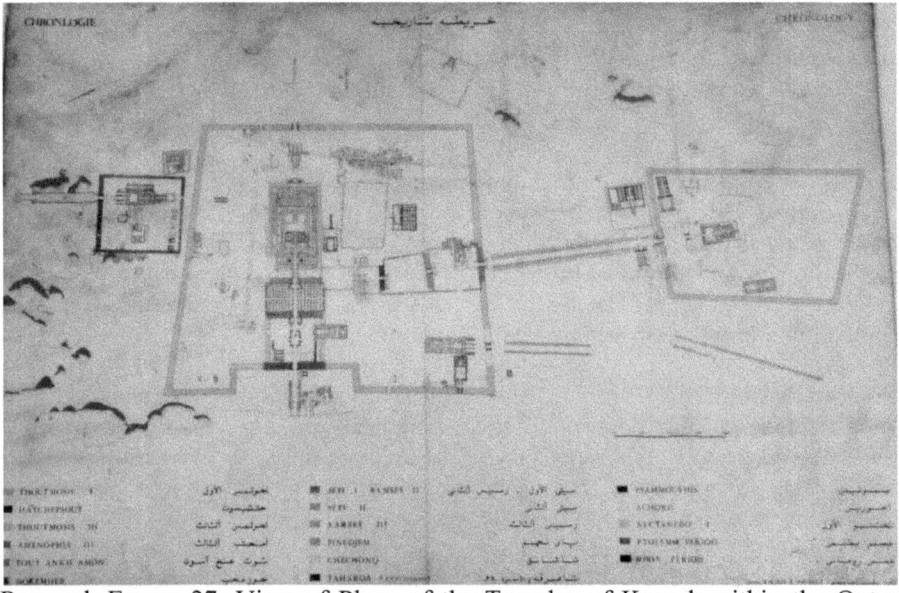

Research Essays 27. View of Plans of the Temples of Karnak within the Outer Enclosure Wall.

RESEARCH ESSAYS ON ANCIENT EGYPT

Research Essays Illustration 28. Dom and Date Palm trees.

Mann (1993: 14) offers an even more penetrating view, when further he described several ways in which the symbolic or the spiritual is expressed through sacred architecture. These are: "First, sacred architecture reflects the structure of the cosmos. Before there were buildings, humanity worshipped the stars and planets, the four elements, the earth, and its animals and plants, as gods. In our progression from caves to modern buildings, the symbolism of this early integration with the cosmos has been central, and still activates the deepest essence within us, the core of our psyche. Initially, sacred monuments were associated with a particular god, goddess, or the natural or supernatural powers they represented. They were aligned by or with the stars or planets in the sky, which represented the god or goddess. They were also geographically oriented and located in places significant to the gods. Some monuments were used by priests or priestesses as observatories to measure the movements of the planets or heavenly bodies they worshipped, while others were sited in accordance with planetary motions. Most megalithic monuments echoed some or all of these functions in their siting, design and function."

Mann continued his explanation: "Second, sacred monuments were organized using primary geometric shapes and proportions, described by number symbolism. Mathematical mysticism or sacred geometry is a profound part of sacred architecture, and it's often mentioned in relation to the Egyptians and Pythagoreans. Pythagoras created a humanistic philosophy which utilized mathematical harmony and proportion as primary tools in daily life, including art, architecture, music, morality and history. He believed that the order inherent in numbers, a number symbolism, creates specific effects on the observer, both psychologically and spiritually. The discovery of the innate meaning of numbers is therefore a primary creative legacy of sacred architecture. The exploration of the numbers and proportions of the sacred brings a higher understanding to architecture."

Next, Mann revealed: "Third, the sacred lives in buildings or monuments in which the structure and decoration follow clear and basic patterns derived from the ancient conception of the four elements, earth, water, air, and fire, the forms of nature and from living energies and the geometries derived from them. Proportion systems amplifying natural rhythms and patterns bring a natural and organic energy and spirituality to sacred architecture – the building contains an elemental as well as a human quality evoking the spiritual."

Conversely, and elsewhere, Mann (1993: 106-07) is of the view: "The creation of sacred buildings echoes the creation of the universe, and both seek to follow similar mathematical laws. Therefore, the Golden Section (phi) is found to govern the growth of plants and animals, and is also the primary proportion found in sacred buildings and monuments. In their use of numbers as a symbolic language, the Egyptians predate and influence Pythagoras and Plato. The Egyptians communicated symbolic astrological and astronomical concepts beyond the actual form of the buildings. Similarly, their hieroglyphical language used symbols instead of mere signs. A sign has a limited meaning, while a symbol evokes correspondences and widens understanding. The Egyptians used their mythology to further understanding because it was more than simple history. Their gods came from the stars, beginning wisdom, understanding and power. Their myths were cosmic myths, describing planetary movements, and brought the mathematical reality of the stars to humanity."

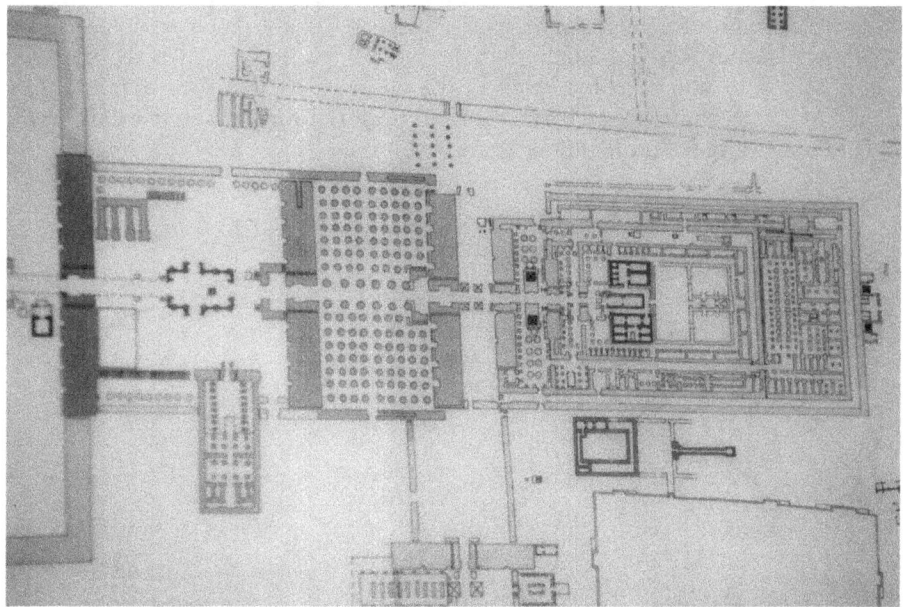

Research Essays 28. Plan of the Temple of Amon-Ra at Karnak.

On the one hand, in evolutionary development of their building and worship practices, Aldred (1980: 145) suggests this explanation: "By the time of the New Kingdom, most of the local divinities had become solarized under the influence of the theologians of Heliopolis, and had attached to themselves the name of Re'Horakhty, the active aspect of the sun-god, so that forms like Amon-re, Sobek-re and Mentu-re are now found. The sun god, however, was worshipped at an altar set in a colonnaded court under the open sky where he was lord. The architecture was divinely inspired and with space for the principal gods, the buildings became complex with small rooms for secondary gods, statues, dim lights, maze of halls, and arrangement of trick doors, as well as stairs to the roof. There were also side rooms for keeping garments, jewelry, and cult objects for the religious ceremonies on altars."

Erman (1907: 40-41) on the other hand, demonstrates his understanding regarding the temple within the enclosure, and the principal gateway with its propylon or pylon. "Behind this gateway lay the first large space, an open court surrounded by colonnades. Here the great festivals were celebrated, in which a large number of citizens were entitled to take part. Behind this court there was a hall supported by columns, the place appointed for all manner of ceremonies, and behind this again lay the holy of holies, the chamber where the statue of the god had his dwelling. In adjoining apartments were the statues of the wife and son of the god. This was the essential part of the temple, naturally there would be various additional chambers to contain the sacred utensils, and for special purposes of the religious cults. A further characteristic of every temple is that from front to rear each apartment was less lofty and light than the preceding. Into the court the Egyptian sun blazed with uninterrupted splendor, in the halls its light was admitted to a modified extent through the entrance and through the windows in the roof; in the holy of holies reigned profound darkness."

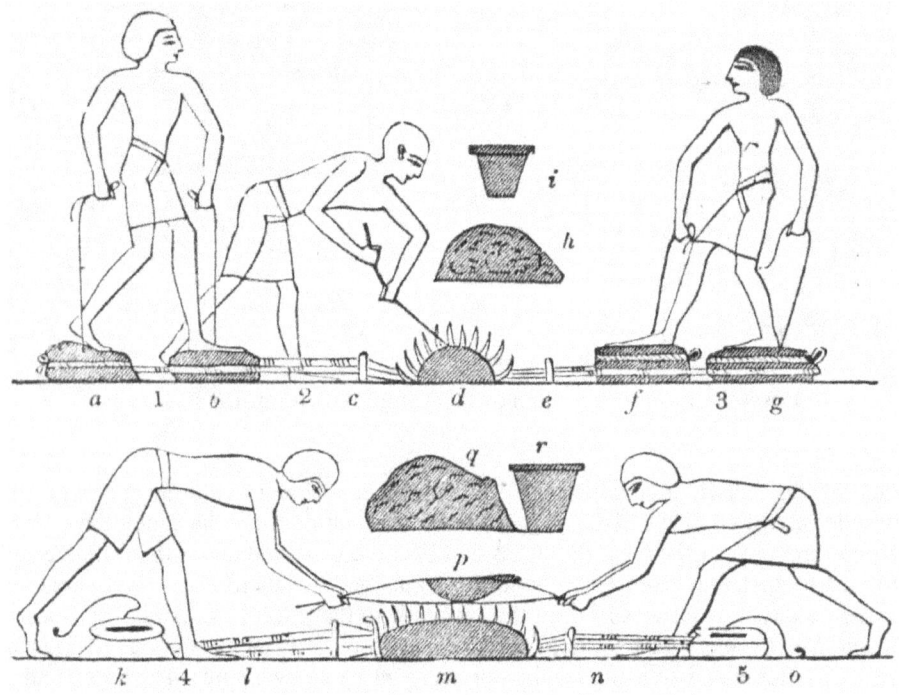

Research Essays Illustration 29. Bellows. Thebes.

All this, notwithstanding, the notion of creating sacred space had to do with divine inspiration, kingly generosity and priestly and professional execution. Still, Margaret Murray in *The Splendor that was Egypt* (1949) (1957: 232-33) makes clear: "The founding of a temple was a religious ceremony, performed by the Pharaoh in person assisted by the goddess Seshat, who was probably represented

RESEARCH ESSAYS ON ANCIENT EGYPT

by the Queen. Each of them held an end of the measuring-cord and marked on the ground the dimensions of the temple. After the measurements had been traced out a sand-bed was made, and on this rough stone blocks were laid to form the foundations. At each corner of the building, and wherever an internal wall touched the outside wall, foundation deposits were placed under the blocks. These deposits consisted of models of all the tools and implements used in the building of the temple, modes of offerings, and scarabs or plaques bearing the name of the royal founder. Even when a temple has been completely destroyed and the foundation blocks removed, it is possible to recover the plan and the name of the founder by means of the foundation deposits. The foundation blocks were scored with lines on the upper surface, which had been smoothed, and on these lines the walls were built. As the walls rose in height earth ramps were built against them, which dragged the stones on rollers. Pillars were built in the same way with ramps. This method of raising blocks of stone to the desired level is as early as the pyramids. It is uncertain whether a temple was built from a plan drawn out by the architect before beginning the work; if so all such plans have perished. If not, then one is confronted with the fact that the architects of those early days were capable of planning a temple or pyramid completely, including the lengths of ramps required, and carrying it through to completion without even a note."

Research Essays 29.   Temple of Amon-Ra at Karnak.   Sphinxes before the Southern Colonnade within the Great Court and with the inner face of the southern half of the First Pylon to the right. The last column of the colonnade is unfinished giving evidence of how these columns were erected before being pounded smooth.

FREDERICK MONDERSON

Libraries were an important part of any temple for the ritual and for scholars who congregated in temples that were considered "Colleges." Some temples had a well, Nilometer, granaries and dwellings for the temple staff. To help meet the needs of the daily rituals, gardens provided fresh flowers for the temple service and food for the staff. Granaries and storehouses were filled with staff-produce, looked-over by large contingents of scribes, overseers and managers in charge of administration. Significant industries or schools of arts and crafts were developed in these structures. Temples were frequently provided with allocations of prisoners-of-wars for work on its lands. They were also recipients of kingly and noble endowments for worship and mortuary cults, and these temples enjoyed tax-free status.

While there were principally god or worship temples, Aldred (1980: 146) elucidates, comparing previous Old and Middle Kingdom structures with New Kingdom mortuary building practices wrote: "The resources that had formerly been devoted to the building of the king's pyramid complexes now went into their mortuary temples, built along the desert margin of the western riverbank at Thebes, the birthplace of their founder Amosis. These were separated from their actual burial places, which from the reign of Tuthmosis I were hewn into the rocky walls of a Wady now known as the Valley of the Kings, about a mile to the west, beneath the dominating peak of a natural pyramid. The tombs themselves were decorated in painted relief, or with walls and ceiling paintings, of scenes from the sacred books that, under the influence of Heliopolis, now governed ideas on the royal destiny …."

In addition to representations of kings, figures of the gods are commonly found. The age also saw a growth of ideas of divinities grouped into triads consisting of a god, his consort and their child. Thus, the concept of the Holy Family with the child was first experienced on the Nile River.

RESEARCH ESSAYS ON ANCIENT EGYPT

Research Essays Illustration 30. Donkey carrying a load of grain sheaves in the Pyramid Age.

Besides the essential nature of the library in every temple for its part in the daily ritual, it was also important in its function as an aid to the temple university in training other priests, government bureaucrats, nobles and physicians. Thus, the library was called the "house" or "room of books."

In clarifying the divine design, spiritual essence and theological intent, Shaw and Nicholson (1995: 285-86) have added the temple was also: "considered to be an architectural metaphor both for the universe and for the process of creation itself. The floor gradually rose, passing through forests of plant-form columns and roofed by images of the constellations or the body of the sky-goddess Nut, allowing the priests to ascend gradually from the outermost edge of the universe towards the sanctuary, which was a symbol of the inner core of creation, the Primeval mound on which the creator-god first brought the world into being."

White (1980: 50-51) on the other hand, offered his comparison showing: "The temple performed the same role in ancient Egypt as the cathedral in mediaeval Europe. It was the dual source of cultural inspiration and physical employment. As in mediaeval Europe, with the exception of the estates of the feudal barons almost the entire ownership of land and property was concentrated in the hands of the king with his chief priests. In theory, the king held the "Black Land" in trusteeship for his fellow gods. His chief priests were therefore his principal tenants, although they gradually became more or less the unchallenged rulers of their own domains - in the way that the Abbot of Tintern or Rievaulx would carry out his ecclesiastic duties while superintending the agriculture, stock-breeding and building-work throughout his wide province. The main temples acted not only as the distributors of their own bounty, but of the royal bounty too. An entire population of civil servants, scribes, policemen, craftsmen, artisans, and artists was fed and clothed from the priestly granaries and storerooms. The chief priests collected taxes on behalf of the king and doled out rewards and necessities as they saw fit. They were thus the instruments and regulators of the state economy and wielded enormous power."

The notion of the king holding the "Black Land" in trusteeship for the other gods is an interesting caveat for it goes to the very heart of the nature of the people who inhabited ancient Egypt/Kemet. Much has been written about Egypt being 90 percent desert and 10 percent fertile land, red and black. Does this mean then that the king did not hold the red land, 90 percent of his domain, in trusteeship? Or does it mean the "Black Land" refers to the black people of Kemet as Theophile Obenga has convincingly argued?

Nevertheless, and thus, it is easier to speak about the ancient Kemet-Egyptian temple, rather than say what it really is, since it meant many things, as well as having a single or several deities worshipped therein. Importantly, regarding the gods, who are generally grouped as a family, in this regard, the following can be said. While Karnak had the Theban Triad of Amon, his wife Mut and their son Khonsu - the sun, earth and moon gods; there were really 16 members of the Theban Ennead and nearly 22 temples, chapels, etc., where worship was conducted in this complex. At the existing temple of Kom Ombo, there were two deities worshipped, Sobek the Crocodile deity and Haroeris, the Elder Horus. This duality may have existed from the earliest times even though the existing temple is of the Graeco-Roman era. At Abydos, on the other hand there were seven deities worshipped in this mortuary temple of Seti I of the 19th Dynasty. The names of these divinities were Horus, Isis, Osiris, Ra-Horakhty, Amon, Ptah and the deified Seti I. At Abu Simbel there were four gods worshipped there including, Ra-Horakhty, Amon, Ptah and Rameses II; while at Edfu and Dendera respectively, Horus and Hathor were worshipped in each. All this notwithstanding, the gods always had a spouse or counterpart, sometimes an offspring. Khnum, the cataract god, had two wives.

RESEARCH ESSAYS ON ANCIENT EGYPT

Research Essays 30. Temple of Amon-Ra at Karnak. The Processional Colonnade with its open umbel capitals beside the ruins of the Hypostyle Hall. To the right openings are remains of Clerestory windows.

Explaining the construct of this divine family relationship, Mariette-Bey addresses this idea of the Trinity, in the following statement: "Egyptian temples are always dedicated to three gods. It is what Champollion calls the Triad. The first is the male principle, the second is the female principle, and the third is the offspring of the other two. But these three deities are blended into one. The father engenders himself in the womb of the mother and thus at once becomes his own father and his own son. Thereby are expressed the un-createdness and the eternity of the being who has had no beginning and shall have no end."

But then, who were these people who were so religiously conscious and engaged in creating such divinely inspired architecture, these ancient Africans resident in the Nile Valley in Northeast Africa? To answer this question, John Jackson (1970: 153), quotes Gerald Massey, author of *A Book of the Beginnings*, Vol. I, p. 4, who wrote: "Egypt is often called Kam, the black land, and Kam does signify black, the name probably applied to the earliest inhabitants whose type is the Kam or Khem of the Hebrew writers."

Even further, Jackson (1970: 153-54) expressed: "It will be maintained in this book that the oldest mythology, religion, symbols, language had their birthplace in Africa, that the primitive race of Kam came thence, and the civilization in Egypt, emanated from that country and spread over the world. The most reasonable view on the evolutionary theory ... is that the black race is the most ancient, and that Africa is the primordial home." Demonstrating this idea further, Jackson (1970: 154) continued: "The Hebrew Scriptures among their other fragments of ancient lore, are very emphatic in deriving the line of Mizraim from Ham or Kam, the black type coupled with Kush, another form of the black. They give no countenance to the theory of Asiatic origin of Noah, Mizraim is the son of Ham, i.e., of Kam, the black race."

Now, to help further understand the concept behind the temple of the nation of ancient Kemet, Egypt, it has to be viewed within the context of the principle of sculptural decoration. On the walls, pictures are arranged symmetrically side by side. Several series of pictures are disposed in tiers one above the other and cover the walls of chambers from top to bottom. The role of the king is thus key as he "presents an offering (a table laden with victuals, flowers, fruits and emblems) and solicits a favor from the god. In his answer the god grants the gift that is prayed for." Thus, decoration of the temple consists of nothing more than an act of adoration from the king. As such, a temple can be either a primordial hill or the "exclusive personal monument of the king by whom it was founded or decorated." In foundation deposits, founders' emblems, tools, food, and blood from sacrificial animals were deposited to ensure blessings to the temple. Deir el Bahari has provided a remarkable example of this phenomenon.

RESEARCH ESSAYS ON ANCIENT EGYPT

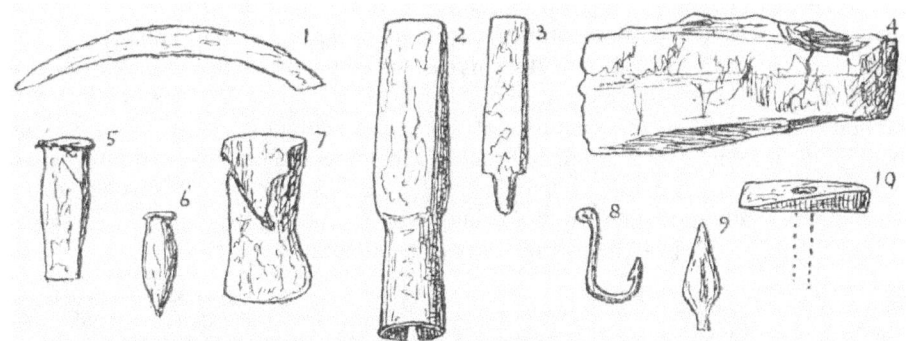

Research Essays Illustration 31. Tools: Blades and hooks.

Anthony Browder (1995: 120) at a later date displays a superimposed figure of Rameses II on the Temple of Luxor; and had this to say of the work of Schwaller de Lubicz who studied that temple with his wife and daughter Lucie. Schwaller de Lubicz "measured, recorded and drew every inch of the temple, including each stone, wall carving and statue." They wrote *Le Temple de l'Homme* (*The Temple in Man*). In this: "Their combined research suggested that the temple was dedicated to the creation of man, and that the floor plan of the temple representative of the anatomical structure of man. Lucie Remy superimposed the skeletal framework of a statue of Rameses II over the floor plan of the temple and discovered some interesting similarities. The open courtyard represents the legs; the hypostyle hall represents the thighs; the peristyle court represents the abdomen and the inner temple represents the head. Within each segment of the temple, activities took place, which related to specific body functions. In the hall the king is generally shown in the pictures on one side and one or more divinities on the other."

"The worship consists of prayers, recited within the temple in the name of the king, and above all, of processions. In these processions which the king is supposed to head, are carried the insignia of the gods, the coffers in which their statues are enclosed, and also the sacred barks which later are generally deposited in the temple, to be brought out on fete days. In the middle concealed under a veil, stand the coffer within which lies the emblem, which no one must see. The processions are commonly held within the temple. They generally ascend the terraces and sometimes spread themselves inside the enclosure away from the prying eyes …. On rare occasions, the processions may be seen leaving the city and winding their way, either along the Nile or along a canal called the Sacred Canal, toward some other city more or less distant. Close to every temple is a lake. In all probability the lake played an important part in the procession and the sacred barks were deposited there, at least while the fete lasted."

FREDERICK MONDERSON

These ancient Africans of Egypt, therefore, were the genesis of their own genius who thought out the fundamental principles of religion, of building, as well as social and ethical practice, and other dynamics of significance for salvation and intellectual and moral development of their people. These 'houses of life,' that crafted the cosmological creation of the particular cult, grew from simple beginnings into huge and complex structures in stone and creative and intellectual manpower. As such then, the temple can be seen as a "royal proscynem, or ex voto that is a token of piety from the king who erected it in order to deserve the favor of the gods. It is a kind of royal oratory and nothing more."

Research Essays 31. Temple of Amon-Ra at Karnak. Twin statues of Amon-Ra and Rameses II just beside the first column at the entrance to the hypostyle hall.

RESEARCH ESSAYS ON ANCIENT EGYPT

Some two hundred years ago, following the American and French Revolutions, Napoleon invaded Egypt in "carrying the war to the British." In the aftermath, the Rosetta Stone was discovered and this led, by 1822, to the decipherment of the ancient language by the Frenchman Jean Jacques Champollion, the Younger. His work led to the birth of Egyptology and increased interest in the ancient culture. Within decades, in furthering that development the discipline of archaeology significantly and systematically began the excavation and restoration of much of the ancient culture that also rescued existing temples and broadened our knowledge of their forms and functions. Today, these excavated and restored edifices teach us much about the culture, builders, function, rituals, art and practical as well as the social and economic dynamics that prevailed therein.

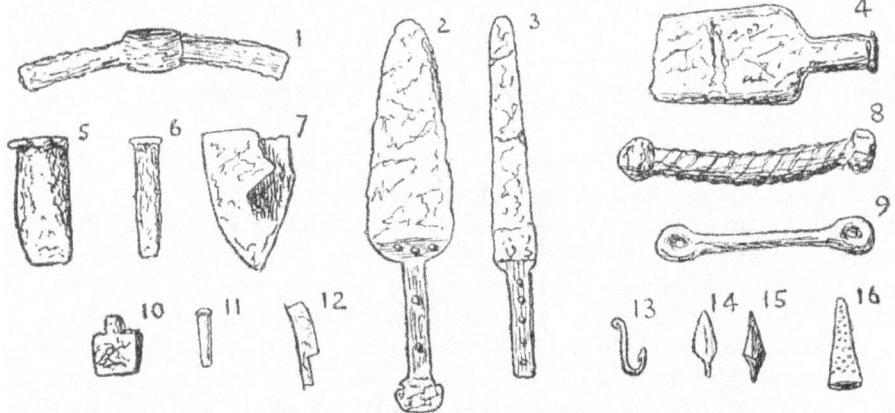

Research Essays Illustration 32. Tools: Rope, chisels, cutting tools, hook, etc.

As such, we now know the climate and geography was instrumental in dictating the types and nature of Egyptian temples. The landscape of Egypt is one of lines, vertical, horizontal or diagonal and thus columns and buildings within temple complexes were vertical or horizontal, roofs were horizontal and pylons were sloping. Much of the lines, terraced elevation and colonnades are manifest in three of the important temples of Deir el Bahari: that of Hatshepsut, Thutmose III and Mentuhotep II. This is so also for Seti I's at Abydos, and the Ramesseum, mortuary temple of Rameses II.

There was little rain in Egypt and hence the sky remained clear and blue and this had something to do with the nature of its architecture. M.A. Murray's *Egyptian Temples,* London: Sampson Low, Marston and Co., Ltd., (1931: 1) explained how the climate impacted upon the psyche and nature of building and other factors of the society. "It is a country" she says, "of violent contrasts; the flat plain and vertical cliffs, the fertile fields and the dreary waste of desert, the brilliant sunshine and the dark shadows, the river which harbored edible fish and murderous crocodile; all these naturally had their effect on the mind of the Egyptian architect and showed themselves in the architecture." The genius of the Egyptian architects is therefore elaborated in works at not only Deir el Bahari, but also, the Ramesseum, naturally Karnak and Luxor, but also at Abu Simbel, Abydos, Medinet Habu and Philae, where the most picturesque structures were built.

Finally, we now know the temple consisted of four parts such as an outer court, an inner court, a vestibule and a shrine or sanctuary. In time however, the temple took on extra dimensions that were a result of the efforts of ruling families who vied with each other to please their god. This extra dimension and literal inundation of its walls is especially true of the Graeco-Roman temples with their structural and artistic innovations.

II. Pre-dynastic Temples

As the Egyptians became religiously conscious at an early time, they equally built temples to worship their deities. These earliest god temples were made of perishable material and are only known from illustrations. Regarding these early temples dedicated to a deity, Murray (1931: 2) tells: "Of temples dedicated to a god none are in existence from the early periods, although the foundations of several are known; e.g., at Abydos there was a temple of Osiris in the Ist dynasty, at Hierakonpolis the temple of the sacred falcon was probably as early, at Bubastis the temple of the cat-goddess is not later than the IVth dynasty, and the shrine of the crocodile-god in the Fayum had very primitive characters." Nevertheless, from these early beginnings they initiated ritual and worship practice that would continue for much of dynastic rule.

III. Old Kingdom Temples

Besides the remaining worship temples Petrie found at Abydos, early temples dedicated to kings can be traced to the Old Kingdom, and are considered a part of the burial apparatus. Naturally, these two types of early temples were different in many respects. Murray's description states: "As the primitive king or chief always had a better house than the common people, so the god who was superior to the king had a better house than the king; the original temple was then merely a finer hut than those used by human beings."

RESEARCH ESSAYS ON ANCIENT EGYPT

Research Essays 32. Temple of Amon-Ra at Karnak. Decorated columns of the Hypostyle Hall with their open umbel capitals and ruins of windows of the Clerestory that let light into the hall.

The earliest temples are those attached to pyramids and other royal burial places, and were intended for the worship of the dead king. Petrie's description of these early structures is as follows: "At first the place of offerings was closely connected with the tomb, as shown by the large steles found at the tombs of the Ist dynasty; and such continue to be the case for the ordinary Egyptian in all times. But the place of offering to the kings was changed at the end of the IIIrd Dynasty. ..."

FREDERICK MONDERSON

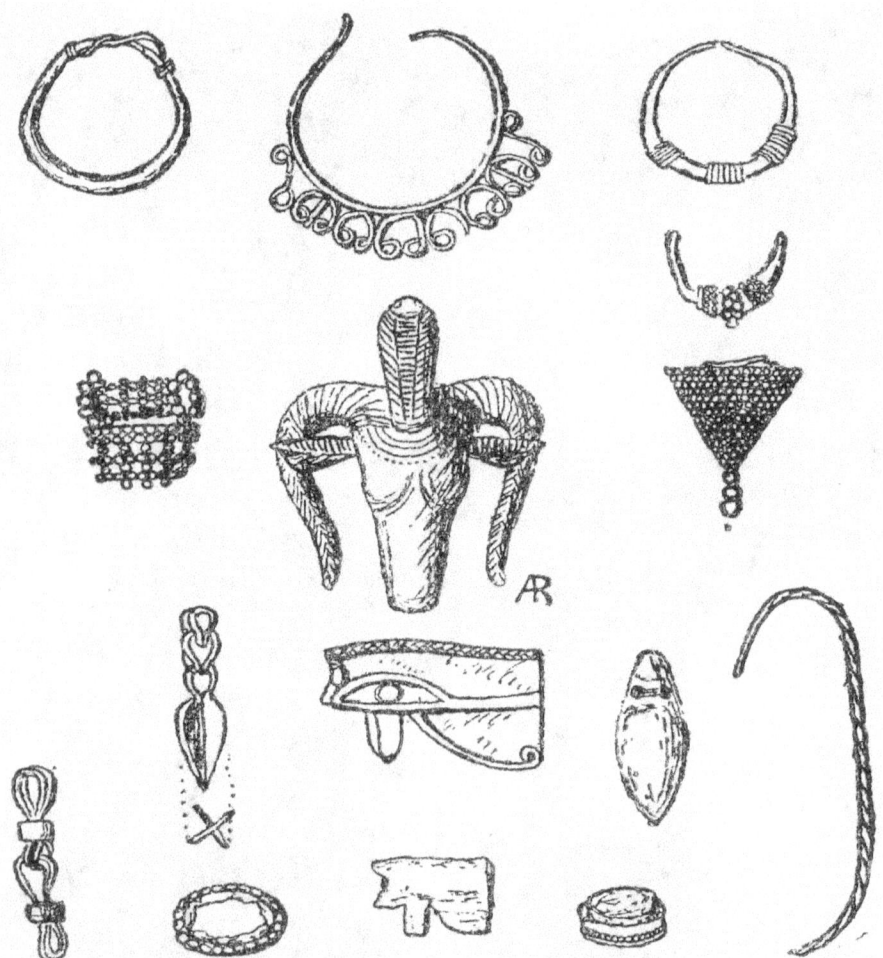

Research Essays Illustration 33. Jewelry, rings, Eye of Horus, etc.

Deiter Arnold in *The Encyclopedia of Ancient Egyptian Temples*, Cairo: The American University in Cairo Press (1993: 242) points out, regarding these early temples: "Despite a lack of finds, it has recently been suggested that monumental temples built of brick began to exist as early as the time of the Unification. Evidence available to date is as follows:

"a)   Late Pre-historic sanctuary of Min of Koptos, with colossal statues of Min (now in Oxford).

RESEARCH ESSAYS ON ANCIENT EGYPT

b) Early Dynastic sanctuary of Satet at Elephantine, built over in the Old Kingdom.
c) Early Dynastic sanctuary of Khentiyimentyu at Abydos, replaced by a brick temple of the Old Kingdom.
d) Primeval mound at Hierakonpolis between the Late Pre-dynastic period and $2^{nd}/3^{rd}$ Dynasty, with decorated granite blocks of Khasekhemwy (now in the Egyptian Museum Cairo). Above it a multiple shrine of brick (Old or Middle Kingdom).
e) Limestone fragments of a shrine of the 2nd or 3rd Dynasty from Gebelin (now in Turin).
f). Limestone fragments of a shrine of Djoser from Heliopolis (now in Turin).
g) The almost completely preserved temple of Harmakhis at Giza (un-inscribed). Other stone temples from the 4th Dynasty onwards are attested by individual finds."

Another point regarding a) Late Pre-historic sanctuary of Min of Koptos, with colossal statues of Min (now in Oxford) does not refer to the color of these statues being black. This is clearly omitted. Anyone reading this has no knowledge of it. However, as Petrie mentions this as an afterthought in his *Religious Life in Ancient Egypt* (1924) it will "disappear" from the record and this is equally why some writers say modern research and writing on Egypt is very much sanitized. We should remember Dr. ben-Jochannan's admonition to young scholars, in which he said: "Get the earliest information and work from there."

The Step-Pyramid had a surviving temple as indicated by Steindorff and Seele in *When Egypt Ruled the East* (1942) (1957: 14) wherein they wrote: "In this new Sakkara necropolis, King Djoser, who opened the Third Dynasty, caused his gifted architect, Imhotep, to erect for him the first royal funeral monument built exclusively of stone. Its central feature is a vast terraced pyramid, which conceals the actual burial vault of the king. The sacred precinct contained in addition to the 'step pyramid' a gigantic mortuary temple with a chamber for the royal statue, tombs for several princesses, an immense festival temple and festival hall adorned with columns of unique design, and many other structures. Though carried out in small-stone masonry, numerous delicate details of design betray that the entire structure was imitated from wooden prototypes."

FREDERICK MONDERSON

IV. Middle Kingdom Temples

Not much has survived of Middle Kingdom temples and those that are identified can only be done so from their faint outlines on the ground. In this respect, Deiter Arnold (1993: 242) says further: "From the Middle Kingdom onwards, coinciding with the reduction in the divine standing of the king and the growing importance of the gods themselves, the gods' primitive shrines were replaced by stone structures (multiple shrines). The growing independence of cult structures led to the development of particular features: separation of sacred and secular architecture, together with a reduction of the temples as a house; axial construction; emphasis on gateways; the sanctuary (naos) often enlarged into a multiple shrine."

However, Edouard Naville and H. Hall discovered the "Temple of Mentuhotep II" of the 11th Dynasty at Deir el Bahari in 1904 and conducted its excavation. It's been described as the oldest surviving at Thebes and the most complete of all Middle Kingdom temples. Hatshepsut's temple was modeled on this structure, transitional from the Old to the New Kingdom, during whose time it was still viable since her temple, instead of being in the center of the cirque is juxtaposed to Mentuhotep's and occupies more of the northern sector of the Deir el Bahari amphitheater. It is a wonderful structure and was richly decorated with a style that was very beautiful, changing beliefs about the art of that period generally thought to be very archaic. This temple of Mentuhotep nevertheless incorporated a pyramid, ramps and colonnades of a hypostyle hall, sanctuary and also tombs of princesses and priestesses. Naturally, it's thought the king was buried there. However, his body has not been found and his tomb has not been positively identified.

V. New Kingdom Temples

With the expulsion of the Hyksos and triumph of Amon, Amon-Ra, at the formation of the New Kingdom, temple building took on a new meaning, becoming more elaborate, complete, picturesque, and built of more varied and durable stone. Here we also see the expansion of temple forms such as the mortuary, processional, and continuation of the valley, sun and rock hewn from earlier periods, as well as barque stations, birth houses, roof temples or chapels, etc. However, of particular significance were the national temples at Thebes. First, we have the temple of Luxor, built by Amenhotep III, and whose principal function was the celebration of the Opet Festival. Later, but more compact and picturesque, it served more esoteric purposes as a university and grand lodge. Next, begun in the Middle Kingdom, Karnak Temple, a principal god or worship

RESEARCH ESSAYS ON ANCIENT EGYPT

temple, experienced its greatest development in the New Kingdom, though in its present form it took 2000 years to complete. Over this expansive period all the elements and dynamics of an Egyptian temple came into play. The following are some features of the Egyptian temple such as found at Karnak, at Thebes, in Upper Egypt.

Now, since the temple was built by the riverside, the King would encounter the following when visiting and disembarking from his sailing craft:

1. Quay for greeting, ceremony and ritual.
2. Canal.
3. Avenue of Sphinxes.
4. Obelisk and statues in front of the entrance as well as obelisks within the structure.
5. Pylon – wall enclosure. This is a gate. The number of entrances varies. Karnak had 4, Luxor 2, Edfu 1 and so on. The temple was also a refuge so that when the doors closed, it was difficult to get in. The idea was to protect the god and then the people inside its walls. On the Pylon were flagstaves that flew flags of the state, nome and principal and subsidiary gods worshipped within.

6. Courts – sometimes a Great Court. Within which you may find:

    a. Altar
    b. Sphinx
    c. Seated and standing statues, kiosks or shrines. Then:
    d. Doors and door posts
    e. Jubilee *Sed Heb* Festival Court and Pavilion
    f. Chapels
    g. Columns or pillars
    h. Portico to another Pylon
    i. Hypostyle Hall
    j. Sometimes second or even third Hypostyle Halls
    k. Adjacent rooms for:
        i. Clothing
        ii. Gold
        iii. Vessels
        iv. Liquid and solid offerings
        v. Library with books of the temple ritual and practice. They provided accumulated knowledge of the temple's role as university that trained students for priestly and bureaucratic work. They also served as training schools

and repositories of competing schools of art and building practice.
l. Subsidiary gods represented in the illustration and in small temples on site.
m. Third Hypostyle Hall
n. The Sanctuary where the God lives
o. Outside a Sacred Lake
p. Quarters for priests, priestesses, stewards, scribes and singing women
q. Schools for art and learning – calendars – measurement
r. Work shops producing cotton, dyes, statuary, and woodwork
s. Pottery, painting, basketry, matting, jewelry of gold and other precious stones, etc. were processed for trade
t. Gardens for pleasure, flowers for the daily temple ritual
u. Nilometer
v. Trees
w. Chapels to other Gods
x. Decorations: Walls – Inside, outside and some ceilings, columns, pylon and enclosure wall in and outside.
y. The Sanctuary and rooms adjacent to the Sanctuary.
z. Kitchens and refractory,

7. In addition there were:

a. Wine Cellars
b. Granaries, store-houses
c. Treasury
d. Altar in the sanctuary or outdoors in the court.
e. There could be a number of halls and minor courts leading to the Sanctuary. There is generally an area or court behind the Sanctuary.
f. Calendar system for festivals, astronomy and Nile Watch to study the river's behavior.
g. Some temples had roof chapels where the god would be taken to celebrate some festival having to do with the sun.

RESEARCH ESSAYS ON ANCIENT EGYPT

Research Essays 33. Temple of Amon-Ra at Karnak. Evidence of repairs to columns of the Hypostyle Hall with their closed bud capitals, abacus and overhead architrave, all decorated.

FREDERICK MONDERSON

In addition, there may be residences for overseers, bakers and bakeries, and also craftsmen who created boulevards, floors, pavements, gates, stelae and untold inscriptions and decorations. Naturally there were feasts and festival celebrated therein. Equally, there were barque stations for the ark of the deity, offering and oblation tables and furniture. Temples possessed ships, harbors, tributary territories, towns, magazines, slaves, cattle, geese, poultry, horses, vineyards, gardens, cultus utensils, as well as guards, archers, and even much more. The temple thus pervaded every aspect of daily life of the ancient Egyptian African.

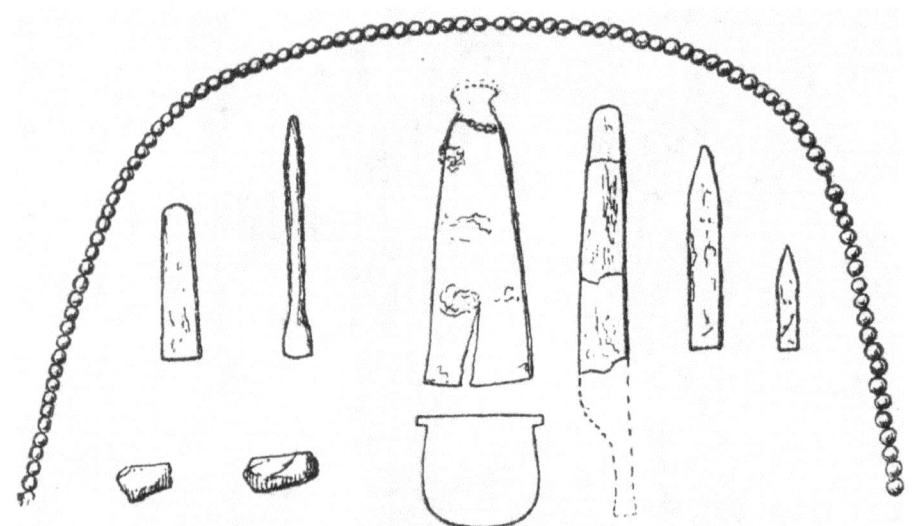

Research Essays Illustration 34. Tools: Chisels, pot, etc.

The Mortuary Temples at Thebes were temples dedicated to the dead king who, upon reaching that state, became a god in his own right. Therefore, by building his temple he was worshipped and remembered. Importantly, Amon left Karnak and crossed the Nile to celebrate the 'Feast of the Valley,' where his priests took the God to visit the mortuary temples or - 'Mansions of Millions of Years,' of these deified kings. Unfortunately, many of these, for the major kings of the New Kingdom, were dismantled after their death to be used as building stones by later builders. However, Medinet Habu, built for Rameses III, is considered the "last major building project of the New Kingdom," and as such, no major emperor came after him to dismantle his temple.

RESEARCH ESSAYS ON ANCIENT EGYPT

The Processional Temples as the "White Chapel," "Red Chapel," and several others, as well as kiosks whether at Karnak, Luxor, etc., were resting places for the god while on the move. These and so much more were all part of the temple retinue. It has been argued, Hatshepsut's "Red Chapel" was in fact, the Sanctuary at Karnak that was dismantled by Thuthmose III who replaced this "Holy of Holies" with his own, subsequently repaired by Alexander's brother, Phillip Arrhidaeus.

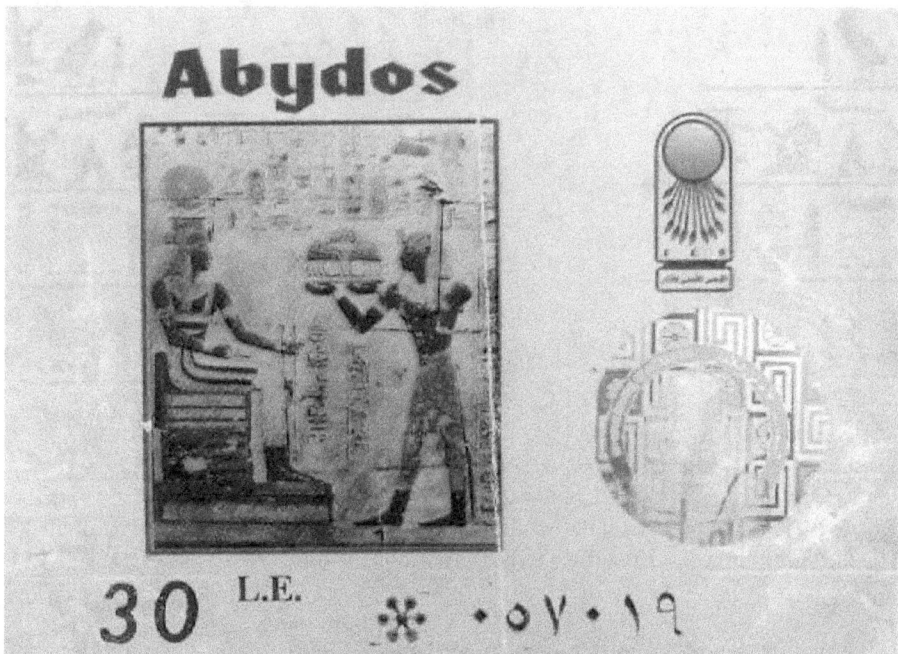

Research Essays Temple Ticket 12. Abydos Temple. Price of entrance is thirty Egyptian Pounds.

FREDERICK MONDERSON

Research Essays 34. Temple of Amon-Ra at Karnak. View of the two obelisks, Hatshepsut's left and that of her father, Thutmose I, right.

Nevertheless, temples appear to have been oriented by the river; the main direction of the stream is to the north, but it naturally varies somewhat and runs occasionally east or west of north. The temples, therefore, also vary in their orientation. The rule, however, is that the temples lie parallel or at right angles to the river, e.g., Luxor and Karnak. This does not discount the axial orientation of the temple along the east/west path of the sun.

In the temples of Thebes, which are almost entirely of the New Kingdom, the lighting of the hypostyle halls was by means of a clerestory. Columns supported

RESEARCH ESSAYS ON ANCIENT EGYPT

the nave of the hall. The temples were richly decorated on the inside and outside. On the outside the wars and struggles of the kings were depicted and on the inside the worship and ritual of the temples were illustrated. Equally too, at Karnak the sanctuary, oriented on the east/west axis, allowed the sun to shine forward on its altar during the morning rising and backwards during the evening setting. Of course the temples at Luxor, Deir el Bahari, the mortuary temples and Abu Simbel had enclosed sanctuaries.

VI. Graeco-Roman Temples

Temples of this period were built by Nubian and Egyptian builders, working to Egyptian specifications dating to the earliest times and were supervised by Greek and Roman overlords. Edfu, Kom Ombo, Esneh, Philae, Kalabsha, etc., were all built with new features over old foundations, decorations and began to be inundated with illustrations depicting the ritual. Barbara Watterson in *The Egyptians* (1997: 223-224) explained: "By the Ptolemaic Period, a more complex, cosmological interpretation of the temple had been developed. As the home of a god, it represented the sky, the rooms on its eastern side equated with the eastern half of the heavens, and those on its western side with the western sky. It was regarded as a cosmic theater in which were enacted the great events pertaining to Egypt and its safety. The temple was also regarded as a representation of the physical world, symbolizing Egypt. The rites carried out therein by the king were designed to maintain the balance between Egypt and the forces of Chaos, an ever-present threat. In the Late and Graeco-Roman Periods, the king was identified with the child of the deity of the temple. Special structures, developed from the sanctuaries which were in earlier periods devoted to the theogamy ritual were built within the temple precinct. The Ptolemaic structures were known as *mammisi*, and in them the birth of the divine child was celebrated annually."

FREDERICK MONDERSON

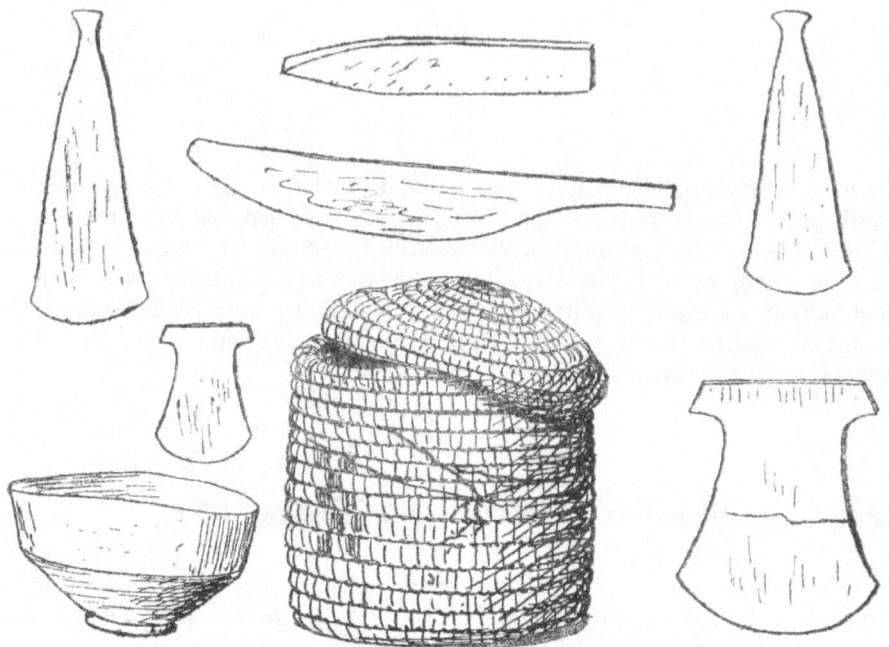

Research Essays Illustration 35. Tools: Basket, axe blades, cutter and chisel.

Even further, Watterson (1997: 224) continued: "The exterior of a temple was concerned with its protection and, by extension, the protection of Egypt, its pylons decorated with reliefs that showed the king smiting Egypt's enemies. Exterior walls were carved with reliefs of battles – usually purposefully orientated in the southern walls contain reliefs depicting Nubian enemies, western walls Libyan enemies and northern walls Asiatic foes. On the exterior walls of many temples are lion-headed gargoyles and round water-spouts intended to remove water, either rain or the water used in rituals, from the roof. They are inscribed with magic formulas, which state that, in spitting out this water, the lions are symbolically spitting out evil away from Egypt – a good example of the Egyptian talent for imbuing something that has practical purpose with magical significance." These temples had enclosed sanctuaries. Fortunately, these two structures have helped preserve much of the cultural and religious history to survive, giving evidence of the much earlier worship and practice. These temples preserved more of the cultural and religious history than all other earlier temples, which were scantily illustrated.

RESEARCH ESSAYS ON ANCIENT EGYPT

Research Essays 35. Temple of Amon-Ra at Karnak. Defaced statue of Queen Hatshepsut just before the Sanctuary.

E.A.E. Raymond's *The Mythological Origin of the Egyptian Temple* tells of the Edfu Documents on the History of the Egyptian Temple. Accordingly, on the walls of Egyptian temples of the Graeco-Roman period are inscribed "numerous ritual texts, among which occurs a series of texts that is found only in a very abbreviated form in certain of the Pharaonic temples." These sources are copies of much earlier material that go back to the earliest conception of the temple. "Those texts make it possible to reconstruct a reasonably complete history of the building of each temple concerned, a picture of the lay-out of the rooms and halls, and their ritual purpose and significance." Here we find the Myth about the Domains and the Temple of the Falcon. This "myth is the contents of the first and second cosmogonical record and of a part of the fifth record which seems to have been originally included in the Sacred Book of the Early Primeval Age of Gods." The Edfu myth is the "unique source that discloses the Egyptian tradition concerning the origin of the sacred domains of the Falcon and the creation of his first temple." Another chapter of *The Mythical Origin of the Egyptian Temple* deals with the Myth about the Origin of the Temple of the Sun God.

"The 3rd, 4th and 5th Edfu cosmogonical records preserve a part of the myth described as the Coming of Re to his Mansion of *Ms-nht*. This myth concerns another period of the mythical age when the lands of the sacred domains were already in existence, and when the primeval houses of the gods were found in places other than the original domain of the Falcon."

These temples had Nilometers, gardens, and ancillary rooms where other gods were worshipped; vestments, materials and texts of the ritual were stored; as well as underground crypts where temple valuables were held.

Smaller and more prolific in decoration, these late period temples added the mammisi, or birth house, where the god was born. The decorations took on a different format as well during this new age in Egypt.

The Egyptian Temple, therefore, represented the philosophical, esoteric, cosmological and theogonic metaphysics of the cultural history of the Nile Valley experience. In that evolution the temple played a vital role in the development of science, building, trade, medicine, art, crafts, mathematics, mummification, astronomy, astrology and a whole lot more. The temple was the center of the intellectual lifeblood of the society and as such, it carried forth the growth and development of the culture with its insistence on religiosity and right behavior based on the philosophical and social axiom of Ma'at, viz., balance, order, goodness, truth, straightforwardness and respect and good judgment. This is what the mind of ancient man in Egypt, Africa, bequeathed to the historical consciousness of humanity.

RESEARCH ESSAYS ON ANCIENT EGYPT

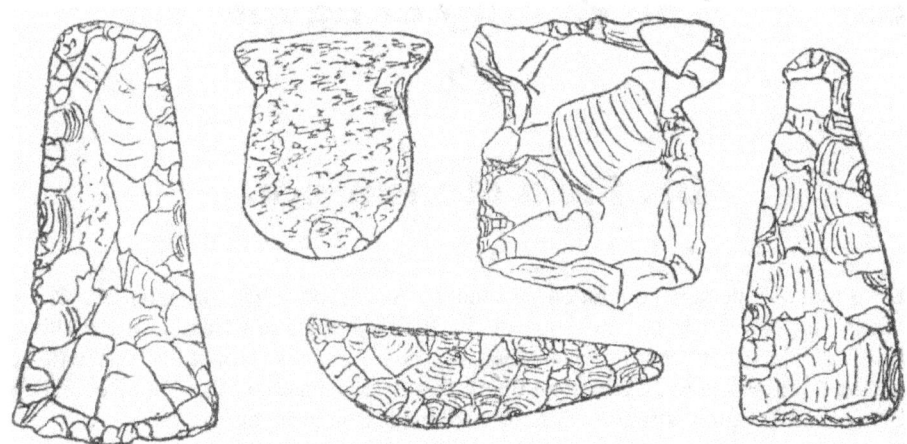

Research Essays Illustration 36. Tools: Stone axes.

References

Arnold, Deiter. *The Encyclopedia of Ancient Egyptian Architecture.* Cairo: The American University in Cairo Press, (1967) 1993.
Erman, Adolf. *Handbook of Egyptian Religion.* London: Constable, 1907.
Shafer, Byron E. (Editor) *The Temples of Ancient Egypt.* London: I.B. Tauris Publisher, (1997) 1998.
Mann, A.M. *Sacred Architecture.* Rockport, Massachusetts: Element, 1993.
Sauernon, Serge. "Temples" in Georges Posener's *A Dictionary of Egyptian Civilization.* London: Methuen and Co., Ltd., (1959) 1962.
Watterson, Barbara. *Gods of Ancient Egypt.* Gloucestershire: Sutton, (1984) 1996.

FREDERICK MONDERSON

8. The History of Egypt
By

Dr. Fred Monderson

Dr. Fred Monderson concluded his lecture series on *Egyptian Civilization* on Wednesday May 12, 19, 26, 2004 at St. John's Recreation Center in Brooklyn, Prospect Place between Troy and Schenectady Avenues. Hopefully this will be repeated in the fall and a powerful thank you goes out to the St. John's Recreation Center and its administration who allowed this lesson to be taught.

Research Essays Illustration 37. Tools: Float and brick-making mold.

The History of Egypt, like so many other histories, is constantly being analyzed, re-evaluated with new propositions and positions established. What is significant, however, the true and definitive history of Egypt has not yet been written! This may be for a number or reasons, primarily because not sufficient information has been found. Strange! New discoveries are still being made. Much of the discoveries of the last 150 years have not been fully and accurately analyzed. The 19th and early 20th Century rush to postulate and publish has led to much mis-diagnosis. The old Adage, "Hurried birds make crooked nests," has resulted in

RESEARCH ESSAYS ON ANCIENT EGYPT

many distortions and many omissions upon which a great deal of the modern interpretation is based. As such, we must constantly re-evaluate what we know. Many of the modern books are very much sanitized, gloss over and do not, among other things, address the blackness of Egypt, which was a fundamental ethnological part of its experience! While black scholars attempt to set the record straight, an increasing number of white scholars attack them with vituperativeness inclandestine that border on malice and vindictiveness. The strategy has been to deny any and all evidence for a black, Negro, African Egypt while affirming no or scant evidence for a South West Asian, Caucasian Egypt. However, when evidence of Black Egyptians are referenced, Hatshepsut for example, the argument generally states "No one knows her color." Yet, when images are presented they are generally of a European or Caucasian example. That is, denying Egypt's blackness yet, affirming her Caucasian ethnicity.

Nonetheless, the admonition of Dr. ben-Jochannan that we "get the oldest materials and work from there," establishes a critical and constructive point of departure for what is at stake and what needs to be done. Bunsen's *Egypt's Place in Universal History* makes known Aahmes-Nefertari was Ethiopian. Hatshepsut has been linked to her progeny, yet critics seek to deny her blackness! This is the indefensible conundrum facing persons who argue for a Caucasian Egypt.

We must not forget Dr. Cheikh Anta Diop, a black Senegalese Egyptologist, recognized by UNESCO as premier in his field, said of African scholars: "We must connect Egypt to Africa much as the west connects with Greece and Rome." Even further he insisted: "The African historian who refuses to include Egypt in African history is either neurotic or an educated fool." We should not forget before the true value of Egypt was realized, Greece and Rome were the foundations of European and Western cultural history. Since Egypt's value has been realized, it has been coveted both in acquisition of artifacts and prognostication of origination and denial of actuality in what Prof. John H. Clarke has expressed is the use of "no logic."

FREDERICK MONDERSON

Research Essays 36. Kashida Maloney of Brooklyn, New York, stands before a broken and repaired statue just outside Luxor Temple.

It should also be pointed out, UNESCO sponsored a symposium in 1974, invited scholars from all over, and determined that Dr. Diop and his associate, Dr. Theophile Obenga were the most prepared of all in attendance, and equally, this institution "Affirmed the fundamental blackness of ancient Egypt."

RESEARCH ESSAYS ON ANCIENT EGYPT

Now, having said all of that, I can say no one knows for sure when the history of Egypt actually began. However, the framework within which the history is recounted uses either the "short" or the "long chronology." The "Short Chronology," some say for convenience sake, begins the First Dynasty at about 3100 or 3050 B.C. The "Long Chronology," on the other hand, begins the First Dynasty at c. 5700 B.C., or thereabouts. Therefore, it is within these time frames one must begin to consider the History of Egypt. Let me say the "Short Chronology" is somewhat more convenient, even though it's been argued such a short list was designed to be more contemporary with Mesopotamian civilization where the history of the west begins. The "Long Chronology" on the other hand, makes Egypt outdistance the other cultures that are purported to have had a significant influence on the Nile Valley experience. This is despite what Dr. Chancellor Williams wrote in the prescript to his book *Destruction of Black Civilization*: *Great Issues of a Race* "What happened to the people of Sumer [originators of Sumerian and Mesopotamian civilization] I hear they were black?" the traveler said to the old man. The old man replied: "They lost their history and were forgotten."

Before we begin, the sources for a history of Egypt need to be discussed so as to arrive at an understanding of these events so long ago.

Archaeology has helped to fill the gaps where records and monuments fall short. Radiocarbon and thermoluminesence dating have also aided the science.

A number of sources have provided the basis of Egyptian chronology. These include slate palettes, maceheads, stela or what we call headstones, and even labels attached to jars found in tombs of the earliest buried kings. The more famous of these early documents is the *Narmer Palette* showing the unification of the northern and southern kingdoms. Much of later pharaonic paraphernalia are evident on this palette, viz., red and white crowns, pharaoh's beard, his tunic, a sandal and sandal bearer, the serekh or palace facade, the Horus hawk, the goddess Hathor, boats, standards, a bull, etc. Then there is the *Bull Palette* showing the king as a bull battering the walls of an enemy. There is also a *Libyan Palette*. The *Narmer Macehead* is the next famous "document" showing the king under a canopy wearing the red crown, his queen nearby and numbers showing captives, men and animals.

FREDERICK MONDERSON

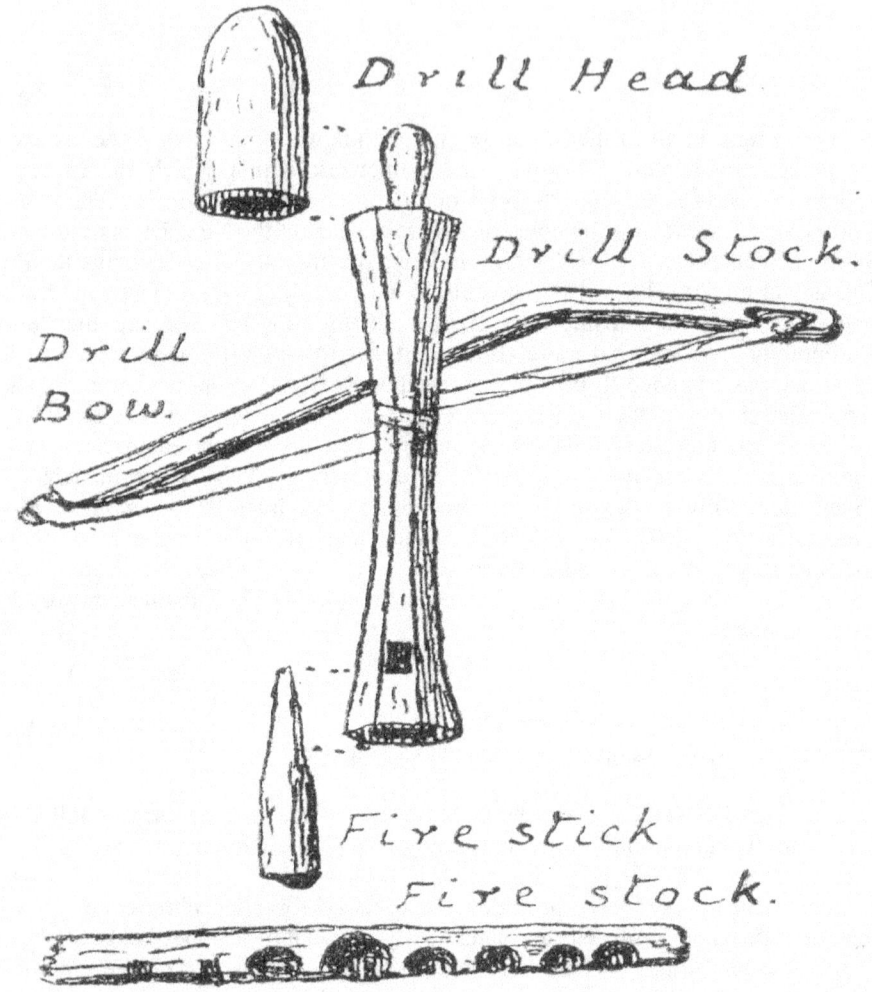

Research Essays Illustration 38. Tools: Drill head, drill bow, drill stock and fire stick and fire stock.

The *Palermo Stone* is the first substantial written document. A slab of black basalt stone, it lists the names of rulers dating from the Old Kingdom back into the Prehistoric Period when the gods ruled Egypt. Ian Shaw in *The Oxford History of Ancient Egypt* reported: "The types of event that are recorded on the Palermo Stone are cult ceremonies, taxation, sculpture, building and warfare – that is precisely the type of phenomena that are recorded on the proto-dynastic ivory and ebony labels from Abydos, Saqqara, and various other early historical sites."

RESEARCH ESSAYS ON ANCIENT EGYPT

Research Essays 37. Temple of Amon-Ra at Karnak. "Girdle Wall" of Rameses II. Goddess Mut, left; Rameses in Blue or War Crown offers a plant to Amon-Ra, center; Rameses offers two bouquets to a defaced deity.

There are King Lists of much later periods. The *Sakkara List* is Old Kingdom; the *Karnak List* is from the 18th Dynasty; and the *Abydos Lists,* of which there are two, one *in situ* at the Temple of Seti I and the other from the Temple of Rameses II also at Abydos, now residing in the British Museum, are of the 19th Dynasty. Stela are the equivalent of tombstones with a biography of the owner that supplies dates and events in the person's life. Tombs, particularly the Mastabas of the Nobles, dating to the Old Kingdom, are inundated with illustrations showing scenes from daily life.

FREDERICK MONDERSON

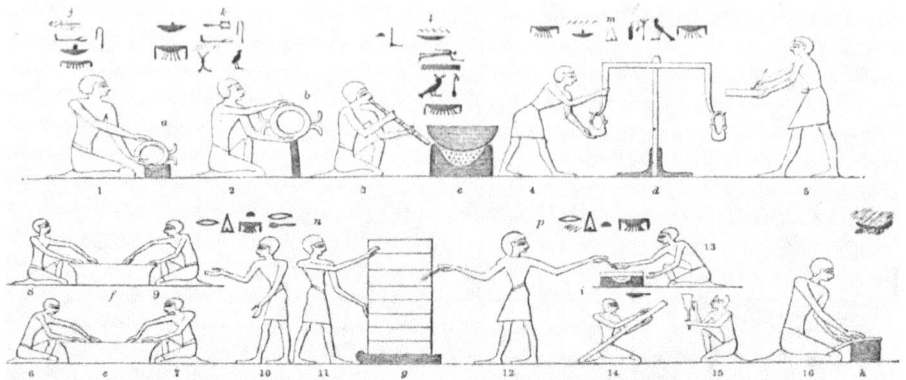

Research Essays Illustration 39. Goldsmiths making jewelry, smelting and weighing gold, superintending and clerks at work. Beni-Hassan.

The Chronology of Ancient Egypt, Etc.

1.	Pre-dynastic	(ben-Jochannan)	6000-3200 B.C.
2.	Archaic	""	3200-2780 B.C.
		Dynasties 1 and 2	
3.	Old Kingdom		2780-2270 B.C.
		Dynasties 3-6	
4.	First Intermediate Period		2270-2100 B.C.
		Dynasties 7-10	
5.	The Middle Kingdom		2100-1675 B.C.
		Dynasties 11-13	
6.	Second Intermediate Period		1675-1600 B.C.
		Dynasties 14-17	
7.	New Kingdom		1600-1090 B.C.
		Dynasties 18-20	
8.	Late Period		1090-527 B.C.
		Dynasties 21-26	
9.	Graeco-Roman Era		332-640 B.C. - A.D
10.	The Religion of Egypt		
11.	The Principal Gods		
	Ra at Heliopolis		
	Ptah at Memphis		
	Osiris at Abydos		
	Amon at Thebes		
12.	Their belief Systems		

RESEARCH ESSAYS ON ANCIENT EGYPT

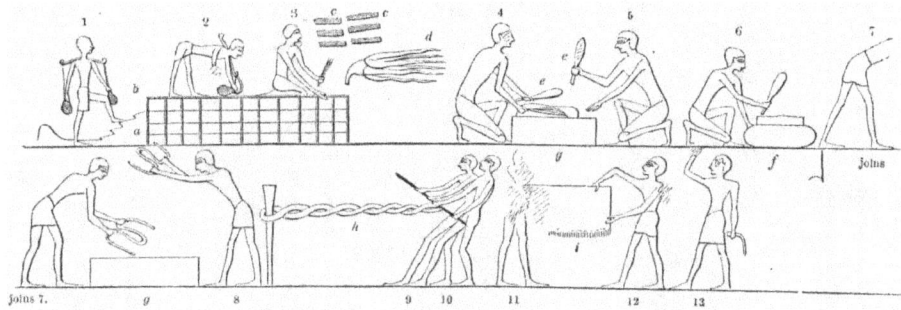

Research Essays Illustration 40. Preparing the flax, beating it, and making it into twine and cloth. Beni-Hassan.

POEM TO AMON-RA

O mighty Amon, the Greatest of the Black African deities, ithyphallic, you were from primeval times, Lord of Gods.
Your creativity radiated over an age, father of the gods, when worshippers praised your hidden nature.
Conquering peoples and places, they brought light and civility to the world, in your immortal name, multitudinous, more numerous, not known. The vanquished contributed wealth filling your treasury and your subjects, victorious in their imperial exploits, erected mansions in glory and praise of your being, Chief of the Great Ennead of the Gods, Self-Begotten, Lord of Heaven, Lord of Earth.
O Dweller in Anu, the Gods ascribe praise to you, maker of things celestial and things terrestrial, for you illuminate Egypt, President of the Apts.

FREDERICK MONDERSON

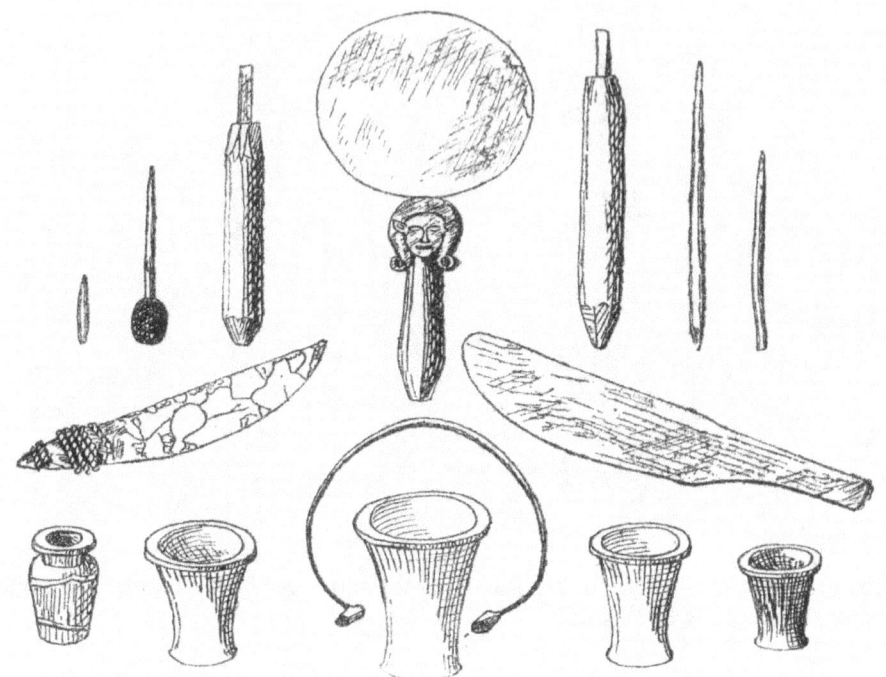

Research Essays Illustration 41. Tools: Mirror, vases, borers, etc.

Beautiful child of Love, from relative obscurity you emerged in the Middle Kingdom and sat on your Sacred Mound of Creation.
That first time, seeking to complete the task of previous gods fallen short, you Created Brilliant Rays, Thunder in Heaven.
Black African rulers of that age imbibed in your inspiration, Lord of the Two Lands.
Mighty in Power, Lord of Awe-inspiring terror, they similarly manifested resolute courage, wisdom, intellect, and creative prowess.
They gained success as Warrior Pharaohs, with mighty souls, all in your name, Fashioner of the Beauty of Kings, Priests and Artisans, O Lord of the Throne of Egypt.
All the Gods are three, Amen, Ra and Ptah and none like thee. Amen is his hidden name; Ra is his face, Ptah his body.

Power made by Ptah, Bull of Heliopolis, kings' architects shaped a society whose blueprint you encouraged in manifold attributes.

RESEARCH ESSAYS ON ANCIENT EGYPT

Research Essays 38. Temple of Amon-Ra at Karnak. "Girdle Wall" of Rameses II. The King offers a plant and two obelisks to Amon-Ra.

Lord of Scepter and Ankh, Frog, Uraeus and Couchant Lion, your symbols include Beautiful Tiaras, Lofty Plumes, and *Ureret, War, Nemes* and *Atef* Crowns.
The prosperity you endowed your adherents generated artistic, scientific and linguistic creations, Lord of the Apts.
These first beneficiaries of your generosity toward mankind, erected temples as chapels simply to glorify your great name, Amon Lord of Thebes, Lord of the Two Lands, Lord of Might, Lord of Food, Bull of Offerings, Kamutef at the head of his Fields.

FREDERICK MONDERSON

Lord of Victuals, Bull of Provisions, the gods beg their sustenance from you, Lord of Fields, banks and plots of ground.

Lord of Truth, Father of the Gods, Maker of Men, Creator of all animals, Black African kings, men of vision, fortitude and tenacity, benefited from an earlier age of African creativity. They synthesized, experimented and with vision and bellicosity bequeathed a creative era where craftsmen, philosophers, priests and kings, were motivated to extol your name to greater heights.
Lord of Radiant Light, you Exist into Eternity as Lord of Heaven, Lord of Earth, Lord of the Gods, Lord of the High Lands and Mountains, Lord of the Joy of Heart, Mighty One of Crowns.
Your Loveliness is in the Southern Sky and Your Graciousness is in the Northern Sky.
Your name is strong, your will is heavy.
Mountains of ore cannot withstand your might, for you set in order the kingdom of eternity unto eternity.

Lord of eternity, creator of everlastingness, you arise in the eastern horizon and set in the western horizon. Born early every day, you overthrew your enemies, steering oar, pilot who knows the water, Lord of the ship of the morning and ship of the evening, master of two stems. Beautiful form fashioned by Ptah, Ox with strong arm who loves strength; you are first in Upper Egypt, Lord of the Land of the Matoi and Prince of Punt.
Lord of Perception who speaks with authority, Lord of the Gods whose shrine is hidden, you are Lord of the Double Crown, Great Hawk who makes festive the body, fair body that makes festive the breast.

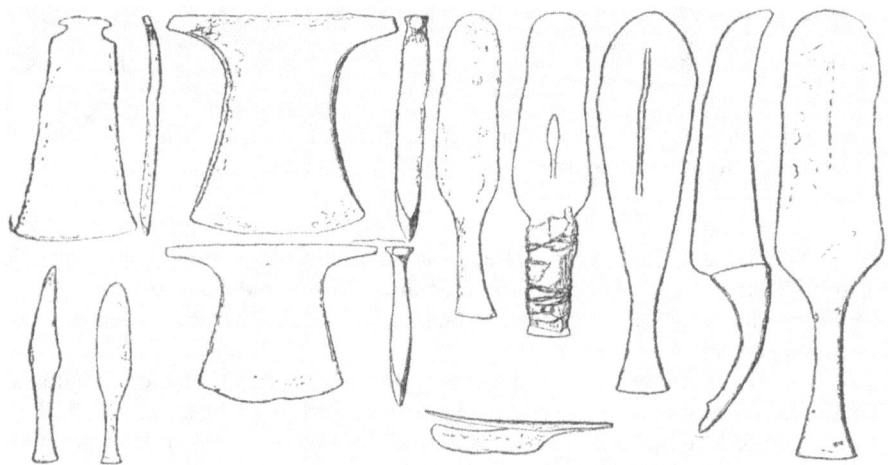

Research Essays Illustration 42. Tools: Axe blades, cutting tools, etc.

RESEARCH ESSAYS ON ANCIENT EGYPT

Research Essays 39. Temple of Amon-Ra at Karnak. "Girdle Wall" of Rameses II. Rameses offers a vessel and a plant to a defaced Goddess.

Beneficent God, you presided over a world as King of Kings.
Lord of the Thrones of the Two Lands, Bull of your Mother, New Kingdom monarchs competed trying to out-do predecessors praising Amon, Greater than Great of the Primordial Deities, who continued to bless his champions.
Chief of Egypt, territorial conquests, ensuing wealth, architectural constructions, and religious and philosophical sonnets, extolled the name of Amon Presider of Karnak, who dwells in the Most Select of Places, in Power and Glory, Invisible and Creative.
As Chief of all the Gods, you fashion the deities, One in his actions as with Gods.
Stablisher of all things, Lord of things that are, you Create all Life, Lord of the *Sektet* Boat and of the *Antet* Boat.

First Born Son of the Earth, Chief of Mankind your Sanctuary at Karnak is a splendid piece of divinely inspired architecture.
Master of the Double Crown, you receive the *Ames* Scepter.

FREDERICK MONDERSON

Lord of the *Makes* Scepter and whip, your precinct, befits the Eternal Spirits of the Theban Triad, Amon, Mut, Khonsu, whose reigns encompassed millennia.
Priests manifested political and theological power from this sacred abode, constructed in stone while similar 'Mansions of Millions of Years' profess Amon's august name, as Source of all Light in Heaven.

Lord of Karnak, King of the South and North, Lord of Things Which Exist, Stablisher of All Creation, You Last Forever, equips all lands, fashioner of all that exists, Just One, Lord of Thebes.

Beautiful boy whom the gods praise, maker of men and stars who illuminates the two lands, you are great of strength, Lord of Might, Chief who made the two lands, the Gods rejoice in your beauty, Amen-Ra, venerated in Karnak.
Lord of the Deeds Case who holds the flail, you are the Heliopolitan, first of his Ennead, who lives daily on truth.
The gods love to gaze at you when the Double Crown rests upon your brow, hawk in the midst of the horizon; you are beloved in the Southern Sky, and pleasant in the Northern Sky, possessor of praise, the Sun of Heaven.

RESEARCH ESSAYS ON ANCIENT EGYPT

Research Essays 40. Temple of Amon-Ra at Karnak. "Girdle Wall" of Rameses II. With a goddess to his rear, Rameses offers three vessels to Amon-Ra.

Lord of Things that are, acting as Judge, Vizier of the Poor Who Takes No Bribes, your intellectual majesty enlightened the world in knowledge of arts and medicine. Your inspiration pioneered astronomy, quarrying, navigation, stone-transportation, agriculture, mathematics, and all gifts of the African mind. Generations of black men and women worship and praise you mighty Amon, King of the Gods, First Born, and Resting upon Ma'at. Amenemenes, Sesostris, then Ahmose, Amenhotep, Thutmose, Hatshepsut, Seti, Rameses, Merenptah and Piankhy, Shabaka, Shabataka, Taharka, were greatest adherents, physical father of these kings, Power of the Gods.

FREDERICK MONDERSON

Amen-Ra the Justified, you give your hands to those you love and assign those you hate to fire.

The Gods love to behold you and they rejoice in your beautiful acts. These divinities acclaim you the Great House and Crown you with Crowns in the House of Fire.
Homage to you, Dweller in Peace for you are Successor to Ra.
Fashioner of Kings and Queens, sole king among the gods, your collective wisdom schooled the Greeks and Romans, the newest converts.
They immersed in your wonderful cultural heritage, praising you with equal zeal and vigor.
Chief of all the Beings of the Underworld, Lord of the Nubians, Governor of Punt, King of Heaven, Amon the great African God, we beseech you, Lord of Eternity, today make enlightening the black culture of Kemet/Egypt, land of the ancestors.
Pour forth your salvation and ingenuity to inspire our people even more as they meet challenges in a new Millennium.

Pre-Dynastic Period I: The Badarian

The time from about 4241 B.C. to about 3100 B.C. is called the Pre-dynastic period in Ancient Egypt. Here, three cultures developed before the dynasties began. They formed the foundations on which the dynasties were able to build the lasting Egyptian civilization in Northeast Africa. The first of these cultures was the Badarian (Ba-da-ri-an), named after a group of cemeteries around Badari on the east bank of the Nile River. This is not far from Aswan in Upper Egypt at the First Cataract. The Badarians were an African people who had a political system that was centralized. Their culture produced a high quality of pottery found when archaeologists dug up their graves. Archaeologists, as you know, are scientists who search for the remains of old cultures. Then they try to write a history of the people based on tools, pots, or other remains left behind. These things tell the archaeologists about the ancient cultures.

Much of the ancient cultural remains of the Badarians were found in graves. They took many objects into the "afterlife" and these were called "goods of the grave." The Badarians believed they needed their tools, pots, food, cosmetics, and so on where they were going after they died and were buried.

RESEARCH ESSAYS ON ANCIENT EGYPT

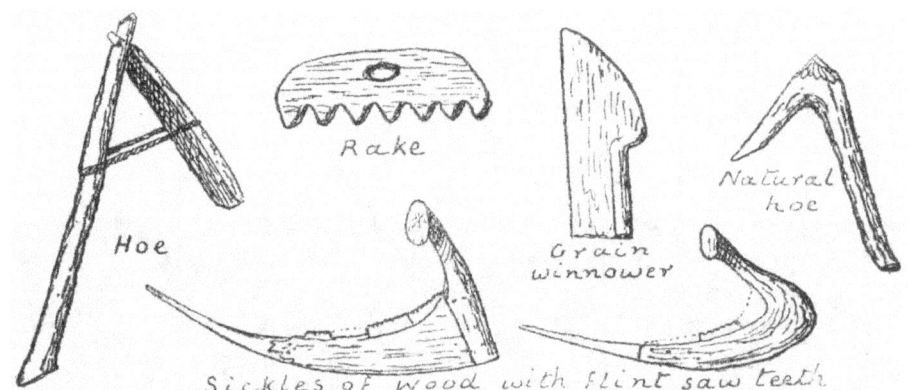

Research Essays Illustration 43. Tools: Rake, hoes, sickles of wood with filing saw teeth and grain winnower.

The graves of the Badarians were rough circular pits about 1.5 meters across and 1 meter deep. In these graves were found cooking pots, baskets, and bone and flint tools. The body was covered with materials made from goat and gazelle skins. Their dress was made from linen or skins, sewn with bone needles. They wore studs for the nose and earrings made of beads and turquoise, a semi-precious stone. The Badarians also wore stone bead necklaces and girdles.

The Badarians had bracelets of ivory, shell, bone and horn. Also, their combs and spoons were made of ivory and bone carved in animal or bird shapes. They decorated their eyes and bodies with green malachite and castor oil was used for cleaning and softening the skin. Other tools included ivory or shell fishhooks and flint arrowheads. These Badarians also used vases made of ivory and stone palettes for grinding cosmetics.

The Badarians were religious and this is evidenced by the care they took with the "goods of the grave." They made ivory statuettes of women to accompany the dead men in whose graves they were placed. Their dead were buried on the side with the bodies in the pre-natal position. Also found in the graves were ivory amulets of hippopotamuses and antelopes that served as hunting charms.

Their economy was based on hunting, fishing, and agriculture and they domesticated, or tamed, animals such as dogs, jackals, goats, cattle and oxen. They lived in mud-brick houses and had polished black, and black-topped polished red or brown pottery. The Badarians had a high quality of pottery. Their bowls had thin walls and were polished red ware, partly blackened. They decorated their pottery with a ripple pattern representing water and stained them with red ochre dye.

FREDERICK MONDERSON

Research Essays 41. Hatshepsut's Temple at Deir el Bahari. From the "Bird's Eye View," from the cliff, end of First Court with First Ramp and Lower Colonnade; Second Court with Second Ramp and Middle Colonnade; Upper Terrace and Upper Colonnade; and beyond Upper Court with Sanctuary against the face of the Mountain. Mentuhotep II's Middle Kingdom Temple is further ahead.

In the remains of the Badarian graves were found small-scale copper implements. Most of this metal has not survived. However, the significance of this metal use means they were beginning to step out of the Stone Age that had characterized man's existence in Africa for hundreds of thousands of years.

RESEARCH ESSAYS ON ANCIENT EGYPT

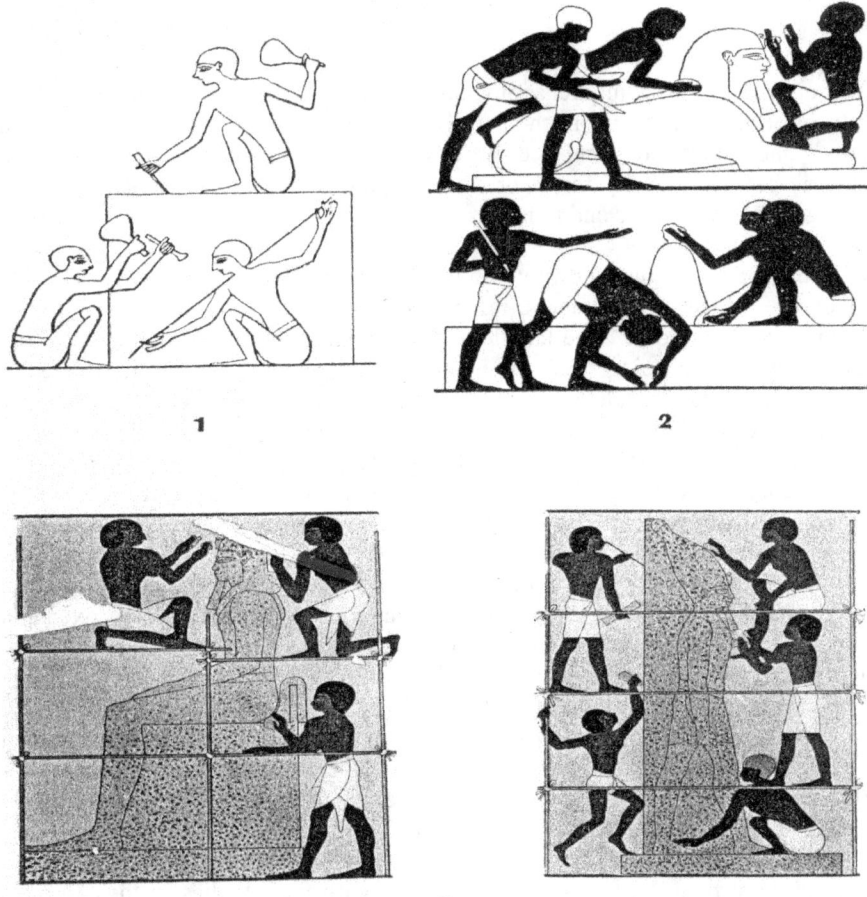

Research Essays Illustration 44: Men dressing stone (1), sculpting a sphinx (2), and making seated and standing colossals of stone (3).

Pre-Dynastic II: The Amratian or Naqada I

The next phase of the Pre-Dynastic culture of ancient Egypt is called the Amratian or Naqada I. The name comes from the sites of el Amrah and Naqada, in Upper Egypt, Northeast Africa. The people of this period built on the earlier cultural gains of the Badarians and this formed a continuing development in the Nile

FREDERICK MONDERSON

Valley civilization. Again, archaeologists were able to write about the Amratians due to information taken from their graves in cemeteries. Pots were most often found. They included burnt red ware with animals, birds, plant shapes and geometric patterns. Many forms or sizes of pottery were used including flasks, bowls, goblets, twin vases and tumblers.

Tools were made of stone and flint and showed the birth of a professional class of toolmakers. There were scrapers, razors, double edged blades, fishtailed knives and lances with wood or bone handles. The cutting edge was saw-like with tiny teeth. Copper was being used for harpoons and pins. They worked in gold, malachite, alabaster, basalt, ivory, bone and hard stone. Weapons were mainly made of stone and flint. The throw stick or boomerang was in use. Ivory carving represented animals such as giraffes, birds, elephants, sheep and hippopotami. Human figures were made of ivory. Pottery figures of women had stumpy arms as handles. There were early signs of tattoo marks on the body. Women wore jewelry of shells, carnelian and coral around the neck. The houses of the Amratians were not different from those of the Badarians. Their huts were in Villages that were sometimes large. During this time dogs, sheep, goats, oxen and pigs were domesticated, or tamed. There was plenty of game, fish and fowl to be caught in the river and the marshes or swamps. Their cooking vessels were made of pottery and such household utensils as plates, cups, bowls, spoons, knives and other vessels were of a high quality. Vases were still being made of stone but they were of all sizes, shapes and very decorative. Agricultural grains were boiled for porridge and baked for bread. Grapes and barley made beverages. These early Africans of Egypt planted flax and had looms for weaving.

The dead were mainly placed in small graves with their bodies in the pre-natal position with enough space left for the goods of the grave. Randall MacIver found evidence of "strongly curled hair" in the graves of the Amratian. Their dead faced south or Upper Egypt or inner Africa. Figurines of women were placed in graves. The methods of burial and things placed in graves shows the continuation of their religious beliefs. Since Egypt received little rains, it's believed the early leaders of the Amratian were rainmakers who were killed, as they grew older. They were probably drowned or cut-up as their powers to bring rain failed. It is interesting that individuals with "strongly curled hair" were also found in the north or Lower Egypt!

RESEARCH ESSAYS ON ANCIENT EGYPT

Research Essays 42. Hatshepsut's Temple at Deir el Bahari. Black-top entrance to the Temple with First and Second Security Posts and the essential features of the structure including two Ramps seeming to join and Lower, Middle and Upper Colonnades.

Pre-Dynastic III: The Gerzean or Naqada II

The Gerzeans or Naqada II people made boats by lashing together bundles of papyrus stalks. Some boats had sails. With the development of fishing the boat-building industry grew. This new vehicle helped to develop trade as the people sought to exchange the surplus goods they had to get things they did not have. This marked the beginning of commerce on the Nile that spread in Africa and elsewhere.

The Gerzean or Naqada II represents the third of the three pre-dynastic culture sequence that set the stage for dynastic Egypt. It is named after el-Gerza in Middle Egypt but also the culture sequence of Naqada II from Upper Egypt. The development of the two earlier periods, the Badarian and Amratian, were continued in this final sequence.

During this period metalworking became a big industry. Copper was worked on a large scale. Gold, lead, silver, malachite, flint and ivory were also used. Stone vases were widely used. Such crafts as ivory carving and shipbuilding began to spread and develop. Egypt now finally entered the metal age, though stone continued in use well into the later periods. Copper mixed with tin made a harder metal called bronze. Most weapons were made with this tough metal. Gold was too soft for weapons. It had a mystical value and was used for religious purposes and decorative jewelry.

Research Essays Illustration 45. Potters making earthenware vases. Beni-Hassan.

In the pre-dynastic period workmen worked in gold, silver, ivory, bone, turquoise, carnelian, lapis lazuli, feldspar and jasper. They also made jewelry from amethyst, button-pearl, amber, agate, onyx, and glass. Ivory, bone, shells and beads also formed part of the jewelry worn by people. The jewelry included necklaces, girdles, bracelets, and a circlet for the head. There were anklets, finger rings and studs for the noses. Amulets of bone, ivory and colored stones were made. They represented the fertility goddess, fishes, birds, hippopotami and crocodiles. The donkey was introduced for overland trade.

There were 42 nomes or small states in all of Egypt. There were 22 in Upper Egypt and 20 in Lower Egypt. Upper Egypt extended from the Aswan frontier to the Apex of the Nile Delta. Lower Egypt extended from the Apex to the Mediterranean. In this early period, many towns built barriers to protect themselves from other towns that constantly made war. This was primarily due to the extensive trade opportunities in the Nile Valley and the wealth generated from it.

There are a number of slate palettes and macehead that record the competition and wars of the time. Each state sought to gain the upper hand over its neighbors owing to the increase in trade and wealth. First the *Battlefield Palette* that shows a Libran victory over other Delta states. Then there is the *Bull Palette* showing the

RESEARCH ESSAYS ON ANCIENT EGYPT

King as a bull goring a foreign enemy. There is also the *Libya Palette* showing cattle, asses, rams and incense trees as part of tribute for a King. Even more important is the *Narmer Palette* showing the King wearing both red and white crowns and he seems to be uniting Upper and Lower Egypt at the beginning of dynastic rule. The *Narmer Macehead* shows the King under a canopy with possibly his wife, Queen Neithhotep. It also records his capture of 120,000 men, 400,000 oxen and 1,200,000 goats. This high number is significant that by the beginning of the First Dynasty these Nile Valley Africans were counting in the millions. Just as significant is the administration and dynamics of moving that much booty.

Narmer came from Thebes in the south, conquered and united Upper and Lower Egypt. He began the First Dynasty and this marked the end of the Pre-Dynastic period. At a later period when Egypt was again divided southerners united the land during the Middle Kingdom, at the start of the New Kingdom and to begin the Twenty-Fifth Ethiopian Dynasty. Later times, in philosophic reflection, the names of Narmer of the First Dynasty, Mentuhotep II of the Middle Kingdom, Kamose and Ahmose of the New Kingdom and we could add Piankhy of the 25th Dynasty who were all linked as uniters of that ancient African kingdom along the Nile River, now known as Egypt.

Research Essays 43. Hatshepsut's Temple at Deir el Bahari. One of the two trees brought by the Punt Expedition and planted in front of the Temple.

The Old Kingdom I

The Old Kingdom lasted from about 2700-2259 B.C. It included the Third to Sixth Dynasties. This period is also called the Pyramid Age. Those large-scale pyramid structures of stone were built at this time. The high level of technology these ancient Africans of Egypt employed enabled their structures to defy time.

King Narmer established the monarchy and feudal relationships at the time of unification inaugurating the First Dynasty. The priesthood justified the divine nature of the kingship. The relationship also defined the role of nobles and nomarchs, or rulers of the nomes, in supporting the system of pharaonic government.

Centralized government remained in effect until the end of the Sixth Dynasty. Social classes continued to grow from the time of unification in the Archaic Period. Their power increased and peaked in the Sixth Dynasty. Some scholars believe this increase in power of the nobles led directly to the end of the Old Kingdom. Position in the social order was based on birth, education and employment. Employment with the government was at central, regional and local levels. Being in the military or a high position in the religious field was also a sought-after social status position.

Architecture is the most predominant feature of the Old Kingdom. It involved a search for more permanent materials. They first worked in wood and mud brick that replaced lashed bundles of papyrus stalks, rush mat-work, palm thatch and wattle and daub mixtures. Then they began using stone for parts of the house subjected to hard wear as lintels, thresholds and doorposts. Soon their architects built more extensively of stone. As such, the pyramids, temples, palaces and mastaba tombs were all built of stone. This material was sometimes quarried from far distances.

First, Imhotep built the Step-Pyramid at Sakkara, for Pharaoh Zoser. Done in the Third Dynasty, it is a reducing sized mastaba tomb with a base of 411 feet east-west by 358 feet north-south. It had a height of two hundred feet. The word mastaba means bench in Arabic. Many of these tombs looked like benches to the Arab workmen who helped in the early excavation, thus the name. The very large mastaba tombs contained hundreds of rooms underground in their substructure.

RESEARCH ESSAYS ON ANCIENT EGYPT

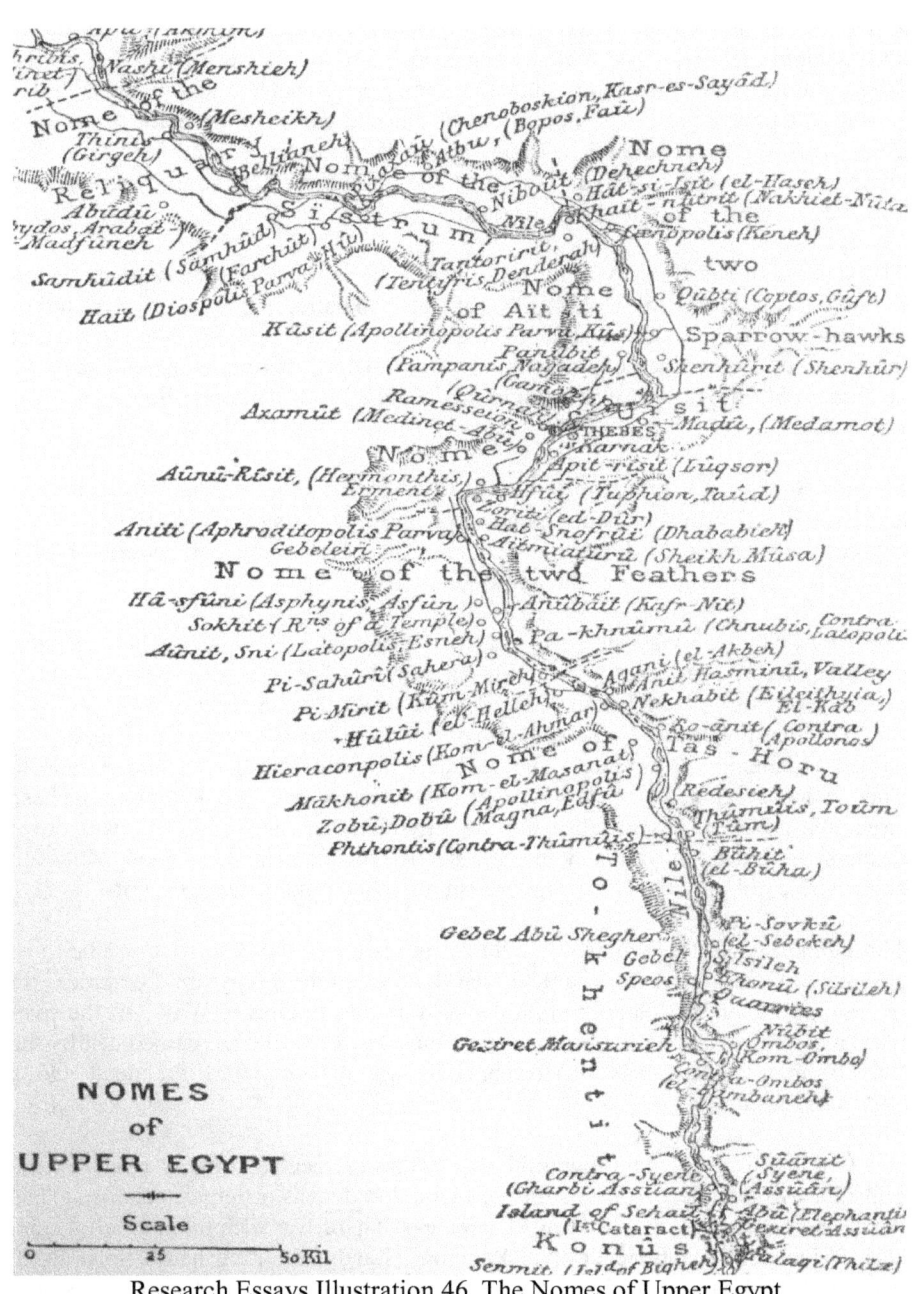

Research Essays Illustration 46. The Nomes of Upper Egypt.

FREDERICK MONDERSON

Zoser's pyramid complex had a tremendous enclosure wall of one-mile perimeter and a height of thirty-three feet. It enclosed buildings that were dwarfed by the Step-Pyramid. The stones were quarried from great distances, sometimes as far as Aswan in Upper Egypt. Their construction showed carvings of "plant forms such as papyrus stalks, pendant leaf capitals and fasciculated columns." This new architecture lent an air of fresh vitality to the buildings. The natural setting was, however, a conflict with ideas of the dead.

The success of the Step-Pyramid encouraged the architects to attempt the Bent-Pyramid at Dashur. Built c. 2600 B.C., it was also called the Southern Pyramid or "Snefru Gleams." It had an approximate angle slope of 54 degrees at the base of the pyramid. Rather than continue upwards to the apex there is a sudden change to an angle of 42 degrees. It was thought this change made the top collapse or it was finished in a hurry.

Pharaoh Snefru built a second pyramid. It was called the Northern Pyramid and also located at Dashur. It had a rising slope of 36 degrees instead of the earlier 53 degrees. The angle of 53 degrees became the normal angle of ascent of later pyramids. This was the first true pyramid.

The Ghizeh Plateau was the stage for the three great pyramids of Khufu, Khafre and Menkaure. The largest pyramid has a height of 756 feet. It is named "Khufu is one belonging to the horizon." The second largest has a height of 708 feet. It is called "Great is Khafra." The smallest of the three has a height of 306 feet. It is named "Menkaure is divine." These builders were father, son and grandson. Their achievements in the 4th Dynasty characterized the Old Kingdom. These structures achieved immortality for the Egyptians in the minds of man, down through the ages. If you add the Sphinx of Ghizeh then these monuments do characterize not only the Old Kingdom but also the permanence of Egypt.

Throughout Egypt there were some 80 pyramids along the Nile River. The three at Ghizeh (Giza), however, characterized the concept of the pyramid complex. In the Pyramid Complex could be found a surrounding Enclosure Wall. At the river there was a Valley Temple. From here a Causeway or walkway, passed nearby the Sun Temple. There was a Mortuary Temple or temple of the dead and a Sacrificial Altar.

In the complex, the Main Pyramid was centrally located. In its rear was the Subsidiary or Smaller Pyramids for the Pharaoh's queens or female relatives. The dead's belongings were stored in Magazines. There was a Sphinx, Obelisk, and also a Heb Sed or Jubilee Festival Pavilion. Lastly, the king had a Solar Boat, deposited in a boat pit. In their view, this vehicle was used to sail across the sky to the next world. In addition, there were mastaba tombs for nobles and officials

RESEARCH ESSAYS ON ANCIENT EGYPT

who served the king. These wished to gain immortality by being buried next to or within the shadows of their god-king. Such was the belief of the Cult of the god-king of the Old Kingdom.

Research Essays 44. Hatshepsut's Temple at Deir el Bahari. Close-up of the two Ramps and Lower, Middle and Upper Colonnades.

These pyramids were not decorated, but nobles' mastabas were early canvases upon which frescoes of daily life and hunting and fishing scenes were lavish within. In the 5th Dynasty, King Teti I had the Egyptian "Bible" or "Pyramid Text" inscribed on his tomb walls. It began with "Rise up O Teti, thou shall not die." These spells were intended to help the king survive in the afterlife. Four other kings of the Fifth and Sixth Dynasty had similar work done on their pyramids.

The Old Kingdom II

Great advances were made in diverse fields of cultural growth. The treatment of medicine expanded in the Old Kingdom lasting from the 3rd through the 6th Dynasties. This medical development can be traced to two reasons. First, the ancient Africans of Egypt had a profound belief in the afterlife. They made special efforts to preserve the body in the religious and philosophical belief that the deceased would return to claim it. The process of preparation was called mummification.

In developing their medical knowledge, diseases of the abdomen, bladder, rectum, eyes and skin were studied. Methods of detecting illnesses based on the visible parts of the body such as the skin, hair, nails and tongue were known. While they practiced surgery and listened to the heart they also knew of the blood circulation. Further, these medical specialists, who were generally priests, treated gallstones, gout and arthritis. They also extracted medicine from plants and minerals.

The gods were considered good to Egypt and they were constantly worshipped and ritualized. In the 5th Dynasty Pyramid of King Teti I the "Pyramid Text" was inscribed on the walls. This Egyptian "Bible" represented the development of Egyptian religious beliefs that were thousands of years old. This lasted for thousands more, thanks to the work of a dedicated priesthood. These were a powerful group who studied the sciences and made progress in the arts. In this endeavor, that body was responsible for conducting various ceremonies and ensuring the administration of justice. Even though they were tax exempt, they themselves also collected taxes especially from the farmers.

RESEARCH ESSAYS ON ANCIENT EGYPT

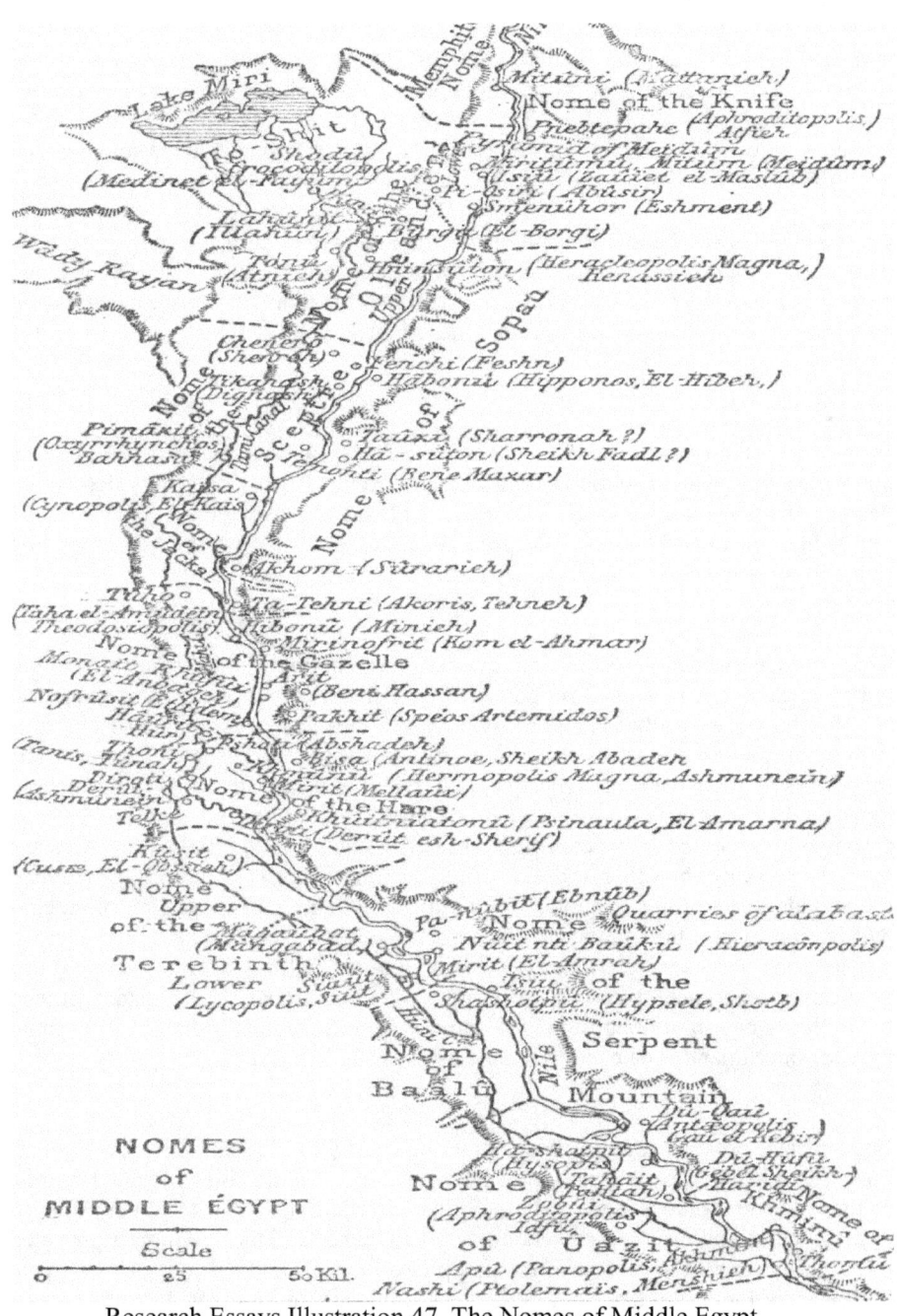

Research Essays Illustration 47. The Nomes of Middle Egypt.

FREDERICK MONDERSON

During the inundation or overflowing of the river, boundary marks of property were washed away. So, the priests provided surveyors who re-surveyed the land and determined where the boundary marks should be placed. By studying the behavior of the river, they also predicted the harvest yield. Taxes were determined based on the height of the Nile. The priests were also responsible for training all branches of civil administration. They also collected tribute for the temples and taught mathematics, astronomy, geometry, philosophy and the arts.

On the walls of tombs, paintings and drawings depicted daily life during the time of the Old Kingdom. Sculpture in relief and in the round developed. Raised and sunk relief showed man, his culture and nature very plainly. This was an age of colossal, or huge, human portraiture. The hieroglyphics depicted drama in the afterlife.

In politics, the power of the nobles increased and threatened the central administration. This resulted in political discontent. Pharaoh Pepi II ruled for 94 years. This is the longest reign in history. At his death during the 6th Dynasty, the Old Kingdom came to an end. Disorder, anarchy, and civil war broke out leading to the First Intermediate Period or Dynasties 7 through 10.

Trade was expanded by land and by sea. Again, merchants exchanged food, crafts, technology, ideas and religion. They were in contact with the Levant and Nubia where they exchanged gold, ivory and other products. Industry bloomed with beautiful and delicate vessels, pottery jars, tables and dishes. The materials they worked included slate, rock crystal, faience, basalt, marble, alabaster and diorite. Such trades as flint-work, papyrus making, jewelry, metalwork, weaving, woodwork, bone and ivory carving and faience, show these Nile Valley Africans expertly working, building and also engaged in carpentry. Agriculture included the swidden or shifting method of cultivation. Methods of irrigation, ploughing and hoeing helped tremendously. They planted barley, corn, wheat, and cereals. These crops were harvested and placed in storage facilities or grain silos. They kept domestic animals of cows, oxen, pigs, sheep and goats. The shaduf, turned by bulls, horses or donkeys helped move water to higher ground. The canal moved water inland. The canal was also used for light boating.

Food meats included mutton, beef, goats and gazelles. Birds eaten were geese, ducks, quail, pigeons or squab, and later chickens. Vegetables included lentils, beans, radishes, onions and garlic. Fruits included figs, dates, grapes, raisins, pomegranates and melons. Bakers made bread, cakes and pies. Animals provided milk, cheese and butter. The fermented juices were wine from grapes, beer from barley and arrack from dates. All this made life bearable for the well-to-do.

RESEARCH ESSAYS ON ANCIENT EGYPT

Research Essays 45. Hatshepsut's Temple at Deir el Bahari. Northern half of the Lower Colonnade with its broken columns to the rear of square pillars.

In summary, these were some of the accomplishments these Northeast African, Nile River, dwellers made some 5000 years ago. Thus, today's African-American youth and adults should recognize, reclaim and speak proudly of their ancestors from the Nile Valley on the African continent.

The Middle Kingdom

The accomplishments of the Old Kingdom were soon lost as the nobles gained more power. Pepi II of the Sixth Dynasty ruled for 94 years and this allowed the increased power of the nobles to threaten the monarchical system. During this pristine and inventive age, all Egyptians wanted to be buried in the shadow of the pharaoh's pyramid. However, with the expanding power of the nobles they chose to be buried closer to their nomes and this generated conflicts in the society and social order. Therefore, the whole system of government that depended upon their support collapsed at the end of the Sixth Dynasty, around 2240 B.C. The civilization thus entered the First Intermediate Period of dynasties seven through ten. This first "Dark Ages" clouded the glitter of classical Egypt.

FREDERICK MONDERSON

The ensuing anarchy of the First Intermediate Period came to an end when the kings of the south again mobilized their forces. These southerners of Thebes were united under a single noble family. They then headed north to subdue and unify the land again as Narmer or Menes had done to begin the First Dynasty. Once again Egypt became a united country, thanks to Thebes, "the fighting province." Thus, the pharaohs Intef and Mentuhotep restored order and began the Middle Kingdom.

Research Essays Illustration 48. The Nomes of Lower Egypt.

The Middle Kingdom was a period of reorganization and expansion of the Egyptian state. The kings Mentuhoteps of the eleventh and Sesostrises or Usertesens, and Amenemhats of the twelfth dynasties restored the greatness of Egypt. Sesostris II broke the power of the nobles and restored internal peace and prosperity. These kings from the south choose Thebes as the cultural,

RESEARCH ESSAYS ON ANCIENT EGYPT

administrative and religious capital of Egypt. During this period, many Africans from Nubia to the south of Egypt entered the country. Many fought in the wars of liberation, unification and expansion. These incoming Nubians called "Pan Grave" people were buried in the pre-dynastic contracted or fetal position. Their heads were placed to the north and their faces to the east or west. Goods of the grave included pottery, jewelry and weapons.

Mentuhotep II of the Eleventh Dynasty was the uniter of the two lands and founder of the Middle Kingdom. He is one of several pharaohs who left evidence of his "black flesh." His statue is in the Cairo Museum. He seemed to make a special effort to portray his "blackness." Later Egyptians linked his name with Menes and Ahmose as unifiers of Egypt. During Mentuhotep's reign, the patron deity of Thebes, Amon, became identified with Ra – the sun god. Amon thus became head of the Egyptian pantheon of gods as Amon-Ra. Interesting, Menes, Mentuhotep and Ahmose, all Thebans, were unifiers of Egypt.

A vigorous foreign policy was pursued in the Middle Kingdom. Expeditions were sent into Nubia, Libya, Sinai and Palestine. Western Asia was also attacked. Gold and other wealth poured into Egypt. Trade was pursued extensively. It was a time of great achievements. This period saw many buildings erected and tremendous intellectual growth and unsurpassed artistic achievements. It was called the period of classical literary accomplishments. Paintings and sculpture depicted the culture in life and death.

The Hieroglyphic language of Middle Egyptian was further developed during this period. It set the stage for even greater literary feats of the New Kingdom. Many literary works and ideas from the old period were copied. Several texts record the exploits and works of the Middle Kingdom, particularly the 12th Dynasty. They tell of the fortresses built to protect trade routes to the south. They also recount punitive expeditions to secure peace. Expeditions were also sent to the quarries and mines were opened in the Sinai. Lastly, the diplomatic relations with Western Asia were recounted.

Soon the Twelfth Dynasty ended. Egypt again failed to continue the tradition of fielding strong and vigorous rulers. The Thirteenth Dynasty with its numerous kings stepped in, yet, could not continue the policies and works of their predecessors. We do know the remains of at least one Sobekhotep was considered Negro or black. Thus, the Thirteenth and Fourteenth Dynasties were weak. As such, Egypt entered the Second Intermediate Period. The country once again became a divided land.

FREDERICK MONDERSON

Research Essays 46. Hatshepsut's Temple at Deir el Bahari. From slightly southeast, view of the Portico to the Sanctuary in the Upper Court.

The New Kingdom

In this Second Intermediate Period, the nobles again fought each other to be pharaoh. Agriculture, trade, arts and religion suffered. Asiatic invaders called Hyksos attacked the weak and divided nation. This was another bleak time in the glorious history of the Nile River civilization of Egypt, called Kemet, the "Black Land," by early Egyptian and classical writers.

The Hyksos formed the 15th and 16th Dynasties. They introduced little, absorbed much and destroyed greatly. Yet still, while they controlled the north there was an alliance with the south that recognized the Hyksos as overlords. After a lengthy period of occupation and strange enough, the Hyksos King Apophis sent a message to the Thebans complaining that the hippopotamuses grazing the Nile at Thebes made so much noise, though 600 miles away in the Delta, he could not sleep. So, "Shut-up your hippos!" Such was insulting war talk and the 17th Dynasty Thebans mobilized and went to war. They waged a protracted war of liberation that expelled the invaders, founded the 18th Dynasty, New Kingdom, and begun imperial expansion into Asia and Nubia. The New Kingdom extended into the 19th and 20th Dynasties. After this, a Third Intermediate Period was ushered in. The Ethiopians conquered Egypt and founded the 25th Dynasty. The 26th Dynasty came from Sais in the North. This was the last local dynasty before the Persians, Assyrians and Persians conquered again. Then after these, the new invaders were the Greeks and finally the Romans. Byzantine rule lasted from 395 to 640. From 640 A.D. onwards, Arabs, Turks, then Mamelukes and finally French and British ruled Egypt, before rule reverted to native Egyptians. Several things could thus be said about Egypt, regarding the Nile River, the Sun, the Desert and permanence of its social and political institutions that characterized this ancient land. All that was developed previously was further crystallized, before the end came. The arts, crafts, agriculture, religion, science, medicine, mummification, quarrying, all got better.

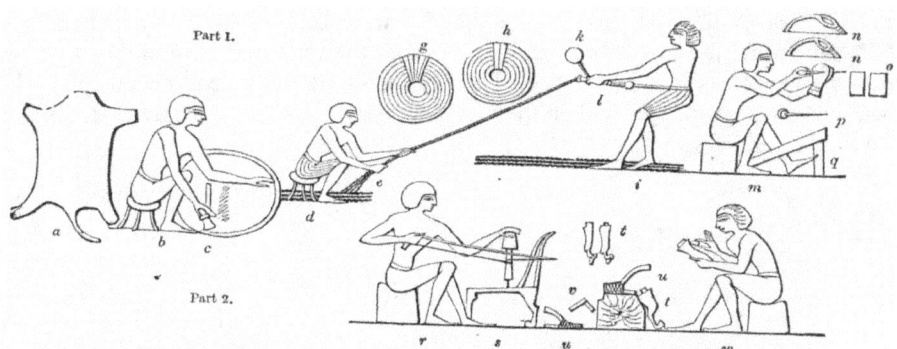

Research Essays Illustration 49. Part I: Cutting and twisting thongs of leather; and Part II: Carpenters plying their trade.

In the arts, schools from different regions of the country competed in the realm of sculpture, painting, boat building, cotton weaving, basketry and matting. The paints, pigments, dyes, inks, and varnishes became even better. More and bigger boats and ships were built to ply the Nile and adjacent waterways. Boring and drilling aided quarrying, gold mining, and iron production while iron and metal work increased. Woodwork, silver and lead production, pottery making, tools and weapons became more pronounced. Domesticated animals and cultivation of food plants improved, as did the culinary arts, their preparation and preservation.

Standards of weights and capacity measurement were refined and irrigation was more extensively pursued to move and store water. Dams, cisterns and wells, water-lifting devices as the shaduf and the water wheel were put to good use. Hieroglyphic, Hieratic and later Demotic writings greatly increased in perfection.

FREDERICK MONDERSON

The Four Principal Gods and Regions

Egyptian religion has intrigued many people as well as been a subject of much discussion, particularly because of the multiplicity of deities in its pantheon. However, this can be easily explained even though it seems rather difficult. While graves of the Prehistoric Period give indication of early religious beliefs, the Pyramids offer the first examples of the permanence of the "house of eternity." The Step-Pyramid built by Imhotep for Pharaoh Zoser of the 3rd Dynasty, was the first philosophic concept of ascending to the heavens and the sun. The "True Pyramids" at Ghizeh followed and then the adjacent mortuary temple that administered to the cult of the dead King. For the much later period, Geoffrey Parrinder in *World Religions* (1975) (1985: 136) explained how New Kingdom tombs in the Valley of the Kings at Thebes were built and decorated to reflect: "The nocturnal journey of the sun-god through the underworld until dawn brings his emergence in the world above. The dead king was believed to accompany the sun-god and to emerge with him in a new dawn – clearly a guarantee of his survival after death."

Research Essays Illustration 50. Man throwing a spear. Beni-Hassan.

RESEARCH ESSAYS ON ANCIENT EGYPT

Research Essays 47. Hatshepsut's Temple at Deir el Bahari. View of the Anubis Shrine (left) and the unfinished "true Northern Colonnade" (right) in the Second Court.

As such, the four principal centers of worship with their cosmogonies and theogonies and belief systems were Ra at Heliopolis, Ptah at Memphis, Osiris at Abydos and Amon-Ra at Thebes manifesting in his temples at Karnak and Luxor. Of course, Amon-Ra was also worshipped in the "Mansions of Millions of Years" or mortuary temples of the respective kings of the New Kingdom across the river in the land of the west. Cosmogonies are stories of the origins of the universe and theogonies are stories of the origins of the gods. However, when we study the Geography of the Gods, interesting questions are posed. Osiris came from Nubia. Wallis Budge tells us Hathor came from the Sudan, and Horus was a blacksmith who "went north." We know the metal age began very early in Africa. Later we see Horus and Hathor as husband and wife. On the *Narmer* Palette, the conqueror has both divinities with him. The Question then is 'Why would he, as a Theban, not be associated with these African Gods?' Like so much, we must apply critical analysis of every aspect of Egyptian history and culture, to correct the grossly distorted record.

Heliopolis' doctrine featured the creator-god Atum who was identified with the sun god Re or Ra. Parrinder (1985: 138) also noted: "Atum was said to have emerged from a chaos of waters, called Nun, and to have appeared on a hill; he procreated, without a consort, the deities Shu (air) and Tefenut (moisture), the former of whom separated the sky from the earth, so that Geb (earth) and Nut (sky) now came into being. A natural procreation was here envisaged, and the same is true of the children of Geb and Nut, the gods Osiris, Isis, Seth and Nephthys, although their cosmic import is initially less clear. Together the nine gods formed the Ennead of Heliopolis, a concept that was afterwards applied to other local groupings and sometimes extended to include more than nine deities. That the physical creation began with the emergence of land from water would seem to be an idea which came naturally to the inhabitants of the Nile Valley, who sometimes saw islands of mud appearing in the Nile."

The Doctrine of Memphis is somewhat different. This Old Kingdom *Memphite Theology* featured Ptah as the creator-god, who was bisexual for he is both father and mother as creator. Accordingly, Parrinder (1985: 139) wrote: "The creation of the world is here said to have been planned by the god's intelligence and to have been implemented by his spoken word – a striking anticipation of the much later Greek doctrine of the divine *logos*. At Hermopolis, on the other hand, the theology of creation had some affinities with the Heliopolitan teaching. Thus creation began; it was said, with the emergence of a primeval hill from the waters of chaos. Four pairs of deities were associated with cosmic qualities – Nun and Naunet with the waters of chaos, Huh and Hauhet with endlessness, Kuk and Kauket with darkness, Amun and Amaunet with invisibility. This Ogdoad consisted of marital couples in which the males and females were conceptually un-discriminated; perhaps four bisexual deities were the original forms. Amun was the head of the Ogdoad, and his name translates as 'The Hidden One.'"

Osiris was a king whose complete history, his life, death and resurrection is known. He was murdered by his evil brother Seth who cut up his body into 13 pieces and scattered it across the land, burying each piece at a particular spot that later became venerated. His head was buried at Abydos and his heart was buried at the Temple of Isis on Philae Island, later in modern times moved to Agilka. He arose from the dead and became judge of the dead and lived in the underworld. His son Horus took his place on earth and ruled as king before the mortal kings who became sons of Horus.

Amon rose to prominence in the Middle Kingdom when his name was associated with four kings named Amenemhat. By the New Kingdom he had emerged as a universal god. He has been called "Amon rich in names" and the poem mentions seventy-five of his names. He was a "Hidden" or mysterious god and the rattling of the winds signaled he was near. He was a creator God, manifested as a snake that renewed itself, and is said to precede the Ogdoad. The *Book of the Dead* describes him as 'eldest of the gods of the eastern sky,' which makes him a solar god. This is further seen when he is syncretized with Re to become Amon-re. He was also a fertility god, sometimes called Amon-Min, 'bull of his mother.' All these gods had temples, priests and disciples who worshipped them. The Kings

RESEARCH ESSAYS ON ANCIENT EGYPT

placated them and built temples and made donations so that they would in turn give these monarchs good fortune.

In another aspect, writing evolved from the earlier slate palettes and culminated in the *Pyramid Texts* on the walls of 5 pyramids during the 5th and 6th Dynasties. Starting with that of Kings Teti and Wenis, this began to reflect this early theology, ritual and mythology. During the Middle Kingdom, the *Pyramid Texts* became transformed into the *Coffin Texts*, because they were written on the sarcophagus or coffins of the dead kings and even nobles. Parrinder again (1985: 137) explained: "From the beginning of the New Kingdom it became customary to give the benefits of such writings to the deceased in quite a different form: the text was written on a roll of papyrus and inserted in the tomb. As compared with the *Pyramid Texts*, both the *Coffin Texts* and the *Book of the Dead* are much wider in their application, for they proffer their privileges to non-royal persons. The use of papyrus as a medium also led to a further innovation: the text was often illustrated with beautifully colored vignettes, as in the papyri of Ani and Hunefer. Much of Ancient Egypt's religious literature is thus funerary in character."

These then are some of the fascinating features that characterized the History of Egypt in ancient times when east was east but there was no west until much later. We now turn to a poem to Osiris to end this chapter.

POEM TO OSIRIS

O Osiris, great immortal with attributes part divine and part human, you are Lord of Being with many names.
Great God, you are the promise of eternity, for the just and those who live by Ma'at's law of right and truth.
Lord of Abydos, you suffered the indignity of death and decapitation, being victimized by conspirators filled with envy.
When the righteousness of your cause reached to heaven, father god Ra dispatched his emissaries to rescue you from the perdition you did not deserve.
They came to shed light on the First among the Westerners, the One God Living in Truth.
You are the Father and Mother of Mankind, Everlasting Soul.
Lord of the Horns with tall Atef-Crown, of good memory in the God's Palace.

Presider over the West, your brother Seth and his evil cohorts plotted your death to seize your throne and legacy, Glorious, Good God!
They entrapped your body through guile and trickery, and into the Nile they discarded your coffin.

FREDERICK MONDERSON

The dastard deed done, the doers of iniquity rejoiced, claiming your legacy, mummy, crown, scepter and whip, great warrior, King of Upper and Lower Kemet/Egypt, King of All the Gods.
When Ra rises everyday and comes to the Under-world, in order to survey this land and also the Countries, you sit there also as he.
The Majesty of Thoth stands near unto you, in order to execute the commands, which proceed from your mouth.
You are king of the Illuminated, prototype of the Dead man, King of Eternity.

Research Essays 48. Hatshepsut's Temple at Deir el Bahari. A surviving broken head of an Osiride Figure of the Queen on the Upper Terrace.

Lord of Rosta, greatly loved on earth, Isis the faithful and loving wife searched the land untiring, for your remains out of honor and duty.
With her sister Nephthys, their lamentations echoed throughout and reached the heavens, triumphant.
Thoth, the personification of intelligence and scribe of the gods, with Anubis assisted the search, Great One contained in Sokhen.
You were great of strength when you overthrow the adversary, Powerful of arms when you slew the foe.
Shining noble at the head of nobles, permanent in high rank, stablished in your sovereignty, you are the beneficent power of the company of the gods, the Lord to whom praises are sung.

RESEARCH ESSAYS ON ANCIENT EGYPT

You put your fear in the enemy and reached the boundaries of them that plotted mischief. Out of fear of reprisal, Seth decapitated and scattered your body in thirteen locations; Beneficent Spirit in the Land of Spirits.
O Noble One with mysterious ceremonies in the temples, the Celestial Ocean Nun offered you water and the sky created air for your nose for contentment of your heart.
Source of the Nile, the north wind journeys southward to you, the plants grow according to your desire and the fields created its food for you.
Lord of the great house in the city of the eight gods, celestial food, you are the beneficent soul among spirit souls.

Mighty One, who appeared in greatness at Abydos, your body was lying as Corpse under the Earth.
August Being, Isis recovered parts at every site and Temples were erected to worship the Just King murdered by evil and jealousy.
Now aided by divine wisdom, One of Many Names, you're the king who guides the land to prosperity, Ruler of Eternity, Eternal Master, Great God of Abydos.
You are very awful in Shashotep, Osiris, King of Gods.
Justified before the entire Ennead, a slaughtering was made for you in the great hall at Herwer.
Before you, the great mighty ones were in terror; these great ones rose from their mats.
Stablisher of truth throughout the two lands, perfect of power in every word, you are Lord to the end of the earth.
Lord of Kerer, with Nephthys, Thoth and Anubis as witnesses Isis performed the ceremony Revivification of Osiris.
Your son Horus at the Bar of Judgment was adjudged your rightful heir and successor.
He assumed the throne reigning as king of the two lands to fulfill the mission of his divine father, to Fill the Land with Excellent Laws.
Powerful leader of every god, you became Governor of Amentet to judge actions of men guided by Ma'at's laws, Ruler of the West.
You are a venerable God, Lord of the Great Dwelling in Sesennou, Lord of Tazoser.

God of all gods, most excellent glorified one; your head was buried at Abydos, your heart at Philae; and you established truth in Kemet/Egypt.
Ceremonies celebrate your birth, life, death, resurrection, and after life, as god who can invest his Body with All Forms as He Wishes.
Throughout Egypt you were worshiped, Prince of Peace, first Cristos, wonderful spirit.

FREDERICK MONDERSON

Men found salvation in your example and purpose for you lived as father, husband, king, betrayed, mutilated, died, revivified, resurrected as deity with power to maintain life indefinitely.

Kings and commoners, worshiped and praised your name, nature, spirit, soul, and divine body while the gods of the provinces are your forms, Primeval God Residing in Tattu, Soul of Ra.

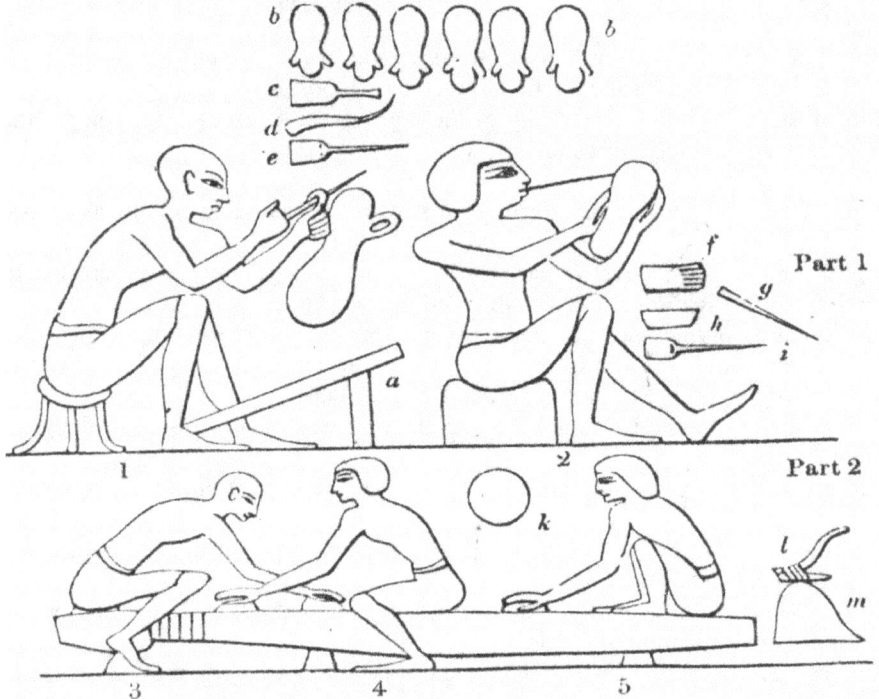

Research Essays Illustration 51. Sandal-makers and men employed in polishing a column. Beni-Hassan.

Master of the Gods, Abydos, throne of your power, is the world's first pilgrimage site, for all seeking your immortality, serene one.

The Great Ennead praised you; the Lesser Ennead loved you, Everlasting King.

All realized there's no empty space on your back.

For millennia adherents imbibed and practiced the Osirian drama recreating your experiences.

Many chose burial near the staircase of the god, or they erected stelae or made pilgrimages for votive offerings as the last rites.

Your holy site immortalized by ten temples, span the duration of dynastic rule.

RESEARCH ESSAYS ON ANCIENT EGYPT

Still Seti's mortuary temple and Osireion at Abydos, birthplace of the sun is a wonderfully magnificent art and architectural testament praising you as God, Lord of the Length of Times in Abydos.

Holy One of the White Wall you have twin souls, bodies and natures.
With the power to be born again you rise on the horizon.
Principles of Abundance in On, Creator of the World, the Heavenly Nile derives its water from you.
Soul of the Sun, the Gods are Joyous at the arrival of Osiris.
The Earth lies upon your arms and its corners upon you even unto the Four Pillars of Heaven.
You stir yourself, the Earth trembles and the Nile comes forth from the sweat of your hands.
Because you rise and stand up, everything whereby man lives, trees and herbs, barley and wheat, is of divine origin, and comes from you.
Lord of the World, you made men and women to be born again.
Lord of the *Seker* Boat and the *Neshmet* boat, these vessels bore your beauty.

Governor of the two companies of gods, praised by your father Keb, beloved by your mother Nut, you established right throughout the two riverbanks.
Admirable in command, heir of Keb in kingship of the two lands, your father entrusted you to lead the two lands to good fortune.
Revered in Ehnas, mighty in Tenent with a great estate in Busiris, you appear on the throne of your father like Ra when he arises on the horizon to give light to those in darkness.
Lord of Eternity in Abydos, Lord of the Great Hall in Hermopolis, abundant in sustenance in Letopolis, the imperishable stars are under your authority.
The height of heaven and earth are open to you, praises are sung in the southern heaven and thanks given in the northern heaven.
Great Mighty One residing in Thinis, Lordship given in Heliopolis, future resurrection, Brother, many found fertile promise in your example.

FREDERICK MONDERSON

Research Essays 49. Hatshepsut's Temple at Deir el Bahari. Close-up of three remaining Osiride Figures of the Queen that escaped destructive agents of her enemies in Thutmose III's backlash. She wears the White Crown, with beard and holds the symbols of power, a whip and flail. The shadow of the author and photographer is in the foreground.

In the resurrection and ascension men and gods shout for joy in the southern sky and adore you in the northern sky.
Thus, with hope of everlasting life, you have the Right to Command in the place of Double Justice, God of the Birth-house, your form is hidden in the temples.

Beneficent One, you are the mighty one of possessions in the shrine.

RESEARCH ESSAYS ON ANCIENT EGYPT

Good God martyred by malice and greed, resurrected, incorruptible, you judge the dead, Mysterious Soul.
Salvation of mankind rested within your bosom, for you possess power to unite bodies and souls.
Another gift of Africa to the world, born again and possessing knowledge, power, and mystery; the father sacrificed, the Black Madonna and Child forever forgiving, salvation is still attainable, Prince of Princes.

Research Essays 49a. Hatshepsut's Temple at Deir el Bahari. Author and photographer Dr. Fred Monderson adjusts his hat but notice the pavement in the Court and on the Ramp towards the Upper Terrace seems immaculately finished.

FREDERICK MONDERSON

9. The Archaeology of Egypt

By

Dr. Fred Monderson

The *Archaeology of Ancient Egypt* is a fascinating subject that first stumbled, and then systematically reclaimed the rich cultural heritage from the misty past in which it lay buried, in the debris of soil and time. As an emerging science, scholars generally date Egyptian archaeology to the beginning of the 19th Century when Napoleon arrived in Egypt and his savants produced their *Description de Egypte* or *The Monuments of Egypt* based on linguistic and visual study of the language and monuments. By the end of the 19th Century archaeology had been placed on a more scientific footing particularly by the work of the tireless and systematic Englishman Flinders Petrie and the boundless energy in the work of the German Auguste Mariette, so that the mist was significantly cleared by then. The 20th Century saw the maturing of the discipline. Nevertheless, in all of this, as the Mighty Sparrow said in one of his songs: "Hurried birds make crooked nests," so the *Story of Egypt* was not correctly told! During the age of African colonization, from 1880 onwards as archaeologists began to simultaneously reclaim ancient Egypt, with all the shenanigans going on, the work of the British archaeologists and so many others, particularly emphasized rapid publication of discoveries to feed the rapidly expanding "penny press" and a public hungry for antiquarian knowledge as Europe manifested its might, militarily, economically, and imperially, globally.

As such, much was said but equally many errors and distortions as well as omissions entered the general body of knowledge and thus misinterpretations under-girded the historical record as to the people, origins and survivals of ancient Egypt. From then to today, as scholars re-examine the "ancient records of the ancient records" generated especially between 1870 and 1930 much remains correct but many things have had to be reinterpreted. Hence, and equally the need for reconstruction in African historiography became necessary, because at the time of interpretation no critical African input was added to authenticate the corpus of new knowledge. Thus, archaeology and anthropology, its sister discipline, had as they say, "some pebbles in their shoes." There was never a broad interpretation of the information using as its cornerstone the full spectrum of the 8 major social sciences, viz., geography, archaeology, anthropology, history, sociology, economics, political science and psychology. Or should I say critical historiographic analysis from credible scholars, were never applied to question the findings and interpretations as put forward by European and American scholars, who were oftentimes biased in arguing from a Eurocentric view of the world.

RESEARCH ESSAYS ON ANCIENT EGYPT

Research Essays Illustration 52. Vases of different sizes and shapes without, with one and with two handles.

Notwithstanding, Egyptian archaeology has helped define and establish parameters of Egyptology by its comprehensive excavation of viable sites and monuments throughout the land. The definition of Egyptology thus includes an understanding of the history, geography and language of ancient Egypt! In this widespread examination, excavation or Archaeology has delved into not just temples and tombs, but cemeteries, and private dwellings and fortified buildings. As such, and moving beyond Roman and Greek periods, structures where towns have remained intact at Koft, Kom Ombo, El Ayandiyeh, and even on the outskirts of Karnak at Thebes, these date to the Middle and New Kingdoms. Towns and private dwellings date from the Twelfth Dynasty at Kahun and at Abydos where remains go back to the earliest times. The town of Tell el-Amarna still standing allowed archaeologists to reconstruct that important city of the religious revolution, though this location suffered tremendously in the reaction to the challenge to Amon's supremacy.

At Tell el Maskhuta the twin towns of Pithom and Rameses established connection with biblical times and events. The two fortresses at Abydos date to the beginnings of Egyptian history. Work of excavation was conducted on the ramparts of El Kab, Kom el Ahmar, el Hibeh, Kuban (Opposite Dakkeh), of Heliopolis, and of Thebes where structures were still standing during the early development of the science of Archaeology.

Archaeology therefore revealed the earliest dwellings made of wattle and daub. Bricks made of mud mixed with sand and chopped straw were molded into oblong forms and dried in the sun. Regarding the art of brick making, Maspero (1914: 4) informed: "A good modern workman will easily turn out 1,000 bricks a day, and after a week's practice he will reach 1,200, 1,500 or even 1,800. The ancient workman whose tools were the same as those of the present day must have obtained equally good results."

An interesting consideration is the soil in which builders had to work. Equally too, the workers were of the poorest class. Today we call them fellahin, individuals who built homes no different from their ancient counterparts. Many of the modern houses, built of concrete are quite different from those of the lower classes, and, are in several stories. For instance, today a father builds his house and a son builds above him and so on and you have the modern multistoried family occupied buildings. This was not so in ancient times. Nevertheless, the private dwellings from the simplest huts to the biggest mansion all had certain features that archaeology has been able to reconstruct. Then we have fortresses built for military purposes and also civic structures designed for Government service and other community activities. Then there was religious architecture as well as tombs, which the early archaeologists were more interested in. Temples as eternal dwelling places for the gods were made of stone. However, the builders did not always use large stone or one stone to build temples.

Maspero (1914: 53) described the type of materials these builders used and the product they produced. "The size varied greatly according to the purpose for which they were intended. Architraves, drums of columns, lintels, and doorjambs were sometimes of very considerable dimensions. The largest architraves known; those above the central aisle of the hypostyle hall at Karnak, average 30 feet in length. Each one represents a solid block of 40 cubic yards and weighs about 65 tons. Generally, however, the blocks are not larger than those in ordinary use among us. They vary from 3 to 4 feet in height, from 3 to 8 feet in length, and from 18 inches to 6 feet in breadth."

Seldom was a temple built of one single type of stone. In fact, variety was sometimes the rule. Again Maspero (1914: 53) explained: "Some temples were built throughout in one kind of stone, but more frequently materials of various kinds and quality are associated, although in unequal proportions. Thus the main buildings of the temple of Abydos are of very fine limestone, while in the temple of Seti I the columns, architraves, jambs, and lintels, all those parts where

RESEARCH ESSAYS ON ANCIENT EGYPT

limestone might not be sufficiently strong, are in sandstone, granite, and alabaster. Similar combinations are to be seen in the temples of Karnak, Luxor, Tanis, Deir el Bahari, Gizeh, and Memphis. At the Ramesseum, at Karnak, and in the Nubian temples, where all these materials are combined, the columns rest on a solid foundation of crude brick. The stone were dressed more or less carefully according to the position they were to occupy."

Research Essays 50. Hatshepsut's Temple at Deir el Bahari. Visitor makes a phone call, perhaps to relate what a wonderful experience the Temple really is.

POEM TO RA – THE SUN GOD

O Ra, King of the Gods, you enjoyed a prominence matched by few divinities.
You emerged at Heliopolis, and once absorbed, you extended your significance throughout dynastic times.
Father of the Gods whose souls are exalted in the hidden place, your symbol is the Disk of the Sun, encircled by serpent Khut, and Ankh, with scepter and tail from your waist.
Self-begotten and Self-born creative vigor, Power of Powers with two uraei, you are a doubly hidden and secret god.
Lord of Eternity, Sovereign of the Gods, you exist forever, Lord of Souls. You possess 14 Kas or life forces, as strength, might, prosperity, food, veneration, eternity, radiance, glory, fame, magic, authority, sight, and hearing and perception, Lord of Heliopolis, Supreme Power.

FREDERICK MONDERSON

Sekhem, begetter of his gods, from Heliopolis, your priests influenced political developments in the Old Kingdom when Pyramid builders incorporated your name into theirs, becoming Son of the Sun, hence the title Son of Ra.
These kings built sun temples with names as 'Favorite Place of Ra' and 'Satisfaction of Ra,' all in Praise of you Lord of Rays. Self-Created, King of Heaven, Great Duration of Life, Lord who advances, you are the Soul that does good to the body.
Governor of his Eye, Lord of Generation, invisible and secret, you are Governor of the Tuat, Double Obelisk God, Lord of the Eastern Bend, and Supporter of the Heavens who dwells in Darkness.
Born as the all-surrounding universe, you send forth the plants in their season, Eternal Essence.

Maker of the Gods, Governor of your circle, Aged One of Forms, Memphis received endowments in the Middle Kingdom in Praise of thee, King of the World. The Priesthood of local gods linked their deity to the Sun God's name Ra, Mighty in Majesty, Vivifier of Bodies.
The Theban triumph merged Amon with Ra assuming all the ancient god's attributes as Maker of Heaven where you are firmly established.
God One from the beginning of time, Mighty One of myriad forms and aspects, Creator of Laws Unchangeable and Unalterable, Lord of Truth your shrine is hidden.
You are the Soul which gives names to his limbs, Body of Khepera, God of Souls who is in the Obelisk.
You are Master of the Spheres who cause the Principles to arise.

Chief of the Earth, Lord of the Gods, Judge of Words, and the glory of Ra manifested in Amon at the Temple of Karnak.
During the New Kingdom, Thebes gloried in the imperial age, and you were Opener of Roads in the Hidden Place, who confers his crown on Pharaoh.
The Ruler of all the Gods, more strong of heart than all those who are in your following, you are maker of gods and men, Creator of Heaven, Earth and the Underworld.
Divine Man-Child, Heir of Eternity, you are Chief of the Gods, Supreme in their Districts, being Crowned King of the Gods, Ram, Mightiest of Created Things.
You Provide the Breath out of your Throat for the Nostrils of Mankind, Fashioner of Himself, and Tonen who produces his members, Supremely Great One.

Provider of the Sovereign Chiefs, Governor of the Holy Circle, Ra as Amon brought victory and fame to those who followed his teachings and praised his name, as Crowner of Pharaoh.

RESEARCH ESSAYS ON ANCIENT EGYPT

Proclaimed King of Earth, Prince of the Tuat, Governor of the Regions of Aukert, Souls in their Circles ascribe your Praises.
Beautiful Being, Rays of Turquoise Light, you are Personification of Right, Truth and Goodness, O Mighty One of Journeys, Lord of the Gods, light of the lock of hair.
Your Emblems secure entrance of the Dead Man into the Kingdom of Osiris.
Chief of the Great Cycle of the Gods, your principles have become your manifestation.
Chief of the Powers inhabiting the holy sphere, you raise your soul, hide your body, shine and see your mysteries.

Creator of Hidden Things, Lord of Heaven, Lord of Earth, for untold ages men praise the Exalted of Souls.
The Maker of Eternity, Ra you sail a Boat of Millions of Years.
In all your glory, you emerge in a Morning Boat *Matet*, becoming strong at Midday.
The day's work done, and weak, you ride the Evening Boat *Semktet*. Confronting your mortal enemy Apep, fishes *Abtu* and *Ant* swim before the Boat of Ra with its defenders at the ready.
United in Numbers, Destroyer of Darkness, Night, Wickedness and Evil, on the dawn of a new day, there are Acclamations of your Rising in the Horizon of Heaven, Only One.
Soul that speaks, rests, creates the developed hidden intellects, you shine in your sphere and hide what it contains, moving luminary.

Ra, Lord of Truth, Lord of the Horizon, Horus of the East, Lord of Fetters of your enemy, protector of hidden spirits, you conquer the fiends of the underworld.
Souls of the East follow and Souls of the West praise you, while you get Support of the Circle of Amenta.
God of Life, King of Right and Truth, you are the World Soul that rested on his High Place.
The Soul who moves onward, Opener of the roads in the Hidden Place, One Alone with many hands, Ra, you are the Great God who lifted up his two eyes.
You address your eye and speak to your head, the spirit that walks, that destroys its enemies, that sends pain to the rebels; you impart the breath of life to the souls that are in their place, Brilliant One who shines in the Waters of the Inundation.

FREDERICK MONDERSON

Research Essays 51. Temple of Luxor. From the southwest, view of the tip of the Processional Colonnade, ruins of the "Ramesseum Front," entrance Pylon, Obelisk and Minaret of Mosque of Abu Haggag, the Patron Saint of Luxor.

Hidden Face, Glorious Creator of Eternity, you make beings come into existence in your creations in the Tuat.
You rise like unto Gold, Great Light Shining in the Heavens illuminating darkness.
Oldest One, Great One, you are Self-begotten, Self-created and Self-produced, the Soul who Departs at his Appointed Time.
You existed forever and would exist for Eternity, Illuminer of Light into his Circle.
Source of Life and Light, Glorious by reason of thy Splendors, you are Joy of Heart within your Splendor.
Mighty One of Victories, Ra, how wonderful was your manifestation among ancient Africans, initiating laudable moral, spiritual and intellectual standards of creative genius, Mighty one whose body is so large it hides its shape, Double Luminary.

Generator of Bodies, True Creative Power of Divine attributes, Sender of Light into his Circle, Ra you rise in the Horizon, and are Beautiful.
So too, Rat, Mistress of the Gods, your female counterpart, Lady of Heaven, Mistress of Heliopolis.
Hathor and Isis are also your companions.
Mightier than the Gods, Glorious Being, Lord of Love, Double Sphinx god, you are Ruler of Everlastingness.

RESEARCH ESSAYS ON ANCIENT EGYPT

God of Motion, God of Light, Lord of Might, you send destruction, fire into the place of destruction and destroy your enemies, Light that is in the Infernal Regions.
Protector of hidden spirits, the Soul that Mourns, the God that Cries, you are the Soul One who avenges his children and who calls his gods to life when he arrives in the hidden sphere.

Aged one of the Pupil of the Utchait, Ra, Lord of the hidden circles, creative force who gathers together all seed, you are manifold in your holy house.
Great One, who rules what is in him, you send forth the stars and make the night light, in the sphere of hidden essences.
Master of the Light, Only One who names the earth by his intelligence, the vessel of heaven, Powerful, Ra in his disk with Brilliant Rays, Lord of Wisdom your precepts are wise.
Lord of Mercy, at whose coming men live, you make strong your double with Divine Food.
Creator of Hidden Things and Generator of Bodies, Enlightener of the Earth, Lord of the Gods who lights the bodies on the horizon, Africans need your continued illumination and Blessings now more than ever.

Research Essays 52. Temple of Luxor. From the west, view of the magnificent Processional Colonnade with its 14 imposing columns with open umbel capitals, abacus and architrave overhead. The walls below, on both sides, depict the voyage from and to Karnak in celebration of the Opet Festival.

FREDERICK MONDERSON

ARCHAEOLOGY

Archaeology has taught us a great deal about ancient Egypt. It has enabled us to delve deep into the prehistoric period, into the palaeolithic period as far back as 300,000 years ago. This has taught us, the Palaeolithic or Old Stone Age is divided into the Lower, Middle and Upper. The Mesolithic represented the Middle Stone Age. The Neolithic period is considered the New Stone Age. This is also the time when farming and settlement began. *Homo habilis* or "true man" made tools to a set and regular pattern and thus overcame his environment, dating back more than a million years. We find evidence of this in Ethiopia and elsewhere in East Africa.

Paleolithic sites in Egypt were found at Merimdeh, Fayum, and Kharga Oasis where hand-axes have been unearthed. Such axes are also found at Thebes dated at 100,000 years. Kom Ombo is also a Paleolithic site. These hand-axes and choppers gave way to man learning to use bone-tools. During this period he also used tools of flint, antler, and ivory. Lance heads and knives were made of all these materials. As tools became more sophisticated he began to become more human, and we see the emergence of early burials and family feelings and relationships. By the end of the Paleolithic Period he began using the bow and arrow, with arrowheads made of various materials and he began to carve animals. There is also a big change in the history of man. He enters the Neolithic period and moves from being a nomadic hunter and gatherer to a sedentary producer of food. In the Palaeolithic Period he hunted and gathered his food, with meats consisting of 90 percent and 10 percent "agri-vegetation." That is, he ate leaves, roots, fruits, shoots, whatever he found growing. Sometimes he even ate grass. He was a "scavenger on nature!" With the change to food production he began to grow crops, domesticated animals and now his diet changed to 10 percent meats and 90 percent "agri-produce." Now he began to "cooperate with nature!" He started building early containers for grain and invented sickles and started winnowing his grain. With this came the emergence of division of labor and specialization of craft. We credit women with beginning agriculture! The "oasis theory" of domestication of animals describes how man came to overcome these creatures. That is, he set up camp near the oasis and as the animals came to water he soon became familiar to them, fed them and so tamed them.

There were three prehistoric or pre-dynastic cultures that emerged in Neolithic Egypt. These were the Badarian, Amratian and Gerzean or Naqada I and Naqada II. The last is called the Proto-dynastic Period.

RESEARCH ESSAYS ON ANCIENT EGYPT

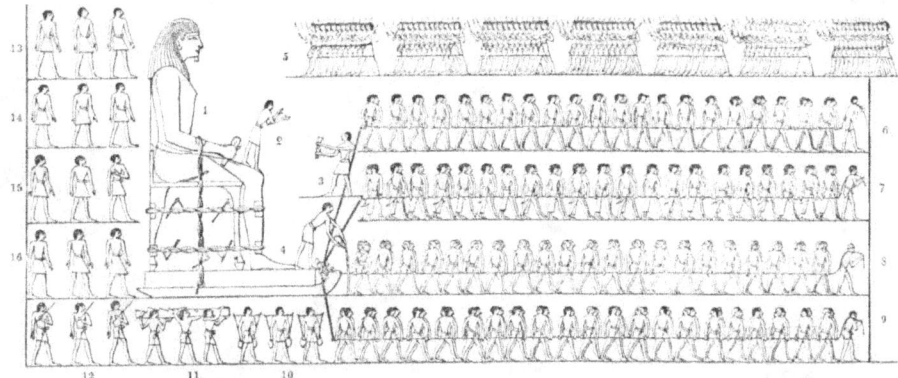

Research Essays Illustration 53. Mode of transporting a colossus from the quarries, from a lithographic drawing of Mr. Bankes.

The Badarian is named after the site of Badari where Flinders Petrie began dating by pottery sequence. At Badari were ivory figurines showing some sort of religious significance. These ancient Africans created and used cosmetic palettes and jewelry was made of shells and turquoise. There was much traveling and trading. Pottery was burnished or burnt. The second sequence is the Amratian found at Merimdeh and Amrah, having beehive huts. A shrine of the local god was found and people seen hunting. A woman sits at a loom and there is a figurine of a dancing lady. The bird lady figurine in the Brooklyn Museum comes from this site. There were male ivory amulets and a woman in a barrel. The mother goddess figurine is transitional to the Gerzean or Naqada period.

During the Gerzean or Naqada II period, we find white incised pottery with a ripple pattern. Here we see the first incised pottery with people and animals, as well as a double shaped pottery. The black topped pottery; burnishing and various designs now emerge. The Naqada site is in Upper Egypt. Petrie also did his sequence dating at Naqada. A tomb from Gebelein nearby shows early representation of boats ushering in the Amratian period. We also have the first clear figures on pottery. A piece of linen fabric from Gebelein is the earliest ever found. There are hippopotamus figurines and a man fishing using a net. Pottery is found *in situ* or on site. The Gerzean pottery represents variety in pottery, stone and alabaster. There is great sophistication in the pottery. Some pottery changed to votive representation. Rock carvings show use of bow and arrows with kilts as garments.

FREDERICK MONDERSON

Research Essays Temple Ticket 13. Dendera Temple. Price of entrance is thirty-five Egyptian Pounds.

The *Dog Palette* in the Louvre Museum shows mythical animals. By the end of the Naqada period there is much fighting for domination and the economic bounty of the land. This led to the formation of the dynastic period. There are many battle scenes. The palettes close this period. They are thus considered "historical documents" for they show much pictographic representation of contemporary events. The "Scorpion king" is a proto-dynastic figure. He is also shown as Horus and in other animal guises. The Dynastic period begins at c. 3200-3150 or sometimes 3050 B.C., by various scholars, with Narmer or Menes conquering the North and uniting the land. Hierakonpolis and Abydos supply much evidence of this early period. Art in registers appear. The *Gebel Arrack* knife that comes from Hierakonpolis has naval battle scenes. Despite the attempts to link it with Mesopotamia, Diop thinks it is clearly African. The painted tomb at Hierakonpolis at 3100 B.C. provides much evidence of the proto-dynastic period. Abydos is thought to be the burial site of Osiris. "King Scorpion" is seen on a macehead from Hierakonpolis. He is seen opening a new canal with scenes of defeated enemies. He is also depicted wearing a White Crown.

The *Narmer Palette* represents the unification of Egypt and the establishment of organization. It begins the First Dynasty. There is some confusion as to the difference between Narmer, Menes and Aha. The *Narmer Macehead* shows him under a canopy purportedly marrying a queen from the north. To some this was a strategic marriage for he chose a wife from his defeated enemies in the North. He

RESEARCH ESSAYS ON ANCIENT EGYPT

united the Red Crown with the White Crown and formed the Red and White Double Crown. That is, the White Crown resting or sitting on the Red Crown. The name of the Red Crown of Lower Egypt is *deshret*; that of Upper Egypt, the White Crown is *hedjet*. The name of the Double Drown of a United Egypt is *pschent*.

Again, it was the discipline of archaeology that lets us reconstruct these cultural developments from a time when there was little or no writing or substantial monuments. We know that the sun and Nile are the two constants of Egypt. They shaped the culture in numerous ways.

Because of its historical, religious and architectural ruins, unlike most other areas, Thebes has attracted a most impressive array of archaeologists and other scholars. Their excavations in temples and tombs, repairing, strengthening, and restoring structures, cataloguing of antiquities and publications of their work, has helped to supply data to make this aspect of ancient history as complete as possible. Much like the Old Kingdom Mastabas, New Kingdom tombs supplied abundant cultural evidence of religious beliefs and social practice. Agricultural exercises, entertainment, war, civil administration and titulary, all interacted in the dynamics of this city of awe, beauty, spiritualism and mystique. Kamil (1984: 141-42) explained how the architects of Thebes' heyday decorated their mortuary structures. "Their tombs are hewn out of solid rock and inscribed with sacred texts from the *Book of the Dead* (developed from the *Coffin Texts* of the Middle Kingdom which were appropriated and revised selections of the *Pyramid Texts* of the Old Kingdom). The smallest tomb is that of Tutankhamon, which was found intact and contained the priceless treasures with which the world is now familiar. The largest belongs to Seti I. It is 100 yards in length and contains fine sculptured wall paintings in perfect preservation."

The temples and tombs of Egypt were very early of greatest importance to archaeologists. When these were laid bare the experts turned to cemeteries where the hot sand preserved many aspects of the ordinary lives and some remains of natural mummification was evident. All this notwithstanding, in 1895, Robert Cust wrote an article entitled "Protest against the Unnecessary uprooting of Ancient Civilizations in Asia and Africa." The behaviors mentioned highlighted the negative side of archaeology and other nefarious practices in Egypt during the 19th Century.

FREDERICK MONDERSON

Research Essays 53. Temple of Luxor. From the southwest, view of papyrus bud columns of the Court of Amenhotep III.

The Archaeology of Ancient Egypt is thus an interesting subject, that lets us see how knowledge of the ancient Egyptian, African, culture unfolded, and helped to shape modern perceptions and understanding of a civilization that has been so influential in erecting buildings, crafting domestic, civic and military implements, and ushering in the practice of science, medicine and so much more. A whole cadre of European scholars was involved in the reclamation, reconstruction and reinterpretation of ancient Egyptian culture and history. There were no Africans involved in this when, during an age as Africa lay prostrate. Thus, there was none of that special criticism that challenged the "European view" of ancient Egypt! All their good works, notwithstanding! Equally, Anthropology also played an important part as a twin adjunct to archaeological reconstruction. As such, then, the following is a chronological listing of the important events of the last two centuries of interest in Egypt.

1. **Pre-Napoleonic Interest**

2. **From Napoleon to Champollion**

3. **Champollion to Mariette**

4. **Mariette to Petrie**

RESEARCH ESSAYS ON ANCIENT EGYPT

5. **Egypt Exploration Fund**

6. **British School in Egypt**

7. **Archaeological Survey of Egypt**

8. **Archaeological Survey of Nubia**

9. **Events to World War I**

10. **Anthropological Implications**

11. **King Tut and Beyond**

12. **The Black Challenge**

13. **Where do we go from here?**

1.   **Pre-Napoleonic Interest** – Before Napoleon's invasion of Egypt, Europe was mostly ignorant of the intricacies of the ancient culture, but from facial features of such monuments as the Sphinx and statues, even accepting Herodotus' description, they accepted Egypt as a black civilization. Count Denon and Count Volney, members of Napoleon's Egyptian entourage, extolled the African nature and blackness of Egypt! Denon painted the sphinx and Volney, in his *Ruins of Empires* (1798), wrote: "The fundamental laws that today govern the universe were developed along the banks of the Nile by the sable skin people we now hold in slavery."

2.   **From Napoleon to Champollion** – Following the discovery of the Rosetta Stone in 1799, in addition to the emerging interest in antiquities, Europe slowly began to pay interest to Egypt and its antiquities and so the race to decipher was on, involving a great many scholars. Equally, the great interest in antiquarian artifacts led to what Brian Fagan depicted in his book of the same name entitled *The Rape of the Nile*.

FREDERICK MONDERSON

Champollion (1790-1832) - *Description of Egypt* – A brilliant linguist who spoke many languages including Coptic, he deciphered hieroglyphics in 1822. Within ten years in 1832 he was dead from overwork. Together with the Italian Rosellini they helped produce *The Description of Egypt* and this opened the floodwaters of European interest in the ancient culture.

Henry Salt (1780-1827) – A British Consul in Egypt, amassed an enormous collection of antiquities and sold it to the British Museum that became the basis of their collection.

Rosellini the Italian - Did early excavation in Egypt around the time of Champollion. He helped produce the *Description of Egypt* together with Champollion.

Giovanni Belzoni (1778-1823) - A circus entertainer who was one of the earliest "raiders of the Egyptian Ark." He did some small-scale digging and clearance of tombs but looted many tombs and acquired more than one collection of antiquities. He was dubbed "The strongman Egyptologist" and was typical of those involved in the "Rape of the Nile" and even destruction of artifacts!

3. **Champollion to Mariette** – This was an age of rampant looting of Egypt. Antiquities hunters ran amok up and down Egypt looking for collector's items and there was no regulation. They also destroyed much of the historical remains. Who really knows what evidence of the blackness of Egypt was destroyed?

David Roberts – Scottish Artist (1786-1864) – Traveled to Egypt and drew many beautiful and colorful pictures of the monuments that encouraged interest in the antiquities. His art showed the monuments, as they lay buried in the sand.

Karl Lepsius 1840s - *Denkmaler* in 24 vols. – He produced a masterful compendium of plans, colorful illustrations, etc., that helped preserve many features now lost owing to recent ravages of time and man.

4. **Mariette to Petrie** – These men moved the discipline from the mist of disorder to order and established scientific foundations in approach to the ancient culture. Petrie spent 50 years in archaeology and produced a very impressive bibliography of his endeavors. Mariette helped found the Cairo Museum of Egyptian Antiquities that preserved the cultural finds and enabled systematic archaeological excavation and restoration of the monuments.

RESEARCH ESSAYS ON ANCIENT EGYPT

Sir Garner Wilkinson - *The Manners and Customs of the Ancient Egypt* – An English scholar who spent many years at Thebes and did extensive recording of texts, illustrations and monuments presenting masterful pieces that are standards of works of study.

Research Essays 54. Temple of Luxor. From the west, another view of the columns of the Court of Amenhotep III.

W.M.F. Petrie (1852-1942) - The "Father of Modern Archaeology." He worked in Egypt actively from 1881-1925, and could boast of "50 years in archaeology." He was probably the most prolific writer of his age, setting Egypt and archaeology on a scientific footing. He did sequence dating at Naqada and identified several sequences of pottery. Besides his many site reports, Petrie established his "Sequence of Prehistoric Remains" and produced "On the Sources of the Alphabet," "The Use of Diagrams," "An early Dynastic Cemetery in Egypt," and "Excavations at Memphis and Hawara in 1911."

These are a paltry sum of his more than 12 pages of bibliographic reference pertaining to his work in Egypt and after.

FREDERICK MONDERSON

5. **Egypt Exploration Fund** 1879-1900 – This was an archaeological society in London, founded by Amelia Edwards and Prof. Stanley Lane-Poole. They encouraged English and American interest in Egypt, raised money and sponsored digs throughout the land. They helped produce and had printed a great many works on different sites, but they all seemed to be devoid of ethnic reference to the blackness of Egypt, as if it was intentional. Whenever such a reference was discovered it was quickly hushed-up or not made much of.

6. **British School of Archaeology in Egypt** and the **Egyptian Research Account** – Adjuncts to the Egypt Exploration Fund with the intent of exploration and publication they also produced many works on excavation of various sites. They produced *Ballas, The Ramesseum, El Kab, Hierakonpolis I and II, El Arabah, Mahasna, Temple of the Kings, The Osireion, Saqqara Mastabas I, Hyksos and Israelite Cities, Gizeh and Rifeh, Athribis and Memphis I, Qurneh and the Palace of Apries (Memphis II)*. All peoples must know of the existence of these important sources. Then there are *Meydum and Memphis III, Historical Studies, The Labyrinth and Gerzeh, Portfolio of Hawara Portraits, Tarkhan and Memphis V, Heliopolis I and Kafr Ammar, Riqqeh and Memphis VI, Tarkhan II, Lahun I: The Treasure and Haragen*. We must also include *Scarabs and Cylinders, Tools and Weapons, Prehistoric Egypt, Lahun II: The Pyramid, Sedment I, Sedment II, The Gospel of St. John, Coptic MS., Tomb of the Courtiers and Oxyrchynchus, Buttons and Design Scarabs, Ancient Weights and Measures, Glass Stamps and Weights, Gurob, Objects of Daily Use, Gerar, Qua and Badari I, Badarian Civilization, Bahrein and Hemamieh, Beth-Pelet I, Corpus of Palestinian Pottery, Qua and Badari III, Antaeopolis (Qua), Beth-Pelet II, Ancient Gaza I, Ancient Gaza II, Ancient Gaza III and Ancient Gaza IV*.

7. **Archaeological Survey of Egypt** – Another British vehicle for archaeological excavation and mapping that published books and reports relative to Egyptian studies, under the auspices of The Egypt Exploration Fund. Their publications, edited by F. LL. Griffith include *Beni Hasan I, Beni Hasan II, El Bersheh I, El Bersheh II, Beni Hasan III, Hieroglyphics from the Collections of the Egypt Exploration Fund, Beni Hasan IV, The Mastaba of Ptahhotep and Akhethetep at Saqqareh, The Rock Tombs of Sheikh Said, The Rock Tombs of Deir el Gebrawi I, The Rock Tombs of Deir el Gebrawi II, The Rock Tombs of El Amarna I, The Rock Tombs of el Amarna II, The Rock Tombs of El Amarna III, The Rock Tombs of El Amarna IV, The Rock Tombs of El Amarna V, The Rock Tombs of El Amarna VI, The Island of Meroe, Meroitic Inscriptions, Five Theban Tombs, The Rock Tombs of Meir I, The Rock Tombs of Meir II, and The Rock Tombs of Meir III*.

RESEARCH ESSAYS ON ANCIENT EGYPT

Another arm of the Fund included the **Graeco-Roman Branch** dealing with papyrus, which published: *The Oxyrhynchus Papyri I, The Oxyrhynchus Papyri II, The Oxyrhynchus Papyri III, The Oxyrhynchus Papyri IV, The Oxyrhynchus Papyri V, The Oxyrhynchus Papyri VI, The Oxyrhynchus Papyri VII, The Oxyrhynchus Papyri VIII, The Oxyrhynchus Papyri IX, The Oxyrhynchus Papyri X,* and *The Oxyrhynchus Papyri XI*. There were also yearly summaries of *Archaeological Reports* Edited by F. Ll. Griffith, as well as listings in the *Journal of Egyptian Archaeology, Sayings of Jesus* and *Fragment of a Lost Gospel, Fragment of an Uncanonical Gospel* by B.P. Grenfell and A.S. Hunt and *The Theban Tomb Series* Vol. I, by Nina de G. Davies and Alan H. Gardiner. Flinders Petrie founded the Journal *Ancient Egypt* in 1914, which aided in publication of his and other scholars' works on Egypt.

8. **Archaeological Survey of Nubia** – With Egypt practically exhausted, scholars now turned to excavate Nubia to determine to what extent she had an impact on Egypt. At least two such reports were produced. Harvard, among several American Universities also did archaeological excavations in Nubia.

9. **Events to World War I** – The two decades from 1895 to 1915 saw enormous advances in the recovery of Egypt, the interpretation of the materials found and a deluge of publication that framed the issue in the minds of Europeans and Americans regarding the origins and peopling of ancient Egypt. We must keep in mind, as early as 1800 of the current era; the German scholar Hegel, perhaps in conspiracy with others began the systematic removal of Egypt from Africa claiming Africa had no history! With that "pronouncement from the mantle of absolute wisdom" of a prominent European scholar, the black role in Egypt began to be diminished and all manner of studies began to be made, many based on faulty data and interpretation. A good source to read that points out the contradictions in European scholarship, yet not really challenged by European scholars, is Cheikh Anta Diop's *African Origin of Civilization: Myth or Reality*, for he outlines all the pros and cons of the arguments. This masterful work needs to be given the serious consideration it truly deserves, for it unmasks the deceit in Egyptological studies masterminded by racist scholarship in Europe and America.

10. **Anthropological Implications** – Anthropology came to the aid of Archaeology and these twin disciplines, to coin a phrase, "skewed the issue" in their determination of whom possibly the ancient Egyptians were. What is interesting is with the deluge of printed books, journals, magazines and newspapers, it's often wondered how did so many people become so hoodwinked

into such great falsehood. After all, following slave trade and slavery, the next phase of non-white subjugation was colonialism and the masters could not countenance and reconcile that the slaves were capable of such intellectual achievements so far back in time before they themselves had become civilized!

This is an aspect of historical evolution. Keep in mind, the mighty Greeks of antiquity, by the end of the 19th Century of our era, were scoring lower on tests than African-Americans who had been out of slavery less than three decades!

Research Essays Illustration 54. Loading and transporting precious cargo.

A great deal of discoveries came under discussion at a multitude of venues. One such place of interest was the *British Association for the Advancement of Science*. One of its principals was the anatomist G. Elliot Smith from Manchester University who worked out of Cairo, Egypt, and examined the mummies of several pharaohs. Some have argued that he was bitter because after he had done his anatomical post mortem examinations of the pharaohs, he was rushed from the room after washing his hands and many of his notes were confiscated. He wrote about Egyptian diffusionism and made the Opening Statement of the "Discussion On the Influence of Egyptian Civilization on the World's Cultures" which W.J. Perry reported on. Smith was Chair of the Committee and did the Report on the "Physical Characters of the Ancient Egyptians" in 1912. The *British Association* met annually, had papers presented and discussed the implications. Yet, how these honest meetings, discussions and debates, etc., disregarded the black element in Egypt; even though these were presented as objective discussions on papers presented, is a mystery to some modern observers. A number of adjunct disciplines were also initiated to fine-tune analysis of the numberless discoveries being made. It's like Prof. Diop said, the African scholar must be multidisciplinary and as Dr. Leonard James taught this writer, the interdisciplinary methodology, now he has a better understanding of the events and documents of the period of 1870-1930, which I have studied intently. To complement archaeology and

RESEARCH ESSAYS ON ANCIENT EGYPT

anthropology, anthropometry, measurement of the skulls, biometrics, and a whole lot more came into service to analyze and compartmentalize and distort and omit the role of blacks in Egypt.

11. **King Tut and Beyond** – The discovery of King Tutankhamon's tomb by Howard Carter in 1922 proved a conundrum for European scholars. Here we had the boy king, with his two painted black statues guarding his tomb that said volumes. Since the press and public were at the tomb when it was opened they could not be destroyed as so many incriminating pieces may have been. We must remember Dr. Zahi Hawass, of the Supreme Society of Antiquities in Egypt has reminded all, "Tutankhamon is the only king we know of with real certainty." This is because he was found in his sarcophagus. Though we recognize all the others, they still have to be re-categorized because they were not so lucky! Recently, however, Queen Hatshepsut's mummy has been identified through archaeological and scientific sleuthing by matching its missing tooth with one found in the Queen's jewel box. Nevertheless, a strange twist has developed in interpreting the meaning of these black statues of Tutankhamon that were replicas of the boy king attired in pharaonic garb and placed just outside of his burial chamber.

Some scholars tell us the statues were painted black for the internment ceremony. Notwithstanding, these statues of King Tutankhamon are not simply guards. They wear the royal headgear and this is significant. How interesting! Nonetheless, where are all the other statues for the numerous embalmed bodies found that should have been painted black for the internment ceremonies? Curiously, right there on the wall beside the statues in the Hall of Tutankhamon, two plaques contradict the claim of blackness for the internment ceremony. Actually there are three plaques. They seem made of bronze and copper. One shows the black base of the surface with the boy king and writing shining through as copper. Another plaque shows the boy king, as a bronze sphinx trampling his enemies. A third shows the boy king, again, painted bronze and trampling other Africans painted black. Are we to believe these vanquished are painted black for the internment ceremony or that their blackness is similar to the black statues of the boy king?

If such is the case, a number of questions and propositions are posed.

a. If the statues were painted black for the internment ceremony; making black so important, then they would be no "Red" or "White" Egyptians in "Heaven."

FREDERICK MONDERSON

b. Of all tombs in existence, why is only one, an intact one at that, shown with such statues? We do know, however, the tombs of Seti I and Amenhotep III contained surviving portions of such statues.

c. Why is black shown to describe other Africans who were not a part of the internment ceremony?

d. We were told one of the wives of Mentuhotep II, Kemsit was painted black but not the others or her servants. Does this mean she was the only one who many have participated in an internment ceremony and gotten to "Heaven?" If so shown and regarded as black, why is Mentuhotep also so shown and not regarded as such?

e. Why is it only wooden statues are painted black? Is it because they show the true color of the Egyptians? Afterall, Herodotus did say they were "burnt of skin!

f. What are we to make of the many small, wooden statues of gods, men and animals painted black in the Cairo Museum?

g. How is it Mentuhotep's statue in the Cairo Museum, discovered in the 1903-04 season, took until 1959 before W. Stephenson Smith's *Art and Architecture in Ancient Egypt* described it as having "black flesh?" Did Petrie, Erman, Maspero, Naville, Ranke, Breasted, Griffith, Davies, etc., not notice such or could not make a similar deduction?

h. By extension, how is it Kurt Sethe could overlook the important Qustol discovery and secreted such in Chicago without any announcement and it was up to Bruce Williams, decades later, to inform all of "The World's Earliest Monarchy" in Nubia?

i. Why did sponsors of the 1970s "King Tut" tour of the United States choose the alabaster bust as its symbol and not the two black statues that depict the boy king in a statelier manner? After the vociferous protest, why did they come back 30 years later with a brown image of the King? Are we to believe, in another 30 years, the next American Exhibit will probably feature one or both statues?

j. We know, contrary to most popular belief, the Egyptians were not white, so why are protestations so vociferous when the blackness of Egypt is raised and articulated and such is not mentioned in "definitive books" by European and American writers? Also, why is it no one questions the unspoken assumption that the ancient Egyptians were white when there is really no evidence to support such?

RESEARCH ESSAYS ON ANCIENT EGYPT

To recap! Another interesting comparison is shown in a room just to the left of the Hall of Tutankhamon. Several cases contain small black wooden statues of kings and gods. One of Amenhotep sits next to a black wooden statue of a panther. Are we to believe the panther is painted black for the internment ceremony? Such a case is away from the beaten path. Nevertheless, its only archaeological sleuthing of unintentional remains of black Egypt that challenges the false house of cards regarding the role of blacks in Egypt.

Research Essays 55. Temple of Luxor. From the west, a further view of columns of the Court of Amenhotep III.

12.   **Those in America** must remember, when the Middle Kingdom temple of Mentuhotep II was discovered in 1903, a statue of the king wearing the *Heb Sed Festival* dress and the Red Crown of Lower Egypt was unearthed, and placed in the Cairo Museum. Despite volumes written about Egypt right after, no one made any commentary about the statue's race! It was not until 1959; 56 years later, that W. Stephenson Smith of Boston in his *Art and Architecture of Ancient Egypt* said Mentuhotep had "black flesh." This revelation, nearly half a century later, was "ground-breaking" and gives some indication of the misinformation that even the white public is subjected to! If this scholar could contend Mentuhotep had "black flesh" why could others not do so?

Pardon this digression! In September 2005, a young female Egyptian guide in the Cairo Museum told this writer: "Mentuhotep was painted black because he was dead. This is what my teacher at the American University in Cairo told me!"

FREDERICK MONDERSON

Imagine, in this day and age such is being taught in Egyptian schools, by western instructors, and fed to visitors by tour guides. From as far back as Petrie's earliest "Min statues" discovered at Koptos and now housed in the Ashmolean Museum in Oxford, to those in a not much visited room in the Cairo Museum, wooden statues were all painted black! All other statues simply reflected the nature of the materials they were made of. Therefore, this is one of the principal ways the Egyptians referred to their skin color. Consider the regular designation, "Red Land, Black Land" as scholars use this dichotomy to describe the fertile land next to the desert encompassing the country of Egypt. However, whenever the gods bequeath Egypt to the king it's always said "I give you the black land" never the red land! However, since Egypt does encompass both red and black lands, does it mean the gods give the "land of the black people" to the king, or only the black half, not the red half? This is a thought that should really be given serious consideration because of the now revealed contradictions in the packaged presentation. In addition, whereas red represents barrenness of the desert, death, and black represents fertility, life, resurrection, can we consider the red in tombs as reference to dead people?

13.   **The Black Challenge** – As they say, "Truth crushed to earth shall rise." Blacks began to become involved in Egyptian studies and to do the critical research that enlightened their people, so long oppressed and kept ignorant in America. As early as the 19th Century, Caribbean interest in Egypt, then fueled by the nationalism of *Marcus Garvey*, blacks began to seek after their cultural history.

W.E.B. DuBois – *The Negro* (1915) and *The World and Africa* (1947); Drusilla Dunjee The *Beautiful Ethiopians* (1926); **Carter Woodson** *The Mis-Education of the Negro* (1932) and *The African Background Outlined*; **J.A. Rogers** – *World's Great Men of Color* and *Sex and Race* I (3 volumes); **Cheikh Anta Diop** *African Origin of Civilization: Myth or Reality, Civilization or Barbarism: An Authentic Anthropology, Cultural Unity of Black Africa,* and *Pre-colonial Black Africa*; **Yosef ben-Jochannan** *Black Man of the Nile and his Family; Africa: Mother of Western Civilization; African Origins of "Major Western Religions;"* **Ivan Van Sertima** *Nile Valley Civilizations; Egypt: Child of Africa; Egypt: Revisited;* **Maulana Karenga, Jacob Carruthers, Tony Browder, Molefi Asante, Wade Nobles**, etc., all produced credible works that exposed the hypocrisy of European scholarship, vis-à-vis, Egypt, together with their American co-conspirators who are just as guilty. We must always remember what **Prof. John H. Clarke**, one of this writer's teachers at Hunter College of the City University of New York, said: "The people who preached racism colonized history!"

RESEARCH ESSAYS ON ANCIENT EGYPT

14.   **Where do we go from here**? – We must visit Egypt, read voraciously, study various disciplines including hieroglyphics, form study groups and continue to teach our young while advocating, *Egypt is African and Black.*

Poem to Thoth

Divine Thoth, how revered is thy name and being, three times great, Trismegistus, majesty.
Rising with Ra in primeval times and Prime Minister of Horus, you are Intelligence of the Gods.
Chief Administrator in the African Hall of Judgment, Lord of the Books, Prince of Laws, you are the Heart of Ra.
The infallibility of your instrumentation and integrity you give the process, determine the faith of millions who enter.

God of Wisdom, their spiritual destiny held in balance in your Ma'atian Psychostasia, Lord of Heliopolis, Patron Divinity of the Learned.
Thoth, as ibis, you were on Narmer's Palette along with Hathor, Lady of Heaven.

You Lord of Hermopolis, who combines with four pairs of gods, are Self-created, Self-produced.
Shrines were constructed at Hermopolis, place of the 'high ground,' at Abydos and elsewhere.
Strength of Gods, you possess Life, Stability, Sovereignty and Dominion, Moon in Heaven, Bull among the Stars, Leader of the Gods, Lordly Ibis you took the place of Horus in the Titulary of Khufu, Letter Writer of the Nine Gods, as Governor of Mankind, you are Lord of Kindliness.
In the Horus/Seth conflict, with words of power you created a cow's head for Isis.

When Osiris became victim to the plot of Seth, Isis and Nephthys lamented the loss of their beloved.
This protestation of sorrow and anguish reached Ra's ears in Heaven.
As father of the gods, Ra dispatched you Thoth and your companion Anubis, to make Osiris True of Voice.
O One of Red Jasper and Quartz, you became emissaries of comfort, intelligence and security providing Isis with magical formulas.
Your Knowledge of Divine speech gave confidence to Isis, and this brought victory to her quest.

FREDERICK MONDERSON

Thus, Thoth, strong deliverer, Scribe of Truth, together with Nephthys and Anubis, you bear witness to the revivification of Osiris, Lord of Goodliness.

When Horus staked his claim in the Imperial Court of the Divinities, Master of Laws you defended him.
Lordly Ibis, your legal mind vindicated his right to mount the Throne of Egypt.
Unquestionably your departed companion Osiris lauded your legalism on his behalf.
Victorious Horus, his mother Isis and aunt Nephthys were equally pleased with your actions, Scribe of the Gods, who sails in his divine boat, and stand among the Lords of Truth, Vicar of Ra.

Your attributes are impressive, Lord of Divine Words.
You gained mastery over your own heart and opened your mouth to bestow life, embracer of heaven.
As Divine Patron of Writing, the arts, astronomy, and science, your origination heralded these gifts of Africa to the world.
Back in ages when Black men and women were founts of creativity and wisdom, your intellect Thoth and the Quintessence of Maat, your counterpart, were great African contributions.

Thoth, as an African divinity of brilliance and integrity, you are Master of Physical and Moral Law.
Your knowledge and power calculated the heavens and the earth, keeping them in equilibrium.
Moon God, symbol of the Equinoxes, your compatriots, the Gods, respect your judgment without question.
For in that august weighing of the hearts of men in the Great Balance, 0 Lord of Divine Words, your findings determine instant Death or Life and Eternal Existence, because you speak truth and are accustomed to Justice. Lord of Khnumu, you record in writing deeds and actions of Gods and men, so continue to Open Your Eye to Give Life.

Thoth you symbolize grace and majesty of the Ibis, and clear-sightedness of the baboon.
Your scales of Balance represent order in every situation, God of Equilibrium, Lord of Ma'at.
You transcribe and interpret the thoughts and aspirations of eternal African spirits who breathe life into creation, 0 Lord of Heaven, Great Deliverer and Creator of Everlastingness; You illuminate the Earth with your Beauty.

RESEARCH ESSAYS ON ANCIENT EGYPT

Great Dom Palm sixty cubits in height, Sweet Well for one that thirsts in the Wilderness, you give prosperity and advancement to mankind who worship you, Patron Divinity of the Learned, who stood in place of Ra.

How interesting these black immortals have destined the talents and intellect of the God Thoth.
Lord of Knowledge and understanding who Possess Power Greater than Osiris and Ra, empower us to cultivate the development of arts, sciences, intellectual growth, and ethical and moral advancement.
This way we can save humanity, within the philosophical construct of the fatherhood of god and the brotherhood of man.

Research Essays 56. Temple of Luxor. In the "Ramesseum Front," the Kiosk of Hatshepsut, usurped by Thutmose III and repaired by Rameses II.

FREDERICK MONDERSON

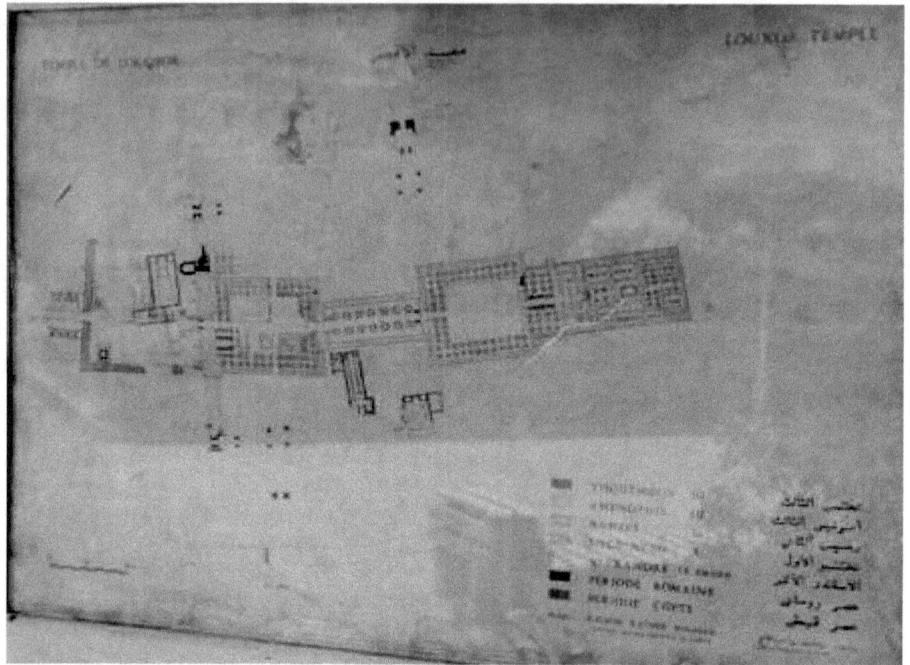

Research Essays 56a. Plan of the Temple of Luxor with names of its builders.

10. The Architecture of Ancient Egypt
By

Dr. Fred Monderson

Dr. Fred Monderson presented the first of his three lectures entitled *The Architecture of Ancient Egypt* at St. John's Recreation Center on Prospect Place, between Troy and Schenectady Avenues, in Brooklyn on Wednesday May 11, 2004. Part II, *The Archaeology of Ancient Egypt* (Wednesday May 18, 2004) and Part III *The History of Ancient Egypt* (Wednesday May 25, 2004) are scheduled for 7:00 to 9:00 PM.

RESEARCH ESSAYS ON ANCIENT EGYPT

Dr. Yosef ben-Jochannan, whom I must give thanks to for showing me the way, has said many things about ancient Egypt. He told me there are 50 countries in Africa; so choose one and specialize in it. Become a specialist, don't be a generalist! So I chose Egypt! He also said check your sources to be accurate, use the oldest materials you can find and dress and behave properly when you enter the temples, respect the culture and don't enter the Sanctuary or "Holy of Holies." In ancient times, only the pharaoh or high priest could enter this sacred space of the god. Further he said, form study groups to discuss this subject, visit Egypt as often as possible and pay particular attention to the architectural layout of the temples. Interestingly enough, we need a different conception to understand the culture and mentality of those ancient Nile Valley Africans of Egypt. As such, you can't properly view Egypt from the prisms of modern conception, unless you have studied it for some time.

The first question one would ask then is 'How were they able to accomplish such architectural feats that have been so impressive down through the ages?' First of all, to answer this, we need to know, for the more lasting monuments, the Egyptians worked in a variety of stone mediums. These stones were quarried and transported from near and distant places. They used wooden sledges and rollers, and ropes and levers were the only means they employed to move the massive stone from the boats, uphill and onto place of erection. They employed bricks to create "the ramp effect," moving things up higher levels. At Karnak Temple builders left evidence of mud ramps on the inner face of the First Pylon. Called away to fight wars of national interest, they were never able to finish this Pylon, and thus the ramp evidence remains.

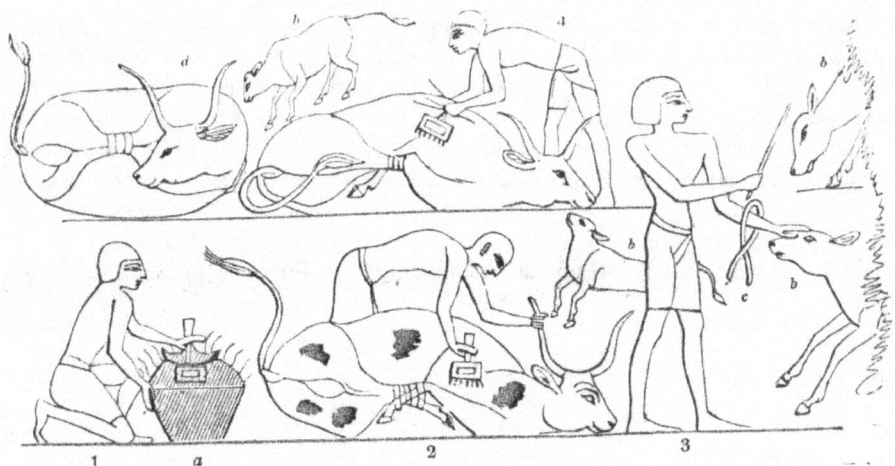

Research Essays Illustration 55. Marking cattle with a hot iron. Thebes.

FREDERICK MONDERSON

Their building tools included the Plumbline; one is seen today to the left on entering the gate at Luxor Temple. This has now been removed. They also used a cubit, measuring line and a leveling staff. Stones were shaped with flint, wooden mallets, hard stone, and copper and bronze tools. They were able to achieve the correct alignment. The Egyptians worked a variety of stone, and precious and semi-precious metals in building and in works of art, whether sculpture or jewelry. Such material of workmanship included gold and silver as well as turquoise, malachite, emerald, carnelian, amethyst, jasper, and lapis lazuli. Stone work was done in limestone, pink and grey granite, basalt, alabaster, syenite, slate, steatite, quartz crystals, sandstone, red quartzite, diorite, marble, serpentine, porphyry and schist. These ancient builders had tremendous patience, access to an enormous work force laid idle by the inundation or overflowing of the river, and tremendous organizational ability that altogether lay behind Egypt's architectural successes.

To get a perception of how we can view the mindset of the ancient Egyptians, Yoyote in Georges Posener *Dictionary of Egyptian Civilization* offered: "According to his individual temperament, modern man can appreciate the geometric beauty and rich decoration of these temples and tombs. He may, however, deplore the apparent excess of a magnificent, but often overwhelming, art. Or again, he may find it difficult to believe that mere animism had the power to inspire such supreme effort and such grandeur. Instead, he seeks in this architecture an inner meaning – a message that provides an answer to our own problems, and he expects to find a guide to practical science or a mystical revelation. The Egyptian built for *themselves*, according to *their* conception of things and for the needs of *their* society. They put all their knowledge, all their creative genius into building temples and tombs, in the same way as modern nations concentrate on improving their industrial capacity." Having established the above, let me now read a poem to the Great God Ptah, divinity of the artisans.

Following a slide show presentation, the following Poem to the God Ptah, was read.

RESEARCH ESSAYS ON ANCIENT EGYPT

Research Essays 57. Ramesseum, Mortuary Temple of Rameses II. View of the Hypostyle Hall with columns and Clerestory (right) and vestibule with Osiride Figures and columns.

POEM TO PTAH

Ptah, Great Architect of the Universe, you were among the earliest African Gods.
At Unification of Kemet, Narmer founded the "White Wall" at Memphis, as his capital in *Aneb-Hetch*, the first nome of the Lower Kingdom.
Lord of the "White Wall," the King built a temple, *Hat-Ke Ptah* at *Khut-Taui*, Horizon of the Two Lands and established worship of your triad Ptah-Sekhmet-Nefertum, later also worshipped at Thebes.
While the fortunes of other gods rose and fell, yours as Patron of Artists, Artisans and Artificers remained not paramount, but consistent, and your festival was celebrated on March 21, Lord of Truth, Great Chief of the Axe.

Lord of the Hidden Throne, whose hidden form is unknown, Powerful One, at Memphis, your High Priest, Great One, Commander of Workmen, was the chief artist of the Royal Court.

FREDERICK MONDERSON

From here, the Great Chief of Artists played a prominent role in state politics, as you Ptah established Ma'at throughout the Two Lands.
Father of Fathers, Power of Powers, you are the Master Architect and Designer of Everything which exists in the World and was employed in the Construction of the Heavens and the Earth, Great of Handicrafts.

Ptah, Disk of Heaven, you illuminate the Two Lands with the Fire of your Two Eyes.
The Theban triad dominated the Middle and New Kingdoms and you, Great Chief of the Hammer, resided in the palace of their abode, with a temple at Karnak.
Father of the Gods, the emblem of your majesty is a close fitting garment, and from an opening in front project your two hands with Scepter, Ankh, and Tet representing power, life, stability.
The *Menat*, symbol of pleasure and happiness, hangs from the back of your neck.

Lord of Thebes, Fire God, while little evidence of Middle Kingdom temples remain, the 18th Dynasty embellished your sanctuary at Karnak and Memphis, the City of Walls.
Ramesside kings were your most ardent champions, O God who Stands upon the Ma'at Pedestal.
Rameses II erected two great sandstone statues at Memphis, one over 10 feet high, in your name.
God of the Beautiful Face in Thebes who created his own image, and fashioned his own Body, you oversaw the construction of that great city, being Chief of All Handicraftsmen and of all Workers in Metal and Stone; God of Wisdom, you understood things before creation.

Very Great God who came into existence in the earliest time, you are the blue-collar god, Master-workman of the Universal Workshop, the Supreme Mind.
Mind and Tongue of the Gods, all things proceeded from you Ptah, Lord of Ma'at, King of the Two Lands.
As a form of the Sun God, Father of Beginnings, you are the Creator of the Eggs of the Sun and Moon.
In this you are the personification of the Rising Sun, artificer in metals, smelter, caster, sculptor, great celestial workman and architect, preparing the primeval elements of earth and water.

God the Father and Son, Lord of Justice, Divine Sculptor, you gave and still give form to all things and beings on earth.
Opener of the Ways, you fashion the Souls of the Dead to live in the Underworld.

RESEARCH ESSAYS ON ANCIENT EGYPT

Research Essays Illustration 56. Male dancers being accompanied by musicians and applauded by females.

As Ptah-Seker, with crook, whip, scepter, crown of disk, plumes, horns and uraei with disks on their heads, the Office of your High Priest existed from the time of the Second Dynasty, though Narmer established your worship at unification.
Great God who came into being in the beginning with two feathers of Ma'at, Lofty Plumes, you rested upon the darkness as King of Eternity, Everlastingness and Lord of Life.
You bring the Nile from its source to make flourish the staff of life and to make grain come forth aged one of Nu.
In same manner you make fertile the watery mass of heaven.

Ptah-Tanen, Disk of Heaven, in peace you light up the world with your brilliant rays.
Ready Plumes, of multitudinous forms, with the Sun and Moon as your eyes, you pass through eternity and everlastingness.

FREDERICK MONDERSON

Builder of your own limbs, maker of your own body, your upper part is heaven; the lower part is the Tuat.
Maker of the Tuat with all of its arrangements, you make to come forth the water on the mountains to give life to all men and women in your name *Ari-Ankh*, Lord of Justice.
Aged one traversing Eternity, Prince of Annu, you judge the dead and give them access to the Field of Peace, Field of Reeds, Field of Grasshoppers.

Ptah, you make all land and all countries.
As you mold gods, men and everything produced Great God who stretched out the heavens; you make your disk to revolve in the body of Nut as you fashion yourself without the help of any other being.
Fully equipped you came forth fully equipped.
The Company of Gods of your Supreme Company praise you; one with many companions.

Ptah-Seker-Asar, Triune God of Resurrection, you Dwell in a Secret Place.
Lord Ta-Tchesetet, pygmy with large baldhead and thick limbs, beetle and plumes, you are the Governor of Everlastingness.
Begetter of Men, Maker of their lives, Creator of all the Gods, you are the Father of the Father of the Gods.
Ptah-Tanen, Babe Born Daily, Aged One on the Borders of Eternity, Lord of Life, Giver of Life at Will, you hear the prayers men make to you.

Research Essays 58.   Ramesseum, Mortuary Temple of Rameses II. A better view of the columns and Osiride Figures within the Porch.

RESEARCH ESSAYS ON ANCIENT EGYPT

The Hapi or Apis Bull, incarnate of Ptah, emerged as the Ptolemaic Serapis in the Memphis Mausoleum or Serapeum of the Greeks, where the great Imhotep was recognized as your son.
From this House of the Aged One, your temple *Aneb-Abt* in Memphis, Men-nefer, the House of the Beautiful Face, you maintain the Balance of the Two Lands.

In this City of "White Wall," Persea and Acacia trees bloom and here reside your female counterpart Sekhmet, sister and wife, mother of your son Nefertum.
This great African Goddess, the Great Lady, Lady of Sa, Queen of Ant, is mighty, strong and violent.
O Holy One, the Lady of Flame, Mighty Lady, Greatly Beloved of Ptah, Lady of Heaven, is Mistress of the Two Lands.
You Gods of Holiness, Bless and Protect African people in the many challenges they face, O Divine Artificer of Creation, Lord of Life of the Two Lands.

The following is a transcript of the main comments of the featured theme:

The Architecture of Ancient Egypt

The architecture of ancient Egypt was its great glory. Beginning with the simplest materials in the pre-dynastic age, the craft of building grew from use of windbreaks, mud and daub to erecting shelters, to unfired then fired brick and finally into the more durable material, stone. Papyrus stalks lined homes and roofs. While the buildings of kings or commoners were constructed of wood and other perishable material, the temples of the gods were made of stone befitting a deity who represented everlastingness. The temple was said to be 'made of fine stone to stand for eternity.' All this notwithstanding, while the dwellings of kings and commoners ascribed to social conventions, the temple of a god was shrouded in symbolism. This reality not only symbolized the eternal nature of the deity, it also represented the notion of the coming into being of that divinity.

Going back to earlier times, according to Yoyote: "A pyramid may perhaps be compared with the primordial rock where the sun was born, and the tunnels in the Valley of the Kings with the passages in the netherworld where the sun regenerated itself." The temple, on the other hand, was a primordial hill from which the god emerged from the waters of chaos at creation. The hypostyle hall with its massive columns was a "forest as at creation." Equally too, since the temple was a fortress for the god-force dwelling within, it had to be equipped with all manner of protective, nurturing, decorative, ritualistic and service paraphernalia to make the god feel comfortably at home, nurtured, satisfied, worshipped and beneficent. As such then, temple architecture came to represent all that was good within the society and hence it was endowed with elaborate buildings and lavish wealth fueled by the successes of imperial warrior pharaohs.

Research Essays Illustration 57. Boat in full sail on the river.

Therefore, the architecture came to embody not simply the quarried stone for the building endowed by pharaoh to house the deity, but so much more. This included the avenue of sphinxes, gates, pylons, propylon, flagstaves and flags, axis or axes depending on whether one or more were employed in the temple, enclosure wall, forecourts and inner courts, doorways, portals, stelae, walls, doors, colonnades, columns, stone drums, capitals, architraves, pavements, floors, roof, shrines, statues, kiosks, sacred lake, obelisks, decorations, gardens, trees, halls, chambers, the Holy of Holies or Sanctuary, altars, sphinxes, standards, libation vases, incense-burners, as well as animals, viz., - cattle, geese, chickens, pigs, horses, donkeys, lions and the implements used by the priests, stewards, priestesses, their kitchens, vine cellars, crypts, bakers, confectioners, store houses, gold and other precious stone houses, treasury, library, craftsmanship, gardens and even more as reflected in the wealth of the priesthood.

RESEARCH ESSAYS ON ANCIENT EGYPT

Thus, the architecture of Egypt was not simply symbolic but also alive, for it fed upon and fed multitudes; or should we say, it fueled social systems engaged in the protection, nurturing, worshipping, and ritualizing of the deity. Ritual, magic and decoration went hand in hand. The "Overseer of the Works," the ritualist and master mason, all cooperated to give life to their building projects. Maspero has pointed out, at Deir el Bahari, a ceremony was performed with white sand laid out, sacrificial animals killed and the blood let to run, tools, the name of the founder, perhaps in a cartouche, was placed there, offerings, breaking of statues, were all part of blessing and providing protection for the temple. They consecrated the living home of the deity. Equally, as in the decoration of tombs, magic was enabled to give life to what was represented.

Research Essays 59. Ramesseum, Mortuary Temple of Rameses II. Rameses kneels to make a Presentation to the enthroned Theban Triad of Amon-Ra, Mut and Khonsu.

Now, to understand the path through the social and politico-religious system just sketched we must trace the architecture of Egypt from the early kingly burials at Abydos as well as the fortresses there at the beginning of the dynastic period; the Memphis "white wall;" Step-Pyramid of Zoser; Snefru's "bent" and "red pyramids;" the "true pyramid" at Ghizeh; the "pyramid complex" concept; the sun temples of the fifth dynasty; and the Middle Kingdom temple at Deir el Bahari, to arrive at New Kingdom and finally Graeco-Roman architecture. Some scholars have argued the pyramid originated in Nubia in the form of silt and even more

FREDERICK MONDERSON

anciently natural wind shaped pyramids. Several of these latter can be seen at Abu Simbel.

By the New Kingdom, principally three types of temples were in use, the god or worship temple such as at Karnak and Luxor, the mortuary temple or "Mansion of Millions of Years," as Hatshepsut's at Deir el Bahari, the Ramesseum and Medinet Habu. The west bank, land of the dead, was littered with mortuary temples of all the New Kingdom pharaohs. Unfortunately, the principal ones tourists visit, Deir el Bahari, Ramesseum and Medinet Habu, are the interesting ones that have withstood the ravages of time and man. Seti's temple at Kurneh has sufficient portions preserved that now, after repairs, is open to visitors; while Merenptah's temple has interesting fragments that is worth the trip. In addition, there was the processional temple, such as the "White Chapel" of Sesostris I, reassembled and now in the Karnak "Open Air Museum," to house the god when he left his main sanctuary. Surviving Kiosks to the Theban Triad as in the Great Court at Karnak and in the "Ramessean Front" at Luxor Temple are other forms of processional temples for worship of the deity outdoors and away from the Sanctuary. However, the Kiosk to Osiris, Isis and Horus are within the temple and near the Sanctuary in the Osirian Complex at Abydos.

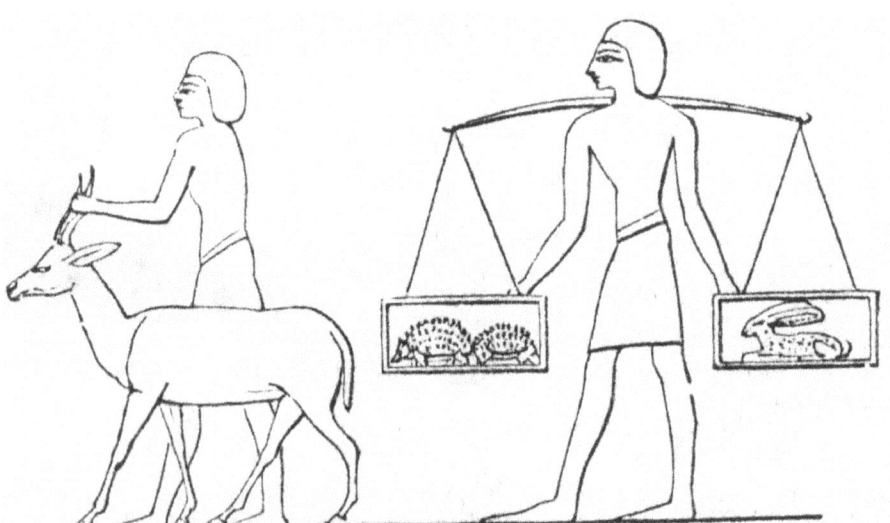

Research Essays Illustration 58. Bringing home the game: A gazelle, porcupines, and a hare. Beni-Hassan.

RESEARCH ESSAYS ON ANCIENT EGYPT

Recognizing the timelessness of this great science, architecture in ancient Egypt has thus been of several forms. These include domestic, civic, military, and religious and mortuary.

Architects began by using the simplest materials such as leaves and branches for windbreaks; they added Nile mud, with leaves to create mud and daub to build the earliest structures. Then they graduated to brick, un-burnt and burnt types. Later they began using stone. The first stone use has been dated to the tomb of King Den of the First Dynasty and King Khasekhemwy of the Second Dynasty. This material, therefore, came into very general use by the Third and Fourth Dynasties.

Now for the types of structures they erected, like all builders, the Egyptian was concerned with the location of his building and how it blended with the environment. In every age as the nature of building construction changed, different challenges faced the architect. The massive pyramid required a different foundation, special orientation than a New Kingdom temple or tomb. Nonetheless, the design was harmonized with the landscape. For the pyramids, the area was cleared to the bare rock before building commenced.

But there were other issues regarding these constructions. Henri Stirlin's edited *Architecture of the World: Egypt* (ND: 131) indicated: "The Egyptian builders considered the problems of organization of work, economy and speedy construction to be of greater importance than questions of mechanics and technical progress, the use of tough materials or more effective tools, or a quest for a more lasting, lighter form of structure." However, while such problems were refined through the ages and with continued practice, no significant changes in construction techniques were made until the XXVth Ethiopian and XXVIth Saite Dynasties and the Graeco-Roman Periods. These changes included "arch vaults, and improved methods of pre-planning foundations and stone-work." Equally, foundations varied according to size of building, wall or even obelisk and according to soil they were erected on. Stirlin (137) again informs: "The general principle was to dig a trench a little wider than the wall to be supported and to line the bottom of it with a thin covering of sand which was stopped from running away by little side walls made of brick. The real foundations were laid in these trenches: stones for the main walls, bricks for the less weighty features. The empty spaces were afterwards filled up with sand." To give an example, to construct walls at Medinet Habu 34 ½ feet wide and 60 feet high, they dug 10 feet deep in the clay's soil. Equally too, at Karnak some foundations as the 8th Pylon, built on clay, were 10 feet deep. On the other hand, at Deir el Bahari in the firmer soil beside the mountain, some walls had a foundation of 20 inches.

FREDERICK MONDERSON

Research Essays Illustration 59. Nubians bringing tribute.

Still, they never misused materials. Again, Stirlin (137) demonstrates: "The actual foundations were often composed of seemingly inadequate materials: small stones, sometimes set edgeways below a first course of large blocks placed lengthways or various elements taken from earlier ruined monuments. Huge squared blocks and drums or half drums of columns were set side by side, caving between them empty spaces unfilled by mortar. This motley collection of masonry frequently shifted ground causing fractures in the lower courses." Significantly, however: "From the twenty-fifth dynasty onwards, and especially during the Ptolemaic period, greater care was taken with regard to foundations: the great temples of later periods were built on proper platforms formed of several layers – up to nine or ten – of well-dressed slabs."

In addition, transportation of stone from distant quarries took place primarily during the inundation period when the river was high and thus, water made these sites easily accessible. Flat bottom boats were generally used. Deir el Bahari temple has a surviving illustration showing two obelisks being transported on these boats drawn by smaller tugs. Lighting also played an important part in their buildings and the clerestory window became an important feature in the New Kingdom temples at Karnak, the Ramesseum and Medinet Habu. The *Akh Menu* Festival Temple of Thutmose III at Karnak seems to have the earliest form of the clerestory. The processional colonnade with the nave higher than the other areas allowed light into the temple's hall. Equally too, roofing and ceilings varied according to temple. Some temples had windows, others did not. Of course, mathematics was an essential part of their construction methods.

RESEARCH ESSAYS ON ANCIENT EGYPT

Research Essays 60.   Medinet Habu, Mortuary Temple of Rameses III. Entrance facade, called a Migdol, with the First Pylon in the rear.

Domestic architecture used primarily the simplest materials, which perished early. Even the palaces of kings were made of simple materials, primarily clay and mud-brick. However, the temples of the gods and burial places of the kings were reinforced with stone. Civic projects, to the extent that they were in pivotal places such as gateways, wharves for landing crafts, public buildings etc., all utilized stone.

Military fortifications were built to garrison forces particularly in foreign lands. Nevertheless, some of the oldest such ruins are found at Abydos and date to the beginning of dynastic times. Here too, in this city, some of the earliest tombs were built for pharaohs of the First and Second Dynasties. These earliest architecture experiments certainly reflected high quality craftsmanship that withstood time and the elements and left evidence of their existence and builders.

Religious architecture included pyramids, mastabas and temples. There were god or worship temples, mortuary temples, kiosks or processional temples as well as chapels. More mortuary than religious, were tombs to house the bodies of kings, queens, nobles and artisans. Poor people were generally buried in sand pits where the dry soil accomplished natural mummification quickly and easily. However, during the Old Kingdom the pyramid combined mortuary and religious structures.

FREDERICK MONDERSON

The mastaba was more mortuary and social as their decoration depicted the owner's status and sometimes daily activities. Some of these were very elaborate with large rooms with lots of decorative scenes proving great usefulness to scholars. As a transitional structure, Mentuhotep II's temple and pyramid at Deir el Bahari is the best example of surviving Middle Kingdom temple architecture. It had a pyramid on a raised platform reached by ramps and a peristyle court and hypostyle hall with many columns.

In the evolution of mortuary architecture, internment changed from the Old Kingdom pyramids and mastabas for kings and queens to tombs for high officials and nobles so that by the New Kingdom, Thutmose I chose to move from the burial on the plains to hidden burial in the Valley of the Kings at Thebes. By the end of the last century, a total of some 65 tombs have been found hidden in this select burial place. On the principle of the kings' internment, there was a separate burial place for other important individuals as named the Valley of the Queens, Valley of the Nobles, and Valley of the Artisans. A great deal of the nation's cultural history is preserved in the painting of these tombs, though much has been desecrated and destroyed.

Every part, feature, utility or location of a type of architecture had its own peculiarity, whether the foundation, floor, ceiling, walls, decoration, quarrying, transportation, each had its own character. Especially important, as one entered a temple the floor got higher and the ceiling got lower approaching the sanctuary. Flower gardens and vines for grapes as well as other plant forms were cultivated in some temples or just beyond their walls enhancing the beauty of the architectural layout. From these gardens flowers were supplied for the daily ritual.

Now let us sketch the history or evolution of building practice from the earliest times. Let us begin with Memphis.

1.   **Memphis – The White Wall** – At unification, Narmer or Menes diverted the Nile River near Memphis, creating a plain of dry land where he founded his administrative and capital city. He built around it an enclosure wall, painted it and hence the title "white wall." This was the first significant civic architectural construction in ancient Egypt. Here he built a temple and established the worship of the God Ptah. While this "white wall" structure has generally disappeared, it noticeably remains in literature and mythology.

RESEARCH ESSAYS ON ANCIENT EGYPT

Research Essays Illustration 60. Conjurers or thimble rig.

2. **Step-Pyramid of Zoser** – By constructing the Step-Pyramid for King Zoser at Sakkara, Imhotep stands large at the beginning of Egyptian architectural history, and for that matter in world history. It was the first significant construction utilizing stone as well as containing a number of new features including the colonnade, standing and engaged columns, the enclosure wall, false entrances, cobra friezes, glazed tiles, multi-story construction, great court, "dummy buildings," a temple for worship, etc. All this, still stands 4,600 years later which says something about construction techniques as well as its builder. Of course, Imhotep was more than an architect, he is considered the "world's first multi-genius." He was an astronomer, mathematician, priest, medical doctor, administrator as Grand Vizier and poet. He has been credited with the saying of the ages: "Eat, drink and be merry, for tomorrow you die." His tomb, thought to be in the Sakkara area, has never been found. For his medical prowess, he was later deified as a god of medicine and praised by the Greeks in their Hippocratic Oath, as the personage Aesculapius.

FREDERICK MONDERSON

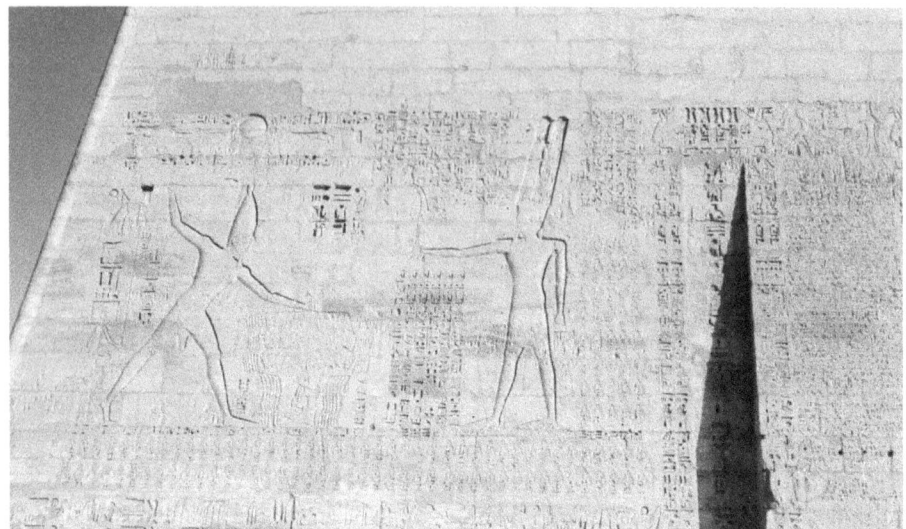

Research Essays 61. Medinet Habu, Mortuary Temple of Rameses III. Rameses smites captives before Amon-Ra who offers him the curved sword on the left side of the Temple's entrance Pylon.

3. **Snefru's Bent-Pyramid** – Snefru, the last king of the Third Dynasty or first king of the Fourth Dynasty built two pyramids and experimented with the true pyramid. The two pyramids are the "Red Pyramid" and the "Bent Pyramid." The "Bent Pyramid" collapsed, but it set the stage for his son Khufu in the Fourth Dynasty to accomplish the "true pyramid at Ghizeh." Rather than ending the Third Dynasty, Snefru also gets credit for beginning the Fourth Dynasty, though in fact the Third and Fourth Dynasties should be fused. It should be reiterated; the idea of the pyramids finds its prototype in the natural pyramids carved in the sand-blown highlands of which some are seen near Abu Simbel temple in the south. There are also pyramids in Nubia that are as numerous as those in Egypt.

4. **The True Pyramid at Ghizeh** – The "True Pyramid" is the highlight of the Pyramid Age. Built to harness the unemployed population at inundation time, as a final resting place for the pharaoh and to awe his contemporaries, it is a masterpiece of architectural accomplishment, building techniques and administrative organization and manpower utilization. Having withstood time, it continues to awe, inspire and amaze attesting to the ingenuity of ancient African architectural creativity. Some have argued it still radiates philosophic, spiritual, theosophic, epistemological and metaphysical power. It is truly an amazing work of architectural construction.

RESEARCH ESSAYS ON ANCIENT EGYPT

5. **The Pyramid Complex** – When we see the Pyramids, say of Ghizeh, in pictures or from a distance, only visible are three triangles against the horizon and flat desert and the inner workings and juxtapositioning of the architectural layout is seldom considered. The Pyramid was housed in a complex. The Pyramid Complex consists of an Enclosure Wall, a Causeway or walkway into the structure, and a Valley Temple where the deceased is first introduced into his final resting place. Moving along this path evident is a Sacrificial Altar and Sun Temple with the king's massive Pyramid in the center of the complex. Off to the right there would be Magazines for storage, a Heb-Sed Festival Pavilion and an open area for the king to run the Heb-Sed race of rejuvenation, at first celebrated after 30 years of rule. There would be "Dummy Buildings" symbolizing the north and south kingdoms of his nation. Before the pyramid there would be Solar Boat Pits with buried boats to ferry him across the sky. There were five pits found near Khufu's Great Pyramid. Off to one side would be smaller pyramids for his female relatives and on the other, Mastaba Tombs for officials and nobles, who wished to be buried in the shadow of his pyramid. Oftentimes there was a God temple within. Beyond the wall were found workmen's dwellings from where they lived, were injured, treated medically, even died and were buried as they labored on those national or civic projects.

Research Essays Illustration 61. Cattle rescued from the inundation. Beni-Hassan.

FREDERICK MONDERSON

6.   **The Sun Temples of the Fifth Dynasty** - The Sun Temples of the Fifth Dynasty sought to emphasize and incorporate a temple to the god as well as one to the king. They generally had an outdoor altar where ceremonies and worship of the Sun God took place.

7.   **Middle Kingdom** – Mentuhotep II's Middle Kingdom temple at Deir el Bahari, the most complete and oldest surviving temple at Thebes, represented a transitional form from Old Kingdom to New Kingdom building practice. It encompassed all the elements of a pyramid on a raised platform with ramp, colonnades, a peristyle court and hypostyle hall with columns, and shrines or Sanctuary up against the face of the mountain. There were also burials of princesses discovered here though no one knows what happened to the king's body. A valley temple lay at the river's edge and this led to the temple. Along this pathway lay a tree-lined Avenue of Sphinxes. In the temple, a statue of the king was found wearing the Heb Sed Festival gear, the Red Crown of the north and his skin painted black; or, as W. Stephenson Smith in *The Art and Architecture of Ancient Egypt* has indicated, Mentuhotep had "black flesh!"

The assumption is that there was also a similar statue of him wearing the white crown and in the same attitude as the other. It would certainly be something if the other statue was found with Mentuhotep wearing the White Crown and painted red! This would certainly put to rest the notion of the "Red Egyptian." This was, however, unlikely since he was black!

8.   **New Kingdom** – The New Kingdom broke with the past and made a separate temple to worship the god and one for the dead king, called his "Mansion of Millions of Years." They also separated the location of their siting. While not absolutely so, worship temples were located on the east bank, "land of the living" and mortuary temples on the west bank, "land of the dead." One scholar believed Seti I conceived of the hypostyle hall at Karnak as a mortuary temple in a worship temple. Then there was a worship temple to Hathor on the west bank near Deir el Medina. Of course there was a third temple called processional where the god rested when traveling away from his main sanctuary. Karnak and Luxor, the Temple of Mut and that of the War god Montu, were typical worship temples of the New Kingdom and situated on the east bank of the Nile, "land of the living," at Thebes. Practically every New Kingdom monarch built a mortuary temple to his deified self. The west bank at Thebes was littered with them. Not many have survived the ravages of time and man. The principal ones visited today are at Deir el Bahari, Ramesseum and Medinet Habu. The temple of Seti I at Gurneh has survived and is currently being repaired, though it is open to visitors.

RESEARCH ESSAYS ON ANCIENT EGYPT

Research Essays 62. Medinet Habu, Mortuary Temple of Rameses III. Rameses smites captives before Ra-Horakhty who offers him the curved sword on the right side of the Temple's entrance Pylon.

The Mortuary Temple of Seti I at Abydos dedicated to Osiris, the god of the dead, is only one of many built here at the home of the judge of the underworld. This is where the ritual drama of the African Judgment took place in the Hall of the Double Maati. Here, the God stood at the Stairway to heaven. The main structure of this temple has survived well and has colonnades and very good colored illustrations. Some scholars have argued that Seti's temple is not simply to the God Osiris but to Seti's predecessor kings whose burial sites are not far off in the desert.

Petrie found 10 successive levels of temples at Abydos dating back to the beginning of dynastic rule. Perhaps there were others of perishable materials of the Prehistoric Period. Nonetheless, this temple of Seti has the best surviving illustrations in all of Egypt today.

9.   **Late Period** – Architectural constructions continued into the Late Period particularly during the XXVth Ethiopian and the XXVIth Saite Dynasties. All the principal worship sites received new construction, reconstructions, repairs, endowments, embellishments, additions, etc., during this period, attesting to Ethiopian and Saite concern and respect for the gods and culture.

FREDERICK MONDERSON

10.   **Greek and Roman Periods** – Building construction never finished during the Greek and Roman periods. In fact, these foreign conquerors added a significant feature of littering the temples with inscriptions that helped retain much of the ancient ritual that were copies of even earlier times. New features also entered the illustrations in terms of how individuals were represented. At Kom Ombo we see Cleopatra's breast exposed. The Mammisi or "birth house" where the god was born was added as a new feature during Roman times. Each temple had one and some had two Nilometers to measure the volume of the river at inundation.

Esna, Edfu, Kom Ombo, Dendera, Philae and Kalabsha are all surviving temples of the Greek and Roman Period built by Egyptian architects along ancient specifications under foreign over-lordship. Kalabsha, however, was first built during the New Kingdom. These temples were built on even earlier sacred foundations taking them back to the earliest times. Clearly there were changes in these temples with the much older ones. However, even with changes they do continue the tradition of building and ritual and worship with basically the same elements and practices.

Now let me wind down and sketch the architectural layout of the temple.

From the Quay at the riverside the pharaoh disembarked when he came to visit the temple. In some cases a canal connected the river to the temple's entrance. In others, an Avenue of Sphinxes led to the First Pylon. At Karnak, for example, we see two small obelisks (one remaining) before the temple while at Luxor there were two seated statues, two regular sized obelisks and four standing statues in front of the pylon. As you enter both the Luxor and Karnak temples the earliest parts are to the rear and the latest parts are first encountered.

At Karnak, an Avenue of Croi-sphinxes, sphinxes with rams' heads with a miniature figure of the king between the paws greet the visitor; all stand on an elevated pedestal, leading to the temple's Pylon entrance. The Pylon is a massive gateway with a tower that was attached to the enclosure wall to block out the temple's doings from the prying eyes and ears of outsiders. This enclosure wall also created the fortress that protected the god and his retinue within. On the Pylon were flagstaves flying flags of the temple's divinity, the national god, the nome and nation.

RESEARCH ESSAYS ON ANCIENT EGYPT

Research Essays Illustration 62. Diverse jobs. Cutting the wheat with a sickle; lining up the asses; loading the animals; emptying the wheat in silos.

Beyond the Pylon is a Great Court where most noble visitors came and this was as far as they got. In this court, there were shrines, kiosks, an altar, sphinxes, statues, colonnades, and much more. At Karnak, a smaller temple of Rameses III was built in the Great Court on the north-south Axis. At the opposite end of the court there is a kiosk to the Theban Triad, Amon, Mut and Khonsu, built by Seti II of the Nineteenth dynasty. A portico led to the Second Pylon. Also, at Karnak, a temple that took 2000 years to build, a Processional Colonnade centered the great hypostyle hall. Beyond this another Pylon led to another Open Court. There was beyond this a Fourth Pylon. Between the Fourth and Fifth Pylons were obelisks erected by Thutmose I, Hatshepsut and Thutmose III. Between the Fifth and Sixth Pylons, Hatshepsut erected two other obelisks. Here Thutmose III erected two pillars highlighting the emblematic papyrus and lotus symbols of the Upper and Lower Kingdoms under unification.

Thutmose III and his father Thutmose I built a Sixth Pylon before the Sanctuary. This warrior pharaoh, Thutmose III, placed Osiride statues and papyrus bundle columns along this path towards the Sanctuary.

Unlike any other New Kingdom sanctuaries, the one at Karnak was open at the east and west ends so the sun could shine through on rising and setting. There was a Sacred Lake nearby so priests could wash themselves before officiating and the god's barge could sail here on festive occasions.

Perpendicular to the original east-west axis, four other pylons were added on a second axis linking the original temple with the god's wife's temple to the south. The gods were generally shown as a family of husband, wife and son. Interestingly, on the east-west axis, the statues face the center of the axis on the Processional Way, while on the north-south axis they face north or parallel along the path of this second axis, not the axis itself as they do with the principal east-west axis. In this national temple, called "the palaces" there were some 22 other temples to various gods and goddesses who were also worshipped at Karnak, besides the Theban Triad of Amon; Mut, his wife and Khonsu, their son.

East of the Sanctuary is a Court of the Middle Kingdom and beyond this Thutmose III built his Festival Temple, the *Akh Menu*. Rameses II came by later and finished the hypostyle hall begun by his grandfather Rameses I and his father Seti I. Then he erected a "Girdle Wall" to enclose the original temple on the east-west axis. He also erected a small temple east of the *Akh Menu*, just inside the eastern gate. There are four gates or entrances to Karnak, though today as in ancient times, the most important one was on the west nearest the river.

Research Essays 63.   Medinet Habu, Mortuary Temple of Rameses III.   Defaced Osiride Figures in the First Court. Notice the small female figure near the foot of the statue.

RESEARCH ESSAYS ON ANCIENT EGYPT

One last thing. Karnak is an open temple so the sanctuary is open. In a closed temple the floor rises and the ceiling lowers as you enter towards the sanctuary. While this phenomenon also applies here, it's just that the "Holy of Holies" is in the open air as opposed to being in a closed location.

Finally, let me close by reading a poem to Imhotep.

Research Essays Illustration 63. An ass fetching the falcon on its back.

FREDERICK MONDERSON

POEM TO IMHOTEP

O Divine Imhotep, you are the greatest of the great Africans, man of wisdom, seer.
Your name, deeds and attributes span millennia.
Adjudged the world's first multi-genius, your intellectual gifts to the world are manifold.
You are famed as High Priest, architect, administrator, astronomer, and mathematician.
Nevertheless, your contributions to helping the living and dying are most revered.

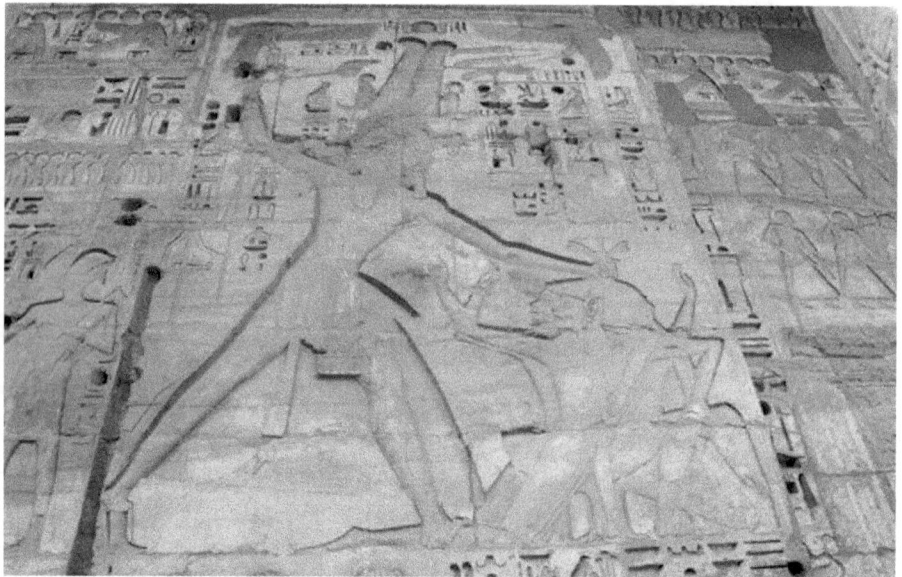

Research Essays 63a. Medinet Habu, Mortuary Temple of Rameses III. Rameses grasps Egypt's enemies by the hair and prepares to administer the death-blow.

As a physician your healing powers remain unparalleled.
As poet, you remind mankind, 'Eat, Drink, be Merry, for Tomorrow You Die.'
As architect your lasting contribution, the Step-Pyramid constructed at Sakkara for Pharaoh Zoser, from the Third Dynasty to today, still this monument remains erect. For five millennia that architectural masterpiece withstood the ravages of time.

RESEARCH ESSAYS ON ANCIENT EGYPT

Acting as prototype for black Egyptian, African, achievements, it is a testimony to your stature and those mountains of black innovations in that age of the intellectual awakening of the world.
Some argue your 'Eat, Drink, be Merry, Tomorrow you Die' a classic admonition of the ages.
This profound philosophical realization early established your reputation as thinker.

Research Essays 64.   Medinet Habu, Mortuary Temple of Rameses III. Pillar and column in the Second Court.

As physician at the court of your esteemed monarch, you defined the parameters of the healing discipline.
Still, not considered the 'father of medicine,' is a boon, for divinity is more your station.
You deserve credit for a profession, the healing art and propagation of life, so essential to humanity's future.

Throughout the land of ancient Kemet temples erected proclaim your healing prowess.
At Karnak, Deir el Bahari, Edfu, Dendera, Kom Ombo, Philae, your name resounds in great reverence.

FREDERICK MONDERSON

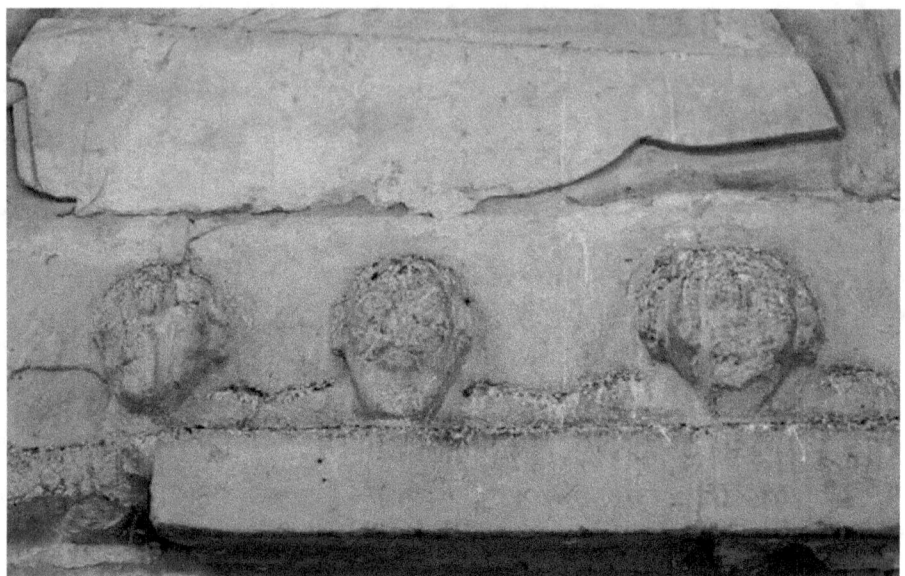

Research Essays 64a. Medinet Habu, Mortuary Temple of Rameses III. Heads of the Egyptians at the time of Rameses III. How interesting that heads or faces of statues always seems to be "purposefully defaced!"

Inscriptions speak of your kinship with Memphite Ptah, black Egyptian, African, God of the Artisans.
You are the third in the Memphite Triad, Son of Ptah, creative.

In troubled times, your accomplishments and exploits are cherished ideals to emulate.
For millennia you under-girded the African art of healing, then praised by the Greeks as Aesculapius, their 'God of Medicine.'

You stand as symbol of blacks entering the medical profession who must marvel, for eons a black, Egyptian, African, has been guardian to their cherished quest, a vocation indeed noble.

All in all, Imhotep, as symbol you manifest the great intellectual, scientific and moral gifts of Africans to advance the cause of humanity.

RESEARCH ESSAYS ON ANCIENT EGYPT

11.   The Power of One

While the song says, "One is a Lonely Number," the Rastaman Bob Marley believed in "One Love," and our ancestors and elders reinforced the view, "Each One, Teach One." Interestingly, and "One More Time," they further tell us, "Each One, Love One," and that we should be "One For All and All For One." In fact, "No One" should be left out. Like the Census, "Everyone" should be counted. However, Let us not turn "One Against the Other," but let us remain "One United People." Importantly, our leaders believed, "No One Should Die at the Hands of Another."

In this country, a current belief holds that "Education is for One and All." Meanwhile, Mr. Moore, during the playing of the National Anthem at school reminded, this cultural symbol professes "One Unity" and that "Opportunity Knocks Only One Time," insisting we be prepared, ready and take advantage of *Fortuna.* The motto of the United States of America, taken from Virgil (*E Pluribus Unum*) is "One from Many." Daniel Webster (1782-1852) advocated: "Liberty, and Union, Now and Forever, One and Inseparable." Even further, Webster noted it is: "One country, One Constitution, One Destiny." Still, President Truman reinforced the view: "If there is One Basic Element in Our Constitution, it is Civilian Control of the Military." Even more, we should be reminded in a Christian nation, the "One Born in a Manger," Jesus, taught "I Am One with the Father," and his coming was so significant, as Adam Clayton Powell professed, "One man split time into B.C. and A.D." Believing in him "One Knows" unquestionably, "There is One God."

We must further remember not "Anyone, or Someone," but "Everyone is Special." We are all "One Human Family." Some are charismatic, diplomatic, revolutionary, nationalistic, and "One Person Can Make a Big Difference." "One Person Can by Forcefulness of his or her Truth; become a Majority." Equally too, "One Person can have a Significant Impact on an Issue," if their name or presence can command, galvanize or influence others. Therefore, philosophical speculation ought to allow us to examine the *"Power of One,"* as a force that has guided and influenced human development and dynamics, particularly as it has unfolded within the context of African historical consciousness and experiences. Still, Jonathan Swift, *On Thoughts of Various Subjects* believed: "We have just enough religion to make us hate, but not enough to make us love one another."

To begin, and despite the significant struggles for "One Man, One Vote," often at election time, many people, frustrated with a political system that has been unresponsive to their needs, are forced to ask "What Will My One Vote do to

FREDERICK MONDERSON

Bring About Change?" This, even after "One King, a man of vision, peace and inspiration, whose ideas helped change a nation," gave his famous "I Have a Dream" speech that "One day this nation will rise up and live out the true meaning of its creed." As a result, this simple yet profound admonition forces us to examine the significance of the "Power of One," and how such a number and concept can have powerful ramifications in social, human, political and intellectual relations.

Research Essays Illustration 64. The Tritura. Thebes.

Such acquiescence has allowed Giuliani, Pataki and Gingrich, Mayor, Governor and Speaker, and now we must be careful Bush the President does not create "One Nightmare" for our city, state and nation. For this will force us to ask, "When is One Plus One, not two?" Sometimes it is best to take it "One Day at a Time," "One By One in the Moonlight," and remember, "One Swallow Don't Make a summer," but "One Blizzard," or "One Hurricane," can devastate and/or paralyze a City, State and Nation.

That year when the Atlanta Braves became World Series champs, one of their ace pitchers, Glavine, shutout the then most powerful and productive team in baseball, the Cleveland Indians, in a "One to Zero" game. Pitching seven and a half innings of shutout ball, all the Braves needed was "One Run" by Dave Justice who homered to bring home the victory to a city and team that came close but could not "ice the cake" on several occasions, in this and in many other sports. Home Run King Hank Aaron was: "One among the Thousands" who witnessed this victory. So the significance of "One Run," like so many other cases of "One," can force people to believe in the *Power of One* and to examine "Oneself."

RESEARCH ESSAYS ON ANCIENT EGYPT

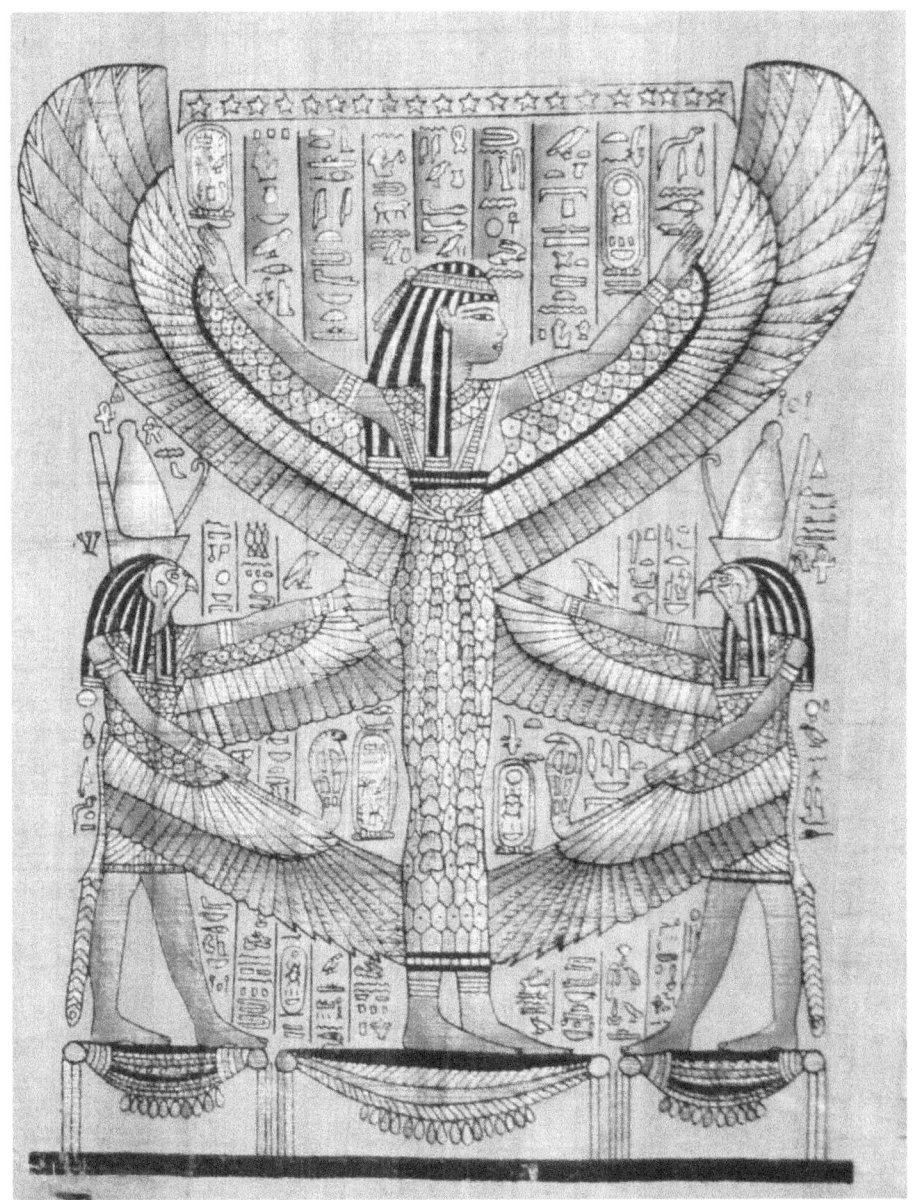

Research Essays Papyrus Art 6. Goddess with wings extended is encircled by two Horuses in Double Crowns and wings with uraei.

One Fall Day, on October 16, 1995, Minister Louis Farrakhan, with a host of dedicated men and women, issued "One Clear Call" and summoned "One Million

FREDERICK MONDERSON

Black Men," to the nation's capital. They came to demonstrate unity, discipline, fortitude and a philosophical orientation that forced many people to take a second look at mobilized black power. We must remember the philosopher Plato reminded us: "You Cannot Conceive the Many without the One." Even further he insisted: "Whether One is or is not, One, and the Others in Relation to Themselves and One Another, All of Them." As we set out for the nation's capital that memorable day, the prayer was: "God Bless us Every One" and I'm pretty sure, for every man on that historic march there was "One Black Woman" who encouraged him, prayed for him and stood majestically to welcome him home. It was like Thomas Mordant (1730-1809) once said: "One Crowded Hour of Glorious Life." So having participated in that tremendous pilgrimage designed to send a most profound message to America and the world, one gets the feeling of being "One Special Person."

So, in this tumultuous gathering of "This One and That One," having heard the cry of: "Come One and Come All," I'm considered "One in a Million," remindful of having participated in William Wordsworth's (1770-1850) glorious assessment of: "One of those Heavenly Days That Cannot Die." For there should be, he added: "One Great Society Alone on Earth, the Noble Living and the Noble Dead." However, not content to sit on my "One Rear," I had to return "One Year Later" to the Day of Atonement, in New York City. Next it was the "One Million Woman March" in Philadelphia and the "One Million Youth March" in Harlem, New York. Not to be left out, I had to attend the "One Million Family March," October 16, 2000. I guess you can call me "One Busy Body" or, "One Concerned Brother" interested in the well-being of his people, "One People." They were "All One and the Same Thing," if we believe Spinoza (1632-1677). A sister who wonders too, like George Coleman (1762-1836) in *Broad Grins* noted: "Thank you, Good Sir, I Owe You One." Then again, if we believe Montaigne the skeptic who said: "Keep Cool: It will be all One a Hundred Years Hence." Nevertheless, Von Bedun (1826-1907) sums it all up: "Unity makes strength, and since we must be strong, we must also be One." In feeling good and thankful, after all those activities, Cervantes' admonition is: "Blessings for the One who Invented Sleep."

RESEARCH ESSAYS ON ANCIENT EGYPT

Research Essays 65. Medinet Habu, Mortuary Temple of Rameses III. View of the Ark at rest with much decorative color remaining.

"One man," O.J. Simpson, held America and the world spellbound for over a year and unleashed a multitude of legal precedents in American jurisprudential litigation. As a result, millions of viewers the world over had a unique opportunity to observe the operational dynamics of "One Nation's Legal System." Millions of dollars were spent and many millions more were made as the trial of the century unfolded, progressed and culminated in a most dramatic fashion. The result, so unexpected, left many people, "All Perhaps One," in an unbelievable state, as the jury rendered its verdict, "One Monkey Don't Stop No Show." All this proves said Napoleon: "There is but One Step from the Sublime to the Ridiculous."

FREDERICK MONDERSON

Research Essays 65a. Medinet Habu, Mortuary Temple of Rameses III. In Blue or War Crown, Rameses holds an ankh, wears a long flowing gown, with apron sporting uraei and above a hawk hovers overhead while further above, uraei signal he's in the temple.

Lead attorney for O.J. Simpson's defense, Johnnie Cochran, masterfully demonstrated how "One Knowledgeable, Skillful and Articulate African American" legal mind could command a courtroom, unleash precedents in this nation's legal system and be rewarded with a verdict that left the whole world

RESEARCH ESSAYS ON ANCIENT EGYPT

spellbound. Mr. Cochran's courtroom flair and forcefulness was particularly significant for in winning his biggest prize and demonstrating great brilliance and intellectual fortitude, he contrasted sharply with "One Other African American," Colin Ferguson. This person, found guilty of a crime on the East Coast, on "One Stormy Night," made a big buffoon of his-self in the courtroom and sought to characterize black men by his amateur behavior. Therefore, Cochran's professionalism became a testimony of the intellectual wellspring of "One African American Mind that was Functional, Challenging, Articulate and Well Meaning." Colin Powell, unlike Jessie Jackson, chose not to be a significant player and "One Presidential Candidate" in a run for the White House. Today this Brother is "One Secretary of State" of the United States. This is the first time "One Black Man" held this position. It does show, as Cervantes (1703-1764) has demonstrated: "Everyone is the son of his own Works."

Research Essays Illustration 65. Two women working the loom.

Marcus Garvey, in his *Philosophy and Opinions*, reminded us that African people worldwide ought to progress under the banner of "One God, One Aim, One Destiny." On the other hand, the country of Guyana in South America holds as its creed, "One People, One Nation, One destiny." Nevertheless, for nationalists, whether Nkrumah, Malcolm X, Paul Robeson, Elijah Mohammed and countless others, this idea of the *Power of One*, remained a beacon of hope, fortitude, and tenacity, as they confronted oppression of African people, and the illness of racism and discrimination. Nkrumah's vision of African Unity was "One Continental Government" strong enough to win Africa respect worldwide.

FREDERICK MONDERSON

At the turn of this century, W.E.B. DuBois created at least four ideas that underscored the *Power of One* as a seed-germ of nationalist determination and struggle. By insisting that "One-tenth" of the black race ought to become doctors, lawyers, teachers, judges, and other professional people, he saw them as being vanguard in the salvation and elevation of African-Americans in this country. By creating the idea of Pan-Africanism, he unleashed a "Philosophy of Oneness of African People Worldwide," to become a significant bulwark against the machinations of European and American colonialism, imperialism and exploitation of "One Race and One Continent." DuBois was visionary enough to realize and clearly state that the "One Most Significant Issue" of the twentieth century was the matter of race, and though we have arrived at the end of this "One Hundred Year Period," the issue seems even more poignant now than ever before. Therefore, we must be careful and remember as in Shakespeare's Hamlet 1, 5 states: "One May Smile and Smile and be a Villain."

Research Essays 66. Medinet Habu, Mortuary Temple of Rameses III. Rameses in Blue or War Crown kneels to Present Ma'at as his name to enthroned Ra-Horakhty.

In his Harvard PhD. dissertation entitled *The Suppression of the African Slave Trade to America* 1638-1880, W.E.B. DuBois articulated a powerful thesis. In the process of his researches, he theorized that in that horrible experience, Africa had lost "One Hundred Million" men, women, and children, in what Dr. Donna Richards, Merimba Ani, came to call the MAAFA, the great enslavement, or the *African Holocaust*. In that experience, time and time again, the notion of "One" seemed to play so significant a role "One" has to agree that the *Power of One* is indeed meaningful.

RESEARCH ESSAYS ON ANCIENT EGYPT

In 1505, "One Bishop," Bartholomew De Las Casas, petitioned "One Pope," to allow the importation of Africans into the New World and thus began "One of the Most Heinous Crimes against the Human Spirit." Additionally, in 1619, "One Dutch Vessel" unloaded a parcel of Africans at Jamestown, North America, and thus in "One Act" began the most horrendous experience of an institution of slavery that created psychological, social, economic and political lacerations upon the enslaved Africans in the New World.

When New England entered the slave trade rum became an important medium of exchange. In the unfolding of this tragedy, those New England entrepreneurs began to exchange 140 gallons of rum for "One Male African," 120 gallons of rum for "One Female African" and 90 gallons of rum for "One young female African" on the verge of puberty. Even more, after centuries of struggle against slavery/racism, we see evidence of its ugliness in the affective and effective dynamics of schools, in the media, in social relations and in government. It reduces us to struggle for every minute we face "One Challenge," every day "One Battle," and every year, "One War." Such a strategy is effective in forcing us to meet the challenges, as Thomas Percy (1728-1811) says: "One Foot on Sea, One Foot on Shore, to One Thing, Constant Never."

Today our people are claiming reparations, because we Blacks in America were denied our "40 Acres and One Mule" after Emancipation. Lest we remain "One-sided" or "One Eyed Jacks," we ought to remember, man is nothing without his woman, or more appropriately, "Behind Every Successful Man There is One Woman." It should not be lost; it was "One African Eve" who started it all, "One Hundred and Fifty Thousand Years Ago." Hetepheres was "One great Queen of Egypt" whose son, grandson and great grandson built the Giza group of pyramids in the Fourth Dynasty. Equally too, Hatshepsut was "One Woman" who challenged male dominance and ruled a great state, the ancient African nation of Kemet, today's Egypt. One woman, Cleopatra, stood against Rome. Later on in African history, Candace, Nzinga, Yaa Asantewaa, and Bottom Belly and Queen Mary from Jamaica and Phyllis Wheatley the American who wrote poetry, Sojourner Truth and Harriet Tubman, who made many forays into the south to free brothers and sisters, and Fannie Lou Hamer who helped politicize the black South, were each "One Cut Above."

Mary McLeod Bethune, the great educator, may have said, "The One Who Learns is the One Who Advances in Life." Equally, "The One Who Does Not Learn is the One Who Falters." And further, "The Ones Who Work to Reach Goals in Life, are the Ones Who Will Enjoy life." Amy Jacques Garvey, Mrs. DuBois, Betty Shabaaz, and Mitta Monderson, each were in time perspective, "One Woman" who contributed significantly to the progress, upliftment and salvation of their people and the human spirit in general. Rosa Parks was "One Revolutionary Female" who sat down and sparked the Civil Rights movement. She refused to further accept racial degradation in transportation as an aspect of wider social inequities in twentieth century America.

Research Essays Illustration 66. Some plants and animals brought back from Paunit or Punt.

In 1968, Shirley Chisholm became "One Black Woman in Congress." Later, Queen Mother Moore, Elsie Richardson, Mrs. Jackie Robinson and Winnie Mandela were each "One Woman" who firmly demonstrated the force of womanhood, "African womanism;" and in the process influenced "men and movements" to help create equality and "Oneness in the Modern World." Therefore, we need recognize in terms of struggle, "Once is not enough," and that we must go "One on One" with the "Young Ones," to teach them their history and culture. For the Old Testament, Ecclesiastes, 1, 4 reminds us, "One Generation passed away, and another Generation Cometh; but the Earth abideth forever." We should teach them, Adelaide A. Proctor's "One by One" description of the minute:

"One by One the Sands are Flowing
One by One the Moments Fall
Some are coming, some are going
Do Not Strive to grasp them all. "

Even further, the young should know, as Thomas Edison said in his Newspaper interview in 1931: "Genius is One Percent Inspiration and Ninety-nine Percent Perspiration." In this we teach the young, not to utter "One Useless Word." They have "Two Eyes to see, One Nose to smell; Two Ears to Listen, One Mouth to speak, and One Brain to Process it All." Teddy Cubia, the poet, once said: "Two Ears can Outlast One Hundred Lips." Equally too, to respect and follow Oscar Wilde's admonition: "To Love Oneself is the Beginning of a Life-Long

RESEARCH ESSAYS ON ANCIENT EGYPT

Romance." Having said as much in Education of Henry Adams he believed "One Teacher Affects Eternity; he can never tell Where his Influence stops."

Research Essays 67. Medinet Habu, Mortuary Temple of Rameses III. The author stands before the feet of two broken seated statues.

In this regard and with some serious work, as we face "One More Century" and "One New Millennium," we can help America live out its true creed, "One Nation, Indivisible with Liberty and Justice for All." We mean "Everyone."

Research Essays Papyrus Art 7. The King stands before Hathor (left) and Presents to Horus as Ra-Horakhty in Double Crown, while the Son of Ra cartouches hang overhead.

Research Essays 67a. Rameses III before enthroned Nile God with Thoth as an ibis at his rear.

RESEARCH ESSAYS ON ANCIENT EGYPT

12. Metals, Men and Materials
By

Dr. Fred Monderson

In ancient Kemet, the Craft of Metallurgy began far back in the pre-historic Badarian culture, between 4500-3600 B.C. For the next three thousand years, metal work advanced civilization fueled by the conventions laid down in this period. The availability of materials allowed ancient man of Egypt, Africa, to experiment and produce wonderful works of art that beautified his person, household, temple and aided his many activities, and as well, advance his trade patterns in his nation. In *Egyptian Metalworking and Tools*, Bernd Scheel argued that the development of trades and crafts were closely connected with social evolution in society. These specializations developed "with the process of settlement, the transition from food-collecting to food-producing economies and the domestication of animals and plants."

Copper was the first metal worked by craftsmen in the Badarian Period. As such, it marked the start of the Metal Age in the land of Kemet/Egypt, North-east Africa. Copper tools and weapons were manufactured simply by open-mold casting. According to Scheel, such gains meant: "melting, casting and smelting metals from ores required a sophisticated pottery industry, which would then have served as a basis for acquiring the technique of producing high temperatures using charcoal and developing smelting furnaces and melting crucibles."

Division of labor and specialization of crafts were early additions in African man's cultural development. In Kemet, industry became so sophisticated, a proliferation of crafts of skilled professionals developed including joiners, carpenters, wood sculptures or carvers and leather workers. There were also stonemasons, quarry workers, stone sculptors and textile workers. Others included barbers, manicurists, doctors, agricultural workers and butchers. They all improved skills and needed tools for their professions.

FREDERICK MONDERSON

Research Essays Illustration 67. Herdsmen and poulterer treating sick animals and geese. Beni-Hassan.

In ancient Egypt, what we call trades or guilds of Medieval Europe and crafts in Medieval Africa, produced leather workers, wood workers, stone workers, potters or metal workers, who were strictly organized. Inspectors or "Overseers of the Workshops," those who supervised standards and quality of work, also handled management and administration dynamics in demands of the state. One authority, Scheel points out: "A workshop could be attached to a temple or a royal palace. Others were attached to the private household of a king's son or to the household of a high official or monarch."

Some workers did not belong to a state-owned palace workshop. They could be part of a private household of the king. At times and as a special honor, the king would have the palace craftsmen do work for private individuals.

The people of ancient Kemet/Egypt made great preparations for the afterlife by building and decorating their tombs as final resting places. Many such tombs showed various scenes and themes with the owners and their families. Such depictions included rural life, fishing, fowling and the desert hunt. Funerary rites and the afterlife were also shown. The wealthy or noble-dead are shown in sport and recreation. Animals such as dogs, donkeys, sheep, goats, gazelles and pigs were depicted. In addition, a wide variety of ducks, geese and even cranes were all part of their funerary offering scenes. They also show such domesticated wild animals as gazelles, oryx, and hyenas.

Most important, these tombs highlighted the professions and various industries. Here we get evidence of many early crafts, pottery making, wine pressing and even circumcision. Wrestling, music and dance, playing board games and even war scenes also decorate the walls of these tombs.

The colorful representations begin with early dynastic tombs such as those of Ti and Ptahhotep at Sakkara, of the Vth Dynasty. Then there is Periankh at Meir and Mereruka at Sakkara; both were of the VI Dynasty. The tombs of Kheti at Beni Hasan, Thehutihotep at el-Bersha and Sarenput II at Aswan, all belong to the Middle Kingdom.

RESEARCH ESSAYS ON ANCIENT EGYPT

By the time of the great Pharaohs of the New Kingdom, the tombs were more elaborate. They provided much more information on mining, smelting, melting, casting and plate production. There are depictions of bowl and shaft furnaces, crucibles, dish bellows, reed blowpipes and molds. Wooden and stone anvils, types of hammers and smoothing and chasing stones are also represented.

The *Tomb of Rekh-mi-re at Thebes* and the *Tomb of Puy-em-re at Thebes* are New Kingdom sources of information for metalworking and tools. The *Tomb of Two Sculptors at Thebes* and the *Rock Tombs of Deir el-Gebrawi* also provide information.

A wide variety of tools represented in tombs and elsewhere depicts specializations that came to show a wide repertoire of professions. Every profession had a different set of tools. They were those who worked in rock such as quarry men, stonecutters, stonemasons, and stone sculptors.

Research Essays Illustration 68. Asiatics bringing tribute.

They used stone, copper and later bronze chisels. Metal picks, wooden mallets and stone hammers. They also used metal wedges as well. Stone workers were in the quarries, transporting the hard stone, sometimes for the full length of the country, polishing and erecting them in civil, religious, mortuary and palace locations. In the fine arts, they made vases of breccia, syenite, quartz, crystal, diorite and alabaster. Slate, basalt and steatite were also worked.

In bead working, drills were used. They were hollow rotating drills and chert drills used in a variety of fields. Bow drills were used in woodworking. Carpentry tools also included axes, adzes, chisels, saws, shavers and hammers. All mallets and hammers had wooden handles. These included everyday and funerary objects. Carpenters made beautiful chairs, stools, chests, draught-boards, scribal palettes, tables, beds, headrests, scales and sticks or staffs. They also made combs, hairpins, boxes and spoons. Agricultural tools such as wooden hoes, plows, and sickles were produced.

Working with metals and other forms of manual labor was difficult and messy work. Most sons followed their fathers in whatever craft they practiced. There was, however, the occasional son who had intellect. His father would not want him to follow in the same line of work. The example of this is told in the story, *Satire of the Trades*. The model here is the youth being encouraged to become a scribe. The scribes were the intellectuals of their day.

Research Essays Illustration 68a. More Asiatics with their tribute.

A father named Khety from the XII Dynasty had the perennial task of speaking to his son Pepi about working hard in school in order that he could become an official. Either cultivate the intellect his father reasoned, otherwise he would become a craftsman and work hard all his life. Khety told his son, he never saw a goldsmith on important business. Interestingly metal workers faced hot furnaces. Their hands were wrinkled and they smelled worse than scraps of fish. Many other trades were just as difficult and unpleasant. Therefore, study hard in school the young lad was told, and he would become a scribe.

The crafts were generally divided into skilled and unskilled workers. The skilled workers were blacksmiths, whitesmiths or finishers. There were also silversmiths, coppersmiths, engravers and gilders. The skilled workers knew about metallurgy, chasing, annealing or casting metals. The unskilled workers started fires, fanned fires by means of blowpipes or bellows, and cleaned and polished vessels. These workers were all paid in grain, bread, cakes, meat, salt, vegetables, dates, sandals, and clothing.

RESEARCH ESSAYS ON ANCIENT EGYPT

Throughout history gold has remained a metal of mystical significance. Including this precious substance, mined in prehistoric times, Petrie (1923: 149) mentions 10 metals and about eighty different minerals and rocks that were known to the Egyptians; of these all but nine are known to have been used. He notes that: "Gold and silver were not only used for jewelry, but also to ornament stone vases with gold brims, handles, and bases, and with silver lids. Gold tips to bows, gold knife handles and gold sheets were made, beads were skillfully burnished over a core of limestone; all these are prehistoric. In the 1st dynasty, the soldering of gold was perfectly executed with the utmost minuteness. Copper was known in very small amounts from the beginning of the prehistoric civilization; but it did not become common for tools till the beginning of the dynasties." In addition to the first two metals, later on, according to *Egyptian Metalworking and Tools*, such metals as "electrum, silver, iron, tin, bronze, lead and platinum were also worked." Without further elaboration he adds, "Traces of nickel, zinc, arsenic, antimony, and cobalt were found in small amounts in metal artifacts." Petrie also mentions bismuth, manganese and tin. So too was mercury. He mentions further: "Casting of metal was usually in open moulds, or else by *cire perdue*; the latter was of extraordinary delicacy, the metal being often only 1/50th of an inch thick. Closed molds, with relief casting, were usual in Syria and the east. Thin copper vessels were hammered out and hammered sheets were built up into statues on a wooden core, secured by lines of nails at the junctions. Wire and chains of copper were well known. Autogenous soldering, with the same metal, was used for jewelry in the 1st dynasty and for copper in the XIXth dynasty. During the Ramesside period of the late New Kingdom, shaft furnaces achieved 1,200 degrees Centigrade (2,200 degrees Fahrenheit) temperatures to work various metals. This intense heat helped to expand tool-making for the various trades."

Research Essays Illustration 68b. Even more Asiatics who look nothing like the ancient Egyptians.

FREDERICK MONDERSON

Metal tools for working leather included hide scrapers, leather-cutting knives, awls and needles. The craftsmen produced leather ropes, writing materials, arrow quivers, kilts and tents. They covered wooden stools, and tied tools like axes, hammers, adzes, and plows to their handles. From the New Kingdom onwards, the chariot and horse equipment produced included harness, saddles and whips. Workers also made sandals. Leatherwork was a highly accomplished craft.

Dressmaking tools included needles, pins, cutting-out knives, and scissors worked by separate fingers. Agricultural tools like bronze hoes, plows and metal-edged sickles were made. Medical instruments, according to A. Lucas, in *Ancient Egyptian Materials and Industries*, included shears, surgical knives and saws in the creations of these ancient craftsmen. There were also different kinds of probes, small hooks and spatulas. All were used in surgery, dentistry, gynecology, and general medicine.

Other metal implements included various knives used as weapons and tools, especially by butchers. Plates were made of copper and bronze.

The *American Journal of Archaeology* XXII (1918: 441-412) reported under: TOOLS AND WEAPONS – "Professor Flinders Petrie has published under the auspices of the British School of Archaeology in Egypt and Egyptian Research Account a work entitled Tools and Weapons. It is concerned particularly with implements from Egypt although many illustrations are drawn from other parts of the world. He discusses in turn the plain blade axe, the socketed axe, the double axe, adzes and picks, the adze and hoe, the lug adze, the hoe, the chisel, the knife, the symmetric knife, the sword, the dagger, the spear-head, the arrow, the throwing-stick, slings and bullets, harpoons, fishhooks, scale armor, rasps and scrapers, artisans' tools, builders' tools, the saw, the sickle, the pruning hook, shears, razors, leather cutters, tweezers, borers, pins and needles, implements for spinning and weaving, agricultural tools, the horse-bit, the spur, stamps for branding, fire-hooks, manacles, fish-spears, flesh-hooks, shovels, ladles, spoons, mortars and pestles, fire-drills, strigils, the bolt, lock and key, pulleys, compasses, chains, and tools used in casting. In conclusion the author comments on the distribution of the different types, pointing out forms peculiar to Egypt, forms unknown in Egypt, and forms which were widespread."

RESEARCH ESSAYS ON ANCIENT EGYPT

Research Essays 68. Medinet Habu, Mortuary Temple of Rameses III. Rameses offers an ape to Amon-Ra and he stands alone in the Blue or War Crown. At right, notice his see-thru flowing dress or galibeah.

In regards tools, R. Engelbach (1961: 139-42) enumerates specifically the ancient Egyptians used: "mason's tools, during the whole of the dynastic period, [that] consisted of chisels, mallets, ball and mauls of diorite for rough dressing the hard rocks, some form of blunt-pointed pick, saw ... plumb-rules, squares, the cord and reel, and tubular drills." The building stones and other rocks included alabaster, basalt, breccia, diorite, dolomite, flint, granite, gypsum, limestone, marble, obsidian, porphyry, quartzite, sandstone, schist and tiff, serpentine, and steatite.

Equally, the tools of the carpenters included "chisels, mallets, double-headed sledge-hammers, adzes, axes, saws, bow-drills, plumb rules and squares." Egyptian timber, though limited was still respectable in acacia, Date palm, Dom palm, Persea, sidder, silicified wood, sycamore, and tamarisk and willow trees. Imported foreign timber, particularly from the Lebanon included ash, beech, box, cedar, cypress, ebony, elm, fir, juniper, lime, oak, pine and yew.

FREDERICK MONDERSON

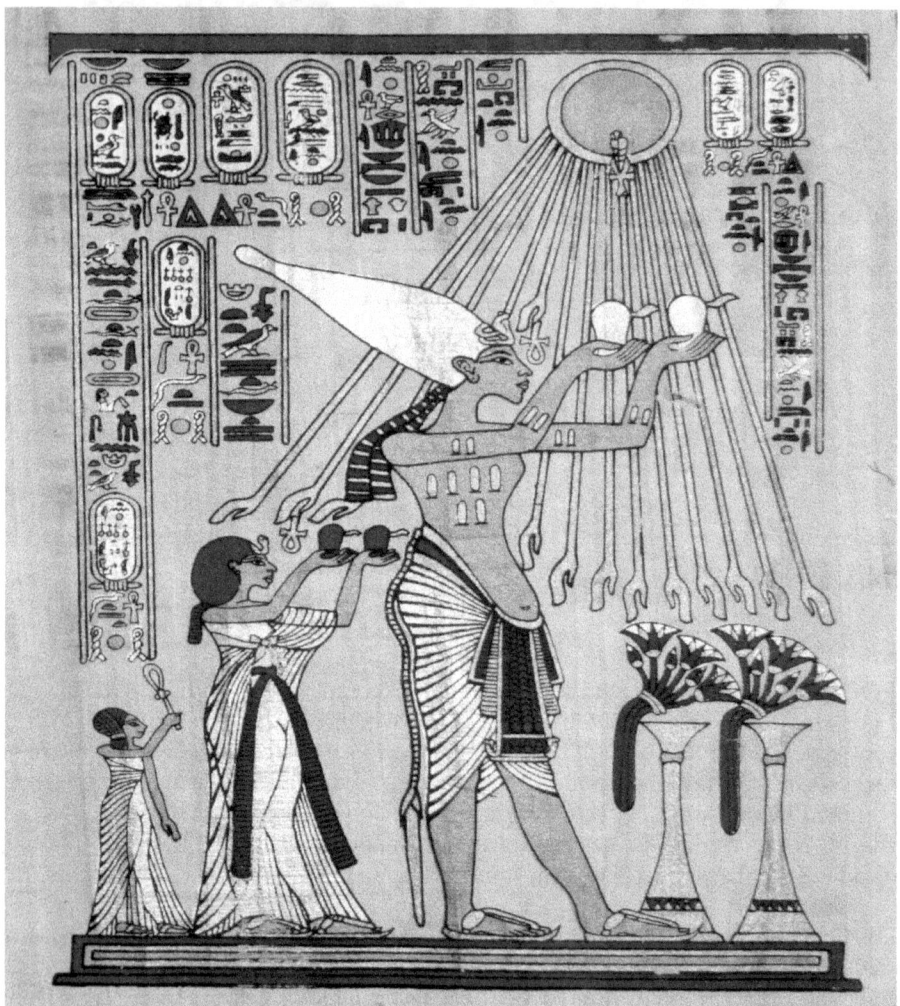

Research Essays Papyrus Art 8. Akhnaton (Ikhnaten) and his wife and child each make a Presentation to the hands of the sun disk, the Aten.

RESEARCH ESSAYS ON ANCIENT EGYPT

Research Essays Illustration 69. Painting of a temple's columned hall with the Bedouin just hanging out. (Breasted 1923)

Not to be outdone, the military was important from the time of Narmer in the first dynasty. Weapons included, as Engelbach (1961: 142) illustrates: "Bow and arrow, spear, a short sword, the scimitar, the battle-axe, many varieties of club, the dagger, the boomerang and other forms of the throw stick; the quarter-staff, the modern Egyptian *nabbut*, which in the Middle Kingdom was shod with a cutting blade, the sling, and the shield." They had also the long and composite bow, clubs, daggers, tubular drills, fire drills, levels, lever, loom and mace-heads. They had no body armor. Chariots were introduced in the New Kingdom, coming from Syria.

The crafts were useful to those ancient Africans of Kemet, along the Nile, who attached an importance to personal hygiene. These early blacks disliked shaggy beards and overall hairiness. So, razors and special toilet implements were used. This repertoire included tweezers, razors and knives. They shaved their faces, necks, armpits, limbs, chests, and pubic regions frequently.

From the metals gold, copper, lead, silver, and tin, four principal alloys were made. These were: copper and tin for bronze and a lead and copper alloy. Gold and silver made electrum, while copper and zinc made brass.

In addition, the dictionary defines minerals as a substance obtained by mining. In that case a number of minerals were also mined in ancient Egypt. These minerals include - *alum*, used in tanning leather, in dyeing and for medical purposes. *Cobalt* was used as an abrasive with drills and saws for working hard stones. *Graphite* was sometimes used in beads. *Manganese-Compounds* were used to implant purple color to glaze and glass. It was also used as an eye-paint.

Mica was used for mirrors, decorating caps, pendant and necklaces. Maspero's *Manual of Egyptian Archaeology* (1926: 277) indicated no diamonds, rubies or sapphires were found in Egypt, but semi-precious stones were found there in abundance. These were: "Amethyst, emerald, garnet, aquamarine, rock-crystal, chrysoprase, the many varieties of onyx and agate, jasper, lapis lazuli, feldspar, obsidian, granite, serpentine, and porphyry; fossiliferous substances such as amber and some kinds of turquoise; animal secretions such as coral, pearls, and mother-of-pearl; metallic oxides such as hematite, oriental turquoise, and malachite." Added to his list were alabaster, Amazon stone, beryl (emerald), calcite, carnelian, chalcedony, coral, jade, jasper, onyx, opal and quartz. Even further Maspero continued: "with the saw, drill, point, and grindstone they worked the stones into a variety of different shapes, hearts, fingers, human limbs, cartouches, serpents, animals, and figures of divinities."

Natron consists of sodium carbonate and sodium bicarbonate. It was used in purification ceremonies, especially the mouth. Also, for the manufacture of glass and glaze, blue and green frits were used as pigments. Again for cooking, in medicine, and for bleaching, salt was used. It was also used for seasoning food, preserving fish and in mummification. *Sulphur* was also used in mummification.

The beauty of the Kemetic state was the lasting political stability it provided. With the exception of the few Intermediate Periods, the government was enduring. Political stability is always important for economic growth, encouraging division

RESEARCH ESSAYS ON ANCIENT EGYPT

of labor, development and specialization of crafts and expansion of trade, aided by river traffic and roads for transportation, where ideas and crafts were spread.

The rich resources of the land, agricultural and mineral, were well exploited by the craftsmen.

Research Essays Illustration 70. Harvest scene. Thebes.

R. Engelbach, in *Introduction to Egyptian Archaeology* (1961: 334) points out: "The building materials: brick, stone, mortar and plaster, were all local; glaze, glass and pottery (wherever they may have originated) were all made in the country from native materials; the metal gold and the silver-alloy, electrum, as also the ores of copper and lead, from which the two latter materials were produced, all occurred in the country; the animal fats and bees-wax were Egyptian products; the pigments were almost entirely naturally occurring materials, or were made from such materials; the precious and semi-precious stones, with few exceptions, were of local origin, as were also the ornamental and monumental stones; the textile fabrics used were woven in Egypt, and baskets, ropes and mats were made from fibers that grew in the country; the skins made into leather were local, and most of the dyes with which the textile fabrics and leather were colored were probably Egyptian, and the foodstuffs, chiefly cereal grains, green vegetables, oil (except for a little olive oil), fruit, honey, meat and fish were all produced in the country." Underscoring that native ingenuity, Engelbach (1961: 334-35) continued: "During the Old Kingdom, alabaster was quarried at Helwan; amethyst was brought either from the eastern or western deserts, in both of which it occurs; a special diorite was brought from the western desert in Nubia; fold gold from Nubia; granite from Aswan; malachite and copper from Sinai; natron from the Wadi el-Natrun, porphyritic rocks from the eastern desert; schist from between Qena and El Quseir, and turquoise from Sinai."

FREDERICK MONDERSON

Research Essays 69. Medinet Habu, Mortuary Temple of Rameses III. In White Crown, Rameses gestures while his cartouche stands nearby.

Clearly, and again, these ancient Egyptian Africans were the genesis of their own genius. They had no one to imitate! Even further, to let all know what is at stake in this African phenomenal creation, Perry (1937: 48-49) quoting Elliot Smith in *The Ancient Egyptians* wrote, that these early Africans: "did a great deal more than merely invent agriculture and devise the earliest statecraft and religion. Not only did they devise the methods of working wood and stone and the art of architecture, they seem also to have been the inventors of linen and of the craft of weaving, of the use of gold and copper, and the making of metal tools and implements. They

RESEARCH ESSAYS ON ANCIENT EGYPT

were the first people to measure the year and to devise a calendar, and later on to substitute for the rough calculation based upon the date of the annual Nile flood the exact measurement based on observation of the sun's movements. They also invented shipbuilding and constructed the first sea-going ships. In a thousand and one of the details of our common civilization the originality of Egyptian civilization is revealed. The art of shaving, the use of wig, the wearing of hats, the invention of the kilt and of the sandal and subsequently of a variety of other articles of dress, many of our musical instruments, chairs, and beds, cushions, jewelry and jewel-cases, lamps - these are merely a few of the items picked at random out of our ancient heritage from the Nile Valley."

Again, in educating the masses of people, we can ask, what's in a word? These are two European writers, and their use of the word OUR is not meant to be representative of humanity in general. It is meant to lay Europe's claim to the African civilization. That is why the struggle continues and we must reiterate, *Ancient Egypt is African and black*!

Research Essays Illustration 71. View of the rapids of the river at Aswan.

Therefore, in applying Egyptian, African, wisdom and ingenuity in the ancient world, Egypt, Kemet, the Nile Valley, harnessed its resources and spoke for emerging Africa. That voice is being heard thousands of years later saying *defend Egypt as African* as the struggle unfolds. And, Africa's sons and daughters have a wonderful cultural heritage to be proud of, worth fighting for today, that heritage beckons us to come explore the physical remains in the temples, tombs and most particularly the Cairo Museum of Antiquities. With this knowledge, we must continue to teach our people, get them involved, make them aware, what is at stake, what is the prize and have them in turn understand and teach *Egypt is African*.

Research Essays 70. Medinet Habu, Mortuary Temple of Rameses III. Illustrations of vessels.

RESEARCH ESSAYS ON ANCIENT EGYPT

13. The Art of Ancient Egypt

By

Dr. Fred Monderson

Introduction: The Art of Ancient Egypt

The Art of Ancient Egypt is one of its most beautiful and enduring accomplishments visible in the country whose artifacts equally adorns museums and private collections worldwide. Egyptian Art can be observed in its technology, burial methods, tomb decorations, buildings, its methods and building techniques, sculptures, paintings, reliefs, steles, quarrying and even river transportation of stone and other materials. Even in its geography art played an important part because in the mythology, the land first emerged from the flood of the inundation. Many of its buildings were based on lines and vertical and horizontal orientation. The location of pyramids, temples and tombs were chosen based on proximity next to some geographical feature. The pyramids were located on a flat plain, temples were built near the river and by the New Kingdom tombs were hidden in valleys of kings, queens, nobles and artisans. The poor were buried in simple tombs in the desert sand. It is interesting that the tombs of the nobles at Aswan were located on the high cliffs. Choice of this spot with its panoramic view of Aswan below highlights the splendid view of nature's canvas below. This choice of these burials is art in a timeless setting and spectacle that the desert has helped to preserve, while the river below helps color the man-made and natural work of art there.

FREDERICK MONDERSON

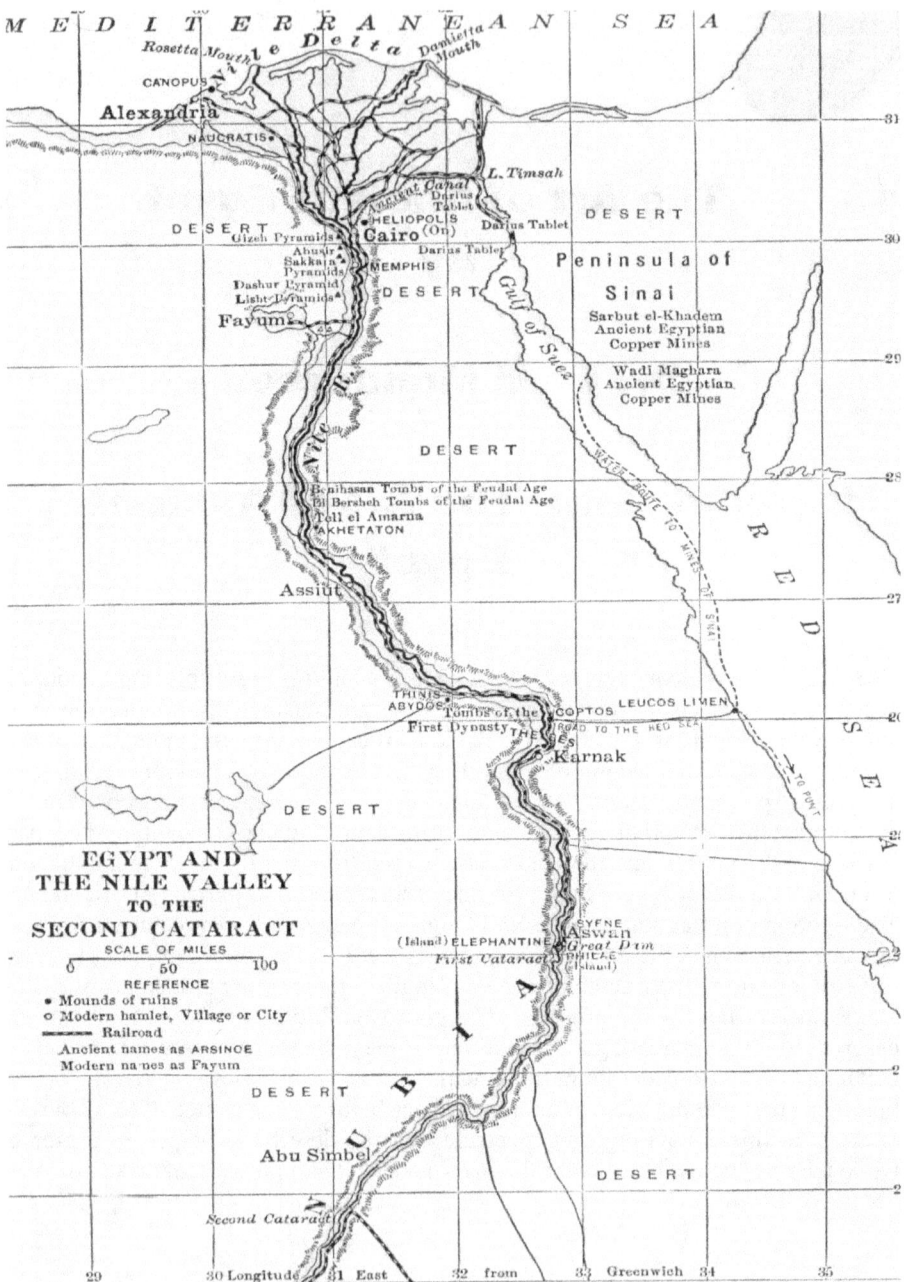

Research Essays Illustration 72. Map of Egypt and the Nile Valley to the Second Cataract.

RESEARCH ESSAYS ON ANCIENT EGYPT

Equally, the Egyptian artist used symbolism in the Hieroglyphic writing, itself art, and in the decoration, and painting and sculpture to emphasize meanings not easily comprehended. Thus, in the artistic development, all the facets of the civilization were thus aided by the craft of the artist who represented every conceivable feature of the culture, building, decoration, writing, statues, steles, etc. Cyril Aldred (1980: 15) in *Egyptian Art* makes the artistic connection between language and culture when he wrote: "The use of symbolic forms in Egyptian art is intimately associated with a characteristic Egyptian culture, the employment of hieroglyphics in a system of writing which has no exact counterpart in other civilizations."

Research Essays 71. Medinet Habu, Mortuary Temple of Rameses III. Rameses faces and prepares to incense two divinities. Notice his long-flowing dress.

Interestingly, their artists' use of color has led to much speculation regarding particularly the skin color of the Egyptians. Historical and archaeological evidence supports the view, by the Old Kingdom they were using the colors red, blue, black, green and yellow imposed on a white background. Long before the prehistoric Badarian, Amratian and Gerzean or Naqada I and Naqada II culture sequence, painting of the flora, fauna, hunting, etc., characterized early man in Africa as well as ancient man in the Nile Valley, as he sought to overcome his environment. However, through the Old, Middle and New Kingdoms and the Late and Graeco-Roman Periods, regional art schools developed that either continued older traditions or innovated techniques that spawned competition and even more creative productions. Throughout, particularly during the dynastic period, kings were major patrons of the arts. While some noble families equally played a role, much of this art is represented in their tombs as the only surviving examples of private endeavors. The temples too played a role in fostering growth, development and expansion of this tangible method of cultural creativity.

Research Essays Illustration 73. A chariot of the New Empire in the Cairo Museum.

Evidence in pre-dynastic graves, as well as monumental structures as the Step-Pyramid, and large mastabas at Sakkara; the group of Great Pyramids at Ghizeh; the Old and Middle Kingdom tombs of the Nobles on the high cliffs at Aswan; the Middle Kingdom Tombs at Beni Hasan; the Middle Kingdom Temple of Mentuhotep II at Deir el Bahari; the New Kingdom worship and mortuary temples at Thebes; the venerated Valley of the Kings, Valley of the Queens, Valley of the Nobles, and Valley of the Artisans with their tremendously colorful tombs; the Late Period temples at Edfu, Kom Ombo, Esneh, Philae, Kalabsha; and equally Abu Simbel, all demonstrate Egyptian Art of the highest quality. Many artifacts from these places and time periods can be viewed in private and public collections worldwide.

RESEARCH ESSAYS ON ANCIENT EGYPT

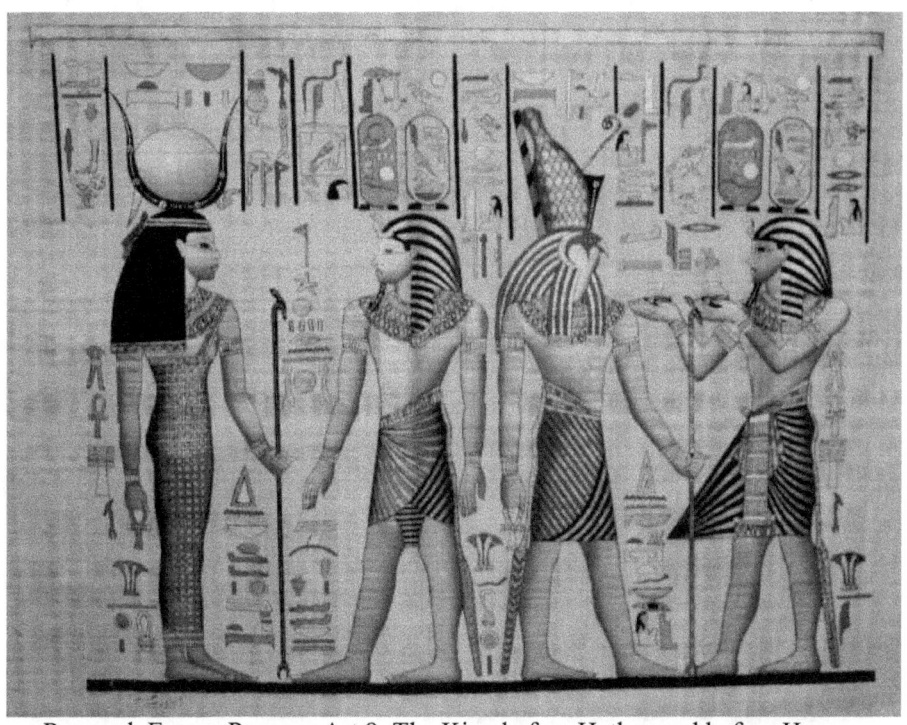

Research Essays Papyrus Art 9. The King before Hathor and before Horus.

The enduring beauty of the statues, sculptures, paintings, papyrus decorations, buildings, sarcophagi, wall decorations and inscriptions, the *Pyramid Texts*, *Coffin Texts*, and the decorated *Book of Coming Forth by Day* (*Book of the Dead*), and hieroglyphic writing are all unmistakable cultural attainments of the highest order. The writing, particularly, is significant for as Richard H. Wilkinson in *Reading Egyptian Art* (1996: 10) notes: "All Egyptian hieroglyphic writing is made up of pictures, yet it is seldom realized that a great deal of Egyptian art is in turn heavily influenced by, and many occasions made up of hieroglyphic words and written signs." Much of this writing is an imitation of nature themes of plants, animals, humans, and the landscape, domestic, civic and military as well as personal objects from every aspect of the society. Other Pharaonic paraphernalia such as crowns, scepters, sandals, rings, bracelets, anklets, girdles, necklaces, armbands, amulets, collars, pectorals, and other more familiar features of jewelry, etc., now decorate museums and attest to the enduring quality and beauty of Egyptian art that so significantly influenced man down through history as well as the modern mindset. And, to think, despite the pernicious and misguided beliefs and interpretations, black African men and women did all this even though today, these ancients and their descendants do not get the full credit for their accomplishments. An interesting aside here is the manner in which this art form influenced western art and ultimately the history of art.

FREDERICK MONDERSON

Research Essays 72. Medinet Habu, Mortuary Temple of Rameses III. While Goddess Mut extends her hand behind Rameses who kneels before enthroned Amon-Ra, Khonsu stands behind his father, the first of the Theban Triad. Notice the Uraeus overhead indicating they're in the temple.

Many modern writers have supplied the most accurately descriptive explanation of the role Egyptian art has played in influencing Greece and western civilization in their art, architecture, sculpture, painting and other forms of artistic cultural expressions and attainments. Indus Khamit Kush in *The Missing Pages of "His-Story"* (1993: 34) indicated: "The celebrated Frenchman Jean-Francois Champollion makes it plain and clear: 'Ancient Egypt taught the arts to Greece, this last gave to them the most sublime development, but without Egypt, Greece would probably never become the classic land of the fine arts. I trace these lines in the face of bas reliefs which the Egyptians executed, with most exquisite fineness of workmanship, seven hundred years before the Christian era,' and what had the Greeks done?'"

RESEARCH ESSAYS ON ANCIENT EGYPT

Research Essays Illustration 74. Harvest scene. Thebes.

Kush notes further, John R. Harris (ed) in *The Legacy of Egypt* (1971: 79) has instructed: "In fact, it is difficult to imagine where it would have been more natural for the Greeks to turn for artistic guidance and inspiration, as well as technical instruction, than to Egypt ... where their philosophers and statesmen had traveled and become acquainted with an age-old culture which had struck them with awe and admiration, and where they had encountered a fully developed artistic tradition which was not only the oldest in the world, but unsurpassed in artistic perfection and technical skill." Kush (1993: 39) continued how: "R.W. Haskins gives a clear illustration of the Egyptian influence on Greek art when he cites a letter written by that world-renowned genius, Jean-Francois Champollion: 'I repeat, once more, Egyptian art owed, only to itself all that it has produced of the great, the pure, and the beautiful and without intending disrespect to those savants who make it part of the religion firmly to believe in the spontaneous generation of the art in Greece, it is evident to me, as it must be to all of the Egyptian monuments existing in Europe that the arts commenced in Greece by a servile imitation of the arts of Egypt, (which were much more advanced than is vulgarly supposed,) at that epoch when the first Egyptian colonies were in contact with the savage inhabitants of Attica, or of the Peloponnesus.'" (*The Arts, Sciences and Civilizations Anterior to Greece and Rome*. A. W. Wilgus, Buffalo, 1844, p. 20).

FREDERICK MONDERSON

Research Essays 73. Mortuary Temple of Seti I at Abydos. Entrance façade of Osiris Temple at Abydos, built by Seti I of the 19th Dynasty.

Further (1993: 41) wrote Kush: "That George R. Gliddon, author of *Ancient Egypt*, depicts the Egyptians with great admiration: "The 'Veil of Isis' ... was lifted by Champollion le Jejune: and the glories of Pharaonic epochs – the deeds of the noblest, the most learned, pious ... and civilized race of ancient days – whose monarchy has exceeded by 1000 years the duration of any of our modern nations – whose works surpass in magnitude, in boldness of conception, accuracy of execution, and splendor of achievement that mightiest labors of any other people ... have, through Champollion's labors ... become familiar to all ...." (*The New World*, Nos. 68-69, Park Benjamin, Ed., J. Winchester, Publish, New York, April, 1843, p. 2).

Nevertheless, Irmgard Woldering in *Egyptian Art in the Time of the Pharaohs* (1962: 11) in the Introduction wrote: "For a long time Egyptian art remained misunderstood by Europeans, since they proceeded from false premises. To those brought up in the Greek school, the Egyptian treatment of form inevitably seemed rigid and primitive. It was thought to possess the clumsiness appropriate to an early stage of development, when men had not yet succeeded in representing in an organic and lively manner the world they saw about them."

Even further (1962: 11) he continued: "Only in the 19th century, when excavations were begun and an abundance of works reached European museums, did it become clear how inadequate this traditional aesthetic approach was in attempting to appreciate the genius of Egyptian art. The relationship between the viewer and the work of art is no doubt always determined by aesthetic considerations, but it must not be forgotten that the image obtained in this way is bound to be a subjective one." He then goes on to express the view, in order to objectively appraise and appreciate Egyptian art one has to be familiar with the history that produced the art. This is sort of akin to an understanding to Flinders Petrie's description of Egyptology as knowing the history, language and geography.

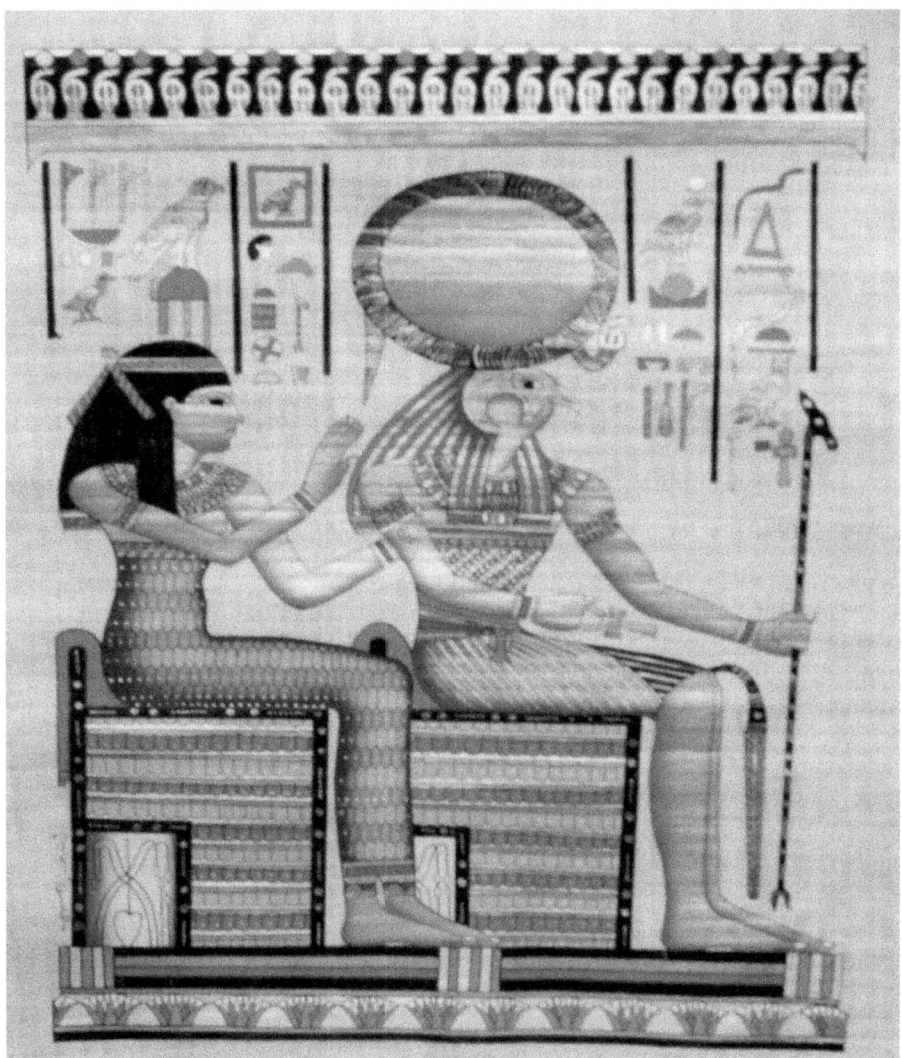

Research Essays Papyrus Art 10. Enthroned Ra-Horakhty sits beside Goddess Hathor.

FREDERICK MONDERSON

Research Essays Illustration 75. The Court of Amenhotep III at the Temple of Luxor, from the northeast, during the Inundation.

Woldering (1962: 11) adds even more in his commentary on the art of Egypt in the statement: "When we look at the monuments, sculptures and reliefs that have been preserved, we are at once struck by their magnificent homogeneity in the expression of form – although we have to bear in mind that, the further back a culture lies in time, the stranger its forms appear to us, and the greater is the tendency to see them as possessing a kind of unity. A close examination of the development of Egyptian art styles reveals that transformation and differentiation took place between one epoch and another, so that, for example, it is possible to distinguish clearly a work of the 3rd millennium B.C. from one of the 2nd millennium B.C. or the Late Period."

ART TO SPREAD THE WORD

Therefore, stepping out of the mist of prehistory, the most significant artistic achievement the Egyptian achieved was the register. The register introduced artistic order from disorder in its representation. All of a sudden, using the register, different themes could be included in the same picture. This was therefore, one of the most revolutionary developments in the history of art. Aside from pottery and personal effects accompanying the dead as "goods of the grave," the earliest and most significant forms of conventional Egyptian art are on slate palettes. The most famous of these is the Narmer Palette. Here the king is shown wearing the White Crown of Upper Egypt and the Red Crown of Lower Egypt. Scholars reasoned that this pharaoh is responsible for uniting the two lands and choosing the united red and white Double Crown. The significance of this artifact is the propaganda role it played in establishing conventions in art and political and social customs.

The Narmer Palette shows the king as monumental in scale to his subjects. It introduced the horizontal register as an art form. This innovation became the dividing line between pre-dynastic and dynastic art. Nonetheless, other early portrayals of the pharaoh, whether in agricultural ceremonials, ritual worship, smiting Egypt's enemies or dancing before the Gods, were symbolic as well as equally serving propaganda purposes.

Art innovations of these beginnings set the stage for the order, stability and unchanging reality of Egyptian Art. Together with the canon, or set of rules, for representing the human figure, Egyptian art changed yet remained traditional and timeless. Classical art, certainly dating to the Old Kingdom, remained the ideal well past the New Kingdom and into the Late Period. The influence of the Greeks after Alexander's conquest in 332 B.C. brought new innovations that still looked to the past for inspiration.

WAYS OF REPRESENTING THE HUMAN BODY

The Egyptians used a Canon of Proportion to represent the human body. This changed slightly from period to period, numbering as much as three forms. In the Old Kingdom or Pyramid Age, 2680-2240 B.C., according to Michalowski, they used 13 divisions for the height of a man. These included "2 for the head, 1 to the armpit, 4 to the fork, 2 to the knee, 4 to the ground." For the position of the figure during the Dynastic Period (3000-30 B.C.), they used a rule that "a vertical line must pass the edge of the wig, or center of the head, the middle of the waist, equidistant between the knees and between the heels."

FREDERICK MONDERSON

Research Essays 74. Mortuary Temple of Seti I at Abydos. Seti in necklace, sash and long flowing gown holds objects as he bows to Amon-Ra, who is all blue!

The New Kingdom began at the expulsion of the Hyksos, Asiatic nomads, who overran Egypt and ruled for a century. The wealth, glamour and opulence of the New Empire built its art upon the earlier developments of the Old and Middle Kingdoms. Even more significant, however, other innovations were made in representing such subjects as birds, animals, fishes, plants, and even the human figure in motion. It's been said, the earliest form of the moving figure dates to the Old Kingdom showing a gazelle being chased. We know Mertisen the artist, who flourished during the Middle Kingdom time of Mentuhotep II, boasted he could portray people in motion. Aldred (1980: 18) quoted Dr. Fisher, lecturer at the New York Metropolitan Museum of Art, who remarked on the notion of representing

RESEARCH ESSAYS ON ANCIENT EGYPT

people in moving postures. He writes "Egyptian statues normally put the left foot or arm forward when a limb has to be advanced. 'They nurse or hold children with the left arm, or carry burdens on the left side. Similarly lions and sphinxes normally show the tail on the right side, corresponding to the rightward orientation of the hieroglyphic image of a lion.' Of course there are exceptions to this rule, such as statues worked as pairs in some balanced arrangement; but the influence of drawing in two dimensions may be seen on the left side to be represented, whereas on the right side both legs are shown, corresponding to the rightward orientation of such figures in relief or in painting."

THE CANON OF PROPORTION

The Canon of Proportion for the human body changed much after the Old Kingdom. The height of a standing figure was divided into 19 units. In *Wisdom of the Ancient Egyptians* (1938) Flinders Petrie gives his own canon of proportion for the human figure. "The head down to the top of the shoulders is 3 units, divided at the top of the forehead and base of the nose. From the shoulders, 4 units to the waist, then 6 to the knees, and thence 6 to the ground."

There was some difference for seated figures in the second canon. These seated figures were "15 squares high. Thus, assigning 19-15 = 4 units to the thighbone. The seat is 5 units over the ground."

As the civilization entered its decline by the later dynasties, they adopted a third canon. Here the figure became "22 1/2 or 22 1/3 units high; of this increase 1/3 unit is in the head, 2 units in trunk and 1 unit in the lower leg."

FREDERICK MONDERSON

Research Essays Illustration 75a. Another view of the Court of Amenhotep III from the North-east near the Mosque of Abu Haggag.

While the Egyptians had Canons of Proportions for the human figure, these were mainly for standing or seated figures. There were also many examples of figures in motion. The long row of wrestlers at Beni Hasan in the XII Dynasty and the dancers, acrobats and workers in action in the XVIII Dynasty, are good examples of depicting people in motion. These representations all show how readily the "instantaneous positions were grouped and reproduced."

THE LIFE OF AN ARTIST

The life of the artist was pleasing yet austere. They made funerary art that was timeless, yet was designed to never be seen by the human eye. Many craftsmen working side-by-side specialized in various crafts, but generally speaking and on the negative side, they were exposed to intense heat, had calloused hands, and many times "smelt like putrid meat." This aside, the strict division of labor aided the creation of beautiful works of art that defied time. Ostraka or broken pottery shred were used as surfaces for sketch or trial pieces and artists sometimes "doodled," leaving illustrated caricatures in addition to their assigned tasks.

There were guilds controlled from the palace or by wealthy nobles as well as the priesthood in temples. In these guilds "one specialist made the designs, another worked in plaster, and another specialized in stone cutting in relief sculpture, in carving statues, in finishing and polishing them, in decorating temple walls, and so on. The jeweler's art also had specialist categories: workers, who washed the gold, did enamel work, and there was even a category of bead stringer. In theory at least, no work was executed entirely by a single artist."

Research Essays Temple Ticket 14. Ticket used by native Egyptians at such places as the Pyramids.

OFFICIAL PORTRAITS

The ruling class comprised the Gods, pharaoh, high dignitaries and the priesthood. Their formal poses were shown in painting, reliefs and statuary. They were shown striding or seated. Nevertheless, the artist was bound to observe the rules of canon when portraying this upper crust of society and this formalism did not change until Akhenaton led the Amarna revolution that gave more emphasis to naturalistic representations.

FREDERICK MONDERSON

Research Essays Illustration 76. The Luxor Temple Processional Colonnade.

The pharaoh especially was shown in an official portrait. Generally shown with all kingly, physical and material accoutrements, any defects or shortcomings he had were concealed by his elaborate costume. "He was a god, a living Horus, and as a divinity his body had always to be represented as timelessly youthful." Again, by Amarna times, human imperfections or wrinkles were shown to represent the complete individual.

The administrative bureaucracy was the second class of artistic models. Because of their closeness with the local people the artist did not adhere strictly to the conventions that bound the first more formal portraits. These latter presented "only the most obvious facial characteristics." In this example, the governors or mayors, were clearly shown, according to Michalowski (187), with "sagging flesh, prominent bellies, and thick legs, but in a dignified posture carrying a staff."

Artistically, the main difference between the way the top two classes, the nobility and the administrative bureaucracy, were represented was in the modeling of the body. Michalowski (188) says further: "The conventions of timeless youth were obligatory for the first group, whereas dignitaries were shown more realistically."

RESEARCH ESSAYS ON ANCIENT EGYPT

Research Essays 74a. Mortuary Temple of Seti I at Abydos. Isis in Double Crown gestures towards Seti I holding objects in both hands.

FREDERICK MONDERSON

The third group of the society comprised a vast array of workers. In the mastaba tombs of the IV and V Dynasties at Sakkara, according to Michalowski (188) there are: "reliefs of laborers, harvesters, herdsmen, and artisans at work in warehouses, fields, pastures, and workshops. There are also fishermen and boat builders, musicians and dancers."

In representing this group, the scribe was free to deviate from the established canon and represent this group more as they were. As a result of this freedom of artistic expression, says Michalowski (189) the ancient Egyptians were able to show how "realistic scenes of common people possess great expressive power."

THE SCRIBE AS A SPECIAL CASE

Scribes were generally shown either in the standing or seated position. The wooden relief figure of the famous third dynasty royal scribe Hesire is now at the Cairo Museum. It stands 44-7/8 inches and was found at Saqqara. He is shown holding his working tools and the SEKHEM rod, emblem of executive officials. The diagram of canon for this Old Kingdom masterpiece in realistic art held "18 rows of squares," as follows: "From top of forehead to base of neck, 2 rows; from neck to knees, 10 rows: from knees to soles of feet, 6 rows. An additional row for the hair above the forehead was not included in the total of 18 rows."

The other posture of scribe was the seated position. The finest known statue of a scribe comes from the V Dynasty and is housed in the Louvre, Paris. Here the subject is shown: "Wearing a loin cloth, he is seated with legs crossed, an open roll of papyrus on his knees, and a reed pen in his right hand. It is made of painted limestone and stands 20 7/8[inch]." At a much later time the scribe was represented in a more obscure way simply as a block statue, with face and writings on the block.

RESEARCH ESSAYS ON ANCIENT EGYPT

Research Essays 75.   Mortuary Temple of Seti I at Abydos.   Seti pours a libation to Amon-Ra as Min, his ithyphallic alter ego.

EGYPTIAN ART AS REALISM

The question is always asked whether there was realism in Egyptian art. If the term realism is defined in broad concepts as denoting, Michalowski (p. 190) says: "the effort to represent a given phenomenon in its most typical form, and the fact recorded by the artist has thus a general significance that every viewer can grasp. In this sense, Egyptian art was certainly realistic."

FREDERICK MONDERSON

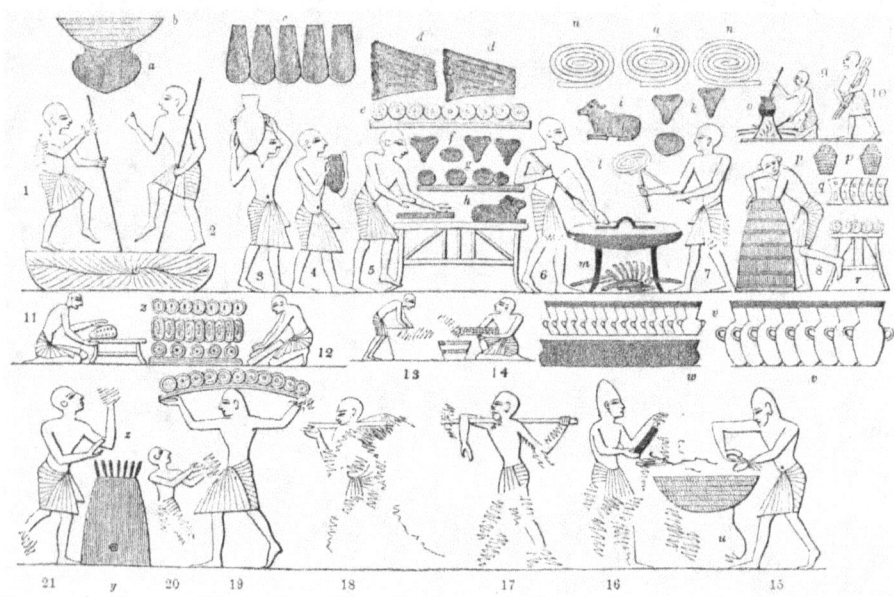

Research Essays Illustration 77. Cooks and Confectioners. In the Tomb of Rameses III at Thebes.

In essence, Egyptian painting and sculpture of the Old Kingdom can be summed up as follows, according to Michalowski in *Art of Ancient Egypt* (No Date: 190-191) who enumerates:

1) The canon was a unique historical phenomenon and has a peculiar indigenous character.
2) It was the result of a lengthy process of observation and experimentation, which culminated in, an art based on the most typical forms of nature; as such, the canon was formulated in terms of certain constant proportions.
3) The aim of the canon was to record phenomenon in the most legible and understandable manner, to reflect reality in both its visual and its social aspects.

RESEARCH ESSAYS ON ANCIENT EGYPT

Research Essays 76. Mortuary Temple of Seti I at Abydos. Seti prepares to incense and pours a libation to enthroned Ra-Horakhty in Double Crown.

4) The canon performed an important function in the ideological superstructure, serving the ruling class by perpetuating the conviction that the existing social function was by glorifying the gods and the Pharaohs.
5) The canon was essential to the maintenance of artistic quality and standards of workmanship.

FREDERICK MONDERSON

THE ART OF ANCIENT EGYPT

On more firm terrain, in Egypt, like elsewhere in Africa, very early man made tools and began to philosophize, paint and plan for the next day's hunt. Drawing animals he hoped to hunt the next day, set him on the path to developing beautiful and realistic human and animal portraiture; as well as initiating other forms of art as painting, sculpture, jewel making, and building boats and architectural structures, all dating to the earliest times. W. Stephenson Smith in *The Art and Architecture of Ancient Egypt* (1989: 25-26) tells us: "Art appears in the Nile Valley as early as the seventh millennium B.C. The earliest productions are the rock-drawings executed on the cliffs bordering the Nile in Upper Egypt and Nubia. The most ancient of these consist principally of geometric designs such as concentric circles or half-circles and net-patterns, or abstract figurations the exact meaning of which is obscure. Representational themes appear later. There are many hundreds of drawings of the animals pursued by the earliest hunters and of weapons and traps .... Drawings of cattle and boats can be definitely associated with the developed Neolithic cultures of Upper Egypt and Nubia, and with the Egyptian pre-dynastic, Nubian C-Group, and later historic cultures."

Hans A. Winkler in *Rock Drawings of Southern Upper Egypt* I (1938: 18) mentions some of the early artistic representation in this part of the Nile Valley. Thus, the art of Egypt, in particular and the Nile Valley in general, can be considered very old and indigenous! "The following animals are represented: gazelle, stag, ibex, antelope, cattle, hare, lion, crocodile, fish, dog, horse. There are men with bow and arrow, with lasso, with staff, with flower, man smelling lotus-flower, man in adoring attitude, Pharaoh on throne, Pharaoh with mace; women; sailing-vessels; Min, Mentu, Taurt, Anubis, Horus the falcon, uraeus." Clearly many of these animals and gods would be incorporated into the hieroglyphic corpus somewhat analogous to William Arnett's view in *The Predynastic Origin of Egyptian Hieroglyphics: Evidence for the Development of Rudimentary Forms of Hieroglyphics in Upper Egypt in the Fourth Millennium B.C.* by the University Press of America, 1982.

RESEARCH ESSAYS ON ANCIENT EGYPT

Research Essays Illustration 78. Front of the state Chariot of Thutmose IV.

Still, much of the Art of Egypt in the Predynastic period can best be viewed from the contents of graves of the Badarian, Amratian and Gerzean or Naqada I and II culture sequence. Guy Brunton's "The Badarian Predynastic Period" in Richard Engelbach's *Introduction to Egyptian Archaeology with special reference to the Egyptian Museum, Cairo*, (2nd Edition. Cairo: Government printing Office, 1961: 19) mentions pottery as their important feature such as deep or shallow bowls, often flat-bottomed and covered with fine ripples. "The Badarian people made linen in small pieces, but their usual clothing was finely tanned leather, sometimes stitched into garments. Their ornaments were ivory bracelets, strings of shells obtained from the shores of the Red Sea, and beads made from colored pebbles. It is probable that their blue-glazed stone beads were not made by the Badarians, but were acquired by trade, since a metal tool had apparently pierced them, and copper colored the glaze. Metal was very scarce in the Badarian Period, and copper beads were worn as precious jewelry. Nose and ear-studs were also found, together with slates, of characteristic form, on which the green eye-paint was ground."

FREDERICK MONDERSON

Research Essays 77. Mortuary Temple of Seti I at Abydos. Ra-Horakhty embraces Seti and makes him an offer.

Regarding the philosophic and aesthetic thoughts behind the forms and purposes of this art, T. Eric Peet (1915: 91) gives three motives for decorative objects among these early people. These are: "for purely artistic motives; a useful purpose; and magical or religious reasons."

In their funerary internments were found items the deceased deemed to be useful in the next life he/she believed in. In addition to food, the contents of which were contained in pottery vessels, personal items including weapons and tools, knife handles, combs, and jewelry represents the earliest forms of the art. Nevertheless, other evidence exists for as Smith (1989: 26) continued: "The sculptured objects

RESEARCH ESSAYS ON ANCIENT EGYPT

which were deposited in the ancient shrine of the southern capital at Hierakonpolis commemorate the victories of the south over the north in the struggle which finally resulted in the subjugation of the Delta which had been ruled from Buto. If we remember that there is no interviewing stage between this transitional period and Gerzean, we can continue to call it Late Pre-dynastic or Proto-dynastic, which is a somewhat better term than Dynasty O, which has also been applied to it."

The statues of Min painted black, found at Koptos and now in the Ashmolean Museum, Oxford, are from this period. Gold, silver, copper, tin and other precious stones were also early forms of adornment. Equally, we see the emergence of various craftsmen who in turn were supervised by masters of the crafts. However, while these specialists may certainly have existed in the Predynastic times, by the start of the dynasties their work began to take on remarkable form. In this regard, Peet (1915: 89) continued: "The discovery of the statue of Khasekhem at Hierakonpolis showed us what the royal sculptor could accomplish in the IInd Dynasty, and the stela of the Serpent King took us back to the Ist, while a series of Predynastic discoveries still continues to furnish us with works of art of an even earlier date." Nonetheless, by the time of the Old, Middle and New Kingdoms when records were being kept more accurately, there is ample evidence of more and better artistic accomplishments.

Research Essays Illustration 79. Twin sentinels of Amenhotep III placed before his temple at Thebes. Notice the size of natives and horses compared to the statues.

FREDERICK MONDERSON

Unquestionably, religion and its adherents, the priesthood, played a key role in the development of Egyptian art. As such, there was a profound mysticism, magic, symbolism and esoteric nature attached to art that shaped the perception relating to and method of Egyptian Art. Cyril Aldred (1980: 11-12) in discussing the character of Egyptian Art wrote: "Egypt, like all the other nations of antiquity, was profoundly influenced by magic, by a belief in the existence of all-pervading, invisible and superhuman forces that had to be propitiated if their aid was to be secured, or neutralized if their enmity was to be avoided. Only continuous worship of these mysterious powers could keep the universe in an equilibrium favorable to the survival of man and his institutions. It was the constant affirmation of the pharaoh, the divine king who presided over the destiny of Egypt and its people that he had restored the harmony (*ma'at*) of an ideal world as it had been established at the First Time, but which could easily be jangled out of tune by human neglect or wrongdoing."

Research Essays 78. Mortuary Temple of Seti I at Abydos. Seti makes a Presentation to enthroned Amon-Ra in plumes. Notice the hawk above the King's head and his cartouches.

RESEARCH ESSAYS ON ANCIENT EGYPT

Aldred (1980: 11-12) goes on to make the connection depicting the priests of Ptah, especially, the creative process and the emergence of art as a discipline and ultimately an industry. Accordingly: "This creativeness was not divorced from the creative process by which the Egyptian universe had come into being and was daily maintained. In historic times the great productive power was the god Ptah of Memphis, the 'Creator' who in his more active and seminal form was depicted as a ram-headed craftsman, fashioning mankind upon his potter's wheel. In a song current in the New Kingdom, he is described as 'making this with his two hands as balm to his heart.' According to the peculiar belief of the ancient Egyptian, Ptah was also the primordial mound of earth that rose from the waters of elemental Chaos and on which all life began, just after the annual inundation of the Nile, a narrow spit of land first emerged from the flood, soon to be covered with vegetation and busy with animal life. Besides the flora and fauna of nature, Ptah, the New Risen Earth, contained within himself all the products from which many under his inspiration could also create things: clay, stone, metals and minerals. It is not surprising, therefore that the High Priest of Ptah should bear the title of Greatest of Craftsmen, and was originally responsible for the design and execution of all Egyptian works of art. Even in later times, when other gods shared the creative power of the demiurge, craftsmen in far-off Thebes, the city of Amun, the god of light and air, still worshipped Ptah in their local shrine and acted as his priests in their leisure hours."

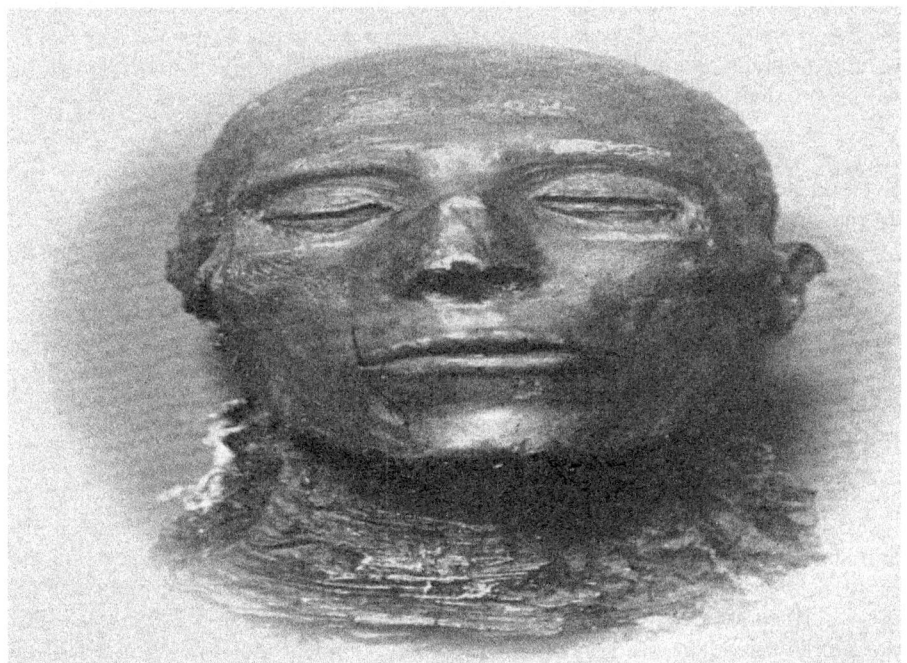

Research Essays Illustration 80. Pretty well-preserved head of Seti's mummy.

FREDERICK MONDERSON

The artist never signed his name to his work, for this was considered blasphemy because of the association of art with religion and the hereafter. In *Art in Egypt*, Gaston Maspero (1912: 299) dealt with the question why the artist did not sign his work. "We should like, indeed, to know what they were called, what was their native city or their condition in life, who had been their first teachers, and by what efforts those geniuses who made the plans of Deir-el-Bahari or the Hypostyle Hall, raised the Pyramid of Chephren, and carved the Seated Scribe in the Louvre, and Thothmes III and the Amanitas at Cairo, the Seti I and the goddesses of Abydos, outstripped the crown of their competitors. The choice that fell on them to undertake these great tasks prove sufficiently that they did not pass unnoticed among their immediate circle, and that they enjoyed in their day the reputation of being the most skillful and most gifted in their craft. Fame was not lacking in them, at least in their lifetime, and among those who surrounded them, but when their generation had passed away, the admiration of the new races was poured out on the Pharaohs or the rich men who had employed them; the memory of the bold craftsmen who dared to design and execute the speos of Abu Simbel was not handed down with his work as was that of Ictinus with the Parthenon. It was thus that, ignorant of the ambition of immortality by fame, the action of which is so powerful among the moderns, the Egyptian masters were for the most part content to observe conscientiously, as they would have done in any ordinary calling, the rules which the teachings of their predecessors had assured them were necessary to the well-being of souls human and divine. When by chance any were born whose inventive minds rebelled against the half technical, half religious education of the workshop, their efforts towards progress or reform had no serious results."

Even further, Maspero (1912: 300) continued: "By refusing details, Egypt gave her art that character of uniformity which strikes us. The personal temperament of the individual is revealed only by almost imperceptible shades of handling, and the majority of visitors carry away with them from museums and ruins the sense of a collective impersonality, slightly varied here and there according to time and place by the greater or lesser degree of skill in the executants. They do not understand what an amount of natural talent and acquired science the unknown authors of great temples and fine sculpture expended, to make themselves more than mere skillful craftsmen."

Nevertheless, Alix Wilkinson (1975: 1) points to names given some of these early craftsmen. "Jewelers were called *neshedi* and *nubi* (the gold man) and *hemu nub* (gold-craftsman). A number of goldsmiths can be identified from tombs, statues and inscribed amulets. Those most likely to have been the actual craftsmen have the simple title Gold Worker; others are called Chief of the Gold Workers of the Estate of Amun. Still more exalted persons, who certainly never touched a

RESEARCH ESSAYS ON ANCIENT EGYPT

blowpipe, but who were responsible for the organization of industry, were those whose title included that of Overseer of the Treasury of Gold and Silver, Overseer of the Gold Land of Amun, Weigher of Amun. Their duties would have been to see that the materials needed for making the treasures for the temples and for the king were available and that the work was carried out as required. Neferronpet, who was Chief of the Makers of Thin Gold, a goldbeater, had his Book of the Dead decorated with gold leaf."

Research Essays 79. Mortuary Temple of Seti I at Abydos. God Anubis embrace Seti, who also touches the divinity. Notice the hawk above Seti's head.

FREDERICK MONDERSON

Research Essays Illustration 81. The Temple of Karnak's Processional Colonnade, during early clearance of the enclosure.

Next, Wilkinson (1975: 3) mentions the method of that delicate, yet aesthetic experience of transferring raw materials into works of art. "Among the processes most frequently illustrated are the preliminaries, weighing, giving out the metal and melting the gold in a crucible over a charcoal fire; then pouring out the molten metal, beating it into sheets and bars with a rounded stone, and polishing it. Gilding is first illustrated in the Old Kingdom tomb of Ibi at Deir el-Gabrawi. Scenes of drilling and polishing beads occur in the Old and New Kingdoms, but the making up of a collar, as distinct from simply holding it up for inspection, is illustrated only in the New Kingdom. In the Old Kingdom an old man is shown making the thread for stringing beads. Glazing may be illustrated in the Old Kingdom tomb of Re-hem at Deir el-Gabrawi, where a collar dripping with the

RESEARCH ESSAYS ON ANCIENT EGYPT

liquid is lifted out of a pot." In addition, Wilkinson (1975: 6-7) writes about the tools and materials utilized by the craftsmen to ply their crafts. "Among the tools which are illustrated are reed pipes, tongs, rounded stones for hammering the metal, stone anvils resting on wooden blocks, crucibles and long rods for lifting them. Moulds used for casting large objects like bronze doors appear in illustrations, but not moulds for small objects. Several of the smaller moulds have however survived, both for casting and for stamping. Casting was usually by the 'lost wax' process, but some small objects were cast solid. The 'lost wax' or *cire perdue* method of casting involved making a model of wax. An outer covering of damp clay was pressed around the model and allowed to dry. When the mould had hardened the wax was melted out and the molten metal poured in to the space it had left."

Clearly there were other types of tools. "The carpenters had saws, but the jewelers did all their piercing and cutting with chisels. The bead-makers used bow-drills and these must also have been available to the goldsmiths. Pointed tools survive which may have been used either for repousse work or for burnishing, and there are measures for gold dust from Naqada dating from the XVIIIth Dynasty, and hammers in Berlin made of serpentine which date from the first century A.D."

Research Essays Illustration 82. Funeral boat or Baris, with shrine.

In addition to the crafts and tools, we are told: "The materials used by the ancient craftsmen were gold and silver, carnelian, lapis lazuli, feldspar, jasper, amethyst, button-pearl, turquoise, amber, agate, onyx and glass imitating colored stones."

FREDERICK MONDERSON

Research Essays Papyrus Art 11. Tutankhamon rides in his chariot and shoots at birds.

Sommers Clarke and R. Engelbach in *Ancient Egyptian Construction and Architecture* Oxford University Press (1930: 200) quote A. Lucas a chemical engineer who wrote about Egyptian metals and materials. He states, in regards to the colors employed in art, the following were used:

"'Most of the Egyptian pigments were naturally-occurring mineral substances, simply powdered.
'The white was generally carbonate lime, but sometimes sulphate of lime.
'The black was carbon, being sometimes soot and sometimes a coarse material, probably powdered charcoal.'
'The grey was a mixture of black and white.
'The red was red ochre, either natural or made by calcining yellow ochre. In Roman times, however, red lead was also employed as well as pink made from madder.
'The browns were all natural ochres.
'The yellows was of two kinds, either natural or made by calcining yellow ochre and the other, which, however, was not used until about the XVIIIth dynasty, was sulphide of arsenic (orpiment), and as this latter does not occur in Egypt, the supply must have been imported.
'The principal blue was an artificial frit, consisting of a crystalline copper-lime-silicate made from malachite, limestone, and powered quartz pebbles, possibly

RESEARCH ESSAYS ON ANCIENT EGYPT

with the aid of natron, though this latter was not necessary. This is known as early as the XIth Dynasty. Another and earlier blue was powdered azurite, a naturally occurring basic carbonate of copper, which was used before the artificial frit was discovered. Still another blue, the occasional use of which has been reported, was a cobalt compound.

'The green used was of two kinds; that employed at first being powdered malachite - a copper ore found in Egypt - and at a later date a green frit, analogous to the blue frit already mentioned.

'The medium with which the colors were put on was water and not oil, with size, gum, or white of egg. It has not yet been definitely established which of the three was used.

'The Egyptian painting was in reality a distemper.'"

Next to jewelry, one of the earliest forms of Egyptian art is the slate palette used for grinding cosmetics. However, they serve an even more historical purpose because they are illustrated pictographic "documents" recounting early and important events. The *Bull Palette*, the *Libya Palette*, the *Narmer Palette* and the *Narmer Macehead*, are all early and enduring fine arts. The funerary evidence, principally from Abydos and Sakkara shows an increase in the goods of the grave and the emerging architecture of king's tombs.

Importantly, by the Third Dynasty, when Imhotep erected the Step-Pyramid at Sakkara, on the outskirts of Memphis, new innovations were made in architecture and art. The colonnade, the Enclosure Wall, Open Court, Heb Sed Pavilion and Court, Dummy Buildings with emphasis on the lotus and papyrus emblems of the Upper and Lower Kingdoms and other facets of kingly paraphernalia became highlighted. Glazed blue wall tiles and illustrations of the "Heb Sed" race within the Step-Pyramid are interesting examples of early artistic accomplishments.

Research Essays 80. Mortuary Temple of Seti I at Abydos. Isis as Hathor offers life to the nostrils of Seti.

RESEARCH ESSAYS ON ANCIENT EGYPT

Research Essays Illustration 83. Villa and Garden of an Egyptian Noble of the Old Kingdom (After Perrot and Chipiez) Breasted (1923).

In addition, the enormous mastaba tombs of the nobles began to be richly decorated, providing the great motivation for artists to ply their skills. At Sakkara, the tomb of Hesi-Ra to the North; tomb of Ti to the West; tombs of Idut, Nebet Khnum-Hotep, Niankh-Khnum, Nefer and Nefer Hent Ptah and Iruka-Ptah to the South; tombs of Mereruka, Kagemni, Thetu and Nefer-Sheshem-Ra, Ankh-Mahor and Nefer Sheshem-Ptah to the East, are all magnificent funerary decorated canvases upon which Egyptian art reached its pinnacle in the old Kingdom. The five pyramids with texts, dubbed the "Pyramid Texts," are those of Unas, Teti,

FREDERICK MONDERSON

Merinre, Pepi I and II, that helped carry the writing to its highest development and set in stone the religious beliefs of this earliest empire along the Nile where art reached enduring heights.

While the 6-story mastaba Step-Pyramid carried architecture to the new frontier of building innovation, the true pyramid at Ghizeh set in stone the more perfect alignment and permanent work of art that today still defies the ravages of time. Strange, the Pyramids of Ghizeh were not illustrated nor painted, though the name of Khufu was found in his great pyramid. On the other hand, some believe the exterior was decorated.

The Art of Egypt in the New Kingdom became more prolific and extensive. In the supremacy of Amon and with imperial wealth flowing into his coffers, art blossomed and bloomed. Regional schools competed extensively, particularly with the Theban School, to produce the timelessness reflected in the paintings, papyrus, glass, pottery, earthenware, statues, architecture, obelisks, jewelry, etc. Decoration in mortuary and worship temples; in the Valleys of the Kings, Queens, Nobles and Artisans, art depicted every aspect of the social, religious and afterlife experiences of the Egyptian. In the worship and mortuary temples, there were statues to complement the colonnades, porches, ramps, doors, walls, shrines, and obelisks. The halls were decorated with praises to the gods as well as the king on the inside and military and other exploits of the king on the outside. While the Sanctuary was often dark and undecorated on the inside; the outside, as at Karnak and Luxor were decorated with episodes of the ritual.

In the Temples of Luxor and Karnak, and many other structures associated with Rameses II, the treaty with the Hittites ending the Battle *of Kadesh* is often depicted on the pylon or other external walls. Rameses' "Girdle Wall" at Karnak is replete with illustrations of the king presenting to, praising and being blest by the gods. The Temple of Mut of the Theban Triad, had hundreds of sculptured statues of the lion-goddess Sekhmet placed there by Amenhotep III. Further, at Luxor, on the west and east walls of the Processional Colonnade, the events surrounding the Opet Festival are depicted. Across the river at Deir el Bahari, statues of the Queen as well as depictions of the Expedition to Punt, recounting of the Queen's "Divine Birth," some would call "Virgin Birth," the Chapels of Hathor and Anubis, the Upper Court, all have powerful examples of Egyptian art. The Kiosk of Seti II in the Great Court at Karnak and the Kiosk of Hatshepsut in the Court of the "Ramesseum Front" at Luxor Temple, usurped by Thutmose II and repaired by Rameses II, were both dedicated to the Theban Triad of Amun, Mut and Khonsu. Both are inundated with the most beautiful sunk reliefs. The "Red Chapel" now reconstructed in the Open Air Museum is a veritable reservoir of compartmentalized picturesque art. The Temple of Abu Simbel has beautiful paintings as also the Temple of Seti I at Abydos decorated by both Seti and Rameses II. The Temple of Seti at Abydos also has a Kiosk in the rear, dedicated to Osiris, Isis and Horus with the most beautiful illustrations. The temple of Rameses II at Abydos, though generally destroyed, yet contains exceptional art. The difference between the two temples, the art of Seti is protected by a roof while those of Rameses are not. The Ramesseum and the Temple of Medinet Habu mortuary structures of Rameses II and Rameses III respectively, carried the art of building, pictographic decoration and hieroglyphic representation to the highest heights and show Egyptian art in its finest features.

However, there was more to the art than architectural representation, and as such the decorative features of painting deserve mention. Von Reben (1902: 42) provides some insights into sculpture, painting, and other aspects of Egyptian "fine arts." First he tells of adding color to this great age of art during the New Kingdom. "A great majority of the Egyptian works of sculpture were cut with marvelous patience in the hardest materials, in variously colored granite, diorite, syenite, and basalt. Limestone and alabaster were rarely employed for colossal or life-size statues, but were used more frequently for works of smaller dimensions; these were also burned in clay with a surface of blue or green glazing, or were cut in more valuable stones, such as agate, jasper, carnelian, and lapis lazuli. Enameled clay idols were manufactured in great numbers; modern museums contain hundreds of these figures of perfectly similar form. The so-called scarabaeus is very common - beetle shaped bodies of clay, or of the above-named stones - with incised figures or hieroglyphics upon their lower surface. Such amulets were perforated and worn as beads, and were placed loosely in the coffins with the mummies."

FREDERICK MONDERSON

Research Essays 81. Mortuary Temple of Seti I at Abydos. Seti offers a plant to Moon God Khonsu with side plat or lock of hair, indicative of youth.

Again, Von Reben (1902: 44-45) continued: "Representation of profane scenes are more varied and are exceedingly interesting; the technicalities of Egyptian art are shown by the cutting of a monolithic palm-column, the polishing of a granite

RESEARCH ESSAYS ON ANCIENT EGYPT

chapel, the painting of walls, the writing of hieroglyphics upon tablets and papyrus, the carving and painting of sphinxes and statues, the making of bricks and walling of brick masonry, the interior of houses, even the plans of dwellings and gardens. Besides numerous tools and the products of manufacturing trades, there may be recognized upon these paintings weavers, rope-makers, the preparers of paper and of linen cloth, ship-builders, carpenters with hand-saw and auger, and the cutters of bows and lances, who employ adzes quite similar to those still in use. Commerce on land and sea is represented by wares, unpacked or in bales, by scales, various kinds of wagons and trading vessels, etc., all shown in the clearest manner possible. Ploughs, sowing and harvesting, the gathering of figs and grapes, the pressing of oil and wine, illustrate the condition of agriculture; while the especial ability of the Egyptian for animal representations is exercised in the hunting scenes of lions, tigers, buffaloes, jackals, and gazelles; by the snarling of birds and fishes in nets, as well as by the admirably characterized figures of apes, porcupines, etc. There are also historical paintings, great battle scenes, the storming of cities, and the triumph of the returning victors, who bring with them booty and prisoners, the nationality of whom is often readily distinguishable by peculiarities of physiognomy and costume. The Egyptian kings appear in superhuman size, either fighting from splendid war-chariots, or striding forward to sacrifice their kneeling enemies, a dozen of whom, seized at once by the hair are decapitated at a blow."

Research Essays Illustration 84. View of Karnak from the south, atop the roof of the Temple of Khonsu of the Theban Triad.

Even further, Von Reben (1902: 47) summarizes his views: "The painting of Egypt existed unchanged for a period of more than two thousand years, with a stability unequalled in the other civilizations of the world. It was perhaps not quite so extensively employed in the ancient kingdom as in later times: paintings can be dated as far back as the third dynasty (3338-3124 B.C.) according to Lepsius, but they were restricted to interior decoration. The walls of the pyramids were

FREDERICK MONDERSON

unadorned by color. After the practice of art had been greatly limited by the invasion of the Hyksos (from the thirteenth to the seventeenth dynasty, 2136-1591 B.C.), it arose with new vigor at the advent of the modern kingdom, especially during the eighteenth and nineteenth dynasties, when the architecture which flourished from Thebes offered a wide field for painted decorations. From that time the walls lost their bareness, and richly colored ornaments were employed over the exterior, enlivening the dead and heavy character of Egyptian buildings and somewhat supplying the deficiency of its exterior development."

For the later period, the Graeco-Roman temples of Isis at Philae, Kalabsha, Kom Ombo, Edfu and Esneh contain more painting, reliefs and sculpture than all surviving earlier Egyptian temples combined. The good thing about this is that they help to record, save and transmit much of the earlier beliefs and practices. By this time, native Egyptian art had entered a decline and there were infusions and innovations made by the conquerors who changed the nature of Egyptian art. Some commentators have argued that the Greeks and Roman brought much needed change and infusion. However, one thing is certain, the early and ancient Africans of Egypt created lasting and picturesque art that was original in its conception and their display in museums worldwide attest to the beauty and timelessness of their creations.

References

Aldred, Cyril. *Egyptian Art: In the Days of the Pharaohs 3100-320 B.C.* New York: Oxford University Press, 1980.
Brunton, Guy in "The Badarian Predynastic Period" in Engelbach, Richard. *Introduction to Egyptian Archaeology with special reference to the Egyptian Museum, Cairo*, 2nd Edition. Cairo: Government Printing Office, 1961.
Clarke, Somers and R. Engelbach. *Ancient Egyptian Construction and Architecture*. Oxford University Press and Humphrey Milford, 1930.
Kush, Khamit Indus. *The Missing Pages of "His-Story."* 1993.
Maspero, Gaston. *Art in Egypt*. New York: Charles Scribner's Sons, 1912.
Michalowski, Kazimierz. *Art of Ancient Egypt*. No Date.
Peet, T. Eric. "The Art of the Predynastic Period." *Journal of Egyptian Archaeology* 2 (1915: 88-94).
Smith, W. Stephenson. *The Art and Architecture of Ancient Egypt*. New York: Penguin Books, (1958) 1981.
Von Reben, Dr. Franz. *History of Ancient Art*. New York: Harper and Brothers Publishers, 1902.
Wilkinson, Alix. *Ancient Egyptian Jewelry*. New York: Methuen and Co., (1971) 1975.
Wilkinson, Richard H. *Reading Egyptian Art*. London: Thames and Hudson, (1992) 1996.

RESEARCH ESSAYS ON ANCIENT EGYPT

Research Essays 82. View of the surrounding terrain in the Valley of the Kings.

Research Essays 82a. Sign indicating all you need to know regarding the "Glory of the Ancient" culture in the Valley of the Kings.

FREDERICK MONDERSON

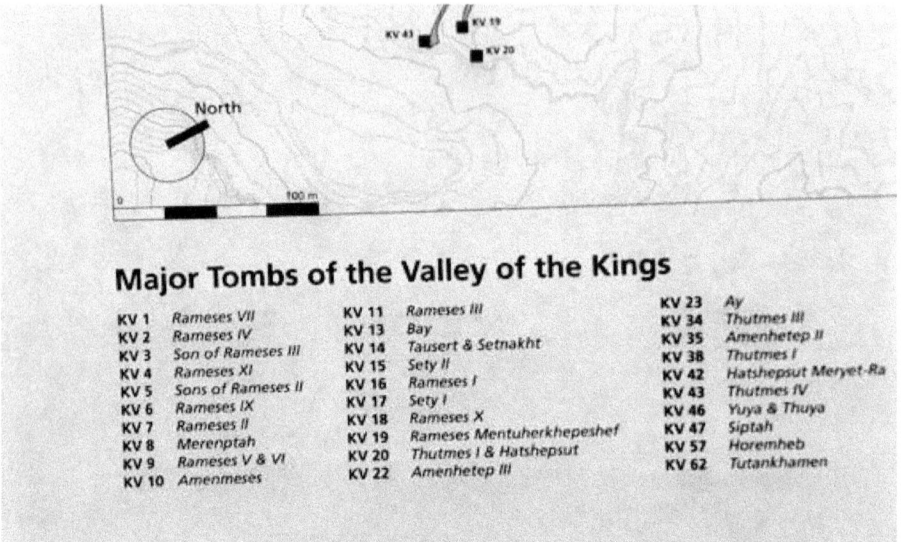

Research Essays 82b. A list of the Major Tombs of the Valley of the Kings.

14. Egyptian Warfare

By

Dr. Fred Monderson

Warfare is a subject caused by many factors, whether it's for land, religion, wealth, spirituality, respect, and intellectualism or for the minds and hearts of a people. In the ancient Nile Valley experience, warfare was principally for domestic pacification of rebellious elements and unification or of an imperialistic nature, to secure political boundaries and booty that became tribute. Up until a century ago, "Nile Valley spiritual warfare" ensued in the "Rape of the Nile" with the acquisition of antiquities as the objective and the propagation of an inaccurate depiction of much of the actual history of that culture. Adorning public institutions and private collections, principally in North America and Europe, the wondrous treasures of a great African civilization stand as prize of an offensive successfully mounted in the cloak of a colonial age and the machinations of "enlightened" and "intellectual imperialism." Those imperial campaigns were part of the effort not simply to acquire artistic treasures but also to prototypically mold

RESEARCH ESSAYS ON ANCIENT EGYPT

and alter history with the intent of maintaining a perennial, unrelenting, subtle yet pernicious, assault on the psyche of Africans at home and in the Diaspora. This *modus operandi* has for the most part been a success and people of African descent must in turn challenge these assaults in a systematic, measured and sustained counteroffensive that frees the mind, educates and elevates the spirit and cultivate a cultural awareness, while being active participants in the molding and creation of history that aims at a corrective with the intent of redeeming Africa and its people in the unfolding drama of historical process. Hence what is needed is a sustained campaign of warfare for the minds and hearts of African people that arms them with a sense of the positive nature of history particularly significant in today's world. As such, it becomes necessary to examine some feature of warfare as it unfolded in Nile Valley experience and who were the principal architects of that early phenomenon that propelled Africa millennia ago.

Warfare in Egypt is as old as the Dynastic period. Prior to the First Dynasty, Egypt experienced cultural growth and prosperity due to the achievements of the Badarian, Amratian and Gerzean accomplishments. This led the strong states, or Nomes, to attack the weaker ones in quest of booty. As a result, fortifications were built to protect various towns and settlements from raids to secure cattle, women, and other wealth. From this period the names Scorpion, Narmer, Menes emerged. From then on and throughout Egyptian history, organized warfare and weaponry changed to meet the times and the development of craftsmanship. Inasmuch, imperial expansion, powerful leadership and the desire to secure resources and establish zones of influence to encourage trade made the Egyptians become more and more warlike.

The Gerzean period, just before the unification of Egypt, has shown the extent to which warfare, whether small-scale or otherwise, persisted. A number of slate "documents" from this period attest to this. First there was the *Battlefield Palette* showing a Libyan victory over states in Lower Egypt. The *Bull Palette* shows the king as a Bull, attacking enemies of the state. The *Libyan Palette* showed cattle, asses, rams, and incense trees as part of tribute for a king, presumably rendered by military conquest.

The famous *Narmer Palette* is decorated on both sides. It shows the king wearing both the Crowns of Upper and Lower Egypt. This regalia is symbolic of his unification of the land. The White Crown of the Upper (Southern) Kingdom conquered the Red Crown of the Lower (Northern) Kingdom. He chose a red and white Double Crown, established the first dynasty and became the King of Upper and Lower Egypt. He also brought peace and stability to the land, a necessary prerequisite for economic and cultural development and expansion. The *Narmer Macehead* shows the king seated with his Queen Neithhotep and recounts his capture of 120,000 men, 400,000 oxen and 1,420,000 goats. These numbers indicate that at c.3100 B.C., these Africans were counting in the millions attesting to their mathematical advances.

FREDERICK MONDERSON

Research Essays Illustration 85. The Funeral Procession – The Mourners. The Oxen dragging the Mummy to his last home; while other members of the funeral entourage bring up the rear

What is more significant, however, in this document regarding his victory over the North, is the size of the booty. In addition, the *Narmer Macehead* does provide room for speculation about the size of the force he used to capture that many men. The size of his army, that of the enemy and the possible size of those who lost their lives on both sides raises even more questions. The possibility exists also, that the final victory is really the culmination of a protracted struggle. This may then mean the size of all combatants and casualties may have been larger.

Another interesting set of questions are: What type of preparation went into this engagement? What was the size and style of weaponry? And even more important, what type of administration went into coordinating this victory?

Existing evidence indicates that throughout Egyptian history, weaponry expanded and improved, as more and more materials were brought under effective exploitation and experimentation. Bunson's *Encyclopedia of Ancient Egypt* (1991) (1999: 168) indicates: "The early kings of Egypt did not preside over a united land in the 1st Dynasty (2920-2770). There is evidence of resistance on the part of various regions. Aha recorded adding territories in the south (probably the area between Gebel es-Silsileh and Aswan). Djer (c. 2900 B.C.) recorded a campaign against the Asiatics in the eastern desert. Perabsen, at the beginning of the 2nd Dynasty (2770 B.C.) made raids into Palestine, probably exploratory expeditions or raids for cattle and other loot. Khasekhemwy (2649 B.C.), the last king of the 2nd Dynasty, secured Egypt's unification, indicating continual or at least intermittent warfare on the Nile up to that point. It is possible that the first

RESEARCH ESSAYS ON ANCIENT EGYPT

settlement at Buhen in Nubia was made in his reign, as Khasekhemwy and his successors had started to penetrate the territories below the First Cataract of the Nile."

Research Essays 83. Valley of the Kings. Tomb of Thutmose III of the 18th Dynasty.

E.A.W. Budge, in *Dwellers on the Nile*, (1972) has provided a description of some weapons of the pre-dynastic Egyptian soldier. These were: "(1) A stout *cudgel* like that used by watchmen in Egypt to-day; (2) a *mace* or *club*, consisting of a short stick with a lump of bitumen on the top of a perforated stone (later copper) head; (3) a *spear* made of wood, with a slice of flint fastened to one end; (4) *bow and arrows*, the latter made of reeds tipped with flints; (5) a large flint *knife* or *dagger*; (6) a *battle-axe* formed by tying a slab of stone or flint to a short stout wooden handle or by fixing it in a cleft in the handle; (7,8) a *curved stick*, similar to that carried by peoples of the Eastern desert today, and a short pike."

From the earliest times each Nome had its own *standard* or totem. Certainly by the Middle Kingdom, the Egyptian soldier defended himself with a shield, which was made of wood or wicker-work covered with hide and sometimes strengthened with a metal rim and bolts. Square-tipped flint arrowheads were carried in leather *quivers* and the *boomerang* was used. Troops were barefoot and wore a kilt.

FREDERICK MONDERSON

Horses and *chariots* were introduced in the New Kingdom. However, there is evidence that there were horses buried in Nubian tombs before the New Kingdom. Nevertheless, the horse was put to great use in the military and in imperialistic ventures of the New Empire.

The army was commanded by the king as the overlord. When there were warrior pharaohs, they personally commanded their troops in the field. Such pharaohs as Mentuhotep and Sesostris in the Middle Kingdom; Ahmose, Thutmose I and III, Amenhotep II and III and Horemheb; Seti I, Rameses I, and Rameses II and III of the New Kingdom; and Piankhy, Shabaka and Taharka of the XXV Dynasty, could be considered warrior pharaohs. They personally led their troops in battle. Otherwise, in the king's absence, the Army was headed by a Commander-in-Chief, a Chief Deputy of the Northern and Southern Corps, General Officers, all with their added bureaucracy. There were town and village levies and internal garrisons. Many positions became hereditary in the emergence of a military caste. Bunsen mentions ordinances, logistical and provisional, and departments who supported the military whether in "barracks" or on the move.

Research Essays Illustration 86. Workmen drilling out stone vessels.

It was the army from the south that helped Narmer subdue the north to unify Egypt at the beginning of dynastic times. Diop identifies Narmer as a Theban, that's from Thebes, today's Luxor. Fifteen hundred years after his push northward, by 1500 B.C., Thebes became the capital of the kingdom and the most dominant city in the world for another millennium, and nicknamed the "fighting province." Four thousand years after Narmer's unification, by comparison, William the Conqueror invaded Britain. Altogether Narmer's victory happened some 5000 years before our time. This was an historic age when the world bowed down to and worshiped

RESEARCH ESSAYS ON ANCIENT EGYPT

black men, black women and black gods and being black was synonymous with creativity, medicine, science, architecture, and warfare as well as ethical and moral behavior. That army helped to maintain the political structure begun in the Archaic Period. They helped support the evolved theocratic state throughout the Old Kingdom, when military activism ensued in Nubia and in Syria and Palestine.

From the Old Kingdom onwards, military activism ensued beyond the borders of Egypt.

Snefru of the Fourth Dynasty sent naval expeditions to the Levant. Wenis of the Fifth Dynasty sent five expeditions to Syria and Canaan.

Breasted's *History of Egypt* (1923: 135) mentions one significant engagement under Pepi I when Uni embarked: "his force, he carried them in troopships along the coast of southern Palestine, and punished the Beduin as far north as the highlands of Palestine. This marks the northernmost advance of the Pharaohs of the Old Kingdom, and is in accordance with the discovery of a Sixth Dynasty scarab at Gezer below Jerusalem, in strata below those dated in the Middle Kingdom."

With that accomplished Pepi turned to Nubia through the "Door to the South" from the Cataracts.

At the end of this period, the wars of the First Intermediate Period, helped create the state of anarchy in the country. This lasted throughout the VII-X Dynasties. Still, while the nation was fragmented and chaos and anarchy reigned, it was the Thebans who kept order in the south and offered resistance to the kings of the IXth-Xth Dynasties. Coupled with this was a respectful reverence held for the king. Breasted mentions: "The great mass of the army employed by the Pharaoh at this time was composed of the free born citizens of the middle class, forming the militia of the permanent force of the nomarch, who at the king's summon placed himself at their head and led them in the wars of his liege-lord. The army in time of war was therefore made up of contingents furnished and commanded by the feudatories. In peace they were also frequently drawn upon to furnish the intelligent power applied to the transportation of great monuments or employed in the execution of public works."

FREDERICK MONDERSON

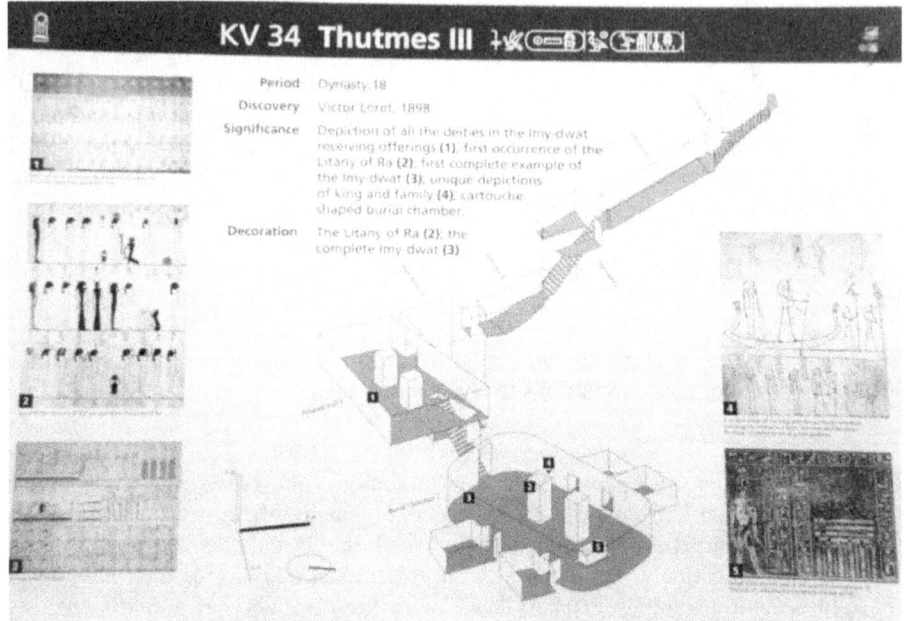

Research Essays 84. Valley of the Kings. Tomb of Thutmose III contains decoration with the *Litany of Ra* and the complete *Imy-dwat*.

As in the Old Kingdom, war continued to be little more than a series of loosely organized predatory expeditions, the records of which clearly display the still unwarlike character of the Egyptian.

"Sehetepibre, a magnate of Amenemhet III's court, left upon his tomb-stone an exhortation to his children that they serve the king with faithfulness, saying among many other things: 'Fight for his name, purify yourself by his oath, and ye shall be free from trouble. The beloved of the king shall be blessed; but there is no tomb for one hostile to his majesty; and his body shall be thrown to the waters.'"

The southern war machine under Intef and Mentuhotep reunited the country after the collapse of the Old Kingdom and the chaos of the First Intermediate Period. It was their army that subdued, expanded and reinforced the reorganization of the Middle Kingdom. Standing armies were held in the Nomes whose Nomarchs held great sway, provided they supplied troops to the national army when called upon. Sesostris was another title of the Middle Kingdom pharaohs who attacked Libya, held Sinai and extended Egyptian control beyond the First Cataract into Nubia. J.A. Wilson in *The Culture of Ancient Egypt* gives a description of this area where the Egyptians were constantly engaged militarily. "The policed frontier of the

RESEARCH ESSAYS ON ANCIENT EGYPT

Middle Kingdom lay at the Second Cataract, but Egyptian interests extended further to the south. The arable and hospitable territory between the Second and Third Cataracts is narrow and inhospitable. South of the Third Cataract the Nile Valley widens out and affords greater possibility for cultivated fields and particularly for pasture-lands for cattle grazing. The Third Cataract itself is hazardous for navigation because of hidden rocks in the rapids .... Nevertheless, that area is worth commercial cultivation. Just south of the Third Cataract and its dangerous rapids lies the modern town of Kerma, possessing a modest agricultural and trading importance and serving as the northern limit of the good land to the south. Under the Middle Kingdom Kerma was an outlying trading post and transshipment point for vessels and land caravans; Egypt maintained a resident colony there for commercial and political advantage, with a fortified trading post known as 'The Walls of Amen-em-het, the Justified.'"

In their interaction with this area, Middle Kingdom Pharaohs left a number of inscriptions at Aswan, and regions to the south. James Henry Breasted's *Ancient Records of Egypt,* Vol. I describes what was undoubtedly an expedition against the Nubians of Wawat, the land to the south of Egypt.

"During the XIth Dynasty, the most important of Mentuhotep's monuments is the relief on the rocks of Shatt el-Regal, near Aswan, where, accompanied by his mother, a lady not of royal lineage, he receives the homage of his vassal, King Intef, who is ushered into the royal presence by Mentuhotep II's chief treasurer, Kheti, with the following inscription: 'year 41, under (the majesty of) Nibkhrure (*Nb-hrw-R*) came the wearer of the royal seal, sole companion, chief treasurer, Kheti, born of Sitre, triumphant; and ships to Wawat ....'"

Again, according to Breasted, the Twelfth Dynasty King Amenemhet I left the following inscription over halfway up to the second cataract. "'Year 29, of the King of Upper and Lower Egypt, Sehetepibre *(Ship-yb-R*, Amenemhet 1), living forever. We came to overthrow Wawat ....'"

FREDERICK MONDERSON

Research Essays Papyrus Art 9. Image of Golden Mask of King Tutankhamun.

The stakes were so high they had no choice. The construction, organization and maintenance of the state, exploitation of the Nile, development of arts and crafts, literacy, trade, religion and science demanded this vigorous action.

In *Ancient Egypt* Jon M. White believes that warfare had become a lucrative trade, during the Middle and New Kingdoms. For, accordingly: "not only were successful officers rewarded with bounties, splendid ceremonial weapons and gold necklaces known as the 'Gold of Valor,' but they also received grants of land from the royal estates. When not on active service with their regiments they were given token posts in the service of the Pharaoh or the nomarchs." Further, he writes: "during the Middle and New Kingdom, the army was recruited at need from the Nomes, each of which raised a levy of between five hundred and a thousand militiamen for specific campaigns."

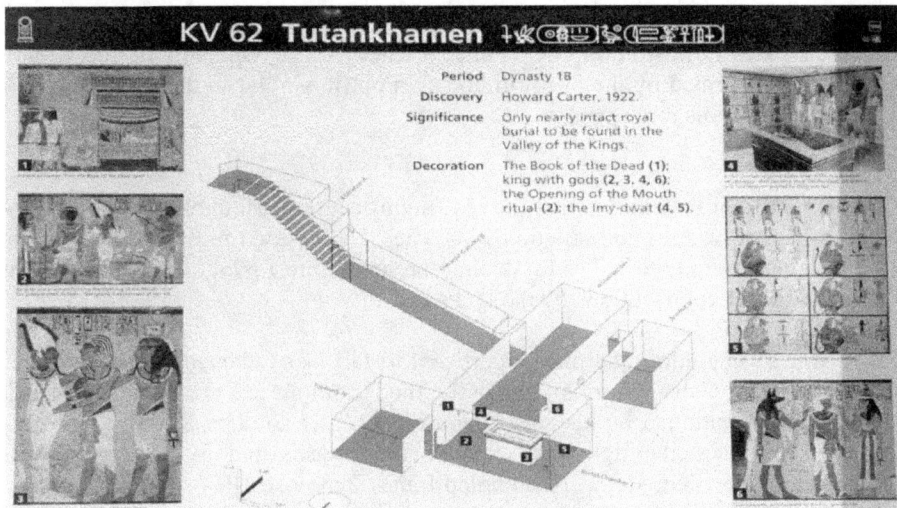

Research Essays 85. Valley of the Kings. Tomb of Tutankhamen contains decoration with the *Book of the Dead, King with Gods,* the *Opening of the Mouth Ritual* and the *Imy-dwat*.

As the Middle Kingdom waned, it was anarchic warfare that resulted in the Second Intermediate Period.

At this time, a more united force of Asiatics called the Hyksos invaded Lower Egypt, established themselves and ruled as the XV and XVI Dynasties. Their occupation was concurrent with the XIII and XIV Dynasty that ruled Upper Egypt. Nevertheless, the Hyksos wreaked havoc in the Valley, destroying much of Middle and Upper Egypt, even though they eventually settled down in the north to be part of the society they had fractured. Still, the southern region accepted them as overlords and paid tribute. However, after an insulting hippopotamus remark, the XVII Theban Dynasty began a protracted war of liberation that lasted for some 50 years in the effort to expel the Hyksos occupiers.

FREDERICK MONDERSON

Research Essays Illustration 87. Funeral Rites – The Opening of the Mouth Ceremony performed by the priest in lion skin outfit, similar to that performed for Tutankhamon in his tomb by Ayi.

Concomitantly, it was shown that the only significant contribution that the Hyksos made to Egypt was the introduction of a type of four-sided military fortification. They were also credited with introducing the horse into Egypt. Today we accept there were other contributions by the Hyksos.

In the war of liberation, the most significant to fall was Sekenenra Tao II, whose mummy, in the Cairo Museum, shows he died from an axe wound to the head. The war was continued by his son, Kamose. Another son and Kamose's brother Ahmose continued the fight and expelled the Hyksos and founded the XVIII Dynasty and New Kingdom. Amenhotep I and Thutmose 1 his son and grandson continued the military adventure, consolidating their positions at home and challenging adversaries abroad. In this fight Thutmose I overran Palestine.

The significance of the Hyksos' sojourn in and expulsion from Egypt was the transformation of the Egyptian military into an effective fighting machine. Egyptian warfare thus became a full time, highly organized and lucrative occupation. Prior to this, in addition to nome recruits, there was an army in the north and one in the south. Now under the New Kingdom, these two armies now had four divisions, Amon, Ptah, Ra and Sutekh or Seth permanently stationed in the north and south. Thus the Egyptians had moved from a conscripted army to a standing army. All this required great and effective administration and Pharaoh found this in the office of the Vizier. Breasted (1923) mentions the functions of the Vizier: "His office was the means of communication with the local authorities, who reported to him in writing on the first day of each season, that is, three times a year. It is in his office that we discern with unmistakable clearness the complete centralization of all local government in all its functions. This supervision of the local administration required frequent journeys and there was therefore an official barge of the vizier on the river in which he passed from place to place. [Air Force Two!]. It was he who detailed the king's bodyguard for service as well as the

RESEARCH ESSAYS ON ANCIENT EGYPT

garrison of the residence city; general army orders proceeded form his office; the forts of the South were under his control; and the officials of the navy all reported to him. He was thus minister of war for both army and navy, and in the Eighteenth Dynasty at least, 'when the king was with the army,' he conducted the administration at home."

Research Essays Illustration 88. Khuenaten worshipping the Solar Disk with his wife Nefertiti and smaller images of his daughters.

Therefore, the realities of imperial expansion created total war.

The great military Pharaohs of the New Kingdom and Empire, were Aahmes, Amenhotep I, Thutmose I, Thutmose III, Hatshepsut, Amenhotep II, Thutmose IV, Amenhotep III, and Haremheb, of the XVIII Dynasty. So too were Rameses I, Seti I, Rameses II, III, IX and XI of the XIXth and XXth Dynasties as well as Piankhy, Shabaka, Shabataka, and Taharka of the XXV Nubian Dynasty, among other fighting pharaohs. They were all powerful rulers, warrior kings who left indelible impressions on their nation state and the African historical landscape. Many were born into warfare, while others had warfare thrust upon them as the unfolding reality and glory of Egypt's place and role in the ancient world manifested itself. "In this time of Egyptian conquest, the army was divided into two great bodies, the Army of the South and the Army of the North: Rameses the Great subdivided it again into four great divisions named after the great gods Ra, Amen, Ptah and Sutekh, the king himself taking command of the division of Amen. The troops were again subdivided into squadrons under captains, and officers of lower ranks, and several regiments were formed of allied troops and mercenaries who were regularly drilled and trained with the Egyptian soldiers." Still, it was a proud time for Mother Africa when ancient was young and modern.

In the New Kingdom, the chariot as a war machine came into being. It gave the Egyptians great mobility and striking speed. This terrorized their adversaries, especially the Syrians who fought two major conflicts with Tuthmose III at Megiddo and later against Rameses II at Kadesh.

Thutmose III distinguished himself at Megiddo by executing an unthinkable strategy of scaling a difficult pass. This seems comparable and tantamount to Hannibal scaling the Alps. Once he was through the pass at Megiddo, at the head of his forces, he caught his adversaries unprepared and was able to effectuate a victory that established his prowess as a military commander.

Throughout Egypt, a number of battle scenes are represented on the monuments to attest to the Pharaohs' exploits. The most prolific military propagandist was Rameses II, and places as the Ramesseum, at Luxor, Karnak, Beit Wali, Derr and Abu Simbel are replete with descriptions of the various wars of this king. His father Seti I depicted his wars in Asia on the north face of the north wall of the hypostyle hall at Karnak.

At Karnak Thutmose III created the Hall of the Ancestors as well as the "Annals" depicting the names of towns he conquered in the Asiatic campaigns. Beside the "Cachette Court" on the north/south axis, there are depictions of pharaonic exploits against the Nubians. The hypostyle hall at Karnak temple is the great glory of Egyptian architecture. This magnificent architectural feat was conceived by Horemhab and begun by Rameses I. It was finished by Seti I and decorated by Rameses II. Breasted III, 81, p. 39 gives a graphic description of the wars fought by Seti I as indicated on the north face of the north wall of the hypostyle hall at Karnak.

RESEARCH ESSAYS ON ANCIENT EGYPT

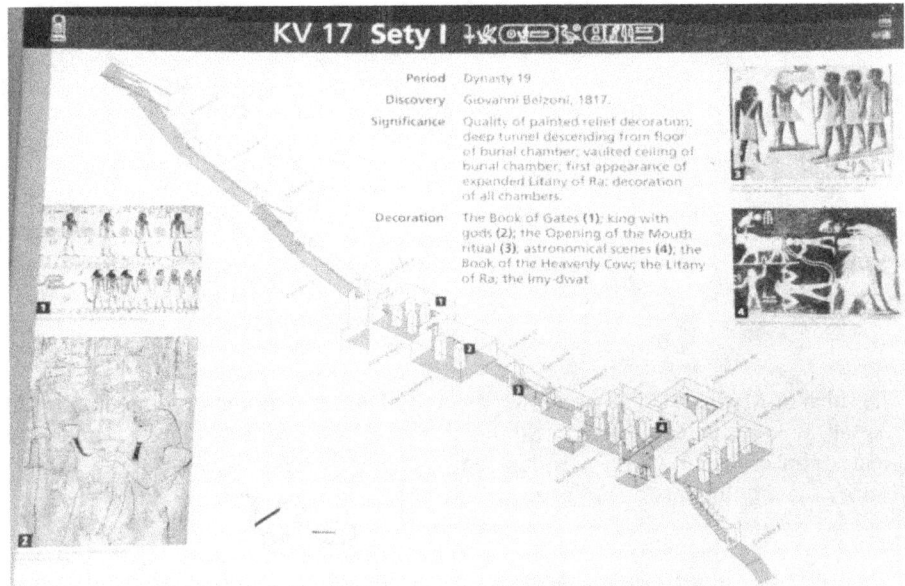

Research Essays 86. Valley of the Kings. Tomb of Seti I contains decoration with the *Book of Gates; King with Gods;* the *Opening of the Mouth Ritual; Astronomical Scenes;* the *Book of the Heavenly Cow,* the *Litany of Ra,* and the *Imy-dwat.*

The Ramesseum or Temple of Rameses

II was erroneously called the Memnonium and the tomb of Osymandyas, of Greek fame. For symmetry of architecture and elegance of sculpture the Ramesseum may vie with any other Egyptian monument. The sculptures are much more interesting than the architectural details but they have suffered over time.

On the north face of the eastern pyramidal tower or propylon is represented the capture of several towns from an Asiatic enemy, called in the hieroglyphic the *Khetas*, now known as the Hittites, whose chiefs are led away in bonds by the victorious Egyptians towards their camp. Several of their towns are introduced into the picture, each bearing its name in hieroglyphic characters, which state them to have been taken in the 4th year of king Rameses II.

At Abu Simbel, both sides of the entrance display kneeling captives.

FREDERICK MONDERSON

The ruins of Medinet Habu were mentioned by Diodorus along with three others at Karnak, Luxor and Ramesseum. Strabo also mentions Thebes' "many temples, the greater part of which Cambyses defaced." The early Christians did much also to destroy the monuments of Egypt as is evident today.

On the walls of the **Great Temple** and **Palace of Rameses III at Medinet Habu**, many scenes of warfare are sculptured. On the front wall the king smites his suppliant captives in the presence of Amen-Ra, who, on the northeast side appears under the form of Ra, the Physical Sun, with the head of a hawk. An ornamental border, representing "the chiefs" of the vanquished nations, Europeans, Asiatic and African, extends along the base of the whole front; and on either side of the oblong court or passage of the center Rameses offers similar prisoners to the deity of the temple who says: "Go, my cherished and chosen, make war on foreign nations, besiege their forts, and carry off their people to live as captives."

RESEARCH ESSAYS ON ANCIENT EGYPT

Research Essays Illustration 89. Head of Amenhotep IV, Khuenaten, Ikhnaton, wearing the Blue or War Crown.

From the palace a dromos of 265 ft. at Rameses III's mortuary temple, Medinet Habu, led to the *Great Temple*, whose front is formed of two lofty pyramidal towers or propyla, with a pylon or doorway between them, the entrance to the first area or propylaeum.

The sculptures over this *First Pylon* refer to the panegyrics of the king, whose name, as at the palace of Rameses II, appears in the center. Those on the west tower represent the monarch about to slay two prisoners in the presence of Ptah-

FREDERICK MONDERSON

Sokar, others being found below and behind the figure of the god. In the lower part is a tablet, commencing with the 12th year of Rameses; and on the east tower the same conqueror smites similar captives before Amen-Ra. Beneath are other names of the conquered cities or districts of this northern enemy; and at the upper part of the propylon a figure of colossal proportions grasps a group of suppliant captives his uplifted arm is about to sacrifice.

Passing through the pylon of the *First Court*, about 110 ft. by 135 ft. there are on the right or north side a row of seven Osiride pillars, and on the left or south side eight circular columns, with bell-formed capitals, representing, not as is erroneously supposed, the full-blown lotus, but the papyrus plant. Next there are two other pyramidal towers with a pylon between them.

On the west tower Rameses III leads the prisoners he has taken to Amen-Ra, who presents the falchion of vengeance, which the king holds forth his hands to receive; and on the east is an inscription beginning with the "eight year of his beloved majesty" Rameses III. It has been translated by M. de Rouge, and contains the names of a large number of the Mediterranean nations of antiquity, including the Pelasgi, the Teucri, the Siculi, the Daunians and the Oscans, who seem to have been confederated against Egypt with the Asiatics.

Luxor, a part of Thebes, signifies "the Palaces" from the temple there erected by Amenhotep III and Rameses II. It also refers to the various temples of visiting gods worshipped at the national temple at Karnak. On the north-west propyla of Luxor Temple a number of battle scenes are recorded on the front of the tower. Many of these are very spirited; and on the western tower is the camp, surrounded by a wall, represented by Egyptian shields, with a guard posted at the gate. Within are chariots, horses, and the spoil taken from the enemy, as well as the holy place that held the Egyptian ark in a tent; instances of which are found on other monuments, as at Abu Simbel. There is also the king's chariot, shaded by a large umbrella or parasol.

RESEARCH ESSAYS ON ANCIENT EGYPT

Research Essays 87. An alabaster factory with its exterior richly illustrated.

Many military expeditions were conducted in Nubia for gold, tribute, trade and for prisoners. In essence then, from the first to the last ages of dynastic Egypt, warfare played an important role in shaping the nature of the culture, its relationships with other states and the remains left by the great ones tell of their military exploits. It can probably be argued also, just as warfare "built" dynastic Egypt, warfare also destroyed it as conquerors from Assyria, Persia, Greece and Rome destroyed it, though some of these made attempts to help preserve what they saw as the greatness of an ancient culture.

REFERENCES

Budge, E.A.W. *The Dwellers on the Nile*. New York: Benjamin Bloom, 1972.
Bunsen, *Encyclopedia of Ancient Egypt*. (1991) 1998.
Breasted, J.H. *A History of Egypt*. Chicago: University of Chicago Press, (1906) 1923.
While, J.M. *Ancient Egypt*. New York: Dover Publications, Inc., 1970.
Wilson, J.A. *The Culture of Ancient Egypt*. Chicago: University of Chicago Press, (1951) 1975.

FREDERICK MONDERSON

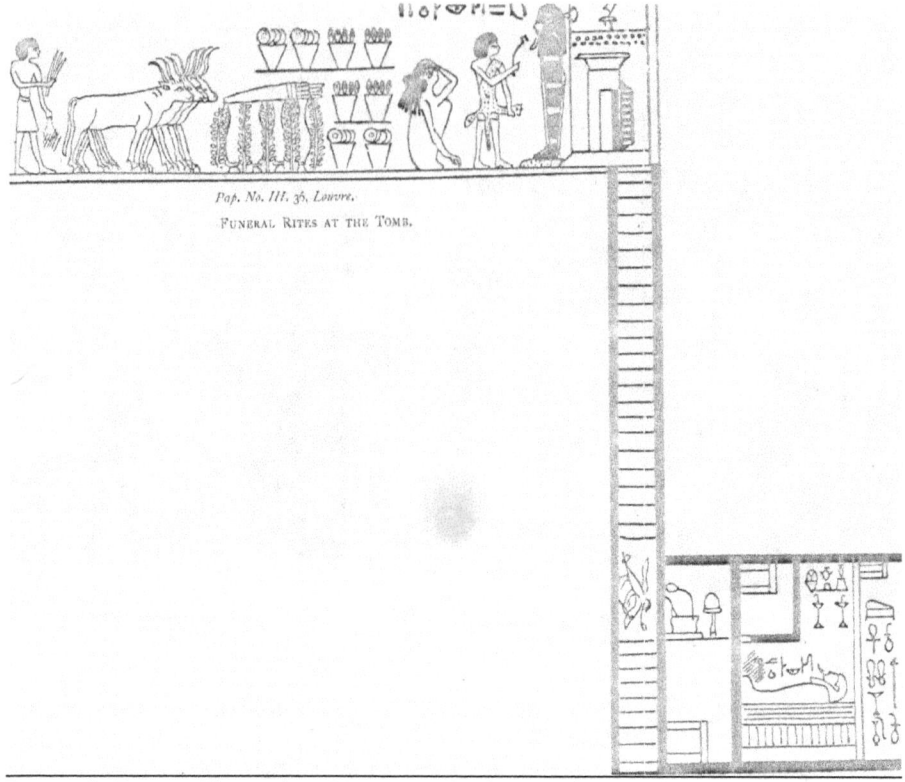

Research Essays Illustration 90. Funeral Rites at the Tomb. The Winged Soul descending a ladder to the Mummy.

15. Egyptian Technology
By

Dr. Fred Monderson

With the passing of time ancient Egyptian technology has retained evidence of its durability, essential essence, utility and esoteric beauty, while resisting the elements and destructive nature of man and time. In this development of high quality and accomplished technology, we see showcased the genius and indomitable spirit of ancient African technological creativity. The craftsmanship that produced Nile Valley accomplishments are evident in ancient Kemetic

RESEARCH ESSAYS ON ANCIENT EGYPT

building constructions, boat-building, tool repertoire, and in a vast array of industries upon which various trades were based. Specializations were manifest in quarrying, transportation, mining, the development of irrigation facilities, and a number of metal-workings. Kemetic craftsmen produced architecture, art, and jewelry of lasting durability the world has come to associate with the eternal nature of ancient African artistic and technical expertise in Egypt. Even further, technology helped to advance the building of canals, dams, dykes and embankments, both to facilitate water storage and as an aid to agricultural enterprise in the land of ancient Kemet.

Ancient Kemet's technological contributions to architectural developments date to the pre-dynastic period when housing structures evolved from the simplest types. In this regard Eric P. Uphill (1988) believed the: "earliest Egyptian dwellings appear to have been simple reed huts or even wind-breaks rather than caves as in Palaeolithic Europe." Those early builders along the Nile were fortunate to have and utilized varied transitional materials that were readily supplied by their environment. As technical skills advanced, patrons and their architects moved to erect structures built of more complex materials and design.

From the earliest times, there were three principal types of materials used for building in ancient Kemet, Egypt. The first of these consisted of various kinds of mud as well as reeds, rushes, papyrus stems and palm ribs and much of this was "cemented" with mud. Such materials were used mainly in domestic structures.

In this early period wood was generally considered a scarce commodity. This notwithstanding, in ancient Egypt/Kemet, "two kinds of planks could be made from two species of palm tree, the date and the dom." In addition: "Acacia (*nilotica*) and tamarisk were other local woods useful for house building. Only later, when very large beams were needed for roofing palaces or making columns and temple flagstaffs, were cedar and other imported woods, used extensively." As early builders innovated, palm fronds, with open and closed buds, and papyrus, influenced the design of column and capital, setting the stage for development of the colonnade, a significant contribution in Africa that appeared as early as 2600 B.C. at Sakkara, and significantly influenced later Egyptian and even Western architecture. Just then, early architects such as Imhotep, building upon the work of their predecessors, with full approval of their monarchs, were free to creatively experiment with points of architectural departure, setting standards for later builders.

The second type of material to evolve in Kemetic technology included a mixture of mud, then wattle and daub. These soon gave way to mud-brick. Soon bricks became an essential component in every building enterprise. So much so, brick making became a highly involved art and generally transmitted as a trade secret.

FREDERICK MONDERSON

Research Essays 88. Part of the rich variety of objects offered for sale at the alabaster factory.

Craftsmen employed wooden molds of various sizes to make the bricks. Large and small wooden molds have been found by archaeologists. The larger ones measured 15.0 X 7.1 X 5.5 inches and the smaller ones 8.7 X 4.3 X 5.5. Some of these old-fashioned techniques are still being used today.

Maspero's *Manual of Egyptian Archaeology* (1926) posited the view that the ancient workman acquired similar results as his modern counterpart who could easily: "turn out 1,000 bricks a day, and after a week's practice he will reach 1,200, 1,500 or even 1,800." Even further he notes distinctions could be made in the finished product since: "bricks from the royal brickyards are occasionally stamped with the cartouche of the reigning sovereign, those from private factories are marked with one or more conventional signs in red ink, a print of the molder's finger, or the maker's stamp."

Of the two kinds of bricks, the most ancient fell into disuse as early as the Sixth Dynasty. Considered small at 8 ¾ X 4 ½ X 5 ¾ inches, it was yellowish and made of sand mixed with a little clay and gravel. The other, fairly large at 15 X 7 X 5 1/2, was black, compact, well molded and made of mud mixed with straw.

RESEARCH ESSAYS ON ANCIENT EGYPT

The Nile generally supplied the needed material and the method of making them was somewhat simple. According to Uphill (1985), who notes regarding this building material: "the best bricks were built with chopped straw, but quite a useful brick could be made by using sand instead. Normally they were simply dried in the sun, although baked clay tiles were used for special functions. Mortar was merely mud of similar constituency to the brick."

The third type of building materials was stone. Evidence seems to indicate one of the earliest individuals to use stone in his building was King Khasekhumi of the First Dynasty. As the art of construction became more sophisticated "houses and domestic buildings and later temples and tombs were built entirely in stone." This changeover to a more durable material had lasting effects on building, mining, commerce and transportation practices. Stone remained a lucrative commodity. Still, in palaces and houses of the wealthy, stone was mainly reserved for "column bases and sometimes door-cases and window grilles .... Wooden column shaft bases could suffer damage from wet rot or insects, and stone bases acted as a protection and were much wider than the wooden shafts."

Ancient technological experimentation in construction of irrigation projects such as dams, dykes, and embankments expanded. Builders next erected fortifications to protect towns and other settlements from hostile neighbors. Such settlements were laid out in a determined pattern. Much later towns and cities with more complex structures and social infrastructures were constructed based on these early beginnings. Fortresses for military and imperial purposes were also erected in areas as Nubia where ongoing military operations were tied to imperial and economic activity. Imperial ventures in Southwest Asia and Nubia also spawned military fortifications for garrisons and to protect supply routes for military ventures.

FREDERICK MONDERSON

Research Essays Temple Ticket 15. Another ticket used by native Egyptians at a temple site. These are naturally less expensive than that paid by foreigners.

The pyramids are the most famous showcases of Egyptian technology. These structures have defied time, the imagination, and been the subject of many commentaries for thousands of years. They amaze both indigenous Egyptians and travelers from far and wide. The pyramid, as theosophical and architectural creations evolved from copying the natural pyramids created by the wind against the land in the desert, many of which are in Nubia and can also be seen at Abu Simbel. The man-made pyramids became the final resting-place for the Pharaoh or God-King after death and having religious, esoteric, philosophical, theological and cosmological implications. This system of belief developed in the Old Kingdom and generated intense construction effort to be buried within the pyramid's perimeter. To repose finally within the shadow of the god king was a noble undertaking, and many aspired to this accomplishment.

RESEARCH ESSAYS ON ANCIENT EGYPT

Research Essays Illustration 91. The Great Temple of Karnak and the Nile Valley at Thebes seen from an airplane.

Herodotus, who visited Egypt in 450 B.C., was one of the first Europeans to comment on the purpose of the pyramids. In his *Histories* he noted it took 100,000 men working twenty years to complete the Great Pyramid. Traditional belief holds, the pharaoh harnessed the unemployed population of ancient Kemet/Egypt during the inundation to build his pyramid. However, when the waters receded and workers returned to their fields, a reduced amount of workers, say, perhaps, 20,000 remained on the site. Such pyramid projects by a pharaoh awed his contemporaries by demonstrating his wealth and power. It also demonstrated an enormous managerial and organization ability to utilize labor in

FREDERICK MONDERSON

quarrying, transportation of huge stones from as far away as Aswan, as well as efficiency and effectiveness in construction techniques. A complimentary medical facility accompanied every project to treat individuals injured on work sites. Let's not forget, facilities for housing workers over the duration were also constructed near work sites.

These logistical dynamics grew out of earlier organization of the Step-Pyramid at Sakkara. Demonstrating architectural continuity, the concept and purpose of the Step-Pyramid grew out of the First and Second Dynasty mastaba tombs of the kings. Mastaba means bench in Arabic. The tombs resembled benches built by Arabs outside their houses, and hence their names. As such, adding one mastaba of decreasing size on top of another rising towards the sun or the heavens raised the Step-Pyramid.

Most people are aware of the Step-Pyramid at Sakkara, built by Imhotep in the Third Dynasty, for his Pharaoh Zoser. It was a masterful feat of achievement initiating an illustrious architectural history. However, Philip Watson (1987) points out the existence of at least three others. He mentions Z. Goneim's 1950 excavation of a second Step Pyramid at Sakkara, built for Pharaoh Sekhemkhet who reigned for only six years. Accordingly, Watson noted the: "essential elements of a seven-stepped pyramid, a paneled enclosure wall and a south tomb comprising a rectangular mastaba built over a deep burial shaft have been identified. There were similarities in the substructure of this pyramid and that of Zoser." Additionally he wrote: "The burial chamber was located along a sloping ramp on the north side which also gave access to one-hundred and thirty-two underground magazines and to four galleries associated with the burial chamber."

RESEARCH ESSAYS ON ANCIENT EGYPT

Research Essays 89. More of the wide assortment of objects offered for sale at the alabaster factory.

Another such structure has been identified at Zawiyet el-Aryan, between Giza and Sakkara. Never finished, it's been called the "Layer Pyramid" and probably belonged to King Khaba. Even further, scholars posited the view that another Step-Pyramid complex might be concealed within the so-called "Great Enclosure at Sakkara." Aerial photographs have revealed this step-pyramid with rectangular outlines to the west of Sekhemkhet's tomb. This is also a Third Dynasty creation.

The Fourth Dynasty experienced the move to create a true pyramid. The pyramid may be explained as a four faced structure, each sloping to the top in diminishing widths culminating in a point reached by all four sides. The pyramid can also be viewed as sitting on the top of an obelisk as a sacred symbol dedicated to the Sun God-Re. An obelisk is, therefore, simply a pyramid upon a high base. The *Bent-Pyramid* at Dashur was built after the *Step-Pyramid* but before the *True-Pyramid*. Snefru was the first king of the Fourth Dynasty though he is traditionally listed as the last king of the Third Dynasty. Importantly, he built the first original *True-Pyramid*. His son and successor Khufu built the great Pyramid at Giza. There were two others built by his son and grandson, Khafre and Menkaure. The Giza-Pyramid group is among the best preserved and most often visited by tourists owing their proximity to the Cairo environs. Together, these buildings enable us to trace the evolution of this building concept affirming the complexity and quality of African construction, this early in time. Some scholars believe there are mysteries contained within the pyramids that will remain forever unknowable.

FREDERICK MONDERSON

A number of smaller Pyramids were built in the Fifth and Sixth Dynasties. Still later, others were constructed in the Middle Kingdom. Nevertheless, most pyramids, regardless of size, were housed in a complex comprising a large expanse of land and numerous other buildings. A priestly bureaucracy, endowed to perpetuate the cult of the monarch served those whose resting-place dominated the complex.

Research Essays Illustration 92. The Weighing of the Soul in the Judgment.

The components of a pyramid complex included: a very tall Enclosure Wall, a Valley Temple, Causeway, or Entranceway, a Sun or Mortuary Temple, a Sacrificial Altar, *Heb-Sed* Festival Pavilion, the Main Pyramid, for the Pharaoh, Subsidiary Pyramids for the Pharaoh's wives and sisters, a Sphinx, an Obelisk, Magazines for storage, the Pharaoh's Solar Bark or Boat generally buried in a pit, and Mastaba tombs for nobles who served the Pharaoh. There was sometimes a god temple within the complex. Khufu had several solar barks in his complex. One of wood was discovered in the 1950s and has been reconstructed and housed in the Boat Museum at the pyramid.

The symbols of these mountains of stone were not the sum total of Old Kingdom technology. Mohamed Saber (ND) points out the discovery of the world's earliest tunnel at Giza. The Pyramid of Khafre had a Valley and Sun or Mortuary Temple. A Causeway that was covered joined these two temples with fine limestone. "It seems that this causeway was used only by the 'Pharaoh' and the chief-priests during the procession from the Valley Temple to the Mortuary one."

RESEARCH ESSAYS ON ANCIENT EGYPT

Therefore, those other persons who wished to move from one side to the other had to make a lengthy detour. This was a distance about three kilometers. Therefore, their planners: "... solved this difficulty by hewing a tunnel under the causeway; it facilitated the connection between the two sides of the causeway .... Needless to say that the discovery of this tunnel caused the astonishment of all people, for it revealed the inventive genius of the ancient architects."

Naturally, with the expansion and cultural apogee of the Egyptian culture, technology reached sophisticated levels in development of civil and religious architecture and domestic and military structures. The arts helped make these technological constructions more beautiful through beautification and experimentation as wealth poured into the state and patrons became more generous with their endowments. Nevertheless, these early experiments set the stage for later breakthroughs in all manner of technological advancements.

Therefore, as we see, technology was extended to facilitate development of arts and craft, statuary, boat building, mining, quarrying and production of medical, military and domestic tools and utilities. So much these early Africans gave to the world, so much they accomplished. So much this can teach us. There is thus a legacy we must claim in defending *Egypt as African*.

REFERENCES

Herodotus. *The Histories*. Trans. by Aubrey de Selincourt. Revised and with an Introduction and Notes by A.R. Burn. New York: Penguin Books, (1954) 1972.
Maspero, Gaston. *Manual of Egyptian Archaeology*. New York: G. Putnam's Sons, 1926.
Saber, Mohamed. *Pyramids and Mastabas*. Cairo: Lehnert and Landrock, Art Publishers, [ND].
Uphill, Eric P. *Egyptian Towns and Cities*. Bucks: Shire Publications, 1988.
Watson, Philip. *Egyptian Pyramid and Mastaba Tombs*. Bucks: Shire Publications Ltd., 1987.

Research Essays 89a. View of the surrounding landscape on the West Bank of the Nile with some evidence of tombs (openings) of people of means.

Research Essays 89b. Scenes from the Tomb of Vizier Rekhmara showing boat-people, individuals bringing gifts and giving out instructions to workers.

RESEARCH ESSAYS ON ANCIENT EGYPT

16. Science in Ancient Egypt/Kemet
By

Dr. Fred Monderson

Today science is in every walk of life in the human experience and it is a wonderful feeling for us to know the first scientist and scientists were black Africans. In fact, science affirms that man first originated in Africa and that all people living on the face of the earth are descendants of a single female who lived in East Africa more than 150,000 years ago. You need science for this and you need science for that. When the mummy of Pharaoh Rameses II began to decay, it was scientists in France who attended to preserve the remains. How interesting, this father, statesman, pharaoh, ruler, warrior, priest, patron of the arts and sciences, would one day be rescued thousands of years later, by a discipline he helped to nurture in its infancy and coming of age. It was that same science that allowed scholars to look into the intestines of this great ruler and determine he had smoked New World tobacco. Here is posited the view he sent sailors to the New World who brought back tobacco, which he smoked sometime before he died. Thus science lets us believe, Africans were in the New World 2800, at least, years before Columbus. Mind-boggling isn't it!

It is reasonable to argue that science in ancient Egypt was developed in a number of areas or disciplines including astronomy, writing, mathematics, geometry, architecture and engineering, navigation, surveying, irrigation and agriculture, as well as in medicine, metallurgy, the science of the mind, physics, and in a whole host of other areas.

Science was developed of necessity to combat the many challenges nature posed in its encounter with the human animal. As a result of meeting those challenges, man in Africa experimented with natural materials of his environment to beat back the frontiers of ignorance and advance the cause of humanity along a path of illustrious achievement. All this was accomplished because Nile Valley inhabitants dared to be creative, inventive, organizational, administrative, adventurous, hardworking and religious. Therefore, with religion, ethics and a sense of fairness as their guide, these ancient Africans of Egypt dared to experiment and praise and ritualize their gods and in this deference were rewarded with fortune, fame, fun and this provided the fundamentals of scientific invention.

FREDERICK MONDERSON

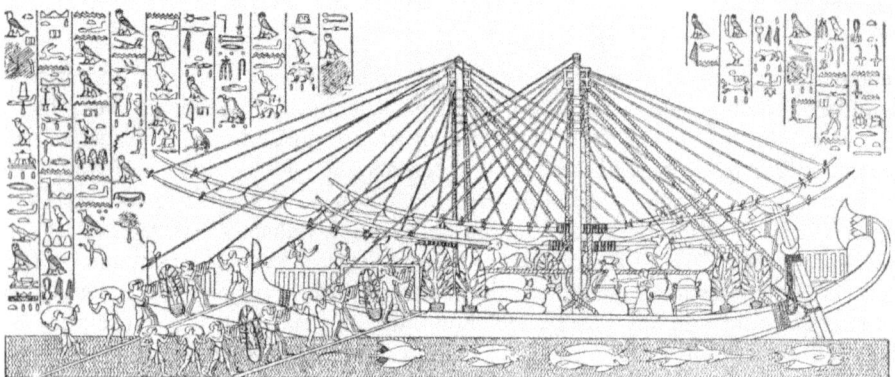

Research Essays Illustration 93. Part of the Fleet of Queen Hatshepsut loading in the Land of Punt.

While we recognize Imhotep as the "father of science," the world's first 'multi genius,' the genre most definitely preceded him. He, however, is the first individual scientist who has stepped out from the mist of history. He became a practitioner of one of the first sciences to be developed, astronomy; for as man emerged in his early state of consciousness, the first blackboard of his learning was the sky and its wonders and he imagined great things as he sat and pondered the heavenly phenomenon. The clear sky of his land afforded the most spectacular view of the dynamics of the workings of the heavens and from here his gods reached out to him. This discipline then aided him in developing the calendar by which he was able to measure time. These endeavors set him and us all on the road to development along the pageantry of human drama still unfolding.

RESEARCH ESSAYS ON ANCIENT EGYPT

Research Essays 90. Still more of the wonderful offering for sale at the alabaster factory.

We can therefore look back to those Nile Valley Africans who were not really the first mental and material inventors. This may have happened further south in Central or South Africa. Nevertheless, in a lengthy trail as such, they simply anchored the race and so emerged from the mist of antiquity equipped for the human and laboratory utility experiments. Therefore as successful practitioners they then bid us go, inquire and experiment, create, and establish conventions to help humanity overcome its fears, adversities and expectations. Do this in the name of science, that Egyptian, African, invention!

FREDERICK MONDERSON

ASTRONOMY

In the evolution of time measurement the Egyptian, African, scientists were innovative, leaders, who left indelible impressions in the minds and hearts of watchers of humanity. In this respect, science as we know it developed in inner Africa and came of age in ancient Egypt, without the regular designation of this discipline being fully applied. However, with the coming of age, the diffusion of knowledge, development of historical consciousness and insights, hindsight and recognition, we see and understand where science came from. Looking up to the heavens and voila, we had astronomy. The first science was the intellectual engagement of the mind. This has enabled Na'im Akbar to argue for "Nile Valley Origins of the Science of the Mind." The ancient Egyptians began it all. Reaffirming Petrie's listing, John Pappademos' "The Newtonian Synthesis in Physical Science and its Roots in the Nile Valley" (1985) (1986: 84-101) points out Egyptian achievement in astronomy as: "The invention of the 365-day calendar, based on astronomical observations; the development of instruments for quantitative astronomical measurement; the Precise alignment of temples and pyramids from astronomical observations; Knowledge of stellar constellations; the writing of astronomy texts; Tables of star culminations and risings; Knowledge of planetary astronomy; Prediction of eclipses; Discovery of the occulations of the stars and planets by the dark side of the half-moon; Discovery that the earth is spherical; Discovery of the obliquity of the ecliptic; Discovery of the precession of the equinoxes; First proof that the angular diameters of the sun and moon are unequal; First use of the Clepsydra (water clock) to measure the angular diameter of the sun; Discovery of the conjunction of the planets with each other as well as with the fixed stars."

The heliocentric theory of the planets' alignment with each other as well as with the sun is another such invention. Then finally, we have "Ptolemy's Almagest. This was the treatise, which became the 'Bible' of world astronomy for over a thousand years. It was written in Alexandria about 150 A.D. by an Alexandrian, in all probability an Egyptian." Pappademos concluded by adding: "each stage in the transmission of this tradition featured the work of scientists (like Aristarchus, Eratosthenes, Alhazen, Copernicus, and Newton himself) who both inherited the work of the past, and made additional contributions of their own."

Equally too, in *Wisdom of the Egyptian* (1940), Prof. Flinders Petrie mentions 10 elements of observational astronomy in the development of Egyptian science. These were the *Observed Year, 360-Day Year, 365-Day Year, 365 ¼ Day Year, Lunar Year, Four Kalendars, Precession, Hieroglyphs of Seasons, Cycle Periods,* and *Early Festivals*. This is after man had measured time in a discontinuous time frame. For example, we have the British 'sen night,' for seven nights; or 'fortnight' for fourteen nights; and Native Americans' 'snows,' for years.

RESEARCH ESSAYS ON ANCIENT EGYPT

Research Essays 91. Kom Ombo Temple to Gods Haroeis and Sobek. Majestic architecture of Kom Ombo's entrance with twin sun disk and twin uraeus on the cornice overhead. Notice the varied capitals and the twin nature of the Temple.

The *Observed Year* marked man's earliest attempts to view time in a consistent manner with a number of days forming a cycle. This continuous flow was aided by establishing a definite position of the sun at rising and setting. Then these early and ancient scientists used some annual phenomenon as a gauge to test it. In the case of Egypt, it was the annual behavior of the Nile River. In this evolution, the river came to regulate the lives, hopes and aspirations and scientific accomplishments of these people.

The *360-Day Year* began from the convenience of twelve months each with 3 - 10-day "weeks." The twelve months were also broken into 3 seasons of 4 months each. The *365-Day Year* was a result of intercalating 5 days, which were named the days of the birth of the gods Osiris, Isis, Seth, Nephthys and Horus. This, after they realized the year was short.

The Egyptians, before 4000 B.C., knew of the *365 ¼-Day Year*. According to Cheikh Anta Diop in, "Africa's Contribution to World Civilization: The Exact Sciences," *Nile Valley Civilizations* (1985) 1986, p. 78, who states: "The Egyptians knew that the civil year of 365 days was ¼ of a day shorter than the solar year. This meant that their civil year slipped steadily backward through the solar year, ½ a day every two years and one day every four years."

FREDERICK MONDERSON

Further, Dr. Diop states: "As early as the fourth millennium B.C., the Egyptians had already created the leap year. However, it is remarkable that they preferred to choose a time-lag of 1,460 years in order to add a whole year instead of adding one day every four years."

Indeed, this time period of 1,460 years is the period, which separated the two "heliacal risings of Sothis." The *Lunar Year* was fixed by the months of the moon. Petrie has shown that: "twelve months of 29.530 days each amounted to 354.36, or 10.88 days short in the year. This calendar also used by the Muslims, amounts to 354 days." Even further, for clarity and comparison, Breasted in his "First Fixed Date in History" (1915) mentions if Muslims celebrated the holy month of Ramadan in April this year, six years later they would celebrate it in June. It is not like our fixed calendar that lets us celebrate July 4th or Christmas on December 25th.

Again, Petrie (1940: 5) has pointed out, Egypt is the only country that has used *Four Calendars*. These were: "(1) a Lunar (Muslim) Calendar in official use, (2) a fixed Seasonal Calendar in agricultural use, (3) a true Calendar in European use, and (4) a Greek Calendar in religious use."

Precession or "precession of the equinoxes" according to John Pappademos in "The Newtonian Synthesis in Physical Science and Its Roots in the Nile Valley," in *Nile Valley Civilizations* (1985) 1986, P.97, refers to the "very slow, cyclic changes in the coordinates of the fixed stars that takes place with a period of some 26,000 years." Some scholars have argued, based on the Precession; to measure one cycle of 26,000 years has meant the existence of another, possibly three. Now, Charles Finch III, MD, has argued for a known second Precession. This then lets us imagine the possibility of a third and fourth, so 52,000, then 78,000 and 104,000 years of Egyptian/African stargazing! Amazing!

Petrie (1940: 5) has further shown: "The date of the Equinox preceded the star date, and this precession of the equinoxes was due to the change of direction of the earth's pole wobbling round the pole of the orbit. Hence the star date of the heliacal rising of Sirius, which was determined on the 1st of Thoth in A.D. 139, had been on 18 Mesore in B.C. 1317, on 6 Mesore in B.C. 2775, on 1 Mesore in 3385, on 24 Epiphi in 4235, on 14 Epiphi in 5705, and on 1 Epiphi in 7471 B.C."

Pappademos has argued further, the precession of the equinox was indeed a "phenomenon." It occurred in three stages. The first stage took place in Egypt, where the successive realignment of the axes of symmetry of various temples

RESEARCH ESSAYS ON ANCIENT EGYPT

noted by Lockyer showed the Egyptians were aware of the change of positions of stars over the course of centuries. (The orientation of Egyptian temples was set with extreme precision by astronomical observations in accordance with their worship of the stars or the sun.) The second stage consisted in the measurements of the rate of rotation of the celestial sphere. Hipparchus (b. circa 190 B.C. d. 125 B.C.) is generally credited with the first measurement, although some have given priority to the Egyptian astronomers.

The third stage consisted in a dynamical explanation of the effect, first given by Isaac Newton in the *Principa*. Pappademos (1986: 84) has noted: "In Isaac Newton's work, there was achieved a synthesis of three lines at the development, each of which started in ancient times. These were astronomy, mathematics, and mechanics. Newton's success rested directly on his predecessors Kepler, Copernicus, Descartes, and Galileo in the fields of astronomy, mathematics and mechanics .... The work of Newton's predecessors would have been impossible without the basis laid centuries earlier in Egypt, so that Egyptian science, after a thousand years, indirectly motivated Newton through his European predecessors such as Kepler, Descartes, Copernicus, and Galileo. Furthermore, Newton was, in addition, directly influenced by ancient Egyptian science."

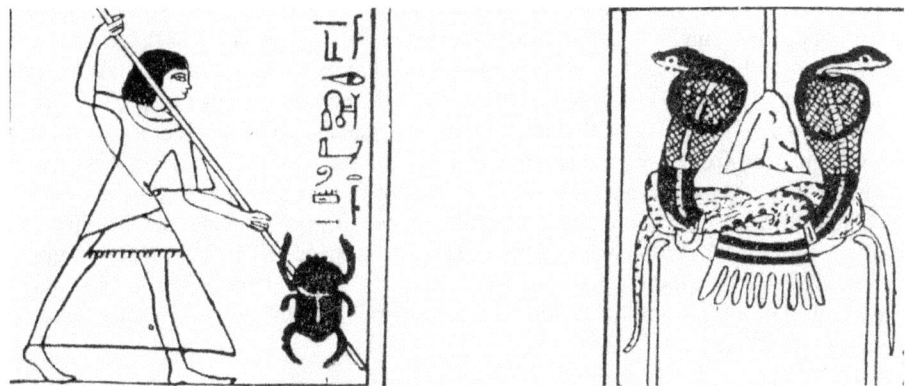

Research Essay Illustration 94. Book of the Dead. Spearing Khepre and Uraei on Guard.

The *Hieroglyphs of Seasons* were based on the 3 seasons of 4 months each. "These were the seasons of *aakhet* written as a growing plant, *pert* as a house sign, and *shemu* with a water sign. These signs obviously refer to the period of growth, November to February, and the living in a house after that from March to June, and the inundation from July to October."

FREDERICK MONDERSON

The *Cycle Periods* range from the 25-year period of the Apis to the 520-year period of the Phoenix. The *Early Festivals* are first shown being celebrated in the IV Dynasty and identify the fixed year, the vague year, and the great and small years. Petrie noted: "The fixed year cannot be anything but that of 365 ¼ days: the vague year must be that of 365 days. Then the other two, of 360 and 354 days, are called the great and small year, and as they only occur in one list they were certainly the least important."

There were some 28-firsts in instrumental astronomy, according to Petrie, including *Sun's altitude, Sun's azimuth, Clepsydra, Plumb-line pendulum, Star observation, Parts of the Body,* and the *Inundation,* among others.

The *Sun's Altitude* was a method of dividing and measuring the sun during the day. "The instrument had a raised end to cast a shadow, and divisions for the hours along a horizontal bar. This was represented as a hieroglyph, with a plumb-line hanging to fix the level of the base on which the hours were read." The *Sun's Azimuth* is the "direction of the sun casting the shadow of an upright stick; or else by a projection from a wall casting a shadow on the wall." The *Clepsydra* was a method of deciding the time by water dropping in and out of a graduated vessel. The *Plumb-Line Pendulum* was probably in use from the very earliest times in ancient Egypt. The known fact is, according to Petrie: "29.157 ins. (the diagonal of the 20.62 ins, cubit), which was the basis of all land measure, is the length which a pendulum would swing 100,000 times in 24 hours, exactly true at Memphis altitude."

RESEARCH ESSAYS ON ANCIENT EGYPT

Research Essays 92. Kom Ombo Temple to Gods Haroeis and Sobek. Another view of the entrance, the wall, Colonnade in the Court and the massive columns, capitals, architrave and twin disks overhead.

Star Observation is recorded in the tombs of Rameses IV and Rameses X in the Valley of the Kings. The outlines of the constellations, according to Petrie, were: "The first step is to lay out, for the first time, as star maps of the XVIII dynasty, by finding the hour meridians, and the pole, of that age on a globe, and transferring them for this map. As the proper motions of the stars amount to a degree or two in the interval, it is of no consequence to lay out nearer than that, especially as we only have whole hours defined, of 15 degrees each."

Lastly, *Parts of the Body* present a puzzling feature in the star list because each star is assigned - both by words and by diagram - to one of seven positions of the body, (1) right arm, (2) right ear, (3) right eye, (4) middle of breast, (5) left eye, (6) left ear, (7) left arm.

The *Inundation* or over-flooding of the Nile River played a very important and crucial role in the development of Egyptian civilization and its science. Moreover, because the river could have various types of impact on the inhabitants of Egypt it came to dominate the lives of all. W.E. Knowles Middleton in *The Scientific Revolution* wrote: "The Nile was also partly responsible for the interest of the Egyptians in astronomy, since they came to associate its flooding with the apparent position of the sun among the stars. But astronomy also had religious uses, for the sun was an object of worship, and the moon and the planets were believed to affect the affairs of men."

FREDERICK MONDERSON

MATHEMATICS

The field of mathematics was a major accomplishment of Nile Valley Africans. The notion of cultural transmission is applicable to upper Nile Valley origins that manifested itself further down the Nile.

While the bone from Ishango dates mathematical concepts in Central Africa to 8000 B.C., one of the earliest and more tangible evidence that has survived in Egypt is the *Narmer Macehead*. Quibell found it with the *Narmer Palette* at Hierakonpolis in Upper Egypt. Enlightening, Petrie credits its meaning as that at the beginning of Egyptian civilization where King Narmer: "records his capture of 120,000 men, 400,000 oxen, and 1,422,000 goats. The signs denoting each decimal place are completely fixed, exactly as they were used during thousands of years afterwards. We must credit therefore that account-keeping up to millions was already developed at the very beginning of the written record that we have."

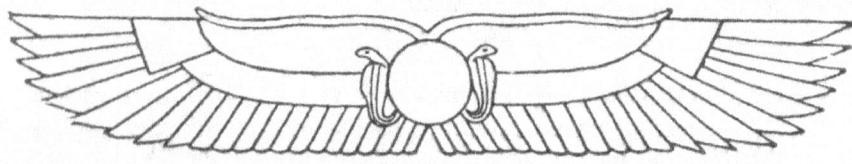

Research Essays Illustration 95. Winged Sun-Disk, a symbol of the Sun-God.

Yet still, and for an even earlier period, Petrie (1940) mentions a stone weight found at the beginning of Amratian or Naqada I civilization that was "carefully wrapped in leather, and put in the hands of the dead." There were 10 other such stones found in the Gerzean or Naqada II civilization. He clarifies (1940: 23-4) this as: "No people require a weight unless they can record the weight. A standard implies that, over a wide area, a people have need of fixed amounts for trading; and that the barter stage of mere agreement on some exchange that may suit both parties is already past. For trade, some sort of tally to record weight is needed, and the foundations of a numerical system are being laid."

Even more, Petrie (1940: 24) continued in explaining how their number system was represented: "The Egyptians started in prehistoric times with an excellent notation, purely decimal, for each place of figures up to millions. Each sign is repeated as often as required up to 9. The unit was commonly written by a stroke, but in detail it was represented by a short piece of rope. The ten was a longer piece of rope, bent. A hundred was a coil of rope. For a thousand, the plant sign is

RESEARCH ESSAYS ON ANCIENT EGYPT

the initial of khaa, a measuring cord. Thus the essential idea of numbering was the length of rope. The finger used for 10,000 seems to be a phonetic rebus. The tadpole for 100,000 is the idea of multitudes. The man with arms raised, for 1,000,000 is the sign of vastness or eternity. All these signs appear on registers of captured cattle before the 1st dynasty, so there was no lack of the means of calculation. A row of totals is found inscribed on a flake of flint of the 1st dynasty, in a scribe's tomb, along with stone palettes for ink, with numbers 40, 320, 88, 60, 44, and 3. Another note of numbers is on a flake of limestone from Meydum, of the IIIrd dynasty."

Still another artifact with numbers is that found in the tomb of Senmut, Hatshepsut's architect who built her Deir el Bahari temple. Gillings (1983: 87) tells of this finding where the: "New York Metropolitan Museum of Art conducted an expedition, obtaining an arithmetical computation on an ostracon that was subsequently translated. This computation consists of three double lines in red and black, showing the answer to the divisions of 2 and 4 by 7, expressed in unit fractions." Added to this, the Rhind Mathematical Papyrus (RMP) and the Ramesseum Mathematical Leather Roll (RMLR) are important sources of Egyptian mathematics. These latter two mathematical documents were discovered at the Ramesseum where a school of learning purportedly existed.

Research Essays 93. Kom Ombo Temple to Gods Haroeis and Sobek. Frontal view of the entrance with the left side dedicated to the Elder (Horus) Haroeis and the right to Sobek, the Crocodile God.

FREDERICK MONDERSON

As the civilization unfolded, the science of numbers became extremely useful in the art of building, quarrying, boat building, as well as artistic measurement and more particularly in irrigation, surveying and measurement of the Nile's inundation through the use of Nilometers. These measuring devices were set up at Abu Simbel, Aswan, Kom Ombo, Edfu, Memphis, etc., and they provided mathematical data regarding the volume of the Nile. This in turn provided a basis for taxation and was used to determine how surveys would be conducted after the inundation removed property marks. Even more importantly, it was linked to astronomy and the calendar. Gillings (1972) (1983: 235-36) puts this in a more succinct perspective in his statement that quotes J.W.S. Sewell "The Calendars and Chronology" in *The Legacy of Egypt*, S.R.K. Glanville, Editor, Oxford University Press, (1963: 97) which stated: "The most important event in Egyptian life was the annual flooding of the Nile River, the inundation period, which coincided with the heliacal rising (just before dawn) of Sirius, the Dog Star, the brightest star in either hemisphere. The first brief appearance of Sirius in the eastern sky was an important event in the Egyptian year. The next morning Sirius would appear some minutes earlier, and so on, so that before long, Sirius would no longer herald the dawn, and some other star would serve this purpose. This measuring of the days by the helical rising of stars gave rise to the system of decans, in which each chosen star would serve its duty of noting the last hour of night for 10 days (or nights), so that there would be 36 decans distributed through the mornings of the year. Of course, not all decans would have been visible on any given night. At the time of the inundation, when Sirius rises helically, 12 decans rise during the night, and thus the "hours" of the summer nights were determined. In winter there would be more decans visible; thus the length of hours varied slightly, both for the seasons and for nighttime and daytime. We see here the origin of the division of the day into 24 hours that is now universally adopted. These two calendars (of 365 and 365 ¼ days) existing side by side from, it is thought, the time of the first pharaoh of Upper and Lower Egypt, was the most scientific organization of calendars which has yet been used by man."

RESEARCH ESSAYS ON ANCIENT EGYPT

Research Essays Illustration 96. Soul with symbols of Life and Breath revisiting the mummied body.

On the question of Egypt and African mathematics, Beatrice Lumpkin's "Africa in the Mainstream of Mathematics History" in *Blacks in Science* (1983: 100) notes in summary: "For thousands of years, Africa was in the mainstream of mathematics history. This history began with the first written numerals of ancient Egypt, a culture whose African origin has been reaffirmed by the most recent discoveries of archaeology. With a longer period of scientific work than any other area of the world, progress in mathematics continued on the African continent through three great periods, ancient Egyptian, Hellenistic and Muslim. The language changed from Egyptian to Greek to Arabic. But the tradition of African science continued, despite change of language. The Renaissance in Europe was triggered by the science and mathematics brought to Spain and Italy by the Moors of North Africa. Although all peoples and continents have played a role in the history of mathematics, the contributions of Africa are still unacknowledged by western historians."

As such then, when we consider the advances made in astronomy, mathematics was certainly a significant corollary. Measuring the calendar, hours, days of the year, cycles of festivals, the 1460-year cycle of Sothis, the precession and so on, African mathematics has been of great importance. Lumpkin again, in a quote referring to the advances the Egyptians made, wrote: "Such precise mathematical

FREDERICK MONDERSON

and astronomical work cannot be seriously ascribed to a people slowly emerging from Neolithic conditions." In a further quote she wrote: "As to mathematics, the Stonehenge discussions have made it necessary to rethink our ideas of what Neolithic people knew. Gillings has shown that the ancient Egyptians could work with their fractions in a most sophisticated way."

Then again, "To those such as Kline, who dismiss all mathematics before the Greeks as less than 'true' mathematics, George Sarton, the Encyclopedist of Science replies: 'It is childish to assume that science began in Greece. The 'Greek miracle' was prepared by millennia of work in Egypt, Mesopotamia and possibly other regions. Greek science was less an invention than a revival."

Gillings (1983: 240-41) also added: "Such aggravated and condemnatory statements by an author of the stature of Professor Kline can only imply that he has not fully informed himself of the extent and nature of either Egyptian or Babylonian mathematics. And this is most surprising, for he knew at least of Neugebauer and Eves, because he lists their books in his work."

"The Exact Sciences in Antiquity alone would have directed his attention to the Rhind Mathematical Papyrus of Chace, et al. In two large volumes, published conveniently in Ohio more than a quarter of a century earlier; the Egyptian mathematics discussed therein most certainly would not have come under the heading of 'the scrawlings of a child just learning how to write.' If then Professor Kline were not familiar with, or was unaware of, the writings of Eisenlohr, Peet, Chace, Struve, Griffith, Schack-Schackenburg, Van der Waerden, Vogel, and others on Egyptian mathematics, then he would have been wiser to omit any reference to this ancient civilization in his "Cultural approach," and to have devoted his opening chapters to the early Greeks, about whose work he was certainly very well informed."

RESEARCH ESSAYS ON ANCIENT EGYPT

Research Essays 94. Kom Ombo Temple to Gods Haroeis and Sobek. Close-up of the intricacies of one of the varied capitals of the Colonnade in the Hypostyle Hall.

"The great accuracy of the dimensions of the pyramids still gives rise to wonder. Geometry, literally the measurement of the land, required a high technology in addition to theoretical mathematics. The famous 'rope stretchers' to whom Democritus compared himself, used special ropes, twisted of many fine strands to assure high stability and constant length. The accuracy of the Egyptian value of pi was 3.16, much closer to the modern 3.14 than the Biblical value of 3.0."

An explanation of "rope stretchers" is provided in Gillings (1983: 238) when he notes: "Even such a sober-minded person as H.W. Turnbull writes: 'Their land surveyors were known as rope stretchers, because they used ropes with knows or marks at equal intervals, to measure their plots of land. By this simple means, they were able to construct right angles, for they knew that three ropes of length three, four and five units respectively, could be formed into a right-angled triangle."

Even further, Gillings (1983: 238) continued: "It is, however, nowhere attested that the ancient Egyptians knew even the very simplest case of Pythagoras' theorem! But Turnbull goes further: 'As Professor D'Arcy Thompson has suggested, the very shape of the Great Pyramid indicates a considerable familiarity with that [sic] of the regular pentagon. A certain obscure passage in Herodotus, can, by the slightest literal emendation, be made to yield excellent sense. It would imply that the area of each triangular face of the Pyramid is equal to the square of the vertical height. If this is so, the ratios of height, slope, and base, can be expressed in terms of the golden section, or of the ratio of a circle to the side of the inscribed decagon."

FREDERICK MONDERSON

An effective irrigation technological strategy, efficient central administration, and the skill of the farmers of ancient Egypt made possible a large food surplus, enough to support mathematicians, teachers and other intellectuals. In turn, these ancient Nile Valley African mathematicians contributed to production by "developing methods of measuring the land through formulas for the areas of rectangles, triangles, circles and even the area of a curved dome. Properties of similar triangles were known and some trigonometry, the equivalent of our cotangent, helped assure a constant slope for the faces of pyramids."

Research Essays Illustration 97. Relief representing Thutmose III making an offering to a God at Gebel Dosha.

"In the case of Euclid, best known of the Alexandrian mathematicians, there is not a shred of evidence to suggest that he was anything other than Egyptian. Euclid's

RESEARCH ESSAYS ON ANCIENT EGYPT

fame is based on his 13 major texts, *The Elements*, a strictly logical deduction of theorems from accepted definitions and axioms. For over 2,000 years these books dominated the teachings of mathematics to the delight of mathematicians and the discomfiture of students. In a similar manner, the *Almagest*, written by another Egyptian, Claudius Ptolemy, c. 150 A.D., dominated astronomy until finally replaced by Copernicus' theory of sun-centered planetary system, c. 1543."

"The *Almagest* (the greatest in Arabic) contains in its 13 books the foundations of spherical trigonometry, a catalogue of 1028 stars and the epicycle of an earth-centered astronomy. By some peculiar racial reasoning, Ptolemy is often described as Egyptian only because his work was of a practical, applied nature, differing in this respect from the strictly theoretical work of Euclid. The fact is that both were Alexandrians and therefore it is highly probable that they were Africans. In Ptolemy's time, Alexandria was already 400 years old and very much a part of Europe."

Research Essays 95. Kom Ombo Temple to Gods Haroeis and Sobek. Twenty-three uraei adorn this ledge above the cartouches.

FREDERICK MONDERSON

MEDICINE

Very early in their history the ancient Egyptians were concerned with their health and developed extraordinary measures to treat such. Two things we must bear in mind created tremendous challenges to the health of inhabitants along the river in the Nile Valley. Second and most important, because these ancient Africans were among the first humans to become conscious of their intellectual, cultural and social capabilities they went to great lengths to invent utilities to make their life experiences and expectancy easy and enjoyable. Even more significant, because their earliest society was isolated from other peoples, their greatest and most far-reaching inventions were original in the truest sense. They had no one to emulate or copy and so writing on a clean slate of human knowledge and experience or *tabula rasa*, made them the earliest creative geniuses. In such areas as dealing with human health as related in medicine as obstetrics, surgery, dental surgery and anatomy and physiology, much of their advances were acquired through trial and error. As such then, modern efforts of criticism are enabled because of an existing documented body of knowledge showing among other things, the ancient Egyptians pioneered in two important areas of health care health care and circumcision.

The priests of Egypt were this culture's earliest intellectuals, a position developed from their responsibility of administering principally to the gods and then the king and nobility, stewards of the state. Because the king was the son of god and himself a god, they were concerned and became guardians of his health so that he could keep the state in equilibrium and be able to procreate and have as many heirs. Thus, in this respect, the priests studied nature and developed a pharmacopeia based on herbs, minerals and animal fats, skins and sinews and even animal and human waste. Today human urine is a credible medicine. Therefore, just as they cared for the living, they ended up caring for the dead and even became involved in their afterlife leading to religious doctrines and documentation that regulated the events of this phenomenon. Very early in the evolution of the priests' functions and responsibilities they developed two practices that, for the rest of time would have the most profound impact on human health.

The first of these was the old adage, "cleanliness is next to godliness." Because the priests administered to the god they had to be clean, washing themselves sometimes three times per day, shaving much of their bodies and wearing only linen clothing while in the temples. In periods of service in the temples they abstained from certain foods such as pigs, fishes and naturally remained free of any sexual contact. Most of the temples had a sacred lake, fed by underground springs connected to the Nile River, where in a rainless country; these individuals washed themselves just as they washed the god, even more so.

RESEARCH ESSAYS ON ANCIENT EGYPT

The god resided in the Sanctuary, a place of utter darkness and the door to that chamber remained locked. Just as in heaven, the chief god was awoken and given his ablutions by his bath attendants, toweled, and anointed with sweet smelling unguents, perfumes, rouge' and even lipstick. All the while, rituals were conducted, songs sang, rattles and tambourines shook and the room incensed. Interestingly, incense was never burned on the altar but in a corner in an incenser.

We know the Egyptian priests were involved in all facets of the intellectual dynamics of the society, but even more important; they were the principal practitioners of mental and physical health, from medicine, within the concepts of specialization in every part of the human body. Obstetrics, gynecology, surgery, ophthalmology, dental surgery and anatomy and physiology played a direct role in their healthcare. Study of the latter subjects of anatomy and physiology played an important part in the development of the practice of mummification, having to do with care of the deceased in the afterlife which they believed was a continuation of their earthly existence.

The god Thoth was the inventor of knowledge, music, writing and even mathematics. He was the Chief Minister to Osiris, God of the Dead and chronographer involved in the construction of the heavens as an assistant to the god Ptah, God of the Artisans, often called the "Blue Collar God."

Thoth was oftentimes represented as a baboon, a man with an ibis head and more often as an ibis bird. We know the peacock was a pretty bird, actually a showoff. However, the ibis was a more majestic creature with a flair and classy style in his walk. As you know the ibis bird has a long beak and a long neck

In the earliest period of the priests' existence, one day an ibis was observed washing itself by the waterside, as we know such creatures do. The ibis was observed taking a beak full of water, turning its long neck and inserting the beak of water into its anus, then shaking itself before passing it out. This led the priests to begin what we would later call colon cleanse. Often times people clean their external body but never do same with their internal structure. Old folks may remember older folks in the old country giving their children "castor oil" every other Sunday to clean them out. Today we call this purging yourself or taking a clean out. This is a powerful tool in physical health.

During the middle ages, an English priest and doctor outlived everyone to the ripe old age of 150 years! When he died the king ordered an autopsy to determine the secret of his long life. It was found he had the cleanest colon one could imagine. He probably cleansed once a week. That in itself is too frequent, but certainly once a month is adequate.

The Egyptians wrote on papyrus, a plant they prepared through a process that enabled them to write and become the earliest literate culture. Much of their medical knowledge was written on papyrus. Very early they began writing medical lore and we know the first physician to stand out from the mist of history was Imhotep, the world's first multi-genius. He was also an architect as his father and grandfather.

In the field of medicine, Egyptian science made advances far ahead of its neighbors. Equally, these ancient African medical men and women were well ahead of their time in examination, treatment and remedies for many illnesses. To treat the sick they used practical experience and magic and made medicine from plants and minerals. This required knowledge of the science of botany, or plant life, and mineralogy which they developed from thousands of years of study.

Imhotep was the first physician who stood out from the mist of antiquity. He lived during the Third Dynasty, c. 2800 B.C. He treated many diseases and wrote books on the state of the art. Many years later he was worshipped as a cult figure and became deified as the Greek God of Medicine, Aesculapius. Many of the diagnoses, especially from the New Kingdom, and reaching back into the Old Kingdom, have come down to us in papyri form. Steindorff and Seele's *When Egypt Ruled the East*, mention eight more or less medical works. "One of these old treatises deals not with human diseases but with veterinary medicine. Of the remaining seven, four are of a diverse nature, containing a mixture of purely medical material and a number of prescriptions or recipes for home uses, that is, cosmetic suggestions such as methods for dying gray hair, and formulas of a magical character." Likewise, "three of the papyri, however are thoroughly homogeneous. One is a treatise on gynecological disorders; another, of which fragments only are preserved, deals with conception, sterility, and the sex of the unborn child; the third is concerned with surgery."

Research Essays Illustration 98. Book of the Dead. Adjusting the sails for smooth sailing.

RESEARCH ESSAYS ON ANCIENT EGYPT

Research Essays 96. Kom Ombo Temple to Gods Haroeis and Sobek. Skyward view of a wonderful contrast of two of the varied capitals below the architrave.

For early knowledge that the ancient Egyptians reached such a high level of medical know-how, we are indebted to Manetho, an Egyptian priest of the third century B.C. During this time the Greek or Ptolemaic Dynasty ruled Egypt. Manetho wrote a *History of Egypt* from the earliest times, beginning when Gods ruled that ancient African country. He grouped the kings into dynasties and began the chronology used by scholars today. Though he made some mistakes in his method, his system of human rulers divided the dynasties into periods. These were I-X, XI-XIX, and XX-XXX dynasties. Modern scholars created the terms Archaic, Old Kingdom, First Intermediate Period, Middle Kingdom, Second Intermediate Period, New Kingdom, Third Intermediate and Late Periods and so on. These scholars, however, found Manetho's divisions and groupings of the dynasties convenient and kept them.

According to Manetho, Athothis, who was the son of Narmer of the First Dynasty, practiced medicine. However, no such records have survived to support this claim. There were implications stemming from this belief. These hold the art of medicine had become highly developed in the millennium of the pre-dynastic Badarian, Amratian and Gerzean cultural developments. This represented accumulation of medical practice dating back thousands of years.

Athothis may be the first physician whose name is recorded in history; however, the first medical person to stand out from the past with distinction was Imhotep who lived about 2800 B.C. Imhotep was the "world's first multi-genius" and

FREDERICK MONDERSON

Chief Physician of King Zoser. He also knew the science of astronomy and mathematics.

His greatest deeds were in the fields of architecture, government and medicine. To recall, he built the Step-Pyramid at Sakkara for King Zoser. It is the world's earliest "tall building" and still stands. This architectural accomplishment attests to the level of technology reached at this early age. Even more of his most lasting works, however, were in the fields of medicine, magic and as a sage or wise man.

As a wise man his ideas were taught from generation to generation. He was described as a "master of poetry" and "patron of the scribes." He is credited with the philosophy of the ages, "Eat, drink and be merry, for tomorrow we die." The *Westcar Papyrus* contains some of his magical feats. However, the *Ebers*, *Oxyrchynchus* and *Edwin Smith Papyri* mention his cures for many illnesses.

Imhotep made great contributions to the gentle art of healing. The Egyptians made him a demi-god and the Greeks made him their God of Medicine, Aesculapius. From the earliest times, temples were built to him at such places as Thebes, Philae, Edfu, and in Nubia. Books were written about him and his profession. A cult grew up around his name and work as a doctor.

There were many after Imhotep whose work as physician has come down to us perhaps by virtue of their work in other fields or survival of their tombs. We know that Hesire a contemporary of Imhotep, whose wooden relief in the Cairo Museum has been a source of numerous commentaries; was a physician, dentist and administrator.

Carole Reeves in *Egyptian Medicine* (1992: 22) points out: "Iry was a chief of court physicians at Giza during the Fourth Dynasty. He was also 'master of scorpions,' 'eye doctor of the palace,' 'doctor of the abdomen,' and 'guardian of the royal bowel movement.' Sekhet-n-Ankh was 'nose doctor' to Pharaoh Sahure (Fifth Dynasty) and successfully cured him of a 'sickness of the upper air passages.' The only Egyptian lady doctor yet known was Peseshet (Fourth or early Fifth Dynasty), whose title, *imy-rt-swnt*, may be translated as 'lady director of lady physicians.'"

The level of medical practice reached by the Egyptians was higher than that of their neighbors in the ancient world. Since the Egyptian doctors were so skilled and specialized, to be treated by one psychologically and physically helped the patient to recover quicker. They also treated kings and queens of other lands. The Egyptian medical men were considered excellent physicians and their services were sought later than the time of the famous Cyrus and Darius of Persia.

RESEARCH ESSAYS ON ANCIENT EGYPT

A Christian writer, Alexandrinus Clemens, living in Alexandria in about 200 A.D., mentions the 42 Books of Thoth, early dynastic priests kept in temples and carried in religious processions. Reeves (1992: 21) wrote: "Six of these books were concerned totally with medicine and dealt with anatomy, diseases in general, surgery, remedies, diseases of the eye and diseases of women. No examples of these books survive nor of the anatomy books said to have been written by Athothis, second Pharaoh of the First Dynasty."

Research Essays Illustration 99. Chapter XXXIX of the Book of the Dead in a Pyramid of Sakkara. Spearing the snake attacking a jackass. From Lepsius' *Denkmaler*.

Further, Reeves (1992: 21) points out: "During the Old Kingdom the medical profession became highly organized, with doctors holding a variety of ranks and specialties. The ordinary doctor or *sinw* was outranked by the *imy-r sinw* (overseer of doctors) the *wr sinw* (chief of doctors), the *smsw sinw* (eldest of doctors) and the *shd sinw* (inspector of doctors). Above all these practitioners was the overseer of doctors of Upper and Lower Egypt. There is evidence that a distinction was made between physicians and surgeons, the latter being known as the 'priests of the goddess Sekhmet.' There were also healers who used purely magical remedies or exorcism."

By the time of the New Kingdom, Egyptian priests fully controlled the practice of medicine. They were general doctors but many specialized on different parts of the body. J.A. Rogers' *World's Great Men of Color* Vol. I, notes regarding specialization among doctors, that: "One ministered to the eye, another to the chest, another to the limbs. None trespassed on the anatomy of the other."
Whereas, Reeves (1992: 22-23) added: "Each specialization of medicine had a patron god or goddess and the physician worked directly under the auspices of his particular deity. Duaw was the god of eye diseases; Taurt was a goddess of

childbirth, as was Hathor. Sekhmet, the lion-headed lady of pestilence, sent plagues all over the land and Horus had power over deadly stings and bites such as those of crocodiles, snakes and scorpions (the most common type of 'everyday' injury appears to have been from bites). The human body was divided into 36 parts and each came under the protection of a god or goddess. The goddess protecting the liver was Isis; that of the lungs was Nephthys; the stomach was the domain of Neith and the intestines belonged to the care of Selket. The House of Life (*Per Ankh*) was the medical study center where doctors were taught and these existed at major cult temples along with centers of healing." Overtime, Rogers noted, these skilled practitioners treated more than 250 diseases. These included: "15 of the abdomen, 11 of the bladder, 10 of the rectum, 29 of the eyes, and 18 of the skin."

These medical specialists knew how to tell a disease by the shape, color or condition of the visible parts of the body. Looking at the skin, hair, nails and tongue, showed how well a person was. They also treated illnesses, according to Rogers, such as "spinal tuberculosis, gall-stones, appendicitis, gout, arthritis, and dental caries." They treated body aches, various fevers, coughing, broken bones, cuts and other types of wounds.

The Egyptians performed surgery, listened to the heart, and thought it the seat of all things. Imhotep it is said knew of the circulation of the blood 4,000 years before it was known in Europe. Further, the Egyptian doctors were familiar with the positions and functions of the stomach, lungs, and other vital organs. They knew the importance of hygiene in the recovery of illnesses. The brain's usefulness, however, was not fully understood. It was easily set aside during the mummification process. Since the Egyptians believed in an afterlife, the art of preserving the body was highly developed. In this, they learned much about anatomy and physiology in preparing for the burial and afterlife.

These ancient Africans of Egypt used herbal remedies. They made medicine from plants and minerals. Accordingly, one writer is quoted as saying: "Historically, African medicine was founded upon holistic intelligences that produced all of the sciences. This pre-Egyptian medical science is believed to be 20,000 and 10,000 years old." Herbal or vegetable medicine often listed in the records of the Egyptians includes castor oil, aloes, coriander, caraway, gentian, and turpentine. "It appears that as early as 6,000 B.C., meadow Saffron was given internally."

They also mention myrrh, juniper, fennel, herbane, linseed, and peppermint .... Iron, soda, lime, salts of lead, sulphate of copper, and magnesia." Other drugs they used came from animal bodies including fats and blood from the ox, lion, and hippopotamus.

Time Life's *What Life Was Like on the Banks of the Nile* (1997: 40) states: "A physician's bedside manner included interviewing patients, palpating abnormalities, examining secretions, and even smelling wounds. Along with aloe, garlic and honey, his medicine chest might contain such items as lead, sandal leather, soot, semen, cow bile, and excrement - both animal and human. Salves and poultices prepared with these distasteful ingredients were intended to make the patient's body so repugnant that the disease – or the demon - would be compelled to find a more suitable host."

Research Essays Illustration 100. Book of the Dead. Chapter XXXIV, Sakkara. Spearing the snake attacking a jackass. From Lepsius' *Denkmaler*.

Hilary Wilson (1993: 170) adds: "In medical papyri the ingredients of prescriptions are sometimes quantified, especially in the case of valuable substances such as spices or incense. The quantities suggested may be given in 10, a mouthful being the equivalent of a modern tablespoon, or by weight. It seems that very small amounts could be accurately weighed against wheat grains or the seeds of the carob tree, both of which are remarkably uniform in size and weight." It is also important that we know where the origins of our neighborhood pharmacy and pharmacists come from.

Cyril Aldred (1961) (1987: 194) in *The Egyptians* says: "A training as a scribe was also a necessary preliminary to a career in such professions as medicine, the priesthood, and art and architecture. A medical student would be apprenticed to a practitioner, almost always his father or some near relative; but an ability to read was necessary for learning the various prescriptions, spells and diagnoses contained in medical papyri, whether the work in question were a quasi-scientific treatise on surgery and fractures such as the Edwin Smith Papyrus, or a specialist work on gynecology such as the Kahun Papyrus, or a mere collection of medico-magic recipes, nostrums, and incantations such as the Ebers Papyrus."

Paul Johnson in *The Civilization of Ancient Egypt* (1987) (1999: 120) writes, the: "Egyptians were the first to use certain well-known drugs which have come in use ever since. Their experience is reflected in Hebrew, Syrian and Persian medical texts, in such classical writers as Theophrastus, Pliny, Dioscorides, Galen and

FREDERICK MONDERSON

Hippocratus, and in Roman Imperial, Byzantine and Arabic medical handbooks, which were in use throughout the Middle Ages, the Renaissance and beyond. The Egyptians had an enduring reputation as expert poisoners, too, springing from their skill with sleeping-potions." He goes on to note there are "eight medical papyri in the British Museum alone, including one on surgical treatment."

Found in a Theban tomb in 1860 and passed into the hands of Georg Ebers in 1873, the papyrus that bears his name *Ebers Papyrus*, contains, Reeves (1992: 49) notes: "876 remedies and mentions 500 substances used in medical treatment." Among these are such remedies including sedatives, hypnotics, expectorants, tonics, astringents, purgatives, diuretics, disinfectants and antibodies.

Reeves says (1992: 49) further: "The Ebers Papyrus describes treatment of and prescriptions for stomach complaints, coughs, colds, bites, head ailments and diseases; liver complaints, burns and other kinds of wounds; itching, complaints in fingers and toes; salves for wounds and pains in the veins, muscles and nerves; diseases of the tongue, toothache, ear pains, women's diseases; beauty preparations, household remedies against vermin, the two books about the heart and veins, and diagnosis for tumors." Ian Shaw's *The Oxford History of Ancient Egypt* informs of other meaningful ways the Ebers Papyrus has been useful to scholars.

Shaw (2000: 11) notes: "Two Egyptian textual records of Sothic risings (dating to the reigns of Senusret II and Amenhotep I) form the basis of the conventional chronology of Egypt, which, in turn, influences that of the whole Mediterranean region. These two documents are a 12th Dynasty letter from the site of Lahun, written on day 16, month 2, of the second season in year 7 of the reign of Senusert III, and an 18th dynasty Theban medical papyrus (Papyrus Ebers), written on day 9, month 3, of the third season of year 9 in the reign of Amenhotep I. By assigning absolute dates to each of these documents (1872 B.C. for the Lahun rising in year 7 of Senusret III, and 1541 B.C. for the Ebers rising in regnal year 9 of Amenhotep I), Egyptologists have been able to extrapolate a set of absolute dates for the whole of the pharaonic period, on the bases of records of the lengths of reign of the other kings of the Middle and New Kingdoms."

RESEARCH ESSAYS ON ANCIENT EGYPT

Research Essays 97. Kom Ombo Temple to Gods Haroeis and Sobek. The Garden at Kom Ombo Temple.

The American Egyptologist Edwin Smith, at Luxor in 1862, acquired the papyrus that bears his name. Reeves (1992: 51) tells us, the *Edwin Smith Surgical Papyrus*: "has been dated at about 1600 B.C. but Old Kingdom words in the text suggest that it was copied from a work written around 2500 B.C., when the pyramids were being built. It was published in 1930 with a translation and commentary by James Henry Breasted and is now housed in the New York Academy of Medicine." Equally, Bob Brier (1994: 62) in *Egyptian Mummies* discusses the Egyptian understanding of the relationship of the brain to the body. He states: "In the Edwin Smith Surgical Papyrus, three specific, traumatic head injuries, so serious that the brain is exposed, are discussed. It is clear that the author of this papyrus was aware of the meningeal membranes surrounding the brain, and of the brain's convolutions." He does add the Egyptians believed "the heart managed the body."

Petrie found the *Kahun Medical Papyrus*, with other Middle Kingdom Papyri, in the town of Kahun in 1889. Consisting of only three pages, it has been variously dated between 2100 and 1900 B.C. It is preserved in the Petrie Museum of Egyptian Archaeology at University College, London. The papyrus is devoted to diseases of women and pregnancy and is possibly the oldest medical papyrus to be discovered. It was first published in 1898, as a hieroglyphic transcript with a translation by F. Ll. Griffith. It deals with treatment of a woman's ruptured womb, possibly the first case of rape and prevention of conception.

FREDERICK MONDERSON

Heinrich Brugsch discovered the *Berlin Papyrus* in a jar during excavation at Saqqara in the early years of the twentieth century. It consists of 279 lines of prescription and has been dated around 1350-1200 B.C. Translated and published by Walter Wreszinski in 1909, it is housed in the Berlin Museum with a fifteen-column papyrus. It contains one of the earliest tests for pregnancy utilizing barley and ember in urine.

The *Chester Beatty Papyrus* VI, housed in the British Museum, is dated around 1200 B.C. and consists of eight columns dealing solely with diseases of the anus. It was translated and annotated by F. Jonckeere in 1947.

Research Essays Illustration 101. Spearing the Gazelle.

Reeves indicated: "The Hearst Papyrus, now in the University of California, dates from about 1550 B.C. and appears to be the formulary of a practicing physician. It is incomplete and contains eighteen columns. A Translation by Walter Wreszinski of the *Hearst Papyrus* and the *London Papyrus* (c. 1350 B.C.) was published in 1912. The *Hearst Papyrus* contains over 250 prescriptions and spells and has a section on bones and bites (notably the hippopotamus bite) and affections of the fingers. It also deals with tumors, burns and diseases of women, ears, eyes and teeth. The *London Papyrus* contains "61 recipes, only 25 of which are medical, the remaining being magical."

Piotr O. Scholz in *Ancient Egypt: An Illustrative Historical Overview* (1977) wrote: "The Egyptians had some idea of hygiene: they practiced circumcision, and that can be considered a hygienic measure. Surgery was successful in the treatment of broken bones. The guidelines for treatment are instructive and the methods correct. Medical instruments, known from temple drawings, came later

RESEARCH ESSAYS ON ANCIENT EGYPT

and corroborate the assertion that medicine was a science of the temples. Egyptian physicians dared to admit in a given case that they could do nothing for the patient. Examination of mummies indicates that Egyptian dentists filled teeth, built simple bridges using gold wire, and treated infected gums."

Reeves (1992: 54) further mentions *The Brooklyn Museum Papyrus*, translated in 1966-67 by Serge Sauernon, which contains "a mixture of magical and rational medicine, particularly with relation to birth and post-partum care. Also included in these papyri is a book of snakebites, describing all the possible snakes to be found in Egypt with a compendium of treatments."

Reeves adds: (1992: 54) even more: "The Carlsberg Papyrus Number VIII, translated by E. Iversen in 1939 and housed in the University of Copenhagen, deals with eye diseases almost identical to those described in the Ebers Papyrus and obstetrics very similar to that in the Kahun, Berlin and Ebers Papyri."

Research Essays 98. Kom Ombo Temple to Gods Haroeis and Sobek. Pharaoh holds the *aba scepter* before Horus in White Crown and Hathor in horns and disk stands behind the god.

Finally, of those important medical treatises, Reeves (1992: 54) again indicates: "The Ramesseum IV and V Papyri are of the same era as the Kahun Papyrus. A translation of both papyri by J.W.B. Barns was published in 1956. Papyrus IV is medico-religious and deals with obstetrics and gynecology. Papyrus V is purely medical and deals mainly with stiffened limbs. The series of obstetrics

FREDERICK MONDERSON

prescription and prognostications in the Carlsberg, Ebers, Berlin and Kahun Papyri are so similar that it is likely that they were all taken from the same source."

In summary, the ancient African peoples along the Nile River, the Egyptians and those throughout the Nile Valley, made significant gains in medicine and treatment of the sick. This was done thousands of years ago. Many of these ideas never reached Europe until much later, and when they did they proved very useful. In fact, Breasted's *History of Egypt* (1905) (1923: 101) notes that many Egyptian medicines: "passed with the Greeks to Europe, where they are still in use among the peasantry of the present day." As we know, Imhotep was the first physician to stand out in history. Later the Greeks made him their God of Medicine. Today, young African-American students especially should try to become medical doctors. When they are qualified they will take the "Hippocratic Oath." It is named after the "Father of Medicine" Hippocrates, who practiced medicine 2300 years *after* Imhotep. They should know, however, that the God Aesculapius, praised in the oath is really Imhotep, an ancestor, from the land of Egypt in Northeast Africa.

The Egyptians held Imhotep in such high esteem because, in addition to his medical skills, they considered him special because he was one of them who became a god. Since the gods were so remote, the locals were glad to identify with someone they had experienced. However, beyond this he was also a sage or wise man, mathematician and architect. A combination of these talents helped him to build the Step-Pyramid for Pharaoh Zoser, of the Third Dynasty.

This was a major accomplishment as it set in motion stone construction and laid the foundation for building the pyramids. In *A Brief History of Science*, A. Rupert Hall and Marie Boas Hall treats this subject. Accordingly, early Egyptian architecture was significantly aided by a: "surplus of labor, combined with an exceptionally complex cult of the dead, created the elaborate tombs and monuments familiar to us as pyramids and obelisks. The colossal size and careful workmanship of these great structures suggest to the modern eye a complex technology." Now we know, "they were built with wedges and stone hammers to split the rock, sledges and ropes to drag the stones to the building sites, ramps from one level to another up which successive courses were hauled, levers to propel the stones into place, and water used to check when all was level. The Egyptians had no wheels or pulleys in the Pyramid Age (from 2700 to 2000 B.C.), and the secret of their success was unlimited manpower, patience, and a strong artistic sense."

RESEARCH ESSAYS ON ANCIENT EGYPT

Research Essays Illustration 102. Book of the Dead. Spearing the snake, in Chapter XXXIX, *Papyrus Musee du Louvre*, 93.

One last thing that particularly has to do with health. We know the Egyptians and Ethiopians were some of the earliest people to practice circumcision. Despite the magico-religious reasons for this procedure, an even more important modern use is explained. Riding along Linden Boulevard, in Brooklyn, New York, there is a sign outside a doctor's office that reads: "Circumcision prevents AIDS." Thus, we can associate the ancient Egyptians with a potent health care practice, that thousands of years later is a powerful antidote to a powerful threat to health care!

NAVIGATION

Navigation is another science the Egyptians mastered very early. Because of the role of the Nile River in their lives boat-building developed in the Predynastic period.

The simplest boats were made of papyrus stalks lashed together and used by the poorest Egyptians. Baines and Malek in *Atlas of Ancient Egypt* (1980) provide the

FREDERICK MONDERSON

following information about how to date the earliest boats. For these river vessels, the: "dating is provided by (1) appearance of the hull, (2) the method of steering, (3) the type of the mast and sail, (4) the vessel's paddles and oars, (5) the disposition of the deckhouses, and (6) unusual features."

In the Predynastic period boats were features on the early pottery from such sources as the Painted Tomb at Hierakonpolis. Some methods of identifying boats from this period included: "(1) sometimes, though not always, sharply upturned prow and stern (even large Nile craft were made mostly of papyrus or similar material); (2) one or more large steering oars; (3) rectangular sail; (4) and (5) paddles in two groups (uninterrupted by central deckhouse); (6) prow decoration of tree branches; (7) standard close to deckhouse."

Research Essays Temple Ticket 16. Imhotep Museum and Sakkara. Price of entrance is sixty Egyptian Pounds.

During the Old Kingdom there were some improvements in ship's layout. These included: "(1) 'classical' Egyptian hull shape (wood now the main building material), often with animal-head prow; (2) several large steering oars, but from 6th Dynasty special steering gear; (3) usually bipod mast, probably trapezoidal sail, usually more tall than wide; (4) from 5th Dynasty oars."

"During the Middle Kingdom, we see (1) higher stern; (2) steering gear operated by a helmsman standing between the massive rudder post and the usually single large rudder oar; (3) single mast, lowered and supported on a forked stanchion when sailing downstream; (4) deckhouse forward of the rudder post."

RESEARCH ESSAYS ON ANCIENT EGYPT

Lastly, in the New Kingdom there were a very: "(1) large range of specialized types; (2) steering gear with usually two rudder oars, operated by a helmsman standing in front of the rudder post; (3) sail more wide than tall; (4) castles forward and aft, with centrally placed deckhouse." And in the late period, there was a tendency towards a higher stern.

While the Nile River and surrounding Mediterranean and Red Seas were plied for everything from trade, war, funerals, fishing, transportation, festivals, etc., there was also some evidence of Atlantic Ocean voyages.

In the *Histories* Herodotus mentions the Pharaoh Necho sent Phoenician sailors, on a three-year voyage to circumnavigate Africa around 600 B.C. Much more important, however, is a letter written to the *Journal of African Civilizations* by the late Dr. Cheikh Anta Diop. He was one of few, and the only Black African scholar who examined the mummy of Pharaoh Rameses II when efforts were made to preserve it some years ago in Paris. Dr. Diop mentions residues of "New World" tobacco found in the intestines of the mummy. Based on this he posited the belief that the Pharaoh may have sent expeditions by ship, to the "New World" and they brought back smoking tobacco. This revelation is significant for the Egyptian science of navigation in the fourteenth century Before Christ.

Ivan Van Sertima has stated, according to Cheikh Anta Diop, "so much radiation was used on Rameses II's mummy, his body turned from brown to almost white."

FREDERICK MONDERSON

Research Essays 99. Kom Ombo Temple to Gods Haroeis and Sobek. God Ra-Horakhty makes a Presentation to the King.

These revelations about science are important for they testify to the fact that Africa has been in the forefront and mainstream of science for any number of utilities.

RESEARCH ESSAYS ON ANCIENT EGYPT

References

Akbar, Na'im. "Nile Valley Origins of the Science of the Mind." *Nile Valley Civilizations*. Edited by Ivan Van Sertima. New Brunswick, New Jersey: Journal of African Civilizations, (1985) 1996.
Breasted, J.H. *A History of Egypt*. Chicago: Chicago University Press, (1905) 1923.
_____. "The First Fixed Date in History." 1915.
Brier, Bob. *Egyptian Medicine*. 1994.
Aldred, Cyril. *The Egyptians*. London: Thames and Hudson, (1961) 1987.
Diop, Cheikh Anta. "Africa's Contribution to World Civilization: The Exact Sciences" in *Nile Valley Civilizations*. Edited by Ivan Van Sertima. New Brunswick, New Jersey: *Journal of African Civilizations*, (1985) 1996.
Gillings, Richard J. *Mathematics in the Time of the Pharaohs*. New York: Dover Publications Inc., (1972) 1981.
Grimal, Nicholas. *The Oxford History of Ancient Egypt*. Oxford at the University Press, 2000.
Hall, A., Rupert and Marie Boas. *A Brief History of Science*.
Johnson, Paul. *The Civilization of Ancient Egypt*. New York: Harper Collins Publishers, (1987) 1999.
Lumpkin, Beatrice. "Africa in the Mainstream of Mathematics History" in *Blacks in Science*. New Brunswick, New Jersey: Transaction Books, 1983.
Middleton, W.E. Knowles. *The Scientific Revolution*.
Pappademos, John. "The Newtonian Synthesis in Physical Sciences and its Roots in the Nile Valley" in *Nile Valley Civilizations*. Edited by Ivan Van Sertima. New Brunswick, New Jersey: Journal of African Civilizations, (1985) 1986: 84-101.
Petrie, W.M.F. *Wisdom of the Egyptians*. London: Bernard Quaritch, 1940.
Reeve, Carol. *Egyptian Medicine*. Shire Publications, 1992.
Shaw, Ian. *The Oxford History of Ancient Egypt*. Oxford at the University Press, 2000.
Steindorff and Seele. *When Egypt Ruled the East*. Chicago: University of Chicago Press, (1942) 1971.
Time-Life. *What Life Was Like on the Banks of the Nile*. Alexandria, Virginia: Time Life Books, 1997.
Wilson, Hillary. *Egyptian Food and Drink*. Bucks: Shire Publications, 1993.

FREDERICK MONDERSON

Research Essays 99a. Kom Ombo Temple to Gods Haroeis and Sobek. Picturesque view of the Peristyle Court and twin entrance to the temple, its massive columns, all against a clear, blue sky in the rear.

Research Essays 99b. Another view of the colonnade of the Court.

RESEARCH ESSAYS ON ANCIENT EGYPT

17. Gold of Egypt
By

Dr. Fred Monderson

Gold has long been an admired, coveted, sought after and presentable mineral. It's been associated with gods, goblets, giving, and go well with gowns, as well as treasured by girls and grandparents. Beyond its beauty there is a mysterious, mystical, some say fertility aspect to gold that makes it appealing to men and women, families, merchants, banks and nations. In fact, the most spectacular archaeological discovery of the twentieth century was that of King Tutankhamon in Egypt's Valley of the Kings and for nearly a century it has captivated the thoughts of man throughout the world. In commenting on this discovery and its symbolism, Yoyotte (1963: 111) expressed the view: "A divine metal, gold conferred divine survival, giving Tutankhamon and to all his kind the eternal life of the sun and the gods. By an extension of this belief, yellow became of great importance in funerary symbolism." Dr. John H. Clarke, on the other hand, says of Tutankhamon, he was "a minor king who got a major funeral." Now, imagine the gold and other precious treasures buried with the major kings as Tuthmose III, Amenhotep III and Rameses II, for example.

Even more important, in the Egyptian experience the descriptive term "Golden Age" came to reflect the fullness of their realization of life's expectations and the society's flowerings. This concept patterned their philosophy after the notion of Ma'at, meaning order, balance, justice, fairness, exactness, permanence, gaiety and even enjoyment. Much of this is explained by White (1963) (1980: 24-25) who wrote, the ancient Egyptians: "did not torment themselves by comparing their present lot with the rosy paradise which they might enjoy if only they introduced pensions and welfare services and abolished the armed forces. Their Golden Age lay not in some hypothetical future, but was anchored in their past, when the gods themselves had reigned upon earth. Their beautifully balanced social system had been a precious gift from on high, and all that men were required to do was to hold the balance with steady grasp. Their object was not, as ours so often is, to transform their social system: they wanted to tamper with it as little as possible. They considered that all change was perilous, as it took society further away from the times when the good gods, after a long hard struggle with their enemies, had ruled so wisely over the valley. It is not surprising, therefore, that 'no people has ever shown a greater reverence for what was termed by them 'the time of the ancestors' or 'the time of the gods'" (Sir Alan Gardiner, *Egypt of the Pharaohs*, p. 56). The Egyptians held that what a man "ought to do was not to nurture

FREDERICK MONDERSON

'progressive' ideals, but to put himself in tune with the rhythm of the universe as it had been established by the gods 'on the first occasion.' As Henri Frankfort puts it, 'The life of man, as an individual and even more as a member of society, was integrated with the life of nature, and the experience of that harmony was thought to be the greatest good to which man can aspire'" (*Ancient Egyptian Religion*, p. 29).

Research Essays 100. Kom Ombo Temple to Gods Haroeis and Sobek. On a wall, twin deities of the Temple, Horus left and Sobek Right.

RESEARCH ESSAYS ON ANCIENT EGYPT

Even more, White (1980: 25) continued: "Life for the Egyptians was here and now. According to King Pittakos of Mytilene, the secret of happiness lies in 'doing the present thing well.' The Egyptians observed this precept, and they were happy. The patient, craftsman-like quality of everything they made - from first to last - is a testimony to it. This is reflected in their buildings, philosophy, religion, crafts, in jewelry, and particularly that of the gold they made. What has come down to us now so wonderfully displayed in Museums worldwide is a fabulous testimony to their creativity."

Africa is the gold continent possessing black, green, but more particularly yellow and red gold. As the mind and computer are to a hand axe, the conception of Africa's gifts of gold to the world is just as vast. Regarding the volume of gold Africa gave to the world is beyond estimation. So much so, from time immemorial this "gold continent," Africa has continued to "gush gold" to the world.

Research Essays Illustration 103. Book of the Dead. With jars and before the monster.

Interestingly enough, this has not always been so. In ancient times when African states dominated and pursued imperialistic policies, the world "gushed gold" to Africa as tribute and trade. Some later argued, as Egypt and other African states floundered, this reality motivated nations with a "score to settle," to invade Africa to collect their gold payments. Millennia later when Africa could not export yellow gold, conquerors took her "black gold." This activity began in the Nile Valley and then moved to West Africa. Throughout it all, however, when the appellation "Golden Age" was attached to a time or culture in Africa, to reiterate, this was not simply a modern designation, or more particularly a cultural attainment. In reality it represented a time when golden ideas ruled and gold played a significant role in the developments of the various states.

FREDERICK MONDERSON

In Ancient Egypt, *Nub* meant gold, and this name comes from Nubia. This was one of Egypt's and ancient Africa's main sources of gold. Petrie in *The Arts and Crafts of Ancient Egypt* (1909: 83) confirms this, but that: "The immediate sources of the metal were in Nubia and Asia Minor. The Asiatic gold was certainly used in the first dynasty, as it is marked by having a variable amount of silver alloy, about a sixth; but looking at the African influence on Egypt it is probable that Nubia was the first source, though whether gold (*nub*) was called from the country (*nub*), or the reverse, is uncertain."

Keating's (1975: 112) *Nubian Rescue*, on the other hand, argues: "In Old Kingdom records of gold is never mentioned in relation to Nubia. Only with the penetration of the Middle Kingdom Pharaohs around 1900 B.C. does the extraction of gold form Wawat and Kush begin to appear in the records. Possibly the mines in Egypt were becoming exhausted or else the demands of the Twelfth Dynasty Pharaohs for gold were on the increase. Whatever the reason, Nubia from now on became Egypt's main source of the precious metal and by the end of the Eighteenth Dynasty gold had become the most important item in the annual tribute sent to Egypt by Kush, as is shown in the tomb paintings of Huy, Viceroy of Kush under the Pharaoh Tutankhamon." Keating (1975: 112) adds further: "One of the richest of the mines in Lower Nubia (Wawat) was in Wadi Allaqi where the Middle Kingdom fortress of Kuban excavated by Emery in 1930, was built to protect the workings. A document which lists the mining areas known to the Egyptians, shows that gold was collected from as far south as Gebel Barkal near the Fourth Cataract; that, however, was much later than the period of the Middle Kingdom forts. In 1928, in a room of the western fort at Semna, Reisner found a pair of scales carved in the form of a palm tree, a wooden cross-beam and two copper pans, while later he obtained from farmers in the vicinity three inscribed and graduated weights for use in such scales."

Woldering (1962) supports the issue (1963: 16) that: "The exploitation of the Nubian gold deposits provided the wherewithal for the rapid development of the goldsmiths' craft. Silver, too, was only available in small quantities on Egyptian soil. It was imported from Asia Minor, especially during the period when Egypt was the leading world power. Copper, which already at an early date supersedes flint as the material used for implements, was obtained from mines in the Sinai Peninsula. The popular turquoise also originates from that area. There is evidence of the use of bronze, an alloy of copper and tin, only from the Middle Kingdom onwards."

This notwithstanding, Petrie (1909: 83-84) gives further insights indicating: "So general was the use of gold for necklaces that the picture of gold collar of beads became the hieroglyphic for gold. Strings of minute gold beads were worn on the ankles in prehistoric times (8000-5000 B.C.). Larger beads were economically

RESEARCH ESSAYS ON ANCIENT EGYPT

made by beating out a thin tube, and then drawing down the ends over a core of limestone. A thin gold finger ring has been found, and a flat pendant with punched dots. But most of the prehistoric gold is seen on the lips of stone vases, overlaying the handles of vases, and forming the wire loops for carrying them. Similarly it was used for covering the handles of flint knives; a sheet of gold was fitted over the flint, embossed with figures of women, animals, twisted snakes, a boat, etc. But the use of thin gold leaf, which adheres to its base, is not found until the pyramid times. At the close of the prehistoric period we meet with a gold cylinder seal engraved with signs. When we remember that it is very rarely than an unplundered grave is discovered, the quantity of gold objects found show that the metal must have been generally used in the ages when commerce developed, before writing was known."

By the time of the Badarian and Amratian and Gerzean or Naqada I and II cultures of pre-dynastic Egypt, gold had become an extremely important mineral. Craftsmanship developed in wood, gold and other types of metalworking. This development was also important because it represented a significant departure from the Stone Age. Maspero (1926: 346-47) pointedly informs: "The idea of overlaying stone or wood with gold was familiar in Egypt before the time of Menes. Many of the earliest stone vases have handles and rims covered with gold leaf, and limestone beads are also overlaid with it. The gold is often mixed with silver. When amalgamated to the extent of 20 per cent it changes its name, and is called electrum. Electrum has a fine pale yellow color, which becomes paler as the proportion of silver is increased, and at 60 percent it is almost white." More important, however, it became highly sought after as a decorative metal.

Murray in *The Splendor that Was Egypt* (1949) (1963: 107) associates the name of gold with one of the earliest and most venerated gods of Egypt, yet this is little known, as if mysterious. She says: "The earliest form of the name is spelt *Setesh* or possibly *Setech* which became hardened into *Setekh*. He had no consort and no offspring, and even to the end he seems to have been independent and aloof. In the early religion he is one of the helpers of Osiris, of whom he had a brother, and he amicably divided the kingdom of Egypt with the Horus-falcon of the invaders; he retaining the south while Horus took the more fertile north. As the chief seat of his worship was the city of Nubt ("the golden") he was known as Nubti, written in the usual way with the sign meaning Gold. Among the early titles of the Pharaoh was one which showed that the king was under the direct protection of the goddesses of the south and north, but when the gods began to dispossess the goddesses in the official religion, the king took a new title compounded of Horus and 'Setekh, thereby placing himself under the protection of the gods of the north and south. The title was Nebui, 'he of the city of Nubt,' while Horus is represented in his usual form of a falcon."

FREDERICK MONDERSON

Research Essays 101. Kom Ombo Temple to Gods Haroeis and Sobek. Khonsu, the Moon God, of the Theban Triad stands majestically, yet defaced.

Margaret Bunson (1991) (1999: 230) has explained in *The Encyclopedia of Ancient Egypt*, under the listing Royal Names: "The titles comprising the five elements used by the kings of Egypt, denoting their connections to the gods, their divine purpose and function. The royal names included the following:

"*Horus name* - the first of the royal names, usually written with a SEREKH alluding to the king as the true representative of the god HORUS on earth.

RESEARCH ESSAYS ON ANCIENT EGYPT

Nebti name - Signifying the king's rule over Upper and Lower Egypt.

Golden Horus name - depicting the royal person as the 'gold of the gods,' the earthly manifestation of the divine ones and their beloved representative.

Nisut-Bit name - the title prefaced by two words meaning king: the Lord of the South, Bit, and Lord of the North, Nisut. This name, considered a king's prenomen, was given to him at his coronation. The prenomen, or first cartouche name, is the most important and frequently used name. In inscriptions the appearance of the prenomen alone indicates which king is meant.

Son of Ra name - the king's actual birth name, denoting his inclusion in a royal line."

Research Essays Illustration 104. Sailing with the Gods, from the Tomb of Rameses IV.

Jean Yoyotte "Gold" in Georges Posener's *A Dictionary of Egyptian Civilization*, London: Methuen and Co., (1963: 111) notes: "Gold was undoubtedly regarded by the Egyptians as one of the most precious substances. But its great value was not at all due originally to purely economic considerations. It was a divine and a royal adornment; it was the brilliant and incorruptible flesh of the Sun and of the gods, which emanated from him. The goddess Hathor was believed to be the incarnation of gold. One of the royal titles was 'Horus of gold.' Divine idols were covered with fine gold when they could not be made entirely of gold. Gold leaf was used to cover the tops of obelisks, temple porticoes, ritual objects and reliefs with particularly sacred representations."

FREDERICK MONDERSON

Regarding this ancient goddess, Hathor of Sudani origin and worshipped throughout the entire land, Lewis Spence in *Myths and Legends of Egypt* (1985) (1986: 164) says of this lady: "She is designated the 'Golden One,' who stands high in the South as the Lady of Teka, and illumines the west as the Lady of Sais." Spence (1986: 164-65) adds more in an effort to: "explain the somewhat paradoxical statement that Hathor is 'mother of her father, daughter of her son' - that she is mother, wife, and daughter to Ra. The moon, when she appears in the heavens before the sun, may be regarded as his mother; when she reigns together with him she is his wife; when she rises after he has set she is his daughter. It is possible that the moon, with her generative and sustaining powers, may have been considered the creative and upholding force of the universe, the great cosmic mother, who brought forth not only the gods and goddesses over whom she rules, but likewise herself as well. It was as the ideal of womanhood, therefore, whether as mother, wife, or daughter, that she received the homage of Egyptian women, and became the patron deity of love, joy, and merry-making, 'lady of music and mistress of song, lady of leaping, and mistress of wreathing garlands.' Temples were raised in her honor, notably one of exceptional beauty at Denderah, in Upper Egypt, and she had shrines without number. She became in time associated or even identified with many local goddesses, and, indeed, it has been said that all Egyptians goddesses were forms of Hathor."

The Bible mentions Hathor as "The Golden Calf."

Commenting further on the precious metal, Petrie (1923: 149) writes: "Gold was used in prehistoric times, but in the earlier dynasties it was always alloyed with silver, which suggests that it came from Asia Minor. Silver was also prehistoric, but down to the XVIIIth dynasty it was almost as rare as gold, and only less valuable by its color and ease of tarnishing. After the Hittites were in full contact with Egypt, silver became less valuable. Gold and silver were not only used for jewelry, but also to ornament stone vases with gold brims, handles and bases, and with silver lids. Gold tips to bows, gold knife handles and sheet gold were made, beads were skillfully burnished over a core of limestone; all these are prehistoric. In the 1st dynasty, the soldering of gold was perfectly executed with the utmost minuteness."

Petrie (1909: 84-85) again, brings us into the dynastic age with his discovery of four serekh or falcon bracelets of the Queen of Zer of the Ist Dynasty at Abydos. This jewelry was attached to part of an arm and had escaped ancient tomb robbers who may have placed it in the discovered location, hoping to return but never did.

Accordingly: "These bracelets show how each separate piece was made to fit its own place in a complex design, and that the latter custom of merely stringing readymade beads was not followed." Describing these bracelets, he wrote: "The bracelet of hawks has the gold blocks alternating with turquoise. The hawks on the gold pieces are all equal, but the sizes of the blocks vary in the height. This is due to their being all cast in the same mold, which was fitted to varying amounts. The surfaces were hammered and chiseled, but not either ground or filed." Alix Wilkinson in his book *Ancient Egyptian Jewelry* recounted the story. He gave a vivid description of the jewelry. He described the first bracelet as: "composed of twenty-nine beads of gold and turquoise representing the royal emblem, a falcon perched above a gateway."

Research Essays 102. Kom Ombo Temple to Gods Haroeis and Sobek. Twin sphinxes in Double Crowns sport uraei and disks overhead.

In regards the second of these, Petrie notes: "The bracelet with spiral beads has the gold spiral formed of a hammered gold wire, thicker at the middle, where it forms the barrel of the beads. This form is imitated in the three dark lazuli beads down the middle. The triple gold balls, on either side of those, are each beaten hollow and drawn into a thread-hole left at each end; so perfectly wrought are they that only in one instance do the slightest ruck of metal remain …."

Wilkinson says further, this: "second bracelet is made of coiled gold wire and lapis lazuli beads ribbed to match them."

Petrie continued: "In the lowest bracelet the hour-glass-shaped beads are of gold, with one of amethyst between each pair. The gold is doubtless cast, being solid. None of these are pierced, but they were secured by tying round a groove at the middle of each bead." Wilkinson adds the: "third bracelet is made of hour glass shaped beads of gold and amethyst with one brown limestone." There was also a: "fourth bracelet with a ball and loop fastening which shows the skill in soldering. The ball is beaten hollow, leaving about a quarter of it open; inside it a hook of gold wire is soldered in without leaving the smallest trace of solder visible. The band round the wrist was formed of very thick black hair plaited with gold wire, which was hammered to exactly the same thickness. We see from these bracelets that casting, chiseling, and soldering were perfectly understood at the beginning of the monarchy." Wilkinson describes this fourth bracelet as having: "beads arranged in two groups. The larger group was on top of the wrist and the shorter underneath, with gold wire and hair twisted together filling in the space at the sides." Other jewelry from this early period included collars, necklaces, earrings, diadems, girdles, pectorals and finger-rings. Many were studded and had precious stones mounted on gold.

A number of burials with gold were discovered at various places which seem to indicate the significance of this sacred and treasured metal. Aldred (1965: 60) says of one such burial: "The owner of a private tomb of Dynasty I at Naga-ed-Der was buried with a rich parure, including a gold circlet, gold beads shaped as snail shells and gold amulets in the form of an oryx and a bull." In addition, Maspero (1902: 357) mentions: "Gold was found in a cemetery near the old metropolis of *This*, where the pottery is similar to that found at Abydos. It comprised a tiny figure of a gazelle, another of a bull, twenty-four large univalve shells as beads, ten large cylindrical beads, besides rings, bracelets and smaller beads."

Research Essays Illustration 105. Book of the Dead. Khepre in a basket and spearing the Crocodile.

RESEARCH ESSAYS ON ANCIENT EGYPT

Research Essays 103. Kom Ombo Temple to Gods Haroeis and Sobek. On a column, Goddess Hathor in the Queen Mother Crown. Notice her right breast exposed.

The sources of Egyptian gold were many, within their borders and the land to the south. Gold mines were located in the high ridges and valleys of Nubia and the pharaoh received a regular income from them. There were also mines in Egypt's eastern desert that was difficult to reach. Breasted's *A History of Egypt: From the*

FREDERICK MONDERSON

Earliest Times to the Persian Conquest (1906) (1923: 6) commented on the geography of this area: "A range of granite mountains parallel with the coast of the Red Sea contains gold-bearing quartz veins, and here and there other gold-producing mountains lie between the Nile and the Red Sea." Adding more clarity to understanding the surroundings, Murray (1969: 41) tells of Thutmose III and some of his works in efforts to exploit this area and its mineral resources. In this respect, she notes the king undertook: "the establishment of a water-station on the way from the Nile Valley to the gold mines in the eastern desert. 'His majesty inspected the hill country as far as the mountains, and he said, 'How evil is the way without water. A traveler's mouth is parched. How shall his throat be cooled? How shall his thirst be quenched, for the Low Land is far away and the High Land is vast? The thirsty man in this fatal country cries aloud. Make haste then, and take counsel for their needs. I will make a supply for preserving their lives so that in after years they will thank god in my name'" A well was dug according to the King's command: "and the water flooded it in very great plenty like the two caves of Elephantine. Then said his Majesty, 'Lo, God has performed my petition, he has brought water for me upon the mountain.'"

In these desolate desert places, White (1970: 111) wrote: "Gangs of laborers were lashed on the whole year round in order to hammer at the quartzite veins in the granite quarries where the metal occurred." This particular work force consisted of criminals and one could well imagine the conditions under which they worked. They literally worked till they died. Perhaps a parallel could be gained from conditions in the lands to the south. Keating (1975: 116-17) also paints a graphic picture of conditions that were similar and related to procuring the precious metal. He wrote about comparing conditions described by Diodorus Siculus of Sicily who visited the area around 50 B.C. as well as Anthony Mills, a modern explorer. "Evidently the method of separating out the gold had changed little in nineteen centuries. As for the mines, which kept the workshops busy, Mills located them by the simple expedient of searching for a road. He found one; wide and well constructed running back from the river into the interior. We followed it over the tops of the stony hills noting the quartz pebbles that littered its length and speculating whether they had fallen from donkey panniers or from baskets carried on human backs. In about two miles white patches of quartz appeared on the surface, scarring the brown flanks of the hills and soon 'I was staring into the first gold mine I had ever seen.' A narrow shaft not 2 feet wide sloped down into darkness at an incredible angle of 50 degrees. It seemed impossible that human beings could ever have worked in it and it seemed even less likely when Mills explained the method of extraction. Wherever the prospectors found a vein of quartz at the surface they followed it in all its twists and turns down through the bedrock until the quartz ran out. Extracting was done by heating the quartz with fires and dousing with cold water when a critical temperature was reached. It had the effect of cracking the quartz and causing it to break away cleanly from the matrix. The mortality from collapsing galleries and heat exhaustion must have been appalling. Mills had located many such mines in the hills roundabout and four workshop sites down by the river. 'Walking back from the mines I became aware of a sharp increase in temperature. The wind had dropped and very soon the air was stifling. How could human beings, I wondered, have endured such working conditions in the heat of a Nubian summer smothered in quartz dust and crouched among blistering fires?'"

Besides the alluvial sands and gravel in Coptos that produced gold, the land of Punt in East Central Africa was also a gold producer. Queen Hatshepsut of the XVIII Dynasty sent an expedition that brought back regular and green gold of Emu from this land. Trade also played an important role in the acquisition of gold in Egypt. In the late 18th Dynasty on the verge of the Amarna heresy, Bill Manley (1996: 65) in *The Penguin Historical Atlas of Ancient Egypt* noted that: "Egypt exported gold, ivory and African trade goods - as well as craftsmen and physicians - in return for silver, copper, timber and various oils."

These advances, nonetheless, as early as the Old Kingdom, Aldred (1965: 120-23) has argued: "At Hierakonpolis, as well as the copper-sheathed statues of Pepy I and his son, Quibell found a magnificent falcon head of gold. This object is surmounted by tall golden plumes and the life-like beady black eyes are formed from a rod of obsidian passing right through the head, its ends being highly polished. The small holes that are pierced round the base of the neck show traces of green copper corrosion and in all probability therefore the head once formed part of a composite statue, being attached to a body of wood or other material by copper nails. The statues of Pepi I and his son are also similar composite statues, since the missing crowns and kilts would have been composed of more perishable material such as gilded plaster. The falcon's head is one of the finest examples of goldsmith's work of the Old Kingdom to have survived and may be dated to the same period of Dynasty VI as the statue of Pepy I." There is therefore evidence the craft of the goldsmith became highly developed during the Old Kingdom.

In fact, gold finds are known of the earlier 3rd Dynasty in the Step-Pyramid of Zoser at Sakkara, built by his architect, Imhotep. Aldred (1965: 76) tells: "In the partly subterranean corridor giving access to the galleries under the pyramid, the excavator, the late Zakaria Goneim, found a deposit of stone and pottery vessels and some mud sealings impressed with the name of the then unknown Sekhem-khet, as well as a cache of jewelry of Dynasty III date. This included twenty-one gold bracelets of varying sizes, a pair of electrum tweezers, a gold necklace and a small gold box which had a lid shaped as a cockle-shell."

FREDERICK MONDERSON

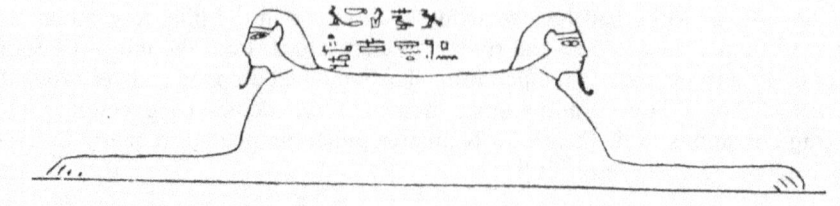

Tomb of Rameses IX. (Musée Guimet, Vol. XVI, Plate 6.)

Chapter XLI. Note 1.

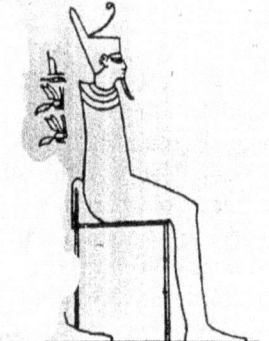

Chapter XLVII.

Leyden Papyrus, No. 16.

Tombeau de Seti I.

Research Essays Illustration 106. Book of the Dead. Vignettes from the Tomb of Rameses IX, Tomb of Seti I, and a Leyden Papyrus.

However, this notwithstanding, not much jewelry has survived from this era and principally what's known of the goldsmith's craft is known from illustrations in tombs.

We do know of the discovery of the tomb of Queen Hetepheres, mother of Khufu, builder of the Great Pyramid at Giza. An intact Old Kingdom tomb, it appears to have been a reburial, perhaps due to some tomb desecration. Scholars have postulated this view, offering that those concerned with the re-interment were afraid to tell Khufu his mother's resting place had been disturbed. She was reburied without his knowing for fear he may have had a temper tantrum.

White (1970: 71-72) mentions the 1925 discovery as: "A wonderful collection of objects was unearthed. There was a canopy, a bed, two chairs and a carrying chair, all sheeted in gold. There were alabaster vessels, a copper basin, copper tools,

RESEARCH ESSAYS ON ANCIENT EGYPT

gold knives and razors, three gold vessels and a gold manicure instrument. There was a toilet box with cosmetics contained in eight little alabaster pots, and a jewel case with twenty silver anklets inlaid with lapis lazuli, carnelian and malachite. Inlaid gold hieroglyphs on the ebony panels of the carrying chair carried the fourfold inscription: 'Mother of the King of Upper and Lower Egypt, follower of Horus, guide of the Ruler, favorite whose every command is carried out for her, daughter of the god (born) of his body, Hetephras.' The excavators had found the tomb of Snefru's wife and Cheops' [Khufu] mother. But although they found the alabaster sarcophagus, they did not find the queen's body. Her viscera were in the Canopic chest, but the sarcophagus was empty."

We also know, from the time of the Old Kingdom's cult endowment, temple and priesthood wealth and power was measured in gold and land. The consolidation of power by the priesthood through endowment and rising power, and autonomy of nobles during the lengthy 94-year reign of Pepi II, contributed to the decline of the Old Kingdom.

Notwithstanding, Woldering (1963: 63) displays an exquisite contemporary: "Gold collar necklace from the tomb of Impse, Old Kingdom, VIth Dynasty. Approx. 2200 B.C. Museum of Fine Arts. Boston. Length 27.5 cm."

In the Middle Kingdom and the New Empire, Syria supplied gold as tribute. Yet still, Nubia remained a powerful source of gold for temple wealth and ornamentation. With the Middle Kingdom's consolidation, reorganization and expansion, a vigorous imperial policy targeted the wealth of Nubia. Much of this booty filled priestly and temple coffers. So much so, Erman (1894: 298) has written: "All of the kings, from the very oldest period, followed the same fatal course; some were more generous than others, as for instance the pious kings of the 5th dynasty; thus even under the Old Empire many temples were rich enough to keep their own military force. The Nubian conquests of the kings of the 12th dynasty opened out those gold districts to Egypt, and the temples received their share of the booty; for instance, the chief treasurer Ychernofret was sent by Usertesen III on a special mission to Abydos: "to erect monuments to his father Osiris, the god of the west, and to adorn the most secret place (i.e. the Holy of Holies) with the gold which His Majesty had brought in victory and triumph from Nubia."

FREDERICK MONDERSON

Research Essays 104. Kom Ombo Temple to Gods Haroeis and Sobek. Goddess of building Seshat, with breast exposed stands next to Horus in Red and White Double Crown.

Mark Lehner, in *The Complete Pyramids* (1997) (1998:175) tells of discoveries made at the giant mud-brick pyramid of Senwosret II of the XIIth Dynasty, where all that was found of the king's remains was a Uraeus. In this piece: "The cobra's body was of solid gold set with green faience, feldspar and carnelian, the head was carved from lapis lazuli with garnet eyes." Even more, Lehner (1998: 176) tells of the "Treasure of Illahun" belonging to the princess Sit-Hathor-Yunet, daughter of Senwosret II and aunt of Amenemhet III. "In 1913 Guy Brunton and Petrie

RESEARCH ESSAYS ON ANCIENT EGYPT

examined the plundered tomb of a princess named Sit-Hathor-Yunet. They found her red granite sarcophagus and Canopic jars, but very little funerary furniture until they discovered a recess, plastered over, containing five boxes, two of which were of inlaid ebony. These contained the princess' necklaces, bracelets, anklets, scarab-rings, mirror, razors and cosmetic containers. This 'Treasure of Illahun' also included a diadem formed of a band of gold adorned with a uraeus similar, though smaller, to that found in the king's pyramid. Her mirror was a disk of silver with a black obsidian handle in the form of an open papyrus, partly plated with electrum, with a face of Hathor. Two pectorals of chased gold inset with semiprecious stones revealed details of the life and death of the princess. One formed the hieroglyphic name of Senwosret II, her father, and the other was the name of Amenemhet III, her nephew."

Underscoring what has been called "culture in captivity," Woldering (1963: 86) again exhibits a: "Gold pendant in the shape of a fish. From Illahun. Middle Kingdom. Approx. 1900 B.C. *Royal Scottish Museum* Edinburgh. Length 3.4 cm." Woldering (1963: 130) further mentions the quality of work of this age, where he states: "Among the most outstanding achievements of Middle Kingdom art are the works produced by goldsmiths. With their exquisite well-blended colors and forms, they testify to the high level of technical expertise and the refined sense of form that existed in this era. Diadems and pectorals are singled out for especially lavish embellishment. Semi-precious stones such as carnelian, amethyst, lapis lazuli, turquoise and jasper are used for inlaying, and give these objects a colorful attractive aspect."

Budge (1972: 8) sums up some accomplishments of the Middle Kingdom. He wrote: "XIIth Dynasty. Many raids in Nubia; that country conquered so far south as the head of the Third Cataract. Raid in Syria. Canal re-made in the First Cataract, and one made to join the Nile and the Red Sea. Gold mines in the Eastern Desert worked, commerce with Punt, Syria and Mediterranean peoples developed, and Egypt becomes very rich. Systematic irrigation introduced and great reservoirs made in the Fayum. Pyramid tombs built at Lisht, Dashur, Illahun and Hawara. Labyrinth built. Great development of literature, the first Recension of the Theban Books of the Dead compiled. End of the Middle Kingdom."

Since very little other sources are available, tombs reveal evidence of the development of the craft of goldsmith. Maspero (1926: 141) explained how these sepulchers were used for a variety of purposes and in this gold was well represented, whether in jewelry or artistic decoration of the walls of tombs. This idea of personal and bodily decoration goes back to the earliest times when gold was found in pre-dynastic graves. Perhaps from this time it takes on its mystical significance. He notes, from the earliest times jewelry and other goods were included with the dead. "Was it a question of how to provide food for all eternity, it was only necessary to draw the different parts of an ox or a gazelle ready prepared for the butcher - the shoulder, the haunch, the ribs, the breast, the heart and liver and the head; but it was also quite easy to represent the history of the animal from a very early period - its birth, its life in the pastures, then the slaughter-house, the cutting up of the creature, and the final offering. In the same way with regard to cakes or loaves, there was no difficulty in depicting the field labor, the sowing, and the harvest, beating out the grain, storing it in the granary, and kneading the dough. Clothing, ornaments and furniture afforded a pretext for introducing spinning and weaving, gold-working and joiner's work."

Research Essays Illustration 107. Book of the Dead. Vignettes of the bird beak, from the *Papyrus of Ani*, *Nicholson Papyrus* and again *Papyrus of Ani*.

With the craft of mummification and the heavy reliance placed on burials, Yoyotte (1963: 111) adds additionally: "The places where statues of the 'double' and the coffin were made were called the 'Houses of Gold.' Some embalmers' workshops and the sarcophagus-chambers of royal tombs were also given this name. The masks, which covered the mummified faces of children, were either covered with gold or painted yellow. For the king and the great nobles, the mask was made of pure gold. Clever goldsmiths used this same metal for fashioning collars, bracelets, finger-stalls, pectorals, and other potent amulets which adorned the embalmed corpse of the king and those whom he favored."

Maspero (1926: 276) provided even more of an explanation: "Beads of agate, carnelian, brown and white quartz, steatite, calcite, and glazed pottery, are found in abundance in the prehistoric graves, while beads of glazed stone, of turquoise, amethyst, lapis lazuli, serpentine, hematite, obsidian, porphyry, silver, gold, and iron are found in somewhat later graves." Even further, Maspero (1926: 291) adds a description of the funerary decoration: "jars deposited in tombs are painted in imitation of alabaster, granite, basalt, bronze and even gold."

RESEARCH ESSAYS ON ANCIENT EGYPT

Research Essays 105.   Kom Ombo Temple to Gods Haroeis and Sobek. On a column, God Sobek, Lord of Ombos.

Maspero (1926: 294-95) continued how: "glass was run into stone molds of the desired size and shape, beads, discs, rings, pendants for necklaces, narrow rods, and plaques bearing figures of men or animals, gods and goddesses. Eyes and eyebrows for stone or bronze statues were made of glass, and so were bracelets for their wrists. Glass was used as an inlay for hieroglyphs, and entire figures, scenes and inscriptions in glass were inlaid in wood, stone, or metal. The mummy-cases of Netemt are decorated this way, and so are the coffins of Iuiya and Thiyu, the grandparents of Akhenaten. They are entirely covered with gold leaf with the exception of the headdress and some details; the inscriptions and the principal part of the decoration are formed of this brilliantly colored enamel which contrasts well with the gold-background."

FREDERICK MONDERSON

Jewelers were called *neshedi* and *nubi* (the gold man) and *hemu nub* (gold-craftsmen). Because it represented wealth and social status, a number of official titles were associated with gold. Among these were "Gold-worker," "Chief of the Gold-workers of the Estate of Amun," "Chief of the Gold-workers," and "Chief of the Gold-workers of Amun." Other titles were "Overseer of the Treasury of Gold and Silver," "Overseer of the Gold Land of Amun," and "Weigher of Amun." Another read "Governor of the Gold Country of Coptos." During the XIXth Dynasty time of Rameses II, the Viceroy of Kush assumed the title: "Governor of the Gold Country of Amon." These many titles are indicative of how important gold was to the economy and culture of Egypt.

Not much was known about the gold-craftsmen themselves. However, their trade was probably hereditary and the secrets passed on from father to son. From the Old Kingdom illustrations indicate dwarfs were principal workers of gold. Still, what is recorded is the: "preliminaries, weighing, giving out the metal and melting the gold in a crucible over a charcoal fire; then pouring out the molten metal, beating it into sheets and bars with a rounded stone and polishing it." Even more, White (1970: 112) added: "Gold was both cast and cold hammered. It was cut and shaped into plaques, foil, leaf, wire, rivets and nails. Silver was scarcer than gold and was therefore reckoned of greater account. It was evidently extremely hard to come by, for very little of it was found even in the tomb of Tutankhamon .... Electrum, a natural alloy of gold and silver, was available in small amounts in Upper Egypt and Nubia. It was known as 'white gold' and highly prized." Naturally, "white gold" was one of the metal mixtures often encountered. In this respect, Maspero (1926: 338) argued: "The noble metals were gold, electrum, and silver; the base metals were copper, iron, and lead, to which tin was added later."

Maspero (1902: 311) had stated earlier: "The gold and electrum came partly from Syria in bricks and rings; and partly from the Sudan in nuggets and gold dust. The process of refining and alloying are figured on certain monuments of the early dynasties. In Old Kingdom bas-relief at Sakkara, we see the gold entrusted to the craftsman for working. In another Middle Kingdom example, (at Beni Hassan) the washing and melting down of the ore is represented and again at Thebes during the New Kingdom, the goldsmith is depicted seated in front of his crucible, holding the blow pipe to his lips and the left hand and grasping the pincers with the right, thus gaining the flame and at the same time making ready to seize the ingot. The Egyptians struck neither gold coin nor medal."

RESEARCH ESSAYS ON ANCIENT EGYPT

Research Essays Illustration 108. Book of the Dead. Chapter XXXIII. From a Papyrus, Leyden Museum, IV. Time to do the Chop-Chop of the snake and cockroach.

Woldering (1963: 208) added the commentary: "Superb works produced by goldsmiths testify to the technical skill and sense of beauty which these craftsmen possessed. Semi-precious stones, pastes and enamel lend a touch of vitality to the glittering gold. The colors are delightful. But XIXth Dynasty embossed gold and silver vessels from Zagazig also merit unqualified admiration." "Bronze mirrors, cosmetic jars and unguent-spoons made of wood, stone or ivory in fanciful shapes give proof of the stylistic refinement and wealth of imagination that existed during this era, which was so exposed to stimulation from outside."

By the New Kingdom the bellows was in general use. It reached a heat intensity of 890 degrees centigrade needed to melt and join copper and gold. Further, the: "Melting point of fine gold is 1,063 degrees centigrade, which allows a good margin for over-heating. For this reason, process may have been used to achieve the fine granulation of the Middle and New Kingdom jewelry, including Tutankhamon's treasure."

Tools used in the metallurgy industry included reed pipes, tongs and rounded stones for hammering the metal. They used stone anvils resting on wooden blocks, crucibles and long rods for lighting them. Molds were used in "lost wax" or *cire perdue* process of casting. White (1970: 110) explained the *cire perdue* process where: "a model of the object is first manufactured by hand or in a mold. It is then coated with clay to form a case or mold. The clay mold is baked, which causes it to harden, and during the baking the beeswax runs away through small vents. Molten bronze is next poured into the empty clay mold. When the metal is cool and set, the clay jacket is broken off and the object emerges complete." In addition, jewelers used chisels for cutting and goldsmiths used bow-drills for making gold beads. Hammers and pointed tools were also available.

Wilkinson in his book on *Ancient Egyptian Jewelry* enumerated precious and semi-precious materials used by the ancient craftsmen for most of dynastic rule that included: "gold and silver, carnelian, lapis lazuli, feldspar, jasper, amethyst and button-pearl." They also used "turquoise, agate, onyx and glass imitating the colored stones." To this we could add beryl, calcite, chalcedony, coral, garnet, hematite, jade, peridot, rock crystal, sard, sardonyx, and turquoise. "Bone, ivory and colored stones were used in making amulets in the form of crouching falcons, symbols of the fertility goddess, fish, birds, hippopotami and crocodiles were also made."

Research Essays 106. Kom Ombo Temple to Gods Haroeis and Sobek. All the Gods, Thoth, Hathor, Bastet, Haroeis, Horus, perform a "Laying of Hands" ritual on the Pharaoh.

Egyptian jewelry included amulets that had a magical or religious significance. In the early dynastic period, amulets were made of sheet gold and represented oryx and bulls.

The Nubian deposits of gold helped in development of the goldsmith craft. Egypt was in contact with this region and Central Africa from the earliest times. The first goldsmiths were dwarfs probably from Central Africa. In the Old Kingdom this profession was often controlled by dwarfs and this is shown in Old Kingdom tomb decorations.

RESEARCH ESSAYS ON ANCIENT EGYPT

From the Old Kingdom, a complete collar was found lying on the top of the IV Dynasty coffin of Babael. It had twenty rows of cylindrical disc-beads of gold, carnelian, steatite, hematite, turquoise and shell. "The semi-circular terminals are of sheet gold." There were two types of collar, the Bat-emblem and the Sah-collar, often made of gold.

Jewelry from the Middle Kingdom, known from tomb decorations, included amulets, anklets, bracelets, collars and diadems. There were also earrings, finger rings and pectorals. The materials were the same as the Egyptian craftsmen had manufactured from the early times.

Research Essays Illustration 109. Book of the Dead. Chapter LVII and LVIII from a Papyrus in the British Museum, No. 9,949 and *Papyrus of Ani*.

The New Kingdom was again a "golden age." This followed a similar designation for the Middle Kingdom. Following the war of liberation and triumph of the Thebans, the New Kingdom became a time of great praise for Amon at Karnak. As New Kingdom imperial warfare ensued, the award of the "Gold of Valor" was given for bravery. One particular individual displayed exceptional bravery. So much so, Murray (1963: 29-30) tells of him: "The story of the campaigns, of the insurrection in the south engineered by Tety the Handsome, of the naval engagement, and of the siege and final capture of the Hyksos stronghold at Avaris, is told with engaging simplicity by the king's namesake, Aahmes, son of Abana. He begins proudly: 'I will tell you, O all ye people, I will inform you of all the honors, which came to me. I was presented with gold seven times in the presence of the whole land; male and female slaves likewise. I was endowed with many fields. The fame of a man valiant in his deeds shall not perish in this land forever."

Successive pharaohs of the XVIIIth, XIXth and XXth Dynasties tried to outdo each other in praising Amon.

FREDERICK MONDERSON

The height of this "golden age" was reached during the reign of Amenhotep III of the XVIIIth dynasty. He experimented with the processional colonnade at Soleb in Nubia; then built one at Karnak and another at Luxor. He constructed the Temple of Mut and placed hundreds of statues of the goddess Sekhmet within. He built a "Palace of Rejoicing," named Malcata, for his Nubian queen, Tiy. He also dug a lake for her to sail the royal barge when she relaxed. It stands to reason he showered jewelry on this beloved queen. Mother of Amenhotep IV, she was shown as her husband's equal and believed the power behind his throne. Woldering (1963: 132) again exhibits: "Head of a statuette of Queen Tiy, a commoner who became consort of Amenhotep III. Painted yew-wood, gold inlays. From Medinet/Gurob, in the Faiyum. New Kingdom, XVIIIth Dynasty, approx. 1360 B.C. Former National Museums, Berlin. Height 10.7 cm."

Naturally he revered his god even more. Murray (1963: 133) recounts how Amenhotep "The Magnificent" described his work: "I made a monument for him who begat me, Amon-Re, Lord of Thebes, making for him the great barge, Amon-Re in the sacred barge, for the Beginning of the River, of new cedar which his Majesty cut in the countries of God's Land; it was dragged over the mountains of Retenu by the princes of all countries. It was made very wide and large, and was adorned with silver and wrought with gold throughout. The great brightness; they bear great crowns; of which the serpents twine along the sides. Flagstaves are set up before it, wrought with electrum; two great obelisks are between them. It is beautiful everywhere."

This monarch was a prolific builder. His experimental Soleb temple notes Murray: "Is furnished with fine white limestone, it is wrought with gold throughout, its floor is adorned with silver, and its portals are of gold."

At Karnak, Murray (1963: 133) wrote, Amenhotep III added: "A very great portal wrought with gold throughout. The Divine shadow as a ram is inlaid with real lapis lazuli wrought with gold and many costly stones; there is no other instance of doing the like. Its floors are adorned with silver. Towers are over against it. Stelae of lapis lazuli are set up, one on each side. Its towers reach the sky like the four pillars of heaven; its flagstaves shine more than the sky, being wrought with electrum."

The religious significance of gold is recounted in literature. In the *Book of the Dead*, chapter one hundred and fifty-five is about placing a *Tet* of gold on the neck of the *Khu*. Chapter one hundred and fifty eight is about putting a collar of gold around the neck of the Khu. Thus, gold could be seen as serving a religious, as well as decorative purpose. Generally, the dead were given collars "Great of Magic," "Collar of the Lord of Eternity," "of Horus," "of Wadjet," "of Nekhbet" and so on to accompany them. Egyptian craftsmen made temple vases, vessels,

RESEARCH ESSAYS ON ANCIENT EGYPT

knives, and razors of gold, ram's heads of gold and gold manicure sets. In the ceremonies, gold was used as part of religious and funerary functions.

In 1908, Theodore Davis discovered a "Gold Tomb" in the Valley of the Kings. It contained cartouches of Queen Tausert, her husband Sethos II and Rameses II. This wonderful cache included a "diadem of rosettes, bracelets, finger-rings, earrings, necklace, scarabs, pendants, plaques and vases."

Research Essays 107. Kom Ombo Temple to Gods Haroeis and Sobek. Horus' Sanctuary in rear of the Temple.

Throughout the historical period, much other fine jewelry of gold was made in the "gold house." Kings such as Akhenaten liked giving away "Collars of Gold." Deserving officials received from the Pharaoh the "Gold of Valor" and "Gold of Praise" as well as "Gold Flies."

At Aswan among the Tombs of the Nobles there is one for Sabni and Mekhu, Old Kingdom nobles. Apparently, Mekhu was sent on a mission to Nubia and natives killed him. Accordingly, Breasted (1923: 141) tells how his son: "Sabni quickly mustered the troops of his domain, and with a train of a hundred asses marched quickly southward, punished the tribe to whom Mekhu's death was presumably due, rescued the body of his father, and loading it upon an ass, returned to the frontier." He was one of the first individuals to receive the "Gold of Praise" for his actions.

Breasted relates another yet later incident of the awarding of this distinction during the reign of Akhenaton and it concerns the appointment of his high priest.

In this, Breasted (1923: 367) relates: "Merire ('Beloved of Re') was appointed by him to the office, coming one day for this purpose with his friends to the balcony of the palace, in which the king and queen appeared in state. The king then formally promoted Merire to the exalted office, saying 'Behold, I am appointing thee for myself to be 'Great Seer' [High Priest] of the Aton in the temple of Aton in Akhetaton .... I give to thee the office saying 'Thou shalt eat the food of Pharaoh, thy lord in the house of Aton.' Merire was so faithful in the administration of the temple that the king publicly rewarded him with "the gold," the customary distinction granted to zealous servitors of the Pharaoh. At the door of the temple buildings the king, queen and two daughters extend to the fortunate Merire the rewards of fidelity, and the king says to the attendants: 'Hang gold at his neck before and behind, and gold on his legs; because of his hearing the teaching of Pharaoh concerning every saying in these beautiful seats which Pharaoh has made in the sanctuary in the Aton-temple in Akhetaton.' It thus appears that Merire had given heed to the king's teachings regarding ritual of the temple, or, as he says, "every saying in these beautiful seats.'"

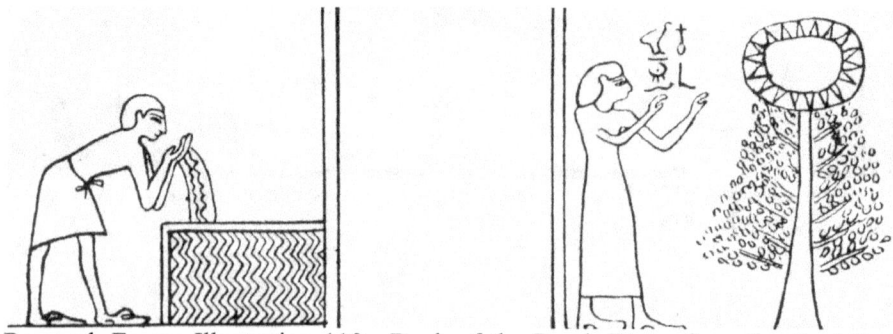

Research Essays Illustration 110. Book of the Dead. Water from the Cool Pool and the Tree with a Halo in Chapter LXI and Chapter LXIV from the *Papyrus du Louvre*, 11,193.

Tribute was an important source of revenue in Dynastic Egypt. Wilson (1975: 184) has written: "Amon-re of Karnak benefited hugely from the foreign tribute. He had promised the victory, and his image accompanied the armies on the march; he received a lion's share of the loot. The purpose of Thutmose III's 'Annals,' carved in the Temple of Karnak and copied from an original leather scroll kept as a field journal, was to state that the pharaoh had fulfilled his share of the contract with the god. For example, Amon was the patron and the senior partner of the exploitation of the gold mines in Nubia and the Sudan. In Thutmose III's thirty-fourth year, Amon received more than 700 Troy pounds of gold from these mines;

RESEARCH ESSAYS ON ANCIENT EGYPT

in the thirty-eighth year about the same; and in the forty-first year somewhat over 800 pounds. This was no slight amount in that day."

White (1970: 111) added even further, regarding the gold: "Vast amounts of it were obtained in tribute from the conquered provinces and it served to buy and perpetuate diplomatic alliances. In the Amarna letters we learn that an early king of Assyria, Ashurn Adinakhi, received a remittance of twenty talents of gold from Amenhotep III, 'the same amount that was sent to the king of Hanigalbat.' From the same source we are informed that Tushratta of Mitanni wrote to Pharaoh as follows: 'Send me so much gold that it cannot be measured. Send me more gold than you sent to my father. In your land, my brother, gold is as common as dust.'"

Trade was another important source of gold and African nations emerged as important trading partners with Egypt. Manley (1996: 65) noted: "Egypt exported gold, ivory and African grade goods - as well as craftsmen and physicians - in return for silver, copper, timber and various oils." Breasted (1923: 136) notes: "Besides gold, the Sudan sent down the river ostrich feathers, ebony logs, panther skins and ivory; while along the same route, from Punt and the countries further east, came myrrh, fragrant gums and resins and aromatic wood."

John A. Wilson's *The Culture of Ancient Egypt* (1951) (1975: 81) added: "The movement of caravans into Nubia and the Sudan and the passage of sailing ships from Egypt to the cedar-bearing areas in Phoenicia were royal enterprises, and we have no indication of any private enterprise outside the frontier. The exploitation of the turquoise and copper mines in Sinai was definitely an activity of the king from the First Dynasty onward, manned by royal officials and policed by the army. On analogy, the exploitation of the gold mines in the eastern deserts must have been a royal monopoly. The production of these two metals would give the palace inestimable economic advantage."

In an assessment of events following the Amarna Period, Budge (1972: 10) summed up the accomplishments of the XIXth Dynasty. He notes how the: "Worship of Amen restored and his priests reinstated. Code of Laws compiled. Wars with Libyans and Nubians and the Hittites and their allies; Egyptians finally compelled to sign a treaty with the Hittites. Gold mines of the Eastern Sudan worked, the rock-hewn temples of Kalabsheh and Abu Simbel made, the Hall of Columns at Karnak and other great buildings constructed. Splendid tombs on the plan of those of the XVIIIth Dynasty hewn in the hills in Western Thebes."

FREDERICK MONDERSON

Research Essays 108. Kom Ombo Temple to Gods Haroeis and Sobek. Sobek's Sanctuary in rear of the Temple.

After Rameses III of the 20th Dynasty, it was practically downhill for Egypt, perhaps some exception with the 25th and 26th Dynasties as there was some revival. However, while the 21st dynasty completed the Temple of Khonsu at Karnak, third of the Theban Triad of Amon, Mut and Khonsu, begun by Rameses III, Sheshonk I founded the 22nd Dynasty and added the Court of the Bubastite in front of Karnak's hypostyle hall.

However, Woldering (1963: 209) notes: "The most important accomplishment of the Libyan period was perhaps the production of large bronze figures. These showed a high degree of technical skill. Inlaying of metals in the metallic ground and engraving were popular means of adding a touch of life to the surface of the figures. This extended down to the very last detail. Inlays of electrum, silver, semi-precious stones, pastes and glass, or a layer of gold leaf were used to give the bronzes color and charm. The grateful statue of Karomama, the consort of one of the Libyan kings from the XXIInd Dynasty, exemplifies the high level of technical perfection and the fine sense of form that were evident in the bronze sculpture of this period."

The Ethiopians of the XXVth Dynasty overthrew the Libyan Dynasty. This former nation had been active participants in Egyptian culture from as early as Williams' discovery at Qustul. Williams found evidence of pre-pharaonic paraphernalia, viz., Nile boat, white crown, enthroned pharaoh, whip and flail, serekh, incense burner, etc., c. 3400 B.C., more than two centuries before they appear in Egypt. In addition, the significance of the Nubian wealth shows, from

RESEARCH ESSAYS ON ANCIENT EGYPT

time immemorial this area has produced gold, precious metals and stones, practically bankrolling Egypt. She has also produced craftsmen of the highest quality. The working of this metal saw the production of exquisite works of jewelry. In the Nubian pyramids and other tombs the craft of the goldsmith continued to produce with distinction we associate with Egypt/Kemet. Some of these memorable and valuable pieces of art are scattered and adorn museums worldwide. They attest to the high level of specialization in gold craftsmanship achieved in Ancient Africa, along the Nile River.

Steindorff and Seele's *When Egypt Ruled the East* (1942) (1971: 195) provide a powerful description of golden vessels depicted in their book and housed in the Cairo Museum of Egyptian Antiquities. Accordingly: "The technical arts were perhaps pre-eminently occupied in Egypt with the manufacture of jewelry and similar ornaments. The technical skill and artistic taste displayed by the goldsmiths are well illustrated by surviving objects from the mortuary equipment of Tutankhamon. Of the great works of art, including the gold bowls and drinking vessels, which were dedicated to the temples by the kings or presented to their followers as marks of favor, of the gold and silver images of the gods which once adorned the temples, only a few examples have survived. Among the noblest creations of the goldsmith's art of all time is the group of vessels assembled .... They belong to the period of the Nineteenth Dynasty, but there is no evidence in their perfection of the decline which had already set in by the middle of the thirteenth century B.C. .... The wonderful wine pitcher of silver with its gold handles in the form of a marvelously modeled wild goat, the smaller jug with engraved flower ornamentation, the gold chalice in the shape of a lotus blossom, and the gold bracelet ornamented with a pair of ducks' heads."

Research Essays Illustration 111. War-Galley; the sail being pulled up during the action. Thebes.

FREDERICK MONDERSON

Finally, Budge (1972: 67-68) adds his commentary on the craft of metallurgy. He wrote: "The articles of jewelry and other decorative objects used as personal ornaments were originally amulets. Among these may be mentioned collars, necklaces and pectorals formed of rows of beads made of semi-precious stones, gold, crystal, etc. The earliest known beads were un-pierced. Under the XIIth Dynasty necklaces were made entirely of scarabs in amethyst, sard, carnelian, agate and lapis-lazuli; at a later time the amulets [Tet, girdle, ankh, scepter] and figures of gods and flies and heads of Hathor, all in gold, were interspersed with the beads. Armlets and bracelets were worn by large numbers of women; the former were usually made of copper, and the latter of gold. A few examples of bracelets or bangles made of flint and glazed Egyptian porcelain, are known. Anklets closely resembled armlets in shape, and were made of copper or gold. Small earrings made of gold inlaid with semi-precious stones were common in early days; in the later periods of Egyptian history they were made very long. The most elaborate examples of them are found in graves of the first five centuries of the Christian era. The varieties of the finger ring are many. The greater number of them was made of gold wire of varying thickness, and the bevel was formed by an inscribed scarab or a plaque, rectangular or oval, on which were carved figures of gods and goddesses or magical inscriptions. Some of the massive gold rings have bevels of cylindrical form, and some have elongated projections in the form of a cartouche with royal names written in it. The finger ring had a special importance in the Other World, and when a man was too poor to afford one in metal he provided himself with one made of plaited grass or straw."

In conclusion, Gold therefore played a significant role in the culture of ancient Egypt from personal decoration and social utility to religious worship to mortuary internment. The craft and craftsmen who produced the wonderful jewelry we have come to associate with ancient Egypt was guarded and well regulated. Old Kingdom evidence dwarfs from Central Africa were principals in working the gold into the beautiful jewelry that decorated the pharaohs, their worthy servants and the implements and objects used in temple worship, since gold was considered a mystical metal associated with the sun god. Gold played an important part both as imperial tribute to Egypt and in its relations with other states for trade and management of good relations. Through it all, Africa to the south of Egypt supplied enormous amounts of gold as it has for millennia. In this latter, one could hardly estimate how much gold Africa actually gave to the world at large. What is unquestioned, the bright and shiny substance has maintained its mysticism from the ancient into the modern world and people still long after this substance of the gods with just as much intensity and zeal then as now.

RESEARCH ESSAYS ON ANCIENT EGYPT

References

Aldred, Cyril. *Egypt to the End of the Old Kingdom.* London: Thames and Hudson, 1965.
_____. *The Egyptians.* London: Thames and Hudson, (1961) 1987.
Breasted, James H. *Ancient Records of Egypt.* 5 Vols. Chicago: University of Chicago Press; London: Luzac and Co; Leipzig: Otto Harraisowitz, 1906-07.
_____. *A History of Egypt: From the Earliest Times to the Persian Conquest.* New York: Charles Scribner's Sons, (1905) 1923.
Budge, E.A.W. *The Dwellers on the Nile.* New York: Benjamin Blom, Inc., 1972.
Erman, Adolf. *Life in Ancient Egypt.* New York: McMillan, 1894.
Keating, Rex. *Nubian Rescue.* New York: Hawthorn Books, Inc., 1975.
Lehner, Mark. *The Complete Pyramids.* London: Thames and Hudson, (1997) 1998.
Manley, Bill. *The Penguin Historical Atlas of Ancient Egypt.* New York: Penguin Books, Inc., 1996.
Maspero, Gaston. *A Manual of Egyptian Archaeology.* (Trans) Amelia B. Edwards. New York; G. Putnam and Sons; London: H. Grevel, and Co., 1902.
_____. *A Manual of Egyptian Archaeology.* New York: G. Putnam and Sons, Inc., 1926.
Murray, Margaret A. *The Splendor That Was Egypt.* New York: Hawthorn Books, Inc., Publishers, (1949) 1963.
Petrie, W.M. Flinders. *The Arts and Crafts of Ancient Egypt.* London and Edinburgh: T.N. Foulis, 1910.
Spence, Lewis. *Myths and Legends of Egypt.* New York: Avenel Books, (1985) 1986.
Steindorff, George and Keith C. Seele. *When Egypt Ruled the East.* Chicago: University of Chicago Press, (1942) 1971.
White, Jon E. Manchip. *Ancient Egypt.* New York: Dover Publications, Inc., New York, 1970.
_____. *Everyday Life in Ancient Egypt.* New York: Perigee Books, (1963) 1980.
Wilkinson, Alix. *Ancient Egyptian Jewelry.* London: Methuen and Co., Ltd., 1971.
Wilson, John A. *The Culture of Ancient Egypt.* Chicago: University of Chicago Press, (1951) 1975.

FREDERICK MONDERSON

Research Essays 108a. Kom Ombo Temple to Gods Haroeis and Sobek. Pharaoh and an assistant make a Presentation to Haroeis, the Elder Horus with Hathor at his rear. Notice the king's and his attendant's see-through gown.

Research Essays 108b. Kom Ombo Temple to Gods Haroeis and Sobek. Beyond the decorated wall, the uraei and disks on the architrave and the majestic columns with their different capitals.

RESEARCH ESSAYS ON ANCIENT EGYPT

Research Essays 108c. Kom Ombo Temple to Gods Haroeis and Sobek. On a column, the king wears the White Crown, necklace, straight beard and long flowing gown as he offers a sphinx to one of the deities of the temple.

Research Essays 108d. Kom Ombo Temple to Gods Haroeis and Sobek. Defaced figures give some understanding of how zealots destroyed much of ancient Egypt.

RESEACH ESSAYS ON ANCIENT EGYPT

18. Pharaonic Taxation

By

Dr. Fred Monderson

All governments depend on taxation to carry out their functions. In ancient Egypt, this was no different. Particularly because of its early emergence, this society set precedents of revenue acquisition and collection that would be imitated down through history. These accomplishments allow Gillings (1972) (1981: 2-3) to laud their significance with the following acclaim: "Well may we express admiration of the wonderful architecture of the Egyptian temples of Karnak and Luxor, at the grandeur and the immensity of the Pyramids and at the construction of their magnificent monuments. Well may we wonder at the government and the economies of a country extending nearly a thousand miles from north to south through which ran the longest river in the then-known world. And well may we marvel at the Egyptians' design of extensive irrigation canals, at their erection of great storage granaries, at the organization of their armies, the building of seagoing ships, the levying and collection of taxes, and at all the thought and effort concomitant with the proper organization of a civilization that existed successfully, virtually unchanged, for centuries longer than that of any other nation in recorded history."

In this remarkable set of milestones, the devising and instituting of a system of taxation was one of the most far-reaching accomplishments the king of Egypt was able to boast. This levy of taxation came to support the ruler, his government, pay its workers and engage various social classes in supporting the system of rulership it pursued. As a result, throughout dynastic rule, a number of laws were enacted and officials were appointed with responsibility for regulating and collecting taxes demanded by the government. Helping to understand this process beginning in the earliest times, Yoyotte (1963: 289-90) explained: "In Egypt, the cradle of civilization, a biennial census of fields and gold was conducted in about 2800 B.C., and in about 2600 B.C. a census of cattle. Taxation was heavy and universal in this country with an advanced bureaucratic system. The treasury invaded every walk of life and was accustomed to use such complex terminology and so involved an accounting system that Egyptologists experience great difficulty in understanding fiscal documents. Pharaoh needed the fine gold, which his high officials brought in procession to the vizier in order to conduct his foreign policy and reward his ministers. He protected his commercial monopoly by imposing customs' duties at the frontiers." The collection process was efficient and stern, and might I add, successful.

FREDERICK MONDERSON

Research Essays 109. Kom Ombo Temple to Gods Haroeis and Sobek. From the rear, both Sanctuaries and the respective aisles of each God.

Whether in the Old, Middle or New Kingdom the state's bureaucracy came to wield extensive and effective power. All of the functions of government as well as taxation came under the office of the Vizier who was likened to the Prime Minister in modern parlance. By the time of the New Kingdom, the duties had become so extensive that the office was split and there were two Viziers. These were Vizier of the Kingdom of Upper Egypt based at Thebes and a Vizier of Lower Egypt based at Memphis and other proximate locations. However, for a number of reasons, the Vizier of the South was the senior of the two. Nevertheless, through all this, taxation remained strictly regulated and the engines that drove the pharaonic system in the Nile Valley culture. Therefore, whatever the mode of payment, whether in labor, food, clothing, metal or animal, or whatever, everything was strictly regulated and failure to pay meant a penalty was imposed. As a result, the collection, processing and safeguarding of the "tax" became an important undertaking; to this end architecture was also oriented toward storage and safeguarding of the tax receipts.

Underscoring the extensive nature of the involved bureaucracy, Breasted (1923: 164) explained, by the time of the Middle Kingdom and later: "The central office of the treasury was still the 'White House,' which through its sub-departments of the granary, the herds, the 'double gold-house,' the 'double-silver house,' and other produce of the country, collected the central magazines and stockyards the annual revenues due the Pharaoh. Whole fleets of transports upon the river were necessary for the conveyance of the great quantities of commodities involved. The

RESEACH ESSAYS ON ANCIENT EGYPT

head of the "White House,' was as before, the chief treasurer, with his assistant, the 'treasurer of the God,' and the vigorous administration of the time is evident in the frequent records of these active officials, showing that notwithstanding their rank, they often personally superintended the king's interests in Sinai, Hammamat, or on the shores of the Red Sea at the terminus of the Coptos road. It is evident that the treasury had become a more highly developed organ since the Old Kingdom. The army of subordinates, stewards, overseers and scribes filling the offices under the heads of sub-departments was obviously larger than before. They began to display an array of titles, of which many successive ranks, heretofore unknown, were being gradually differentiated. Among these appear more prominently than heretofore the engineers and skilled artisans who were exploiting the mines and quarries under the administrative officials. Such conditions made possible the rise of an official middle class." Murray (1963: 57) also noted: "Many of these officials were scribes or clerks in the government offices, for there was a vast amount of writing to be done in regard to taxation owing other peculiarities of the country. Taxes were paid in kind, chiefly corn, flax, or farm animals. As agriculture depended entirely on the inundation, the assessment for taxation varied from year to year, and these calculations had to be made locally. A census of farm animals was made every second year, and this again was made locally. To do all this required local organizations, and the country was then divided into [forty-two] nomes or provinces, each with its own governor (known as 'the First under the King'), its own assessors, tax-collectors and all other officials necessary for government."

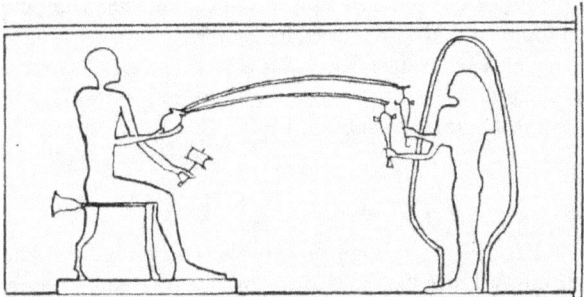 

Research Essays Illustration 112. Book of the Dead. Vignettes of pouring the refreshment found at Sakkara in Lepsius' *Denkmaler* and Lanzone's *Egyptian Dictionary*.

So extensive were the responsibilities of this individual, the administration of justice also fell under the functions of the Vizier. Breasted (1923: 164-65) continued his commentary: "Justice, as in the Old Kingdom, was still dispensed by the administrative officials; thus a treasurer of the god boasts that he was one 'knowing the law, discreet in exercising it.' The six 'Great Houses' or courts of justice, with the vizier at their head, sat in *Ithtowe*. There was besides a 'House of Thirty,' which evidently possessed judicial functions, and was also presided over by the vizier, but its relations to the six 'Great Houses' is not clear. There was now more than one 'Southern Ten,' and 'Magnates of the Southern Tens' were frequently entrusted with various executive and administrative commissions by the king."

Petrie (1923: 45) contrasted the national administration and explained how the two local administrations functioned: "The management of the country districts was left to the chief men, known as *saru* (captains or chiefs), who were similar to the *sheykhs* of the *meglis*, or council, at present. They were independent of the royal service; they judged suits relating to contracts, the division of property, wills, and sales (the present *quid* court). They issued orders, to be countersigned by the Director of the South, and administered by royal officials. They settled the corvee and local taxation. They had thus the regulation of local assessment, levied on them in blocks by the king. It seems that they were co-opted. They were thus two systems interlocking: locally, the landowners in council and their chiefs of the nome; centrally, the vizier and his corner-men observing affairs, and with the execution of the local acts in their own hands."

"In the Old Kingdom as the monarchy and feudal system was set up, taxation became the principal means by which the relationship supported itself. In a 3-tiered society, the lower class bought into the societal structure and as they struggled to find their place, the system of taxes came to determine obligation and expectation in a land blest by the gods, engineered by artistic and technological innovations, and watered by the majestic Nile River. Nevertheless, in addition, to the monarchy, nobility and lower classes there emerged a priestly class who were religious adherents and the intellectual brain thrust who were pivotal in training to organize and maintain the system of taxation in ancient Egypt."

Pointing to the significance of a Civil Service beginning in the Old Kingdom, and looking at a plan of noble burials within the proximity of the pharaoh's tomb, Aldred (1987: 88-89) noted: "The presence of the tombs of high officials in close proximity to those of their kings emphasizes the importance of such men in the life and government of Egypt. Land in Egypt was made suitable for cultivation as much by seasonal organized effort on a large scale as by natural conditions. This circumstance favored the emergence of technocrats who directed labor, determined the right moment for raising dams and piercing dykes, cutting canals and re-defining boundaries. They organized the collection and storage of harvests, and decided how much of it was to be allocated to imposts and to the next season's seed. Apart from the companions of the king, who assisted him in his administrative duties and in the affairs of his household, there were the two chancellors in charge of the Red and White Treasuries, as the store-houses of Lower and Upper Egypt were designated from their natural colors. The collection and distribution of supplies of all kinds from wine and oil to corn and honey were under their direction and that of the two Comptrollers of the Granaries. The distribution of supplies to the temples, and to a privileged elite of courtiers and officials, was administered from the Office of the Overseer of the King's Bounty."

Research Essays 110. Kom Ombo Temple to Gods Haroeis and Sobek. On a rear wall, colossal sculpture and accompanying inscriptions. Notice the 10 crocodiles sacred to Sobek.

The Middle Kingdom was known for its efforts at consolidation, reorganization and expansion. So it stands to reason the system of taxation also received its due treatment to remain consistent with changes in the broader society. However, in this regard not much evidence of taxation has come down to us. Much of what we know is from New Kingdom sources.

FREDERICK MONDERSON

In the New Kingdom, as the state expanded, taxes became more extensive and complex. Added to the collection process was foreign tribute from the nation's imperialistic ventures. With this new reality came the expansion of bureaucratic size and functions. Equally too, as the nation became more militaristic, levy for military service became a form of taxation. Nevertheless, military service had become a form of luxury and sought-after profession that offered a chance of adventure, honor and reward.

The principal forms of taxes were those levied on products and on labor. The state imposed heavy burdens and land-food rents on the wealthy. There were taxes on geese and other animals, on date palms and there were taxes on rights of passage over certain lands and ferries for water transport. Taxes also took the form of tribute exacted from conquered peoples and states. In addition, there were taxes at respective sites such as Abydos, Thebes, etc. It is believed that the Egyptian craftsmen and traders also had to pay some form of taxes, especially in times of war. However, the main forms of taxes were of 3 types. These were taxes on officials, taxes on agricultural produce and taxes as tribute from foreign vassal states.

Research Essays Temple Ticket 17. Sakkara New Tombs. Price of entrance is thirty Egyptian Pounds.

RESEACH ESSAYS ON ANCIENT EGYPT

Research Essays Illustration 113. Spearing the Hippopotamus.

From the earliest times, Egypt has been an agricultural society dependent on the Nile River. The Inundation season lasted for four months. The height or size of the flood determined the expected yield of the harvest. In his commentary, Kees (1961) (1977: 52) has argued: "The control and utilization of the flood-waters of the Nile was effected in a number of ways: by the building of dykes to protect certain parts of the countryside from flooding, such as gardens and villages; by the construction of enclosed areas or 'basins' to hold the flood-waters which would be released at the right moment by piercing of the dams; by the laying out of canals for distributing and conducting water from the 'basins' for irrigation purposes; and finally for sinking wells and using the shaduf, a water-raising appliance, for the irrigation of gardens." In addition, to aid this effort, the Egyptian engineers who were concerned with surveying and numbers, had to rely on their Nile gauges or Nilometers to help them measure the volume of the river.

The Nilometers were placed strategically as at Semnah in Nubia. One can be seen from the high ground at Abu Simbel. There is another at Elephantine, Egypt's southern border, two on the Island of Philae, and one at Memphis in Middle Egypt. There were two at Edfu, Temple of Horus. There is another in the well at Kom Ombo. There was probably one at Thebes, and so on. These instruments enabled the priestly engineers to measure and predict high or low Nile, and plan accordingly. In the *Dwellers on the Nile*, E. A. Wallis Budge explained what the Nilometers were. According to him, the Nilometer is a: "pillar or slab, standing in a sort of well. It is cut into a scale divided into cubits (the cubit is 21 1/3 inches), and kirats (the kirat is 1/24th part of a cubit)." A flood too high could mean destruction and one too low could mean famine. The ideal was between twenty-five and twenty-six and a half inches.

The Nile flood removed all land boundary marks. Importantly, this meant that surveyors had to re-survey and demarcate the land on an annual basis. This surveying required the use of arithmetic and geometry. As a result, knowing or predicting the extent of the river's rise enabled the inspectors to determine what the size of taxation should be. This revenue in turn was based on the projected yield in crops produced by farmers. Of course different lands, based on proximity to source of water, yielded different qualities and quantities of produce, thus, having different grades of taxes. In this regard, Kees (1977: 53) noted: "The value of the land depended upon whether it was reached by the normal inundation, could be irrigated artificially, contained springs or lay beside a canal. In assessing annual taxes the state took into consideration the varying productivity of the arable land and also the estimated yield of the harvest. Varying land values necessitated a complicated system of assessment and even exercised an influence upon land laws .... Floodwater had to be kept away from riparian land and from village enclosures, but it could cover all the land between the boundaries of the villages and edge of the desert. It was there that the retreating flood-waters remained the longest in pools."

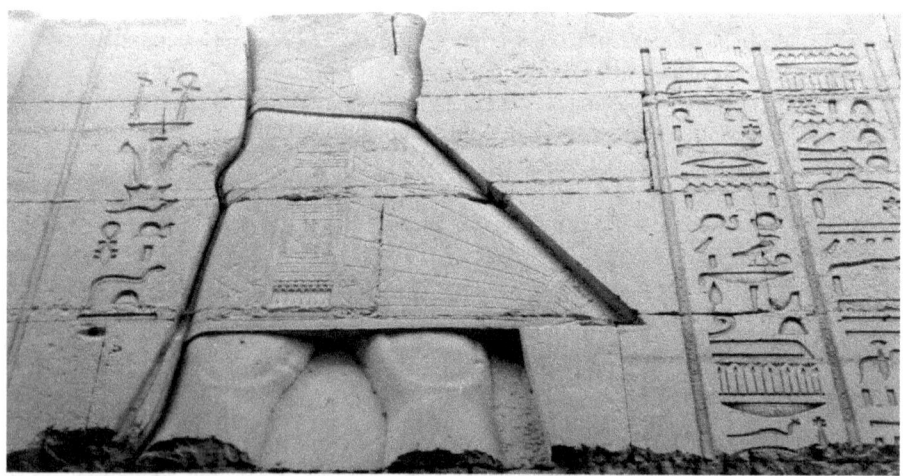

Research Essays 111. Kom Ombo Temple to Gods Haroeis and Sobek. Some scholars believe, from the makeup and decoration of the Apron, this depiction is probably that of Imhotep, builder of the Step-Pyramid at Sakkara.

Even further, Kees (1977: 53-54) continued: "In the days of basin-irrigation the felaheen distinguished between *rei*-fields which were covered by the flood and

RESEACH ESSAYS ON ANCIENT EGYPT

sharaki-land which required artificial irrigation. The ancient Egyptian division of land into what was called 'lowland' and 'upland' apart from the 'islands' that were occasionally the subject of special mention, yet did not correspond exactly to these two categories. According to evidence from the New Kingdom it is clear that the bulk of arable land was classed as 'upland' with the result that the Greeks translated the Egyptian word simply as 'mainland' or 'corn-bearing land.' 'Upland' was therefore, not always *sharaki*-land even though inscriptions from the feudal period of the first Intermediate Period make it appear that to conduct Nile-water to the 'upland' was regarded as typical: 'I made upland into marsh, I let the Nile flood the fallow land' and 'I brought the Nile to the upland in your fields so that plots were watered that had never known water before.' Upland was, therefore, contrasted apparently with 'lowland;' it was such land as could be denied flooding when the inundation fell below normal, but which was normally productive, and consequently, taxable. Real *sharaki*-land was used for orchards and vegetable gardens."

Research Essays Illustration 114. Manner from the Tree Goddess, in Lepsius' *Todtenbuch*.

The regulation of taxation based on the river's bounty is very old. It dates back to the earliest organized society of the first dynasty or earlier. All lands were registered and taxed except those owned by the temples, and in special circumstances consideration was given to others. The temple group, because of their special functions of service to the state was generally declared tax-exempt. Nevertheless, Wilson (1975: 271-72) adds: "The question whether these vast ecclesiastical properties were tax free or not is still far from clear. We possess a large scroll from the Twentieth Dynasty, giving certain notations of the government tax-assessors on fields for about one hundred miles in Middle Egypt. Unfortunately, this mass of detail is not completely intelligible, because the system of notation is too abbreviated for us, so that we cannot tell whether the figures given are the measures of grain assessed per unit of land or are some kind of data which the assessor would later use to fix the tax. These are the government tax collectors, and many of the lands are the stated property of the temples. The editor of this document notes that Herodotus and Diodorus, as well as Genesis 47: 26, carry a tradition that the priests of Egypt were free from taxation and quotes a text of Persian times indicating that the temples were exceptionally forced to pay dues in time of hardship, but then concludes that the temple privileges were partially only. He suggests that the priests themselves and the temple personnel were exempt from forced labor and that the charters of temple immunity forbade civil officials from violating this exemption, but that the temple lands were subject to government taxes. This is a decided amelioration of the situation, since tax-free lands running between 12 and 30 percent of the arable acreage would have been a crushing burden. On the present evidence, the privilege of the temples was confined to an immunity from the corvee which burdened the rest of Egypt." Nobles' estates were registered and the size of their households counted. The taxes they paid were "in kind" and amounted to one-fifth of produce. Today we call this the "20% bracket." It was better explained by Petrie (1923: 57) who indicated: "All land, except that held by the priests, was assessed annually for taxation, varying according to the height of the Nile and the amount of crop which could be raised. This regulation of dues by the extent of inundation dates from the 1st dynasty, if not earlier, as the height is minutely recorded to a sixteenth of an inch for every year in the national annals. This certainly would not be done without a serious purpose. Not only land was registered but estates, and the number of persons living on each holding. The taxes were, of course, in kind, and amounted to a fifth of the produce. As we have seen, these were not centralized, but were retained locally to pay the administration and the army. There was also a sort of professional income tax paid by officials, entirely in the hands of the vizier; this tax was remitted by Horemheb, apparently to gain the support of the civil service and weaken the position of the vizier, whom he may have thought dangerous, after the feebleness and confusion of the Aten party.'"

The general public was taxed on products. There were food dues of baskets of vegetables; fruits, eatables, bread and fodder supplies made to the registry office. There was a tax on animals. There was also a tax on linen, yarn and cordage, on leather, as well as common and precious metals. Kees (1977: 89) explains; in the Old Kingdom animals were an integral part of not just taxes but also festivals, and that the bulls were prized animals for these latter celebrations. He uses later records to show what was the value of such animals. This is supplied from records of the Ramesside period, where: "According to quality, a bull fetched from 30 to 120 *deben* of copper, a *deben* being an Egyptian weight of about 91 grams; a donkey fetched about 40 *deben* and a goat only 2. In considering the trade in cattle we must remember that the temples needed a large number of sacrificial animals and that the bull was regarded as the best for slaughter."

RESEACH ESSAYS ON ANCIENT EGYPT

Research Essays 112. Kom Ombo Temple to Gods Haroeis and Sobek. Even further, this colossal relief also depicts a person of great importance.

We are lucky that such evidence has survived from the Old Kingdom. Kees continued: "The endowment lists of the Sun Temple of Niuserre of Dynasty V recorded for a single festival the following sacrificial animals: 10 fat oxen, 1 (ordinary) ox, 1 oryx-antelope or 2 fat oxen, 100 oxen and 2 oryx-antelopes - a real hecatomb. Such were the expenses entailed by ceremonial public festivals at which food had to be provided for more than 100,000 persons. From a document of Sheshonk I we learn that the modest-sounding donations of a single ox for the daily sacrifice in the temple of Arsaphes at Heracleopolis necessitated that the high priest, who was also the nomarch, should contribute two months supply of sacrificial oxen (about 60 annually) and that every class right down to the shepherds, gardeners and stonemasons had to contribute according to their means. In the light of this knowledge we can calculate the economic consequences of the colossal endowments that Rameses III made for the Theban temples alone for their permanent possession - 421,362 head of oxen and small cattle and in addition as a special gift, perhaps for breeding purposes, 297 bulls. He further donated 45,544 head of cattle of various kinds to the Heliopolitan temples, 10,047 to those at Memphis and 13,433 to other temples. Although the sacrifices ultimately served as the food for the priests and for the vast crowds attending the festivals, such a voluntary contribution in kind was, nevertheless, a very heavy burden on agriculture for the benefit of certain privileged classes."

Research Essays Papyrus Art 12. Queen presents two jars to enthroned Hathor.

The tax on leather was a by-product of cattle rearing. Kees (1977: 90) again explained: "The Egyptian state demanded tax on all raw materials and all commercial products, a matter in which it served as the teacher of the Ptolemies. As in the case of the output from the manufacture of lines, so part of the production of hides was obviously liable to the tax; the nomarch as chief priest had claims on the payment received for the hides of sacrificial animals. It was for this reason that protective ordinances in the Old Kingdom freed certain endowments or temple estates from the hide-tax."

RESEACH ESSAYS ON ANCIENT EGYPT

There was a poll tax and levy of laborers for cultivation and harvesting of royal lands. In fact, Murray (1963: 60) explained the conundrum farmers found themselves in trying to meet these demands as well as tending for themselves. "The Crown had of course large estates, but the greater part of the land was in private hands. This was now registered with great exactness and was placed under the control of the State, whether it was arable land, orchards, vineyards, or even gardens. In practice the result was that all landholders merely leased their land from the State, with this anomaly, that the lessee was bound to the land but the State could dismiss the tenant at will. The farmer was forced to remain at the place where he was registered; and for permission to work his farm he had to cultivate the land, sow, reap, and transport his crop at his own expense. The state made a pretense of regarding the house and the agricultural implements as the private property of the farmer, but it could at anytime sell them up as payment to itself for arrears of taxes."

From the earliest times the king was associated with the inauguration of some public works. These ranged from digging or opening the irrigation canals, dykes, basins and, even an artificial lake. These water-troughs ran parallel to the Nile and would trap the inundated water when the river retreated. The trapped water was used in time of need to decrease the long wait until the next inundation. Therefore, the pharaoh's role in the ceremonial opening or construction of these facilities became important. Maspero (1926: 44) offers the view: "An early bas-relief, now at Oxford shows one of the kings of the Archaic Period, in full state, pick in hand, breaking the sod for a new canal or some public work, while an attendant holds a basket." Wilson (1975: 62) adds regarding the interest of the king, since: "His government had a definite interest in the annual height of the Nile and the consequent prosperity of the land. The early royal annals give a measurement for each year, which can only be the height of the River above or below some fixed datum. Prosperity belonged to the Pharaoh and had to be credited to his divine activity on behalf of his land; adversity was probably ascribed to the hostile activity of other gods, whom the Pharaoh would have to propitiate in order to rescue his land."

FREDERICK MONDERSON

Research Essays 113. Edfu Temple of Horus the Falcon. Defaced King and his Queen make a Presentation to falcon image of the Temple while Horus stands before them in Double Crown.

Digging and maintenance of irrigation canals and embankments were a part of the corvee system. Kees (1977: 52-53) points out the importance of this function in the creation of a title with requisite responsibilities. "The fertile Nile mud, which is nevertheless poor in nitrogen content, collected in these 'basins.' One of the oldest administrative titles in the nomes of Lower Egypt and one which was later to be held in high esteem as an historical survival was that of 'canal-digger.' The official bearing this title was certainly empowered by virtue of his appointment to conscript temporary labor for such work. He is the predecessor of the historical nomarch; while the *Strategos*, his descendant in Graeco-Roman times was far more occupied with irrigation works than with military affairs." The priests, on the other hand, ritualized the ceremony in a way of blessing the enterprise and to ensure its success.

The importance of maintaining the canals, dykes, and embankments in a workable state should be mentioned. This irrigation helped to create a checkerboard pattern of stored water running vertical and horizontal to the Nile. As such, Maspero (1926: 45) explained: "The ancient canals were generally straight, but occasionally some slight irregularity in the ground would turn them out of their course, and they would form immense curves. The dykes that traverse the plain intersect the canals at intervals and divide the valley into basins, which retain the water during the months of the inundation. These dykes are generally of earth, though sometimes of baked brick, as in the province of Girgen. The embankment at Kosheish is very exceptional; it is constructed of worked stone, and was made by Menes, the first king of the First Dynasty, for the benefit of his new city of Memphis. This system of dykes began near Silsilis, and extended to the sea, keeping close to the Nile throughout its course, except at Beni Suef, where it threw out an arm in the direction of the Fayum. It crossed the rocky barrier of the Libyan Mountains near Illahun and sinuous gorge, which possibly was artificially deepened and then widened into a fanlike network of many ramifications. The inundation retreated after having watered the province and the water nearest the Nile returned by the way it came, while the remainder found its way into a series of lakes, the largest which is known to-day as the Birket el Karun." These measures extended the arable land space under cultivation. This feature also served as a waterway for light sailing craft that could move people and supply inland. They provided useful water when the Nile's volume was low. There was also a tax for passage across such lands owned by the king.

Petrie (1923: 62-63) informed further: "There were taxes on the river traffic, on all that went up the Nile at Schedia, north of Alexandria, and on the products of the south where they passed Hermopolis. These are much like the Khedivial River tolls at the railway bridges, which were put on to drive trade to the railways. Goods brought in from the Red Sea were met by a duty at the entry on the Nile valley. The tariff of Koptos has been preserved and shows that the tax was farmed out here, and needed to be placed on public record to prevent extortion. The dues were mainly personal, on Red Sea sailors, and on women, mostly only of few shillings, and trivial taxes on conveyance."

Just as any other aspect of government disappeared during the intermediate periods, breakdown in central administration, taxes and the whole collection paraphernalia associated with it also suffered.

At the end of the Old Kingdom the malady of disorganization affected taxes. Wilson (1975: 107) paints a picture of the anarchy that ensued in the First Intermediate Period and quotes the Prophet Ipu-wer. The wise man is quoted as saying: "Why really, the land spins as does a potter's wheel. The robber is (now) the possessor of riches .... Why really, all maidservants make free with their tongues. When their mistresses speak, it is burdensome to the servants .... Why really, the ways [are not] guarded roads. Men sit in the bushes until the benighted (traveler) comes, to take away his burden and steal what is upon him. He is presented with blows of a stick and slain wrongfully .... Ah, would that it were the end of men, no conception, no birth! Then the earth would cease from noise, without wrangling! ... Why really, the children of nobles are dashed against the walls. The (once) prayed-for children are (now) laid out on the high ground .... Behold, noble ladies are (now) cleaners, and nobles are in the workhouse. (But) he who never slept on a plank is (now) the owner of a bed .... Behold, the owners of robes are (now) in rags. (But) he who never wove for himself is (now) the owner

FREDERICK MONDERSON

of fine linen .... If three men go along a road, they are found to be two men: it is the greater number that kills the lesser .... All these years are civil strife: a man may be slain on his (own) roof, while he is on the watch in his boundary house."

Again, Wilson (1975: 107-08) continued, mentioning the Prophet Nefer-rohu who added: "This land is helter-skelter, and no one knows the result .... I show thee the land topsy-turvy. That which never happened has happened. Men will take weapons of warfare, so that the land lives in confusion. Men will make arrows of metal, beg for the bread of blood, and laugh with the laughter of sickness .... I show thee the son of a foe, the brother of an enemy, and a man killing his (own) father. Every mouth is full of 'Love me!' and everything good has disappeared .... Men take a man's property, away from him, and it is given to him who is from outside. I show thee the possessor in need and the outsider satisfied .... I show thee the land topsy-turvy .... I show thee the undermost on top .... It is the paupers who eat the offering-bread, while the servants jubilate .... The land is completely perished, so that no remainder exists, not (even) the black of the nail survives from what was fated."

Research Essays 114. Edfu Temple of Horus the Falcon. As the King prepares to incense the Goddess he looks to his rear at Anubi figures holding aloft an image of the God.

These conditions naturally impacted on the tax-collection process and Wilson (1975: 108) explained this further by saying: "For one thing, they are talking about the breakdown of that central government in which the god-king was accepted as all-powerful. That cherished mystery of the divine nature of the pharaoh had been

RESEACH ESSAYS ON ANCIENT EGYPT

cheapened through competition for rule. 'Behold now,' said Ipu-wer, 'it has come to a point where the land is despoiled of the kingship by a few irresponsible men. Behold now, it has come to a point where (men) rebel against the (royal) uraeus, which made the Two Lands peaceful. Behold, the secret of the land, whose limits are un-know (able), is laid bare. The Royal Residence may be razed within an hour …. The secrets of the King of Upper and Lower Egypt are laid bare.' This is still highly symbolic language, but Ipu-wer makes himself clearer: 'Why really, Elephantine, the Thinite nome, and the [shrine] of Upper Egypt do not pay taxes because of [civil] war …. What is a treasury (good) for without revenues?' Such taxes as are paid are raided by anybody from the government treasury: 'The storehouse of the king is a (mere) come-and-get-it for everybody, and the entire palace is without its taxes.' Nefer-rohu points out that fewer tax-paying sources mean a heavier burden on those who are left to the palace: 'The land is diminished, (but) it's administrators are many; bare, (but) it's taxes are great; little in grain, (but) the (tax)-measure is large, and it is measured to overflowing.'"

Research Essays Papyrus Art 13. Tutankhamon sits enthroned and being attended by his queen.

FREDERICK MONDERSON

Research Essays 114a. Native Egyptian Antiquities Guide Shawgi Abed El Rady stands beside the back wall in the "Corridor of Victory" at Edfu Temple.

Nonetheless, by the time of the XVIII Dynasty taxes for the general masses were more widespread and extensive. The power and size of the temple holdings, however, had expanded, yet their tax-exempt status remained in effect. The period of imperial expansion intensified into Nubia, Palestine and Syria. The end result was a massive inflow of wealth to the state, which gave ever-increasing amounts

RESEACH ESSAYS ON ANCIENT EGYPT

to the temples and priesthood. Gardiner (1961) (1974: 296-97) adds to the discussion on taxation by mentioning: "The great Wilbour papyrus in the Brooklyn Museum, dated in year 4 of Rameses V, is a genuine official document of unique interest. Its main text records in four consecutive batches covering a few days apiece the measurement and assessment of fields extending from near Crocodilopolis (Medinet el-Fayum) southwards to a little short of the modern town of El-Minya, a distance of some 90 miles. The fields, of which the localization and the acreage are given in every case, are classified under the heads of the different land-owning institutions, these proving to be the great temples of Thebes, Heliopolis, and Memphis, then after them a number of smaller temples mainly in the vicinity of the plots owned by them, and lastly various corporate bodies too different and too problematic to be mentioned here. These assessments are reckoned in grain and clearly refer to taxes; they are presented in two distinct categories, according to the owning institutions were themselves liable or as the liability rested upon the actual holders or cultivators of the soil. The latter type of paragraph is the more interesting since it names a multitude of different properties or tenants, including whole families, men of Sherden race, and sometimes even slaves; in one singe paragraph, for example, we find side by side, dependent upon the temple of Sobk-Re of Anasha and localized near a place named the Mounds of Roma, plots each of ten arouras occupied by the well-known overseer of the treasury, Kha'emtir, by a certain priest, by temple-scribe, another scribe, by three separate soldiers, by a lady, and lastly by a standard-bearer."

The Treasury Department, under the Vizier and an extensive host of officials was busy by the New Kingdom. These administrators managed the numerous storehouses, granaries and stables of the state. The taxes they collected were in turn redistributed. This satisfied the state's obligations of wages, etc., due "in kind" produce.

Maspero (1926: 42-43) offers commentary on civil architecture designed as storehouses of collected tax revenue. This form of architecture could be found throughout the land since taxable revenue collection occurred at both the civil and religious structures. "Taxes were collected in kind, and Government officials were paid on the same system. Monthly distributions were made to the workpeople of corn, oil, and wine, while from end to end of the social scale, each functionary, in return for his services, received cattle, stuffs, manufactured goods, and certain qualities of copper or precious metals. It was, therefore, necessary that the fiscal authorities should have command of vast storehouses for the reception of the taxes demanded of the people. Each class of goods had its separate quarter walled in, and protected by vigilant guards. There were large stables for the cattle; cellars where the amphorae were piled in regular layers or hung in rows on the walls, each with the date of the vintage written on the side; and oven-shaped granaries where the grain was poured in through a shuttered opening in the roof, and taken out through a trap near the ground."

FREDERICK MONDERSON

Again, Maspero (1926: 43) mentions such remains discovered by archaeologists. "At Thuku (identified with Pithom by M. Naville) the store-chambers are rectangular, of various sizes, and have no direct connection with each other; the wheat was both put in and taken out at the top."

"At the Ramesseum the thousands of Ostraca and jar-stoppers scattered over the place prove that the ruinous brick buildings immediately behind the temple contained the stores of wine belonging to the god. These chambers are long vaulted passages placed closely side by side, and were originally surmounted by a platform. Philae, Ombos, Daphnae, and most of the frontier towns of the Delta possessed store-houses of this kind, and many more will be discovered when a systematic search is made for them."

Research Essays 115. Edfu Temple of Horus the Falcon. Second part of the previous frame where the image of the God is hoisted by Anubi-like figures.

The Pharaohs of the New Kingdom seized lands in Nubia as far as the third through sixth cataracts. Here the Nubian goldfields were located. A Viceroy or "Prince of Kush and Overseer of the Southern Lands" was appointed to administer this region. J.A. Wilson's book *The Culture of Ancient Egypt*, explained the Prince of Kush's domain extended from: "El Kab in Upper Egypt to the Southern frontier of the Empire which, from the time of Thutmose III was located in the District of Karoy, in the region of Napata."

The Viceroy's functions were extensive. They included the exploitation of the mines, the encouragement of free flow of trade and stamping out any forms of

RESEACH ESSAYS ON ANCIENT EGYPT

rebellion. From this area would be sent to the Treasury Department at Thebes: "Gold, either in the form of dust packed in sacks or in the rings which were the nearest approach to coin known to the ancient Egyptians; various kinds of cattle; male and female slaves; and the ships laden with ivory, ebony, and every other beautiful product of the land in addition to the yield of the harvest."

A similar kind of duty was imposed on the lands to the north, Palestine and Syria.

From Palestine came useful wood, the conifers, which were highly valued in an almost treeless Egypt. Here they were used for "buildings and manufacture of large and small articles of furniture, chests, small dishes and the like." It was an impressive sight, according to Wilson, when the: "Chiefs of Retenu and all the northern lands came from the ends of the earth, bowing in humility, bearing their tribute on their backs." Wilson continued, mentioning how pictures of tribute bearing foreigners became a: "favorite subject chosen for the wall paintings used in the decoration of their tombs by the dignitaries in charge of the reception of the tribute."

More importantly, however, was the tribute from Syria. From this region the payment included "male and female slaves who were assigned to work in the construction of temples and public buildings or to labor in mines and quarries; horses and chariots; great numbers of all kinds of cattle, sheep and goats."

In addition, the tribute from the "north-land" of Syria included "rarer animals such as elephants and bears; incense, oil, wine and honey; ivory and desirable metals, including gold, copper and lead; semi precious stones, especially lapis lazuli and rock crystal." The tax also numbered countless manufactured products of Syrian craftsmanship, including gold and silver pitchers, some of which were remarkably executed in the form of animal heads."

Therefore, taxation provided a significant source of revenue in ancient Egypt. In its management, a huge bureaucracy grew up around it. These early civil servants were paid in kind. What is more important, however, is the effective administration of the system.

FREDERICK MONDERSON

Research Essays Papyrus Art 14. Ma'at kneels before enthroned Hathor in Queen Mother Crown comprising a vulture headdress, and atop a mortar, horns and a sun disk.

Therefore taxation began a whole history of African administrative functions in major social systems of this and other societies. Thus, it is clear, when given a chance, Africans can administer large bureaucratic systems.

In this, Breasted (1923: 237-38) offers the view: "The great object of government was to make the country economically strong and productive. To secure this end, its lands, now chiefly owned by the crown, were worked by the king's serfs, controlled by his officials, or entrusted by him as permanent and indivisible fiefs to his favorite nobles, his partisans and relatives. Divisible parcels might also be held by tenants of the untitled classes. Both classes of holdings might be transferred by will or sale in much the same way as if the holder actually owned the land. The people of both classes held other royal property, like cattle and asses, subject, like the lands, to an annual assessment for its use. For purposes of taxation all lands and other property of the crown, except that held by the temples, were recorded in the tax-registers of the White House, as the treasury was still called. All "houses" or estates and the "numbers belonging thereto were entered in these registers. On the basis of these, taxes were assessed. They were still collected in naturalia: cattle, grain, wine, oil, honey, textiles and the like. Besides the cattle-yards, the 'granary' was the chief sub-department of the White House, and there were innumerable other magazines for the storage of its receipts. All the

RESEACH ESSAYS ON ANCIENT EGYPT

products, which filled these repositories, were termed 'labor;' the word employed in ancient Egypt as we use 'taxes.' If we may accept Hebrew tradition as transmitted in the story of Joseph, such taxes comprised one fifth of the produce of the land. It was collected by the local officials, whom we have already noticed, and its reception in and payment from the various magazines demanded a host of scribes and subordinates, now more numerous than ever before in the history of the country. The chief treasurer at their head was under the authority of the vizier, to whom he made a report every morning, after which he received permission to open the offices and magazines for the day's business."

Research Essays 116. Edfu Temple of Horus the Falcon. With multiple images above, the King gestures to an image of a falcon with seated divinities and (below) the King Presents to a falcon and the God aloft with lions in attendance as the Queen sports the Red Crown with Hathor patting her back.

Even further, Breasted (1923: 238-39) continued: "The collection of a second class of revenue, that paid by the local officials themselves as a tax upon their offices was exclusively in the hands of the viziers. The southern vizier was responsible for all the officials of Upper Egypt in his jurisdiction from Elephantine to Siut; and in view of this fact, the other vizier doubtless bore a similar responsibility in the North. This tax on the officials consisted chiefly of gold, silver, grain, cattle and linen; the mayor of the old city of El Kab, for example, paid some 5,600 grains of gold, 4,200 grains of silver, one ox and one 'two year old' into the vizier's office every year, while his subordinates paid 4,200 grains of silver, a bead necklace of gold, two oxen and two chests of linen. Unfortunately the list from which these numbers are taken, recorded in the tomb of the vizier Rekhmire at Thebes, is too mutilated to permit the calculation of the exact total of this tax on all the officials under the jurisdiction of the southern vizier; but they paid him annually at least some 220,000 grains of gold, nine gold necklaces, over 16,000 grains of silver, some forty chests and other measures of linen, one hundred and six cattle of all ages and some grain; and these figures are short by probably at least twenty per cent. of the real total. As the king presumably received a similar amount from the northern vizier's collections, this tax on the officials formed a stately sum in the annual revenues. We can unfortunately form no estimate of the total of all revenues."

Still, Breasted (1923) offers even more: "Of the royal income from all sources in the Eighteenth Dynasty the southern vizier had general charge. The amount of all taxes to be levied and the distribution of the revenue when collected were determined in his office, where a constant balance sheet was kept. In order to control both income and outgo, a monthly fiscal report was made to him by all local officials, and thus the southern vizier was able to furnish the king from month to month with a full statement of prospective resources in the royal treasury. The taxes were so dependent, as they still are, upon the height of the inundation and the consequent prospects for a plentiful or scanty harvest, that the level of the rising river was also reported to him. He held also all the records of the temple estates, and in the case of Amon, whose chief sanctuary was in the city of which the vizier was governor, he naturally had charge of the rich temple fortune, even ranking the High Priest of Amon in the affairs of the god's estate. As the income of the crown was, from now on, so largely augmented by foreign tribute, this was also received by the southern vizier and by him communicated to the king. The great vizier, Rekhmire depicts himself in the gorgeous reliefs in his tomb receiving both the taxes of the officials who appeared before him each year with their dues, and the tribute of the Asiatic vassal-princes and Nubian chiefs."

RESEACH ESSAYS ON ANCIENT EGYPT

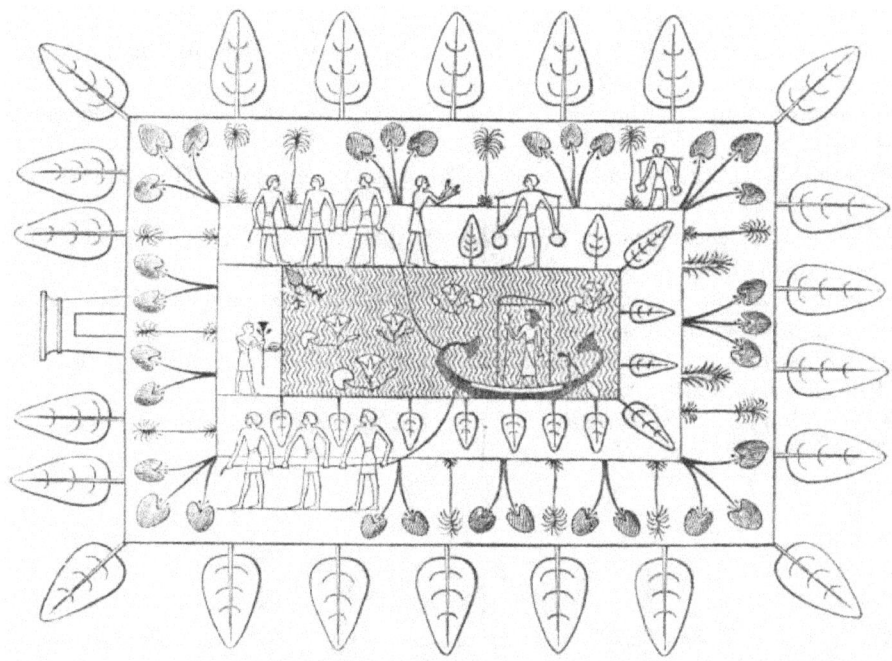

Research Essays Illustration 115.　Pleasure-boat towed round a pond.　Thebes.

Thus, we see, taxation, taxes and methods of collection and subsequent disbursement, played a significant role in the society of ancient Nile Valley Egypt. It helped in the administration of the country, helped ensure its economic production and viability, and established parameters that were easily duplicated throughout history.　This is another significant contribution that Africa has bequeathed to the world and its implications for societal growth and advancement has been phenomenal. Hence, the old adage, "There's taxes, taxes and more taxes" finds its origins in ancient Africa.　Perhaps one of the songs the boatman sang when he sailed the majestic Nile River was probably an earlier version of the famous adage: "Taxes, Death and Trouble."

References

Aldred, Cyril. *The Egyptians*.　London: Thames and Hudson, (1961) 1987.
Breasted, James H. *A History of Egypt*. New York: Charles Scribners' Sons, (1905) 1923.
Gardiner, Alan. *Egypt of the Pharaohs*. New York: Oxford University Press, (1961) 1974.
Gillings, Richard J. *Mathematics in the Time of the Pharaohs*. New York: Dover Publications Inc., (1972) 1981.

FREDERICK MONDERSON

Kees, Hermann. *Ancient Egypt: A Cultural Topography*. Chicago: The University of Chicago Press, (1961) 1977.

Maspero, Gaston. *A Manual of Egyptian Archaeology*. New York: G. Putnam's Sons, 1926.

Murray, Margaret. *The Splendor That Was Egypt*. New York: Hawthorn Books, Inc., (1949) 1963.

Petrie, W.M.F. *Social Life in Ancient Egypt*. Boston/New York: Houghton Mifflin Company, 1923.

Yoyotte, Jean in Georges Posener's *A Dictionary of Egyptian Civilization*. London: Methuen and Co., Ltd., 1963.

Weigall, Arthur E.P. *A Guide to the Antiquities of Upper Egypt*. New York: The MacMillan Co., 1910.

Wilson, John A. *The Culture of Ancient Egypt*. Chicago: The University of Chicago Press, (1951) 1975.

Research Essays 116a. Edfu Temple of Horus the Falcon. Pharaoh offers two vases to Amon as Min while Horus sits enthroned with Isis at his rear who seems to be saying "I've got your back, Brother."

RESEACH ESSAYS ON ANCIENT EGYPT

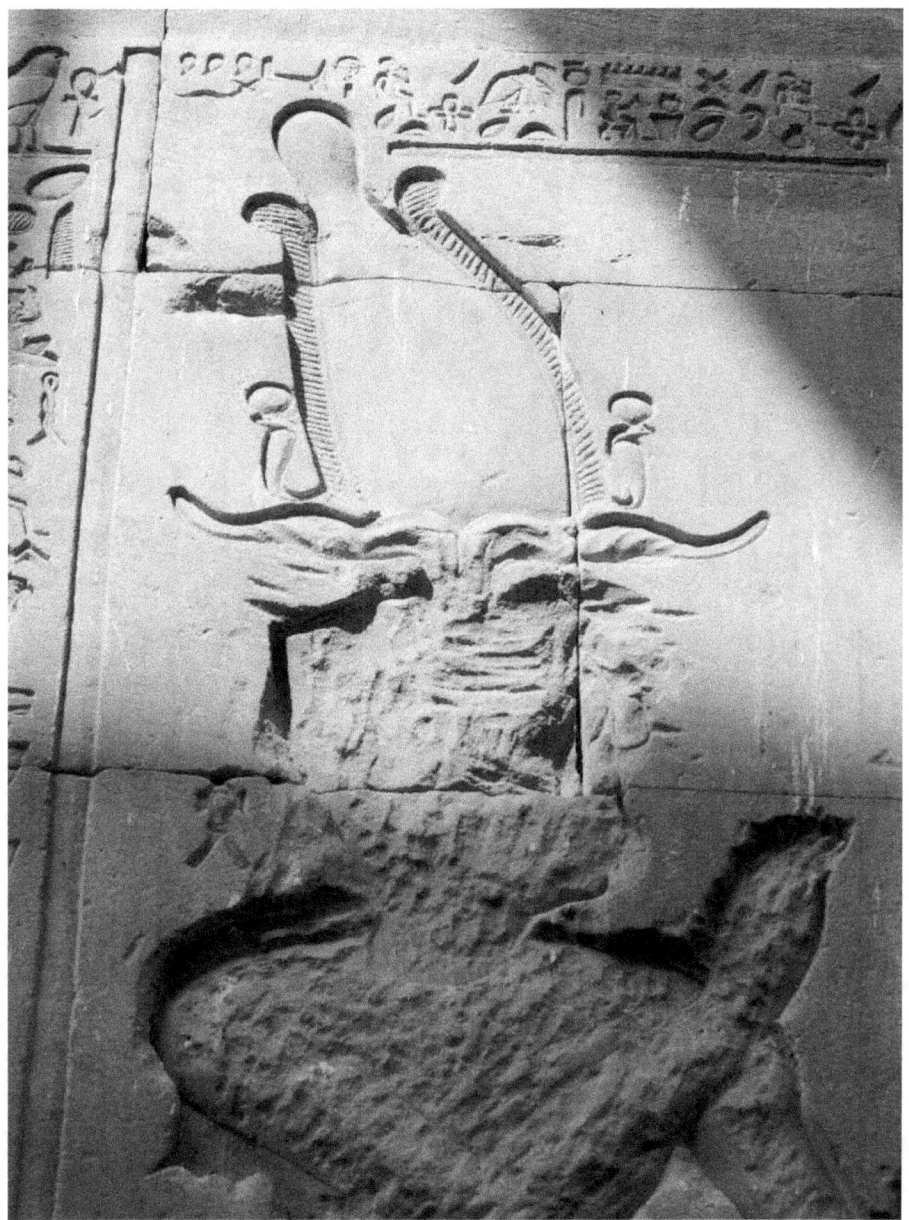

Research Essays 116b. Edfu Temple of Horus the Falcon. Defaced figure wearing the Osiris Crown with horns, White Crown with feathers and Uraei with disks.

FREDERICK MONDERSON

Research Essays 116c. Edfu Temple of Horus the Falcon. Colossal figure of Horus wearing the Double crown and holding scepter and ankh.

RESEACH ESSAYS ON ANCIENT EGYPT

19. PHARAOH THEN AND NOW
BY

Dr. Fred Monderson

The position of Egyptian head of state has been powerful and influential for the longest; yet still, different from ancient to modern times. Whereas, in ancient times, the ruler of Egypt was considered the Son of god, he himself a God on earth; in modern times, some have argued that individual has thought himself a god. While in ancient times, pharaoh was powerful, he was also benevolent. In ancient times his benevolence towards his subjects, was shaped and dictated by his being answerable to the higher gods; in modern times the all-powerful ruler was answerable to no one. The ancient king ruled through a divine mandate whereas that he be shepherd to his people; the modern ruler established the parameters of his power through a ruthless apparatus that checked the aspiration of his people.

An even fuller understanding of the role of the ancient ruler is mentioned in "Kingship: Kingship in the Ancient Mediterranean World" by Cristiano Grollanelli (1987) and Pietro Mander (2005) in *Encyclopedia of Religion* (2nd Edition) by Editor-in-Chief Lindsay Jones, Vol. 8, New York: Thomson/Gale, 2005: 5163) who saw the king as "one who would fulfill the concept of *maat*, thereby annihilating *isfit* at the same time. The word maat conveys the idea of an all-pervading cosmic order: it is the principle according to which the universe had been created. The world lost touch with this principle, and therefore no longer corresponded to its original state of order. The opposite of *maat*, *isfit* (defect) conveys the sense of disorder that comes into being wherever and whenever the relationship with the creator principle is lost: illness, crime, misery, war, lies – everything, in short, that makes history – are all episodes of *isfit*. The pharaoh, helped by the two cosmic forces *sia* (knowledge) and hu (word), can restore the primeval "wealth" that conforms to *maat*. He is, consequently, one of the three poles of a triad formed with the god and the concept *maat*. When he identifies himself with the latter, he becomes 'one with the god,' and his will cannot but be good."

Thus, to accomplish this state of goodness, in ancient times the king was assisted by a noble class and bureaucrats who administered a social order dictated by the principles of *maat*, viz., balance, justice, fairness, order, social equilibrium; in modern times, with no similar "accountability to a higher authority," "kingly counterparts bilked the people" systematically through systems of nepotism, cronyism and corruption while employing a system of repressive measures.

FREDERICK MONDERSON

With the exception of a couple of ancient work actions, for non-payment of just dues; nothing from this time compares with the modern revolutionary uprising of the people against the establishment as we witnessed recently in Egypt. Again, the king was he who made the "realization of *maat* possible. As the opponent of *isfit*, the pharaoh was also the defender of the poor."

As such, these two examples characterize loving benevolence and arrogant omnipotence in rule from the same seat of power at different times. However, while a comparison with modern development in that nation has just been sketched, this essay concerns the King in Ancient Egypt, as such …

To begin, sometime around 3200 B.C., using the "short chronology," Narmer, king of Upper Egypt began the earliest systematic mobilization of a military force, sailed north and conquered Lower Egypt, and unified the state of Kemet, Tawi, today's Egypt. Now, while the White Crown as kingly paraphernalia characterized the Upper Kingdom; and the Red Crown that of the Lower Kingdom; Narmer chose a red and white Double Crown to symbolize a unified land. His title thus became King of Upper and Lower Egypt.

Dispensing prerogatives to loyalists, he established a noble class that assisted and supported a monarchical system upon which their social status depended. Narmer consolidated the military, established the structure of its machinery and utilities of its weaponry. Next he consolidated the position of the old gods then built them temples, establishing principles for their worship and endowment; to which he himself adhered. Now, having established peace, security and justice in the land; the three classes of nobles, professional bureaucrats and common people, free and slave, prospered in the pursuit of economic, cultural, artistic and scientific endeavors because the order believed in a system of judgment in the afterlife. Thus, maintaining heavenly and earthly equilibrium, society's wealth from top to bottom expanded and all benefitted.

In contrast, according to modern claims, that ancient workable model was reversed, so much so, those in the lowest rungs of the social order often felt themselves on a treadmill, struggling, while predominantly wealth flowed upward enriching the ruler and those in association and alignment with his and their aspirations.

RESEACH ESSAYS ON ANCIENT EGYPT

Research Essays 117. Edfu Temple of Horus the Falcon. Image of Thoth, God of writing and intellect as he does his recording.

In many discussions the question arises as to where and when the notion of kingship arose and what were the motivating principles of this phenomenon that has played such a significant role in statecraft and nation building from ancient to modern times. Even more, whether the origin is mortal or divine the impact on civilization's progress has been unquestioned. Nevertheless, now thanks to the University of Chicago's Bruce Williams' important "Qustul discovery," the question seems settled, the notion and actuality of kingship is African in origin, or more appropriately, Nubian. From the discovery at Qustul, Mr. Williams has been able to trace and date the world's earliest monarchy at c. 3400 B.C. or *Nile Year* 840. He showed that the paraphernalia of kingship found more than 200 years later in Egypt, viz., enthroned pharaoh with white crown, whip and flail, Serekh, palace facade, incense burner, Nile boat, etc., was first evident in Nubia centuries

FREDERICK MONDERSON

earlier. Such an occurrence confirms Prof. John Clarke's theory of the "rehearsal stage for civilization" that manifested itself two centuries later in Egypt. Therefore, the implications and manifestations of concomitant theology, cosmology, monarchy, religion and spirituality are clearly African; for this is where God first approached man in showing his unbounded love for humanity in a contract or covenant simply requiring recognition, worship and ritual. In this he conferred a tremendous responsibility on the conscience of this African man with the admonition to advance the cause of humanity within the construct of the fatherhood of god and the brotherhood of man.

Today, millennia later, the essence of that admonition seem the only ingredient helping keep lit the flame of human existence in a world now tremendously mechanical, calculated, selfish, greedy and punitive. Yet, the responsibility of guarding the destiny of the human family is a charge well borne within the humanistic bosom of the African. It is reflective of the first act, of that "first occasion," when the African was instructed to be the shepherd of his community, nation, and ipso facto, the future of humanity, in the metaphysical and spiritual interest of the gods.

In that divinely cosmological metamorphosis, the Gods first ruled, and then demi-gods apprenticed the king. In seeking to understand this phenomenon, Murnane (1983: 46) helps in untangling the mist of the relationship and responsibility of the monarch of this Nile Valley state. He wrote: "In theory, the king's position was simple. Although born a mortal and retaining throughout his life all the human frailties, he was infused with godly power from the moment the hereditary kingship passed to him. By virtue of this office he was a god on earth, the living nexus between the divine and mortal spheres of activity. He alone could effectively worship the gods, standing before them as a son to his parents. Through him, moreover, was maintained the cosmic harmony that the Egyptians called *Ma'at*. Of the ritual scenes carved on temple walls, one of the most frequently encountered is the representation of the king offering *Ma'at* - shown as a tiny seated goddess, with her characteristic feather headdress - to the gods; and sometimes - to emphasize the king's role as the guarantor of Ma'at - the hieroglyphs that make up the king's own name are substituted for the goddesses' image. To the ancient Egyptians, whose idea of right order was a blessed un-eventfulness in natural affairs, this was the ruler's most important function."

In support of this theological construct, a comparison and contrast was made with the other ancient nations. Here, Budge (1969, I: 3) expressed the view: "The Egyptians, however acted in a perfectly logical manner, for they believed that they were a divine nation, and that they were ruled by kings who were themselves gods incarnate; their earliest kings, they asserted, were actually gods, who did not disdain to lie upon earth, and to go about and up and down through it, and to mingle with men. Other ancient nations were content to believe that they had been brought into being by the power of their gods operating upon matter, but the

RESEACH ESSAYS ON ANCIENT EGYPT

Egyptians believed that they were the issue of the great God who created the universe, and that they were of direct divine origin. When the gods ceased to reign in their proper persons upon earth, they were succeeded by a series of demi-gods, who were in turn succeeded by the Manes, and these were duly followed by kings in who were enshrined a divine nature with characteristic attributes. When the physical or natural body of a king died, the divine portion of his being, i.e., the spiritual body, returned to its original abode with the gods, and it was duly worshipped by men upon earth as a god and with the gods. This happy result was partly brought about by the performance of certain ceremonies, which were at first wholly magical, but later partly magical and partly religious, and by the recital of appropriate words uttered in the duly prescribed tone and manner, and by the keeping of festivals at the tombs at stated seasons when the appointed offerings were made, and the prayers for the welfare of the dead were said."

This belief is again reinforced by Robert Bauval and Adrian Gilbert's *The Orion Mystery* (1995: 180) in their explanation that the Egyptians termed the time of the transition for the gods the first "golden age" or *Tep Zeti* which translates loosely as the "First Time." Herein, the Egyptians believed: "the system of cosmic order and its transference to the land of Egypt had been established a long time before by the gods. Egypt had been ruled by a race of gods for many millennia before it was entrusted to the mortal yet divine line of pharaohs. The pharaohs were the sacerdotal connection with the gods and, by extension represented the link with the First Time; they were the custodians of its established laws and wisdom. Everything they did, every action, every move, every decree had to be justified in terms of the First Time, which served as a sort of covenant of kingship, to abide by and to explain their actions and deeds. This was true not only for the king and his court but applied to all natural events: the movement of the celestial bodies, the unexplained phenomena of nature and the ebbing and rising waters of the Nile. It would not be an exaggeration to say that everything a pharaoh did was connected with the First Time; hence, the careful re-enactment of mythical events which could be either cosmic or secular or both combined in a duality by the power of symbols and rituals. It is not surprising that this blissful First Time was invariably referred to as the Time of Osiris."

FREDERICK MONDERSON

Research Essays 118. Cairo Museum of Egyptian Antiquities. A black goose. The Goose is also symbolic of Amon-Ra.

However, Mercer argued and Bauval and Gilbert (1995: 75-76) explained: "The dead king would be reborn as a star and that his soul was believed to travel into the sky and become established in the starry world of Osiris-Orion, the god of the dead and of resurrection: 'The Dog Star was identified with Sirius; Orion was identified with Osiris .... It is not surprising to find an identification of Osiris with Orion ... [for] one of the central themes of the Pyramid Texts was the complete identification of the dead king with Osiris ....'" Even more of an elaboration is provided by Petrie (1923: 36) who tells of a XIIth Dynasty description of the death of the king: "'the god entered his horizon, the king flew up to heaven and joined the sun's disc; the follower of the god met his maker. The palace was silenced and in mourning, the great gates were closed, the courtiers crouching on the ground, the people in hushed mourning.' Three thousand years later, it is said: 'Upon the death of a king the Egyptians generally lament with a universal mourning, rend their garments, shut up the temples, inhibit sacrifices, and all feasts and solemnities for the space of seventy-two days; they cast dust likewise upon their heads, and gird themselves under their breasts with a linen girdle; and thus men and women, two or three hundred sometimes in a company, twice a day go about singing mournful songs in praise of the deceased king ... they neither eat flesh, nor anything baked or heated by the fire, and abstain from wine and all sumptuous fare.'"

McMahan (1998: 40) adds also: "The Pyramid Texts make it clear that the pharaoh was expected, on his death, to become one of the stars. 'You shall bathe in the starry firmament .... The imperishable stars have raised you aloft. You shall reach the sky as Orion, your akh shall be as effective as Sothis; be powerful,

RESEACH ESSAYS ON ANCIENT EGYPT

having power; be strong, having strength; may your akh stand among the gods as Horus who dwells in Iru.' Sothis was the Egyptian name for Sirius the Dog Star. The brightest star in the heavens, every year it appeared below the horizon for 70 days, then reappeared in late June as the herald of the annual Nile flood."

In discussing this heavenly metamorphosis of the king upon his death, Petrie (1924: 85) says even further: "The soul of the king at death was believed to fly to heaven in the guise of a falcon. As the emblem of the king, it was always represented standing above the royal ka name; this was originally a figure of the wooden palace of a chief, with his name on the door, and the falcon-king within it was shown above, like the pattern inside a bowl being drawn resting on the top of it. The chief place of falcon worship was about the old capital of Southern Egypt, at Hierakonpolis and the neighboring Apollinopolis or Edfu. Other cities, from Philae on the south to Tentyra on the north, worshipped the hawk; below that, it was only sacred at Heliopolis in connection with the sun and Horus. Thus the worship was essentially southern. The bird continued to be honored until the Gnostic age, when it represented the souls of the just."

Now, with upon the king's death and burial, the coronation of the new king took place generally at New Year or on some important festival. Cristiano Grollanelli (1987) and Pietro Mander (2005: 5164) continued: "The ritual involved cultic practices in the dual shrines of the royal ancestral spirits of Pe and Nekhen, and it culminated in the placing of the two crowns of Upper and Lower Egypt on the pharaoh's head. A further important kingly ritual was the Sed festival, which took place once or several times during a pharaoh's reign. This renewal of the kingly power was held on the anniversary of the pharaoh's coronation. It included a procession; the offering of gifts to the gods; pledges of loyalty by the king; visits to shrines; the dedication of a field to the gods by the pharaoh, who twice ran across it in the four directions of the compass, first as king of Upper, then Lower Egypt; and the shooting of arrows by the king in these four directions, symbolically winning control of the whole universe."

FREDERICK MONDERSON

Research Essays 119. Cairo Museum of Egyptian Antiquities. One of two wooden statues of Tutankhamon dressed in gold and painted black to represent his color, in the living position.

Therefore, in that divine, demi-god, human coming of age, the King of Egypt came to inherit many hats throughout his lifetime, as Prince, Pharaoh, and "God." We know his protocols would later include 5 names, viz., *Horus, Golden Horus, Suten Bat, Two Ladies,* and *Son of Ra.* Yet, Dr. ben-Jochannan attributed 9 names to the king. The customary five; and also when the king functions as high priest, celebrating certain festivals, head of the army, and another, the "Prefect God." Of course he was also father of the nation. Still, there were others. In all this, the name "pharaoh," signifying "great house" (as we use "White House" to signify the President or the government) is not found used before the New Kingdom. In explaining this idea of protocol, Steindorff and Seele (1957: 84-85) give as an example of the king's five names, Thutmose III, who was the: "Horus: Mighty Bull, Appearing in Thebes; the Two Ladies: Enduring of Kingship; the Horus of gold: Splendid of Diadems; the King of Upper and Lower Egypt: Enduring of Form is Re [Menkheperre]; the Son of Re: Thoth is Born [Thutmose]." Of all these names, the last one alone was the original one which was given to the king at birth and by which he was known before the beginning of his reign; the other four were all adopted upon his accession to the throne and were often amplified by the addition of supplementary epithets in the course of his reign. In official intercourse and in letters addressed to him by foreign rulers, the king was addressed by the "Great name" which he bore as 'King of Upper and Lower Egypt' and which was enclosed when written in hieroglyphic, like the personal name given at birth as the 'Son of Re,' in an elliptical cartouche. In daily life there was a tendency to avoid the mention of the king by name; instead he was referred to by various titles or circumlocutions such as 'His Majesty' or the 'Good God,' while it was customary to say 'one commanded' for 'the king commanded.'"

Thus, in his multi-functionality and responsibilities the king became the embodiment of the nation, the good king, divine monarch, soul of the nation, the ancient precursor to "*L'etat, c'est, moi,*" which in fact he was. So much so, Diop (1974: 138) in his "Argument for a Negro Origin" notes: "The concept of kingship is one of the most impressive indications of the similarity in thinking between Egypt and the rest of Black Africa. Leaving aside such general principles as the sacrosanct nature of kingship and stressing one typical trait because of its strangeness, we shall single out the ritual killing of the monarch. In Egypt, the king was not supposed to reign unless he was in good health. Originally, when his strength declined, he was really put to death. But royalty soon resorted to various expedients. The king was understandably eager to preserve the prerogatives of his position, while undergoing the least possible inconvenience. So he was able to transform the fatal judgment into a symbolic one: from then on, when he grew old, he was merely put to death ritualistically. After the symbolic test, known as the 'Sed Festival,' the monarch was supposedly rejuvenated in the opinion of his people and was once again deemed fit to assume his functions. Henceforth, the 'Sed Festival' was the ceremony of the king's rejuvenation: ritualistic death and revivification of the ruler became synonymous and took place during the same ceremony."

Regarding this Deification of the King who "went to Osiris," and was sometimes worshipped alive in the Sed Festival, Petrie (1923: 16-17) says: "The earliest scene of it shows the king dressed in a close-fitting garment like Osiris, holding the flail and crook of Osiris, seated in a high shrine approached by steps. Before him are captives dancing in an enclosure. This is of Narmer-Mena. A little later, king Den is shown on the same high throne, and another crowned king is performing the

FREDERICK MONDERSON

ritual dance before him, which belongs to the coronation ceremonies. In the earlier scene is a woman seated in a covered litter. The apparent interpretation of it is that the king was deified as Osiris, and the successor married the heiress, was crowned, and performed the ritual dances. The tightly clad Osiride figures of the king are associated with Sed-festivals throughout history. The ending was that of the king's life; in African custom the kings were killed after a term of years, as in Ethiopia and now further south; then in historic times this was commuted to the Osirification of the king at the appointment of his successor, while he lived on to his natural death, as the living Osiris."

Petrie (1923: 17-18) identified and explained where evidence of this ceremony was found particularly in the vicinity at Thebes. "The chapel of Sonkh-ka-ra for the ceremony, with the cenotaph sarcophagus, and parts of the statue, were found on the top of one of the peaks at Thebes, and apparently another chapel, for Senusert II, stood on the highest rock at Lahun. An Osiride figure of one of the Mentuhoteps was found buried in a pit at Deir el Bahari, probably representing the burial of the king when he became Osiris. The period of this deification seems to have been connected with the end of a week of change of Sothis rising, or thirty years, and most of the dates of festivals known agree with this period. It was thus the Osirification at the Sed feast of Hatshepsut which constituted her apotheosis, and so gave rise to the worship of her, and to her statues, while she was still reigning. Under the Ptolemies, deification began in the sixteenth year of Philadelphus. Ptolemy Soter was deified after his death. In Roman times, the emperors had their own worship as chief of the state; this, and their deification after death, was purely Roman, but it would harmonize with their position in Egypt. More Egyptian in theory was the deification of the drowned Antinous as Osiris-Antinous 'worshipped there [in his temple] as a god by the prophets and priests of the South and of the North as well as the people of Egypt.' At Arsinoe there was a temple of Jupiter Capitolinus, where the birthdays of the Emperors of Rome were kept."

RESEACH ESSAYS ON ANCIENT EGYPT

Research Essays Illustration 116. A party of guests, to whom wine, ointment, and garlands are brought. Sweet-smelling cones are on their heads, as a sort of perfume ointment. From Thebes, and now in the British Museum.

Even further, Diop (1974: 38) continued: "The monarch, the revered being par excellence, was also supposed to be the man with the greatest life force or energy. When the level of his life force fell below a certain minimum, it could only be a risk to his people if he continued to rule. This vitalistic conception is the foundation of all traditional African kingdoms, I mean, of all kingdoms not usurped." This idea cannot be considered as applying to today's Egypt.

As an aside, regarding Mentuhotep II whose statue, discovered at Deir el Bahari in the Heb Sed mode, and as has been argued by "professors at the American University in Cairo, "he was painted black for the funerary ceremony" as opposed to W. Stephenson Smith's "black flesh." Tutankhamon is similarly painted "for the funerary ceremony."Evidence of the same black statue was found in the tombs of Seti I and Amenhotep III. Are we to believe these monarchs, returning to the divine essence of the source of their being, would "misrepresent themselves" by being painted "black?" Would they not portray their true color as the god met his god?

This notwithstanding, again Petrie (1923: 37-38) argued: "The theory of a divine kingship was thus greatly limited; but as the Egyptian did not consider his gods to be omniscient, or free of infirmities, there was little incongruity in accepting the royal divinity. Probably the greatest scope of the king was in his initiative; the regulations of affairs, the enterprise of public works, the management of foreign relations, all gave scope, and there is express mention of the king's initiative in Aahmes I building a memorial of Teta-shera, and Hatshepsut erecting her obelisks.

FREDERICK MONDERSON

Seti I also visited the mines, and gave orders for the cistern and temple at Wady Abad because he noticed the difficulty of the work there."

Research Essays 120. Cairo Museum of Egyptian Antiquities. The other statue of the boy-King that adorns the entrance to the gallery that houses his treasure.

Still, Williams' discovery aside and that of the Scorpion King, one of the earliest pictorial representations of Egyptian kingship comes from the *Narmer Palette*. Here Narmer is shown as a conqueror from Upper Egypt, the South. Diop described him as Theban, meaning similar in color to Mentuhotep, Aahmes-Nefertari, her husband-brother and son, Aahmes and Amenhotep I, Thutmose I, Tutankhamon, and the rest. In his first significant recorded act, the monarch

RESEACH ESSAYS ON ANCIENT EGYPT

subdued the North, Lower Egypt, and in a process of creating national harmony, united the two lands under one kingdom. However, while the double crown was composed of red and while (Lower and Upper) the pharaoh was King of Upper and Lower Egypt, the south having prominence in the political dispensation. On the *Narmer Macehead* we see the king enthroned with his wife, Queen Neithhotep, nearby. Their son Aha followed his father to the throne as Pharaoh. Narmer's victory ended the divisive and destructive pre-dynastic wars, established protocols of the monarchy and laid the groundwork for subsequent economic pursuits and other forms of harmony that encouraged constructive development in the state.

In awe of reverence and with his inherited powers, Narmer set up the monarchy as the form of government. Next, the administrative system that characterized the parameters of dynastic rule in Egypt was set up. As conqueror who led the army from the South, he also defined the nature and role of the army in internal and external relations. It is believed he also defined the type of weaponry the army used, and especially, the weapons and emblems we came to associate with the king. In addition, the *Bull Palette* and the *Libyan Palette* are some artifacts relating to the person and activities of the king.

In addition, more evidence of Egyptian kingship, besides the *Narmer Palette* and *Macehead*, comes from the various *King Lists*. Not that many, but those that have survived provide significant information enabling scholars to practically account for every ruler from Narmer to Cleopatra. While the lists for the most part are of the early dynasties, the later periods provide sufficient corroborating evidence that the entire history of the kings is clearly established. Ian Shaw and Paul Nicholson in the *Dictionary of Ancient Egypt* (1995: 152) mention: "Several such lists exist, although only that in the temple of Sety I (1294-1279 B.C.) at Abydos, listing seventy-six kings from Menes to Sety himself, remains in its original context. A second list, from the nearby temple of Rameses II (1279-1213 B.C.), is now in the British Museum, and an earlier example from the temple of Amun at Karnak, listing sixty-two kings from Menes to Thutmose III (1279-1425 B.C.), is now in the Louvre. The Sakkara Tablet, an example of a private funerary cult of the royal ancestors, was found in the tomb of a scribe called Tenroy; it lists fifty-seven rulers from the IST Dynasty until the reign of Rameses II. Another private example of king list was found in the tomb of Amenmessu at Thebes (TT373; c. 1300 B.C.), where the deceased is shown worshipping the statues of thirteen pharaohs."

Even further Shaw and Nicholson (1995: 53) continued: "The hieratic papyrus known as the Turin Royal Canon, compiled in the 19th Dynasty, and the basalt stele known as the Palermo Stone, dating from the end of the 5th Dynasty, are valuable records, although both are incomplete, much of the Turin Canon having been lost in modern times. There are also a few much briefer king lists, such as a graffito at the mining and quarrying site of Wady Hammamat, dated palaeographically to the 12th Dynasty (1985-1795 B.C.), which consists of the names of five 4th Dynasty rulers and princes." To this must be added the work of the Greek Egyptian priest Manetho (323-245 B.C.) who wrote a *History of Egypt* that has only survived in fragments commented on by ancient writers. His most lasting contribution however, has been the division of the History of Egypt into dynasties or rule by houses or families of kings. Gardiner (1974: 46) provides insights into Herodotus who was, of course, an earlier commentator on Egypt in his book, *The Histories*, c. 450 B.C., with Book II, *Euterpe*, devoted to Egypt. Then came Diodorus Siculus and the Jewish historian Josephus who flourished around A.D. 70, together with Sextus Julius Africanus (early 3rd century A.D.), and Eusebius (early 4th century A.D.) as well as the compiler George the Monk, known as Syncellus (c. A.D. 800) who all helped in the transmission of Manetho's works through their commentaries.

Nonetheless, at the early time of the Archaic Period of Dynasties I and II, the regalia of pharaonic protocols were many. These included crowns and insignia, the sacred symbol of the Uraeus upon the king's brow, together with whip, flail, crook, scepter, mace, sickle-shaped sword, and pectoral. Also, part of the pharaoh's insignia included a talisman, amulets, precious stones, magic jewels, necklaces, tunic, girdle, beard, tail, and sandals. Explaining this phenomenon, Erman (1894: 61) tells us: "The royal insignia were very complex even in the time of the Old Empire; in later times they were essentially the same, though more splendid in appearance. In the later period special importance was attached to the front piece of the royal skirt, which was covered with rich embroidery, uraeus snakes were represented wreathing themselves at the sides, and white ribbons appeared to fasten it to the belt. If, according to ancient custom, the Pharaoh wore nothing but this skirt, it was worn standing out in front in a peak, which was adorned with gold ornamentation. Usually, however, the kings of the New Empire preferred to dress like their subjects, and on festive occasions, they put on the long transparent dress under as well as the full over dress, the short skirt being then worn either over or under these robes."

All this notwithstanding, the crowns of Egypt were the embodiment of power. There were about 5 principal crowns, each for a specific purpose or region. In fact, there were actually 23 crowns listed at the temple of Hathor at Dendera. One each is on the eastern and western outer face of the temple and another on a column on entering the pronaos to the right. The crowns of Egypt included the Red Crown of the Lower Kingdom with its traditional religious capital at Behedet near Tell-el-Bel-Amon. Its heraldic plant was the papyrus. On the other hand, the White Crown represented the Upper Kingdom with the royal residence at Ombos near modern Naqada. It is generally thought the heraldic plant was the lotus. At unification the red and white crowns were united in the Red and White Double Crown, though they were worn individually at different times and occasions. Nonetheless, the entire repertoire of the king's insignia with the crowns remained constant throughout dynastic rule. Steindorff and Seele (1957: 84) explained the difference between the principal crowns worn by the king, each with its respective

RESEACH ESSAYS ON ANCIENT EGYPT

designation. "The royal headdress consisted of a whole collection of crowns: the white crown of Upper Egypt; the red crown of Lower Egypt; the double crown, a combination of the red and white crowns, which symbolized in the person of the king the 'uniter of the Two Lands' and therefore the ruler of all Egypt; the blue crown, a cap of cloth or leather which the king often wore on the battlefield; the linen kerchief which covered the head and extended in front over the shoulders and chest in two broad lappets, while it ended behind the head in a sort of queue hanging below the back of the neck."

All these items of royal paraphernalia represented the full panoply of pharaonic symbolism, each contributing to the esoteric, magical mystique of the King of Egypt, who was both man and god.

Today, however, the ruler simply wore a western-style suit.

In addition, the king had his personal priests and his family, viz., mother, sons, wives, daughters, harem, and noble companions who all had a role to play in the dynamics and totality of the king's responsibilities to the nation and the gods. The issues of the "players" surrounding the king were such, Erman (1894: 53-54) provides an interesting scenario of the dynamics of kingship amidst intrigue and statesmanship. He pointed out: "Around the king were the old counselors who had served his father, and whom the clerks and officials were accustomed blindly to obey, as well as the generals with the troops in their pay, and the priesthood with their unlimited power over the lower classes. In the small towns the old rich families of the nobility, residing in their countryseats, were nearer to the homes of the people than the monarch dwelling in his distant capital. The king was afraid to offend any of these powerful people; he had to spare the sensitive feelings of the minister; discover a way of gratifying the ambition of the general without endangering the country; watch carefully that his officers did not encroach on the rights of the nobility; and above all keep in favor with the priests. It was only when the king could satisfy all these claims, and understands at the same time how to play off one party against another, that he could expect a long and prosperous reign. If he failed, his chances were small for there lurked close to him his most dangerous enemies, his nearest relatives."

FREDERICK MONDERSON

Research Essays Papyrus Art 15. Tutankhamon and his wife out hunting in the marshes (left) and he being embraced by her (right).

This is interesting! Even further, Erman (1894: 54) continued: "There always existed a brother or an uncle, who imagined he had a better claim to the throne than the reigning king, or there were the wives of the late ruler, who thought it a fatal wrong that the child of their rival rather than their own son should have inherited the crown. During the lifetime of the king they pretended to submit, but they waited anxiously for the moment to throw off the mask. They understood well how to intrigue, and to aggravate any misunderstanding between the king and his counselors or his generals, until at last one of them, who thought himself slighted or injured, proceeded to open rebellion, and began the war by proclaiming one of the pretenders as the only true king, who had wrongfully been kept from the throne. The result was always the same; the others admired the boldness of their rival and hastened to imitate it, until there were as many pretenders as there were parties in the kingdom. It made little difference who won in the fight; he made his way to the throne through the blood of his opponents, and then began a struggle with those who had helped him. If he possessed good luck and energy he was able to clear them out of his way; otherwise he became a tool in the hands of those around him, who, at the first sign of independence, would cause him to be murdered and place a more docile ruler on the throne in his place."

RESEACH ESSAYS ON ANCIENT EGYPT

Research Essays 121. Cairo Museum of Egyptian Antiquities. Bronze plaque of the boy-King striking a lion.

He also had others with which to contend. For example, Rawlinson (1898: 288-89) pointed out how the kings were particularly fearful of their subjects, the priests. "The kings lived always in a considerable amount of awe of the priests. Though claiming a certain qualified divinity themselves, they yet could not but be aware that there were diverse flaws and imperfections in their own divinity - 'little rifts within the lute'- which made it not quite a safe support to trust to, or lean upon, entirely. There were other greater gods than themselves - gods from whom their own divinity was derived; and they could not be certain what power or influence the priests might not have with these superior beings, in whose existence and ability to benefit and injure men they had the fullest belief. Consequently, the kings are found to occupy a respectful attitude towards the priests throughout the whole course of Egyptian history, from first to last; and this respectful attitude is especially maintained towards the great personages in whom the hierarchy culminates, the head officials, or chief priests, of the temple which are the principal centers of the national worship - the temple of Ra, or Tum, at Heliopolis, that of Phthah at Memphis, and that of Ammon at Thebes. According to the place where the capital was fixed for the time being, one or other of these three high-priests had the pre-eminence; and, in the later period of the Ramesside, Thebes having enjoyed metropolitan dignity for between five and six centuries, the Theban High-Priest of Ammon was recognized as beyond dispute the chief of the sacerdotal order, and the next person in the kingdom after the king."

The dynamics of such intrigue aside, on the *Narmer Palette*, the king is shown with his sandal bearer. He is also shown smiting the enemy with his mace and as a true conqueror, with captives. The raised relief sculpture of the palette shows him as a colossal figure in relationship to his subjects. This colossal representation of the kingly person remained an art form throughout Egyptian history.

Once again, Williams' discovery aside, perhaps underscoring his relationship with the divine, Narmer established a shrine for the God Ptah at Memphis and began the official practice of religious worship and ritualization. Much of this became well established by the first and second Thinite Dynasties from *This*, near Abydos, also site of the "tomb of Osiris." *This* is the site where Petrie discovered 10-levels of temples dating back to the beginning of dynastic rule. He found evidence that Narmer of the first dynasty and Khufu of the fourth dynasty worshipped there.

Next, the king's role as builder was shown with several projects, including the major "white wall," he built at Memphis. After unification, for economic and strategic reasons, this city was chosen as the nation's new administrative capital. As Pharaoh he was responsible for the inspection of public works such as irrigation projects of canals, basins, embankments, wells and lakes. These contained the much-needed waters essential in Egypt after the Inundation Season. Records depict the king, after the first dynasty, inspecting the frontier and establishing his authority by "going round the wall" and "uniting the lands of Upper and Lower Egypt."

Consistent with his divine heritage and cognizant of the existence of good and evil, the head of the Egyptian state assumed the function of head of the army, chief administrator, and high priest who performed religious functions on behalf of the state.

RESEACH ESSAYS ON ANCIENT EGYPT

Research Essays 122. Cairo Museum of Egyptian Antiquities. Bronze plaque of the boy-King smiting his Nubian enemies who are painted black as he is shown previously.

According to the religious beliefs, these rituals were especially important. J. Manchip White's *Ancient Egypt* offers commentary that explains one of the roles and functions of the king. He wrote: "The enemy whose onslaughts Pharaoh resisted was not only the host of Libyans, Nubians, Beduins and Asiatics who lurked on Egypt's physical boundaries, but also the spiritual enemy in the shapes of Seth and Apophis." This cosmological belief held that the: "powers of darkness, though constantly vanquished, attempted ceaselessly to overthrow Egypt by blighting the crops, obstructing the flow of the Nile, causing floods or preventing the sun from rising." As such, the pharaoh unceasingly worshipped and ritualized the Gods or was in turn ritualized as their earthly manifestation. He was the Gods' "man on the ground," who did the earthly work for the divinities.

FREDERICK MONDERSON

To accomplish such an assignment by the king, or his assignees or subordinates, of placating the gods, and in comparative analogy, Petrie (1924: 25) comments on Clemens' view of "a temple in living order." He wrote: "The porticoes, vestibules and groves are constructed with great splendor; the halls are adorned with many columns; the walls are perfectly splendid with rare stones and brilliancy of color; the sanctuary shines with gold, silver and electrum, and with a variety of glittering stones from India or Ethiopia, and the adytum is hung with curtains of gold tissue. If you enter the circuit of the holy place, and, hastening to behold what is most worthy of your search, you seek, the statue of the deity, one of the priests, who performs the rites there, steps forward to introduce you to the object of his worship, looking upward with a grave and reverent fact, as he chants the paean hymn in the native tongue."

The ritual of the temple, generally practiced several times per day, remained essentially traditional and unchanged. Again, Petrie (1924: 28-29) explained how the ceremony was conducted throughout the day, with the king officiating as part of his functions as the Gods' representative on earth, or as a god worshipping himself as well as the other gods. "The whole course of daily service began with the series of actions each carried out with a long speech. This may not have been entirely aloud, as there are long prayers and adorations recited inaudibly by the priest in the Coptic service. So, anciently, much may have been recited mentally, or by "intention." First the incense was offered, to perfume the whole sanctuary. Then the priest opened the chapel and saluted the god with many protestations, and chanting hymns. Sand was sprinkled on the floor. Then the sacred vessels were taken, and the daily toilet of the god performed. Twice, water was sprinkled over the statue, which was then clothed in linen bands, white, green, red, and brown. Then the statue was anointed, and painted with green paint under the eyes, and black on the eyelids. Then the food was placed before the god. The food and the linen could next day be offered to the statues of dead persons, which were placed in the temple. Thus a man often secured his own offerings, and insured his own benefit by making an endowment to the god, which could not be revoked. The copying of domestic service is obvious. The house was fumigated, the floor sanded; then the master was awakened. He was washed, dressed, had the preservative eye paints put on, and then partook of his morning meal. Processions were the great external part of the worship. The barque of the god was carried, just as a noble was carried, on a stand supported on two long poles, which rested on the shoulders of the two rows of priests. At other times, it might be the emblem of the god, such as the sacred head of Osiris that was carried."

The idea of the king worshipping himself is generally considered a New Kingdom phenomenon. Perhaps it is Ramesside! We look for this at the Temple of Seti I at Abydos that is dedicated to multiple gods. In fact, the seven shrines are for the seven deities situated from right to left, Horus, Isis, Osiris, Ra Horakhty, Amon,

RESEACH ESSAYS ON ANCIENT EGYPT

Ptah and Seti deified. These were the gods of the Osiris cycle, Horus, Isis and Osiris; the three great gods of Egypt Amon, Ptah and Ra-Horakhty; and a deified Seti. After Hatshepsut's temple at Deir el Bahari, this is one of the first such surviving temples principally dedicated to multiple gods. Hatshepsut's temple at Deir el Bahari is dedicated principally to Amon and secondarily hosts Shrines to Hathor and Anubis, as well as having an altar to Ra-Horakhty. In addition, the Queen also had a chapel where she and Tuthmose I and Thutmose III were worshipped. However, Rameses II's temple at Abu Simbel is dedicated, again, to the three great gods of the New Kingdom, Amon, Ra-Horakhty, Ptah and that deified king Rameses II. Later, during Graeco-Roman times the surviving temple at Kom Ombo was dedicated to twin deities, Horus and Sobek. This latter and several other temples are dedicated to particular gods, or may have shrines to other deities but not the king. Karnak is a good example. It is a worship temple dedicated to the Theban Triad of Amon, Mut and Khonsu, though each had his own temple. Equally, there are a host of other deities worshipped there and that is why it is called the 'Palaces.' Still, though the kings built there at Karnak, no one king is worshipped at this shrine.

Research Essays Illustration 117. A party of guests entertained with music and the dance.

Even more, prior to Ramesside times, no king is shown being worshipped as a deified person. Nevertheless, Petrie (1924: 103-04) does, however, supply surviving Ramesside evidence of clear-cut examples of the king being worshipped as a god. He states: "The best evidence for the worship of the living king before Osirification is in the Harris papyrus where Rameses IV represents Rameses III as enjoining people to bow to Rameses IV, serve him always, adore him, implore him and magnify his goodness, as they do to Ra. As Rameses IV was under thirty years old at the time, he cannot yet have been Osirified, even as co-regent. There was a lesser claim of divine descent; this was enforced by each generation claiming direct divine paternity, by the father impersonating the god. The idea still continued to Greek times, as seen by the tales of their divine paternity of Alexander from Zeus Ammon, quoted by Plutarch and others and elaborated into a tale. The Persian conquerors were naturally disliked, yet Darius, 'while he was alive, gained the title of a god, which none of the other kings ever did; and when he was dead, the people allowed him all those ancient honors due and accustomed to be done to the former kings of Egypt after their deaths.'"

Further, records indicate, the "spiritual potency of the king, on which the well-being of his subjects depended, was enhanced by the purity of his breeding. Theoretically the actual blood of the sun god had been transmitted by Horus into the royal veins." This caused the priesthood, one of whose realm of concern was succession, to take great pains in ensuring prolific procreation for the Pharaoh. As far as possible, they permitted few marriages outside the royal family. This way divinity was kept "all in the family."

The Pharaoh ruled by *Ma'at,* a philosophy and social and ethical practice of justice. In the afterlife and in front of Osiris, Thoth, Anubis, Isis, and Nephthys he was judged based on his actions while on earth. So, he structured his rule to bring about the ideal - "Justice was defined as 'what Pharaoh loves,' wrongdoing as 'what Pharaoh hates.'" He was the rule of law in the state and the final refuge of appeal. Few cases, however, reached this level of litigation. That is because the judges were admonished to be fair, impartial and just, these matters were settled there. In contrast, in modern times the ruler controlled and dictated the judicial process to the absence of fairness and impartiality.

In time, Pharaoh Amenemhat III ruled in the Twelfth Dynasty, during the Middle Kingdom. A high official in his service spoke to his children and summed up what was a universal belief throughout Egypt regarding his master, as well as the symbol of Pharaoh. "'He is the God Ra whose beams enable us to see. He gives more light to the Two Lands than the sun's disc. He makes the earth more green than the Nile in flood. He is the Ka (i.e. the guardian spirit). He is the god Khnum who fashions all flesh. He is the goddess Bast who defends Egypt.'"

RESEACH ESSAYS ON ANCIENT EGYPT

Research Essays 123. Cairo Museum of Egyptian Antiquities. Part of the ushabti entourage Tutankhamon took with him to the otherworld.

Further, continued this source: "... whoever worships him is under his protection. But he is Sekhmet, the terrible lion goddess, to those who disobey him. Take care not to defy him. A friend of Pharaoh attains the rank of Honored One, but there is no tomb for the rebel. His body is thrown into the river. Therefore listen to what I tell you and you will enjoy health and prosperity.'"

Therefore, in order to understand how the king came to enjoy this status, respect and engendered such awe, we need to create a framework to examine why the Pharaoh came to epitomize the lifeblood of Egypt and Nile Valley cultural and philosophical experience. First, the religious character of the king is indicated in *Hastings Encyclopedia of Religion and Ethics*, Vol. VII (1915: 711-715) wherein is discussed the: "conception of monarchy which is composed of purely theological elements and based solely upon the assimilation of the king to the gods who are the makers of the world and the mythical founders of Egyptian society." Taken together, therefore, the names of the king in their totality, "constitutes the nature of the pharaoh and of the royal attributes."

The king's divine lineage extends deep into the prehistoric period. In this examination we find: "the old 'sky-god' source of life and death, of rain and heavenly fire. Among his names that of Heru symbolized conventionally by the hawk, has given rise to the so-called 'hawk names,' which appear among the most ancient forms of royal names with which we are acquainted - viz., the series of names from the monuments belonging to the Thinite period (1st and 2nd dynasties). These show when set in order, that the reigning king is a form or emanation upon this earth of the Supreme Being - or, more exactly one of the 'souls' of that being."

FREDERICK MONDERSON

In the theological evolution of the religious thought and practice, the 'sky god' was replaced by the 'sun god.'"

"When the king is called 'the two Horus,' or the 'Horu-Siti,' we see a reminiscence of the system which divided the world into two halves, each with its Supreme God, in heaven and on earth. Similarly, the religion of the sky-goddess Nuit, who was believed to have produced the world, first by her own activity and later by union with the earth-god Sibu, gave the king the name of 'son of Nuit,' or 'eldest son of Sibu.' This prepared the way for the assimilation of the Pharaoh to Ra, then to Osiris, according to the successive theologies reversing the order of the first cosmogonies, have made Ra the son of Nuit, or, on the other hand, the father of Sibu and Nuit, and the grandfather of Osiris. In the last form the Pharaoh is the successor of Osiris, as the direct descendant of Horus, son of the pair Isis-Osiris."

Even further, we learn an: "Outstanding characteristic of the king has always been that he was either an incarnation of the god who made the world or his son (in the literal sense of the word, not symbolically, or by a mystic adoption, but by real dilation). The king of Egypt has thus never been merely a representative or interpreter of the Supreme God, or his 'vicar;' either he is the god himself, manifest upon the earth in human body in which is incarnate one of the souls of the god, or he is the god's own son." The article continued: "This form of the affiliation best known to us is the title of Sa Ra, 'son of the sun,' which was inaugurated as early as the middle of the Vth dynasty, under the influence of the priesthood of Heliopolis, and persisted as long as the Pharaonic protocol was in existence."

"This divine descent was, as a rule, proved by the ordinary genealogy. From ancestor to ancestor, the reigning king was able to trace back his lineage to the fabulous Menes, or Mini, the legendary founder of the first human dynasty, and from him he went back through the mythical reigns of Menes as far as Horus, son of Isis, and son and avenger of his father Osiris, the first king-god of the valley of the Nile."

But in certain exceptional cases of which we possess three or four historical examples the king boasts of being procreated directly by the god. It's stated: "in order to establish legitimacy indisputably, the Pharaoh seems to have claimed the testimony of a more direct and recent intervention of the Supreme God. Thus (1) in the temple of Luxor for Amenhotep III, (2) in the temple of Deir-el-Bahari for Hachopsitu, and (3) at Erment for Caesarian, the bas-relief tell how the god himself descended to the earth in order to have union with the queen and himself beget the little prince who should one day reign over Egypt. They also show the birth of the divine scion, the magic charms which accompanied him, and the benediction of the god upon the new-born child when it was presented to him."

RESEACH ESSAYS ON ANCIENT EGYPT

"They felt that the kingship must be the final result of all that legendary Egypt had known of divine domination or, rather, that it meant the total heritage of all that the world contained of the forces belonging to the beneficent gods. Hence the walls of the temples show the king as heir and adopted son of all the great deities of the national pantheon in succession - the great feudal gods of the Nile Valley and the chief elementary or starry gods."

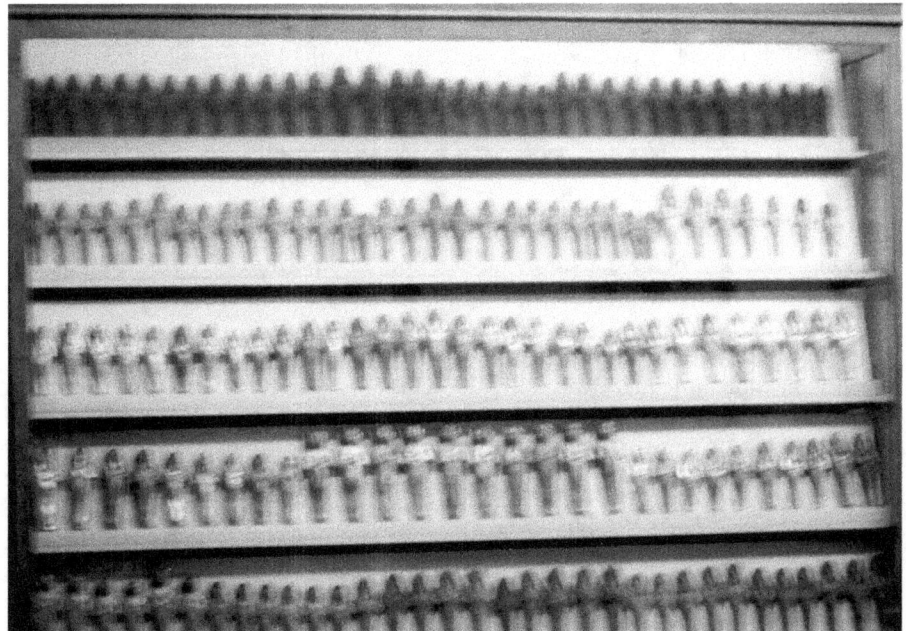

Research Essays 124. Cairo Museum of Egyptian Antiquities. More of the ushabti entourage Tutankhamon took with him to the next world.

The king is well-beloved son
He addresses the gods 'father'

"In the case of the goddesses, they make the young king their veritable son by giving him milk from their breast in token of adoption. Even this accumulation of divinity seemed insufficient to the Egyptians to constitute their god-king completely."

Still, the philosophical transformation is another issue facing the new king. Even more we are told: "The true Pharaoh does not exist, theologically speaking, until he has received at Heliopolis, all the magico-religious consecrations which transform him into a living incarnation of Ra, the sun-god, creator of the world. The elaborate series of ceremonies employed to accomplish that transformation is well known to us today through: (1) the historical inscriptions, such as that of the celebrated Ethiopian conqueror Piankhy, (2) the ritual published in the Pyramid texts, (3) the bas-reliefs and special enactments of the solar temples of Abusir, (4) the extracts from anointing and coronation scenes sculptured in the great temples, chiefly at Thebes, (5) the statues and statuettes commemorating coronations (notably at Karnak), and (6) the descriptive scenes telling of the 'jubilee' feasts of habsedu. Finally the Thinite monuments discovered at Abydos provide evidence that the whole of this ceremonial was already established, in its essential elements, at the Thinite period. Even under the 1st dynasty there appeared scenes of that distant epoch similar to those found in the Greek period upon the walls of the temple of Edfu or other sanctuaries built in Egypt by the Ptolemies."

THE ROYAL TITLES

The king, then, is a being constituted by all that, in this world, religion could know of divine forces, governing powers, magic resources, and super-terrestrial science.

"The king of Egypt had at least five names in the classical period: (1) 'birth-name,' which is his human name, expressing the relation of the reigning dynast to one or another of the great provincial gods of Egypt (e.g., Thuthmose = 'Thoth had fashioned him;' Amenhotep = 'he is united to Amen'); this is the name which is preceded by the epithet 'son of the sun' (Se Ra) in the inscriptions; (2) the coronation name, preceded by the affirmation of kingship over the world of the north and world of the south by the heraldic figuration of the Reed and the Bee; this name (chosen by the astrological colleges of priests according to horoscopic indications) materialized, somehow or other, the aspect and attributes of the particular solar soul that came to transform the young prince into a god on the day of his anointing; it was sometimes a long motto expressing the role or the energies of Ra in this world (e.g., 'Ra is the lord of the cosmos,' 'Great are the successive becomings of Ra'); (3) the hawk name (i.e. sky-god name; this was enclosed in a kind of panel or rectangle representing a facade of a palace, and surmounted by a hawk, divine Horu; (4) a name called in archaeology 'name of the vulture and uraeus,' which reached to the extreme frontiers of Egypt, from El Kab to Buto; (5) a name, often incorrectly called 'golden hawk name,' which, preceded by the figure of a hawk perched on a sign of gold (nub), declares in reality that the king is the heir to the stellar powers who share the two astrological halves of the universe."

RESEACH ESSAYS ON ANCIENT EGYPT

Research Essays 125. Cairo Museum of Egyptian Antiquities. Sphinx statue of Queen Hatshepsut.

Other names

Heir of the war-like gods, he is called "Powerful Bull" (*Nib iri khitu*), or "Resplendent in his glorious appearings' (*Nib khau*). Some of these names expressing the virtues or forces of the kingship bear a curious resemblance to those which describe (or designate) the kings of certain monarchies in black Africa (e.g. the sovereigns of Dahomey or Benin) and it would be worthwhile to draw up a list of the possible comparisons. None of these epithets should be regarded (as they too often are) as arising from vanity or grandiloquence, for each corresponds theologically to a very precise definition of a function or force belonging to one or other of the great gods of Egypt."

"Good god"

"Double Palace"

"Sublime Gate"

"Great Dwelling" (= the royal Residence), the equivalent of which is found in the royal title-list of certain black monarchies of W. Africa. The Egyptian term *pir-ao* has become the word 'Pharaoh,' which served throughout the classical world to designate the king of Egypt."

EARTHLY COUNTERPART OF GODS

The sovereign is a singularly complex person, whose body contains even more souls (*biu*), doubles (*kau*), and 'shadows' (*haibit*) than that of ordinary men.

These are frequently figured beings formed by the gods in heaven, or beings suckled at birth by the fairies, or accompanying the king (but distinct from him) in coronation and procession scenes.

The king is a living epitome of all that is divine in the Nile Valley.

"First, he is in every function an earthly image of the various gods, and performs their legendary activity on the earth. In his justice he is Thoth, in his power he is Ra; like the first divine masters of the divine valley, he destroys the enemies of the work done by the ancient gods when they assisted Ra in the conflict against darkness and in the organization of the .... This view, the very beginning of dualism originated in the primitive cosmogony, and was later transformed by the Osirian legend into the myth of the conflict between the partisans of Horus and the bad spirits who were the friends of Set. The Pharaoh is thus heir to the powers and qualities of the good gods, whose powers are symbolized by, and materialized in, the various names."

The organized theologies ascribed to the royal person a thousand different roles, implying a thousand traditional moral duties and magical powers. Some of these duties concern war, and perhaps may seem somewhat brutal for our taste; others are as noble as modern thought could desire. Scenes and texts display the king 'as a bull young, ardent, and resistless, which tramples down under its hoofs the enemies of Egypt' (*Hymn of Thuthmose* III), the 'rebels.' Some of the other names are, 'accursed;' the 'children of ruin;' as a 'devouring lion;' as a Sudan leopard; or

RESEACH ESSAYS ON ANCIENT EGYPT

as a hawk which tears and rends the foreign nations with beak and claws (The Thinite palettes). To each of these representations there is attached a role formerly played by the national gods, which the king assumed when he ascended the throne of Horus. The lion, the griffin, the bull, the hawk, and the sphinx are all aspects of powers he possesses.

The King is therefore, "Lord of all order and truth." It is said: "Ra and his friends, the gods, organized the world; their final purpose was the reign of order and the triumph of good. Egypt and its people were the land and people chosen and beloved by the gods; it was, therefore, essential that the son of the gods should be able to bring the work to a successful issue, and this enterprise demanded that strangers, the ungodly enemies of Egypt, and all that was hostile to the ultimate triumph of the good should be destroyed or subdued."

It should also be pointed out, after his spiritual and philosophic roles; the king's next most important role was as defender of the realm. From the time of Narmer when he conquered Lower Egypt and established unification, all through the Archaic Period, the Old Kingdom actions against the Asiatic Bedouins, the Middle Kingdom unification, consolidation and expansion with punitive actions against enemies north and south; in the War of Liberation to expel the Hyksos and establishment and maintaining the New Kingdom; wars of Thutmose I, III, Amenhotep; the Ramesside kings - Seti, Rameses II, Rameses III; the Ethiopians, Piankhy, Shabaka, Taharka, etc., the king was always a warrior pharaoh. Here he defended his nation against internal and external tangible enemies as opposed to the role he performed in his spiritual responsibility to the gods and country. Therefore, the Kingship of Egypt was quite a responsibility in ancient times when the world was just coming into vogue, and the Nile Valley was aflame with the thoughts, aspirations and accomplishment of ancient Africans of Egypt, in northeast Africa.

In contrast, the equivalent of the king of Egypt, the contemporary ruler, Hosni Mubarak, who came to power through military action and ruled for some three decades, according to recent claims governed through *Isfit* rather than *Ma'at*. His iron-fisted tenure stifled the aspirations of the people, condoning imprisonment, murder, brutality and repression, while his cohorts and he gorged themselves financially at the public trough. As the governing elite were fattened, the people became leaner, their travails and burdens increased. In all this, the universality of Hosni Mubarak's name spread across the land on streets, hospitals, you name it. Soon the people's animosity, contravening the ancient love for the ruler, began to fester as they cried out from under the oppression and unjust condition of their experiences. Like all boiling states of affairs, the contents spilled over the container and the people revolted in the streets as they would have never done to an ancient ruler whose watch word was *Ma'at* and adherence to his divinely dictated rule in harmony with the well-being of the society in mind.

FREDERICK MONDERSON

In conclusion, the King of Egypt was both man and god. He possessed extraordinary powers when rightfully ordained. His principal function was to worship and ritualize the gods, defend Egypt, keep the country in equilibrium and reign as a good king. He had to be a statesman, priest, politician, diplomat, warrior and astute and generous. Only then was he able to subdue the forces that threatened his nation, domestic and foreign, material and spiritual, ecclesiastic and secular. When able to do all these things, the nation prospered and great national projects were undertaken, arts and crafts, science and medicine, building and engineering, theology and cosmogony and astronomy and astrology as well as learning, were pursued and thus the culture has left us great evidence of its accomplishments. In modern times as the head of state allowed disequilibrium to gain prominence the society degenerated into discord and the people revolted, an act inconsistent with the longstanding divine mission of a great African nation that has given the world so much in material invention and ethical and social responsibility.

Research Essays Papyrus Art 16. Horus in double crown holds the hands of his Queen.

RESEACH ESSAYS ON ANCIENT EGYPT

References

Bauval, Robert and Adrian Gilbert. *The Orion Mystery*. New York: Crown Trade Paperbacks, (1994) 1995.
Budge, E.A.W. *Gods of the Egyptians*. Vol. I. New York: Dover Publications, Inc., (1904) 1969.
"The King" in *Encyclopedia of Religion and Ethics* Vol. 15. New York: C. Scribner's Sons, 1915.
Erman, Adolf. *Life in Ancient Egypt*. New York: Macmillan, 1894.
Gardiner, Sir. Alan. *Egypt of the Pharaohs*. New York: Oxford University Press, (1961) 1974.
Grollanelli, Cristiano and Pietro Mander. "Kingship: Kingship and the Mediterranean." *Encyclopedia of Religion*, 2nd Edition. New York: Thomson/Gale, 2005.
McMahan, Ian. *Secrets of the Pharaohs*. New York: Avon Books, 1998.
Murnane, William J. *The Penguin Guide to Ancient Egypt*. New York: Penguin Books, 1983.
Petrie, Sir Flinders. *Social Life in Ancient Egypt*. Boston and New York: Houghton Mifflin Company, 1923.
_____. *Religious Life in Ancient Egypt*. London, Bombay, Sydney: Constable and Company, Ltd., 1924.
Rawlinson, George. *Ancient Egypt*. New York: G. P. Putnam's Sons, 1893.
Shaw, Ian and Paul Nicholson. *The Dictionary of Ancient Egypt*. New York: Harry N. Abrams, Inc., Publishers, 1995.

Research Essays Illustration 118. Geese brought and numbered. British Museum – from Thebes.

FREDERICK MONDERSON

Research Essays 125a. View of part of the Cairo Museum front from the garden, where this is the only place photographs can now be taken, no more photographs in the Museum; you have to check your camera as you enter the security zone.

RESEACH ESSAYS ON ANCIENT EGYPT

Research Essays 125b. Grounds of the Cairo Museum of Egyptian Antiquities. Ptah and Sekhmet flank Rameses II comprising the Memphis Triad.

FREDERICK MONDERSON

20. The Conspiracy Against Ancient Egypt
By

Dr. Fred Monderson

I. INTRODUCTION

For centuries an argument has held that the ancient Egyptians and people of the Nile in the earliest antiquity were black and only the moderns with their racism have argued against, proffering a fabricated view. Herodotus and many other ancient writers described the "Colchians, Egyptians and Ethiopians" in the same terms, by today's standards, black. Some critical scholars have argued that the displacement of "Black Egypt" occurred at the start of the 19th Century. The distinction or process of "removing blacks from Egypt and Egypt from Africa" was begun in the "Age of Hegel" and his contemporaries and continued by many European and American scholars of like mind for much of the 19th and 20th Centuries. This, however, was not the universal European or American view of Egypt. Nevertheless, along with this strategy, the geographical notions of "Middle East" and "Africa South of the Sahara" were created to reinforce the distancing of Egypt from Africa.

Consider, interest in Egypt and Egyptian antiquities had been creeping and began to mount following the discovery of the Rosetta Stone, during Napoleon's sojourn in that country, at the end of the Eighteenth Century. This development was at the height of the Slave Trade of Africans to the Americas. Contemporary scholarship of that time went to great lengths to debunk ancient African accomplishments, while glorifying its descent into the inhumane conditions practiced in the institutions of slave trade and slavery. Nonetheless, this "crime against humanity," while perpetrated by Christian Europe, prompted the *Philosopher* Baron de Montesquieu to declare: "It must either be affirmed that we are not Christians or that the Negroes are not men." This was indeed a risky proposition because a great deal of un-Christian behavior was practiced and legal sanction used to legitimize an inhuman treatment of the African in the institution of New World Slavery! Notwithstanding, critical analysis of that contention and by extension in a comparative manner, if we apply Aristotle's syllogism, a logical tool of analysis, to the U.S. Declaration of Independence of 1776 which says: "We hold these truths to be self-evident that all men are created equal;" we find an inherent contradiction in this statement.

RESEACH ESSAYS ON ANCIENT EGYPT

Research Essays 126. Cairo Museum of Egyptian Antiquities. Kneeling statue of Queen Hatshepsut.

The syllogism has three parts consisting of a major premise, a minor premise and a logical conclusion. If the Declaration of Independence, which is today accepted as "a true and living document" from back then and has not changed, but affirmed 'all men are created equal' while blacks were enslaved in America, then it inherently argued blacks were not men! Now, in that climate of thinking and reality supporting the status quo, it was difficult to credit blacks with being the creators of such a magnificent Egyptian civilization in antiquity. Of course, as early as 1798, the iconoclast Count Volney would not conform and wrote, in essence, the "people we enslave today because of their frizzled hair and sable skin,

FREDERICK MONDERSON

on the banks of the Nile invented the arts and sciences that govern the universe." Herein then is the contradiction! As a result, all manner of stratagems were resorted to, "to paint this Ethiopian white!" Pardon the pun, but I mean, "Egyptian."

In the process of historical distortion, the conspiracy against ancient Egypt has long employed a multi-pronged strategy including removal of precious artifacts from the African continent to the other continents, particularly Europe, the Americas and Australia, where principally Europeans live. Following the "naked" and then "enlightened imperialism," another form, "intellectual imperialism" as well as "spiritual warfare" was cloaked in diplomacy, archaeological excavation and hurried publication of findings reinforcing the "Caucasian Egyptian" claim, as well as initiating efforts of preservation of monuments when more artifacts were removed. Brian Fagan has called this operation *The Rape of the Nile*! Coupled with this, destruction of valuable information by unwitting native and foreign collaborators, and distortion of critical literary, pictographic and artifactual remains were standard practices for much of the Nineteenth Century and quite frankly for much of the Twentieth Century too. As things unfolded, credible critical and constructive critique in commentary was omitted from the emerging reservoir of knowledge that began to reach a crescendo, while pandering to a developing 'Penny Press' feeding an unquenchable European and American hunger for ancient Egyptian news and artifacts. No one dared challenge the juggernaut of "Pied Pipers" who oftentimes misled others as well as their own people, whether through prejudice or out of sheer ignorance.

Even more important, in the emergence of credible black scholarship and other literary expressions, a systematic onslaught was made to eviscerate and distort their research findings. *Ipso facto*, black scholars of note, even their white counterparts, who wrote "correctly" about ancient Egypt were dismissed, their work minutely and infinitesimally analyzed, criticized and ridiculed and marginalized for daring to connect ancient Egypt and Africa and Africans. The purpose and intent of such attacks are clear, because the Afrocentric pioneers in critical commentary attacked the hegemonic pillars of white supremacy and its intended or un-intended historical distortion through inaccuracy, purposely or otherwise, bent on elevating Europe and Europeans and denigrating Africa and Africans.

For years fellow students, friends and colleagues have raised the specter of the noses in Egyptian statues that have been broken because they portray a close affinity to the likeness of Nubians and other Africans south of Egypt. Nine out of ten of these noses were destroyed in this manner and this cannot have all been accidental. Without question, many ancient writers have commented on that likeness and Herodotus in particular has said in his work *The Histories*, Book II, *Euterpe*, that the "Egyptians, Colchians and Ethiopians have thick lips, broad

RESEACH ESSAYS ON ANCIENT EGYPT

noses and are burnt of skin" meaning black. This was a visual observation on the part of the "Father of history," who was also dubbed one of the earliest anthropologists in history, based on his human, floral and faunal descriptions that are attributed great credibility. This observation, however, came at the end of Egyptian history. Nonetheless, he was among the people, and wrote about what he heard and saw. As such then, the following quotation is of particular interest for two reasons that will soon become readily apparent.

John David Wortham in *The Genesis of British Egyptology 1549-1906* University of Oklahoma Press at Norman, (1971: 93) has boldly asserted: "Great progress was made during the nineteenth century in the study of Egyptian mummification. Augustus Bozzi Granville, a physician and a student of Coptic, undertook the earliest nineteenth-century dissection of a mummy at his London home in 1825. From his detailed dissection he correctly concluded that the ancient Egyptians were Caucasians. He also succeeded in clearing up many erroneous ideas about the embalming process. Among the things, he proved the correctness of Herodotus' assertion that the ancient Egyptians had, when preparing a cadaver for burial, extracted the pituitary through the nostrils."

The first part is particularly erroneous because in 1992 David O'Connor of the Philadelphia Museum told this writer: "The Egyptians were not white!" Therefore, they were not Caucasian! This is clearly a distortion of the history. Even more important, Wortham asserts that Herodotus was correct in his views about mummification. This was told to him! Naturally, he probably never saw mummification in progress. However, he did observe the people among whom he walked and with whom he talked. Yet Wortham refuses to uphold Herodotus' eyewitness account that the "Egyptians, Colchians and Ethiopians have thick lips, broad noses and are burnt of skin" meaning black. This, then, is what we call scholarship of convenience. And so the misrepresentation has continued. However, if the pituitary of the mummy was extracted through the nostrils, still even more,
Why break the noses of statues, for unless every statue is broken, then the theosophical, spiritual, or religious intent becomes meaningless. This treatment must also be applied to every painting, illustration, etc., representative of the individual seems hardly likely the Egyptians wanted a disfigured individual standing before his god!

By 1825, just three years after Champollion's decipherment of Hieroglyphics the science had barely evolved and the authenticity of the mummy dissected, the conditions under which the study was done and the lack of critical review of the process, question the rock solid founding of "white Egyptian" or "Caucasian." This could very well be the operation set out to prove the findings.

The question of omission as well as distortion has also been significant to the controversy surrounding ancient Egypt and, interestingly enough, the whole question is still taboo today. Many have argued the critical nature of the problem and perhaps within another century, Egypt and Egyptian studies will be all white!

FREDERICK MONDERSON

However, through African and African American scholars, in trail of Diop, et al., and together with the modicum of whites who care, this fight for African historiography reconstruction is far from over!

In a critical retort, the current writer has insisted that all people, black and white, go beyond the nose and be more knowledgeable about the archaeology, anthropology, history, anthropometry, geography, language, biometrics, and use of diagrams. This then raises the stakes in the discussion. Equally, in the disciplines of art and architecture, religion of ancient Egypt, their theosophy, metaphysics and their impact on science, navigation, medicine, and mathematics as well as literature and linguistics, all can provide the potent armaments in the battle for ownership of ancient Egypt as research continuously unfolds regarding these ancient Africans.

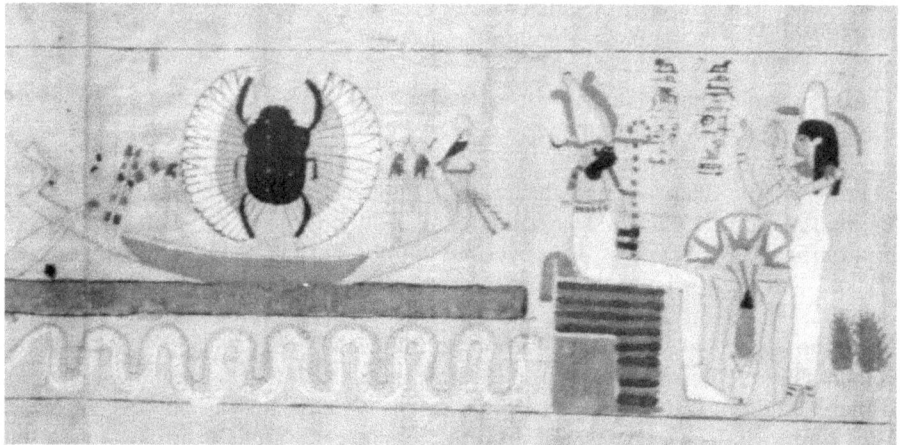

Research Essays 127. Cairo Museum of Egyptian Antiquities. Papyrus of deceased female making a salutation to the enthroned image of Osiris, God of the Dead, painted black; while to his rear Khepre sails his boat above the great serpent.

II.   THE NOSE JOB

Recently this writer visited the Metropolitan Museum of Art in New York City to observe the Egyptian collection and was impressed by the wonderful display the museum houses. On the other hand, the question of "Nose" caught my attention because several statues seemed to have had their noses broken. Strange it seemed that these statues were made of the hardest, most durable stones and yet the noses were broken. I remember years ago as a student that my professor said that the

RESEACH ESSAYS ON ANCIENT EGYPT

"noses were broken because in ancient Egypt in the mummification ceremony the brain was removed through the nostrils." Importantly, one has a tendency to believe one's professors, without realizing either the professor was schooled in another discipline or was ignorant of the facts, though he was teaching the subject. This can happen! Of course one expects the mummy's nose to be broken but not a statue detached from the mummification process. The statues were made before the corpse's demise. Imagine, upon the death of an individual of note, traversing the entire nation, finding every statue made in honor of that individual and breaking its nose! Naturally, one had to do this for every painting and raised and sunk relief portrayal, otherwise the argument easily collapses because the intent is not complete. It seems very probable only statues found were destroyed. Those yet to be discovered and those discovered in an aura of fanfare are not destroyed!

The noses of Tutankhamon's statues, that of Mentuhotep II, the thousands found in the "Cachette Court," that found in the *Wadjit* were not broken, but found as when interred by the ancients. The nose of the Memphis statue of Rameses II is not broken nor is the noses of the seated statues at Abu Simbel. Perhaps only statues mainly in Western museums have broken noses, for the most part.

If we argue the exception proves the rule, here's an example of a "nose job. Rosalie David, in *Discovering Ancient Egypt* (New York: Facts on File, 1993, pp. 182-83) presents two photographs of heads whose noses, pointed, but not affected in any manner. The caption to the first reads: "A plaster head from the cemetery at Mallawi (Near Beni Suef), the location of a Roman garrison. The head, originally placed over a mummy, dates to the Roman Period (2nd century A.D.). Such representations seem to have been in use here for only about eighty years." The second photograph's caption reads as follows: "This plaster head of a woman from the cemetery at Mallawi (2nd century A.D.) depicts the contemporary hairstyle and jewelry of that period, when tomb robbery had led to the custom of representing jewelry on the mask instead of placing it in the tomb." Now, let us again compare another photograph between pages 160 and 161 that reads: "A colossal figure of Nefertari, favorite queen of Rameses II, as the goddess Hathor. This decorates the façade of her rock-cut temple at Abu Simbel. With the Great Temple, this was rescued by the UNESCO salvage campaign." This statue is pretty much preserved but the nose and mouth is disfigured! As I said, one has to wonder if plaster could remain intact over millennia but granite could be broken and this sets one to thinking, "Is there a conspiracy against Ancient Egypt?"

FREDERICK MONDERSON

Research Essays Papyrus Art 17.   Goddess Hathor holds the hand of Queen Nefertari.

Case in point. In all probability, nearly all the statues in the Cairo Museum have their noses intact and perhaps mainly those statues in European and American public display museums have statues with broken noses. The statues discovered in the "Cachette Court" between 1903-04, were placed there by the ancients; who, rightly should have, but, probably did not break noses! In the fanfare of the discovery with every one present, it would have looked suspicious if noses were broken all of a sudden. These statues were delivered to the Cairo Museum as the ancients had placed them! Even further, a good example is made of the "double

RESEACH ESSAYS ON ANCIENT EGYPT

statue of Neferhotep found in the northern part of the *Wadjyt* under the obelisk of Hatshepsut." This statue is displayed in a photograph at Karnak Temple in the position of how the ancients had placed it. The nose is intact. Therefore, if the argument for the broken nose is upheld, then this statue, *in situ*, should have had its nose broken. This exception does prove the rule and it should also contradict Wortham's one mummy contention in addition to the arguments against his "flawed experiment in 1825!"

Consider also only the best pieces were chosen as "gifts" to foreign museums by individuals conducting excavations. It is reasonable to assume, statues of important Egyptians/Kamites with "questionable noses" would have been "doctored" before being placed in their cases to justify the professor's false or incorrect statement! Equally, there were always more than one statue of an individual, but it seems like only those statues portraying African features are for the most part broken, and those with European features are preserved.

In the Metropolitan Museum, I noticed that the noses of statues of earliest Egyptian history, made of granite, one of the hardest of stones, were generally broken in most museum displays, here and elsewhere. In contrast, the noses of sunk and raised reliefs on "talatat stones" in the Open Air Museum at Karnak Temple and elsewhere tell a different story. In this regard, Cheikh Anta Diop makes an interesting point in his *African Origins of Civilization: Myth or Reality*. He has argued, while statues in museums could be "doctored," the Sphinx, in full view, could not be tampered with as it demonstrates the image of an African persona.

To develop our argument further, Gay Robbins, in *The Art of Ancient Egypt* (1997: 24) points out there were two types of stone materials used by Egyptian sculptors. Soft stone consisted of limestone, calcite, sandstone, schist, greywacke and hard stone consisted of quartzite, diorite, granodiorite, granite and basalt. In this, she says: "Stone was the major building material for free-standing and rock-cut temples and tombs. It was also used to make statues, stelae, offering tables, libation bowls, vessels and other ritual equipment." Even further, Robbins (1997: 24) continued: "Soft stones were usually covered with a thin layer of plaster and painted. Although paint was sometimes applied to harder stones, it would seem that much of the stone was left visible, and that the color of the stone was often chosen for its symbolism. Black stones like granodiorite referred to the life-giving black silt brought by the Nile inundation. Thus they symbolized new life, resurrection and the resurrected god of the dead, Osiris, who is often shown with black skin. A range of colors – red, brown, yellow, gold – was associated with the sun, so that stones of these colors, such as red and brown quartzite and red granite, carried a solar symbolism. Green stones referred to fresh, growing vegetation, new life, resurrection and Osiris, who can also appear with green skin."

FREDERICK MONDERSON

Research Essays Temple Ticket 18.   Mit Rahina Museum. Price of entrance is thirty-five Egyptian Pounds.

Since the Egyptian religion was essentially solar based, can their use of red, "associated with the sun," be the reason they painted themselves, generally, red to be identified with this solar phenomenon? Perhaps, and this raises a whole lot of other serious questions.

Nevertheless, as I toured the display at the Met I realized that statues or busts or faces of the Graeco-Roman period with rather aquiline noses were intact. What raised a "red flag" is that busts of many of these statues were oftentimes made of plaster, perhaps *Paper Mache*, and were probably so well-preserved because they portrayed European images. On the other hand, Egyptian statues of hard stone that portrayed African images were broken. Imagine plaster thousands of years old being more durable than the hardest stone! If these two mediums were exposed to the elements, then plaster would dissipate in a relatively short time whereas stone would remain, seemingly forever. This got me to thinking! The stone head of Rameses II's colossal seated statue at the Ramesseum or even the seated one at Luxor's entrance, even the seated statues at Abu Simbel, lying open in the elements for thousands of years have not changed, yet so many concealed stones have been broken or destroyed in some form or fashion!

RESEACH ESSAYS ON ANCIENT EGYPT

Research Essays Illustration 119. Part 1. Fowling scene. Part 2. Spearing fish with the bident.

On the way to the Cafeteria at the Met I passed through the Medieval European period and noticed statues with the most aquiline noses imaginable, really thin and long, all were well-preserved in these displays. Time did not permit a determination of the nature of the material used. One thing seemed certain, the most durable and indurable materials portraying European noses seems to outlast the most durable materials portraying African noses, and one has to wonder whether there was and still is a conspiracy regarding ancient Egypt. That is because, since the argument for the breakage is not credible, when subjected to close scrutiny. However, there is no question the noses of the most ancient Egyptians differed from those surviving of the Graeco-Roman period and certainly than those of the European Medieval Period when they were very aquiline.

Equally, the noses of many mummies, particularly those of the Kings are not always broken which begs the question of 'why break the nose of a statue and not the mummy?' It seems for the most part, the nose breaking phenomenon was primarily a modern.

III.   THE HAIR

Hair is an interesting topic in ancient Egypt. Yet, it's hardly dealt with in the multitude of books on this subject.

As early as 1905 Randall-McIver commented on the 'strongly curled hair' he found in his study of the cemeteries of El Amrah, an Upper Egyptian pre-dynastic site. Goodwin said the "curly hair" was really a wig! How ridiculous! We must, however, remember Count Volney's description. It is interesting that not much

FREDERICK MONDERSON

has been said about hair in Dynastic and Predynastic graves. In the Cairo Museum of Egyptian Antiquities there is a case on the second floor displaying Egyptian wigs. This is a one of a kind exhibit, because to my recollection there are no other displays housing wigs, "Afro-Wigs." In view of the "destruction of Egyptian monuments" this "find" was discovered in the "Deir el Bahari cache" amidst great fanfare and, as such, was preserved.

Let me add, recently Dr. Zahi Hawass has called for a re-evaluation of the identities of all the mummies based on the fact only Tutankhamon was found in his sealed tomb. Such a call, however, does not disprove who those other pharaohs are said to be, it is simply an effort to be absolutely clear who they actually are based on the Tutankhamon yardstick. Since, Queen Hatshepsut's mummy has been identified through a broken tooth!

Now, all kinds of conflicting deductions have been made regarding the ethnicity and function of the two replica statues placed before his burial chamber. In as much as these statues were placed in this location it may very well be a burial practice to place such figures of the occupant with their respective function in this location. In fact, the tombs of Seti I, Amenhotep I and Rameses III have revealed remains of such statues. Using Hawass' Tutankhamon yardstick, every other pharaoh may have had such figures as part of the funerary ritual. Being of wood, their tombs not discovered sealed whether through nature or malicious intent these figures could have been destroyed or rotted, in ancient or modern times, because they show the true color of the ancient Egyptians. Let us not forget UNESCO's 1974 Conference underscored the "fundamental blackness of ancient Egypt."

However, another important point needs to be made. Even if we accept the Cairo University's Professor's contention that the "statues were painted black for the funeral ceremony," it still raises the most important question that is still contradictory. The Egyptians believed the afterlife would last much longer than the earthly existence. This is similar to their belief that the home of the god should be more durable than that of a domestic residence. Now, if the deceased was embarking on a journey of a lifetime would he or she not dress appropriately? Would that person go to such an engagement as make-believe or a real person? Diop reminded us, the Egyptians painted themselves red to simply be distinguished from other Africans. Could it not be that black was really their true color? Why would an imitation statue be dressed in royal paraphernalia and placed to guard the interred King Tutankhamon?

Returning to the issue of the hair, according to "**IMPORTANT ARCHAEOLOGICAL DISCOVERIES IN EGYPT**" published in the London *Times* Thursday, August 4, 1881, from Cairo July 24, 1881, regarding the great Deir el Bahari discoveries of New Kingdom monarchs of the above year: "Fifteen enormous wigs for ceremonial occasions form a striking feature of the Deir-el-Bahari collection. These wigs are nearly 2 ft. high, and are composed of

RESEACH ESSAYS ON ANCIENT EGYPT

frizzled and curled hair. There are many marked points of resemblance between the legal institutions of ancient Egypt and of England. For instance, pleadings must be "Traversed," "confessed and avoided" or demurred to. Marriage settlements and the doctrines of uses and trusts prevailed in ancient Egypt, but the wearing of these wigs was not extended to the members of the legal profession, but was reserved exclusively for the princess of the blood and ladies of very high rank." Yet, they have not shown us any of these brothers, I mean pharaohs, wearing these big Afros!

Importantly, such a significant find is encapsulated in a simple description. In the case of Wortham above, it was a single sentence before he moved on.

Pardon this digression. In the case of the single study done by Granville in 1825, a number of factors can be considered.

1. This early in the 19th Century studies of this type could have been considered "primitive" and not generally done in a scientific setting.

2. The mummy he dissected was probably not of royal lineage. The study was done 3 years after Champollion's decipherment of Hieroglyphics and so the discipline of Egyptology was very young.

3. According to Diop's *African Origins: Myth or Reality*, Champollion's letters to his brother based on his pristine and unprejudiced observations, clearly indicated the Egyptians were African and black, not Caucasian.

4. Wortham goes from the specific to the general, a sort of "one sparrow, so its summer" supposition.

5. There was probably hardly any "credible criticism" of the study at the time it was done.

Equally, a similar argument is made for the Old Kingdom, Fifth Dynasty, seated scribe now in front and center in the Louvre Museum. This individual is shown with blue eyes, therefore the argument is made, "See, the Egyptians had blue eyes." Such an argument also goes from the specific to the general. It utilizes deductive as opposed to inductive reasoning. We do know, in many instances, the Egyptians inlaid eyes, with whatever material, depending on the situation. The question never delves into very much, such as 'Are the eyes of the Louvre Scribe inlaid?' One could easily ask, 'How many other statues had blue eyes?' 'Is this statue a fabrication?' and so on!

FREDERICK MONDERSON

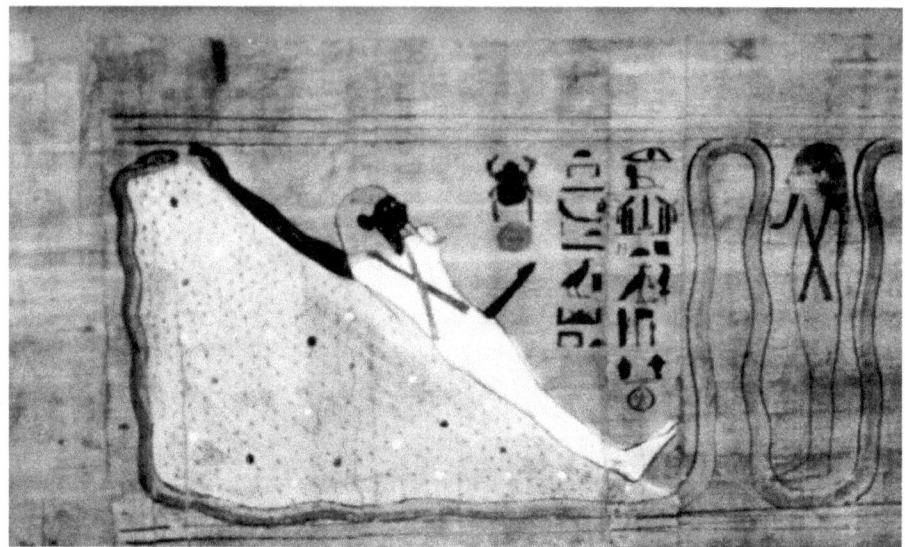

Research Essays 128. Cairo Museum of Egyptian Antiquities. The Great God Geb painted black and in reposed position on a hill encircled by the serpent.

That's all part of the omission and distortion syndrome in the "conspiracy against ancient Egypt."

Nonetheless, many of the images of the Old Kingdom and later, show people who seem to be wearing "black hair" as opposed to the long flowing type. When this latter is shown, it seems to be in the form of a wig that is basically a covering of the head. All evidence seems to show, in ancient times, from noble to fellahin all wearing "wigs" of "black hair." The question is why? We know Nefertiti was Syrian and white. Are we to expect her to wear a "black hair" or "white hair" wig?

Notwithstanding, in a final commentary in this section, we turn to H.K.S. Bakry's *A Brief Study of Mummies and Mummification* (Cairo 1965) where he gives insights on the hair of some New Kingdom pharaohs whose mummies were recovered in the two 19th Century "Caches" discovered at Thebes.

He begins (1965: 21) with Ahmose (Amosis I) of the 18th Dynasty, who reigned c. 1575-1550 B.C. "His body is covered with black resinous material and his hair is rather long, dark brown and curly." Then (1965: 23-24) he gives Thutmose II, also of the 18th Dynasty (1510-1490 B.C.) and states: "The crown of the head is bald, but there is curly hair on the temples, nearly five inches long and dark brown." For Amenhotep II, son of Thutmose III, (1436-1413 B.C.) he states: "His hair is brown and curly like that of his son and successor, Thutmose IV, but Amenhotep has a lot of grey hair on his head." For Thutmose IV (1413-1405 B.C.) he states: "The hair

RESEACH ESSAYS ON ANCIENT EGYPT

is curly, dark brown and about six and a half inches in length." Need I say more on this?

One thing is remarkable and often not commented on. The New Kingdom Pharaohs' height varied from five feet to five and a half feet, not generally taller. Thutmose III was 5 feet 1 inch tall! This shows that height is not a principal hallmark of greatness.

Added for further clarification, the following is a 1961 Publisher's Note that is appended to Hope (1962: xxi) who wrote nearly two centuries ago about ancient Egyptian costumes: "The ancient Egyptians were descended from the Ethiopians, and while their blood remained free from any mixture with that of European or Asiatic nations, their race seems to have retained obvious traces of the aboriginal Negro form and features. Not only all the human figures in their colored hieroglyphics display a deep swarthy complexion, but every Egyptian monument whether statue or bas-relief presents the splay feet, the spreading toes, the bow-bent shins, the high meager calves, the long swinging arms, the sharp shoulders, the square flat hands, the head, when seen in profile, placed not vertically but obliquely on the spine, the jaws and chin consequently very prominent, together with the skinny lips, depressed nose, high cheek bones, large un-hemmed ears raised far above the level of the nostrils, and all the other peculiarities characteristic of the Negro conformation. It is true that the practice prevalent among the Egyptians of shaving their heads and beards close to the skin (which they only deviated from when in mourning) seldom allows their statues to show that most undeniable symptom of Negro extraction, the woolly hair; the heads of their figures generally appearing covered with some sort of cap, or, when bare, closely shaven. In the few Egyptian sculptured personages, however, in which the hair is introduced, it uniformly offers the woolly texture, and the short crisp curls of that of the Negroes; nor do I know a single specimen of genuine Egyptian workmanship, in which are seen any indications of the long sleek hair or loose wavy ringlets of Europeans or Asiatics. The black streak, which, in the masks or faces carved and painted on the cases of the mummies, is carried from the outside corner of the eye-lids to the temple, seems to denote that anciently, as to this day, the natives of Egypt were in the habit of artificially deepening the hue and increasing the length of their eye lashes, by means of some species of pigment."

If one writer could observe such characteristics, why can't others see the same features? Of all the scientific studies done on the mummies, with all the measurements taken, none have come close to such a description or finding. Does it mean such studies - physical, craniometrical, biological, are for the most part, flawed?

FREDERICK MONDERSON

IV. THE STATUES – STONE VERSUS WOOD

a. **Stone** – This medium was exploited from the earliest times in depicting the gods, pharaohs and sometimes nobles. All manner of stone was used for sculpture, soft as well as hard. It is understandable that there would be some losses in recovered material but when all of the hardest stone statues, particularly those on display in Western Museums, seems to have this problem, one has to wonder. We must also remember as Gay Robbins pointed out above, stone statues are not painted; the color of the stone is the representative color of the statue. However, wood is painted. It seems the artists went to great lengths to show the people by painting wood to convey an unmistaken message!

As a freshman student in college we were told of the *Ad hominem* argument that is generally fleeting and upon closer inspection it begins to fall apart, a straw man. For example, one must consider the context of the color of stone or material used in representing the individual depicted. In the late 1970s around the bicentennial celebrations of American independence, the Tutankhamon exhibit toured the United States. Naturally choice pieces comprised the collection. Significantly, the symbol representative of the boy king was not the famed gold mask, which seems to be on the cover of more books on Egypt and the ancient world than any other single representation. The symbol representing the Tutankhamon exhibit in the United States for that historic tour was the alabaster bust of the young king.

Research Essays Papyrus Art 18. Attended by Thoth and Amun, Isis sits in the papyrus field nursing Horus as two goddesses stand nearby.

RESEACH ESSAYS ON ANCIENT EGYPT

Now, try to remember Danny Kay's famous children's song, "The King's New Clothes." In all the hoopla during the parade, people waving, drums drumming, intellectuals, all commenting on how well the suit fitted the king. It stands to reason, perhaps, some of those fat bureaucrats standing and cheering as the king went by probably said to their associates or persons nearby, the suit looks so good, I must have one! Fortunately, it was a youngster who saw through the farcical facade that the king was naked!

Now, fast forward to the parade and again all the farcical hoopla and here comes the symbol, that little black boy is jolted because, not knowing that alabaster is a white material, he opines, the king is white! Shame is cast on American organizers who perpetuated the myth of a white King Tut on the little black boy, and on so many other little black boys and girls. This applies even to white boys and girls, scattered across the globe, who never did, or probably would never see the life-like statue of the boy-king, but would hear of his name, King Tut. They would never know that Tutankhamon had himself represented as similarly a little black boy. That is the nature of what this essay is all about, 'The Conspiracy Against Ancient Egypt!'

In the Cairo Museum, the same two life-like black statues of Tutankhamon are shown with left foot forward in a moving, living position. At the entrance of the gallery housing his treasures, they are never really seen and some visitors probably don't care as they rush into the hall to view the gold and other wealth of his funerary furniture.

Just to the right of these statues on a wall are two plaques made of bronze. One shows the young King Tutankhamon colored bronze slaying an enemy and the other, the King in the same material as a sphinx crushing his Nubian enemies who are painted black like the statue. If the Nubians are represented as they are, black, then the King is represented not as bronze but as black. Get the point! Let us not forget, contrary to popular misguided "spin" that the statue was painted black for the funerary ceremony, the king represented himself as he wanted to be seen in the next world and the life-like statues guarding his dead body are exact replicas of himself, dressed in kingly attire. Let us not forget, Dr. Zahi Hawass clarified that Tutankhamon is the only king whose identity is certain because his tomb was found intact. In all probability, similarly painted statues may have been similarly situated before other pharaohs' burial chambers and been the victims of the destroyer's hands.

FREDERICK MONDERSON

Research Essays 129. Cairo Museum of Egyptian Antiquities. Another image of Osiris painted black in his shrine as he receives supplication of a deceased female. Other deities are in the background. Why is the God painted black and not the woman, "painted black for the funeral ceremony as in the case of King Tutankhamon?"

b. Wood – While statues seem to be made from a wide variety of stone material that give no indication regarding the ethnicity of the people represented, it is a whole lot different with wooden statues. First and foremost, because of its nature not too many wooden statues have been recovered showing facial features. A valid argument has been made that wooden statues have been "doctored in basements" of western museums. This treatment is not reserved exclusively for wooden statues but also for any artifact that gives credence to the blackness of Egypt. It goes without saying that those images that have survived of black Egyptians, King Tutankhamon, Mentuhotep II, Queen Aahmes Nefertari, Thutmose I, etc., "could not be destroyed" because of their prominence or possibly fanfare at the time surrounding their discovery. Despite this, in face of their images, their blackness is still denied through all forms of ridiculous subterfuges. In view of this, one has to give some credence to the notion of a 'conspiracy against ancient Egypt.'

The Cairo Museum has a room on the second floor that houses displays of small wooden statues painted black. Some are pharaohs and some are of animals. One particular statue of interest is the black-panther, beside an Amenhotep also painted black. These understandably are "survivors." However, if the panther is painted black to represent its color then it's a powerful given that the pharaoh represented juxtaposed and similarly painted is also black. There are also a great many Osiris

RESEACH ESSAYS ON ANCIENT EGYPT

statues of wood and painted black in this room. These are housed high above the cases near the ceiling or in some obscure place, and thus, out of sight of the most casual visitor. If we look at all the wooden statues of people or animals they are either painted or not. The greatest majority of those painted are either in the traditional red or black. If, therefore, any panther, goose, bird or Nubian is painted black and that portrays such, why then would any Egyptian god, king or regular person painted black, not be such.

On October 7, 2010 this writer entered the Hall of Tutankhamon on the second floor of the Egyptian Museum as a local guide was addressing a group of visitors. He began by describing the differences between the two statues in that one wore the white crown and the other a cloth headdress. Both headdresses were signs this was indeed a royal depiction. Two things caught the passing observer. First he said, "The black skin does not mean the king was Nubian." Second, that the statues were guards placed before the King's burial chamber. How interesting that the statues painted black does not represent the color of the king, yet, nearby on a wall plaque the king is shown in bronze attacking Nubians painted black. Are we to believe black is the color of the Nubians but bronze is the color of the king? Why would statues of the king painted black be considered mere guards yet be wearing crowns of the Upper and Lower Kingdoms?

Research Essays 130. Ghizeh Plateau. The Sphinx of Ghizeh in its majestic splendor against the wonderful blue sky.

A young Egyptian female guide in the Cairo Museum once told this writer in September 2005, the Pharaoh Mentuhotep II, whose *Heb Sed* Festival statue was found at Deir el Bahari and painted black, was so painted for the funeral ceremony. Let's be clear, the *Heb Sed* Festival is about rejuvenation and has nothing to do with the funeral ceremony. When I questioned her about this she told me her teacher at the American University in Cairo taught her this! Two things are readily apparent here. First, Professors at the American University in Cairo seem to be teaching the strange history of Egypt which their students, acting as guides, are propagating on unsuspecting visitors in their tours. This augurs well with gullible and ill-educated European visitors to the Cairo Museum who choose to see themselves represented in the culture of ancient Egypt. Equally, for the most part, they never read a book about Egypt before they get there or purchase one while there. One has to wonder about the Professors' intent, the fact of misinformation being disseminated and their students or "disciples" perpetuating this false information right there in the heart of the culture. Obviously, in this day and age, she probably did not know of W. Stephenson Smith's *Art and Architecture of Ancient Egypt* (1959), wherein the author says Mentuhotep II had "black flesh." She did not know that by wearing the Red Crown of Lower Egypt, it's postulated that the Pharaoh, in all probability, wore the White Crown in another statue not discovered and this had nothing to do with his death ceremony per se, but represented his kingship over the north and south, as part of the Heb Sed rejuvenation ceremony. After all, in the desert and fertile land contrast, red is desolate and death while black, is fertile and life-giving.

Equally and important too, there are too few black Egyptian guides in the museum, who could give a different view than the false one presented to visitors by the Egyptian guides, similar to the young lady referred to above. I noticed one such person on my October 7, 2010 visit to the Museum.

Another important insight is appended here. Though the Pharaoh Mentuhotep's temple was discovered in 1904, and his statue displayed in the Museum, no writer for more than fifty years had the audacity to comment that he had "black flesh" as did Smith. Does this mean that all the books written about Egypt between 1904 and 1959 have been falsified or had pertinent information omitted? This is a classic case of omission and distortion! It must certainly have taken "marbles" for Smith to proclaim Mentuhotep II had "black flesh!"

Pressing the young lady further, and mentioning that Osiris was often represented black, she said "I have never seen Osiris painted black!" Imagine being a guide in the Cairo Museum and never seen Osiris painted black. There are many examples on papyrus and in wooden statues. Just then I realized she had an agenda. As a guide she did not know Osiris was known as the "Great Black!" Interesting, the people who argue vehemently and inclandestine against the Afrocentrists have never taken on the likes of this young lady or recanted their falsity, nor have they challenged professors the likes of John David Wortham. This may simply be that these preachers of falsity uphold and vehemently defend the false notion that the Egyptians were white!

RESEACH ESSAYS ON ANCIENT EGYPT

Research Essays Papyrus Art 19. Hunting in the mashes with the wife and child as fishes swim in the river nearby.

Once again, the people who argue in this vein, that the deceased was colored black for the death ceremony seem to forget that in the designation "Red Land, Black Land," red stands for the desert and its deathlike appearance while black represents life and regeneration. Osiris the God of the Dead is generally portrayed as black or even green but hardly red, and certainly not white, even though he was dead. This is because he represented rebirth or life and the best example of this is black. Additionally, when the god says to the king, "I give you the Black Land," does he mean he does not give him that part of Egypt referred to as the Red Land? Or, is it that the god meant he gave pharaoh the whole land that is representative of the people, as Theophile Obenga says, the "black land" refers to the country and black people.

V.   IMAGES

Queen Aahmes-Nefertari was the founder and ancestress of the 18th Dynasty and in the portrait in the British Museum she is shown as a "Coal Black Ethiopian." She married her brother, Aahmes, as was customary at that time. If she was black, then it goes without saying that her brother was also black and so must have been her father and mother. If their parents are considered, so too must have been the

FREDERICK MONDERSON

other brother Kamose who led the expulsion of the Hyksos following his father Sekenenra's death in the fighting. Let us still not forget, these people were Thebans from the south or Upper Kingdom and not from the Delta or north or Lower Kingdom where their racial origin could be questioned!

Research Essays 131. Ghizeh Plateau. Causeway to the Great Pyramid of Khufu of the 4th Dynasty.

In the third volume of Bunsen's four volume work *Egypt's Place in Universal History* (1879: 112-113) he writes of this important Queen regarding her name in the Temple of Amon at Karnak. He writes: "Over this inscription is the royal scutcheon of the king, and on each side of it that of his wife. She is the illustrious heiress with whom we became acquainted when making our researches about the 17th Dynasty – the Princess AAHMES NEFRU-ARI (the good, glorious woman). Her titles are : "Royal Wife, Mother, Daughter, Sister." She was, consequently, the daughter of a Theban king, or one allied with Ethiopian blood. The historical representations describe her as black, unlike all the other Egyptian races. It is easy to understand in those days Theban families intermarried with Ethiopian princes; for it was from the South only that they received any support and reserves during the struggle with the Shepherd Kings. It is probable that the Ethiopian ancestress, on the mother's side, received some provinces as her dowry : at all events, a portion of the country paid tribute to Amosis. Nefru-ari, then , as an heiress : her husband reigned in her right, and took the name of "Young Moon," perhaps, in consequence of this inheritance; at any rate, it had reference to her, and was afterwards dropped. The monuments prove that no queen was ever held in such honor as this Aahmes. She is styled "Divine Spouse of Amon;" she enjoys the distinction of the barque of the Gods; and sits beside her son, Amenophis I [Amenhotep I], as if sharing equal rank with him, the reigning sovereign."

RESEACH ESSAYS ON ANCIENT EGYPT

This family relationship is underscored in **"THE ROYAL MUMMIES OF DEIR-EL-BAHARI."** *The Academy* 35 No. 891 (June 1, 1889: 383-384) as indicated: "Among other genealogical emendations, Prof. Maspero makes out Queen Aah-hotep (the famous Queen Aah-hotep of the Boulak jewels) to be the wife, not of Kames, as hitherto believed, but of Sekenen-Re, and the mother of both Kames and Aahmes I."

Please appreciate the humor here in this example. On one occasion the respected Dr. Yosef ben-Jochannan was giving a lecture. At the end, during the question and answer period, a lady came over and complained to the Brother about her son. She is quoted as saying: "Dr. Ben, I don't know what to do about this boy, he is the black sheep in the family!" Dr. Ben quickly responded: "Well lady, you are black, your husband is black, and so what type of sheep do you expect to have?" Therefore, if Sekenenra and Aah-hotep (Tetisheri) produced a "black sheep" in Nefertari, then what type of ewe and ram were they? Ha. Ha.

Sometimes we run into pertinent information without marking the appropriate reference and later this poses a problem. I do remember encountering a 19th Century reference in the British Journal *Academy* of a report done by Prof. Sayce. There he says he entered a tomb of a nobleman and the occupant is shown in a painting on the wall worshipping Tuthmose I painted black! This revelation never seemed to be repeated and is a classic example of the omission creating distortion in this subject. Just as this piece of critical information is omitted from subsequent records, it stands to reason that other information just as critical is often also omitted, perhaps destroyed because it challenges the myth of a white Egypt. Hence, we must adhere to Dr. Ben's dictum, as researchers "Get the oldest information and work from there!"

Research Essays 132. Ghizeh Plateau. The Pyramid of Khafre viewed from the desert.

FREDERICK MONDERSON

A subject not often talked about and since these days one cannot take photos in the tombs then the prima facie evidence, cannot be presented unless taken previously in earlier days. The subject discussed is sculpture in the Tomb of Rameses III that is akin to that of Seti I, New Kingdom Monarchs of the 19th and 20th Dynasties.

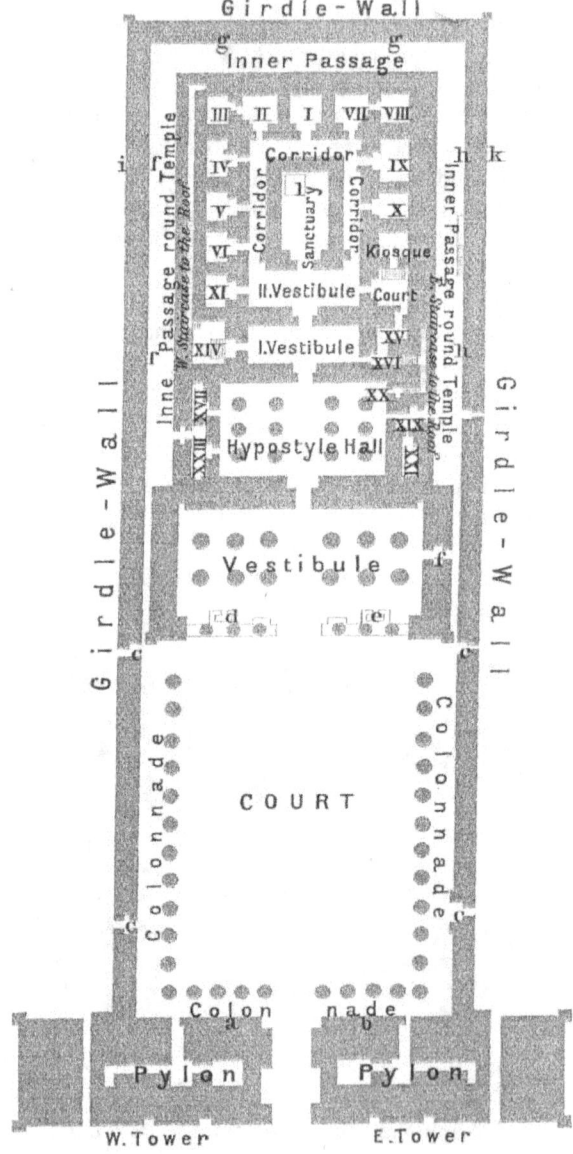

Temple of Horus at Edfu

RESEACH ESSAYS ON ANCIENT EGYPT

The following is presented in Murray's *Handbook for Egypt* (1888: 483-485) and provides a description of the Tomb of Rameses III, No. 11, in the Valley of the Kings, commonly called *Bruce's* or *The Harper's Tomb*. "This tomb was discovered by the English traveler Bruce, hence one of its names. The other appellation is derived from the famous picture in one of the chambers of the men playing the harp. The execution of the sculptures is inferior to that in No. 17 [Seti I's], but the nature of the subjects is more interesting."

Regarding: SCULPTURE in the Tomb of Rameses III.

"This tomb is much defaced, and the nature of the rock is unfavorable for sculpture."

"The subjects in the first passage, after the recess to the right, are similar to those of Seti's and are supposed to relate to the descent to Amenta. The figure of Truth, and the other groups in connection with that part of them, is placed in a square niche. The character of the four people in the first hall differs slightly from those of the former tomb."

"Four Blacks clad in African dresses, being substituted instead of the Egyptians, though the same name, Rot, is introduced before them."

The following description is provided to give some insights on the disposition of a temple's architectural layout so the reader can understand how events therein played itself out in the ritual and processions.

"A, The entrance hall opens to the light of day. B - The hall from which the religious processions started. C and D contained altars where prayers were recited as the processions passed. In the hall E were the four barks and which often played so conspicuous a part in the processions. The chamber F was a laboratory for the preparation of perfumes. In G, the consecrated products of the earth used in the ceremonies were collected. H and I were for offerings and libations. J was the treasury of the temple. In the chamber K, the vestments were deposited with which the statues of the gods were draped. Prayers were recited in the chapel L. The court M was used for the collection of offerings and the limbs of the victims slaughtered at the sacrifice. N was another place for deposit, and in O, P, and Q, the king consecrated special offerings. The walls of the corridor R were used for the sculptured pictures representing the motif of the temple. S, the chamber where Isis was consecrated to Osiris. T, the chamber consecrated to Osiris. U was sacred to Osiris-On-nophris, who restored youth to his body and imparted vigor to his

FREDERICK MONDERSON

limbs. In the chamber V the work of resurrection was completed. In X, and Y, Hathor was worshipped. The chamber Z is the axis of the temple, and the principal divinity was adored there under the most comprehensive titles. Lastly, in the chambers, A, B, C, D, a special worship is paid to Pasht, considered as the fire that vivifies; to Horus, considered as the light which has conquered darkness, and the terrestrial Hathor." After Mariette in B.L. Wilson's "The Temples of Egypt" 1888.

Research Essays 133. Ghizeh Plateau. The massive stone supports and architraves within the vicinity of the pyramids.

Regarding distortion and omission as a method for falsifying history we are quite aware that among arguments, one holds the Egyptians did not know of the arch! They probably did not know of McDonalds! Every time I'm in the rear of the Ramesseum I question whether the structure I'm seeing is an arch and am I the only one who has seen this structure though it's been there for ages. As if that is not enough to dispel this argument, the following is a 19th Century reference of **EGYPT EXPLORATION FUND**. *The Academy* 44 No. 1104 (July 1, 1893: 17-18) "**The Excavations at Dayr el Bahari**" which states inter alia: "The western door leads to a long hall, with well-preserved sculptures of gigantic proportions, showing Hatasu and Thothmes III making offerings to Amon. Next to it is an open court limited on the north by the mountain, on the east by the remains of a chamber with columns. From that court one enters into a small rock-cut chapel, the funeral chapel of Thothmes I. The ceiling, well painted in blue

RESEACH ESSAYS ON ANCIENT EGYPT

with yellow stars, is an Egyptian arch." This description predates the previous statement since Hatshepsut is of the 18th Dynasty and Rameses is of the 19th Dynasty. We hear the same thing about the Zodiac as being a foreign importation and so on as the 'Conspiracy against Ancient Egypt' continues but "Truth crushed to earth shall rise."

Even more important, Ptah the Creator God was a pygmy from central Africa. Are we to believe the ancient Egyptians were foreigners to Africa, Caucasian from the Caucus on the Russian steppes, and notwithstanding, their creator, one of their highest Gods, came from Central Africa? Hathor was Sudani, according to Budge. Oftentimes Amon or other gods are described as being exceedingly happy when they come from "God's Land," Africa proper. Will someone please tell Wortham that the gods of the "Caucasian Egyptians" came from "God's land," in Black Africa! We are also told in the literature, after Ra made the world and two principal gods, the first people he made were Nubians. See how the cookie crumbles or the house of cards tumbles!

Research Essays 134. Columns adorn a Carpet Factory on road from Sakkara.

FREDERICK MONDERSON

Research Essays Illustration 120. While the deceased Ani and his wife enter Osiris' Hall of Judgment, Anubis adjusts the scale, Thoth records, Am-Mit, eater of the dead, waits, and the Gods of the jury sit overhead.

VI.   THE STUDIES

Many studies are done to prove the "non-African" nature of the ancient Egyptians. More correctly, these studies are done to "prove the Caucasian origins of the Egyptians;" just as extensive studies were done in the 19th Century to prove man originated in Europe! But this is to no avail. In the nineteenth century a great many studies were done about the Egyptians but none really proved conclusively that they were White! A good example of one such study pertained to: **"THE ROYAL MUMMIES OF DEIR-EL-BAHARI."** *The Academy* 35 No. 891 (June 1, 1889: 383-384).

"It was during the summer of 1886 that Prof. Maspero resigned his Egyptian appointment; and the opening of the royal mummies closed his official labors. On June 1, in the presence of the Khedive and a select company of Egyptian and foreign notabilities, the mummies of Rameses II (XIXth Dynasty) and Rameses III (XXth Dynasty) were formally un-bandaged. Next followed, on June 9 the un-bandaging of Sekenen-Ra (XVIIth Dynasty) and Aahmes 1 (XVIIIth Dynasty); and subsequently, during the interval which elapsed between the arrival of M.

RESEACH ESSAYS ON ANCIENT EGYPT

Grebaut and the departure of Prof. Maspero, the rest of the Deir-el-Bahari Pharaohs, with the single exception of Amenhotep I, were duly opened. Each body in succession was carefully unwrapped and measured by Prof. Maspero, M. Bouriant, M. Insinger, and Dr. Fouquet, assisted by M. Mathey in the capacity of chemical analyst. These measurements, which are calculated on the French metrical system, give the lengths of the hand, foot, arm, forearm, etc.; various diameters of the skull; the circumference of head, shoulders, and waist; the length of the orbit of the eye, and the distance between the two orbits; the width of the mouth, length of nose and chin, circumference of pelvis, facial angle, etc. etc.; all having been twice taken and verified. Even the position of the orifice of the ear has been noted, and one learns with no little interest that, in at least one instance – e.g. that of the Princess Sit-Kames - this orifice is parallel with the root of the nose and somewhat above the line of the eye, precisely as we see it represented in Egyptian statuary."

Seriously, I don't think any other race of people have been so microscopically studied as the black race to disprove them black! Even more, another quote is appropriate here.

"The King Ra Kha-em-uas, whose name, at all events in this form, is unknown, is identified by Prof. Maspero with Rameses XII, the contemporary and predecessor of Her-Hor, and by M. Grebaut, with Rameses IX. Among other genealogical emendations, Prof. Maspero makes out Queen Aah-hotep (the famous Queen Aah-hotep of the Boulak jewels) to be the wife, not of Kames, as hitherto believed, but of Sekenen-Re, and the mother of both Kames and Aahmes I. He also, with infinite skill, based on an exhaustive study of a vast number of scattered inscriptions, reconstructs the framework of the XXIst Dynasty - thus, for the first time, presenting a satisfactory solution of one of the most difficult problems in Egyptian history."

FREDERICK MONDERSON

Research Essays 135. Memphis Museum. The alabaster Sphinx of Memphis that adorns the grounds of the museum.

Research Essays 135a. Suten Bat title of the Pharaoh with symbol of Ma'at, goddess of goodness.

RESEACH ESSAYS ON ANCIENT EGYPT

Research Essays Papyrus Art 20. Egyptian birds nest in a beautiful tree.

Besides the repetition here, two things should be mentioned. First, all this measurement and even the great Maspero could not indicate that, whatever said, Queen Aah-hotep and King Sekenen-Re produced Kames and Aahmes I, but give us no color of these personalities. Yet, Queen Aahmes-Nefertari who is akin to that group is pictured as a "Coal Black Ethiopian." So what does this make her brothers and father and mother?

Second, all the above measurements, notwithstanding, when Prof. Diop asked for a miniscule piece of the mummies to do his own study to show that they were black, he was denied. Still, he was able to secure some specimens elsewhere for his studies. Such meticulous research as Dr. Diop had done was instrumental at the 1974 United Nations' Conference on Egypt that affirmed the "fundamental blackness" of ancient Egyptian civilization!

VII.   THE WRITINGS

I.   THE ANCIENTS

Homer, one of the earliest writers of Europe refers, in the *Iliad*, to the Greek gods and their connection to Ethiopians "Jupiter today, followed by all the gods Receives the sacrifices of the Ethiopians" and again, "Yesterday to visit holy Ethiopia Jupiter betook himself to the ocean shore."

In his *Histories*, Book II, *Euterpe*, Herodotus stated: "The Colchians, Egyptians and Ethiopians have broad noses, thick lips, woolly hair, broad noses and are burnt of skin." On the other hand, G. Mokhtar in the official report of the 1974 United Nations Conference on the Nile Valley, as given in *Ancient Civilizations of Africa* Vol. II (London: Heinemann Educational Books, Ltd., 1981, p. 68) states, in replying to Prof. Vercoutter's question of how precisely Herodotus had defined the Egyptians as Negroes Dr. Cheikh Anta Diop responded: "Herodotus referred to them on three occasions in speaking of the origin of the Colchians, in speaking of the origin of the Nile floods, and in discussing the oracle of Zeus-Amon." Even further, Kamit Kush in *The Missing Pages of His-Story* (1993: 54) quotes Mokhtar (p. 62) that "Professor Diop went on to speak of the evidence provided by ancient written sources, pointing out that Greek and Latin authors described the Egyptian as negroes. He referred to the testimony of Herodotus, Aristotle, Lucian, Apollodorus, Aeschylus, Achilles, Tacitus, Strabo, Diodorus Siculus, Diogenes Laertius and Ammianus Marcellinus."

John D. Baldwin's *Pre-Historic Nations* (Harper and Brothers, New York: 1898, p. 276) as quoted in Indus Kamit Kush's *The Missing Pages of History* (p. 47) wrote: "Diodorus Siculus adds to his statement that the customs, religious observances, and letters of the ancient Egyptians closely resembles those of the Ethiopians, 'the colony still observing the customs of their ancestors."

Xenophanes, an Ionian by birth, wrote according to Bertrand Russell, *A History of Western Philosophy* (New York: Touchstone Books, Simon and Schuster, 1972, p. 40) as quoted in Kamit Kush (p. 46), "The Ethiopians make their gods black and snug-nosed; the Thracians say theirs have blue eyes and red hair." This view was also echoed by Dr. Victor Robinson in *The Story of Medicine* (New York: Albert and Charles Boni, 1936, p. 38) again quoted by Kush who states: "... the gods of

RESEACH ESSAYS ON ANCIENT EGYPT

the Ethiopians are swarthy and flat-nosed, the gods of the Thracians are fair-haired and blue-eyed." The gods of the Egyptians were no different and this forces us to question Wortham's contention that the Egyptians were Caucasians, and if so, why would they worship Black Gods?

II. THE MODERNS

Count Volney in *The Ruins of Empire* (1791) (1833: pp. 16-17) noted: "There a people, now forgotten, discovered, while others were yet barbarians, the elements of the arts and sciences. A race of men now rejected from society for their sable skin and frizzled hair, founded on the study of the laws of nature, those civil and religious systems which still govern the universe."

George Glidden in *Ancient Egypt: The New World*, (New York: J. Winchester, 1843: p. 59) stated: "the advocates of the African origin of the Egyptians cling to the superior antiquity of the pyramids at Meroe, as a proof of the origin of civilization in Ethiopia, and its consequent descent into Egypt ...." While not subscribing to this view himself, he states the "advocates" were Champollion Figeac and Rosellini, the Italian.

Herein is an important conundrum facing people who insist on the "Caucasian" origin of the Egyptians. Great store is given to the work and efforts of Herodotus and Champollion but when they say the Egyptians were Black nobody pays any attention. How sad!

a. **Wilhelm Hegel** - While contemporary with our time, Prof. Jacob Carruthers has quite eloquently pointed out how Hegel had not only removed Africa from being a part of history but also began the process of removing Egypt and Egyptians from Africa. Obviously, Hegel was probably not aware or unconcerned about Champollion the Younger's description of the ancient Egyptians and other Africans and the level of their cultural accomplishments alongside his comparison of the accomplishments of, as he said, "our ancestors" or the "Blond beasts." Strange, that the notion of "our ancestors" as they refer to Europeans in this work is equally incorrect when European writers refer to the ancient people of the Nile Valley as "our ancestors." Ideas die hard and as such we have the debacle that now pervades the discipline of the history of the Nile Valley cultural experience. Again, let's not forget Goethe's statement about how Germans corrupt other people's culture!

b. **Samuel Cartwright** - was described as "the banana skin physician," who equally, was an apologist for slavery in the ante-Bellum south. His book, *Slavery and Ethnology* was published in 1857, that epoch-making year and decade when

FREDERICK MONDERSON

Dred Scott was enshrined on the wrong side of American history and jurisprudence. In that work Samuel Cartwright wrote: "The Nilotic monuments furnish ample evidence that blacks (Negroes) were slaves along the banks of the Nile from time immemorial." What did he know? He probably never heard of Champollion the Younger or read his reports. His work had scant if any referents, was certainly not scientific and most assuredly was apologetic for slavery. The philosopher Immanuel Kant said: "act as if your work or words can become a universal axiom." However, these arguments have a tendency to fall apart upon closer scrutiny and revelation of new and sometimes even older information. Need I say more!

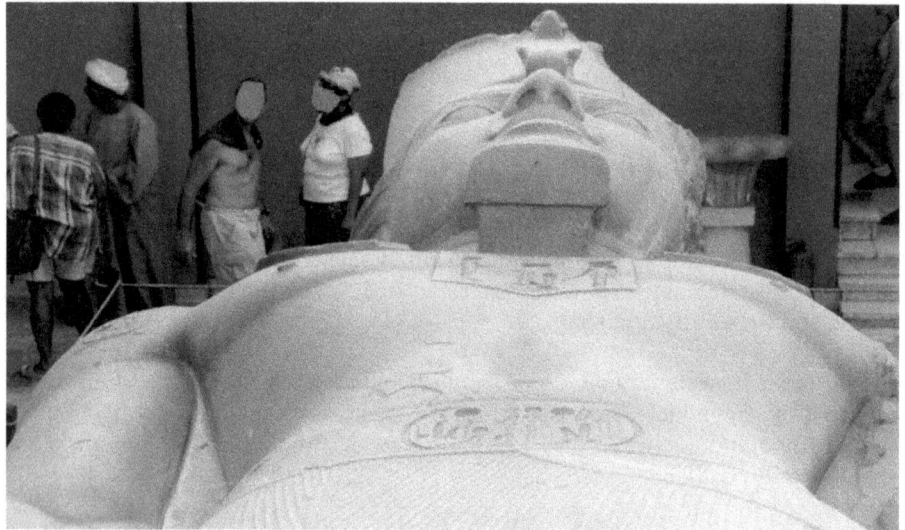

Research Essays 136. Memphis Museum. Visitors mill around the fallen colossal statue of Rameses II around which the Memphis Museum is built. Notice the uraeus on his brow, the beard and the cartouche and dagger at his waist.

c. The distinguished **Gaston Maspero** certainly did little to dispel the distorted misinterpretation of this aspect of a discipline he was so versed in. His Cairo Museum place cards in the display cases shaped the interpretation of the exhibits to this day. His description of the 19th Dynasty Nobleman Maherpra as being "Negroid but not Negro" has gone a long way to color the misinterpretation and misrepresentation of the ethnology of the ancient Egyptians. Since Maspero falls between Augustus Bozzi Granville and John David Wortham and the latter claims "Egyptians were Caucasian" and the former that Maherpra was "Negroid not Negro," could we then conclude the Nobleman was a "Negroid Caucasian." Or, should we entertain Cheikh Anta Diop's statement that "we reach the absurd conclusion that Negroes are basically whites."

RESEACH ESSAYS ON ANCIENT EGYPT

Research Essays 136a. The Statue upturned with the pharaoh shown wearing the Nemes Headdress and with the uraeus on his forehead and cartouche on the arm. His nose is not broken!

It's strange that of all the untold numbers of books written about ancient Egypt so little ever address the real facts of the case as it is raised in this selection. Such

FREDERICK MONDERSON

vivid descriptions are made about these ancient Egyptian Africans, but they seem so couched in misleading language it's hard to locate them.

A case can be made to compare different writers on the same topic. I use as an example, Beethoven, the German musical genius, whom it was argued, had "Moorish" blood implying he was Negro, African or had what we would call African-American features. Authorities differ on the "racial Origin" of this musical great. However, writing in *Sex and Race* vol. III, J. A. Rogers (1944: 306) supplies *Notes on Beethoven* showing that: "Beethoven was German and because his portraits are usually shown with a white tone and abundant hair nearly every one thinks of him as white." Rogers' beliefs on Beethoven's color based on commentary supplied by the musical genius' biographers that are included here as follows. Fanny Giannatasio del Rio "mulatto;" May Byron "swarthy;" Alexander Wheelock Thayer "negroid;" Frederick Hertz "negroid;" Brunold Springer "negroid;" Brunold Springer "negro;" Emil Ludwig "dark."

Why then would these writers use different words to describe the same person who is considered "negro?" It's the same with Maspero's definition of Mahepra that others may call the nobleman "negro." We must remember Mahepra is important because his papyrus says: "We came from the foothills of the Mountain of the Moon where the God Hapi [Osiris] dwells!!!" Also, let us consider all attempts to locate the ancient Egyptians are based on speculation. Yet, one seated scribe's statue with inlaid eyes out of thousands of such workers; one dissected mummy out of millions done by an Englishman in an age when Britannia ruled the world. Still, they disregarded the monumental sphinx and Maherpra's pinpointing not only the Egyptians' origins but also that of Hapi (Osiris).

To continue, two things are also raised in the following. First, in **EGYPT EXPLORATION FUND. THE EXCAVATION OF THE TEMPLE OF QUEEN HATASU AT DEIR-EL-BAHARI.** *The Academy* 45 No. 1137 (February 17, 1894: 153-154).

Luxor: Jan. 10, 1894.

We are told: "So far, the main finds of the latter class have been beads, scarabs, and figurines, made of the famous blue-glazed ware. Good Demotic and Coptic *Ostraka* are frequent, and there is much refuse from rifled mummy pits of the XXIInd Dynasty. Some coffins and mummies have been found lying loose among the upper layers of *debris*: one fine case belonged to Namen-Kenkhet-amen, a relative of Osorkhon II and Takelothis; another contains a very finely rolled mummy, for whose reception it was not originally intended; a third is early Coptic, and shows on the front of the outer cloth representations of wine and corn in the hands, while below is the sacred boat of Osiris and over the heart a swastika."

RESEACH ESSAYS ON ANCIENT EGYPT

This must shock Hitler's master race theorists as well as that erudite German school beginning with Hegel! So here we have ancient African use of this master-race symbol aeons ago. The patron saint of Germany, a black African general, also wears this symbol.

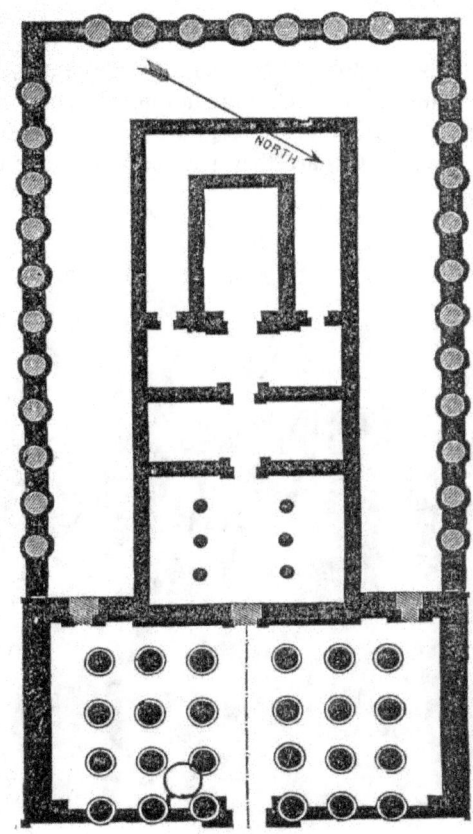

**Temple of Esneh, with restorations
By Grand Bey.**

Secondly, and this is significant because Dr. ben-Jochannan often told us the people were colored red by the henna plant. It states here in the above reference: "The last toilette of some royal ladies of the XXIst Dynasty was, for instance, most elaborate, the wrinkles caused by the process of mummification being filled up with some kind of enamel, the skin colored with ochre, the cheeks and lips rouged, and false eyes introduced under the shriveled and half-open lids; thus giving a horribly life-like appearance to the faces, as shown in the auto-type illustrations

FREDERICK MONDERSON

from Herr Brugsch's photographs." The ochre here is the Henna plant. Imagine the numerous individuals in the Rekhmire tomb, working, all dead, 'Are they painted red with Henna?' The "false eyes," are they reminiscent of the "Louvre Scribe who has blue eyes?" Or, are they painted red as the "chosen people" in association with a solar deity?

Research Essays 136b. Items for sale on grounds of the Memphis Museum.

RESEACH ESSAYS ON ANCIENT EGYPT

Research Essays Temple Ticket 19. Cairo Museum of Egyptian Antiquities. Price of entrance is sixty Egyptian Pounds.

Even further, elsewhere in East Africa, the anthropologist Mary Leakey and her husband Louis between 1935-1951 (*Nile Year* 6175-6191) discovered and catalogued 186 rock-painting sites. This extensive gallery supplied 1,600 individual scenes, over a 500-square-mile area in Tanzania. Through Mary Leakey's (1983: 86) work, "Tanzania's Stone Age Art," we are helped in understanding an archaeological study of man's distant past in Africa, that brings to us the startling conclusion: "Those long-ago works of art tell us, for example, that Stone Age man in Africa wore clothing, had a variety of hairstyles, hunted, danced, sang, played musical instruments, and may even have known the secret of fermenting spirits."

The interesting point is, for these early East African painters, in many respects similar to those of the Tassili artists, painting materials were of principal concern. Their choice of colors is interesting for: "the predominant red was made from ocher, which is derived from iron ore. Black probably came from manganese, and bird droppings may have provided the basis for the white." So even these peoples removed from Egypt loved "predominant red." Many figures, even those represented by the Tassili frescoes show red in their paintings. Are we to believe these people are also Egyptians?

FREDERICK MONDERSON

Research Essays 136c. Another of the booths offering memorabilia for sale on the grounds of the Memphis Museum.

Another significant point is developed from the following quote. Budge (1969, II: 22-23) explained how: "The worship of Amen-Ra was introduced into Nubia by its Egyptian conquerors early in the XIIth Dynasty, and the inhabitants of that country embraced it with remarkable fervor; the hold which it had gained upon them was much strengthened when an Egyptian viceroy, who bore the title of 'royal son of Cush,' was appointed to rule over the land, and no efforts were spared to make Napata a second Thebes. The Nubians were, from the poverty of their country, unable to imitate the massive temples of Karnak and Luxor, and the festivals which they celebrated in honor of the Nubian Amen-Ra, and the processions which they made in his honor, lacked the splendor and magnificence of the Theban capital; still, there is no doubt that, considering the means which they had at their disposal, they erected temples for the worship of Amen-Ra of very considerable size and solidity. The hold which the priesthood of Amen-Ra of Thebes had upon the Nubians was very great, for in the troublous times which followed after the collapse of their power as priest-kings of Egypt, the remnant of the great brotherhood made its way to Napata, and settling down there made plans and schemes for the restoration of their rule in Egypt; fortunately for Egypt their designs were never realized." So, whatever happened to these Egyptians since they were so different from the Nubians? Why have they vanished? Also, if "fortunately for Egypt their desires were never realized" is true, what are we to say of the Persian, Assyrian, Greek, Roman, Christian, Arab, and all others.

RESEACH ESSAYS ON ANCIENT EGYPT

Research Essays 137. Memphis Museum. Anubis sits atop a granite sarcophagus on the grounds of the Museum.

Dr. ben-Jochannan has often pointed out, soldiers on the move never carry their women but intermingled with the women they meet in the cities or countries they invade and garrison. Are we to believe, Egypt at the crossroads, invaded by so many foreign armies never experienced any admixture so much so, the ancient and modern Egyptians are practically the same?

FREDERICK MONDERSON

Equally, we are also told from inscriptions at Abu Simbel Temple of Rameses II, of 200,000 or so soldiers who rebelled against Psammetichus settled in Nubia, in that age, Ethiopia. So where are these foreigners in Nubia? I mean these red Egyptians who were so different from the African Nubians! In anthropometrical studies done by Myers, he claims no difference between ancient and modern Egyptians. Yet, the above two groups of Egyptians settled among the Nubians and we see no difference today. Yet, Egypt, at the crossroads of the ancient world was conquered by Hyksos, Persians, Assyrians, Greeks and Roman as well as infused by various peoples as conquered slaves, then the Muslim invasion of 640 and the Mamelukes and all other foreign conquerors as the French, English, and everyone else who came, invaded and without question certainly did damage to the culture. Thus, that there is no difference between the ancient and modern Egyptians is a laughable conclusion.

Kush quotes W.E.B. DuBois in *The World and Africa* (New York: International publishers, 1965, p. 106) who wrote: "We conclude, therefore, that the Egyptians were Negroids, and not only that, but by tradition they believed themselves descended not from the whites or the yellows, but from the black peoples of the south. Thence they traced their origin, and toward the south in earlier days they turned the faces of their buried corpses."

Even more, when the statue identified as the "Sheikh el Beled" was discovered, arguments were made that the ancient and modern Egyptians were so alike there was no change, despite the many centuries of admixture Egypt underwent. In a parallel case, with the significant incursions of these "different Egyptians" who moved into Nubia how come they are not distinct from the other Africans? We know Sesostris left an army in the Caucus who were the Colchians and that element is pronounced in that environment today. Hannibal had an army in Italy for two decades and this affected the population of southern Italy, Sicily, for millennia to come. Therefore, perhaps we can ask how really different were the Egyptians from the other Africans south of Egypt? Prof. Diop's simple explanation is that the Egyptians painted themselves red so as to be distinguished from other Africans. We also know, red as well as gold had a divine connotation and since the Egyptians considered themselves special, why not paint themselves with the divine color, red. However, with the divine color red, these ancient Africans could not foretell the modern conception of race and racism and the impact it would have on people relationships. The only answer surrounding this issue of the implication of the "red" color of the Egyptians, seems it's all part of the 'Conspiracy Against Ancient Egypt.'

RESEACH ESSAYS ON ANCIENT EGYPT

Research Essays 137a. Memphis Museum. Ptah, great god of Artisans and Memphis, a bald-headed dwarf, or pygmy.

VIII. ARGUMENTS FOR ORIGINS

The arguments for origins and ethnicity of the Egyptians have principally centered on external influences and ipso facto they could not be black. The last half and particularly the last quarter of the 19th Century has witnessed a full court press of theories of the origins of the Egyptians that were primarily based on speculative linguistic evidence coupled with migration factors that for all but the seasoned linguist seem convincing. However, the substantive cultural features such as architecture, the earliest significant culture manifestation in any cultural development seem lacking in the places of supposed origins. In a modern comparison, the Australians of today possess cultural affinity that links them with England and British culture; so too do the Americans. Germans, Italians and many who migrated to America brought and have retained their cultural connections with their ancient homelands. However, the foreigners who supposedly migrated and advanced Egyptian civilization have not left any significant cultural remains of their homeland. Nor do we see these remains in their place of origins, especially in the Southwest Asia and European Caucasus. Yet still, these spurious ideas have persisted, been preserved in mothballs and trotted out ever-so-often, despite the fact that reputable scholars are not "Concerned with physical origins but cultural accomplishments." However, there is clear evidence of Central African ideas and motifs and even contemporary survivals linking modern Africa with their ancient antecedents in Egypt.

IX. CONTEMPORARY VIEWS

The contemporary approach is one of "don't ask, don't tell," as it relates to the race of the ancient Egyptians; yet, modern books, despite the avalanche of recent research are tremendously sanitized that "the issue is really a non-issue." We ought not to forget Dr. ben-Jochannan's admonition. "Get the earliest research material and work from there," as it falls upon us as participants in African historiographic reconstruction to do what we must to set the record straight.

The African world is awake and its scholars are seriously challenging the misrepresentations, distortions and omissions systematically implanted by pseudo-scientists, racists and all who are ignorant of the fact of the glorious role Africans have played not only in Africa but globally. Clearly history has to be and is being rewritten placing Africa in her respectful place at the head in the order and narrative of humanity's global and triumphant experience.

RESEACH ESSAYS ON ANCIENT EGYPT

Research Essays 138. The Step-Pyramid of Sakkara built by Imhotep for Pharaoh Zoser, 3rd Dynasty, 2600 B.C. This structure remains standing and intact, attesting to its architectural magnificence and the construction genius of its builders.

Research Essays 138a. Memorabilia for sale on grounds of Sakkara, home of the Step-Pyramid.

FREDERICK MONDERSON

Research Essays 138b. Another of the vendors plying his wares in the grounds of the Memphis Museum.

X.   References

Bakry, H.K.S. *A Brief Study of Mummies and Mummification.* Cairo: 1965
Diop, Cheikh Anta.   *The African Origin of Civilization: Myth or Reality.* Brooklyn, New York: Lawrence Hill Book Co., (1955) 1974.
Herodotus. *The Histories.* Translated by Audrey de Selincourt. New York: Viking Penguin, Inc. (1954) 1972.
Kush, Indus Kamit. *The Missing Pages of His-Story.* D and J. Books, Inc., Laurelton, New York: 1993.
Robins, Gay.   *The Art of Ancient Egypt.* Cambridge, Massachusetts. Harvard University Press, 1997.
Smith, W. Stephenson.   *The Art and Architecture of Ancient Egypt.* Boston: Museum of Fine Arts, 1959.

RESEACH ESSAYS ON ANCIENT EGYPT

Research Essays Papyrus Art 21. The golden mask of King Tutankhamon.

FREDERICK MONDERSON

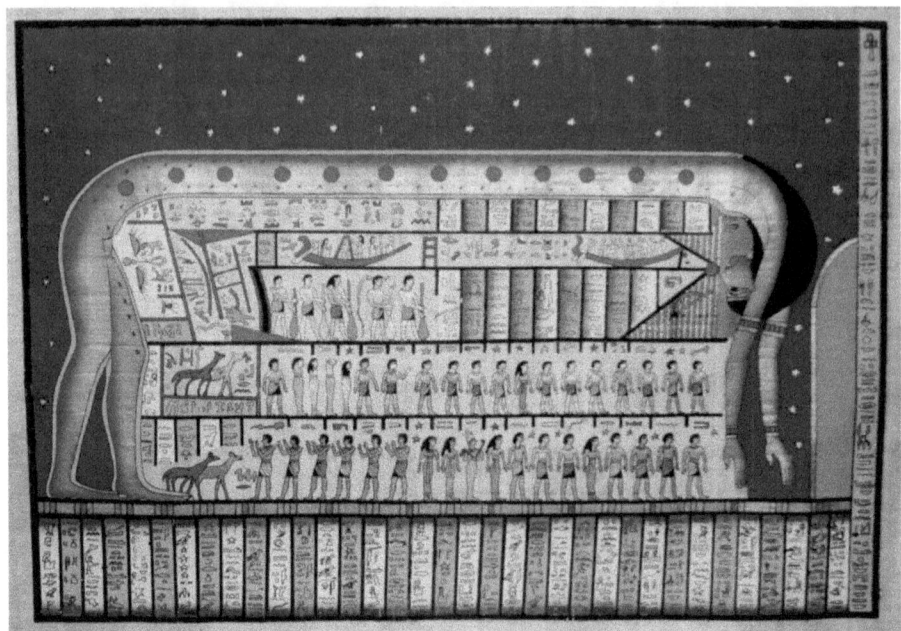

Research Essays Papyrus Art 22. Goddess Nuit spanning the heavens where she gives birth to the sun in the morning and swallows it up at evening time.

Research Essays 138c. Memphis Museum. Side view of the Sphinx of Memphis.

RESEACH ESSAYS ON ANCIENT EGYPT

21. Suggestions for Further Reading

ben-Jochannan, Yosef A.A. *Black Man of the Mile and his Family.* New York: Alkebu-Lan Publishers, 1972.
_____. *Africa: Mother of Western Civilization.* New York: Alkebu-Lan Publishers, 1970.
_____. *African Origins of the Major Western Civilizations.* New York: Alkebu-Lan Publishers, 1971.
Bernal, Martin. *Black Athena.* 2 Vols. New Brunswick, New Jersey. Rutgers University Press, 1987.
Carruthers, Jacob H. *Mdw Ntr: Divine Speech.* New Jersey: Red Sea Press, 1995.
_____. *Intellectual Warfare.* Chicago: Third World Press, 1999.
DeGraaf-Johnson, J.C. *African Glory.* Baltimore, MD.: Black Classics Press, (1954) 1986.
Diop, Cheikh Anta. *Civilization or Barbarism.* Brooklyn, New York: Lawrence Hill Books, (1981) 1991.
_____. *Pre-Colonial Black Africa.* Westport, Connecticut: Lawrence Hill and Co., 1987.
_____. *African Origins of Civilization: Myth or Reality.* Brooklyn, New York: Lawrence Hill Book Co., (1955) 1974.
_____. *The Cultural Unity of Black Africa.* Chicago: Third World Press, (1959) 1987.
DuBois, W.E.B. *The Negro.* New York: Oxford University Press (1915) 1970.
Finch, Charles III. *Echoes of the Old Darkland.* Decatur, Georgia: Khenti, Inc., (1991) 1996.
Jackson, John. *Introduction to African Civilizations.* Secaucus, New Jersey: The Citadel Press, 1970.
Johnson, J.C. *African Glory.* Baltimore, MD.: Black Classics Press, (1954) 1986.
Karenga, Maulana and Jacob Carruthers. *Kemet and the African Worldview.* Los Angeles: University of Sankore Press, 1986.
Kush, Indus Khamit. *The Missing Pages of "His-Story."* Laurelton, New York: D and J Books, 1993.
Rogers, J.A. *World's Great Men of Color.* 2 Vols. New York: Macmillan, 1972.
_____. *Sex and Race.* 3 Vols. New York: Helga Rogers, 1967.
Van Sertima, Ivan. *Nile Valley Civilizations.* Journal of African Civilizations, Inc. New Brunswick, New Jersey: Transaction Publishers, (1985) 1986.
_____. *Egypt Child of Africa.* New Brunswick, New Jersey: Transaction Publishers, (1994) 1995.
_____. *Egypt: Revisited.* New Brunswick, New Jersey: Transaction Publishers, 1989.
_____. *Great African Thinkers: Cheikh Anta Diop.* New Brunswick, New Jersey: Transaction Books, (1986) 1987.

FREDERICK MONDERSON

_____. *Great Black Leaders: Ancient and Modern*. New Brunswick, New Jersey: Journal of African Civilizations, 1988.
_____. *Blacks In Science: Ancient and Modern*. New Brunswick, New Jersey: Journal of African Civilizations, Ltd., Inc., 1983.
_____. *Black Women in Antiquity*. New Brunswick, New Jersey: Journal of African Civilizations, Ltd., Inc., ((1984) 1986.
Williams, Chancellor. *Destruction of Black Civilizations*. Chicago: Third World Press, 1970.
Woodson, Carter G. *The Mis-Education of the Negro*. Trenton, New Jersey: Africa World Press, (1990) 1993.
_____. *The Education of the Negro*. Brooklyn, New York: A and B Books Publisher, (1919).

Research Essays 138d. Memphis Museum. Remains of columns on the grounds of Memphis Museum.

Comparing EGYPTIAN CHRONOLOGY

(Dr. A.A. ben-Jochannan *Black Man of the Nile*, 1972

(William J. Murnane *The Penguin Guide to Ancient Egypt*, 1983)

RESEACH ESSAYS ON ANCIENT EGYPT

Predynastic 6000-3200 B.C.	Predynastic 5000-3300 B.C.
Badarian	Badarian 5000-4000 B.C.
Amratian................... (Naqada 1)	Amratian 4000-3500 B.C.
Gerzean................... (Naqada I and II)	Gerzean 3500-3300 B.C.
Archaic Period 3200-2780 B.C.	Archaic Period 3050-2686 B.C.
Old Kingdom 2780-2270 B.C.	Old Kingdom 2613-2181 B.C.
First Intermediate Period	First Intermediate Period
Middle Kingdom 2100-1675 B.C.	Middle Kingdom 2040-1782 B.C.
Second Intermediate Period 1675-1600 B.C.	Second Intermediate Period 1782-1570 B.C.
New Kingdom 1600-1090 B.C.	New Kingdom 1570-1070 B.C.
Third Intermediate Period	Third Intermediate Period
Late Period 713-332 B.C.	Late Period 527-332 B.C.
Graeco-Roman Period 332 B.C.-640 A.D.	Graeco-Roman Period 332 B.C.-395 A.D.

The Comparing of Egyptian Chronologies is designed to give the reader some insights into how scholars have viewed this important subject. The dates presented here represent those of the "Short Chronology," whereas at the end of the 19th Century the "Long Chronology" was in vogue. The "Long Chronology" moves certainly the earliest period back by nearly two thousand years. However, the period from the New Kingdom onward is generally more stable for it coincides with other "Middle Eastern" dates of societies on the move. Nevertheless, we should not be unmindful that some scholars have argued use of the "Short Chronology" is more political for it synchronizes with Mesopotamian dates. Notwithstanding, the two scholars' works chosen above is contemporary, though Murnane is newer than ben-Jochannan and is the generally accepted working model among most scholars today.

FREDERICK MONDERSON

Research Essays 138e. Memphis Museum. Side view of colossal statue of Rameses II and remains exhibited in and outside of cases as two ladies stroll along enjoying the view.

RESEACH ESSAYS ON ANCIENT EGYPT

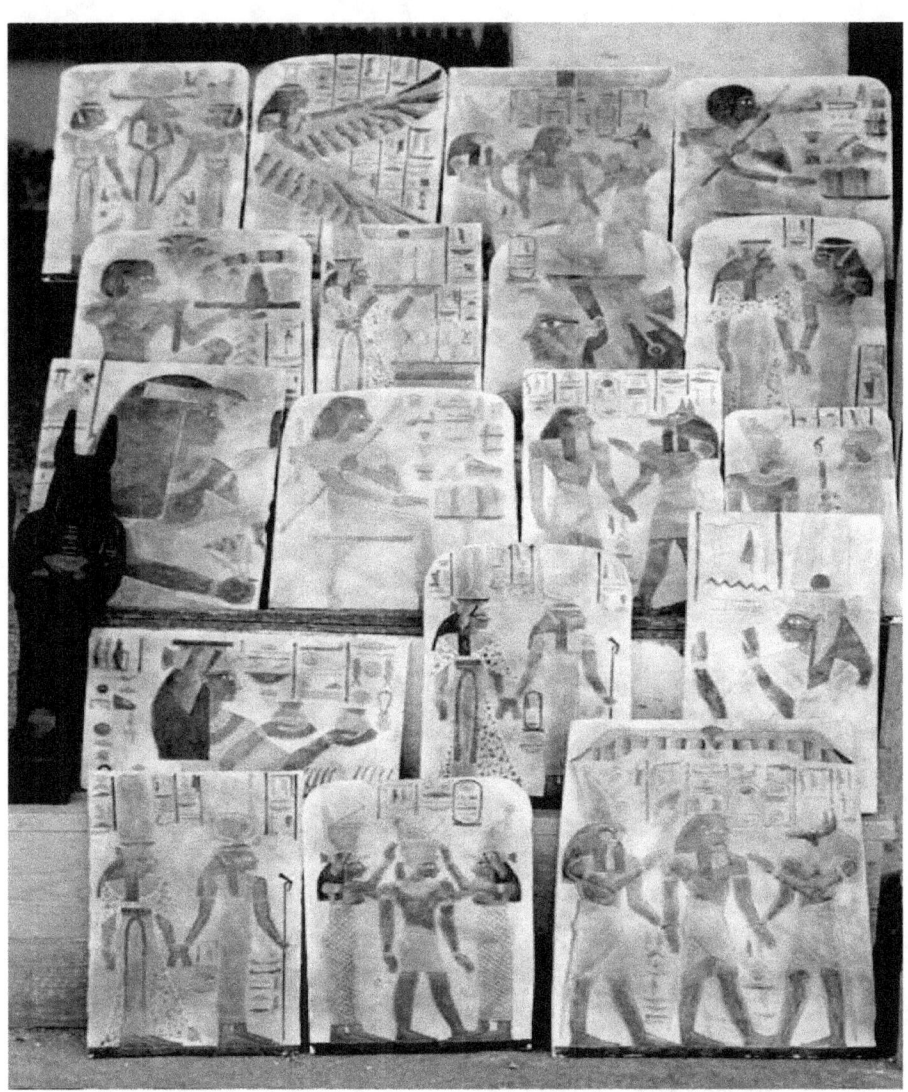

Research Essays 138f. Artifacts for sale outside of Theban sites.

FREDERICK MONDERSON

Research Essays 139. Images of figures from a tomb at Sakkara. Interestingly, it's always the face that is attacked and one has to ask why!

INDEX

Abu Simbel 44, 46
    Gods of 44, 46
Abydos, temples 286
Aegyptopithecus 32
African Americans writers and historians 133
Africans in the New World 344
Ahmes-Nefertari 477, 544, 547, 557
Akh Menu 288
Aldred, Cyril 137, 141, 144, 384
    (1980) *Egyptian Art* 161, 165, 169, 322, 331, 347
    (1961) (1987) *The Egyptians* 417, 440-441, 467-468
Almagest, the 408
Am-Mit, a woman 131
Amun (Amen, Amon) 144-145
    Symbols of 203
Amrah, el "strongly curled hair" 537
Amratian Culture 211-213
Anatomists who studied ancient Egypt 87-88
"Ancient Records of Ancient Records" (1870-1930) 240
Animals as art motifs 298

RESEACH ESSAYS ON ANCIENT EGYPT

Anthropoidea 34
Archaeological Survey of Egypt 256-257
Archaeological Survey of Nubia 257
"Argument for a Negro Origin" Diop, 66
Aristotle
    Physiognomonica 90
Army 324
Arnett, William
    (1982) *The Predynastic Origin of Egyptian Hieroglyphics: Evidence for the Development of Rudimentary Forms of Hieroglyphics in Upper Egypt in the Fourth Millennium* B.C. 299
Arnold, Deiter
    (1993) *The Encyclopedia of Ancient Egyptian Temples* 180, 182
Art of Egypt 355
Asante, Molefi 262
Australopithecus Africanus 32,
Australopithecinae 36
Australopithecus Paranthropus 36
Australopithecus Robustus 32,
Badarian Culture 209-210, 249
Baedeker
    (1929) *Baedeker's Guide to Egypt* 43,
Baines and Malek
    (1980) *Atlas of Ancient Egypt* 422-424
Bakry, H.K.S.
    (1965) *Brief Study of Mummies and Mummification* 540-541
Baldwin, John D.
    (1898) *Prehistoric Nations* 76, 559
Barber's tools 313
Bartholomew De Las Casas 260
Basic traits of early man 38
Basic traits of early sites 38
Battle of Kadesh 36
Battle Scenes 330
Beethoven, Ludwig
Belzoni, Giovanni 44, 254
ben-Jochannan, Yosef A.A. (Dr Ben) A.A. 26, 30, 52, 63, 69, 87, 114, 262, 266, 564, 567-570, 571
"" Admonition (Dictum) "Get the oldest materials and work from there!" 572, 579
"" Chronology of Ancient Egypt 200-201
"Black pharaohs" 87
Blacks in Science 354
Black statues of Min 301
Blyden, Edward Wilmot 30
Boats 422-424

Book of the Dead 251
Books of
    Am Duat 57, 124
    Dead or *Coming Forth by Day* 121, 124, 130-131, 139
    Gates 47, 105,
    Khun Anup 57
    Knowing the Appearance of Ra 57
    Maa-Khere 57
Books of Thoth, forty-two 361
Breasted, James H. 106-107
    (1906) (1923) *History of Egypt* 368, 370, 373, 421, 437, 465-466, 466-467, 486, 487, 488,
    Ancient Records of Egypt
    Ancient Times
    The Development of Religion and Thought 83
    (1915) *First Fixed Date in History* 351
Bricks 337
Brier, Bob
    (1994) *Egyptian Mummies* 418
British School of Archaeology in Egypt 256
British Association for the Advancement of Science 225
Brodeur, Arthur G.
    (1931) *The Pageant of Civilization* (Preface)
Brother Abdul "Master of Karnak" 43, 61, 69
Brooks, Lester
    (1971) *Great Civilizations of Ancient Africa* 80, 82
Browder, Anthony 262
    Nile Valley Contribution to Civilization 74, 174
Brugsch-Bey, Karl Heinrich
    (1902) Egypt Under the Pharaohs 97
Budge, E.A.W. 99
    (1905) *Egyptian Heaven and Hell* 138-139
    (1900) (1991) Egyptian *Religion* 119-120
    (1934) *From Fetish to God in Ancient Egypt* 124, 125-126, 127, 142
    (1894) *The Mummy* 83
    (1972) *Dwellers on the Nile* 366, 446, 459, 470-471
    Egyptian Magic 83
    Book of the Dead 83
    Egyptian Hieroglyphic Dictionary 83, 84
    (1969 I) Gods of the Egyptians 497
    (1969 II) "" "" 567
Building materials 267
Bunson
    (1991) (1999) Encyclopedia of Ancient Egypt 365, 433-434
Burckhardt 34

RESEACH ESSAYS ON ANCIENT EGYPT

"Cachette Court" 456
Cadogan
    (2002) *Cairo, Luxor, Aswan* 74,
Cairo Museum 54, 60, 65, 86
Cairo Museum statues painted black 87
Calendars, 4 349
Calendars and chronology 353
Canon of Proportion 331, 331, 332-333, 340-341
Carruthers, Jacob 30, 59, 262
    Mdw Ntr: Divine Speech 43
Cartwright, Samuel
    (1857) *Slavery and Ethnology* 560
Cataract dynamics 325
Ceboidea 34
Centers of religious worship 231
Cercopithecoidea 25
Champollion, Jean Francois 54, 94, 254, 325
Chapels
    "Red" 187
    "White" 187
Chronology 191, 493
    "Long Chronology" 197
    "Short Chronology" 197
Chronology of Egypt 364
Cire Perdue process 445
Clarke, John Henrik 28, 30, 74, 76, 113, 262
Clarke, Sommers and R. Engelbach
    (1930) *Ancient Egyptian Construction and Archaeology* 309-310
Classical writers
    Ammianus Marcellus 92
    Aristotle 90
    Diodorus Siculus 91
    Diogenes on Zeno 92
    Herodotus 90
    Homer 89
        Homer
        The *Iliad* 89
        The *Odyssey* 89

Cochran, Johnny 258
Coffin Texts 118
Colors 352-353
Components of a Pyramid complex 344-345
Copernicus 357, 360
Cosmological interpretation of the temple 189
Cosmology of Egypt 231

FREDERICK MONDERSON

Craft of Metallurgy 305
Crafts 305
Crafts, Themes of 306, 307
Cranial Capacity 33
Crowns 287, 320
    Ureret, War, nemes and *Atef* 177
    deshret –Red Crown 251
    hedjet – White Crown 251
    pschent – United Double Crown 219
Cultural contributions of ancient Egypt 63, 64
Daily temple ritual 115
Dart, Raymond 30
Dating of Boats 368-369
Dating methods 34
    C-14 34
    Potassium Argon 34
    Thermoluminesence 34
    Dendochronology 34
David, Rosalie
    (1993) *Discovering Ancient Egypt* 454
Davidson, Basil
    "Whose Roots?" 76
Davis, Theodore 398
Deir el Bahari "cache" 468, 473-474
Delaney, Martin 30
Denon, Count 30
De Rogue 105
Diop, Cheikh Anta 30, 31, 87, 89, 90, 95, 157, 195, 196, 262, 424
    (1974) *African Origins of Civilization: Myth or Reality* 81, 93
""   "Africa's Contribution to World Civilization: The Exact Sciences" 396
""   "Egyptians painted themselves red ..." 570
Diop and Rameses II 369-370
Diop at the UN Conference
Diseases 221
Divine nature of esoteric religion 116-117
Divisions of the Army 328
Division of Labor 292
Doxey, Denise M.
    (2001) *The Oxford Encyclopedia of Ancient Egypt* 145,
Dr. Fred 69
DuBois, W.E.B. 30, 111, 262
    (1896) *Suppression of the Slave Trade to America* 1638-1880
    (1915) *The Negro* 111
    (1946) *The World and Africa* 111, 569-570
Dunjee, Drusilla 30

RESEACH ESSAYS ON ANCIENT EGYPT

Dynamics of pyramid work 340
Dynasties
    XVIII 40,
Dynastic Periods 360, 361
Dyropithecus 32
Early architecture, early 336, 367
Early pyramid features 342
Early man in Africa 23,
Early tool making materials 30
Egypt Exploration Fund 256
Egyptian art 323
Egyptian Calendar 76
Egyptian doctors, hierarchy 361
Egyptian fine arts 315
Egyptian jewelry 382
Egyptian l'etat c'est moi 109
Egyptian monotheism 107, 121
Egyptian painting
Egyptian pharmacopeia 416
Egyptian Research Account 256
Egyptian science 392, 426
Egyptian taxation 464, 489
Egyptian technology 390
Egyptian temple, business of 135
Egyptian temple, origin of 136
Egyptian timber 269
Egyptian trinity 171-172
Elements, the 407
Emery, Walter
    (1961) *Archaic Egypt* 83
Engelback, R.
    (1961) *Introduction to Egyptian Archaeology with special Reference to the Egyptian Museum* 138, 315, 316, 343
Erman, Adolf 97-98
    (1894) *Life in Ancient Egypt* 443
    (1907) *Handbook of Egyptian Religion* 160, 166-167
Ethiopia 61
Euclid's elements 357
Fagan, Brian
    (1975) *The Rape of the Nile* 254
Festivals 42
    Opet 42, 43, 45,
Festival ritual 115-116
"Fields of
    Elysian" 132
    Peace" 132

Reeds" 132
Finch, Charles
    (1988) *Great Black Leaders: Ancient and Modern* 82
Foods of Egypt 224
Fossil grounds 32

Research Essays 139a. Two images of Noblemen from Sakkara holding their staff and Aba Scepter. Notice the little figure beside the staff of authority.

Forty-two books of Thoth 361
Foundation, temple 168
Frankfort, Henri
    (1946) (1961) *Ancient Egyptian Religion* 128-129
Gardiner, Alan
    (1961) *Egypt of the Pharaohs* 480-481
Garvey, Marcus 32
    Philosophy and Opinions 259
Gerzean Culture 214-215
Gebel Arrack knife 250
Ghizeh Plateau 41,
Gigantopithecus 32
Gilbert
    (1995) 497, 498
Gillings

RESEACH ESSAYS ON ANCIENT EGYPT

    (1972) (1983) *Mathematics in the Time of the Pharaohs* 405, 406, 464,
"Girdle Wall of Rameses II" 62
Glanville, S.R.K.
    (1963) *The Legacy of Egypt* 355
Gliddon, George
    (1843) *Ancient Egypt: The New World* 76
God in earliest times 100-101
God of creation 125
God's land in Black Africa 553
Gods
    Amon 42, 58, 70
    Amon-Ra 51
    Anubis
    Haroeis (Elder Horus) 37
    Horus 37, 51, 58
    Isis 51, 58,
    Khnum 40,
    Min 70
    Osiris 51, 70
        "The Great Black" 71
    Ptah 58
    Ra-Horakhty 51, 58,
    Sobek 37
    Seti 58
    Thoth 410
Goodwin, C.W.
    (1873) 139-140, 141-142
Gold 379
Gold awards 454
Gold of Egypt 428
Golden Calf 380
Gold, melting 391-392
Gold work 309, 384
Gold workers' title 448
Graeco-Roman Branch 257
Greaves, Kersey 30
Greek inheritance from Egypt 61, 62
Grollanelli and Mander 493, 499, 560
Haag, Michael
    (2000) *Cairo, Luxor, Aswan* 89
Hall, A. Rupert and Marie Boas Hall
    A Brief History of Science 421
    "Hamitic Hypothesis" 25
Hansberry, William Leo 111-112
Harris, J.E.
    (1981) *Pillars in Ethiopian History* 111-113

FREDERICK MONDERSON

Harris, John R.
    (1971) *The Legacy of Egypt* 284
Hatshepsut 350
Hawass, Zahi 259
Hegel, Wilhelm 560
Helical rising of Sothis 348
Herodotus 90, 559
Hierakonpolis 530
Hieroglyphics of seasons 350
Higgins, Godfrey 30
"Hippocratic Oath" 367
Hippocrates 369
Hominoidea 34, 36
Homo erectus 33
Homo habilis 32, 33, 39, 24824, 25, 29,
Hope (1962) on Egyptian costumes 541
Hotels
        Oberoi 47
        Old Cataract 47
        New Cataract 47
"House of Life" 364
Household cults and state gods 115
Huggins, John 21
Hyksos "dare" 228
Hypostyle Hall at Karnak 52
Imhotep 216, 411, 413
Instrumental Astronomy 399
Jackson, John G.
    (1970) *Introduction to African Civilization* 172
James, Leonard 134
James, George G.M. 134
Johnson, Paul
    (1987) (1999) The *Civilization of Ancient Egypt* 417
Johnston, Sir Harry 114
Junker, Herman 97,
Kamit Indus Kush 69
    "*Missing Pages of His-Story*" 63
Karenga, Maulana 262
Karnak 69
Keating
    (1975) *Nubian Rescue* 431, 440
Kees, Herman
    (1961) (1977) *A Social History of Ancient Egypt* 470, 471, 471-472, 473, 474, 475, 477

RESEACH ESSAYS ON ANCIENT EGYPT

Research Essays 139b. Goddess Mut is the principal figure with portion of the White Crown visible to the right, from a tomb at Sakkara.

Kenyapithecus wickeri 32
Khety and Son Pepi 267
Kingdoms:
    Middle 41,
    New 41,
    Old 41
King Lists
    Abydos 197
    Karnak 197
    Sakkara 197
Kings 42
    Aahmes Preface,
    Akhenaten (Amenhotep IV, Ikhnaton) 42
    Alexander 42
    Amenhotep I
    Amenhotep III 42, 51
    Aye 51
    Court of 43
    Horemhab (Horemheb) 42
    Menes (Narmer) 51
    Mentuhotep II 226, 227, 545
        "Black flesh" 226, 285
    Merenra 138

Pepi I 138
Pepi II 138
Rameses II 42, 43
    "Girdle Wall" 55
Rameses III 51
    Gifts to Amon's temple 475
Seti I 42, 51
Seti II 42

Teti (Teta) 138
Thutmose I 69
Thutmose II
Thutmose III
Thutmose IV
Tutankhamon (Tutankhaten) 259
Unas 138

Kingly endowments to temples 386
Kitchener Garden 36
Knowledge 47
Kush, Khamit Indus
    (1993) *The Missing Pages of "His-Story"* 75-76, 160, 325, 326, 327, 559
Leakey, Louis and Mary 32, 566
Lehner, Mark
    (1997) (1998) *The Complete Pyramids* 443, 444
Length of the year 348
Lepsius, Karl
    (1852) *Discoveries in Egypt, Ethiopia and the Peninsula of Sinai in the Years 1842-1848* 95, 255
Linnaean classification 27
"Locks" 47
Loret and Gaillard 104
Lotus Memorial 36
Lucas, Alfred
    Ancient Egyptian Materials and Industries 310
Lumpkin
    (1983) *Blacks in Science* 404, 405
Luxor architectural wonders 315
Ma'at 192-193
Mahepra 65
Maintenance of divine order 129
Malcolm X 28
Manetho
    History of Egypt 411
Manley, Bill
    (1996) *The Penguin Historical Atlas of Ancient Egypt* 440, 455

RESEACH ESSAYS ON ANCIENT EGYPT

Mann, A.T.
    (1993) *Sacred Architecture* 162, 163, 165
"Mansions of Millions of Years" 51, 186
Mariette, Auguste 96-97
Mariette, Bey 171
Maspero, Gaston 98, 561
    (1891) "Creation by voice"
    (1891) *Creation By Voice* 147-148
    (1902) *Manual of Egyptian Archaeology* 449
    (1912) *Art in Egypt* 348
    (1926) *Manual of Egyptian Archaeology* 314, 432, 446, 447, 449, 476, 477, 483
Maspero on bricks 241
Maspero on materials 242-243
Massey, Gerald 22, 134
    Book of the Beginning 172
Mausoleum of Aga Khan 36
McMahan (1998) 499
Medical works 359
Memphis 41
Memphite Theology 232
Metals 391
Methods of dating 42
    C-14 - 42
    Dendochronology 42
    Potassium Argon 42
    Thermoluminesence 42
Michalowski, K.
    (ND) *Art of Ancient Egypt* 331, 338, 339, 340
Middle Kingdom
Military pharaohs 374
Min of Koptos 115
Mines of Nubia 376
Minerals 309
Mokhtar, G.
    (1981) *Ancient Civilizations of Africa* 478
Montesquieu
    Spirit of the Laws 74, 527
Move, adapt or die 25,
Mummification 127
Murnane, William J.
    (1983) *The Penguin Guide to Ancient Egypt* 496
Murray's
    (1888) *Handbook for Egypt* 89, 550, 551
Murray, Margaret

(1949) (1963) *The Splendor That Was Egypt* Preface, 77-79, 167, 432, 437-438, 476
(1931) *The Temples of Egypt* 135, 177, 178
Myth of Europe and Asia in Africa 22,
Narmer Macehead 364
"″″″″" Palette 171, 189, 203, 219, 288, 320
Na'im Akbar
    Egyptian Origin of the Science of the Mind 349
Name for gold 375
Names of craftsmen 305
Names, Kings
    Horus 433
    Nebti 433
    Golden Horus 433
    Nisut-Bit 433
    Son of Ra 433
    Napoleon/Monuments of Egypt 433
Narmer, Menes 135, 215, 216
Narmer Macehead 197, 215
Naville, Edouard 102, 182
"Near man" 32, 39
Nefertari 36
Negative Confessions 131, 133-134
New Kingdom
Newton's predecessors 349
"Newtonian Synthesis in Physical Science" 395
Nile Valley 51
"Nile Valley Origins of the Science of the Mind" 395
Nilometer 37, 38
Nobles, Wade 262
    Kemet and the African Worldview 228
Nomes of Egypt 215
Obenga, Theophile 30, 171
    "Black Land" 171
O'Connor, David Preface, 69
O'Connor, David "Egyptians were Not White!" 531

Old Kingdom 216
Old Kingdom painting and sculpture 296
Open Air Museum (Karnak) 56
    Free at Luxor 56
Open Mold Casting 264
Origins of Egyptian hieroglyphs 298
Oreopithecidae 34
Osei, G.K. 127

RESEACH ESSAYS ON ANCIENT EGYPT

Osiris 232
    "Painted black" 86, 546
Osireion 51

Research Essays 139c. Sign identifying Tombs of Nobles at Sakkara, open to visitors including Nefer-her-En-Ptah, Ruka-Ptah, Niankh-Khnum, Khnum-Hoteb all needing special tickets of 30 Egyptian Pounds each to visit.

Palettes 310
    Battlefield

Bull 197, 215, 353, 364
Dog 250, 353, 364
Libya 197, 215, 353, 364.
Narmer 197, 215, 251, 329, 330, 353, 364
"Pan Grave people" 227
Pappademos, John
    (1985) (1986) *Newtonian Synthesis in Physical Science and its Roots in the Nile Valley* 349, 350, 351
Papyrus
    Berlin 418
    Brooklyn Museum
    Carlsberg Number VIII
    Chester Beatty 418
    Ebers
    Edwin Smith 417
    Hearst 419
    Hunefer 65, 131
    Kahun Medical 418
    London 419
    Narmer
    Oxyrchynchus
    Turin 131
    Westcar
Parrinder, Geoffrey
    (1975) (1985) *World Religions* 230
Parts of the Body
Peet, T. Eric 110
    (1915) 344
Percy, Thomas 261
Perry, W.J.
    (1937) *The Growth of Civilization* 30, 76, 317-318
Petrie, W.M. Flinders 98, 255-256
    (1924) *Religious Life in Ancient Egypt* 181, 396, 397, 398, 473, 478, 499
    (1923) *Social Life in Ancient Egypt* 395, 396, 397, 398
    (1918) *Tools and Weapons* 310, 466-467
    (1940) *Wisdom of the Egyptians* 332-333
    (1909) *The Arts and Crafts of Ancient Egypt* 431, 435, 436
Pharaonic paraphernalia 324
Pharaonic portrait 335
Philosophers
    Dua Khety 57
    Meryukare 57
    Ptahhotep 57
Pliopithecoidea 34
Poem to Amon-Ra 201-207

RESEACH ESSAYS ON ANCIENT EGYPT

Poem to Imhotep 290-292
Poem to Ptah 267-272
Poem to Ra- The Sun God 243-247
Poem to Thoth 263-265
Pongidae 36
"Power of One" 293-303
Pre and Proto-dynastic 322
Proconsul 32
Professors
    Rosellini
    Naumann
    At the American University in Cairo 70
Prosimil 34
Psychostasia
Ptah 143
Ptolemy, Claudius 360
Ptolemy's Almagest 350
Pyramids 2, 19, 275
Pyramid
    Bent, Snefru 282
    Complex 283
    "True" 282-283
Pyramid Texts 220, 221
Pythagoras 165
Queens
    Aahmes-Nefertari 70
Ra 142
Ramapithecus 24, 26
Rameses II
    "Girdle Wall"
Rameses II and Queen Nefertari 44
Ramesseum Mathematical Leather Roll (RMLR)
Randall-MacIver 105
Rawlinson, Canon George
    (1893) *Story of the Nations: Egypt 100, 136-137*
Raymond, E.A.E.
    The Mythological Origin of the Egyptian Temple 190-191
Redford, Donald
    (2001) *The Oxford Encyclopedia of Ancient Egypt*
Reisner, Dr. 103-104
Reeves, Carol
    (1992) *Egyptian Medicine* 414, 415, 417, 418, 421
Reid 133
Representing pharaoh's body
Rhind Mathematical Papyrus (RMP)
Robbins, Gay

(1997) *The Art of Ancient Egypt* 84, 535
Roberts, David 254
Robinson, Victor
    (1936) *The Story of Medicine* 559
J.A. Rogers has shown in 262
    (1944) *Sex and Race* Vol., I, II Preface, 114, 563
    (1972) *World's Great men of Color* 415
Rosetta Stone 54, 176
Rosellini
    Description of Egypt 254
Royal Mummies of Deir el Bahari 554
Ruffle 97
Russell, Bertrand
    (1972) *History of Western Philosophy* 559
Sacred architecture
Sacred building equals sacred universe
Sakkara
Salt, Henry 254
Satire of the Trades 308
Schweinfurth 104
Scholars on the anatomy of the Ancient Egyptians 104-105
Sauernon 161-162
Scepters
    Ames
    Makes
Scheel, Bernd
    Egyptian Metalworking and Tools 305, 309
Scholz, Piotr O.
    (1997) *Ancient Egypt: An Illustrative Historical Overview* 420
Schools of art
Science in ancient Egypt 392
Science of astronomy 395
Scientific writers
Sekenenra, Kamose and Ahmose
Sekhem rod
Semi-precious stones 314-315
Senmut
Seven positions of the body
Seven Wonders of the World
Sewell, J.W.S. "The Calendars and Chronology" 403
Shabaka Stone 43
Shafer, Byron E.
    (1998) *Temples of Ancient Egypt* 1362
Shaw, Ian
    (2000) *The Oxford History of Ancient Egypt* 198

RESEACH ESSAYS ON ANCIENT EGYPT

Shaw, Ian and Paul Nicholson
    (1995) *The British Museum Dictionary of Ancient Egypt* 152, 170, 417
Shawky Abdel (Guide at Luxor) 52
Simpson, O.J. 257
Site entrance fees 71
Sites
    Mesolithic 248
    Neolithic 248
    Palaeolithic 248, 249
Sivapithecus 32
Smith, G. Elliot
    The Ancient Egyptians 30, 76-77, 107
Smith, W. Stephenson
    (1959) *The Art and Architecture of Ancient Egypt* 65, 86, 284, 342, 344-345, 546
Sobekhotep 227
Spence, Lewis
    (1985) (1986) *Myths and Legends of Egypt* 435
Spinoza 257
Statues of Min 345
Steindorff and Seele
    (1942) (1971) *When Egypt Ruled the East* 411, 458
Stirlin, Henri
    Architecture of the World: Egypt 240, 241
Stone 396
Stones and rocks 269
Stone Age 40
Stone Age diet 41
Sun temples 284
Swastika 567-568
Tablets
    Abydos 51, 58
Technicalities of Egyptian art
Temple architectural layout 551
Temple, essential parts
Temple wealth
Temples
    Abu Simbel 568
    Abydos of Rameses II
    Abydos of Seti I 63, 72, 73
        Gods at 171
    Beit Wali 46
    "Coca Cola"
    Deir el Bahari 70
    Dendera 286
    Edfu 47, 48, 64, 71, 286

"Corridor of Victory" 48, 71
Esneh 48, 286
Gerf Hussein 34
Isis of Philae 6, 71, 72
"Kiosk of Trajan"
Kalabsha 46, 286
Karnak (*Ipet Isut*) 287
    Beautification 51
Kom Ombo 46, 47, 48, 286
Luxor (*Southern Isut*) 53, 54
Medinet Habu
Mut
Nefertari 46
Philae 46
Temples, features of 313

Texts
    Coffin 121, 130, 139, 251
    Pyramid 121, 130, 138, 251
    Thoth 145-147

Theban Ennead 171
Themes, of crafts 306, 307
Time Life
    (1997) *What Life Was Like on the Banks of the Nile*
    Tools
    Tomb decoration

Tombs
    Rekh-mi-re 265, 307
    Puy-em-ra 265, 307
    Two Sculptors at Thebes 265, 307
    Rock Tombs at Gebrawi 265, 307

Tool making materials 40
Tools of carpenters 311
Tools of masons 311
Tombs at Sakkara 354
Tombs of the Valley of the Kings 362
Tourist Police
Training of scribes
"True man" 32, 39
"True, True man" 33
Tunnel, the first 390
UNESCO's "fundamental blackness of ancient Egypt 196, 538
Uphill, Eric P.
    (1988) *Egyptian Towns and Cities* 384
Valleys
    Artisans 281

RESEACH ESSAYS ON ANCIENT EGYPT

    Eastern 280
    Kings 280
    Nobles 280
    Queens 280
    Western
Van Sertima, Ivan 30, 33, 90, 92, 115, 262
    (1989) *Egypt Revisited* 115
    (1983) 404
Viziers 465
Volney, Count 92
    (1791) *Ruins of Empires* 77, 254, 560
Von Bedun (1826-1907)
Von Reben (1902) 357-360
Wadjyt
Wages, kinds of 308, 482-483
Warfare in Egypt 363
Warrior pharaohs
Watson, Philip
    (1987) Egyptian Pyramid and Masta Tombs 87-388
Watterson, Barbara
    (1984) (1996) *The Gods of Ancient Egypt* 159
    (1997) *The Egyptians* 189, 190
Weapons of predynastic soldiers 312, 366
Weigall, Arthur 105
    Flights into Antiquity
Western, European and American historiography
White, Jon
    (1970) *Ancient Egypt* 371-372, 430, 439-440, 442-443, 450, 455
    (1963) (1980) *Everyday Life in Ancient Egypt* 170-171
"White Wall" 281
Wilkinson, Alix
    (1975) *Ancient Egyptian Jewelry* 348-349, 349-350, 436450
Wilkinson, Richard H.
    (1966) *Reading Egyptian Art* 324
Wilkinson, Sir Garner
    (1875) *The Manners and Customs of Ancient Egypt* 95, 255
Williams, Chancellor
    Destruction of Black Civilization 197
Wilson, Hillary (1993) 416-417
Wilson, J.A.
    (1951) (1975) *The Culture of Ancient Egypt* 369-370, 455, 456, 472, 478-479, 479-480, 484
Wilson, Robert Forest
    (1924) *The Living Pageant of the Nile* 160
Winkler, Hans A.
    (1938) *Rock Drawings of Southern Upper Egypt* I 342

FREDERICK MONDERSON

Woldering, Irmgard
    (1962) (1963) Egyptian *Art in the Time of the Pharaohs* 327, 328, 431, 443, 445-446, 450, 457
Woodson, Carter G. 30, 111, 262
    (1932) (1993) *The Mis-Education of the Negro* 94,
Wordsworth, William (1770-1850) 256
Wortham, John David.
    (1971) *The Genesis of British Egyptology* Preface 530, 539
Yoyotte 267, 273
    (1963) *A Dictionary of Egyptian Civilization* 428, 434, 447, 464
Zinjanthropus Boise 36, 39
Zoser 217, 219

Research Essays 140. On a trip to a Nubian Village at Aswan, a tumultuous turnout welcomed African American visitors and these folks followed them to the waterside.

RESEACH ESSAYS ON ANCIENT EGYPT

Research essays 140a. Two images of Anubis painted blue are looked over by two "Eye of Horus" in the Tomb of Senufer, taken back in 2003.

Research Essay 140b. Sennufer stands before Thoth and other gods, one wearing the red and white Double Crown in the tomb of Sennufer, picture taken back in 2003.

FREDERICK MONDERSON

Research Essays 141 a and b. Two statues of very hard stone are included to give an example of broken noses.

www.ingramcontent.com/pod-product-compliance
Lightning Source LLC
Chambersburg PA
CBHW070004010526
44117CB00011B/1421